AS Statistics

Mark Brace
Anthony Eccles
Bob Francis
Michael Ling
Roger Porkess
David Smart
Phil Stockton
Alastair Summers
Sidney Tyrrell

Series Editor: Roger Porkess

The Publishers would like to thank the following for permission to reproduce copyright material:
Photo credits: © Photo Central/Alamy, p.4; © Eric Cahan/Corbis, p.92; BDI Images, pp.125, 134; Emma Lee/Life File, pp.146, 164; Nigel Shuttleworth/Life File, p.156; Colin Taylor Productions, p.178; © Graham Ella/Alamy, p.267; Hein von Horsten/Gallo Images/Getty Images, p.343; Agence France Presse/Hulton Archive/Getty Images, p.351
Acknowledgements: Data and diagrams in Exercise 2B question 6 (pages 74–75), Exercise 2C question 4 (page 84) and Exercise 2D question 1 (page 85) reproduced by permission of Manchester United Supporters' Club France; Suduko puzzle on page 266 reproduced by permission of *The Independent on Sunday*.
MEI examination questions are reproduced by permission of OCR.
Every effort has been made to trace all copyright holders, but if any have been inadvertently overlooked the Publishers will be pleased to make the necessary arrangements at the first opportunity.

Although every effort has been made to ensure that website addresses are correct at time of going to press, Hodder Murray cannot be held responsible for the content of any website mentioned in this book. It is sometimes possible to find a relocated web page by typing in the address of the home page for a website in the URL window of your browser.

Hodder Headline's policy is to use papers that are natural, renewable and recyclable products and made from wood grown in sustainable forests. The logging and manufacturing processes are expected to conform to the environmental regulations of the country of origin.

Orders: please contact Bookpoint Ltd, 130 Milton Park, Abingdon, Oxon OX14 4SB. Telephone: (44) 01235 827720. Fax: (44) 01235 400454. Lines are open from 9 a.m. to 5 p.m., Monday to Saturday, with a 24-hour message-answering service. Visit our website at www.hoddereducation.co.uk.

First published in 2007 by
Hodder Murray, an imprint of Hodder Education,
a member of the Hodder Headline Group,
an Hachette Livre UK Company
338 Euston Road,
London, NW1 3BH

Impression number 10 9 8 7 6 5 4 3 2 1
Year 2012 2011 2010 2009 2008 2007

Cover photo by Cocoon/Digital Vision/Getty Images
Illustrations on pages 55, 83, 215 and 356 by Barking Dog Art; all others by Tech-Set
Typeset in 10.5pt Minion by Tech-Set, Gateshead, Tyne and Wear
Printed in Malta

A catalogue record for this title is available from the British Library.

ISBN: 978 0340 94052 5

Contents

Introduction

This book covers the MEI AS Statistics course which is examined by OCR. The course is designed for those needing statistics to support other subjects and students are not expected to be taking AS or A Level Mathematics alongside it. Consequently the emphasis is on the use of statistics rather than any underlying mathematical theory.

There are three units: Z1 (Chapters 1 to 7), Z2 (Chapters 8 to 13) and Z3 (Chapters 14 to 17). The content of Z1 is exactly the same as that of the MEI AS unit, Statistics 1, allowing students to switch between AS Statistics and AS Mathematics at an early stage in either course. The text of the Z1 chapters is almost the same as those for *Statistics 1* but all the exercise questions are new. All the material in the remaining chapters, those covering Z2 and Z3, is completely new.

Each chapter begins with an article from a fictional local newspaper, the *Avonford Star*. Much of the information that we receive from the media is of a broadly statistical nature. In this book you are encouraged to recognise this and shown how to evaluate what you are told. Other examples are built around contexts that arise in the wide variety of subjects that use statistics: psychology, sociology, biology, geography, business, etc.

The approach and style of this book mean that it will be found helpful and useful by a very large number of students, not just those following the particular course for which it has been written.

The authors of this book would like to thank the many people who have helped in its preparation and particularly those who read early versions of their chapters. We would also like to thank OCR who have given permission for their questions to be used in the exercises.

Roger Porkess
Series Editor

Key to symbols in this book

? This symbol means that you may want to discuss a point with your teacher. If you are working on your own there are answers in the back of the book. It is important, however, that you have a go at answering the questions before looking up the answers if you are to understand the mathematics fully.

! This is a warning sign. It is used where a common mistake, misunderstanding or tricky point is being described.

This is the ICT icon. It indicates where you should use a graphic calculator or a computer.

e This symbol and a dotted line down the right-hand side of the page indicates material which is beyond the criteria for the unit but which is included for completeness.

☆☆ Harder questions are indicated with stars. Many of these go beyond the usual examination standard.

Unit 1

1 Exploring data

A judicious man looks at statistics, not to get knowledge but to save himself from having ignorance foisted on him.

Carlyle

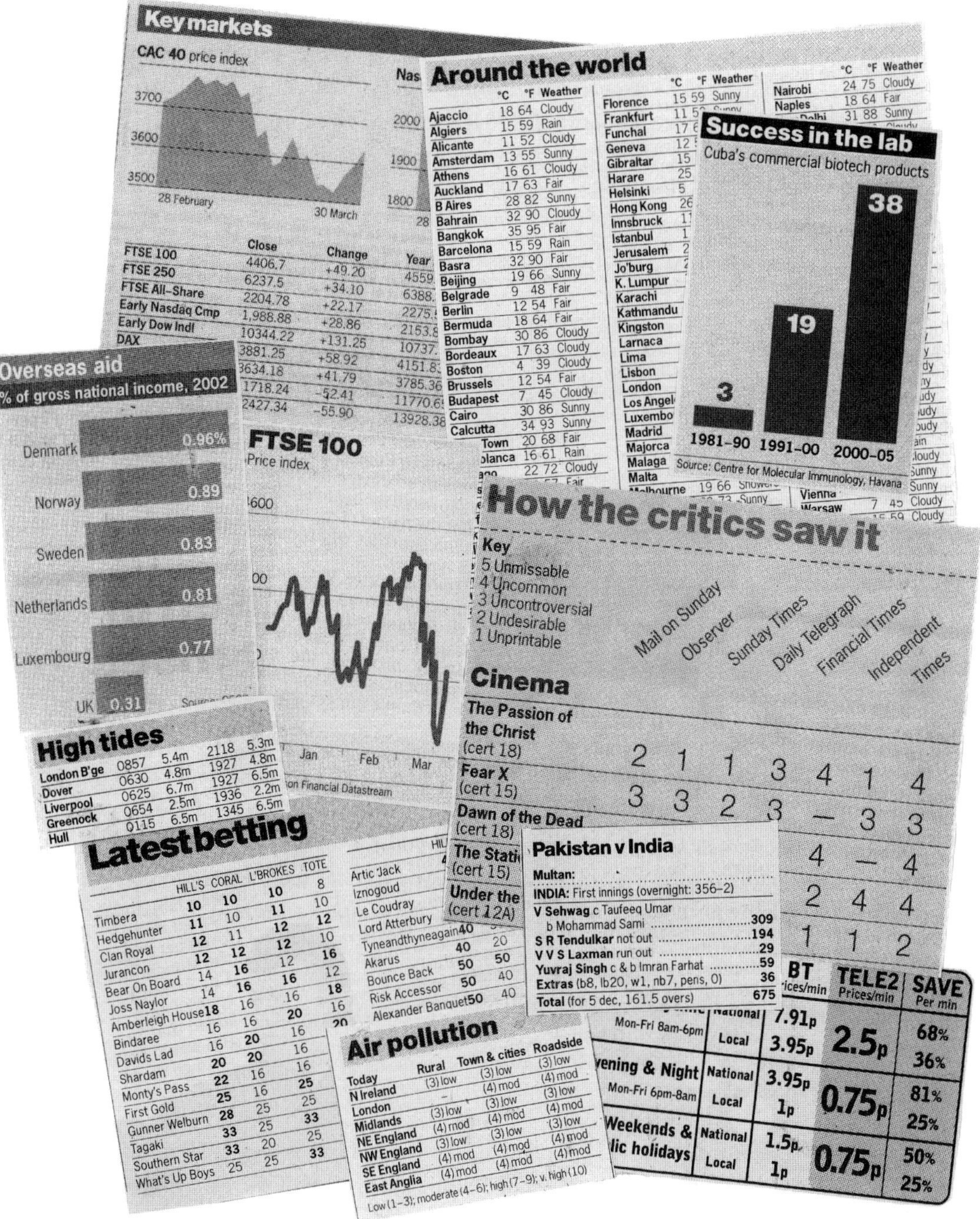

Key markets

CAC 40 price index

	Close	Change	Year
FTSE 100	4406.7	+49.20	4559.
FTSE 250	6237.5	+34.10	6388.
FTSE All-Share	2204.78	+22.17	2275.
Early Nasdaq Cmp	1,988.88	+28.86	2153.8
Early Dow Indl	10344.22	+131.25	10737.
DAX	3881.25	+58.92	4151.8
	3634.18	+41.79	3785.36
	1718.24	-52.41	11770.6
	2427.34	-55.90	13928.38

Around the world

	°C	°F	Weather
Ajaccio	18	64	Cloudy
Algiers	15	59	Rain
Alicante	11	52	Cloudy
Amsterdam	13	55	Sunny
Athens	16	61	Cloudy
Auckland	17	63	Fair
B Aires	28	82	Sunny
Bahrain	32	90	Cloudy
Bangkok	35	95	Fair
Barcelona	15	59	Rain
Basra	32	90	Fair
Beijing	19	66	Sunny
Belgrade	9	48	Fair
Berlin	12	54	Fair
Bermuda	18	64	Fair
Bombay	30	86	Cloudy
Bordeaux	17	63	Cloudy
Boston	4	39	Cloudy
Brussels	12	54	Fair
Budapest	7	45	Cloudy
Cairo	30	86	Sunny
Calcutta	34	93	Sunny
Town	20	68	Fair
blanca	16	61	Rain
Florence	15	59	Sunny
Nairobi	24	75	Cloudy
Naples	18	64	Fair
Delhi	31	88	Sunny
Melbourne	19	66	Showers
Warsaw	7	45	Cloudy

Frankfurt, Funchal, Geneva, Gibraltar, Harare, Helsinki, Hong Kong, Innsbruck, Istanbul, Jerusalem, Jo'burg, K. Lumpur, Karachi, Kathmandu, Kingston, Larnaca, Lima, Lisbon, London, Los Angel, Luxembo, Madrid, Majorca, Malaga, Malta, Vienna

Success in the lab

Cuba's commercial biotech products

1981–90: 3
1991–00: 19
2000–05: 38

Source: Centre for Molecular Immunology, Havana

Overseas aid

% of gross national income, 2002

Denmark 0.96%
Norway 0.89
Sweden 0.83
Netherlands 0.81
Luxembourg 0.77
UK 0.31

FTSE 100

Price index

Jan Feb Mar

Source: Thomson Financial Datastream

High tides

London B'ge	0857	5.4m	2118	5.3m
Dover	0630	4.8m	1927	4.8m
Liverpool	0625	6.7m	1927	6.5m
Greenock	0654	2.5m	1936	2.2m
Hull	0115	6.5m	1345	6.5m

How the critics saw it

Key
5 Unmissable
4 Uncommon
3 Uncontroversial
2 Undesirable
1 Unprintable

Cinema

	Mail on Sunday	Observer	Sunday Times	Daily Telegraph	Financial Times	Independent	Times
The Passion of the Christ (cert 18)	2	1	1	3	4	1	4
Fear X (cert 15)	3	3	2	3	–	3	3
Dawn of the Dead (cert 18)					4	–	4
The Stati (cert 15)					2	4	4
Under the (cert 12A)					1	1	2

Latest betting

	HILL'S	CORAL	L'BROKES	TOTE
Timbera	10	10	10	8
Hedgehunter	11	10	11	10
Clan Royal	12	11	12	12
Jurancon	12	12	12	10
Bear On Board	14	16	12	16
Joss Naylor	14	16	16	12
Amberleigh House	18	16	16	18
Bindaree	16	16	20	16
Davids Lad	16	20	16	20
Shardam	20	20	16	
Monty's Pass	22	16	16	
First Gold	25	16	25	
Gunner Welburn	28	25	25	
Tagaki	33	25	33	
Southern Star	33	20	25	
What's Up Boys	25	25	33	

	HIL	
Artic Jack	4	
Iznogoud		
Le Coudray		
Lord Atterbury		
Tyneandthyneagain	40	
Akarus	40	20
Bounce Back	50	50
Risk Accessor	50	40
Alexander Banquet	50	40

Pakistan v India

Multan:

INDIA: First innings (overnight: 356–2)

V Sehwag c Taufeeq Umar b Mohammad Sami	309
S R Tendulkar not out	194
V V S Laxman run out	29
Yuvraj Singh c & b Imran Farhat	59
Extras (b8, lb20, w1, nb7, pens, 0)	36
Total (for 5 dec, 161.5 overs)	675

Air pollution

Today	Rural	Town & cities	Roadside
N Ireland	(3) low	(3) low	(3) low
London	–	(4) mod	(4) mod
Midlands	(3) low	(3) low	(3) low
NE England	(4) mod	(4) mod	(4) mod
NW England	(3) low	(3) low	(3) low
SE England	(4) mod	(4) mod	(4) mod
East Anglia	(4) mod	(4) mod	(4) mod

Low (1–3); moderate (4–6); high (7–9); v. high (10)

		BT Prices/min	TELE2 Prices/min	SAVE Per min
Mon-Fri 8am-6pm	National	7.91p	2.5p	68%
	Local	3.95p		36%
Evening & Night Mon-Fri 6pm-8am	National	3.95p	0.75p	81%
	Local	1p		25%
Weekends & Public holidays	National	1.5p	0.75p	50%
	Local	1p		25%

Source: *The Guardian* 2004

The cuttings on page 3 all appeared in one newspaper on one day. Some of them give data as figures, others display them as diagrams.

How do you interpret this information? Which data do you take seriously and which do you dismiss as being insignificant or even misleading?

To answer these questions fully you need to understand how data are collected and analysed before they are presented to you, and how you should evaluate what you are given to read (or see on the television). This is an important part of the subject of statistics.

In this book, many of the examples are set as stories within a fictitious local newspaper, the *Avonford Star*. Some of them are written as articles; others are presented from the journalists' viewpoint as they sort through data trying to write an interesting story. As you work through the book, look too at the ways you are given such information in your everyday life.

AVONFORD STAR

Another cyclist seriously hurt.
Will you be next?

On her way back home from school on Wednesday afternoon, little Denise Cropper was knocked off her bicycle and taken to hospital with suspected concussion.

Denise was struck by a Ford Transit van, only 50 metres from her own house.

Denise is the fourth child from the Springfields estate to be involved in a serious cycling accident this year.

The busy road where Denise Cropper was knocked off her bicycle yesterday

After this report the editor of the *Avonford Star* commissioned one of the paper's reporters to investigate the situation and write a leading article for the paper on it. She explained to the reporter that there was growing concern locally about cycling accidents involving children. She emphasised the need to collect good quality data to support presentations to the *Star's* readers.

? Is the aim of the investigation clear?
Is the investigation worth carrying out?
What makes good quality data?

The reporter started by collecting data from two sources. He went through back numbers of the *Avonford Star* for the previous two years, finding all the reports of cycling accidents. He also asked an assistant to carry out a survey of the ages of local cyclists; he wanted to know whether most cyclists were children, young adults or whatever.

 Are the reporter's data sources appropriate?

Before starting to write his article, the reporter needed to make sense of the data for himself. He then had to decide how he was going to present the information to his readers. These are the sorts of data he had to work with.

Name	Age	Distance from home	Cause	Injuries	Treatment
John Smith	45	3 km	skid	Concussion	Hosp. Outpatient
Debbie Lane	5	75 km	hit kerb	Broken arm	Hosp. Outpatient
Arvinder Sethl	12	1200 m	lorry	Multiple fractures	Hosp. 3 weeks
Marion Wren	8	300 m	hit each other (both)	Bruising	Hosp. Outpatient
David Huker	8	50 m		Concussion	Hosp. overnight

There were 92 accidents listed in the reporter's table.

Ages of cyclists (from survey)

66 6 62 19 20 15 21 8 21 63 44 10 44 34 18
35 26 61 13 61 28 21 7 10 52 13 52 20 17 26
64 11 39 22 9 13 9 17 64 32 8 9 31 19 22
37 18 138 16 67 45 10 55 14 66 67 14 62 28 36
9 23 12 9 37 7 36 9 88 46 12 59 61 22 49
18 20 11 25 7 42 29 6 60 60 16 50 16 34 14
18 15

This information is described as *raw data*, which means that no attempt has yet been made to organise it in order to look for any patterns.

Looking at the data

At the moment the arrangement of the ages of the 92 cyclists tells you very little at all. Clearly these data must be organised so as to reveal the underlying shape, the *distribution*. The figures need to be ranked according to size and preferably grouped as well. The reporter had asked an assistant to collect the information and this was the order in which she presented it.

Tally

Tallying is a quick, straightforward way of grouping data into suitable intervals. You have probably met it already.

Stated age (years)	Tally	Frequency
0–9	𝍸 𝍸 |||	13
10–19	𝍸 𝍸 𝍸 𝍸 𝍸 |	26
20–29	𝍸 𝍸 𝍸 |	16
30–39	𝍸 𝍸	10
40–49	𝍸 |	6
50–59	𝍸	5
60–69	𝍸 𝍸 ||||	14
70–79		0
80–89	|	1
⋮		
130–139	|	1
Total		92

Extreme values

A tally immediately shows up any extreme values, that is values which are far away from the rest. In this case there are two extreme values, usually referred to as *outliers*: 88 and 138. Before doing anything else you must investigate these.

In this case the 88 is genuine, the age of Millie Smith, who is a familiar sight cycling to the shops.

The 138 needless to say is not genuine. It was the written response of a man who was insulted at being asked his age. Since no other information about him is available, this figure is best ignored and the sample size reduced from 92 to 91. You should always try to understand an outlier before deciding to ignore it; it may be giving you important information.

Practical statisticians are frequently faced with the problem of *outlying observations*, observations that depart in some way from the general pattern of a data set. What they, and you, have to decide is whether any such observations belong to the data set or not. In the above example the data value 88 is a genuine member of the data set and is retained. The data value 138 is not a member of the data set and is therefore rejected.

Describing the shape of a distribution

An obvious benefit of using a tally is that it shows the overall shape of the distribution.

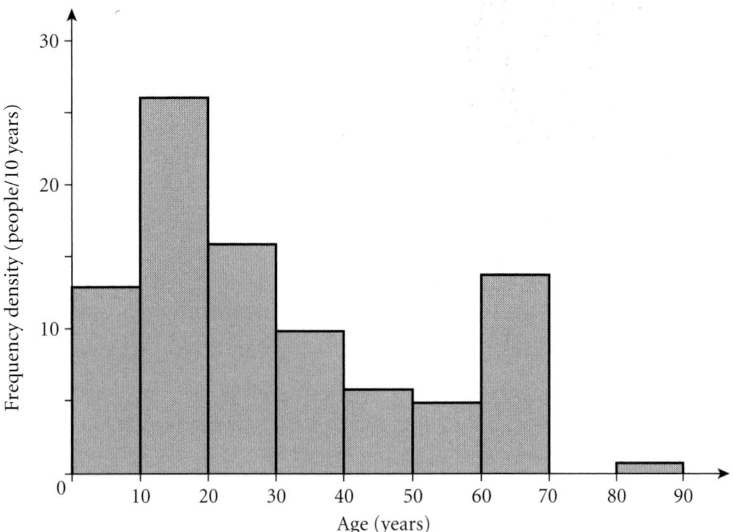

Figure 1.1 *Histogram to show the ages of people involved in cycling accidents*

You can now see that a large proportion (more than a quarter) of the sample are in the 10 to 19 year age range. This is the *modal* group as it is the one with the most members. The single value with the most members is called the *mode*, in this case age 9.

You will also see that there is a second peak among those in their sixties; so this distribution is called *bimodal*, even though the frequency in the interval 10–19 is greater than the frequency in the interval 60–69.

Different types of distribution are described in terms of the position of their modes or modal groups, see figure 1.2.

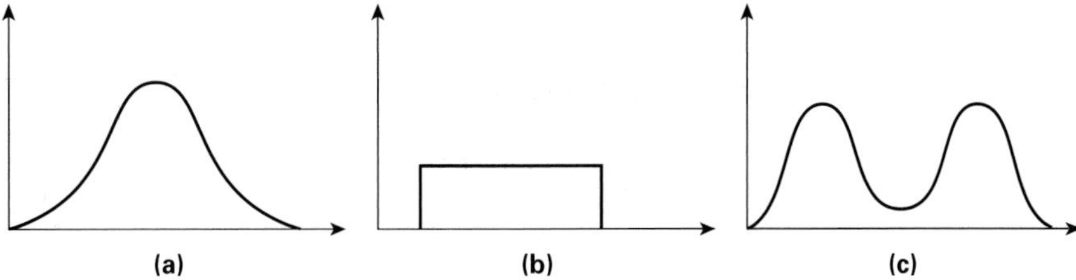

Figure 1.2 *Distribution shapes:*
(a) *unimodal and symmetrical* **(b)** *uniform (no mode but symmetrical)* **(c)** *bimodal*

When the mode is off to one side the distribution is said to be *skewed.* If the mode is to the left with a long tail to the right the distribution has positive (or right) skewness; if the long tail is to the left the distribution has negative (or left) skewness. These two cases are shown in figure 1.3.

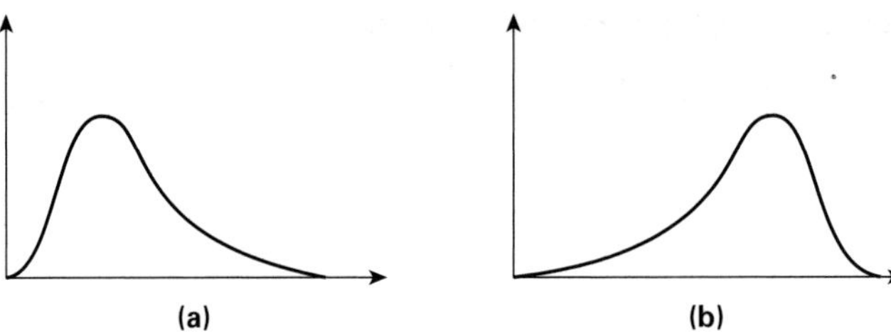

Figure 1.3 *Skewness:* **(a)** *positive* **(b)** *negative*

Stem-and-leaf diagrams

The quick and easy view of the distribution from the tally has been achieved at the cost of losing information. You can no longer see the original figures which went into the various groups and so cannot, for example, tell from looking at the tally whether Millie Smith is 80, 81, 82, or any age up to 89. This problem of the loss of information can be solved by using a *stem-and-leaf diagram* (or *stemplot*).

This is a quick way of grouping the data so that you can see their distribution and still have access to the original figures. The one below shows the ages of the 91 cyclists surveyed.

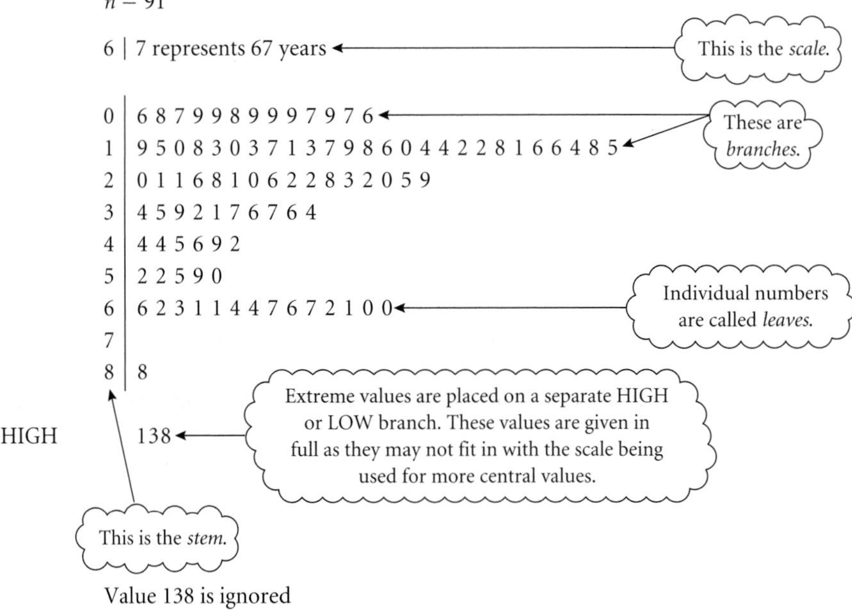

Figure 1.4 *Stem-and-leaf diagram showing the ages of a sample of 91 cyclists (unsorted)*

? Do all the branches have leaves?

The column of figures on the left (going from 0 to 8) corresponds to the tens digits of the ages. This is called the *stem* and in this example it consists of 9 branches. On each branch on the stem are the *leaves* and these represent the units digits of the data values.

As you can see above, the leaves for a particular branch have been placed in the order in which the numbers appeared in the original raw data. This is fine for showing the general shape of the distribution, but it is usually worthwhile sorting the leaves, as shown in figure 1.5.

$n = 91$

6 | 7 represents 67 years

0	6 6 7 7 7 8 8 9 9 9 9 9 9
1	0 0 0 1 1 2 2 3 3 3 4 4 4 5 5 6 6 6 7 7 8 8 8 8 9 9
2	0 0 0 1 1 1 2 2 2 3 5 6 6 8 8 9
3	1 2 4 4 5 6 6 7 7 9
4	2 4 4 5 6 9
5	0 2 2 5 9
6	0 0 1 1 1 2 2 3 4 4 6 6 7 7
7	
8	8

Note that the value 138 is left out as it has been identified as not belonging to this set of data.

Figure 1.5 *Stem-and-leaf diagram showing the ages of a sample of 91 cyclists (sorted)*

The stem-and-leaf diagram gives you a lot of information at a glance:

- The youngest cyclist is 6 and the oldest is 88 years of age
- More people are in the 10–19 year age range than in any other 10-year age range
- There are three 61-year-olds
- The modal age (i.e. the age with the most people) is 9
- The 17th oldest cyclist in the survey is 55 years of age.

If the values on the basic stem-and-leaf diagram are too cramped, that is, if there are so many leaves on a line that the diagram is not clear, you may *stretch* it. To do this you put values 0, 1, 2, 3, 4 on one line and 5, 6, 7, 8, 9 on another. Doing this to the example results in the diagram shown in figure 1.6.

When stretched, this stem-and-leaf diagram reveals the skewed nature of the distribution.

$n = 91$

6 | 7 represents 67 years

0*	
0	6 6 7 7 7 8 8 9 9 9 9 9 9
1*	0 0 0 1 1 2 2 3 3 3 4 4 4
1	5 5 6 6 6 7 7 8 8 8 8 9 9
2*	0 0 0 1 1 1 2 2 2 3
2	5 6 6 8 8 9
3*	1 2 4 4
3	5 6 6 7 7 9
4*	2 4 4
4	5 6 9
5*	0 2 2
5	5 9
6*	0 0 1 1 1 2 2 3 4 4
6	6 6 7 7
7*	
7	
8*	
8	8

You must include all the branches, even those with no leaves.

Figure 1.6 *Stem-and-leaf diagram showing the ages of a sample of 91 cyclists (sorted)*

? How would you squeeze a stem-and-leaf diagram? What would you do if the data have more significant figures than can be shown on a stem-and-leaf diagram?

Stem-and-leaf diagrams are particularly useful for comparing data sets. With two data sets a back-to-back stem-and-leaf diagram can be used, as shown in figure 1.7.

represents 590   9 | 5 | 2   represents 520

9	5	1 7
2	6	0 2 3 5 8
5 3 0	7	1 2 5 6 6 7
9 7 5 1 1	8	3 5
8 6 2 1	9	2

Note the numbers on the left of the stem still have the smallest number next to the stem.

Figure 1.7

? How would you represent positive and negative data on a stem-and-leaf diagram?

EXERCISE 1A

1 The prices of two-bedroom terraced houses sold in the same street are recorded below. The prices are in thousands of pounds.

130 140 125 129 120 99 175 119 108 103 130 110

(i) Display the data on a sorted stem-and-leaf diagram.
(ii) Comment on the distribution.

2 The weekly earnings, in pounds, of a sample of fifteen Year 12 students are recorded below.

20 18 15 4 28 22 0 28 31 42 28 30 90 80 34

(i) Display the data on a stem-and-leaf diagram with ten branches.
(ii) Comment on the shape of the distribution.

3 The populations in 2002 of 14 countries are given below.

Country	Population in millions
Austria	8
Belgium	10
Denmark	5
Finland	5
France	59
Germany	82
Greece	11
Ireland	4
Italy	58
Netherlands	16
Portugal	10
Spain	39
Sweden	9
UK	59

(i) Display the data on a sorted stem-and-leaf diagram.
(ii) Comment on the distribution.

4 A biologist collects ten small crustaceans and measures their lengths in millimetres. She then collects a second set of similar crustaceans but only selects ones that have parasites on them. The lengths are given below.

Set 1	7.6	10.6	9.0	6.0	8.8	10.3	6.2	7.3	5.5	11.6
Set 2	5.3	6.0	6.6	5.5	5.2	7.1	7.3	4.0	8.8	7.5

(i) Display the data on a back-to-back sorted stem-and-leaf diagram.

(ii) Comment on the two sets of data.

5 A poultry farmer is experimenting with food additives to promote growth in young birds. He use two groups of birds. One group eat food with additives and the other set eat ordinary feed. The weights, in kilograms, of the birds in the two groups at age 4 months are given below.

Feed with additives

1.79 1.82 1.85 1.72 1.87

1.86 1.85 1.90 1.86 1.91

Ordinary feed

1.81 1.74 1.61 1.72 1.73

1.78 1.83 1.72 1.70 1.83

(i) Display the results on a back-to-back sorted stem-and-leaf diagram.

(ii) Comment on the results.

6 The heights of the world's 14 highest mountains are recorded below.

Name of mountain	Height in feet
Annapurna	26 545
Broad Peak	26 401
Cho Oyu	26 906
Dhaulagiri	26 795
Everest	29 029
Gasherbrum I	26 470
Gasherbrum II	26 362
K2	28 251
Kangchenjunga	28 169
Lhotse	27 940
Makalu	27 766
Manaslu	27 781
Nanga Parbat	26 657
Shisha Pangma	26 398

(i) Round each height to 3 significant figures and then display it on a sorted stem-and-leaf diagram using stems going up in steps of 500 feet.

(ii) Comment on the distribution.

(iii) A climber has climbed K2 and wants to climb Everest next.
Calculate, using
(a) the rounded values **(b)** the raw data
the increase in height of Everest from K2 as a percentage of K2's height.

7 A lepidopterist (someone who studies moths and butterflies) counts the number of moths she catches in her moth trap over 14 nights in June and July one summer. She also records the temperature to be normal (N) or cold (C).

Number of moths	9	28	16	25	12	23	29	21	30	17	23	14	21	18
Temperature: N or C	C	N	C	N	C	N	N	C	N	C	C	C	N	N

(i) Display the data using a back-to-back sorted stem-and-leaf diagram with four branches on the stem.

(ii) What conclusions should she reach with regard to the temperature?

8 A psychology teacher asks her students to test the hypothesis that music hinders learning to spell.
A group of 12 students from Year 12 are asked to learn 24 nonsense words in a timed silent session. A similar group of students are asked to learn the same nonsense words in the same time but have music playing while they try to remember them. The numbers of correct spellings are recorded below.

Without music

8 10 7 8 10 3
10 11 9 8 9 12

With music

12 11 13 18 14 22
11 13 14 15 11 19

(i) Display these data on a back-to-back sorted stem-and-leaf diagram using three branches: 0–9, 10–19 and 20–29.

(ii) Now display these data on a back-to-back sorted stem-and-leaf diagram using five branches each covering five possible scores: 0–4, 5–9, 10–14, 15–19 and 20–24.

(iii) Does this extended stem-and-leaf diagram make the shape of the distribution easier to see?

(iv) Comment on the two sets of results.

(v) What implications does this have for students trying to learn while listening music?

Categorical or qualitative data

Chapter 2 will deal in more detail with ways of displaying data. The remainder of this chapter looks at types of data and the basic analysis of numerical data.

Some data come to you in classes or categories. Such data, like these for the members of the Select Committee for Education and Employment, are called categorical or qualitative.

L L L C L   L L L C L   LD C L L C   L LD

C = Conservative; L = Labour; LD = Liberal Democrat
Members are listed alphabetically.
(Source: *www.parliament.uk* August 1999)

Most of the data you encounter, however, will be numerical data (also called quantitative data).

Numerical or quantitative data

Variable

The score you get when you throw an ordinary die is one of the values 1, 2, 3, 4, 5 or 6. Rather than repeatedly using the phrase 'The score you get when you throw an ordinary die', statisticians find it convenient to use a capital letter, X, say. They let X stand for 'The score you get when you throw an ordinary die' and because this varies, X is referred to as a *variable*.

Similarly, if you are collecting data and this involves, for example, noting the temperature in classrooms at noon, then you could let T stand for 'the temperature in a classroom at noon'. So T is another example of a variable.

Values of the variable X are denoted by the lower case letter x, e.g. $x = 1, 2, 3, 4,$ 5 or 6.

Values of the variable T are denoted by the lower case letter t, e.g. $t = 18, 21, 20,$ $19, 23, \ldots$.

Discrete and continuous variables

The scores on a die, 1, 2, 3, 4, 5 and 6, the number of goals a football team scores, 0, 1, 2, 3, … and British shoe sizes $1, 1\frac{1}{2}, 2, 2\frac{1}{2}, \ldots$ are all examples of *discrete variables*. What they have in common is that all possible values can be listed.

Distance, mass, temperature and speed are all examples of *continuous variables*. Continuous variables, if measured accurately enough, can take any appropriate value. You cannot list all possible values.

You have already seen the example of age. This is rather a special case. It is nearly always given rounded down (i.e. truncated). Although your age changes continuously every moment of your life, you actually state it in steps of one year, in completed years, and not to the nearest whole year. So a man who is a few days short of his 20th birthday will still say he is 19.

In practice, data for a continuous variable are always given in a rounded form.

- A person's height, h, is given as 168 cm, measured to the nearest centimetre; $167.5 \leqslant h < 168.5$
- A temperature, t, is given as 21.8°C, measured to the nearest tenth of a degree; $21.75 \leqslant t < 21.85$
- The depth of an ocean, d, is given as 9200 m, measured to the nearest 100 m; $9150 \leqslant d < 9250$

Notice the rounding convention used here: if a figure is on the borderline it is rounded up. There are other rounding conventions.

Measures of central tendency

When describing a typical value to represent a data set most people think of a value at the centre and use the word *average*. When using the word average they are often referring to the *arithmetic mean*, which is usually just called the *mean*, and when asked to explain how to get the mean most people respond by saying 'add up the data values and divide by the total number of data values'.

There are actually several different averages and so, in statistics, it is important for you to be more precise about the *average* to which you are referring. Before looking at the different types of average or *measure of central tendency*, you need to be familiar with some notation.

Σ notation and the mean, $\bar{x}$

A sample of size n taken from a population can be identified as follows.

The first item can be called x_1, the second item x_2 and so on up to x_n.

The sum of these n items of data is given by $x_1 + x_2 + x_3 + \ldots + x_n$.

A shorthand for this is $\sum_{i=1}^{i=n} x_i$ or $\sum_{i=1}^{n} x_i$. This is read as the sum of all the terms x_i when i equals 1 to n.

So $$\sum_{i=1}^{n} x_i = x_1 + x_2 + x_3 + \ldots + x_n.$$

Σ is the Greek letter, '*sigma*'.

If there is no ambiguity about the number of items of data, the subscripts i can be dropped and $\sum_{i=1}^{n} x_i$ becomes $\sum x$.

$\sum x$ is read as 'sigma x' meaning 'the sum of all the x items'.

The mean of these n items of data is written as $\overline{x} = \dfrac{x_1 + x_2 + x_3 + \ldots + x_n}{n}$

where $\overline{x}$ is the symbol for the mean, referred to as '*x-bar*'.

It is usual to write $\overline{x} = \dfrac{\sum x}{n}$ or $\overline{x} = \dfrac{1}{n}\sum x$.

This is a formal way of writing 'To get the mean you add up all the data values and divide by the total number of data values'.

In the survey at the beginning of this chapter the mean of the cyclists' ages,

$\overline{x} = \frac{2717}{91} = 29.9$ years.

However, a mean of the ages needs to be adjusted because age is always rounded down. For example, John Smith gave his age as 45. He could be exactly 45 years old or possibly his 46th birthday may be one day away. So, each of the people in the sample could be from 0 to almost a year older than their quoted age.
To adjust for this discrepancy you need to add 0.5 years on to the average of 29.9 to give 30.4 years.

Note

The mean is the most commonly used average in statistics. The mean described here is correctly called the *arithmetic mean*; there are other forms, for example, the geometric mean, harmonic mean and weighted mean, all of which have particular applications.

The mean is used when the total quantity is also of interest. For example, the staff at the water treatment works for a city would be interested in the mean amount of water used per household ($\overline{x}$) but would also need to know the total amount of water used in the city ($\sum x$). The mean can give a misleading result if exceptionally large or exceptionally small values occur in the data set.

There are two other commonly used statistical measures of a typical (or representative) value of a data set. These are the median and the mode. A fourth measure is the mid-range.

Median

The median is the value of the middle item when all the data items are ranked in order. If there are n items of data then the median is the value of the $\frac{n+1}{2}$th item.

If n is odd then there is a middle value and this is the median. In the survey of the cyclists we have

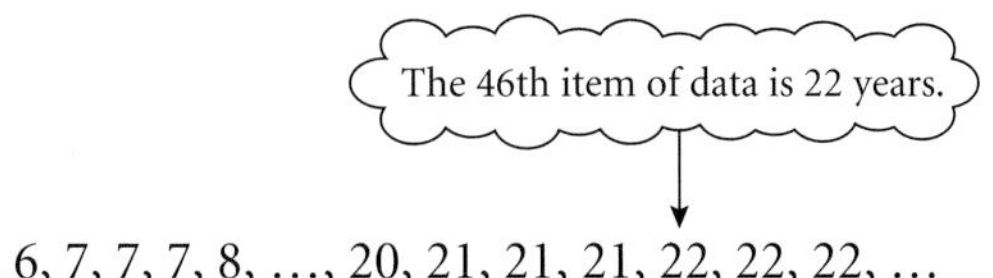

The 46th item of data is 22 years.

6, 6, 7, 7, 7, 8, …, 20, 21, 21, 21, 22, 22, 22, …

So for the ages of the 91 cyclists, the median is the age of the $\frac{91+1}{2} = 46$th person and this is 22 years.

If n is even and the two middle values are a and b then the median is $\frac{a+b}{2}$.

For example, if the reporter had not noticed that 138 was invalid there would have been 92 items of data. Then the median age for the cyclists would be found as follows.

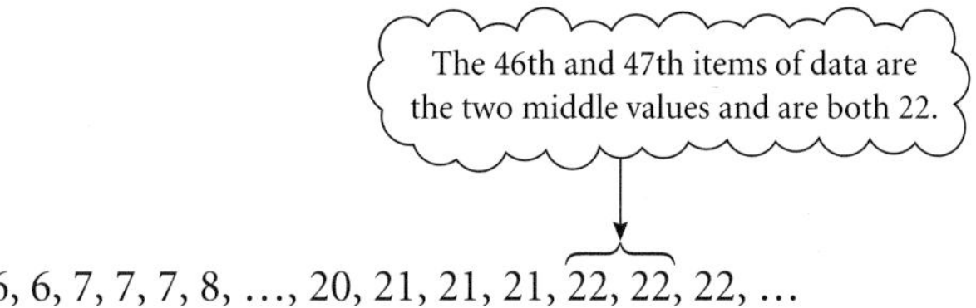

The 46th and 47th items of data are the two middle values and are both 22.

6, 6, 7, 7, 7, 8, …, 20, 21, 21, 21, 22, 22, 22, …

So the median age for the cyclists is given as the mean of the 46th and 47th items of data. That is, $\frac{22+22}{2} = 22$.

It is a coincidence that the median turns out to be the same. However, what is important to notice is that an extreme value has little or no effect on the value of the median. The median is said to be resistant to outliers.

The *median* is easy to work out if the data are already ranked, otherwise it can be tedious. However, with the increased availability of computers, it is easier to sort data and so the use of the median is increasing. Illustrating data on a stem-and-leaf diagram orders the data and makes it easy to identify the median. The median usually provides a good representative value and, as seen above, it is not affected by extreme values. It is particularly useful if some values are missing; for example, if 50 people took part in a cross country race then the median is halfway between the 25th and 26th values. If some people failed to complete the course the mean would be impossible to calculate, but the median is easy to find.

In finding an *average* salary the median is often a more appropriate measure than the mean since a few people earning very large salaries would have a big effect on the mean but not on the median.

Mode

The *mode* is the value which occurs most frequently. If two non-adjacent values occur more frequently than the rest, the distribution is said to be *bimodal*, even if the frequencies are not the same for both modes.

Bimodal data usually indicate that the sample has been taken from two populations. For example, a sample of students' heights (male and female) would probably be bimodal reflecting the different average heights of males and females.

For the cyclists' ages, the mode is 9 years (the frequency is 6).

For a small set of discrete data the mode can often be misleading, especially if there are many values the data can take. Several items of data can happen to fall on a particular value. The mode is used when the most probable or most frequently occurring value is of interest. For example, a dress shop manager who is considering stocking a new style would first buy dresses of the new style in the modal size, as she would be most likely to sell those ones.

Mid-range

The *mid-range* is the value midway between the upper extreme and the lower extreme values in the data set.

For the cyclists' ages the mid-range is $\frac{(6 + 88)}{2} = 47$ years.

The mid-range is easy to calculate but only useful if the data are reasonably symmetrical and free from outliers; for example, ages of students in a school class. A single outlier can have a major effect on the mid-range; for example, the mid-range of the cyclists' ages is increased by ten years by the inclusion of the 88-year-old, Millie Smith. By comparison, the mean is increased by 0.6 years, the mode and the median remain unchanged.

Which average you use will depend on the particular data you have and on what you are trying to find out.

The measures for the cyclists' ages are summarised below.

Mean	29.9 years	(adjusted = 30.4 years)
Mode	9 years	
Median	22 years	
Mid-range	47 years	

? Which do you think is most representative?

EXERCISE 1B

1 Find the mean, mode, median and mid-range for these data sets.

(i) The scores obtained in a playground game

0 5 4 4 1 3 3 3 5
3 2 3 3 0 6 6 1 3
4 1 0 3 4 5 7 0 4

(ii) The times, in minutes, taken by one person to complete 16 different Sudoku puzzles

26 25 28 27 31 36 34 122
29 29 17 39 22 18 38 20

(iii) The number of different fish species seen on different days on a diving trip in the Red Sea

25 44 47 40 30 32 10 12 27 22 45 29 33 35 28
28 51 52 40 30 25 18 34 52 35 34 42 26 18 23

2 For each of these sets of data find

(a) the mean, mode, median and mid-range

(b) state, with reasons, which you consider to be the most appropriate form of average to describe the distribution.

(i) The number of a particular alcopop drink bought by different people in a nightclub one evening.
The nightclub manager wants to know how many to keep in stock to cover a typical night's drinking.

0 5 6 5 3 0 5 5 3 4 0 3 4 4 2 4 0 2 0

(ii) The length, in metres, of fronds of the brown seaweed *Himanthalis elongata,* commonly called thongweed, found in one place.
A marine biologist is comparing its length in different locations.

1.9 4 7 7.7 8.1 5 5.6 1.9 5.2 7.5
5.8 6.6 6.3 3.9 4.6 4.9 6 4.5 7.4 6.9

(iii) A cricketer's scores so far this season.
The team captain wants to know whether to play him in an important match.

25 10 4 0 0 6 0 6 0 2 3 5 109 0 121

(iv) The weight, in pounds, of fish caught during an angling match.
The secretary of the angling club wants to publish the names of the top half of the list as 'Best anglers' in the club newsletter.

4 12 8 4 7 9 21 6 10 9 7 5 17 6 10 19

(v) The numbers of applicants for a history course at a university during recent years.
The admissions tutor wants to advise the department on how many places to make available next year.

25 25 24 11 24 28 30 34 24 27 33 12 15 13 26

(vi) The weight, in kilograms, of bananas eaten per day by the chimpanzees at a zoo.
The zoo-keeper wants to advise the management on how many bananas to buy.

12.5 14.8 14.0 14.8 11.9 13.7 14.4 15.2 12.7 15.0 13.4 12.8

Frequency distributions

You will often have to deal with data that are presented in a frequency table. Frequency tables summarise the data and also allow you to get an idea of the shape of the distribution.

EXAMPLE 1.1

Claire runs a fairground stall. She has designed a game where customers pay £1 and are given 10 marbles which they have to try to get into a container 4 metres away. If they get more than 8 in the container they win £5. Before introducing the game to the customers she tries it out on a sample of 50 people. The number of successes scored by each person is noted.

5	7	8	7	5	4	0	9	10	6
4	8	8	9	5	6	3	2	4	4
6	5	5	7	6	7	5	6	9	2
7	7	6	3	5	5	6	9	8	7
5	2	1	6	8	5	4	4	3	3

The data are discrete. They have not been organised in any way, so they are referred to as raw data.

Calculate the mode, median, mid-range and mean scores. Comment on your results.

SOLUTION

The *frequency distribution* of these data can be illustrated in a table. The number of 0s, 1s, 2s, etc. are counted to give the frequency of each mark.

Score	Frequency
0	1
1	1
2	3
3	4
4	6
5	10
6	8
7	7
8	5
9	4
10	1
Total	50

With the data presented in this form it is easier to find or calculate the different averages.

The mode score is 5 (frequency 10).

As the number of items of data is even, the distribution has two middle values, the 25th and 26th scores. From the distribution, by adding up the frequencies, it can be seen that the 25th score is 5 and the 26th score is 6. Consequently the median score is $\frac{1}{2}(5 + 6) = 5.5$.

The mid-range score is $\frac{1}{2}(0 + 10) = 5$.

Representing a score by x and its frequency by f, the calculation of the mean is shown in this table.

Score, x	**Frequency, f**	$x \times f$
0	1	$0 \times 1 = 0$
1	1	$1 \times 1 = 1$
2	3	$2 \times 3 = 6$
3	4	12
4	6	24
5	10	50
6	8	48
7	7	49
8	5	40
9	4	36
10	1	10
Totals	50	276

So $\bar{x} = \frac{\sum xf}{n}$ ($n = \sum f$)

$= \frac{276}{50} = 5.52$

The values of the mode (5), the median (5.5), the mean (5.52) and the mid-range (5) are close. This is because the distribution of scores does not have any extreme values and is reasonably symmetrical.

EXERCISE 1C

1 The number of smooth newts in different ponds during Spring in 2003 were recorded. The results are shown in the table

Number of newts, x	Number of ponds, f
0–3	0
4	4
5	8
6	6
7	10
8	9
9	5
10	5
11+	0

(i) State the mode.
(ii) Find the median.
(iii) Calculate the mid-range.
(iv) Calculate the mean using the statistics functions on your calculator.

2 The table gives the results of a survey into the amount of pocket money some 10-year-old children receive. The figures are rounded to the nearest 50p.

Pocket money, £x	Number of children, f
1.00	2
1.50	6
2.00	5
2.50	4
3.00	2
3.50	0
4.00	0
4.50	0
5.00	1

(i) State the mode.
(ii) Find the median.
(iii) Calculate the mid-range.
(iv) Estimate the mean using the statistics functions on your calculator.
(v) The parents of a 10-year-old are trying to decide how much pocket money to give their child. State, with reasons, the most appropriate form of average to help them.

3 The financial controller of a haulage company keeps a record of the number of hours, to the nearest hour, worked by the drivers in the company, all of whom receive the same hourly pay.

Hours worked, x	Number of drivers, f
$\leqslant 34$	0
35	12
36	34
37	25
38	46
$\geqslant 39$	0

(i) State the mode.
(ii) Find the median.
(iii) Estimate the mean using the statistics functions on your calculator.
(iv) State, with reasons, the most helpful form of average for the financial controller.

4 A school records the number of GCSE passes (grades A*–C) gained by a Year 11 class.

Number of GCSEs, x	Number of students, f
0–2	0
3	1
4	6
5	8
6	6
7	2
8	4
9+	0

(i) State the mode.
(ii) Find the median.
(iii) Calculate the mid-range.
(iv) Calculate the mean using the statistics functions on your calculator.
(v) State which of the averages is the most representative measure to give to prospective parents.

5 A seedsman is growing a new variety of seed to sell to a garden centre. He measures the heights, to the nearest millimetre, 5 days after they have germinated. The results are given below.

Height of seedlings, x	Number of seedlings, f
$\leqslant 7$	0
8	21
9	44
10	35
11	35
12	15
$\geqslant 13$	0

(i) State the mode.
(ii) Find the median.
(iii) Calculate the mid-range.
(iv) Calculate the mean using the statistics functions on your calculator.
(v) State which of the averages gives the seedsman the most useful information.

6 An ornithologist carries out a survey to see how many eggs thrushes are laying in order to help find the reason thrushes are declining in numbers. The vertical line chart below shows the number of eggs found in thrush nests.

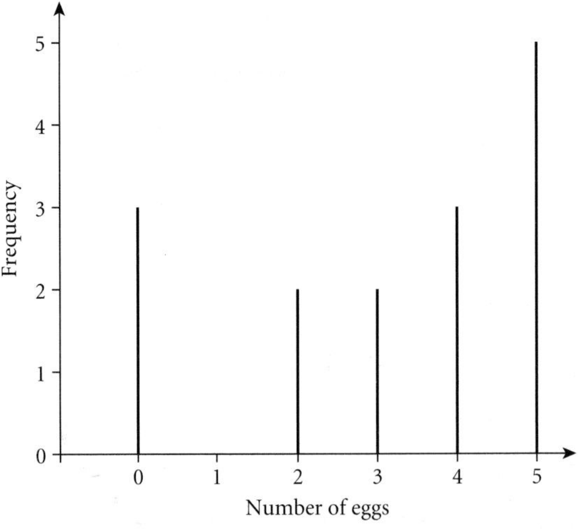

(i) State the mode, median and mid-range.
(ii) Calculate the mean using the statistics functions on your calculator.
(iii) State which of the averages is the most helpful measure.

Grouped data

Grouping means putting the data into a number of classes. The number of data items falling into any class is called the *frequency* for that class.

When numerical data are grouped, each item of data falls within a class interval lying between *class boundaries*.

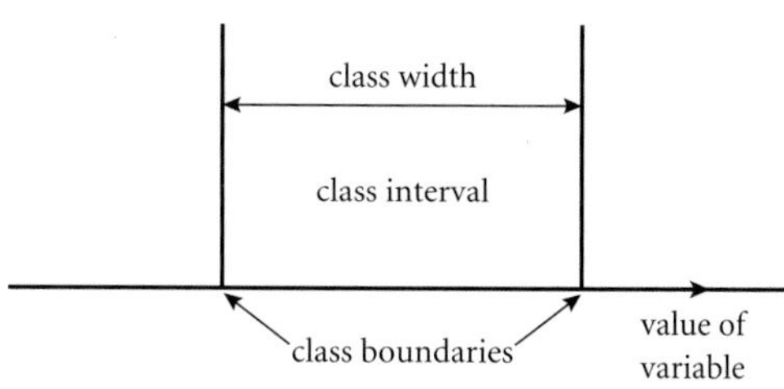

Figure 1.8

You must always be careful about the choice of class boundaries because it must be absolutely clear to which class any item belongs. A form with the following wording:

How old are you? Please tick one box.

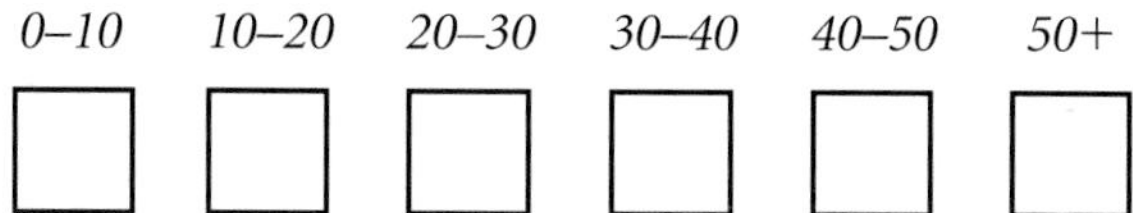

would cause problems. A ten-year-old could tick either of the first two boxes.

A better form of wording would be:

How old are you (in completed years)? Please tick one box.

0–9 10–19 20–29 30–39 40–49 50+

☐ ☐ ☐ ☐ ☐ ☐

Notice that this says 'in completed years'. Otherwise a $9\frac{1}{2}$-year-old might not know which of the first two boxes to tick.

Another way of writing this is:

$$0 \leqslant A < 10 \quad 10 \leqslant A < 20 \quad 20 \leqslant A < 30$$
$$30 \leqslant A < 40 \quad 40 \leqslant A < 50 \quad 50 \leqslant A$$

Even somebody aged 9 years and 364 days would clearly still come in the first group.

Another way of writing these classes, which you will sometimes see, is

0–, 10–, 20–, … , 50–

What is the disadvantage of this way?

Working with grouped data

There is often a good reason for grouping raw data.

- There may be a lot of data.
- The data may be spread over a wide range.
- Most of the values collected may be different.

Whatever the reason, grouping data should make it easier to analyse and present a summary of findings, whether in a table or in a diagram.

For some *discrete data* it may not be necessary or desirable to group them. For example, a survey of the number of passengers in cars using a busy road is unlikely to produce many integer values outside the range 0 to 4 (not counting the driver). However, there are cases when grouping the data (or perhaps constructing a stem-and-leaf diagram) are an advantage.

Discrete data

At various times during one week the number of cars passing a survey point was noted. Each item of data relates to the number of cars passing during a five-minute period. A hundred such periods were surveyed. The data are summarised in the following frequency table.

Number of cars, x	Frequency, f
0–9	5
10–19	8
20–29	13
30–39	20
40–49	22
50–59	21
60–70	11
Total	100

From the frequency table you can see there is a slight negative (or left) skew.

Estimating the mean

When data are grouped the individual values are lost. This is not often a serious problem; as long as the data are reasonably distributed throughout each interval it is possible to *estimate* statistics such as the mean, knowing that your answers will be reasonably accurate.

To estimate the mean you first assume that all the values in an interval are equally spaced about a mid-point. The mid-points are taken as representative values of the intervals.

The mid-value for the interval 0–9 is $\frac{0 + 9}{2} = 4.5$.

The mid-value for the interval 10–19 is $\frac{10 + 19}{2} = 14.5$, and so on.

The $x \times f$ column can now be added to the frequency distribution table and an estimate for the mean found.

Number of cars, *x* (mid-values)	**Frequency, *f***	$x \times f$
4.5	5	$4.5 \times 5 = 22.5$
14.5	8	$14.5 \times 8 = 116.0$
24.5	13	318.5
34.5	20	690.0
44.5	22	979.0
54.5	21	1144.5
65.0	11	715.0
Totals	100	3985.5

The mean is given by

$$\bar{x} = \frac{\sum xf}{\sum f}$$

$$= \frac{3985.5}{100} = 39.855$$

The original raw data, summarised in the above frequency table, are shown below.

10	18	68	67	25	62	49	11	12	8
9	46	53	57	30	63	34	21	68	31
20	16	29	13	31	56	9	34	45	55
35	40	45	48	54	50	34	32	47	60
70	52	21	25	53	41	29	63	43	50
40	48	45	38	51	25	52	55	47	46
46	50	8	25	56	18	20	36	36	9
38	39	53	45	42	42	61	55	30	38
62	47	58	54	59	25	24	53	42	61
18	30	32	45	49	28	31	27	54	38

In this form it is impossible to get an overview of the number of cars, nor would listing every possible value in a frequency table (0 to 70) be helpful.

However, grouping the data and estimating the mean was not the only option. Constructing a stem-and-leaf diagram and using it to find the median would have been another possibility.

? Is it possible to find estimates for the other measures of centre?
Find the mean of the original data and compare it to the estimate.

The data the reporter collected when researching his article on cycling accidents included the distance from home, in metres, of those involved in cycling accidents. In full these were as follows.

3000	75	1200	300	50	10	150	1500	250	25
200	4500	35	60	120	400	2400	140	45	5
1250	3500	30	75	250	1200	250	50	250	450
15	4000								

It is clear that there is considerable spread in the data. They are continuous data and the reporter is aware that they appear to have been rounded but he does not know to what level of precision. Consequently there is no way of reflecting the level of precision in setting the interval boundaries.

The reporter wants to estimate the mean and decides on the following grouping.

Location relative to home	**Distance, d, in metres**	**Distance mid-value, x**	**Frequency (number of accidents), f**	$x \times f$
Very close	$0 \leqslant d < 100$	50	12	600
Close	$100 \leqslant d < 500$	300	11	3 300
Not far	$500 \leqslant d < 1500$	1000	3	3 000
Quite far	$1500 \leqslant d < 5000$	3250	6	19 500
Totals			32	26 400

$$\bar{x} = \frac{26\,400}{32} = 825 \text{ m}$$

A summary of the measures of centre for the original and grouped accident data is given below.

	Raw data		**Grouped data**
Mean	$25\,785 \div 32 = 806$ m	Mean	825 m
Mode	250 m	Modal group	$0 \leqslant d < 100$ m
Median	$\frac{1}{2}(200 + 250) = 225$ m		
Mid-range	$\frac{1}{2}(5 + 4500) = 2252.5$ m		

Which measure of centre seems most appropriate for these data?

The reporter's article

The reporter decided that he had enough information and wrote the article below.

AVONFORD STAR

A council that does not care

The level of civilisation of any society can be measured by how much it cares for its most vulnerable members.

On that basis our town council rates somewhere between savages and barbarians. Every day they sit back complacently while those least able to defend themselves, the very old and the very young, run the gauntlet of our treacherous streets.

I refer of course to the lack of adequate safety measures for our cyclists, 60% of whom are children or senior citizens. Statistics show that they only have to put one wheel outside their front doors to be in mortal danger. 80% of cycling accidents happen within 1500 metres of home.

Last week Denise Cropper became the latest unwitting addition to these statistics. Luckily she is now on the road to recovery but that is no thanks to the members of our unfeeling council who set people on the road to death and injury without a second thought.

What, this paper asks our councillors, are you doing about providing safe cycle tracks from our housing estates to our schools and shopping centres? And what are you doing to promote safety awareness among our cyclists, young and old?

Answer: Nothing.

Is it a fair article? Is it justified, based on the available evidence?

Continuous data

For a statistics project Robert, a student at Avonford College, collected the heights of 50 female students.

He constructed a frequency table for his project and included the calculations to find an estimate for the mean of his data.

Height, h cm	Mid-value, x	Frequency, f	xf
$157 < h \leqslant 159$	158	4	632
$159 < h \leqslant 161$	160	11	1760
$161 < h \leqslant 163$	162	19	3078
$163 < h \leqslant 165$	164	8	1312
$165 < h \leqslant 167$	166	5	830
$167 < h \leqslant 169$	168	3	504
Totals		50	8116

$$\bar{x} = \frac{8116}{50}$$
$$= 162.32 \text{ cm}$$

Note: Class boundaries

His teacher was concerned about the class boundaries and asked Robert 'To what degree of accuracy have you recorded your data?' Robert told him 'I rounded all my data to the nearest centimetre'. Robert showed his teacher his raw data.

163	160	167	168	166	164	166	162	163	163
165	163	163	159	159	158	162	163	163	166
164	162	164	160	161	162	162	160	169	162
163	160	167	162	158	161	162	163	165	165
163	163	168	165	165	161	160	161	161	161

Robert's teacher said that the class boundaries should have been

$157.5 \leqslant h < 159.5$

$159.5 \leqslant h < 161.5$, and so on.

He explained that a height recorded to the nearest centimetre as 158 cm has a value in the interval 158 ± 0.5 cm (this can be written as $157.5 \leqslant h < 158.5$). Similarly the actual values of those recorded as 159 cm lie in the interval $158.5 \leqslant h < 159.5$. So, the interval $157.5 \leqslant h < 159.5$ covers the actual values of the data items 158 and 159. The interval $159.5 \leqslant h < 161.5$ covers the actual values of 160 and 161 and so on.

?

What adjustment does Robert need to make to his estimated mean in the light of his teacher's comments?

Find the mean of the raw data. What do you notice when you compare it with your estimate?

You are not always told the level of precision of summarised data and the class widths are not always equal, as the reporter for the *Avonford Star* discovered. Also, there are different ways of representing class boundaries, as the following example illustrates.

EXAMPLE 1.2

The frequency distribution shows the lengths of telephone calls made by Emily during August. Choose suitable mid-class values and estimate Emily's mean call time for August.

SOLUTION

Time (seconds)	Mid-value, x	Frequency, f	xf
0–	30	39	1170
60–	90	15	1350
120–	150	12	1800
180–	240	8	1920
300–	400	4	1600
500–1000	750	1	750
Totals		79	8590

$$\bar{x} = \frac{8590}{79}$$

$$= 109 \text{ seconds (3 s.f.)}$$

Notes

1 The interval '0–' can be written as $0 \leqslant x < 60$, the interval '60–' can be written as $60 \leqslant x < 120$, and so on, up to '500–1000' which can be written as $500 \leqslant x \leqslant 1000$.

2 There is no indication of the level of precision of the recorded data. They may have been recorded to the nearest second.

3 The class widths vary.

EXERCISE 1D

1 As part of a small mammals survey, an ecologist measures the length of the woodmice caught in a local wood. The results are shown in the table below.

Length, x (mm)	Frequency
$155 < x \leqslant 160$	4
$160 < x \leqslant 165$	5
$165 < x \leqslant 170$	10
$170 < x \leqslant 175$	10
$175 < x \leqslant 180$	9
$180 < x \leqslant 185$	13
$185 < x \leqslant 190$	12
$190 < x \leqslant 195$	2
$195 < x \leqslant 200$	0

Using suitable mid-class values, estimate the mean length of the woodmice in this survey.

2 A group of sixth-form students are carrying out a survey of pebbles on a beach. The length of each pebble is measured and recorded. The data are set out in the table below.

Length of pebbles, x (mm)	Frequency
$5 < x \leqslant 10$	3
$10 < x \leqslant 15$	7
$15 < x \leqslant 20$	16
$20 < x \leqslant 25$	12
$25 < x \leqslant 30$	15
$30 < x \leqslant 35$	12
$35 < x \leqslant 40$	9
$40 < x \leqslant 45$	8
$45 < x \leqslant 50$	4

(i) Comment on the spread of the data.

(ii) Estimate the mean of the grouped data by choosing suitable mid-interval values.

3 Piaget carried out tests on children for *conservation* of volume. A child who can *conserve* knows that when liquid is poured from a short fat beaker into a tall thin beaker there is still the same amount of liquid, despite appearances. A psychologist obtains the following experimental results.

Age, A (years)	% children who have just learned to conserve	Total % of children who can conserve
$A \leqslant 6$	0	
$6 < A \leqslant 6\frac{1}{2}$	3	
$6\frac{1}{2} < A \leqslant 7$	7	
$7 < A \leqslant 7\frac{1}{2}$	28	
$7\frac{1}{2} < A \leqslant 8$	42	
$8 < A \leqslant 8\frac{1}{2}$	15	
$8\frac{1}{2} < A \leqslant 9$	5	

(i) Copy and complete the table.

(ii) Estimate the mean age at which a child can first conserve.

4 The managing director of a large company wants to compare the monthly pay, £p, of the shop floor employees in two branches A and B. The finance departments of the branches provide these data.

Branch A

Salary range (£)	Number of employees
$400 < p \leqslant 600$	6
$600 < p \leqslant 800$	7
$800 < p \leqslant 1000$	9
$1000 < p \leqslant 1200$	10
$1200 < p \leqslant 1400$	14
$1400 < p \leqslant 1600$	10
$1600 < p \leqslant 2000$	7

Branch B

Salary range (£)	Number of employees
$400 < p \leqslant 600$	12
$600 < p \leqslant 800$	10
$800 < p \leqslant 1000$	9
$1000 < p \leqslant 1200$	7
$1200 < p \leqslant 1400$	7
$1400 < p \leqslant 1600$	6
$1600 < p \leqslant 2000$	4

(i) Estimate the mean monthly pay for each branch.

(ii) Compare the means and comment.

5 The house prices below have been obtained from local newspapers in North London and an area in Scotland. The results are for three-bedroom properties.

London

Price, p, in £1000s	Number of houses
$290 < p \leqslant 300$	12
$300 < p \leqslant 310$	10
$310 < p \leqslant 320$	8
$320 < p \leqslant 330$	0
$330 < p \leqslant 340$	2
$340 < p \leqslant 350$	1

Scotland

Price, p, in £1000s	Number of houses
$110 < p \leqslant 120$	1
$120 < p \leqslant 130$	5
$130 < p \leqslant 140$	8
$140 < p \leqslant 150$	13
$150 < p \leqslant 160$	8
$p \leqslant 170$	4

(i) Estimate the mean house price to the nearest £1000 for each area and compare them.

(ii) In the next year, the mean prices in London will rise by 10% and in Scotland by 4%. Calculate the mean house price to the nearest £1000 for both areas in a year's time.

6 A trading standards officer checks the weight of Ryeflake biscuits sold in packets that are supposed to contain 225 g. These are the results.

Weight, x (g)	Frequency (number of packets)
$223 \leqslant x < 224$	3
$224 \leqslant x < 225$	8
$225 \leqslant x < 226$	14
$226 \leqslant x < 227$	15
$227 \leqslant x < 228$	18
$228 \leqslant x < 229$	8

(i) Estimate the mean weight of the packets.

(ii) What would you expect the trading standards officer to say?

(iii) What advice would you give the company?

Measures of spread

In the last section you saw how an estimate for the mean can be found from grouped data. The mean is just one example of a *typical value* of a data set. You also saw how the mode and the median can be found from small data sets. The next chapter considers the use of the median as a *typical value* when dealing with grouped data and also the *interquartile range* as a *measure of spread.* In this chapter we will consider the range, the mean absolute deviation, the mean square deviation, the root mean square deviation, the variance and the standard deviation as measures of spread.

Range

The simplest measure of spread is the *range.* This is just the difference between the largest value in the data set (the upper extreme) and the smallest value (the lower extreme).

Range = largest − smallest

The figures below are the prices, in pence, of a 100 g jar of Nesko coffee in ten different shops.

161 161 163 163 167 168 170 172 172 172

The range for this data is

Range = 172 − 161 = 11p.

Be careful not to confuse the range, a measure of spread, with the mid-range, a measure of central tendency.

The mid-range for these data is $\frac{161 + 172}{2} = 166.5$p.

EXAMPLE 1.3

Ruth is investigating the amount of money students at Avonford College earn from part-time work on one particular weekend. She collects and orders data from two classes and this is shown below.

Class 1

10	10	10	10	10	10	12	15	15	15
16	16	16	16	18	18	20	25	38	90

Class 2

10	10	10	10	10	10	12	12	12	12
15	15	15	15	16	17	18	19	20	20
25	35	35							

She calculates the mean amount earned for each class. Her results are

Class 1: $\bar{x}_1 = £19.50$
Class 2: $\bar{x}_2 = £16.22$

She concludes that the students in Class 1 each earn about £3 more, on average, than do the students in Class 2.

Her teacher suggests she look at the spread of the data. What further information does this reveal?

SOLUTION

Ruth calculates the range for each class: Range (Class 1) = £80
Range (Class 2) = £25

She concludes that the part-time earnings in Class 1 are much more spread out.

However, when Ruth looks again at the raw data she notices that one student in Class 1 earned £90, considerably more than anybody else. If that item of data is ignored then the spread of data for the two classes is similar.

One of the problems with the range is that it is prone to the effect of extreme values.

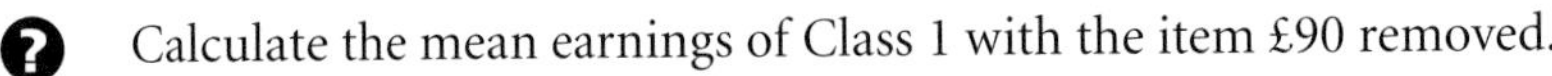

Calculate the mean earnings of Class 1 with the item £90 removed.

What can you conclude about the effect of extreme values on the mean?

The range does not use all of the available information; only the extreme values are used. In quality control this can be an advantage as it is very sensitive to something going wrong on a production line. Also the range is easy to calculate. However, usually we want a measure of spread that uses all the available data and that relates to a central value.

The mean absolute deviation

Kim and Joe play as strikers for two of Avonford's local football teams. They are hoping to be picked for the Avonford Town team who are due to play nearby Newton St Mary's in a friendly match. The team manager is considering their scoring records.

Kim's scoring record over ten matches looks like this:

0 1 0 3 0 2 0 0 0 4

Joe's record looks like this:

1 1 1 0 0 2 1 1 2 2

The mean scores are, for Kim, $\bar{x}_1 = 1$ and, for Joe, $\bar{x}_2 = 1.1$.

Looking first at Kim's data consider the differences, or *deviations*, of his scores from the mean.

Number of goals scored, x	0	1	0	3	0	2	0	0	0	4
Deviations $(x - \bar{x})$	-1	0	-1	2	-1	1	-1	-1	-1	3

To find a summary measure you need to combine the deviations in some way. If you just add them together they total zero.

Why does the sum of the deviations always total zero?

The mean absolute deviation ignores the signs and adds together the *absolute deviations*. The symbol $|d|$, tells you to take the positive, or absolute, value of d.

For example $|-2| = 2$ and $|2| = 2$.

It is now possible to sum the deviations

$$1 + 0 + 1 + 2 + 1 + 1 + 1 + 1 + 1 + 3 = 12,$$

the *total of the absolute deviations.*

It is important that any measure of spread is not linked to the sample size so you have to average out this total by dividing by the sample size.

In this case the sample size is 10. The *mean absolute deviation* $= \frac{12}{10} = 1.2$.

The mean absolute deviation from the mean $= \dfrac{1}{n}\sum|x - \bar{x}|$

For Joe's data the mean absolute deviation is

$$\tfrac{1}{10}(0.1 + 0.1 + 0.1 + 1.1 + 1.1 + 0.9 + 0.1 + 0.1 + 0.9 + 0.9) = 0.54$$

The average number of goals scored by Kim and Joe is similar (1.0 and 1.1) but Joe is less variable (or more consistent) in his goal scoring (0.54 compared to 1.2).

The mean absolute deviation is an acceptable measure of spread but is not widely used because it is difficult to work with. The *standard deviation* is more important mathematically and is more extensively used.

Sum of squares

An alternative to ignoring signs is to square the differences or deviations. The sum of the squares of the deviations is known as the *sum of squares* and is denoted by S_{xx}.

For n data values $x_1, x_2, \ldots, x_n$

$$S_{xx} = (x_1 - \bar{x})^2 + (x_2 - \bar{x})^2 + \ldots + (x_n - \bar{x})^2$$

$$= \sum_{i=1}^{n}(x_i - \bar{x})^2 \text{ which is often abbreviated to } \sum(x - \bar{x})^2.$$

It can be shown that S_{xx} is equivalent to $\sum_{i=1}^{n} x_i^2 - n\overline{x}^2$ or $\sum x^2 - n\overline{x}^2$. This alternative formulation may be easier to work with, depending on the nature of the data.

The equivalence of the two forms of S_{xx}, the sum of the squares of the deviations is given in the appendix on page 444.

The mean square deviation and root mean square deviation

The mean of the *sum of squares* is a measure of spread called the *mean square deviation* (*msd*). The square root of this gives the *root mean square deviation* (*rmsd*).

To find the mean square deviation of a data set

- find the sum of squares $\qquad S_{xx} = \sum(x - \overline{x})^2$ or $\sum x^2 - n\overline{x}^2$
- find their mean $\qquad msd = \dfrac{S_{xx}}{n}$.

So the root mean square deviation (*rmsd*) is given by $\sqrt{msd} = \sqrt{\dfrac{S_{xx}}{n}}$.

? Look carefully at both methods for calculating the mean square deviation. Are there any situations where one method might be preferred to the other?

For Kim's data, where $\overline{x} = 1$

- find the sum of squares

$$\begin{aligned} S_{xx} = \sum(x - \overline{x})^2 &= (0 - 1)^2 + (1 - 1)^2 + (0 - 1)^2 + \ldots + (4 - 1)^2 \\ &= 1 + 0 + 1 + 4 + 1 + 1 + 1 + 1 + 1 + 9 \\ &= 20 \end{aligned}$$

or

$$\begin{aligned} S_{xx} = \sum x^2 - n\overline{x}^2 &= 0^2 + 1^2 + 0^2 + \ldots + 4^2 - 10 \times 1^2 \\ &= 0 + 1 + 0 + \ldots + 16 - 10 \\ &= 20 \end{aligned}$$

- find their mean

$$msd = \frac{S_{xx}}{n} = \frac{20}{10} = 2.$$

So the $rmsd = \sqrt{msd} = \sqrt{2} = 1.41$ (to 3 s.f.).

(In terms of ease of computation, for Kim's data there is little difference between the two methods of computing S_{xx}.)

? How might you set your working out in a table?

For data given as a frequency distribution, the corresponding approach is given by

- find the sum of squares $S_{xx} = \sum(x - \bar{x})^2 f$ or $\sum x^2 f - n\bar{x}^2$
- find their mean $msd = \dfrac{S_{xx}}{n}$.

So the *rmsd* is given by $\sqrt{msd} = \sqrt{\dfrac{S_{xx}}{n}}$.

For Joe's data we use the frequency distribution of his scores and set out the working in a table.

x	f	xf	$(x-\bar{x})^2 f$	$x^2 f$
0	2	$0 \times 2 = 0$	$(0 - 1.1)^2 \times 2 = 2.42$	$0 \times 2 = 0$
1	5	$1 \times 5 = 5$	$(1 - 1.1)^2 \times 5 = 0.05$	$1 \times 5 = 5$
2	3	$2 \times 3 = 6$	$(2 - 1.1)^2 \times 3 = 2.43$	$4 \times 3 = 12$
Totals	10	11	4.90	17

Hence $n = \sum f \Rightarrow \bar{x} = \dfrac{\sum xf}{n} = \dfrac{11}{10} = 1.1$

- find the sum of squares
$$S_{xx} = \sum(x - \bar{x})^2 f = 4.9$$
or
$$S_{xx} = \sum x^2 f - n\bar{x}^2 = 17 - 10 \times 1.1^2 = 4.9$$
- find their mean
$$msd = \frac{S_{xx}}{n} = \frac{4.9}{10} = 0.49.$$

So the *rmsd* is given by $\sqrt{msd} = \sqrt{\dfrac{S_{xx}}{n}} = \sqrt{0.49} = 0.7$.

Comparing this to the *rmsd* of Kim's data (1.41), you can see that Joe's goal scoring is more consistent (or less variable) than Kim's. This confirms what was found when the mean absolute deviation was calculated for each data set.

The variance and standard deviation

In the last section you worked with the mean square deviation and the root mean square deviation as measures of spread. Here we explore related ideas which give rise to measures of spread called the *variance* and *standard deviation*.

In deriving the *msd* you divided the sum of squares of the deviations from the mean, S_{xx}, by n, representing the mean of the squares of the deviations. The variance and standard deviation are based on dividing S_{xx} by $n - 1$. The reason for this is that in calculating S_{xx} there are only $n - 1$ independent values of $(x - \bar{x})$ since $\sum(x - \bar{x}) = 0$. When all but one of these deviations have been calculated by subtracting $\bar{x}$ from each x value, the final value of $(x - \bar{x})$ may be deduced from the fact that $\sum(x - \bar{x}) = 0$.

Consider a data set of five values, namely 2, 7, 8, 11 and 12, then $\bar{x} = \frac{40}{5} = 8$.

The first four corresponding deviations from the mean are:

$$2 - 8 = -6, \quad 7 - 8 = -1, \quad 8 - 8 = 0 \quad \text{and} \quad 11 - 8 = 3.$$

The final deviation from the mean must be 4 to make the sum of the deviations zero. The final deviation, $12 - 8$, could be found directly but this is *not* necessary. The final deviation is *dependent* on the previous $n - 1$ deviations, so there are just $n - 1$ *independent* deviations.

Calculation of the *variance* (s^2) *and standard deviation* (s) follow similar lines to those for the mean square deviation and root mean square deviation, but using a divisor of $n - 1$.

To find the variance of a data set

- find the sum of squares $\quad S_{xx} = \sum(x - \bar{x})^2 \quad or \quad \sum x^2 - n\bar{x}^2$
- divide by $n - 1$ $\quad s^2 = \frac{S_{xx}}{n - 1}$.

So the standard deviation $\quad s = \text{variance} = \sqrt{\frac{S_{xx}}{n - 1}}$.

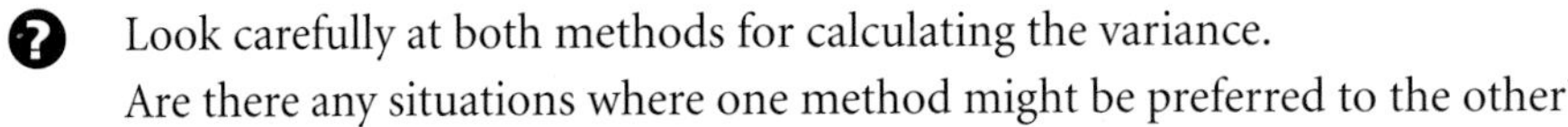

Look carefully at both methods for calculating the variance.
Are there any situations where one method might be preferred to the other?

For Kim's data:

- find the sum of squares $\quad S_{xx} = 20$
- divide by $n - 1$ $\quad s^2 = \frac{S_{xx}}{n - 1} = \frac{20}{9} = 2.22$ (to 3 s.f.).

So the standard deviation, $s = \sqrt{\frac{S_{xx}}{n - 1}} = \sqrt{2.22\ldots} = 1.49$ (to 3 s.f.).

For data given as a frequency distribution, the corresponding approach is given by

- find the sum of squares $\quad S_{xx} = \sum(x - \bar{x})^2 f \quad or \quad \sum x^2 f - n\bar{x}^2$
- divide by $n - 1$ $\quad s^2 = \frac{S_{xx}}{n - 1}$.

So the standard deviation, $s = \sqrt{\frac{S_{xx}}{n-1}}$.

Looking at Joe's data again.

x	f	xf	$(x - \bar{x})^2 f$	$x^2 f$
0	2	$0 \times 2 = 0$	$(0 - 1.1)^2 \times 2 = 2.42$	$0 \times 2 = 0$
1	5	$1 \times 5 = 5$	$(1 - 1.1)^2 \times 5 = 0.05$	$1 \times 5 = 5$
2	3	$2 \times 3 = 6$	$(2 - 1.1)^2 \times 3 = 2.43$	$4 \times 3 = 12$
Totals	10	11	4.90	17

Hence $n = \sum f \Rightarrow \bar{x} = \frac{\sum xf}{n} = \frac{11}{10} = 1.1$

- find the sum of squares $\quad S_{xx} = 4.9$
- divide by $n - 1$ $\quad s^2 = \frac{S_{xx}}{n-1} = \frac{4.9}{9} = 0.544$ (to 3 s.f.).

So the standard deviation, $s = \sqrt{\frac{S_{xx}}{n-1}} = \sqrt{0.544\ldots} = 0.738$ (to 3 s.f.).

Comparing this to the standard deviation of Kim's data (1.49), you can see that Joe's goal scoring is more consistent (or less variable) than Kim's. This is consistent with the previous conclusions when comparing the variability in their scoring record.

In practice you will make extensive use of your calculator's statistical functions to find the mean ($\bar{x}$), root mean square deviation (*rmsd*) and standard deviation (s).

Most calculators represent the mean by $\bar{x}$, but care must be taken when reading off either the root mean square deviation or the standard deviation. The symbols σ, σ_x or σ_n are sometimes used to represent the root mean square deviation, whilst S, s, σ_{n-1} or $\hat{\sigma}$ are sometimes used to represent the standard deviation.

The following examples involve finding or using the *rmsd* or *standard deviation.*

EXAMPLE 1.4

The following information relates to a sample of raw data.

$$n = 60, \qquad \sum x = 960, \qquad \sum x^2 = 18\,000.$$

Find the mean, root mean square deviation and standard deviation.

SOLUTION

$$\bar{x} = \frac{\sum x}{n} = \frac{960}{60} = 16$$

$S_{xx} = \sum x^2 - n\bar{x}^2 = 18\,000 - 60 \times 16^2 = 2640$

Root mean square deviation, $rmsd = \sqrt{\dfrac{S_{xx}}{n}} = \sqrt{\dfrac{2640}{60}} = \sqrt{44} = 6.63$ (to 3 s.f.)

Standard deviation, $s = \sqrt{\dfrac{S_{xx}}{n-1}} = \sqrt{\dfrac{2640}{59}} = \sqrt{44.745\,76\ldots} = 6.69$ (to 3 s.f.)

Note

Since n is fairly large, there is little difference between the values of the *rmsd* and s.

EXAMPLE 1.5

The following information relates to a frequency distribution.

$\sum f = 1000, \qquad \sum xf = 6100, \qquad \sum x^2 f = 42\,260.$

Find the mean, root mean square deviation and standard deviation.

SOLUTION

$n = \sum f = 1000,$

so $\bar{x} = \dfrac{\sum xf}{n} = \dfrac{6100}{1000} = 6.1$

$S_{xx} = \sum x^2 f - n\bar{x}^2 = 42\,260 - 1000 \times 6.1^2 = 5050$

Root mean square deviation, $rmsd = \sqrt{\dfrac{S_{xx}}{n}} = \sqrt{\dfrac{5050}{1000}} = \sqrt{5.05} = 2.25$ (to 3 s.f.)

Standard deviation, $s = \sqrt{\dfrac{S_{xx}}{n-1}} = \sqrt{\dfrac{5050}{999}} = \sqrt{5.055\ldots} = 2.25$ (to 3 s.f.)

Note

Since n is very large, the values of *rmsd* and s are equal, correct to 3 s.f. This illustrates the idea that as n gets larger, the values of the *rmsd* and s converge.

EXAMPLE 1.6

As part of her job as quality controller, Stella collected data relating to the life expectancy of a sample of 60 light bulbs produced by her company. The mean life was 650 hours and the *rmsd* was 8 hours. A second sample of 80 bulbs was taken by Sol and resulted in a mean life of 660 hours and *rmsd* 7 hours.

Find the overall mean and *rmsd*.

SOLUTION

Overall mean:

Mean of first sample × first sample size.

Mean of second sample × second sample size.

$$\overline{x} = \frac{\overline{x}_1 \times n + \overline{x}_2 \times m}{n + m}$$

Overall $\sum x$.

Total sample size.

$$\overline{x} = \frac{650 \times 60 + 660 \times 80}{60 + 80}$$

$$= \frac{91\,800}{140} = 655.71\ \dots$$

$$= 656 \text{ hours (3 s.f.)}$$

For Stella's sample the *msd* is 8^2. Therefore $8^2 = \dfrac{\sum x_1^2}{60} - 650^2$.

For Sol's sample the *msd* is 7^2. Therefore $7^2 = \dfrac{\sum x_2^2}{80} - 660^2$.

From the above Stella found that $\sum x_1^2 = (8^2 + 650^2) \times 60 = 25\,353\,840$ and $\sum x_2^2 = 34\,851\,920$.

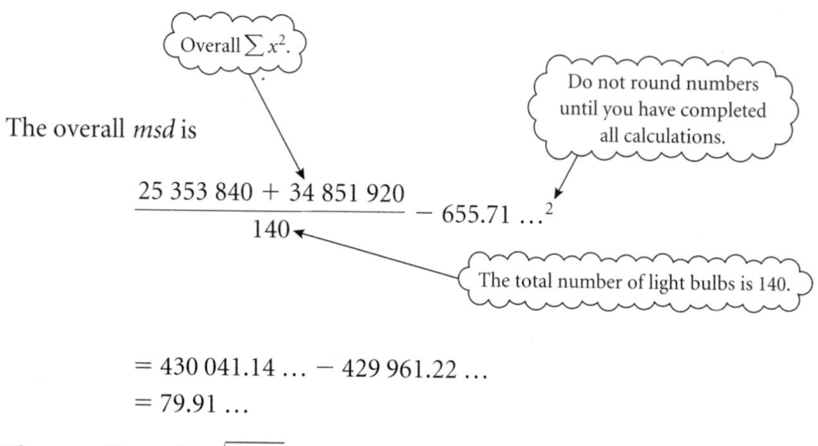
Overall $\sum x^2$.
Do not round numbers until you have completed all calculations.
The total number of light bulbs is 140.

The overall *msd* is

$$\frac{25\,353\,840 + 34\,851\,920}{140} - 655.71\ \dots^2$$

$$= 430\,041.14\ \dots - 429\,961.22\ \dots$$

$$= 79.91\ \dots$$

The overall *rmsd* is $\sqrt{79.91\ \dots} = 8.94$ hours (3 s.f.)

? Carry out the calculation above using rounded numbers. That is, use 656 for the overall mean rather than 655.71 …. What do you notice?

The standard deviation and outliers

Data sets may contain extreme values and when this occurs you are faced with the problem of how to deal with them.

Many data sets are samples drawn from parent populations which are normally distributed. In these cases approximately:

- 68% of the values lie within 1 standard deviation of the mean
- 95% lie within 2 standard deviations of the mean
- 99.75% lie within 3 standard deviations of the mean.

You will learn more about the normal distribution in *Statistics 2*. If a particular value is *more than two standard deviations from the mean* it should be investigated as possibly not belonging to the data set. If it is as much as three standard deviations or more from the mean then the case to investigate it is even stronger.

The 2-standard-deviation test is one of several ways of defining outliers. It is a way of identifying those values which it might be worth looking at more closely. They should only be discarded if found to be invalid.

In an A level German class the examination marks at the end of the year are shown below.

35 52 55 61 96 63 50 58 58 49 61

The value 96 was thought to be significantly greater than the other values. The mean and standard deviation of the data are $\overline{x} = 58$ and $s = 14.9$. The value 96 is more than two standard deviations above the mean:

$58 - 2 \times 14.9$	$58 - 14.9$	mean	$58 + 14.9$	$58 + 2 \times 14.9$	
$= 28.2$	$= 43.1$	$= 58$	$= 72.9$	$= 87.8$	96

Figure 1.9

When investigated further it turned out that the mark of 96 was achieved by a German boy whose family had moved to Britain and who had taken A level German because he wanted to study German at university. It might be appropriate to omit this value from the data set.

Calculate the mean and standard deviation of the data with the value 96 left out. Investigate the value using your new mean and standard deviation.

The times taken, in minutes, for some train journeys between Hereford and Shrewsbury were recorded as shown.

56 61 57 55 58 57 5 60 61 59

It is unnecessary here to calculate the mean and standard deviation. The value 5 minutes is obviously a mistake and should be omitted unless it is possible to correct it by referring to the original source of data.

EXERCISE 1E

1 A group of sixth-form students want to investigate whether the growth of a seaweed called *pelvicia canaliculata* is affected by the environment in which it grows. Two samples were collected, one from an exposed position and the other from a sheltered position. The length, in millimetres, of the longest frond on each piece of seaweed was measured and recorded.

Length of longest frond in sheltered position	Length of longest frond in exposed position
8	3.5
10	2
11	1
9	1
13	3
9	1
8	3
9	2.5
12	1
14	2.52

Calculate the mean length and the standard deviation of each set of data. Comment on your results.

2 A company which manufactures floppy disks is concerned that the quality of disks produced is substandard. They take a sample of disks and assess the number of bad sectors they each contain. The following data are recorded for a random sample of disks.

Percentage of bad sectors, p	Mid-interval value	Number of disks
$0 < p \leqslant 20$	10	2
$20 < p \leqslant 40$		5
$40 < p \leqslant 60$		12
$60 < p \leqslant 80$		8
$80 < p \leqslant 100$		7

(i) Copy and complete the table and calculate the mean and the standard deviation of the data.

(ii) A sample of disks is taken from a different batch on a different day. Both samples have the same mean. The standard deviation of the second sample is half the standard deviation of the first sample. What does this indicate about the quality of the two sets of disks?

3 A car manufacturer has two speedometers to choose from. Below are the results of tests using the speedometers at a speed of 40 miles per hour.

Test	1	2	3	4
Speedometer A	40.6	41	42.2	39.6
Speedometer B	38.9	41.5	40.8	43.2

Calculate the mean and root mean square deviation for each speedometer and comment.

4 A winegrower holds a wine tasting evening to see which of her two new wines is the more popular. She asks six people to taste the wine and give each wine a score between 1 and 5. A score of 5 means the taster liked the wine. The results are given below.

Taster	1	2	3	4	5	6
Wine 1	4	4	3	4	2	4
Wine 2	5	4	2	1	5	4

(i) Calculate the mean and the standard deviation for each wine.

(ii) Compare people's reactions to the two wines.

5 In a survey of the number of hours, x, worked per day, the results for 14 students are summarised by $\sum x = 126$ and $\sum x^2 = 1230$.

(i) Calculate the mean number of hours worked and the standard deviation.

Another set of data from 9 different students has a mean of 6.78 hours and a standard deviation of 2.048 hours.

(ii) Find

(a) the total number of hours worked by all 23 students

(b) the mean number of hours worked by them

(c) the overall standard deviation for the 23 students.

6 A market gardener grows two varieties of potato, King Edward and Desiree, to sell to a supermarket. She wants to analyse the weights, w grams, of the potatoes for each type. Below are the results for samples of each type.

Weight of potato, w (g)	**Mid-interval value**	**King Edward**	**Desiree**
$0 < w \leqslant 100$	50	6	5
$100 < w \leqslant 200$		8	8
$200 < w \leqslant 300$		13	12
$300 < w \leqslant 400$		15	5
$400 < w \leqslant 500$		9	7
$500 < w \leqslant 600$		5	5

(i) Copy and complete the table.

(ii) For each type of potato, estimate the mean and standard deviation.

(iii) Give reasons to say which variety is better for selling to the supermarket.

7 A psychologist wants to test which out of the '*look and say*' and the '*phonic*' methods of teaching reading is better. The '*look and say*' method is when the words are written on cards and the child learns the shape of the word. Using '*phonics*' involves building up the word from the sounds the letters make. He uses a test of 20 words and records the number of correctly read words. He tests six children at a school using the '*look and say*' method and six similar children at a school using the '*phonic*' method. His results are shown in the table.

'Look and say'	9	11	12	13	14	9
'Phonic'	12	12	16	14	15	14

(i) Calculate the mean and standard deviation of the reading score for each method.

(ii) Which method is better for these children?

8 A frequency diagram for a set of data is shown below.

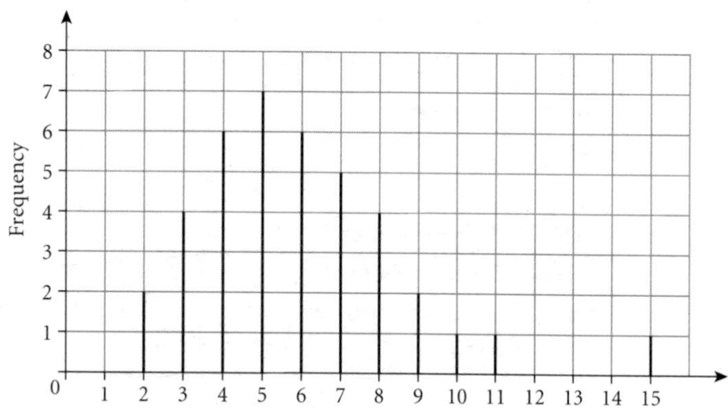

(i) Find the median and the mode of the data.

(ii) Given that the mean is 5.95 and the standard deviation is 2.58, explain why the value 15 may be regarded as an outlier.

(iii) Explain how you would treat the outlier if the diagram represents

(a) the ages (in completed years) of children at a party

(b) the sums of the scores obtained when throwing a pair of dice.

(iv) Find the median and the mode of the data after the outlier is removed.

(v) Without doing any calculations state what effect, if any, removing the outlier would have on the mean and on the standard deviation.

(vi) Does the diagram exhibit positive skewness, negative skewness or no skewness? How is the skewness affected by removing the outlier?

[MEI]

9 A small business has 12 employees. Their weekly wages, £x, are summarised by $\sum x = £2501$ and $\sum x^2 = £525\,266.8$.

(i) Calculate the mean and the standard deviation of the employees' weekly wages.

A second business has 17 employees. Their weekly wages, £y, have a mean of £273.20 and a standard deviation of £23.16.

(ii) Find $\sum y$ and show that $\sum y^2 = £1\,277\,432.25$.

(iii) Now consider all 29 employees as a single group. Find the mean and the standard deviation of their weekly wages.

[MEI]

AVONFORD STAR

Human computer has it figured

Avonford schoolboy, Simon Newton, astounded his classmates and their parents at a school open evening when he calculated the average of a set of numbers in seconds while everyone else struggled with their adding up.

Mr Truscott, a parent of one of the other children, said, 'I was still looking for my calculator when Simon wrote the answer on the board'.

Simon modestly said when asked about his skill 'It's simply a matter of choosing the most suitable code'.

The Avonford Star wants to know 'What is the secret of your code, Simon?'

Without a calculator, see if you can match Simon's performance. The data is repeated below.

Send your result and how you did it into the Avonford Star. Don't forget – no calculators!

Number	Frequency
3510	6
3512	4
3514	3
3516	1
3518	2
3520	4

Simon gave a big clue about how he calculated the mean so quickly. He said 'It's simply a matter of choosing the most suitable code'. Simon noticed that subtracting 3510 from each value simplified the data significantly. This is how he did his calculations.

Number, x	$y = x - 3510$	Frequency, f	$y \times f$
3510	0	6	$0 \times 6 = 0$
3512	2	4	$2 \times 4 = 8$
3514	4	3	$4 \times 3 = 12$
3516	6	1	$6 \times 1 = 6$
3518	8	2	$8 \times 2 = 16$
3520	10	4	$10 \times 4 = 40$
Totals		20	82

$$\text{Average (mean)} = \frac{82}{20} = 4.1$$

3510 is now added back. → $3510 + 4.1 = 3514.1$

Linear coding

Simon was using *linear coding* to ease his arithmetic.
Coding is used for two reasons:

- to simplify messy arithmetic
- to convert between different units.

Consider again Robert's data on the heights of female students.

Height, h (cm) mid-points	**Frequency, f**
158.5	4
160.5	11
162.5	19
164.5	8
166.5	5
168.5	3
Total	50

The arithmetic involved in calculating the mean and the standard deviation can be simplified considerably as follows:

The h values are replaced by x values, which are found by

(i) subtracting 158.5 from the h values,

then further simplifying the resulting values, 0, 2, 4, 6, 8 and 10, by

(ii) dividing by 2, giving 0, 1, 2, 3, 4 and 5.

Height, h (cm) mid-points	x	**Frequency, f**	xf	x^2f
158.5	$158.5 - 158.5 = 0 \div 2 = 0$	4	0	0
160.5	$160.5 - 158.5 = 2 \div 2 = 1$	11	11	11
162.5	$162.5 - 158.5 = 4 \div 2 = 2$	19	38	76
164.5	$164.5 - 158.5 = 6 \div 2 = 3$	8	24	72
166.5	4	5	20	80
168.5	5	3	15	75
Totals		50	108	314

$$\bar{x} = \frac{108}{50} = 2.16 \text{ cm}$$

$$s^2 = \frac{314 - 50 \times 2.16^2}{49} = 1.6473 \ldots$$

$$s = 1.28 \text{ cm}$$

In this example the data has been *coded* as $x = \dfrac{h - 158.5}{2}$.

From this, $h = 2x + 158.5$

$\therefore\ \bar{h} = 2\bar{x} + 158.5$ and $s_h = 2s_x$.

You can now find the mean and standard deviation of the original data.

$$\bar{h} = 2 \times 2.16 + 158.5 = 162.8 \text{ cm}$$
$$s_h = 2 \times 1.28 = 2.56 \text{ cm}$$

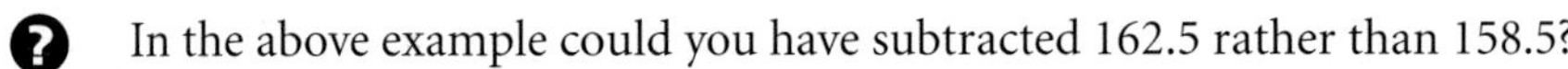

In the above example could you have subtracted 162.5 rather than 158.5?

The following example illustrates how linear coding can be used to convert between units.

EXAMPLE 1.7

For a period of ten days during August the mean temperature in Gresham, Oregon, was 80° Fahrenheit. The standard deviation during that period (in degrees Fahrenheit) was 0.7°F. Find the mean temperature and the standard deviation in degrees Celsius.

SOLUTION

The conversion formula is $c = \dfrac{5(f - 32)}{9}$

$\left(\text{which can be written as } c = \dfrac{5f}{9} - \dfrac{160}{9}\right)$.

So $\quad \bar{c} = \dfrac{5 \times 80}{9} - \dfrac{160}{9} = \dfrac{240}{9}$

$$= 26\tfrac{2}{3}\text{°C} \quad \text{or} \quad 26.7\text{°C}$$

Subtracting 32 does not affect the spread so the standard deviation is

$$s_c = \tfrac{5}{9} \times s_f = \frac{5 \times 0.7}{9} = 0.4\text{°C}$$

The coded values are easy to calculate, even without a calculator!

In general, if the coded value, x, is given by a linear equation (or code) of the form $x = \frac{y - a}{b}$, then the original value, y, can be found using the equation $y = a + bx$. And, if $\bar{x}$ and s_x are the mean and standard deviation of the coded x values, then $\bar{y}$ and s_y, the mean and the standard deviation of the original data, the y values, can be found using $\bar{y} = a + b\bar{x}$ and $s_y = bs_x$.

Look back at Robert's data on the heights of female students and check that Robert used $a = 158.5$ and $b = 2$ to code his data.

EXERCISE 1F

1 A physics student has obtained the following set of temperatures. They are measured in degrees Celsius.

25 56 45 98 67 55 −40 −22

(i) Calculate the mean and standard deviation of the temperatures.

(ii) Calculate the mean temperature in degrees Kelvin. (0° Celsius is 273° Kelvin and 100° Celsius is 373° Kelvin.)

(iii) Find the standard deviation of the set of temperatures in degrees Kelvin.

2 A motorcycle dealer takes a sample of the specialist bikes he has for sale. Their prices are as follows.

£5500	£6700	£7500	£8600
£12 850	£6500	£12 500	£11 350

(i) Calculate the mean and the standard deviation of these prices to the nearest pound.

The dealer now has to convert the prices into euros as he is considering selling bikes in Europe.

(ii) Using 1 euro = £0.67, calculate the rate of exchange for pounds into euros to the nearest cent and call this a.

(iii) Using the coding $E = aP$ where E represents the cost in euros and P represents the cost in pounds sterling, calculate the mean price and the standard deviation in euros to the nearest euro.

3 Two infant schools, P and Q, send children to the same primary school. Both infant schools teach their students to read but the primary school find that those children from school Q score more highly on standard tests than those from school P. They find that to be fair to students from school P, their scores, x, have to be adjusted using the rule $y = 1.1x + 10$. This makes the means and standard deviations of the children's scores from the two schools the same.

The mean mark for the students from school P is 40 and the standard deviation is 6.

Calculate the mean mark and the standard deviation for the students from school Q.

4 A company make a board game for teenage children. However, they find that younger children like to play too but are disappointed that they always get low scores and lose. The company decide to produce a simple rule so younger children can increase their scores and compete with older children. Trials are carried out where many children play the game and send their scores into the company. The scores are summarised below.

	Mean score	Standard deviation
Young players	35	3
Teenage players	60	6

The company decide to multiply the younger person's score by 2 and subtract 20.

(i) Investigate, using suitable calculations, whether the rule the company is using is fair or not.

(ii) Suggest a better rule.

5 A random sample of 50 television advertisements was taken and their lengths, x seconds, were recorded. The distribution is illustrated by the histogram below.

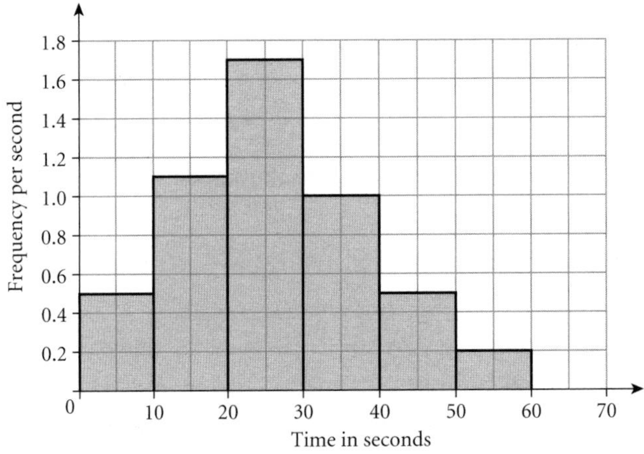

(i) Show that the frequency in the 0–10 class interval is 5. Find the remaining frequencies. Hence illustrate the data by a cumulative frequency graph.

(ii) Use your cumulative frequency graph to find the 10th and 90th percentiles. What proportion of the data lies between these two times?

(iii) Calculate estimates of the mean and standard deviation of the length of advertisements.

It was later found that the times recorded within each interval were in fact at the upper class boundary for that interval.

(iv) State, with a reason, how this information would affect your answers to part **(iii)**.

[MEI]

6 Over a period of time, a teacher recorded the number of times, x, each of the 20 students in the mathematics class was absent. The distribution was as follows.

Number of times absent, x	0	1	2	3	4	5	6	7	8	9	10	11 or more
Number of students, f	4	6	3	2	0	2	0	1	1	0	1	0

$\sum f = 20 \qquad \sum fx = 53 \qquad \sum fx^2 = 299$

(i) Illustrate the data using a suitable diagram.

(ii) State the mode and find the median for the data set.

(iii) Calculate the mean and the standard deviation of the data set.

During this period of time, there were 30 mathematics lessons. The teacher needs to analyse the distribution of the number of times each student was *present* during the 30-lesson session.

(iv) Without creating a new frequency distribution, deduce values for the mean and standard deviation of the numbers of times students were present. Describe the shape of the new distribution.

There are 12 boys and 8 girls in the class. The mean of the numbers of times boys were *absent* was 3, and the standard deviation was also 3.

(v) Show that the mean of the numbers of times girls were absent is 2.125.

(vi) Find the standard deviation of the numbers of times girls were absent.

[MEI]

EXERCISE 1G MIXED EXERCISE

1 A study of rats was conducted to find out whether environmental inputs could affect brain growth. A researcher took a group of 24 rats at birth and randomly assigned them to one of two groups. The first group was raised in a stimulating environment with toys etc. but the rats in the other group lived alone in dimly lit cages. All the animals received the same diet. After 90 days the weight of each rat's cortex was weighed in grams. The results are shown below.

Group 1 Stimulating environment	2.4	2.2	2.3	3.3	2.1	2.0	2.4	2.1	2.2	2.2	2.4	2.0
Group 2 Unstimulating environment	1.9	1.7	1.7	1.6	1.8	1.8	1.9	1.7	2.0	1.6	1.7	1.9

(i) Find the mean, median and modal values for each group of rats. Give your answers to 2 decimal places.

(ii) Comment on the results.

(iii) Calculate the standard deviation for each group.

(iv) Comment on the standard deviations.

(v) What conclusion would the researcher reach?

2 George records the time he spends per day surfing the internet for the first three weeks of May. The times, given to the nearest minute, are as follows.

0	26	13	5	18	12	35
24	61	16	10	26	15	0
0	73	21	17	16	42	32

(i) Illustrate the data using a sorted stem-and-leaf diagram with eight stems. Comment briefly on the shape of the distribution.

(ii) Find the mode, median and mean, commenting on their relative usefulness as measures of central tendency for this data set.

(iii) Calculate the standard deviation and hence find any outliers.

(iv) George's Dad claims that he is spending too much time on the internet. He tells George to reduce his usage so that the mean daily time for May is 20% less than the current mean.
What is the maximum total time George can spend surfing the internet for the remaining 10 days of May?

[MEI]

3 One day Sarah does ten practice laps at a go-kart track. Her mean lap time is 21.6 seconds.
Another day her mean time for fourteen practice laps is 21.5 seconds.

(i) Calculate the mean time in seconds for all 24 laps. Give your answer to 2 decimal places.

(ii) The median lap time for all 24 laps is 23.0 seconds and, when the times are rounded to the nearest second, the mode is 24.0 seconds.
Comment on the shape of the distribution for all 24 laps and explain how an extra lap time of 29.0 seconds would affect the mean, mode and median.

4 A sports coach is organising trials so he can choose the best runners for the 100-metre race in the district sports event. Each child runs three trials and the coach calculates the mean time for each child. The boys' times, in seconds, are given below.

David	Ravin	Stephen	Henry	Ahmed	Mark
17.5	16.9	17.9	18.2	16.9	18.5
18.0	17.2	18.3	17.9	17.2	17.8
17.8	17.0	18.1	18.1	17.1	18.1

(i) Calculate the mean time for each boy.

(ii) Which three boys should the coach choose?

The coach also has the girls' results but has lost some of the individual times.

Sally	Heidi	Comfort	Angela	Ketaki	Lois
18.4	21.5	17.2	19.1	18.2	20.0
18.2	?	17.2	19.2	17.9	19.2
?	20.5	?	19.3	17.6	?
Mean 18.4	Mean 20.8	Mean 17.2	Mean ?	Mean ?	Mean 19.2

(iii) Calculate the missing times.

5 A biologist is investigating whether the morphology of *Nucella lapillus*, commonly called the dog whelk, is affected by different levels of exposure. Samples were collected from an exposed and a sheltered shoreline where the *Nucella lapillus* are found. The height and apertures, in millimetres, of each dog whelk were recorded for both samples and the height to aperture ratio calculated.

The aperture is where the foot protrudes from the shell. The whelk clings to the rock using its foot. The foot is the only part of the whelk that is not protected by the shell.

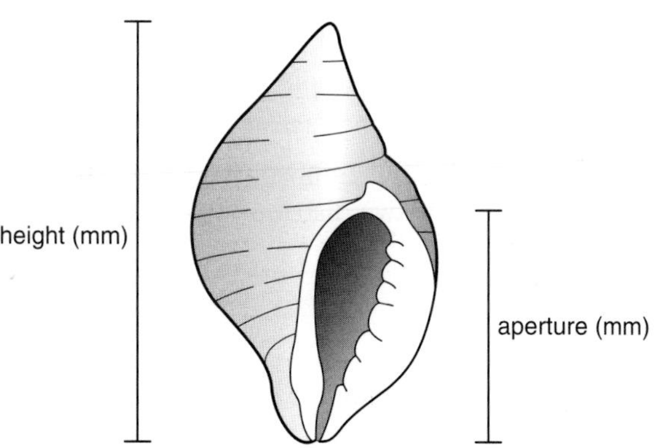

Nucella lapillus

Results for the *Nucella lapillus* height to aperture ratio on the sheltered shore

$$\sum x = 130.41, \quad n = 70, \quad \sum x^2 = 244.69$$

Results for the *Nucella lapillus* height to aperture ratio on the exposed shore

$$\sum x = 113.71, \quad n = 70, \quad \sum x^2 = 189.32$$

(i) Calculate the mean length to aperture ratio for each sample and suggest why there might be a difference.

(ii) Calculate the standard deviation for each sample of length to aperture ratios. Comment on the results.

6 A boys' school displays a list of the names and ages of all former students who died in the First and Second World Wars. The school has summarised the data in this table.

Age at death	Number of former students who died in WW1	Number of former students who died in WW2
17	4	0
18–20	32	9
21–24	15	23
25–28	8	17
29–32	8	8
33–40	5	7
41–50	2	3

First World War	Second World War
Minimum age at death = 17	Minimum age at death = 18
Maximum age at death = 47	Maximum age at death = 48

(i) State the mid-values of the intervals in the table.

(ii) Estimate the mean age at death in each of the two World Wars, giving each answer to the nearest whole year.

(iii) Calculate the mid-range age at death in each of the two World Wars.

(iv) Explain why the mid-ranges are not particularly close to the means.

(v) Comment on the two distributions.

Historical note

For most of the First World War, the minimum age for joining the army was 18 but this was reduced to 17 in 1918, just before the end of the war. However, throughout the war many brave boys gave false ages and joined up before they were 18.

7 The figures in the table below are the ages, to the nearest year, of a random sample of 30 people negotiating a mortgage with a bank.

29 26 31 42 38	36 39 49 40 32	33 31 33 52 44
45 35 37 38 38	32 34 27 61 29	32 30 38 42 33

Copy and complete the following stem-and-leaf diagram. Use the diagram to identify two features of the shape of the distribution.

$n = 30$

4 | 4 represents 44 years

2* |
3 |
3* |

Find the mean age of the 30 people. Given that 18 of them are men and that the mean age of the men is 37.72, find the mean age of the 12 women.

[MEI]

8 The first paragraph of the children's book *Stig of the Dump* contains 107 words. The number of letters per word is summarised in the following table.

Word length (x)	1	2	3	4	5	6	7	8	9	10
Frequency (f)	2	15	30	23	14	12	6	1	3	1

$\sum f = 107, \sum fx = 443, \sum fx^2 = 2183.$

(i) Illustrate the distribution of word lengths by a suitable diagram.

(ii) State the mode, median and mid-range of the data. What feature of the distribution accounts for the different values of these quantities?

(iii) Calculate the mean and standard deviation of the data. Hence identify the outliers and discuss briefly whether or not they should be excluded from the sample.

A passage of an adult fiction book was analysed in a similar way. The mean number of letters per word was 5.07 and the standard deviation was 2.62.

(iv) Compare the word lengths in the two passages of writing, commenting briefly on the differences.

[MEI]

KEY POINTS

1 Categorical data are non-numerical; discrete data can be listed; continuous data can be measured to any degree of accuracy and it is not possible to list all values.

2 Stem-and-leaf-diagrams (or stemplots) are suitable for discrete or continuous data. All data values are retained as well as indicating properties of the distribution.

3 The mean, median, mode or modal class and the mid-range are measures of central tendency.

- The mean, $\bar{x} = \dfrac{\sum x}{n}$; for grouped data $\bar{x} = \dfrac{\sum xf}{n}$.
- The median is the mid-value when the data are presented in rank order; it is the value of the $\dfrac{n+1}{2}$th item of n data items.
- The mode is the most common item of data. The modal class is the class containing the most data, when the classes are of equal width.
- The mid-range $= \frac{1}{2}$(minimum data value + maximum data value).

4 The range, mean square deviation, root mean square deviation, variance and standard deviation are measures of spread or dispersion.

- The range = maximum data value − minimum data value.
- The sum of squares $S_{xx} = \sum(x - \bar{x})^2$ *or* $\sum x^2 - n\bar{x}^2$; for grouped data $S_{xx} = \sum(x - \bar{x})^2 f$ *or* $\sum x^2 f - n\bar{x}^2$.
- The mean square deviation, $msd = \dfrac{S_{xx}}{n}$.
- The root mean square deviation, $rmsd = \sqrt{msd} = \sqrt{\dfrac{S_{xx}}{n}}$.
- The variance, $s^2 = \dfrac{S_{xx}}{n-1}$.
- The standard deviation, $s = \sqrt{\text{variance}} = \sqrt{\dfrac{S_{xx}}{n-1}}$.

5 An item of data x may be identified as an outlier if $|x - \bar{x}| > 2s$; that is, if x is more than two standard deviations above or below the sample mean.

6 If data, represented by the variable x, are coded as $y = a + bx$, then the mean ($\bar{y}$) and standard deviation (s_y) of the coded data are

$$\bar{y} = a + b\bar{x} \text{ and } s_y = bs_x.$$

2 Data presentation and related measures of centre and spread

A picture is worth a thousand numbers.

Anon

AVONFORD STAR

Avonford top e-mail users league

Of a sample of 600 people surveyed in Avonford, 480 had their own e-mail address. They gained access to the Web via their own computers or through cable television. 95 people used their mobile phones to send and receive e-mails. 46 respondents sometimes used Avonford's Cyber Cafe. Samples were also taken in other towns of similar population size.

Of a sample of 720 people surveyed in Downlee only 29% had their own e-mail address.

Avonford residents' use of the Web varied from less than 1 hour per week to 12 hours per week. 50% of those who had their own e-mail address spent at least 8 hours on line each week compared to 20% of Downlee e-mailers.

Avonford's Mayor said today, 'This is very encouraging. I am optimistic that good use will be made of Avonford's own Web page.' Avonford's Web page can be found at www.avonford.town.ac.uk

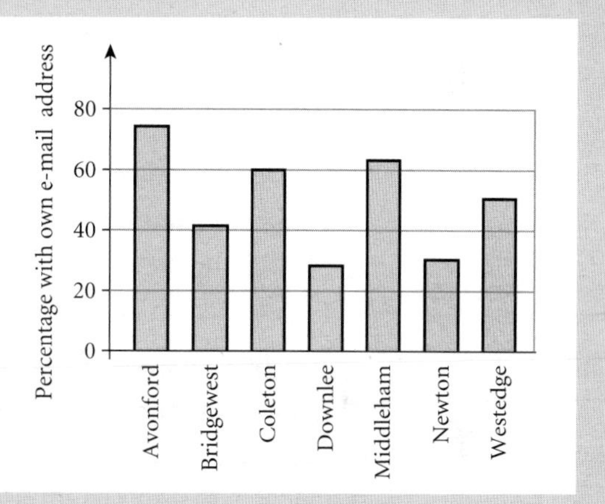

? How many Downlee residents have their own e-mail address?
How many Avonford residents use the Web for at least eight hours per week?

Some of the data the *Avonford Star* used in the article came from this table.

Town	Avonford	Bridgewest	Coleton	Downlee	Middleham	Newton	Westedge
Sample size	660	500	884	720	994	600	813
% with own e-mail	73	41	60	29	62	33	50

Most raw data need to be summarised to make it easier to see any patterns that may be present. You will often want to draw a diagram too. The *Avonford Star* used the table above to construct the first diagram.

In Chapter 1 you saw some ways of illustrating data. For example, a frequency distribution table makes it immediately obvious where data are concentrated or if there are extreme values that need consideration. You also saw how data could be represented using a stem-and-leaf diagram. This method allows you to retain individual data values and at the same time present a picture of the distribution.

You will often want to use a diagram to communicate statistical findings. People find diagrams a very useful and easy way of presenting and understanding statistical information.

Bar charts and vertical line charts

It is best to use bar charts to illustrate categorical data and vertical line charts to illustrate discrete data, although people on occasion use them the other way round. The height of each bar or line represents the frequency.

If bars are used there should be gaps between the bars. The widths and areas of the bars have no significance, but all the bars should be the same width to avoid distorting the picture of the data.

The political parties of the members of the Select Committee for Education and Employment, August 1999 (see page 14) are represented in the bar chart shown in figure 2.1. It is immediately obvious that the Labour party has a majority membership of this committee.

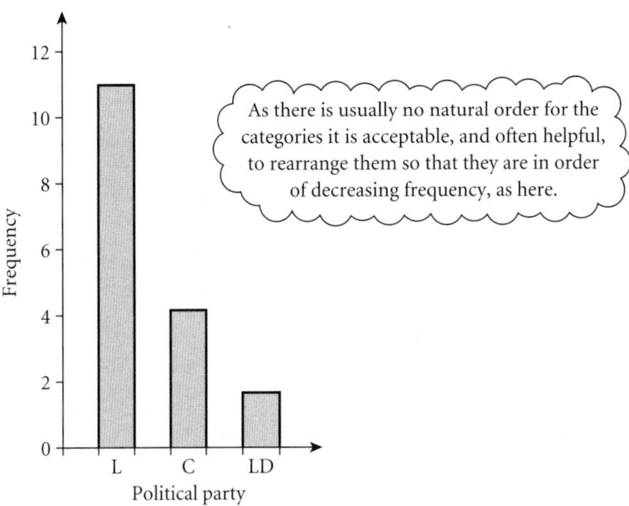
Frequency
0
2
4
6
8
10
12
L
C
LD
Political party
As there is usually no natural order for the categories it is acceptable, and often helpful, to rearrange them so that they are in order of decreasing frequency, as here.

Figure 2.1 *A bar chart illustrating categorical data*

Rachel plays cricket for the Avonford Amazons Cricket Club. During her first season, in which she batted and bowled for the team, she summarised her batting record in the following diagram.

Even though a bar chart might be used in this example, a line chart is preferable as it shows quite clearly that the scores can only take integer values.

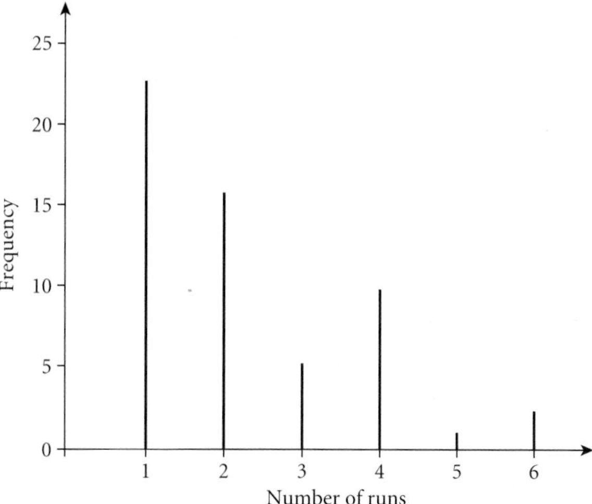

Figure 2.2 *A vertical line chart illustrating discrete data*

There are many different ways of drawing bar charts. The bars can be horizontal or vertical. The bars can also be subdivided. A compound bar chart is shown in figure 2.3. Often there is no single right way of displaying the information; what is most important is that it should be easy to follow and not misleading.

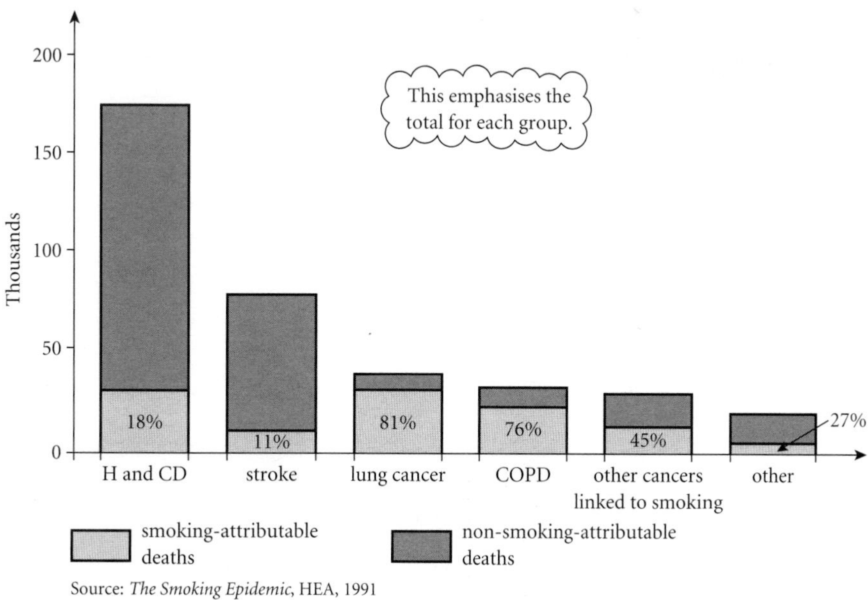

Figure 2.3 *Compound bar chart showing smoking- and non-smoking-attributable deaths*

Figure 2.4 shows a multiple bar chart comparing the level of sales of three products of a company over a period of four years. Note that there is a gap between the information for each year.

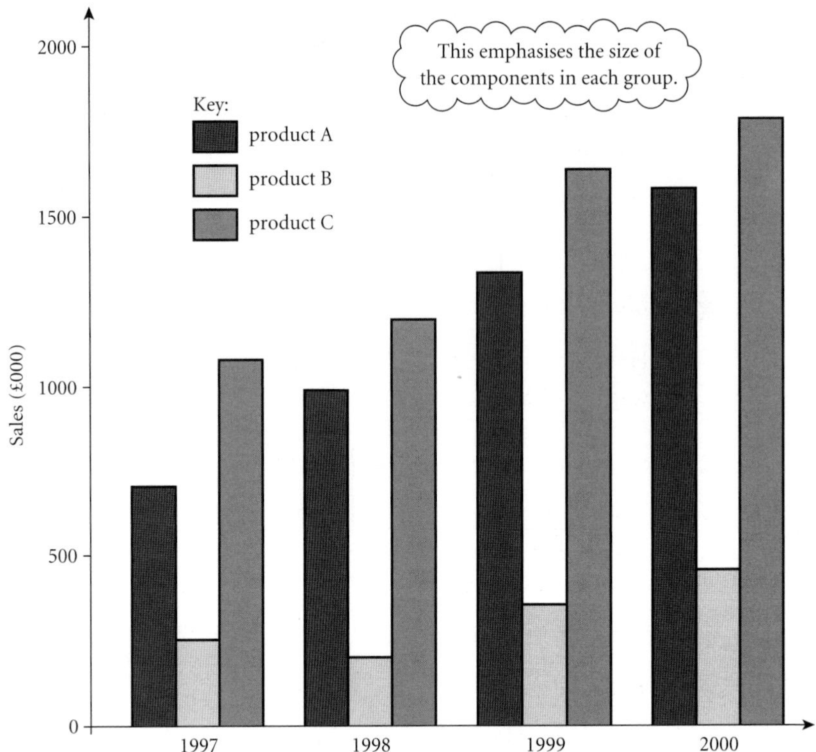

Figure 2.4

Pie charts

A pie chart can be used to illustrate categorical (or qualitative) data or it can be used to illustrate discrete or grouped continuous data. Pie charts are used to show the size of constituent parts relative to the whole.

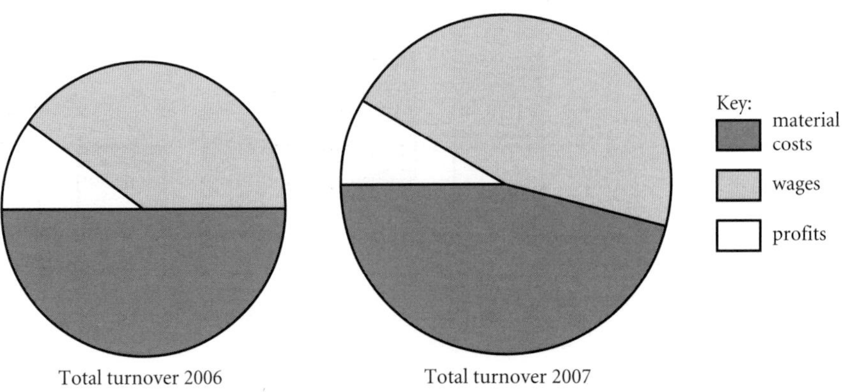

Figure 2.5

Avonford Electronics increased their turnover from £1 800 000 in 2006 to £2 400 000 in 2007. The pie charts show the division of the money between wages, material costs and profits.

The increase in total turnover from 2006 to 2007 is reflected in the larger area of the second pie chart.

The values of the data are proportional to the areas of the pie charts and not proportional to the radii.

For example: Area of chart 2 $= \frac{4}{3} \times$ area of chart 1

? Measure the radii of the pie charts. Are they consistent with the data?

How can you see from these pie charts that proportionally more is spent on wages in 2007 than in 2006?

Has the actual amount spent on wages increased?

Some statisticians feel that in most cases a bar chart is a better choice. Why do you think this is?

EXERCISE 2A

1 (a) State whether the data described below are categorical or numerical and, if numerical, whether discrete or continuous.

(b) State what you think would be the most appropriate method of displaying the data.

(i) The number of items in the shopping basket used to calculate the retail price index
(ii) The colours of puppies born to dogs at a dog-breeding kennels
(iii) The weights of pebbles found on a beach by geography students
(iv) The number of rosettes won by a show jumper during one season
(v) The sizes of football boots worn by Manchester United football team
(vi) The number of mobile phones lost each week in the UK
(vii) The times taken for different surgeons to carry out an appendectomy operation
(viii) The total number of days employees are absent in a week
(ix) The scores in a gymnastics competition at the Olympics
(x) The lengths of flex attached to electric kettles

2 The data below are for two schools in the same town.

Lea School		Harper School	
Number of students in Years 7, 8, 9	480	Number of students in Years 7, 8, 9	780
Number of students in Years 10, 11	320	Number of students in Years 10, 11	520
Number of students in Years 12, 13	100	Number of students in Years 12, 13	300
Total number of students	900	Total number of students	1600

(i) The data for Lea School are illustrated on a pie chart of radius 6 cm. What radius should be used for Harper School?

(ii) Draw both pie charts.

3 A sociologist employs a market research company to survey how people with different jobs spend their time over a week. The market research company give the results as the table below. All figures are hours per week.

Type of job	Time spent working	Time spent at leisure	Time spent with family
Teacher	60	4	20
Postman	45	10	30
Sky TV technician	40	14	25
Part-time doctor's receptionist	20	10	40

(i) Display this information as a compound bar chart.

(ii) State which is easier to read, the data table or the bar chart, and say why.

(iii) Criticise the data the market research company gave the sociologist and suggest how the survey could be improved.

4 A farmer is comparing the crops grown at each of his two farms. The table shows the numbers of acres of the crops grown in 2005.

Crop	Wood Farm	High Oak Farm
Set aside	80	150
Potatoes	100	250
Linseed	100	250
Wheat	120	500
Barley	200	600
Rapeseed	300	750

(i) Calculate the ratio of the radii needed to draw pie charts to display this information.

(ii) Use a spreadsheet to draw the pie charts.

5 As part of a school's Physical Education A Level, students had to do a study of a role model in a particular sport. Here are the choices for the classes of 2003 and 2004.

Role model	Sport	2003	2004
Michael Vaughan	Cricket	3	1
John Terry	Football	3	2
David Beckham	Football	3	2
Tiger Woods	Golf	2	1
Carlos Spencer	Rugby	2	1
Johnny Wilkinson	Rugby	3	2

(i) Draw two pie charts to show this information. The larger one should have a radius of 6 cm.

(ii) Draw a multiple bar chart to show this information.

6 Jane O'Hara is head of mathematics in a school. She asks all 600 students to write down the names of a famous mathematician. The results are shown below.

Name of mathematician	Number of students who wrote the name down
Albert Einstein	177
Pythagoras	123
Isaac Newton	220
Jane O'Hara	45
Andrew Wiles	12
Stephen Hawking	10
Others	13

(i) What type of chart would be appropriate to display these data?

(ii) What additional information might have been obtained?

Histograms

Histograms are used to illustrate continuous data. The columns in a histogram may have different widths and it is the area of each column which is proportional to the frequency and not the height. Unlike bar charts, there are no gaps between the columns because where one class ends the next begins.

Continuous data with equal class widths

A sample of 60 components is taken from a production line and their diameters, d mm, recorded. The resulting data are summarised in the following frequency table.

Length (mm)	Frequency
$25 \leqslant d < 30$	1
$30 \leqslant d < 35$	3
$35 \leqslant d < 40$	7
$40 \leqslant d < 45$	15
$45 \leqslant d < 50$	17
$50 \leqslant d < 55$	10
$55 \leqslant d < 60$	5
$60 \leqslant d < 65$	2

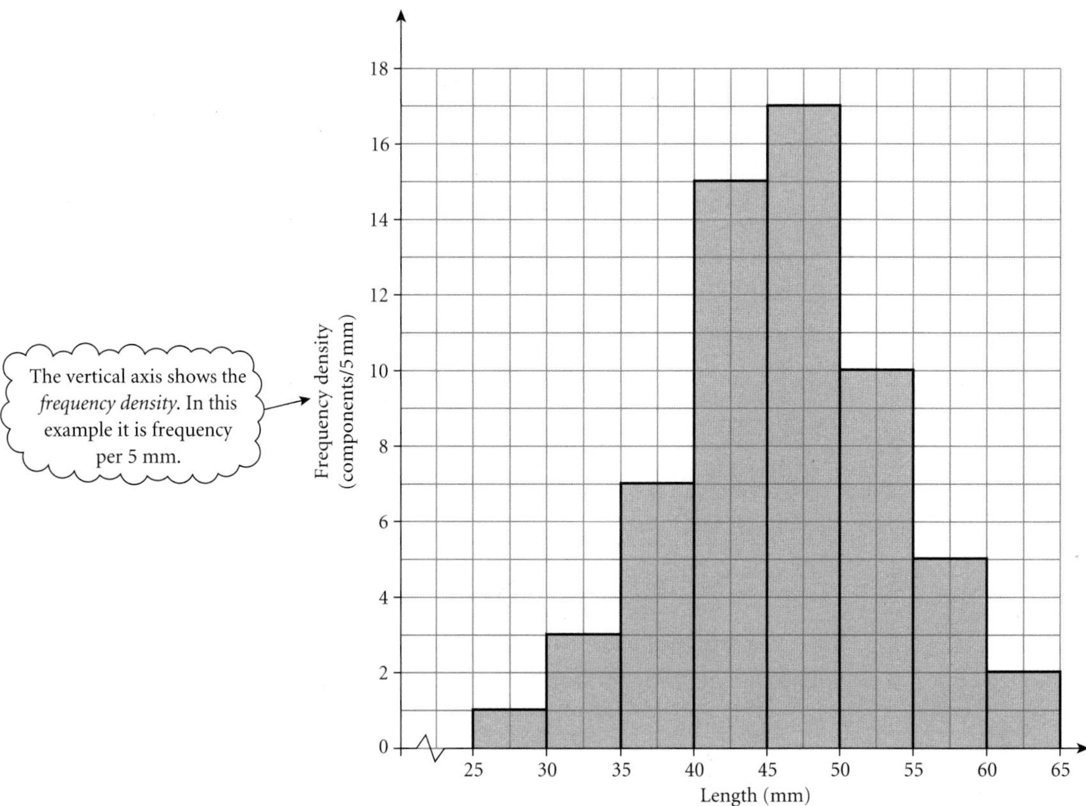

Figure 2.6 *Histogram to show the distribution of component diameters*

The class boundaries are 25, 30, 35, 40, 45, 50, 55, 60 and 65. The width of each class is 5.

The area of each column is proportional to the class frequency. In this example the class widths are equal so the height of each column is also proportional to the class frequency.

The column representing $45 \leqslant d < 50$ is the highest and this tells you that this is the modal class, that is, the class with highest frequency per 5 mm.

? How would you identify the modal class if the intervals were not of equal width?

Labelling the frequency axis

The vertical axis tells you the frequency *density*. Figure 2.8 looks the same as figure 2.7 but it is not a histogram. This type of diagram is, however, often incorrectly referred to as a histogram. It is more correctly called a frequency chart. A histogram shows the frequency density on the vertical axis.

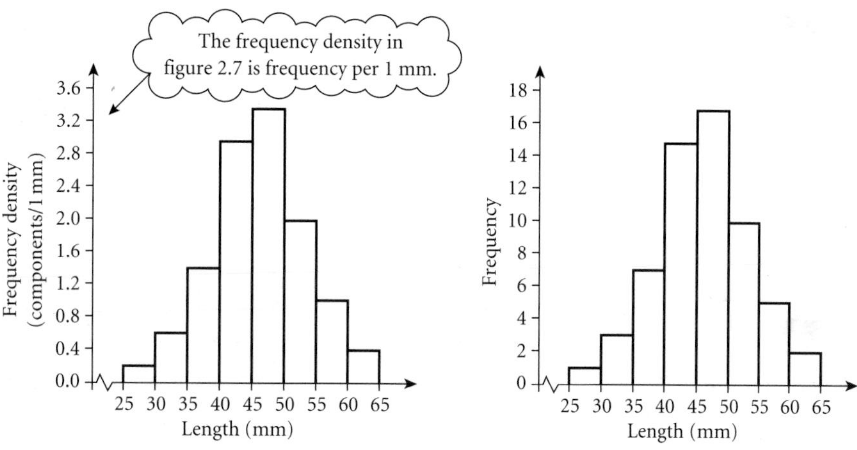

Figure 2.7 **Figure 2.8**

The units which you choose for the frequency density are particularly important when the class widths are unequal, as you will see in the next example.

Continuous data with unequal class widths

The heights of 80 broad bean plants were measured, correct to the nearest centimetre, ten weeks after planting. The data are summarised in the frequency table.

Height (cm)	Frequency	Class width (cm)	Frequency per 2 cm
$7.5 \leqslant x < 11.5$	1	4	$\frac{1}{2}$
$11.5 \leqslant x < 13.5$	3	2	3
$13.5 \leqslant x < 15.5$	7	2	7
$15.5 \leqslant x < 17.5$	11	2	11
$17.5 \leqslant x < 19.5$	19	2	19
$19.5 \leqslant x < 21.5$	14	2	14
$21.5 \leqslant x < 23.5$	13	2	13
$23.5 \leqslant x < 25.5$	9	2	9
$25.5 \leqslant x < 28.5$	3	3	2

Most of the classes are 2 cm wide so it is convenient to take 2 cm as the *standard width.*

The first class is twice the standard width; consequently the height of this column on the histogram is half the given frequency. The last class is $\frac{3}{2}$ times the standard width so the height of the column is $\frac{2}{3}$ of the given frequency. The area of each column is proportional to the class frequency.

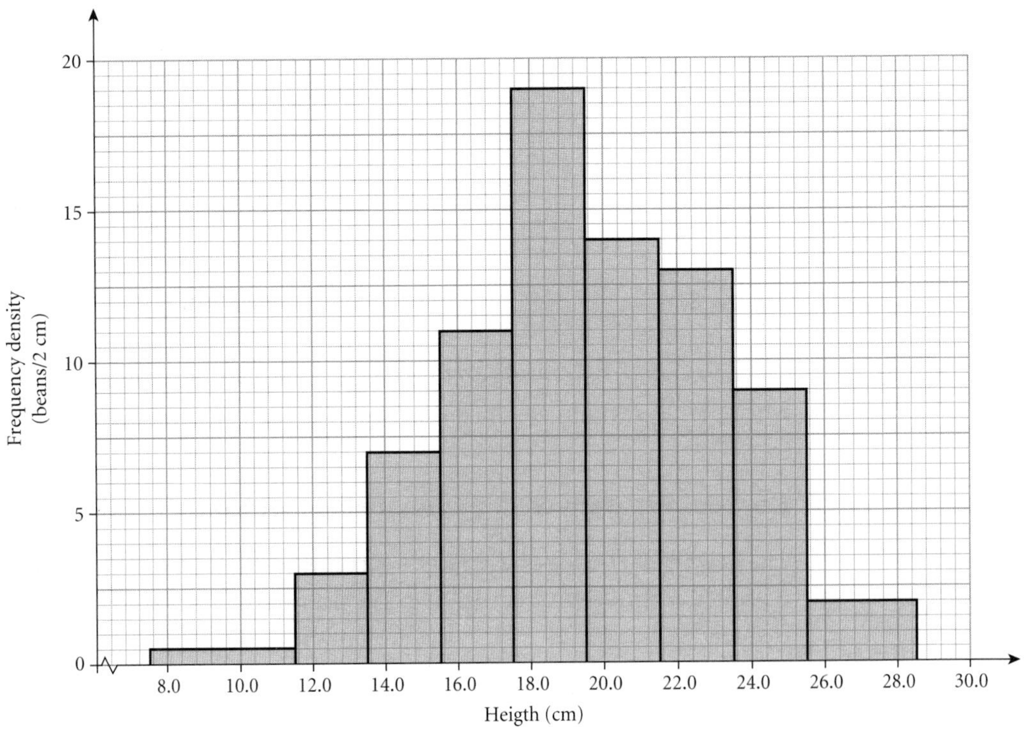

Figure 2.9

Discrete data

Histograms are occasionally used for grouped *discrete* data. However, you should always first consider the alternatives.

A test was given to 100 students. The maximum mark was 70. The raw data are shown below.

10	18	68	67	25	62	49	11	12	8
9	46	53	57	30	63	34	21	68	31
20	16	29	13	31	56	9	34	45	55
35	40	45	48	54	50	34	32	47	60
70	52	21	25	53	41	29	63	43	50
40	48	45	38	51	25	52	55	47	46
46	50	8	25	56	18	20	36	36	9
38	39	53	45	42	42	61	55	30	38
62	47	58	54	59	25	24	53	42	61
18	30	32	45	49	28	31	27	54	38

Illustrating this data using a vertical line chart results in this diagram.

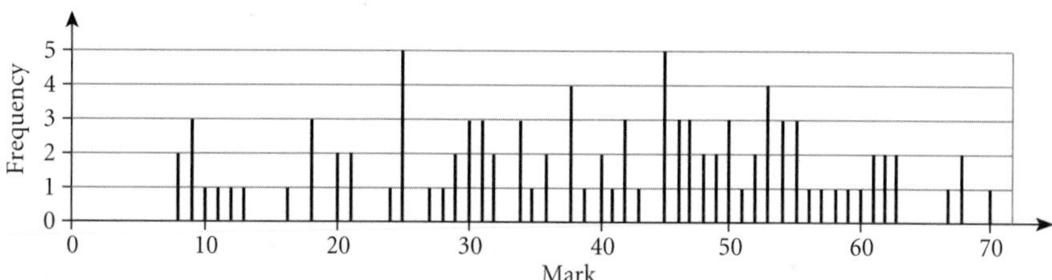

Figure 2.10

Figure 2.10 fails to give a clear picture of the overall distribution of marks. In this case you could consider a bar chart or, as the individual marks are known, a stem-and-leaf diagram, as in figure 2.11.

$n = 100$

2 | 5 represents 25 marks

0	8 8 9 9 9
1	0 1 2 3 6 8 8 8
2	0 0 1 1 4 5 5 5 5 5 7 8 9 9
3	0 0 0 1 1 1 2 2 4 4 4 5 6 6 8 8 8 8 9
4	0 0 1 2 2 2 3 5 5 5 5 5 6 6 6 7 7 7 8 8 9 9
5	0 0 0 1 2 2 3 3 3 3 4 4 4 5 5 5 6 6 7 8 9
6	0 1 1 2 2 3 3 7 8 8
7	0

Figure 2.11

If the data have been grouped and the original data have been lost, or are otherwise unknown, then a histogram may be considered. A grouped frequency table and histogram illustrating the marks are shown below.

Marks, x	Frequency, f
0–9	5
10–19	8
20–29	14
30–39	19
40–49	22
50–59	21
60–70	11

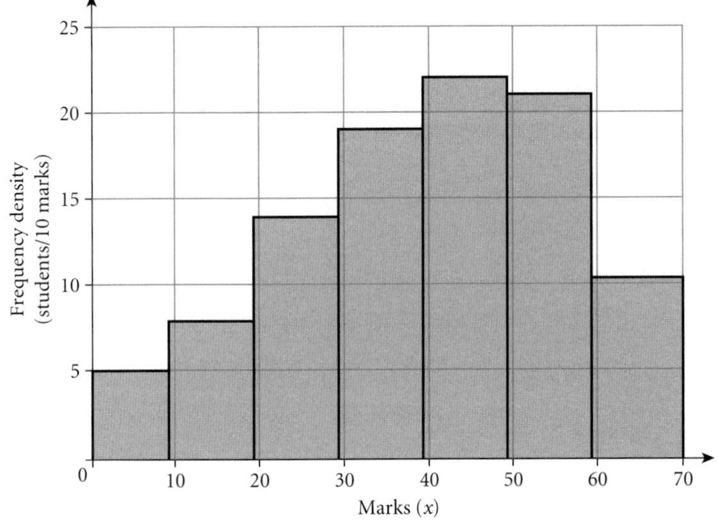

Figure 2.12

Note

The class boundary 10–19 becomes $9.5 \leqslant x < 19.5$ for the purpose of drawing the histogram. You must give careful consideration to class boundaries, particularly if you are using rounded data.

? Look at the intervals for the first and last classes. How do they differ from the others? Why is this the case?

Grouped discrete data are illustrated well by a histogram if the distribution is particularly skewed as is the case in the next example.

The first 50 positive integers squared are:

1	4	9	16	25	36	49	64
81	100	121	144	169	196	225	256
289	324	361	400	441	484	529	576
625	676	729	784	841	900	961	1024
1089	1156	1225	1296	1369	1444	1521	1600
1681	1764	1849	1936	2025	2116	2209	2304
2401	2500						

Number, n	Frequency, f
$0 < n \leq 250$	15
$250 < n \leq 500$	7
$500 < n \leq 750$	5
$750 < n \leq 1000$	4
$1000 < n \leq 1250$	4
$1250 < n \leq 1500$	3
$1500 < n \leq 1750$	3
$1750 < n \leq 2000$	3
$2000 < n \leq 2250$	3
$2250 < n \leq 2500$	3

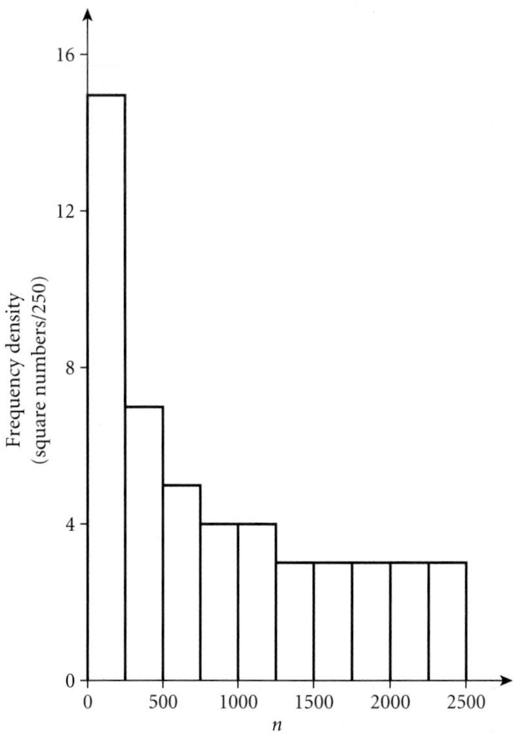

Figure 2.13

The main points to remember when drawing a histogram are:

- Histograms are usually used for illustrating continuous data. For discrete data it is better to draw a stem-and-leaf diagram, line graph or bar chart.
- Since the data are continuous, or treated as if they were continuous, adjacent columns of the histogram should touch (unlike a bar chart where the columns should be drawn with gaps between them).
- It is the areas and not the heights of the columns that are proportional to the frequency of each class.
- The vertical axis should be marked with the appropriate frequency density (*frequency per 5 mm* for example), rather than frequency.

EXERCISE 2B

1 The following data were given on the Chicago Bulls Basketball Team official website. They give the 2005–2006 roster for the players together with their heights in feet and inches. 7–1 means seven feet and one inch. There are twelve inches in a foot.

Number	Player	Height
3	Tyson Chandler	7–1
2	Eddy Curry	6–11
34	Antonio Davis	6–9
9	Luol Deng	6–8
21	Chris Duhon	6–1
51	Lawrence Funderburke	6–9
7	Ben Gordon	6–3
44	Adrian Griffin	6–5
24	Othella Harrington	6–9
12	Kirk Hinrich	6–3
5	Andres Nocioni	6–7
15	Jannero Pargo	6–1
52	Eric Piatkowski	6–7
35	Jared Reiner	6–11
30	Frank Williams	6–3

(i) Convert all the heights into inches and construct a histogram using class intervals of $73 < \text{height} \leqslant 75$, $75 < \text{height} \leqslant 77$, $77 < \text{height} \leqslant 78$, $78 < \text{height} \leqslant 79$, $79 < \text{height} \leqslant 81$, with the last one being $81 < \text{height} \leqslant 85$.

(ii) Comment on the shape of the histogram.

(iii) Calculate an estimate of the mean height, to the nearest inch, of this baseball team.

2 A horticulturist is growing a new variety of dwarf sunflowers. After three weeks she records their height, h, to the nearest centimetre.

(i) Copy and complete the table below and construct a histogram to show the distribution.

Height (cm)	Class boundaries	Class width	Frequency	Frequency density
10–19	$9.5 \leqslant h < 19.5$	10	1	
20–29	$19.5 \leqslant h < 29.5$	10	2	
30–39	$29.5 \leqslant h < 39.5$	10	5	
40–49	$39.5 \leqslant h < 49.5$	10	10	
50–69	$49.5 \leqslant h < 69.5$	20	10	

(ii) How many sunflowers did the horticulturalist grow?

(iii) Estimate the median height of a sunflower and mark it on your histogram as a vertical line. What can you say about the areas on either side of the line?

3 A student measures the lengths of 20 pencils. He then puts the information into a grouped table. He tells a friend 'You can use the grouped data to give you a very good estimate of the mean.' She disagrees.

The actual lengths, in millimetres, of the pencils are as follows.

80	85	90	99	86	95	95	102	107	128
138	145	152	162	168	88	140	125	157	155

(i) Make a table using the class intervals $79.5 < \text{length} \leqslant 99.5$, $99.5 < \text{length} \leqslant 119.5$, $119.5 < \text{length} \leqslant 129.5$, $129.5 < \text{length} \leqslant 159.5$ and $159.5 < \text{length} \leqslant 169.5$ and calculate an estimate of the mean length.

(ii) Calculate the mean length from the raw data.

(iii) What is the percentage error?

(iv) Is the friend justified in her opinion that using the grouped data results in a poor value for the mean?

4 A market research firm is to conduct a survey of consumer spending at a local supermarket. The firm wants various age groups to be represented.

The amount spent, £x, by each of the 100 customers sampled is summarised in the following table.

Amount spent, £x	Number of customers
$0 \leqslant x < 10$	6
$10 \leqslant x < 20$	16
$20 \leqslant x < 30$	35
$30 \leqslant x < 50$	18
$50 \leqslant x < 75$	15
$75 \leqslant x < 100$	10

(i) Illustrate the spending patterns by a histogram, drawn on graph paper.

(ii) Calculate estimates of the mean and standard deviation of the amount spent.

[MEI, *part*]

5 This table shows the distance, to the nearest mile, travelled by double glazing sales representatives on one day.

Distance (miles)	Class boundaries	Class width	Frequency	Frequency density
20–59			160	
60–79			20	
80–99			100	
100–119			200	
120+			0	

(i) Copy and complete the table and then plot the histogram.

(ii) Comment on the number of miles travelled by double glazing sales representatives and estimate the mean and median miles travelled per day. Comment on these results.

6 These diagrams show the number of hits on the French Manchester United Supporters' Club website, for one-hour periods through the day on three days in June 2005.

Thursday, 23 June 2005: an ordinary Thursday

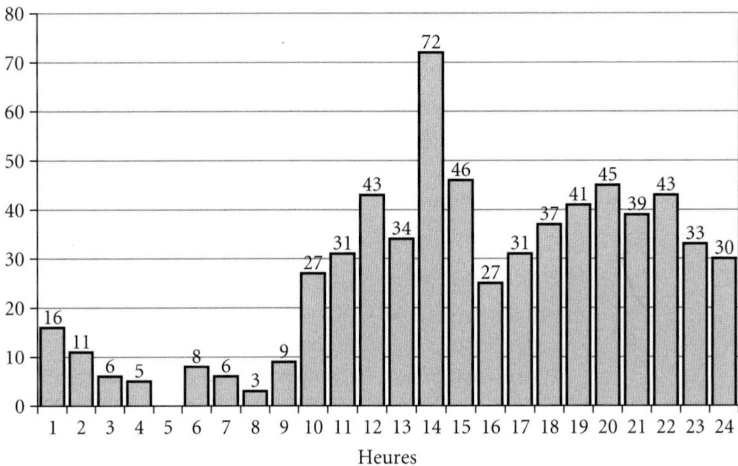

Sunday, 26 June 2005: an ordinary Sunday

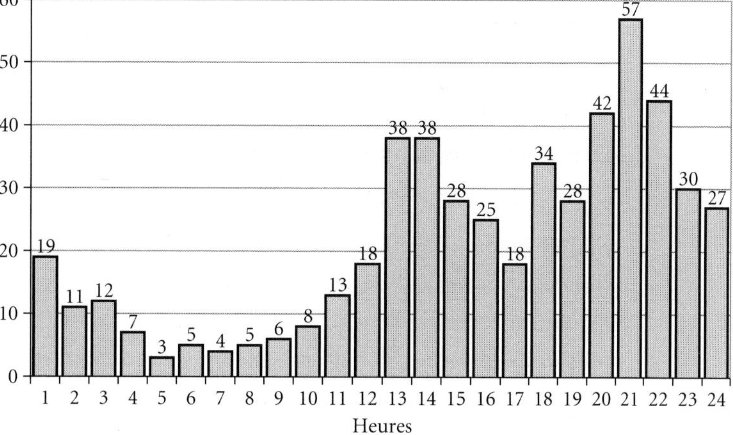

Thursday, 14 July 2005: a Bank holiday in France

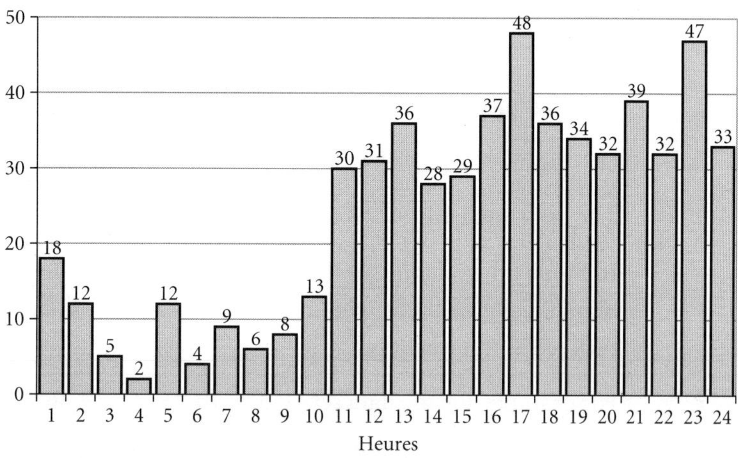

(i) Comment on these commercially produced charts.

(ii) Comment on when the hits occur on each of the days illustrated.

Measures of central tendency and of spread using quartiles

You saw in Chapter 1 how to find the median of a set of discrete data. As a reminder, the median is the value of the middle item when all the data items have been ranked in order.

The median is the value of the $\frac{n+1}{2}$th item and is half-way through the data set.

The values one-quarter of the way through the data set and three-quarters of the way through the data set are called the *lower quartile* and the *upper quartile* respectively. The lower quartile, median and upper quartile are usually denoted using Q_1, Q_2 and Q_3.

Quartiles are used mainly with large data sets and their values found by looking at the $\frac{1}{4}$, $\frac{1}{2}$ and $\frac{3}{4}$ points. So, for a data set of 1000, you would take Q_1 to be the value of the 250th data item, Q_2 to be the value of the 500th data item and Q_3 to be the value of the 750th data item.

Quartiles for small data sets

For small data sets, where each data item is known (raw data), calculation of the middle quartile Q_2, the median, is straightforward. However, there are no standard formulae for the calculation of the lower and upper quartiles, Q_1 and Q_3, and you may meet different ones. The one we will use is consistent with the output from some calculators which display the quartiles of a data set and depends on whether the number of items, n, is even or odd.

If n is *even* then there will be an equal number of items in the lower half and upper half of the data set. To calculate the lower quartile, Q_1, find the median of the lower half of the data set. To calculate the upper quartile, Q_3, find the median of the upper half of the data set.

For example, for the data set $\{1, 3, 6, 10, 15, 21, 28, 36, 45, 55\}$ the median, Q_2, is $\frac{15 + 21}{2} = 18$. The lower quartile, Q_1, is the median of $\{1, 3, 6, 10, 15\}$, i.e. 6. The upper quartile, Q_3, is the median of $\{21, 28, 36, 45, 55\}$, i.e. 36.

If n is *odd* then define the 'lower half' to be all data items *below* the median. Similarly define the 'upper half' to be all data items *above* the median. Then proceed as if n were even.

For example, for the data set $\{1, 3, 6, 10, 15, 21, 28, 36, 45\}$ the median, Q_2, is 15. The lower quartile, Q_1, is the median of $\{1, 3, 6, 10\}$, i.e. $\frac{3 + 6}{2} = 4.5$. The upper quartile, Q_3, is the median of $\{21, 28, 36, 45\}$, i.e. $\frac{28 + 36}{2} = 32$.

The definition of quartiles on a spreadsheet may be different from that described above. Values of Q_1 and Q_3 in the even case shown above are given as 7 and 34 respectively on an *Excel* spreadsheet. Similarly, values of Q_1 and Q_3 in the odd case shown above are given as 6 and 28 respectively.

ACTIVITY

Use a spreadsheet to find the median and quartiles of a small data set.
Find out the method the spreadsheet uses to determine the position of the lower and upper quartiles.

EXAMPLE 2.1

Catherine is a junior reporter at the *Avonford Star*. As part of an investigation into consumer affairs she purchases 0.5 kg of lean mince from 12 shops and supermarkets in the town. The resulting data, put into rank order, are as follows:

£1.39 £1.39 £1.46 £1.48 £1.48 £1.50 £1.52 £1.54 £1.60 £1.65 £1.68 £1.72

Find Q_1, Q_2 and Q_3.

SOLUTION

139	139	146	148	148	150	152	154	160	165	168	172
1	2	3	4	5	6	7	8	9	10	11	12

Q_1 has position $\frac{6+1}{2} = 3\frac{1}{2}$. Value = £1.47.

Q_2 has position $\frac{12+1}{2} = 6\frac{1}{2}$. Value = £1.51.

Q_3 has position $\frac{6+1}{2} = 3\frac{1}{2}$ from the top. Value = £1.63.

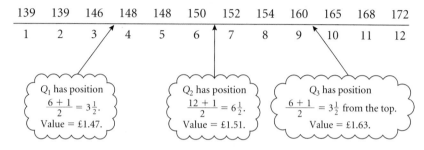

In fact, the upper quartile has a value of £1.625 but this has been rounded up to the nearest penny.

You may encounter different formulae for finding the lower and upper quartiles. The ones given here are relatively easy to calculate and usually lead to values of Q_1 and Q_3 which are close to the true values.

What are the true values?

Interquartile range or quartile spread

The difference between the lower and upper quartiles is known as the *interquartile range* or *quartile spread*.

Interquartile range (IQR) = $Q_3 - Q_1$.

In Example 2.1 $IQR = 163 - 147 = 16$p.

The interquartile range covers the middle 50% of the data. It is relatively easy to calculate and is a useful measure of spread as it avoids extreme values. It is said to be resistant to outliers.

Box-and-whisker plots (boxplots)

The three quartiles and the two extreme values of a data set may be illustrated in a *box-and-whisker* plot. This is designed to give an easy-to-read representation of the location and spread of a distribution. Figure 2.14 shows a box-and-whisker plot for the data in Example 2.1.

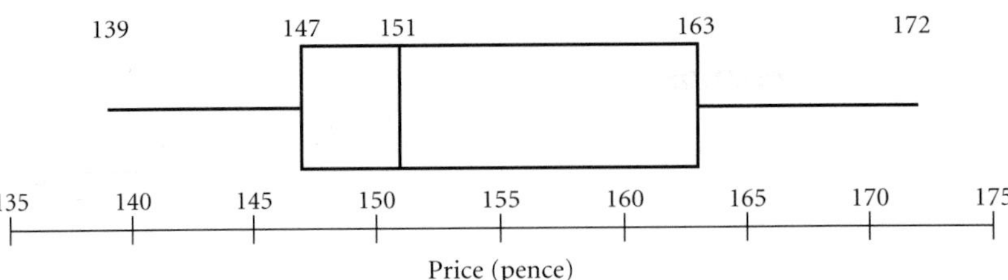

Figure 2.14

The box represents the middle 50% of the distribution and the whiskers stretch out to the extreme values.

Outliers

In Chapter 1 you met a definition of an outlier based on the mean and standard deviation. A different approach gives the definition of an outlier in terms of the median and interquartile range (*IQR*).

Data which are more than $1.5 \times IQR$ beyond the lower or upper quartiles are regarded as outliers.

The corresponding boundary values beyond which outliers may be found are

$$Q_1 - 1.5 \times (Q_3 - Q_1) \quad \text{and} \quad Q_3 + 1.5 \times (Q_3 - Q_1).$$

For the data relating to the ages of the cyclists involved in accidents in Avonford discussed in Chapter 1, for all 92 data values $Q_1 = 13.5$ and $Q_3 = 45.5$.

$$\begin{aligned} \text{Hence} \quad Q_1 - 1.5 \times (Q_3 - Q_1) &= 13.5 - 1.5 \times (45.5 - 13.5) \\ &= 13.5 - 1.5 \times 32 \\ &= -34.5 \\ \text{and} \quad Q_3 + 1.5 \times (Q_3 - Q_1) &= 45.5 + 1.5 \times (45.5 - 13.5) \\ &= 45.5 + 1.5 \times 32 \\ &= 93.5 \end{aligned}$$

From these boundary values you will see that there are no outliers at the lower end of the range, but the value of 138 is an outlier at the upper end of the range.

Figure 2.15 shows a box-and-whisker plot for the ages of the cyclists with the outlier removed. For the remaining 91 data items $Q_1 = 13$ and $Q_3 = 45$.

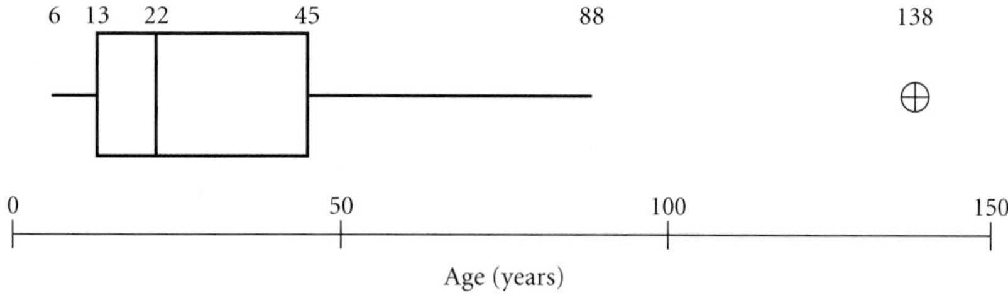

Figure 2.15

From the diagram you can see that the distribution has positive or right skewness. The ⊕ indicates an outlier and is above the upper quartile. Outliers are usually labelled as they are often of special interest. The whiskers are drawn to the most extreme data points which are not outliers.

Cumulative frequency curves

When working with large data sets or grouped data, percentiles and quartiles can be found from *cumulative frequency curves* as shown in the next section.

AVONFORD STAR

Letters to the editor

Dear sir,

I am a student trying to live on a government loan. I'm trying my best to allow myself a sensible monthly budget but my lecturers have given me a long list of textbooks to buy. If I buy just half of them I will have nothing left to live on this month. The majority of books on my list are over £16.

I want to do well at my studies but I won't do well without books and I won't do well if I am ill through not eating properly.

Please tell me what to do, and don't say 'go to the library' because the books I need are never there.

Yours faithfully,
Sheuli Roberts

After receiving this letter the editor wondered if there was a story in it. She asked a reporter to carry out a survey of the prices of textbooks in a large shop.
The reporter took a large sample of 470 textbooks and the results are summarised in the table.

Cost, C (£)	Frequency (No. of books)
$0 \leqslant C < 10$	13
$10 \leqslant C < 15$	53
$15 \leqslant C < 20$	97
$20 \leqslant C < 25$	145
$25 \leqslant C < 30$	81
$30 \leqslant C < 35$	40
$35 \leqslant C < 40$	23
$40 \leqslant C < 45$	12
$45 \leqslant C < 50$	6

He decided to estimate the median and the upper and lower quartiles of the costs of the books. (Without the original data you cannot find the actual values so all calculations will be estimates.) The first step is to make a cumulative frequency table, then to plot a cumulative frequency curve.

Cost, C (£)	Frequency	Cost	Cumulative frequency	
$0 \leqslant C < 10$	13	$C < 10$	13	
$10 \leqslant C < 15$	53	$C < 15$	66	← See note 1.
$15 \leqslant C < 20$	97	$C < 20$	163	← See note 2.
$20 \leqslant C < 25$	145	$C < 25$	308	
$25 \leqslant C < 30$	81	$C < 30$	389	
$30 \leqslant C < 35$	40	$C < 35$	429	
$35 \leqslant C < 40$	23	$C < 40$	452	
$40 \leqslant C < 45$	12	$C < 45$	464	
$45 \leqslant C < 50$	6	$C < 50$	470	

Notes

1 Notice that the interval $C < 15$ means $0 \leqslant C < 15$ and so includes the 13 books in the interval $0 \leqslant C < 10$ and the 53 books in the interval $10 \leqslant C < 15$, giving 66 books in total.

2 Similarly, to find the total for the interval $C < 20$ you must add the number of books in the interval $15 \leqslant C < 20$ to your previous total, giving you $66 + 97 = 163$.

A cumulative frequency curve is obtained by plotting the upper boundary of each class against the cumulative frequency. The points are joined by a smooth curve, as shown in figure 2.16.

In this example the actual values are unknown and the median must therefore be an estimate. It is usual in such cases to find the *estimated* value of the $\frac{n}{2}$th item. This gives a better estimate of the median than is obtained by using $\frac{n+1}{2}$, which is used for ungrouped data. Similarly, estimates of the lower and upper quartiles are found from the $\frac{n}{4}$th and $\frac{3n}{4}$th items.

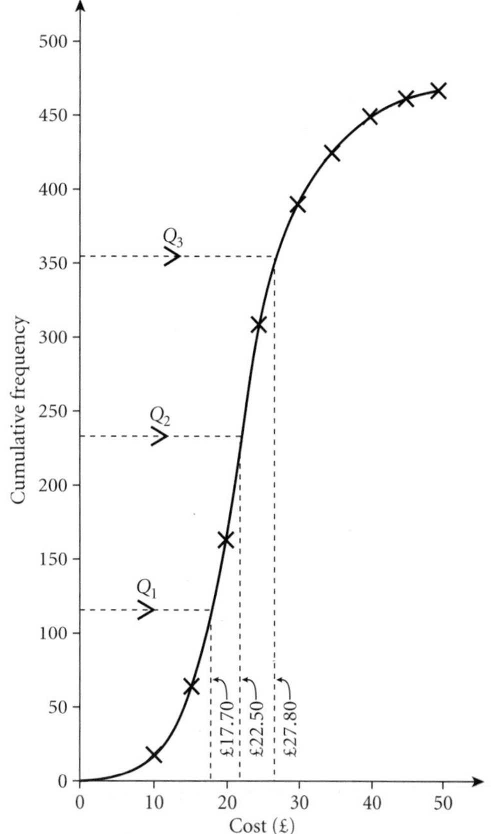

Figure 2.16

The 235th $\left(\frac{470}{2}\right)$ item of data identifies the median which has a value of about £22.50. The 117.5th $\left(\frac{470}{4}\right)$ item of data identifies the lower quartile, which has a value of about £17.70 and the 352.5th $\left(\frac{3}{4} \times 470\right)$ item of data identifies the upper quartile, which has a value of about £27.70.

Notice the distinctive shape of the cumulative frequency curve. It is like a stretched out S-shape leaning forwards.

What about Sheuli's claim that the majority of textbooks cost more than £16? Q_1 = £17.70. By definition 75% of books are more expensive than this, so Sheuli's claim seems to be well founded. We need to check exactly how many books are estimated to be more expensive than £16.

From the cumulative frequency curve 85 books cost £16 or less. So 385 books or about 82% are more expensive.

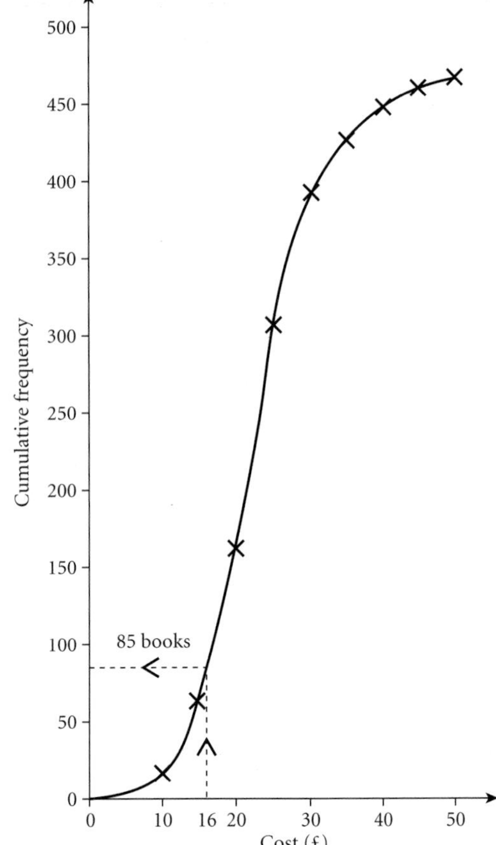

Figure 2.17

You should be cautious about any conclusions you draw. This example deals with books many of which have prices like £9.95 or £39.99. In using a cumulative frequency curve you are assuming an even spread of data throughout the intervals and this may not always be the case.

Box-and-whisker plots for grouped data

It is often helpful to draw a box-and-whisker plot. In cases such as the above when the extreme values are unknown the whiskers are drawn out to the 10th and 90th percentiles. Arrows indicate that the minimum and maximum values are further out.

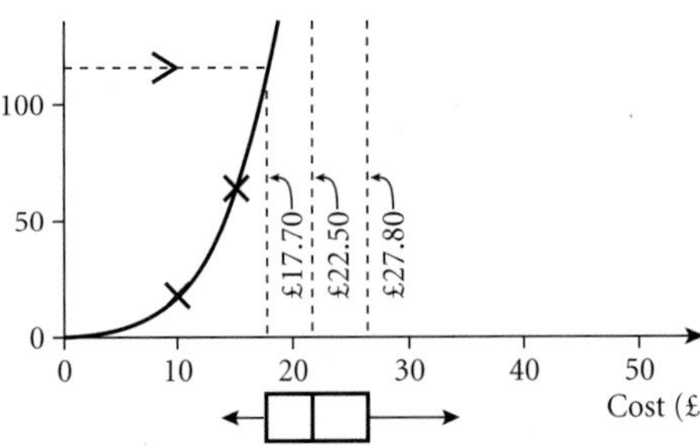

Figure 2.18

EXERCISE 2C

1 A quadrat is a square grid. It is placed at random on the ground by throwing and the number of the required species is then counted and recorded.

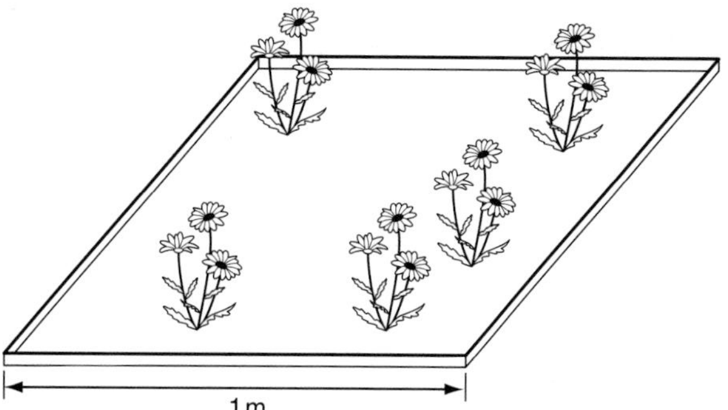

The following data are the number of daisy plants found in each quadrat by biology students on a field trip.

3	6	1	0	0	4	8	2	4
3	5	1	13	8	4	2	9	0

(i) Find the median number of daisy plants.

(ii) Find the lower and upper quartile values and the interquartile range.

(iii) Identify any outliers.

2 The two box-and-whisker plots below show the Geography results for a class at the end of Year 10 and then after their mock GCSE examinations in Year 11.

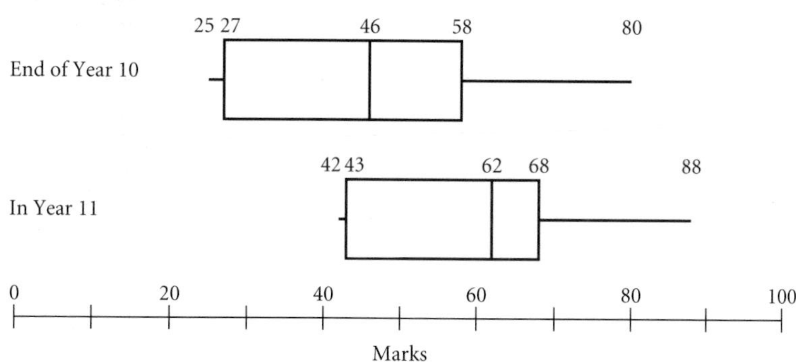

(i) Write down three differences between the two sets of results.

(ii) Give a possible explanation for the differences.

3 Two dog breeders are comparing the number of Newfoundland puppies in the litters they have bred over the last five years.

Breeder 1	0	5	6	6	8	4	6	7	7	6
Breeder 2	8	5	7	5	8	5	7	7	10	

(i) For each breeder

(a) find the median number of puppies

(b) find the lower and upper quartile values and the interquartile range

(c) identify any outliers.

(ii) State which breeder is more successful and give reasons.

4 The table shows the numbers of paid-up Manchester United French Supporters' Club members in August 2005.

Age (years)	Frequency
0–9	0
10–19	8
20–29	18
30–39	7
40–49	3
50–59	3
60+	0

(i) Construct a cumulative frequency table for these data.

(ii) Draw a cumulative frequency graph.

(iii) Use your graph to estimate the median and the interquartile range of the ages.

(iv) Comment on the distribution.

5 The number of minutes of recorded music on a sample of 100 CDs is summarised below.

Time (t minutes)	Number of CDs
$40 \leqslant t < 45$	26
$45 \leqslant t < 50$	18
$50 \leqslant t < 60$	31
$60 \leqslant t < 70$	16
$70 \leqslant t < 90$	9

(i) Illustrate the data by means of a histogram.

(ii) Identify two features of the distribution.

[MEI]

MIXED EXERCISE

1 The four bar charts show the distribution of shares for a top UK football team over two years. *Corporate* investors are companies and businesses that buy shares in another company.

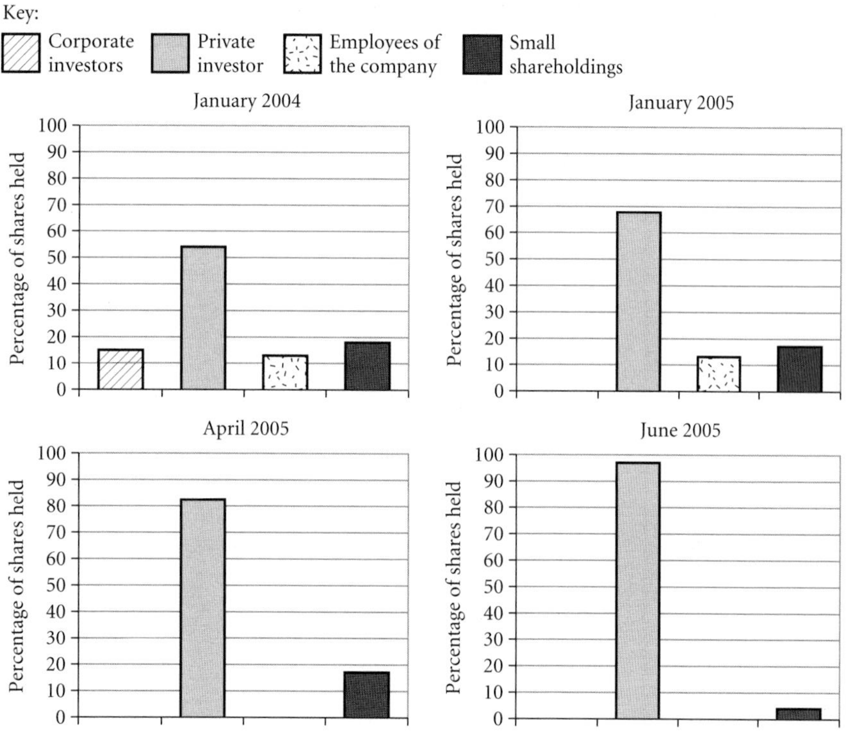

Describe the changes in the ownership of the shares of the football club. In 2005 the company was no longer being quoted on the stock exchange in London as over 97.5% of the shares were owned by one person.

2 A company making industrial ovens checks the temperatures for a sample of ovens. The temperature that is checked is meant to be 300°C. The actual temperatures, to the nearest degree, for 78 ovens are given in the table.

Actual temperature in °C (mid-interval value)	Number of ovens
296	2
297	3
298	6
299	8
300	40
301	10
302	8
303	0
304	0
305	1

(i) Calculate the mean and standard deviation of these temperatures.

(ii) Illustrate the data on a histogram.

(iii) Mark clearly on the histogram the mean temperature and the temperatures that are two standard deviations either side of the mean.

(iv) The specification says that all oven should operate within 2° of the required temperature. What conclusions should the company draw from the sample data?

3 The cumulative frequency graph illustrates the distribution of the weights, x kg, of 150 newly-born babies in a hospital's maternity unit.

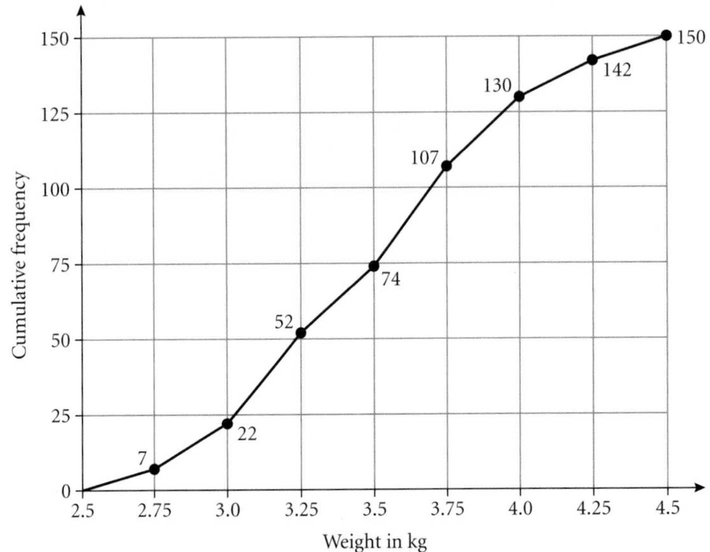

(i) Use the cumulative frequency graph to estimate the median and interquartile range.

(ii) Draw a box-and-whisker plot for the data.

(iii) Copy and complete the following frequency table. Hence calculate an estimate of the mean weight of the 150 babies.

Weight of baby (kg)	Frequency
$2.50 < x \leqslant 2.75$	7
$2.75 < x \leqslant 3.00$	15
$3.00 < x \leqslant 3.25$	
$3.25 < x \leqslant 3.50$	
$3.50 < x \leqslant 3.75$	
$3.75 < x \leqslant 4.00$	
$4.00 < x \leqslant 4.25$	
$4.25 < x \leqslant 4.50$	

During the same period of time, 18 babies were born in the special care baby unit of the hospital. The mean weight of all 168 babies was found to be 3.35 kg (to 3 significant figures).

(iv) Calculate an estimate of the mean weight of the 18 babies in the special care unit.

(v) What effect will the addition of the 18 extra data items have on the median and on the interquartile range? Explain your reasoning.

[MEI]

4 The magazine *Nearly Eighteen* has a website, on which it recently ran a pop trivia quiz with ten questions. The results of the first 1000 entries were analysed. The numbers of questions answered correctly, x, are illustrated by the frequency diagram.

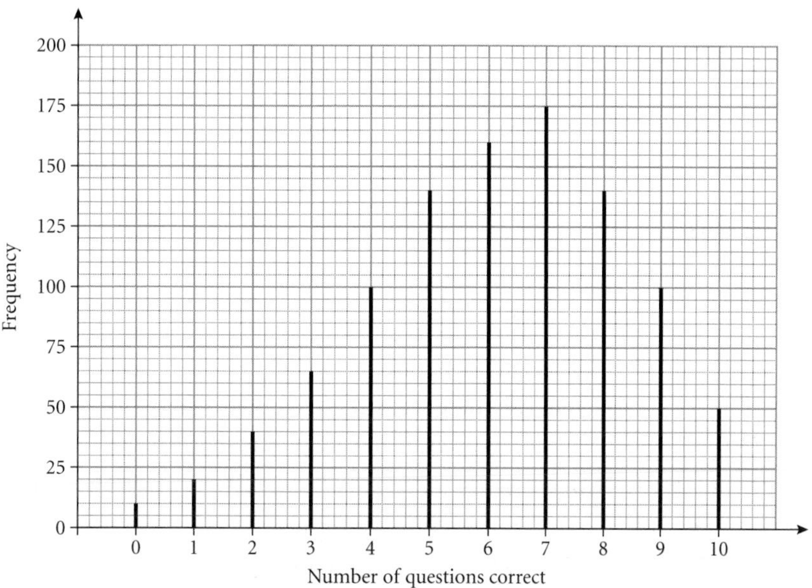

$$n = 1000 \qquad \sum fx = 6100 \qquad \sum fx^2 = 42\,260$$

(i) Find the mode and the median of the data, and describe briefly the shape of the distribution.

(ii) Illustrate the data using a box-and-whisker plot.

(iii) Calculate the mean and standard deviation of the data.

Each question in the quiz was in fact of the multiple choice variety, with four possible answers. Three points are awarded for a question answered correctly, and one point is deducted for a question which is not answered correctly.

(iv) Show that, if x questions are answered correctly, the number of points, y, is given by

$$y = 4x - 10$$

(v) Hence find the mean and standard deviation of the number of points scored.

[MEI]

5 A motoring magazine carried out a survey of the value of petrol-driven cars that were five years old. In the survey, the value of each car was expressed as a percentage of its value when new. The results of the survey are summarised in the following table.

Percentage of original value (x)	**Number of cars**
$15 \leqslant x < 20$	4
$20 \leqslant x < 25$	12
$25 \leqslant x < 30$	18
$30 \leqslant x < 35$	13
$35 \leqslant x < 40$	6
$40 \leqslant x < 45$	5
$45 \leqslant x < 55$	2

(i) Draw a histogram on graph paper to illustrate the data.

(ii) Calculate an estimate of the median of the data.

(iii) Calculate estimates of the mean and standard deviation of the data, giving your answers correct to 2 decimal places. Hence identify any outliers, explaining your method.

A similar survey of 60 diesel-driven cars produced a mean of 34.2% and a standard deviation of 11.7%.

(iv) Use these statistics to compare the values of petrol and diesel cars five years after they were purchased as new.

[MEI]

6 The cumulative frequency curve shows the lengths of telephone calls from my house during the first six months of last year.

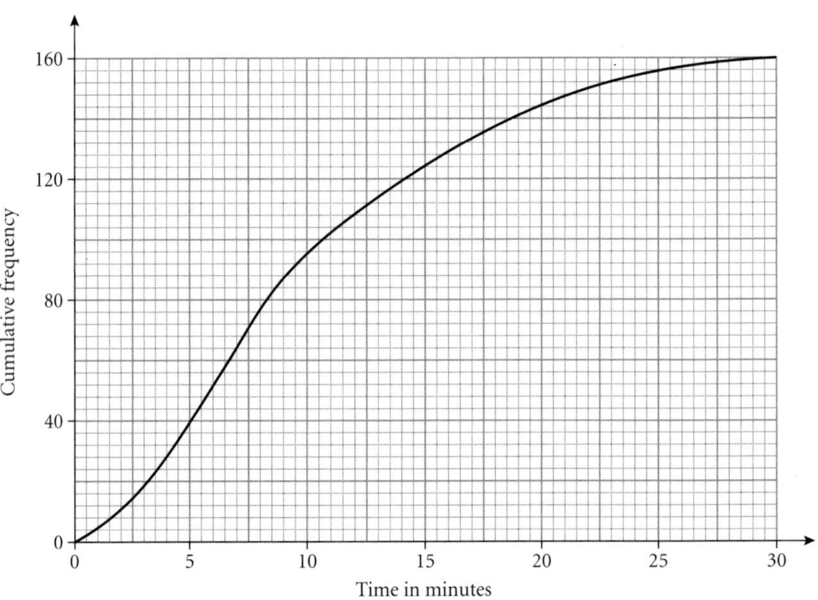

(i) Find the median and interquartile range.

(ii) Construct a histogram with six equal intervals to illustrate the data.

(iii) Use the frequency distribution associated with your histogram to estimate the mean length of call.

(iv) State whether each of the following is true or false.

(a) The distribution of these call times is negatively skewed.

(b) The majority of the calls last longer than 6 minutes.

(c) The majority of the calls last between 5 and 12 minutes.

(d) The majority of the calls are shorter than the mean length.

[MEI]

7 A farmer gathers apples from his orchard. The apples are graded according to their diameter, measured in millimetres.
The histogram shows the distribution of diameters of a sample of the apples. The scale on the vertical axis represents the frequency density (that is, frequency per mm).

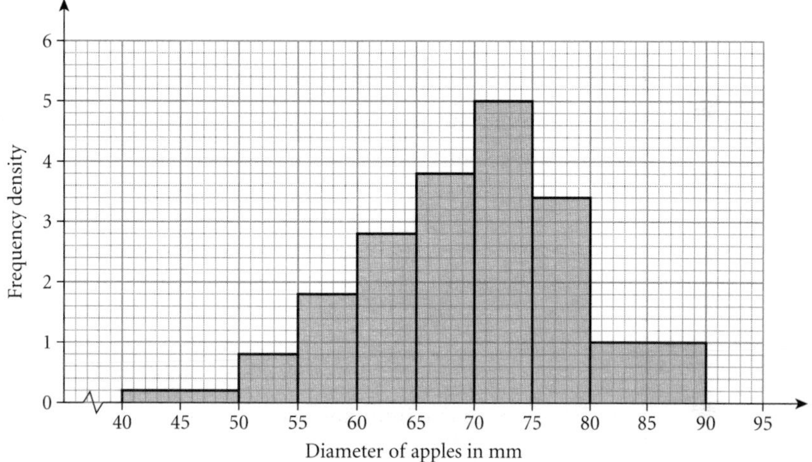

(i) How many apples are there in the modal class?

(ii) Show that the sample contains 100 apples.

(iii) Calculate an estimate of the mean diameter of apples in the sample. Explain why your answer is only an estimate.

(iv) Find an estimate of the median diameter.

(v) Describe the shape of the distribution.

(vi) The standard deviation is approximately 9 mm. State, with reasons, the number of apples you regard as outliers.

[MEI]

8 In a survey of TV viewing habits, the 29 students in a Year 11 class were asked how long they had spent watching TV after school the day before. Four students had not watched any TV, but the times spent watching TV by the other 25 were as follows.

Number of hours	Number of students
0 to 1	5
1 to 2	7
2 to 3	8
More than 3	5

(i) Explain why the classification '0 to 1, 1 to 2, 2 to 3' in the first column of the table is unclear. Suggest a clearer classification.

Assume that no-one in the class watched more than 6 hours of television.

(ii) Illustrate the data in the table by a histogram. Show your scales clearly.

(iii) Calculate estimates of the mean and standard deviation of the numbers of hours spent watching TV *by all 29 students.*

A national survey of 5000 students in Year 11 produced the following data for the time spent watching TV on a particular day.

Number of hours	Percentage of students
0	8.3
0 to 1	19.4
1 to 2	29.2
2 to 3	23.6
More than 3	19.5

(iv) The survey reported that the mean time spent by the students watching TV was 2.1 hours. Calculate an estimate of the mean time spent watching TV by those students who watched for more than 3 hours.

[MEI]

KEY POINTS

1 **Vertical line charts:**
- commonly used to illustrate discrete data
- vertical axis labelled frequency.

2 **Histograms:**
- commonly used to illustrate continuous data
- horizontal axis shows the variable being measured (cm, kg, etc.)
- vertical axis labelled with the appropriate frequency density (per 10 cm, per kg, etc.)
- no gaps between columns
- the frequency is proportional to the area of each column.

3 For a small data set with n items,
- the median, Q_2, is the value of the $\frac{n+1}{2}$ th item of data.

If n is even then
- the lower quartile, Q_1, is the median of the lower half of the data set
- the upper quartile, Q_3, is the median of the upper half of the data set.

If n is odd then exclude the median from either 'half' and proceed as if n were even.

4 Interquartile range (IQR) $= Q_3 - Q_1$.

5 When data are illustrated using a cumulative frequency curve the median, lower and upper quartiles are estimated by identifying the data values with cumulative frequencies $\frac{1}{2}n$, $\frac{1}{4}n$ and $\frac{3}{4}n$.

6 An item of data x may be identified as an *outlier* if it is more than $1.5 \times IQR$ beyond the lower or upper quartile, i.e. if $x < Q_1 - 1.5 \times (Q_3 - Q_1)$ or $x > Q_3 + 1.5 \times (Q_3 - Q_1)$.

7 A box-and-whisker plot is a useful way of summarising data and showing the median, upper and lower quartiles and any outliers.

3 Probability

If we knew Lady Luck better, Las Vegas would still be a roadstop in the desert.

Stephen Jay Gould

AVONFORD STAR

A library without books

If you plan to pop into the Avonford library and pick up the latest bestseller, then forget it. All the best books 'disappear' practically as soon as they are put on the shelves.

I talked about the problem with the local senior librarian, Gina Clarke.

'We have a real problem with unauthorised loans at the moment,' Gina told me. 'Out of our total stock of, say, 80 000 books, something like 44 000 are out on loan at any one time. About 20 000 are on the shelves and I'm afraid the rest are unaccounted for.'

That means that the probability of finding the particular book you want is exactly $\frac{1}{4}$. With odds like that, don't bet on being lucky next time you visit your library.

Librarian Gina Clarke is worried about the problem of 'disappearing books'

How do you think the figure of $\frac{1}{4}$ at the end of the article was arrived at? Do you agree that the probability is *exactly* $\frac{1}{4}$?

The information about the different categories of book can be summarised as follows.

Category of book	Typical numbers
On the shelves	20 000
Out on loan	44 000
Unauthorised loan	16 000
Total stock	80 000

On the basis of these figures it is possible to estimate the probability of finding the book you want. Of the total stock of 80 000 books bought by the library, you might expect to find about 20 000 on the shelves at any one time. As a fraction, this is $\frac{20}{80}$ or $\frac{1}{4}$ of the total. So, as a rough estimate, the probability of your finding a particular book is 0.25 or 25%.

Similarly, 16 000 out of the total of 80 000 books are on unauthorised loan, a euphemism for *stolen*, and this is 20%, or $\frac{1}{5}$.

An important assumption underlying these calculations is that all the books are equally likely to be unavailable, which is not very realistic since popular books are more likely to be stolen. Also, the numbers given are only rough approximations, so it is definitely incorrect to say that the probability is *exactly* $\frac{1}{4}$.

Measuring probability

Probability (or chance) is a way of describing the likelihood of different possible *outcomes* occurring as a result of some *experiment.*

In the example of the library books, the experiment is looking in the library for a particular book. Let us assume that you already know that the book you want is on the library's stocks. The three possible outcomes are that the book is on the shelves, out on loan or missing.

It is important in probability to distinguish experiments from the outcomes which they may generate. Here are a few examples.

Experiments	Possible outcomes
• Guessing the answer to a four-option multiple choice question	A B C D
• Predicting the stamp on the next letter I receive	first class second class foreign other
• Tossing a coin	heads tails

Another word for experiment is *trial.* This is used in Chapters 6 and 7 of this book to describe the binomial situation where there are just two possible outcomes.

Another word you should know is *event.* This often describes several outcomes put together. For example, when rolling a die, an event could be 'the die shows an even number'. This event corresponds to three different outcomes from the trial, the die showing 2, 4 or 6. However, the term event is also often used to describe a single outcome.

Estimating probability

Probability is a number which measures likelihood. It may be estimated experimentally or theoretically.

Experimental estimation of probability

In many situations probabilities are estimated on the basis of data collected experimentally, as in the following example.

Of 30 drawing pins tossed in the air, 21 of them were found to have landed with their pins pointing up. From this you would estimate the probability that the next pin tossed in the air will land with its pin pointing up to be $\frac{21}{30}$ or 0.7.

You can describe this in more formal notation.

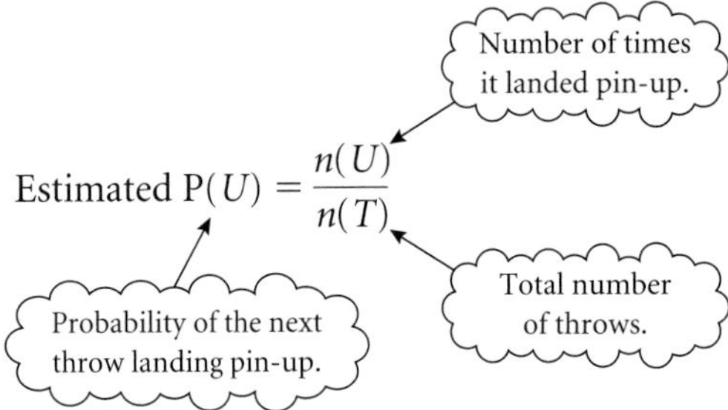

Theoretical estimation of probability

There are, however, some situations where you do not need to collect data to make an estimate of probability.

For example, when tossing a coin, common sense tells you that there are only two realistic outcomes and, given the symmetry of the coin, you would expect them to be equally likely. So the probability, P(H), that the next coin will produce the outcome heads can be written as follows:

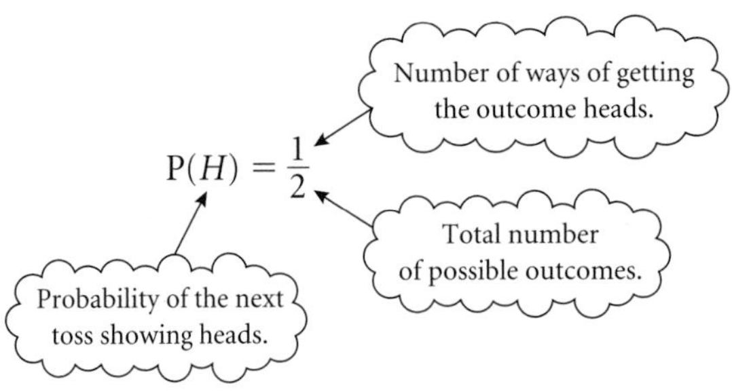

EXAMPLE 3.1

Using the notation described above, write down the probability that the correct answer for the next four-option multiple choice question will be answer *A*. What assumptions are you making?

SOLUTION

Assuming that the test-setter has used each letter equally often, the probability, P(*A*), that the next question will have answer *A* can be written as follows:

$$P(A) = \frac{1}{4}$$

Answer *A*.

Answers *A*, *B*, *C* and *D*.

Notice that we have assumed that the four options are equally likely. Equiprobability is an important assumption underlying most work on probability.

Expressed formally, the probability, P(*A*), of event *A* occurring is:

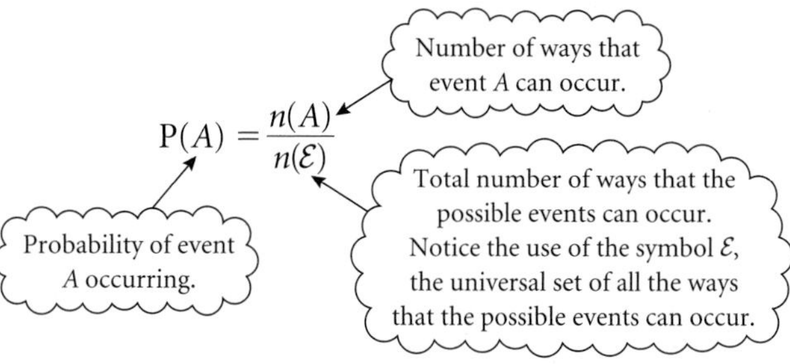
Number of ways that event A can occur.
P(A) = n(A)/n(ℰ)
Probability of event A occurring.
Total number of ways that the possible events can occur. Notice the use of the symbol ℰ, the universal set of all the ways that the possible events can occur.

Probabilities of 0 and 1

The two extremes of probability are *certainty* at one end of the scale and *impossibility* at the other. Here are examples of certain and impossible events.

Experiments	Certain events	Impossible events
• Rolling a single die	The result is in the range 1 to 6 inclusive	The result is a 7
• Tossing a coin	Getting either heads or tails	Getting neither heads nor tails

Certainty

As you can see from the table above, for events that are certain, the number of ways that the event can occur, $n(A)$ in the formula, is equal to the total number of possible events, $n(\mathcal{E})$.

$$\frac{n(A)}{n(\mathcal{E})} = 1$$

So the probability of an event which is certain is one.

Impossibility

For impossible events, the number of ways that the event can occur, $n(A)$, is zero.

$$\frac{n(A)}{n(\mathcal{E})} = \frac{0}{n(\mathcal{E})} = 0$$

So the probability of an event which is impossible is zero.

Typical values of probabilities might be something like 0.3 or 0.9. If you arrive at probability values of, say, -0.4 or 1.7, you will know that you have made a mistake since these are meaningless.

$$0 \leqslant \mathrm{P}(A) \leqslant 1$$

The complement of an event

The complement of an event A, denoted by A', is the event *not-A*, that is the event 'A does not happen'.

EXAMPLE 3.2

It was found that, out of a box of 50 matches, 45 lit but the others did not. What was the probability that a randomly selected match would not have lit?

SOLUTION

The probability that a randomly selected match lit was

$$\mathrm{P}(A) = \frac{45}{50} = 0.9.$$

The probability that a randomly selected match did not light was

$$\mathrm{P}(A') = \frac{50 - 45}{50} = \frac{5}{50} = 0.1.$$

From this example you can see that

$$P(A') = 1 - P(A)$$

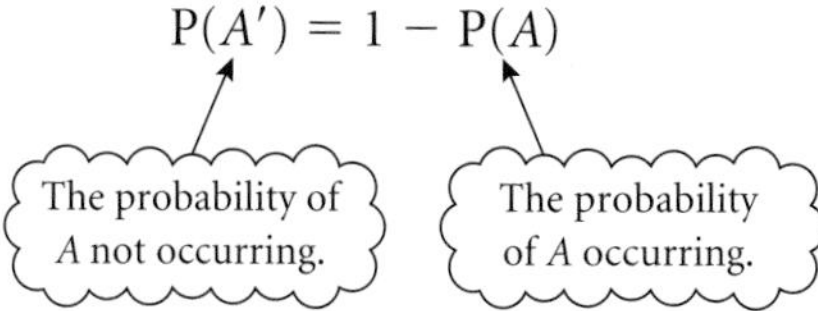

This is illustrated in figure 3.1.

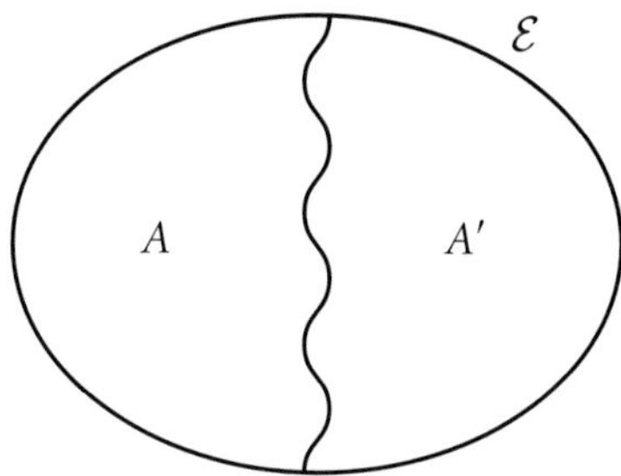

Figure 3.1 *Venn diagram showing events A and not-A (A′)*

Expectation

AVONFORD STAR

Avonford braced for flu epidemic

Local health services are poised for their biggest challenge in years. The virulent strain of flu, named Trengganu B from its origins in Malaysia, currently sweeping across Europe is expected to hit Avonford any day.

With a chance of one in three of any individual contracting the disease, and 120 000 people within the Health Area, surgeries and hospitals are expecting to be swamped with patients.

Local doctor Aloke Ghosh says 'Immunisation seems to be ineffective against this strain'.

How many people can the Health Area expect to contract flu? The answer is easily seen to be $120\,000 \times \frac{1}{3} = 40\,000$. This is called the *expectation* or *expected frequency* and is given in this case by np where n is the population size and p the probability.

Expectation is a technical term and need not be a whole number. Thus the expectation of the number of heads when a coin is tossed 5 times is $5 \times \frac{1}{2} = 2.5$. You would be wrong to go on to say 'That means either 2 or 3' or to qualify your answer as 'about $2\frac{1}{2}$'. The expectation is 2.5.

The idea of expectation of a discrete random variable is explored more thoroughly in Chapter 4. Applications to the binomial distribution are covered in Chapter 6.

The probability of either one event or another

So far we have looked at just one event at a time. However, it is often useful to bracket two or more of the events together and calculate their combined probability.

EXAMPLE 3.3

The table below is based on the data at the beginning of this chapter and shows the probability of the next book requested falling into each of the three categories listed, assuming that each book is equally likely to be requested.

Category of book	Typical numbers	Probability
On the shelves (S)	20 000	0.25
Out on loan (L)	44 000	0.55
Unauthorised loan (U)	16 000	0.20
Total ($S + L + U$)	80 000	1.00

What is the probability that a randomly requested book is *either* out on loan or on unauthorised loan (i.e. that it is not available)?

SOLUTION

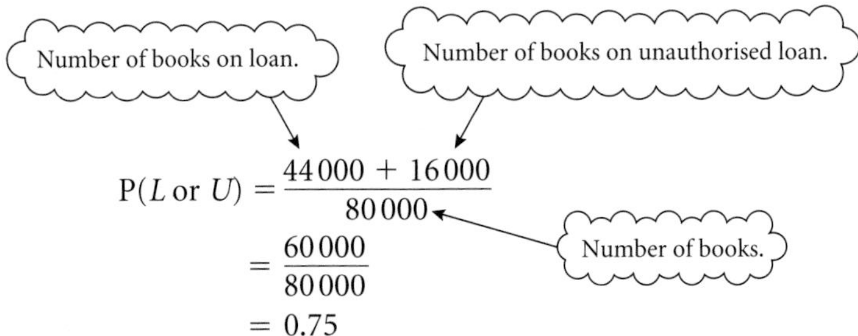

$$P(L \text{ or } U) = \frac{44000 + 16000}{80000} = \frac{60000}{80000} = 0.75$$

This can be written in more formal notation as

$$P(L \cup U) = \frac{n(L \cup U)}{n(\mathcal{E})}$$

$$= \frac{n(L)}{n(\mathcal{E})} + \frac{n(U)}{n(\mathcal{E})}$$

$$P(L \cup U) = P(L) + P(U)$$

Notice the use of the *union* symbol, ∪, to mean *or*. This is illustrated in figure 3.2.

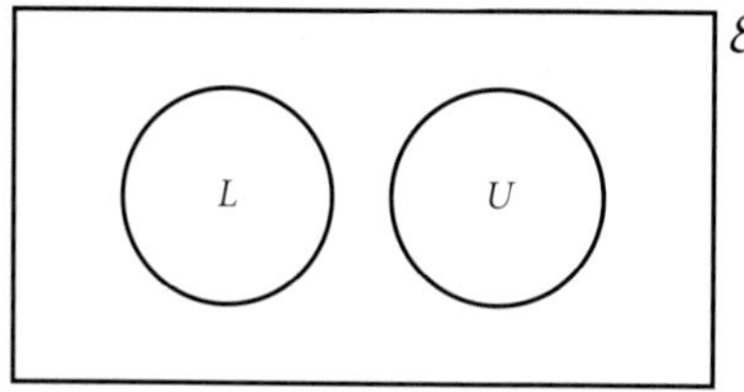

Key: L = out on loan
U = out on unauthorised loan

Figure 3.2 *Venn diagram showing events L and U. It is not possible for both to occur.*

In this example you could add the probabilities of the two events to get the combined probability of *either one or the other* event occurring. However, you have to be very careful adding probabilities as you will see in the next example.

EXAMPLE 3.4

Below are further details of the categories of books in the library.

Category of book	Number of books
On the shelves	20 000
Out on loan	44 000
Adult fiction	22 000
Adult non-fiction	40 000
Junior	18 000
Unauthorised loan	16 000
Total stock	80 000

Assuming all the books in the library are equally likely to be requested, find the probability that the next book requested will be either out on loan or a book of adult non-fiction.

SOLUTION

$$\text{P(on loan)} + \text{P(adult non-fiction)} = \frac{44\,000}{80\,000} + \frac{40\,000}{80\,000}$$
$$= 0.55 + 0.5 = 1.05$$

This is clearly nonsense as you cannot have a probability greater than 1.

So what has gone wrong?

The way this calculation was carried out involved some double counting. Some of the books classed as adult non-fiction were counted twice because they were also in the on-loan category, as you can see from figure 3.3.

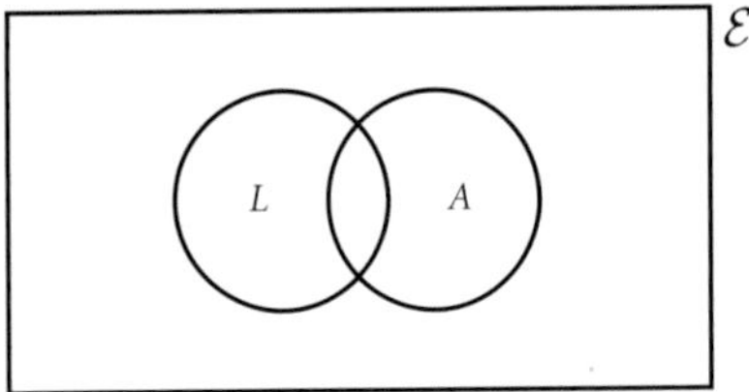

Key: L = out on loan
A = adult non-fiction

Figure 3.3 *Venn diagram showing events L and A. It is possible for both to occur.*

If you add all six of the book categories together, you find that they add up to 160 000, which represents twice the total number of books owned by the library.

A more useful representation of these data is given in the two-way table below.

	Adult fiction	Adult non-fiction	Junior	Total
On the shelves	4 000	12 000	4 000	20 000
Out on loan	14 000	20 000	10 000	44 000
Unauthorised loan	4 000	8 000	4 000	16 000
Total	22 000	40 000	18 000	80 000

If you simply add 44 000 and 40 000, you *double count* the 20 000 books which fall into both categories. So you need to subtract the 20 000 to ensure that it is counted only once. Thus:

Number either out on loan or adult non-fiction

$$= 44\,000 + 40\,000 - 20\,000$$
$$= 64\,000 \text{ books.}$$

So, the required probability $= \dfrac{64\,000}{80\,000} = 0.8.$

Mutually exclusive events

The problem of double counting does not occur when adding two rows in the table. Two rows cannot overlap, or *intersect*, which means that those categories are *mutually exclusive* (i.e. the one excludes the other). The same is true for two columns within the table.

Where two events, A and B, are mutually exclusive, the probability that either A or B occurs is equal to the sum of the separate probabilities of A and B occurring.

Where two events, A and B, are *not* mutually exclusive, the probability that either A or B occurs is equal to the sum of the separate probabilities of A and B occurring minus the probability of A and B occurring together.

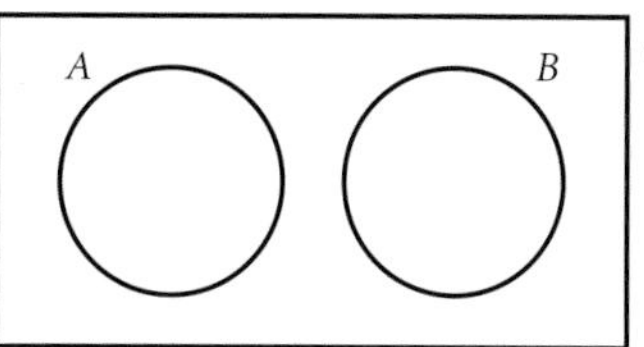

(a) *Mutually exclusive events*

(b) *Not mutually exclusive events*

Figure 3.4

$P(A \cup B) = P(A) + P(B)$

$P(A \cup B) = P(A) + P(B) - P(A \cap B)$

Notice the use of the intersection sign, ∩, to mean *both … and …*.

EXAMPLE 3.5

A fair die is thrown. What is the probability that it shows

(i) Event A: an even number

(ii) Event B: a number greater than 4

(iii) Event $A \cup B$: a number which is either even or greater than 4?

SOLUTION

(i) Event A:

Three out of the six numbers on a die are even, namely 2, 4 and 6.

So $P(A) = \frac{3}{6} = \frac{1}{2}$.

(ii) Event B:

Two out of the six numbers on a die are greater than 4, namely 5 and 6.

So $P(B) = \frac{2}{6} = \frac{1}{3}$.

(iii) Event $A \cup B$:

Four of the numbers on a die are either even or greater than 4, namely 2, 4, 5 and 6.

So $P(A \cup B) = \frac{4}{6} = \frac{2}{3}$.

This could also be found using

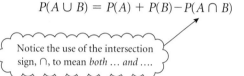

$$P(A \cup B) = P(A) + P(B) - P(A \cap B)$$

$$P(A \cup B) = \frac{3}{6} + \frac{2}{6} - \frac{1}{6}$$

$$= \frac{4}{6} = \frac{2}{3}$$

This is the number 6 which is both even and greater than 4.

EXERCISE 3A

1 The personnel department of a company decides to find out the proportions of the staff who are married and unmarried. There are 80 staff members in total. 20 are men, of whom 18 are married; 15 of the women are single.

(i) Copy and complete this table.

	Married	Unmarried	Total
Men			
Women			
Total			80

(ii) Suggest two reasons why the personnel department might find this information useful.

(iii) An employee is selected at random to show a visitor round the company. What is the probability that the person is

(a) a married man

(b) a single woman

(c) a single man

(d) a married person?

2 A farmer's daughter has to make up a probability question for her maths homework. This is her question.

On a farm there are 36 animals which are either cows or goats. 20 animals are all brown and the rest are all white. There are 10 white goats and 4 brown cows.

(i) *Draw a suitable table to show the data.*

(ii) *An animal is chosen at random. What is the probability that it is*

(a) *a white animal*

(b) *a cow*

(c) *brown and is not a cow?*

What are the correct answers?

3 A geography lecturer is trying to decide on a date for a field trip. It will be in either March or October. She looks at the weather for March and October the previous year.

Weather		Number of days in March	Number of days in October
Dry	Hot	0	5
	Medium	8	9
	Cold	10	10
Wet	Hot	0	2
	Medium	11	5
	Cold	2	0

She selects a day at random. Based on last year's weather data where necessary, what is the probability that her chosen day is

(i) in October

(ii) in March and not cold

(iii) not cold

(iv) dry?

4 The Venn diagram shows details of children in a co-educational school.

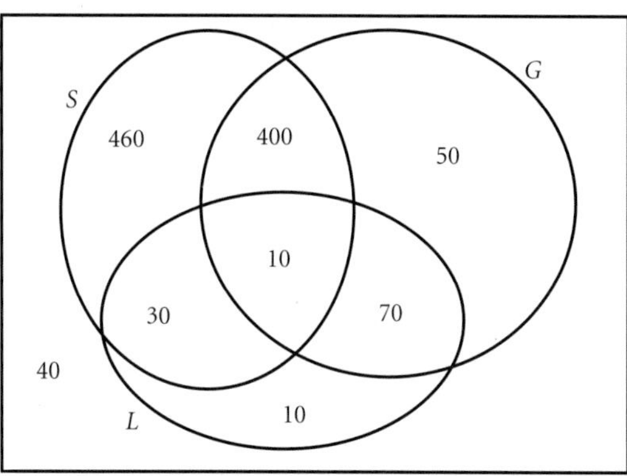

Key: G = girls in the school
S = children who can swim
L = children who are left handed

(i) How many left-handed children are there?

(ii) How many girls cannot swim?

(iii) A boy is selected at random. What is the probability that

(a) he can swim

(b) he is left-handed?

(iv) A girl is selected at random. What is the probability that

(a) she is left-handed

(b) she is left-handed and can swim?

5 Sandra has 60 different vitamin pills in the same bottle. Each pill contains at least one of the vitamins A, B and C.

12 pills have vitamin A only.
7 pills have vitamin B only.
11 pills have vitamin C only.
7 pills have vitamins A and B only.
8 pills have vitamins B and C only.
6 pills have all three vitamins.

(i) How many pills have vitamins A and C only?

(ii) Draw a Venn diagram to show this information.

(iii) How many pills contain vitamin A?

(iv) Sandra selects a pill at random. What is the probability that it contains exactly two vitamins?

6 Students on a particular degree course have three main options to choose from. These are Computing in Society (C), Pascal Computer Language (P) and Basic Computer Skills (B). However, they do not have to choose any of these options. In 2007 the following information is obtained.

- There are 125 students on the course.
- 12 students study both Computing in Society and Pascal Computer Language but not Basic Computer Skills.
- 41 students study both Computing in Society and Basic Computer Skills but not Pascal Computer Language.
- 18 students study just Computing in Society.
- $n(\text{C} \cap \text{P} \cap \text{B}) = 5$
- $n(\text{P} \cap \text{B}) = 9$
- $n(\text{P}) = 31$
- $n(\text{B}) = 57$

(i) Draw a Venn diagram to show this information.

(ii) How many students did not choose any of these three options?

(iii) Find the probability that a randomly selected student studies just two options from the three above.

(iv) Find the probability that a randomly selected student studies just one option from the three above.

7 An animal sanctuary categorises its animals in various ways, including:

- Animals that had been badly treated by their owners, B
- Dogs, D
- Animals which have been at the sanctuary for at least a month, M.

One day there are 385 animals in the sanctuary.
There are 189 dogs, 45 of which had been badly treated by their owners but have been there for less than a month.
80 dogs have been at the sanctuary for more than a month but had not been badly treated.
126 animals (not dogs) that had not been badly treated have been at the sanctuary for more than a month.
22 cats have been at the sanctuary for less than a month and had been badly treated.
There are 254 animals that have been at the sanctuary for more than a month.
Also there are 35 dogs that have been there for more than a month and had been badly treated.

(i) How many animals are not dogs?

(ii) How many animals are not dogs, had been badly treated and have been at the sanctuary for at least a month?

An animal is selected at random.

(iii) Find the probability that it is a dog that had been badly treated.

(iv) Find the probability that the animal is not a dog and has been at the sanctuary less than a month.

8 A company decides to support a local hospice and wants to raise money for a new extension. The fund-raising committee decide to run a lottery. There is be a first prize of £100, a second prize of £50 and a third prize of £25. There are 3000 tickets costing £1 each. The tickets were printed for free. People can only buy one ticket each. All the tickets are sold.

(i) What is the probability of winning a prize?

(ii) What is the probability of not winning a prize?

(iii) How much money does the company raise for the hospice?

(iv) How many tickets had to be sold before any money was raised for the hospice?

The following year the committee decide to increase the prizes to £200, £100 and £50 and sell 5000 tickets. They also allow people to buy as many tickets as they wish.

(v) If all the tickets are sold, how much will they raise for the hospice?

The committee feel they are not raising enough money. They have to choose from the following two options.

Option A	One prize of £500	5000 tickets costing £1 each	Sell all the tickets
Option B	Prizes of £500, £100 and £50	3000 tickets costing £2 each	Sell all the tickets

(vi) How much money would be raised by each option and which option is the better one?

(vii) If only half the tickets are sold, which option is better now?

(viii) Under which scheme is a ticket holder more likely to win a prize?

The probability of events from two trials

AVONFORD STAR

A Chance in a Million

I don't know whether Veronica, 14, saw a black cat last Saturday morning, or six magpies, or what, but it was certainly her lucky day.

Not only did her one and only ticket win her the top prize of £100 in the raffle at Avonford Summer Fair but later in the afternoon she received another £50 when her programme number came up in the programme draw.

Veronica said, 'To be honest, I didn't even know there was a programme draw. I was just about to throw mine away when they announced the winning number. I couldn't believe it – two wins in one day. It must be a chance in a million.'

This story describes two pieces of good fortune on the same day. Veronica said the probability was about $\frac{1}{1\,000\,000}$. What was it really?

The two events resulted from two different experiments, the raffle and the programme draw. Consequently this situation is different from those you met in the previous section. There you were looking at two events from a single experiment (like the number coming up when a die is thrown being even or being greater than 4).

The total sales of raffle tickets were 1245 and of programmes 324. The draws were conducted fairly, that is each number had an equal chance of being selected. The table below sets out the two experiments and their corresponding events with associated probabilities.

Experiment	Events (and estimated probabilities)
Raffle	Winning with a single ticket: $\frac{1}{1245}$
	Not winning with a single ticket: $\frac{1244}{1245}$
Programme draw	Winning with a single programme: $\frac{1}{324}$
	Not winning with a single programme: $\frac{323}{324}$

In situations like this the possible outcomes resulting from the different experiments are often shown on a *tree diagram.*

EXAMPLE 3.6

Find, in advance of the results of the two draws, the probability that

(i) Veronica would win both draws

(ii) Veronica would fail to win either draw

(iii) Veronica would win exactly one of the two draws.

SOLUTION

The possible results are shown on the tree diagram in figure 3.5.

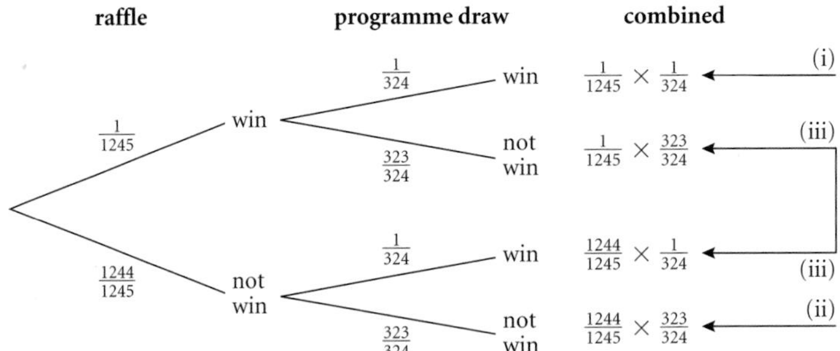

Figure 3.5

(i) The probability that Veronica wins both

$$= \frac{1}{1245} \times \frac{1}{324} = \frac{1}{403\,380}$$

This is not quite Veronica's 'one in a million' but it is not very far off it.

(ii) The probability that Veronica wins neither

$$= \frac{1244}{1245} \times \frac{323}{324} = \frac{401\,812}{403\,380}$$

This of course is much the most likely outcome.

(iii) The probability that Veronica wins one but not the other is given by

$$= \frac{1}{1245} \times \frac{323}{324} + \frac{1244}{1245} \times \frac{1}{324} = \frac{1567}{403\,380}$$

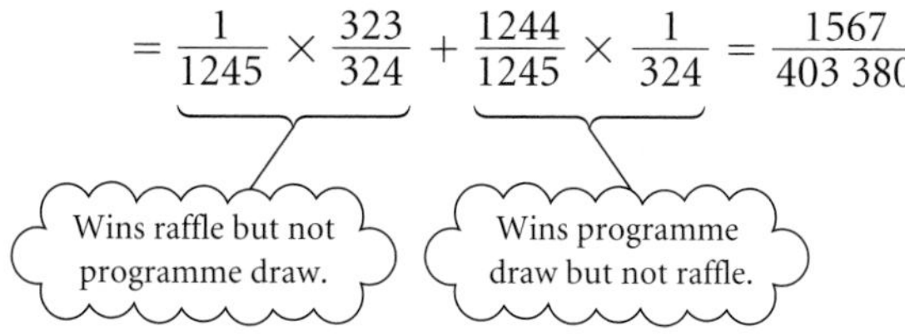

Look again at the structure of the tree diagram in figure 3.5.

There are two experiments, the raffle and the programme draw. These are considered as *First, Then* experiments, and set out *First* on the left and *Then* on the right. Once you understand this, the rest of the layout falls into place, with the different outcomes or events appearing as branches. In this example there are two branches at each stage; sometimes there may be three or more. Notice that for a given situation the component probabilities sum to 1, as before.

$$\frac{1}{403\,380} + \frac{323}{403\,380} + \frac{1244}{403\,380} + \frac{401\,812}{403\,380} = \frac{403\,380}{403\,380} = 1$$

EXAMPLE 3.7

Some friends buy a six-pack of potato crisps. Two of the bags are snake flavoured (S), the rest are frog flavoured (F). They decide to allocate the bags by lucky dip. Find the probability that

(i) the first two bags chosen are of the same flavour

(ii) the first two bags chosen are of different flavours.

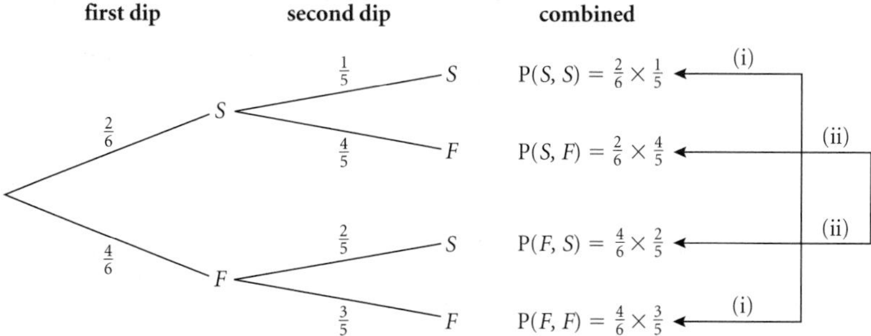

Figure 3.6

SOLUTION

Note: $P(F, S)$ means the probability of drawing a frog bag (F) on the first dip and a snake bag (S) on the second.

(i) The probability that the first two bags chosen are of the same flavour

$$= P(S, S) + P(F, F) = \frac{2}{6} \times \frac{1}{5} + \frac{4}{6} \times \frac{3}{5}$$

$$= \frac{1}{15} + \frac{6}{15}$$

$$= \frac{7}{15}$$

(ii) The probability that the first two bags chosen are of different flavours

$$= \mathrm{P}(S, F) + \mathrm{P}(F, S) = \tfrac{2}{6} \times \tfrac{4}{5} + \tfrac{4}{6} \times \tfrac{2}{5}$$
$$= \tfrac{4}{15} + \tfrac{4}{15}$$
$$= \tfrac{8}{15}$$

Note

The answer to part (ii) above hinged on the fact that two orderings (*S* then *F*, and *F* then *S*) are possible for the same combined event (that the two bags selected include one snake and one frog bag).

The probabilities changed between the first dip and the second dip. This is because the outcome of the second dip is *dependent* on the outcome of the first one (with fewer bags remaining to choose from).

By contrast, the outcomes of the two experiments involved in tossing a coin twice are *independent*, and so the probability of getting a head on the second toss remains unchanged at 0.5, whatever the outcome of the first toss.

Although you may find it helpful to think about combined events in terms of how they would be represented on a tree diagram, you may not always actually draw them in this way. If there are several experiments and perhaps more than two possible outcomes from each, drawing a tree diagram can be very time-consuming.

Calvin, a keen gambler, writes a regular article in the *Avonford Star* entitled 'Calvin's Tips'. This is one of them.

AVONFORD STAR

Calvin's Tips

I was playing roulette last night. The first time I bet on my lucky number 7 and lucky it was. I then put all my winnings on my other lucky number, 4. That came up too so I collected my winnings and moved off to a poker table.

When I came back later I found my friend Katy still at the roulette table, looking very cross. 'My lucky number is 17 and I have tried it 40 times and not once has it come up,' she explained. 'I'm jinxed. I would have expected to win twice by now and that would make me £32 up not £40 down.'

I know I was lucky, but was Katy really that unlucky? Did she have good reason to think herself jinxed?

A roulette wheel has 37 numbers marked on it (0, 1, 2, 3, …, 36) so the probability that your number comes up on any roll is $\frac{1}{37}$.

On one roll,

$$\mathrm{P(win)} = \tfrac{1}{37} \quad \mathrm{P(not\ win)} = 1 - \tfrac{1}{37} = \tfrac{36}{37}.$$

On 40 rolls,

$$\mathrm{P(no\ wins)} = \tfrac{36}{37} \times \tfrac{36}{37} \times \tfrac{36}{37} \times \ldots \times \tfrac{36}{37} = \left(\tfrac{36}{37}\right)^{40}$$
$$= 0.334.$$

So no wins in 40 rolls is not particularly unlikely. Katy has no reason to think herself jinxed.

The probability of Calvin's outcome is $\frac{1}{37} \times \frac{1}{37} = 0.000\,73$. This is a low probability and he is quite right to think himself lucky.

The odds offered by most casinos for a single number are 35–1, meaning that if you bet £1 you win £35 and get your £1 back.

So on one roll the expectation of your winnings is

$$£\left(35 \times \tfrac{1}{37} - 1 \times \tfrac{36}{37}\right) = -2.7\text{p or a } 2.7\text{p loss.}$$

On 40 rolls Katy could expect to lose $40 \times 2.7\text{p} = £1.08$.

In fact she had lost £40 so perhaps she was entitled to think that luck was not on her side, but her statement that she should be £32 in profit was certainly not accurate.

EXAMPLE 3.8

AVONFORD STAR

Is this justice?

In 1991, local man David Starr was sentenced to 12 years' imprisonment for armed robbery solely on the basis of an identification parade. He was one of 12 people in the parade and was picked out by one witness but not by three others.

Many Avonford people who knew David well believe he was incapable of such a crime. We in the *Star* are now adding our voice to the clamour for a review of his case.

How conclusive, we ask, is this sort of evidence, or, to put it another way, how likely is it that a mistake has been made?

Investigate the likelihood that David Starr really did commit the robbery.

SOLUTION

In this situation you need to assess the probability of an innocent individual being picked out by chance alone. Assume that David Starr was innocent and the witnesses were selecting in a purely random way (that is, with a probability of $\frac{1}{12}$ of selecting each person and a probability of $\frac{11}{12}$ of not selecting each person). If each of the witnesses selected just one of the twelve people in the identity parade in this random manner, how likely is it that David Starr would be picked out by at least one witness?

$$\begin{aligned} \text{P(at least one selection)} &= 1 - \text{P(no selections)} \\ &= 1 - \tfrac{11}{12} \times \tfrac{11}{12} \times \tfrac{11}{12} \times \tfrac{11}{12} \\ &= 1 - 0.706 = 0.294 \text{ (i.e. roughly 30\%).} \end{aligned}$$

In other words, there is about a 30% chance of an innocent person being chosen in this way by at least one of the witnesses.

The newspaper article concluded:

AVONFORD STAR

Is 30% really the sort of figure we have in mind when judges use the phrase 'beyond reasonable doubt'? because if it is, many innocent people will be condemned to a life behind bars.

This raises an important statistical idea, which you will meet again in Chapter 7, about how we make judgements and decisions.

Judgements are usually made under conditions of uncertainty and involve us in having to weigh up the plausibility of one explanation against that of another. Statistical judgements are usually made on such a basis. We choose one explanation if we judge the alternative explanation to be sufficiently unlikely, that is if the probability of its being true is sufficiently small. Exactly how small this probability has to be will depend on the individual circumstances and is called the *significance level*.

Somebody on trial is assumed innocent until shown to be guilty beyond reasonable doubt; reasonable doubt must mean a very small probability that the person is innocent.

EXERCISE 3B

1 At a busy airport in the UK the security staff search the bags of 1 in 20 passengers, chosen at random. 45% of passengers are actually carrying a prohibited item, such as a penknife, scissors or a toy gun.

(i) Draw a tree diagram showing all the possible outcomes when a passenger goes through the security check, and the probability of each.

(ii) What is the probability of a passenger being found to have a prohibited item by the security staff?

(iii) Find the probability that a passenger has their luggage searched and is found not to have a prohibited item.

(iv) Given that 32 000 passengers go through the airport every day, how many out of those searched are not carrying prohibited items?

2 The probability of a middle-aged man in the UK having gallstones is 1 in 6. For middle-aged women it is 1 in 3. In a particular town, the ratio of middle-aged men to middle-aged women is 2 to 3.

(i) Draw a tree diagram to show the probability of men and women having gallstones.

A middle-aged person from the town is selected at random.

(ii) Find the probability that the person is a woman who has gallstones.

(iii) Find the probability that the person is a man who does not have gallstones.

30% of people who have gallstones go on to develop problems.

(iv) What is the probability that the person selected has gallstones and will go on to develop problems?

3 Mr Brown travels to work by train. If he catches the 7.00 am train, the chance of him getting to work on time is 95%. If he catches the 7.10 am train, he has a 20% chance of being late and, if he catches the 7.20 am train, he has a 50% chance of being late for work. The probabilities of him catching these trains are shown in the table below.

Time of train	Probability of catching train	Probability of being on time for work
7.00 am	0.8	0.95
7.10 am	0.15	
7.20 am	0.05	

(i) Copy and complete the table and then draw a tree diagram to show this information.

(ii) Find the probability that, on a randomly selected day,

(a) he catches the 7.10 am train and is late for work

(b) he is on time for work.

Mr Brown's boss makes employees who are late buy cakes for the morning coffee break.

(iii) What is the probability of Mr Brown buying cakes?

(iv) Comment on Mr Brown's punctuality.

4 A health report for a distant country states that one third of chickens carry a particular type of bacteria. The bacteria carried by half of these chickens are resistant to the antibiotics that the chickens are fed. 10% of the people who eat chickens with resistant bacteria will fall ill. 0.01% of those that fall ill will need hospital treatment.

(i) This tree diagram illustrates the situation when a randomly selected chicken is eaten. Copy and complete it with the probabilities.

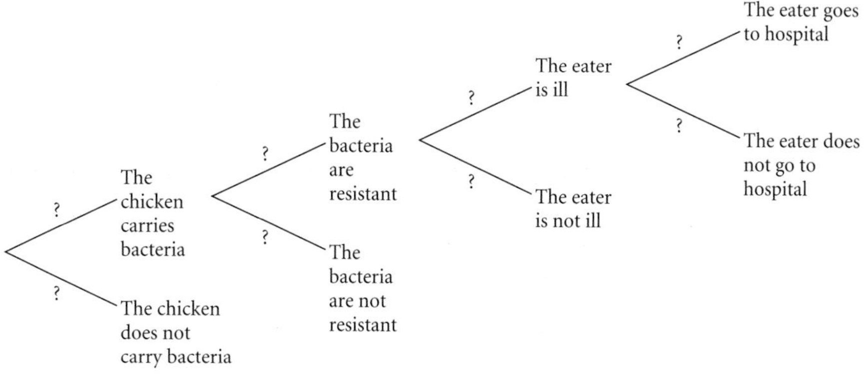

(ii) What is the probability of a person not becoming ill after eating chicken?

(iii) What is the probability of a person going to hospital after eating chicken?

(iv) If one million people eat chicken one day, how many are likely
(a) to become ill
(b) to end up in hospital?
(v) The report was based on a sample of 150 chickens. Comment on the sample and relate it to these results.

5 A company has one office in the centre of Paris and the other in the centre of Lyon. $\frac{2}{3}$ of the company's employees work in Paris. In the Paris office $\frac{1}{4}$ of the employees live in the city centre and the rest live in the suburbs. In the Lyon office $\frac{3}{8}$ of the employees live in the city centre and the rest live in the suburbs. The personnel department are interested to know where the employees live to help them target their advertising for new jobs.
(i) Draw a tree diagram to show this information.

An employee is selected at random.
(ii) What is the probability that the person
(a) lives in the centre of Paris
(b) lives in the suburbs of Paris
(c) lives in the centre of Lyon or Paris?
(iii) Should the advertising target those living in inner cities or suburbs?

6 One patient in twenty thousand is infected by a dangerous bacterium when in hospital. 99.5% of those who contract the infection will survive.
(i) Find the probability that a randomly selected patient
(a) is not infected by the dangerous bacterium
(b) is infected and does not survive.

After national publicity about the cleanliness of wards, one group of hospitals decides to employ ward matrons to run the wards and supervise the cleaning. Six months later, the rate of patients in these hospitals being infected had dropped to one patient in one hundred and fifty thousand and earlier detection means that 99.7% who contract the infection will survive.
(ii) Find the probability that a randomly selected patient at a hospital in the group
(a) is not infected by the dangerous bacterium
(b) is infected and does not survive.

7 Shaldon High School has two AS mathematics classes, called East and West, East and West each have 15 boys and 5 girls.
The East class chooses three students at random to represent it on the MCC (Mathematics Consultative Committee).

(i) Copy and complete the probability tree diagram to show all the possible choices of boys and girls from the East class.

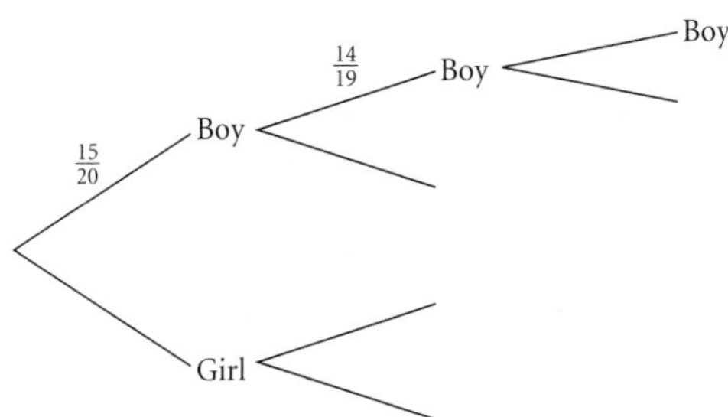

(ii) Find the probability that the East class is represented by

(a) three boys

(b) two boys and one girl.

The West class also chooses three students at random to represent it on the MCC, so that the MCC has six students altogether.

(iii) Find the probability that the MCC contains

(a) one girl and five boys

(b) at most one girl.

[MEI, *part*]

8 Wendy is an amateur weather forecaster. She classifies the weather on a day as either wet or fine. From past records she suggests that

- if a day is wet then the probability that the next day is wet is 0.5
- if a day is fine then the probability that the next day is fine is 0.8.

In a particular week, it is wet on Monday.

(i) Draw a probability tree diagram for wet or fine days on Tuesday, Wednesday and Thursday.

(ii) Find the probability that Tuesday, Wednesday and Thursday all have the same weather.

[MEI, *part*]

9 A test of proficiency can be taken up to three times by each of a large group of people. No-one who passes takes the test again.
60% of those attempting the test for the first time pass, as do 75% of those attempting it for the second time, and 30% of those attempting it for the third time.

(i) Find the probability that a randomly chosen person fails at all three attempts.

(ii) Find the probability that a randomly chosen person fails at the first attempt but passes at either the second or third attempt.

(iii) Write down the probability that a randomly chosen person passes the test.

[MEI, *part*]

Conditional probability

AVONFORD STAR

Local man dies of heart attack

Mr Paul Strangelove, 47, of Dunrobbin Close, collapsed while out shopping late yesterday afternoon. He was rushed to hospital but found to be dead on arrival.

What is the probability that somebody chosen at random will die of a heart attack in the next 12 months?

One approach would be to say that, since there are about 300 000 deaths per year from heart and circulatory diseases (H & CD) among the 57 000 000 population of the UK,

$$\text{probability} = \frac{\text{Number of deaths from H \& CD per year in UK}}{\text{Total population of UK}}$$

$$= \frac{300\,000}{57\,000\,000} = 0.0053.$$

However, if you think about it, you will probably realise that this is rather a meaningless figure. For a start, young people are much less at risk than those in or beyond middle age.

So you might wish to give two answers:

$$P_1 = \frac{\text{Deaths from H \& CD among over-40s}}{\text{Population of over-40s}}$$

$$P_2 = \frac{\text{Deaths from H \& CD among under-40s}}{\text{Population of under-40s}}$$

Typically only 1500 of the deaths would be among the under-40s leaving (on the basis of these figures) 298 500 among the over-40s. About 25 000 000 people in the UK are over 40, and 32 000 000 under 40 (40 years and 1 day counts as over 40). This gives

$$P_1 = \frac{\text{Deaths from H \& CD among over-40s}}{\text{Population of over-40s}} = \frac{298\,500}{25\,000\,000}$$

$$= 0.0119$$

and $$P_2 = \frac{\text{Deaths from H \& CD among under-40s}}{\text{Population of under-40s}} = \frac{1500}{32\,000\,000}$$

$$= 0.000\,047.$$

So somebody in the older group is over 200 times more likely to die of a heart attack than somebody in the younger group. Putting them both together as an average figure resulted in a figure that was representative of neither group. (The figures used in this section are approximated from those supplied by the British Heart Foundation who had themselves used a number of official sources.)

But why stop there? You could, if you had the figures, divide the population up into 10-year, 5-year, or even 1-year intervals. That would certainly improve the accuracy; but there are also other factors that you might wish to take into account.

- Is the person overweight?
- Does the person smoke?
- Does the person take regular exercise?
- Etc.

The more conditions you build in, the more accurate will be the estimate of the probability.

You can see how the conditions are brought in by looking at P_1:

$$P_1 = \frac{\text{Deaths from H \& CD among over-40s}}{\text{Population of over-40s}} = \frac{298\,500}{25\,000\,000}$$

$$= 0.0119$$

You would write this in symbols as follows:

Event G: Somebody selected at random is over 40.
Event H: Somebody selected at random dies from H & CD.

The probability of someone dying from H & CD given that he or she is over 40 is given by the conditional probability $\mathrm{P}(H \mid G)$ where

$$\mathrm{P}(H \mid G) = \frac{n(H \cap G)}{n(G)}$$

$$= \frac{n(H \cap G)/n(\mathcal{E})}{n(G)/n(\mathcal{E})}$$

$$= \frac{\mathrm{P}(H \cap G)}{\mathrm{P}(G)}.$$

$\mathrm{P}(H \mid G)$ means the probability of event H occurring *given that* event G has occurred.

This result may be written in general form for all cases of conditional probability for events A and B.

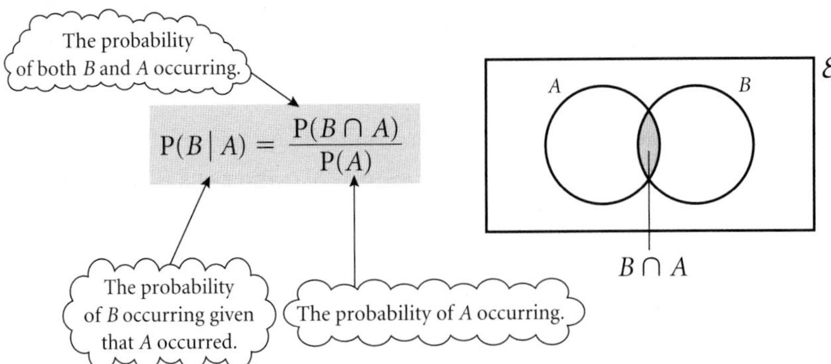

Conditional probability is used when your estimate of the probability of an event is altered by your knowledge of whether some other event has occurred. In this case the estimate of the probability of somebody dying from heart and circulatory diseases, $P(H)$, is altered by a knowledge of whether the person is over 40 or not.

Thus conditional probability addresses the question of whether one event is dependent on another one. If the probability of event B is not affected by the occurrence of event A, we say that B is *independent* of A. If, on the other hand, the probability of event B is affected by the occurrence (or not) of event A, we say that B is *dependent* on A.

If A and B are independent, then $P(B \mid A) = P(B \mid A')$ and this is just $P(B)$.

If A and B are dependent, then $P(B \mid A) \neq P(B \mid A')$.

As you have already seen, the probability of a combined event is the product of the separate probabilities of each event, provided the question of dependence between the two events is properly dealt with. Specifically:

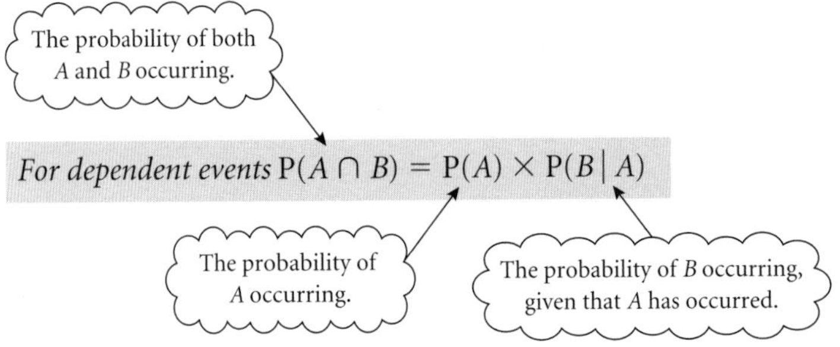

When A and B are independent events, then, because $P(B \mid A) = P(B)$, this can be written as

For independent events $P(A \cap B) = P(A) \times P(B)$

EXAMPLE 3.9

A company is worried about the high turnover of its employees and decides to investigate whether they are more likely to stay if they are given training.
On 1 January one year the company employed 256 people (excluding those about to retire). During that year a record was kept of who received training as well as who left the company. The results are summarised in this table:

	Still employed	Left company	Total
Given training	109	**43**	152
Not given training	60	**44**	104
Total	169	**87**	256

Find the probability that a randomly selected employee

(i) received training

(ii) did not leave the company

(iii) received training and did not leave the company

(iv) did not leave the company, given that the person had received training

(v) did not leave the company, given that the person had not received training.

SOLUTION

Using the notation T: The employee received training
S: The employee stayed in the company

(i) $\mathrm{P}(T) = \dfrac{n(T)}{n(\mathcal{E})} = \dfrac{152}{256}$

(ii) $\mathrm{P}(S) = \dfrac{n(S)}{n(\mathcal{E})} = \dfrac{169}{256}$

(iii) $\mathrm{P}(T \cap S) = \dfrac{n(T \cap S)}{n(\mathcal{E})} = \dfrac{109}{256}$

(iv) $\mathrm{P}(S|T) = \dfrac{\mathrm{P}(S \cap T)}{\mathrm{P}(T)} = \dfrac{\frac{109}{256}}{\frac{152}{256}} = \dfrac{109}{152} = 0.72$

(v) $\mathrm{P}(S|T') = \dfrac{\mathrm{P}(S \cap T')}{\mathrm{P}(T')} = \dfrac{\frac{60}{256}}{\frac{104}{256}} = \dfrac{60}{104} = 0.58$

Since $\mathrm{P}(S|T)$ is not the same as $\mathrm{P}(S|T')$, the event S is not independent of the event T. Each of S and T is dependent on the other, a conclusion which matches common sense. It is almost certainly true that training increases employees' job satisfaction and so makes them more likely to stay, but it is also probably true that the company is more likely to go to the expense of training the employees who seem less inclined to move on to other jobs.

How would you show that the event T is not independent of the event S?

In some situations you may find it helps to represent a problem such as this as a Venn diagram.

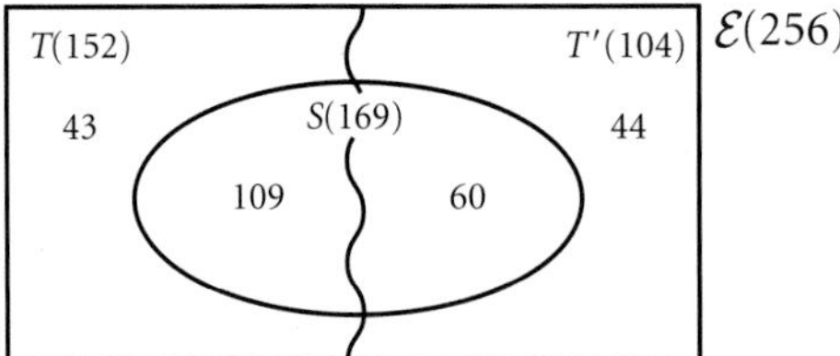

Figure 3.7

What do the various numbers and letters represent?
Where is the region S'?
How are the numbers on the diagram related to the answers to parts **(i)** to **(v)**?

In other situations it may be helpful to think of conditional probabilities in terms of tree diagrams. Conditional probabilities are needed when events are *dependent*, that is when the outcome of one trial affects the outcomes from a subsequent trial, so, for dependent events, the probabilities of all but the first layer of a tree diagram will be conditional.

EXAMPLE 3.10

Rebecca is buying two goldfish from a pet shop. The shop's tank contains seven male fish and eight female fish but they all look the same.

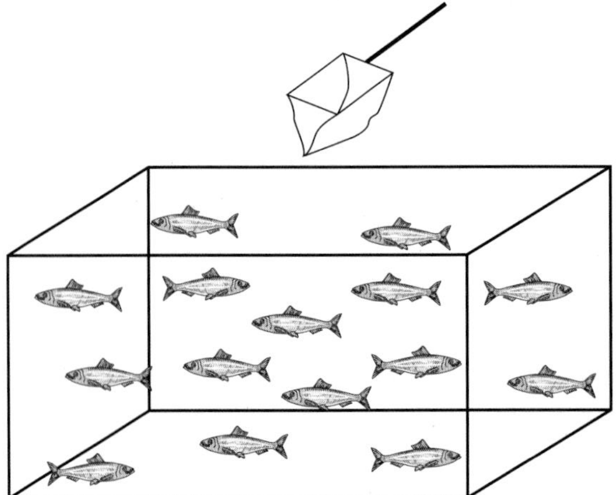

Figure 3.8

Find the probability that Rebecca's fish are

(i) both the same sex

(ii) both female

(iii) both female given that they are the same sex.

SOLUTION

The situation is shown on this tree diagram.

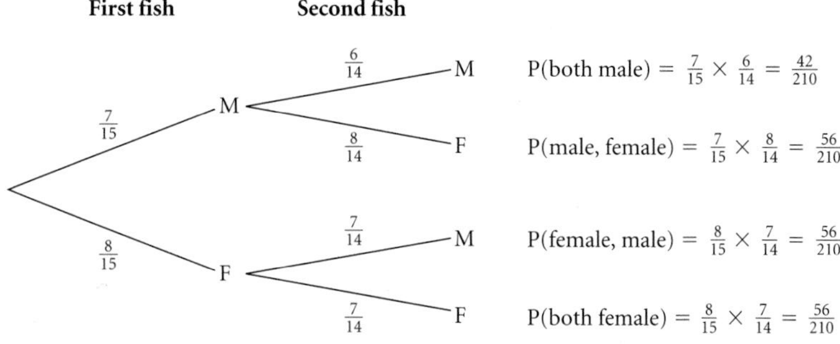

Figure 3.9

(i) P(both the same sex) = P(both male) + P(both female)

$$= \frac{42}{210} + \frac{56}{210} = \frac{98}{210} = \frac{7}{15}$$

(ii) P(both female) $= \frac{56}{210} = \frac{4}{15}$

(iii) P(both female | both the same sex)

$$= \text{P(both female and the same sex)} \div \text{P(both the same sex)} = \frac{\frac{4}{15}}{\frac{7}{15}} = \frac{4}{7}$$

This is the same as P(both female).

The ideas in the last example can be expressed more generally for any two dependent events, A and B. The tree diagram would be as shown in figure 3.10.

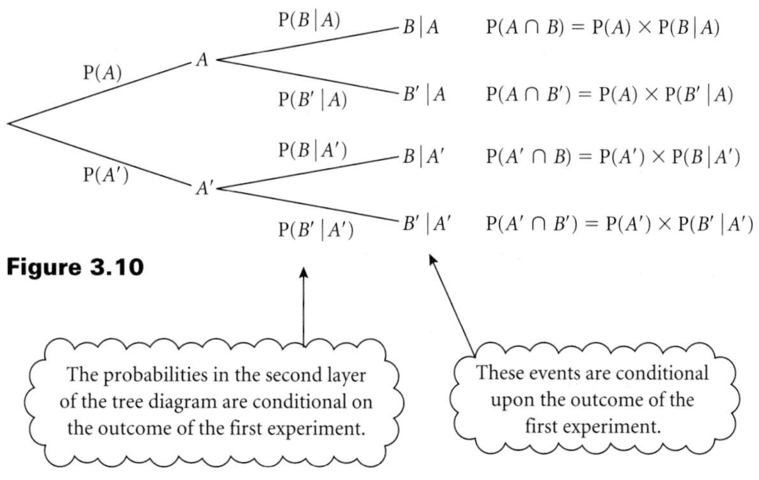

Figure 3.10

The tree diagram shows you that

- $\mathrm{P}(B) = \mathrm{P}(A \cap B) + \mathrm{P}(A' \cap B)$
  $= \mathrm{P}(A) \times \mathrm{P}(B \mid A) + \mathrm{P}(A') \times \mathrm{P}(B \mid A')$
- $\mathrm{P}(A \cap B) = \mathrm{P}(A) \times \mathrm{P}(B \mid A)$
  $\Rightarrow \mathrm{P}(B \mid A) = \dfrac{\mathrm{P}(A \cap B)}{\mathrm{P}(A)}$

? How were these results used in Example 3.10 about the goldfish?

EXERCISE 3C

1 A charity in Africa rescues orphaned baby elephants. The probability of an orphan surviving its initial ordeal, once it has been rescued, is 0.6. For those that survive the initial ordeal, the probability of then reaching adulthood is 0.7. The probability of an adult elephant being successfully returned to the wild is 0.9.

(i) Draw a tree diagram to show this information.

(ii) An orphaned elephant is rescued. Find the probability that it

(a) is successfully returned to the wild

(b) reaches adulthood but is not successfully returned to the wild.

(iii) What proportion of those rescued orphan elephants that do not survive die as a result of the initial ordeal?

2 A budget airline sells seats in different categories and at different prices.

Early sales:	20%	90% at reduced price
Normal sales:	70%	60% at reduced price
Late sales:	10%	50% at reduced price

(i) Draw a tree diagram showing the time seats were sold and whether the seats sold at full or reduced prices.

(ii) A ticket holder is selected at random. Find the probability that the person's ticket is

(a) a normal ticket that was sold at a reduced price

(b) a ticket that was sold at full price.

(iii) Given that a ticket is reduced, what is the probability that it was an early sale?

3 A market gardener has a stock of *nigella* seeds. She plants 80% in her greenhouse but does not have room for the remaining 20% so plants them outside. The chance of a seed germinating in the greenhouse is 60% and for seeds planted directly into the garden it is only 20%. Seedlings that have germinated in the greenhouse have a 90% chance of surviving to become mature plants and those that have germinated outside in the garden only have a 40% chance of surviving to become mature plants.

(i) Illustrate this information on a tree diagram.

(ii) Find the probability of a *nigella* seed not becoming a mature plant.

(iii) Given that the plant survived to maturity, find the probability that it was grown in a greenhouse.

4 Some geography students are carrying out fieldwork. They make a list of all the properties in their local town. Then they classify them according to type and age. There are 503 properties in total.

	Type of housing		
Age	**Detached**	**Semi-detached**	**Terraced property or a flat**
Pre-1850	5	13	90
1850–1914	5	15	85
Inter-war	10	45	35
Post-war	30	60	15
Modern	15	45	35

A property is selected at random from the list.

(i) Find the probability that it is

(a) detached

(b) detached and built after 1914

(c) built before 1915 and semi-detached.

(ii) Given that the property is semi-detached, what is the probability of it not being modern?

5 A fruit machine has three small windows, in each of which a picture appears. When the fruit machine is played, pictures appear independently in each of the windows with the following probabilities.

Picture	Lemon	Orange	Cherry	Bell
Probability	0.4	0.3	0.2	0.1

(i) Find the probabilities that the three windows will display

(a) three bells

(b) a lemon, orange and cherry, in that order

(c) three different *fruits*, in any order (a bell is *not* a fruit).

(ii) Given that the windows display three fruits, find the conditional probability that they are all different.

For a stake of 10 pence, which is not returned, prize money is given for the following combinations.

3 lemons	50 pence	3 oranges	£1
3 cherries	£2	3 bells	£5

(iii) What is the probability of *not* winning a prize?

(iv) In one week the fruit machine is played 1000 times. How much profit would the machine be expected to make? [MEI]

6 I have three book tokens to give away to a class consisting of six boys and seven girls. I decide to write the 13 names on pieces of paper and to draw three at random to determine who gets the tokens.
Suppose that I *do not* replace the pieces of paper after drawing, so that nobody can win more than one token. Find, correct to 3 decimal places, the probability that

(i) all three tokens are awarded to boys

(ii) tokens are awarded to at least one boy and to at least one girl.

Now suppose I *do* replace the pieces of paper after drawing, so that it is possible for somebody to win more than one token. Find, correct to 3 decimal places, the probability that

(iii) all three tokens are awarded to boys

(iv) all three tokens are won by the same person

(v) there is someone who wins exactly two tokens.

[MEI]

7 A practical music examination can be taken once or twice. Those candidates who fail it on the first occasion take it a second time.
For those having their first attempt, 25% pass with distinction and 45% gain an ordinary pass. For those taking the examination for a second time, the corresponding figures are 5% and 70% respectively. The tree diagram illustrates the situation.

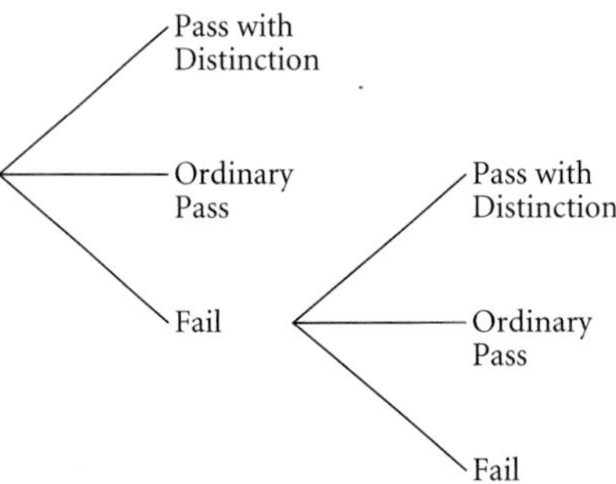

(i) Find the probability that a randomly chosen candidate

(a) fails the examination

(b) passes the examination (with or without distinction).

(ii) Given that a randomly chosen candidate passes the examination, find the probability that he or she passes with distinction.

(iii) Jill and Jo are two randomly chosen entrants for the examination. Find the probabilities that

(a) both pass (with or without distinction), but just one of them needs a second attempt

(b) Jill gets a better result than Jo.

[MEI]

8 New-born babies are tested for a mild illness which affects 1 in 500 babies. The result of a test is either positive or negative. A positive result suggests that the baby has the illness. However, the test is not perfect:

- for babies with the illness, the probability of a positive result is 0.99
- for babies without the illness, the probability of a negative result is 0.95.

A new-born baby is chosen at random and tested for the illness.

(i) Copy and complete this probability tree diagram to illustrate the situation.

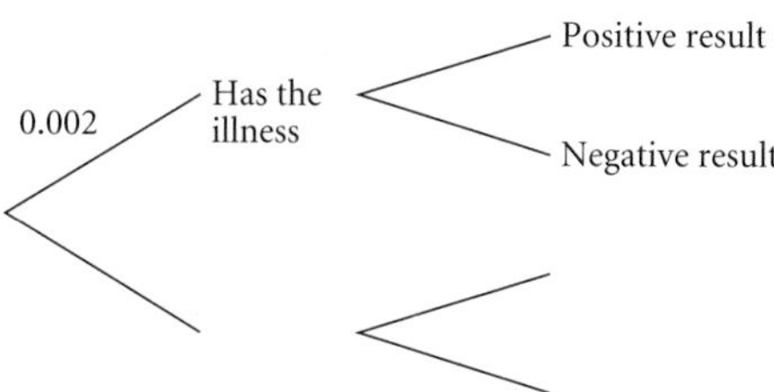

(ii) Find the probability that

(a) the result is positive

(b) the test gives the correct diagnosis.

(iii) Given that the result of a test is positive, show that the conditional probability that the baby has the illness is 0.038 (correct to 3 decimal places).

Comment on the test in the light of this value being so low.

It is required to raise the probability found in part **(iii)** by improving the testing process. To achieve this, it is intended to increase the probability of negative results for babies who do *not* have the illness from its current value of 0.95 to p.

(iv) Find the value for p that would raise the probability in part **(iii)** to 0.5.

[MEI]

9 In a certain city, there are just two political parties, the Red Party and the Blue Party. Each year one person from each party seeks to be elected as mayor of the city. If the city has a Red Party mayor one year, the probability that it has a Red Party mayor the next year is 0.5. If the city has a Blue Party mayor one year, the probability that it has a Blue Party mayor the next year is 0.7.

In the year 2004 the mayor belongs to the Blue Party.

(i) Illustrate the possible outcomes for mayor in the years 2005, 2006 and 2007 on a probability tree diagram.

(ii) Find the probability that

(a) the mayors in 2005 and 2006 belong to the same party

(b) the mayor in 2007 belongs to the Red Party

(c) the mayor for just one of the three years after 2004 belongs to the Blue Party.

(iii) Find the conditional probability that the mayor in 2005 belongs to the Red Party, given that the mayor in 2007 belongs to the Red Party.

[MEI]

KEY POINTS

1 The probability of an event A,

$$P(A) = \frac{n(A)}{n(\mathcal{E})},$$

where $n(A)$ is the number of ways that A can occur and $n(\mathcal{E})$ is the total number of ways that all possible events can occur, all of which are equally likely.

2 For any two events, A and B, of the same experiment,

$$P(A \cup B) = P(A) + P(B) - P(A \cap B).$$

Where the events are mutually exclusive (i.e. where the events do not overlap) the rule still holds but, since $P(A \cap B)$ is now equal to zero, the equation simplifies to:

$$P(A \cup B) = P(A) + P(B).$$

3 Where an experiment produces two or more mutually exclusive events, the probabilities of the separate events sum to 1.

4 $P(A) + P(A') = 1$

5 $P(B|A)$ means the probability of event B occurring given that event A has already occurred.

$$P(B|A) = \frac{P(A \cap B)}{(A)}$$

6 The probability that event A and then event B occur, in that order, is $P(A) \times P(B|A)$.

7 If event B is independent of event A, $P(B|A) = P(B|A') = P(B)$.

4 Discrete random variables

An approximate answer to the right problem is worth a good deal more than an exact answer to an approximate problem.

John Tukey

AVONFORD STAR

Traffic chaos in town centre – car-share scheme to go ahead

In an attempt to reduce the volume of traffic coming into and going out of Avonford town centre at peak times Avonford Council are to promote a car-share scheme.

Council spokesman, Andrew Siantonas, told the *Star*, 'In a recent traffic survey we found that there were far too many cars with only the driver in the car. We need to take action now to reduce the number of vehicles travelling through the town centre in the early morning and late afternoon. The Council have put aside a sum of money to fund a car-share scheme.

Interested drivers will be put in touch with one another using a central database. An advertising campaign is to start in the next few weeks. In six months time we will conduct another survey to measure the success of the scheme.'

? How would you collect information on the volume of traffic in the town centre?

A traffic survey, at critical points around the town centre, was conducted at peak travelling times over a period of a working week. The survey involved 1000 cars. The number of people in each car was noted, with the following results.

Number of people per car	1	2	3	4	5	>5
Frequency	560	240	150	40	10	0

? How would you illustrate such a distribution?
What are the main features of this distribution?

The numbers of people per car are necessarily discrete. A discrete frequency distribution is best illustrated by a vertical line chart, as in figure 4.1. This shows you that the distribution has positive skew, with the bulk of the data at the lower end of the distribution.

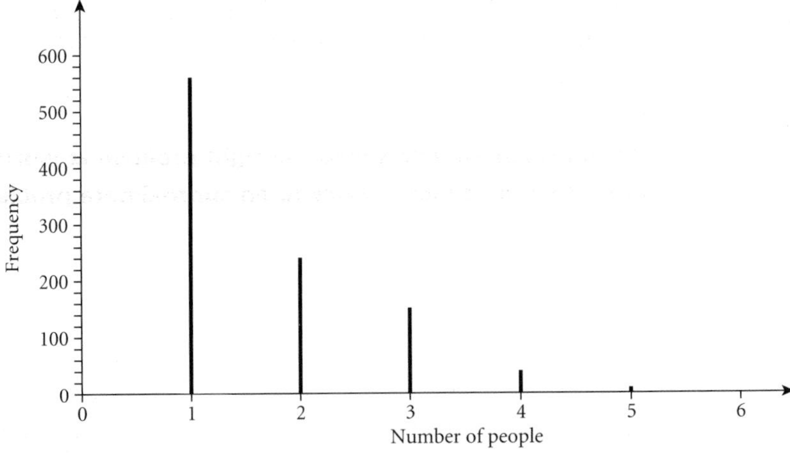

Figure 4.1

The survey involved 1000 cars. This is a large sample and so it is reasonable to use the results to estimate the *probabilities* of the various possible outcomes: 1, 2, 3, 4, 5 people per car. You divide each frequency by 1000 to obtain the *relative frequency*, or probability, of each outcome (number of people).

Outcome (Number of people)	1	2	3	4	5	>5
Probability (Relative frequency)	0.56	0.24	0.15	0.04	0.01	0

Discrete random variables

You now have a *mathematical model* to describe a particular situation. In statistics you are often looking for models to describe and explain the data you find in the real world. In this chapter you are introduced to some of the techniques for working with models for discrete data. Such models are called *discrete random variables.*

The model is *discrete* since the number of passengers can be counted and takes positive integer values only. The number of passengers is a *random variable* since the actual value of the outcome is variable and can only be predicted with a given probability, i.e. the outcomes occur at random.

Discrete random variables may have a *finite* or an *infinite* number of outcomes.

The distribution we have outlined so far is finite – in the survey the maximum number of people observed was five, but the maximum could be, say, eight, depending on the size of car. In this case there would be eight possible outcomes. A well known example of a finite discrete random variable is the *binomial distribution*, which you will study in Chapter 6.

On the other hand, if you considered the number of hits on a website in a given day, there may be no theoretical maximum, in which case the distribution may be considered as infinite. A well known example of an infinite discrete random variable is the *Poisson distribution*, which you will meet in Chapter 8.

The study of discrete random variables in this chapter will be limited to finite cases.

Notation and conditions for a discrete random variable

A discrete random variable is usually denoted by an upper case letter, such as X, Y, or Z. You may think of this as the name of the variable. The particular values that the variable takes are denoted by lower case letters, such as r. Sometimes these are given suffixes $r_1, r_2, r_3, \ldots$. Thus $P(X = r_1)$ means the probability that the discrete random variable X takes a particular value r_1. The expression $P(X = r)$ is used to express a more general idea, as, for example, in a table heading.

Another, shorter way of writing probabilities is $p_1, p_2, p_3, \ldots$. If a finite discrete random variable has n distinct outcomes $r_1, r_2, \ldots, r_n$, with associated probabilities $p_1, p_2, \ldots, p_n$, then the sum of the probabilities must equal 1. Since the various outcomes cover all possibilities, they are exhaustive.

Formally we have:

$$p_1 + p_2 + \ldots + p_n = 1$$

or $$\sum_{k=1}^{n} p_k = \sum_{k=1}^{n} P(X = r_k) = 1.$$

If there is no ambiguity then $\sum_{k=1}^{n} P(X = r_k)$ is often abbreviated to $\sum P(X = r)$.

Diagrams of discrete random variables

Just as with frequency distributions for discrete data, the most appropriate diagram to illustrate a discrete random variable is a vertical line chart. Figure 4.2 shows a diagram of the probability distribution of X, the number of people per car. Note that it is identical in shape to the corresponding frequency diagram in figure 4.1. The only real difference is the change of scale on the vertical axis.

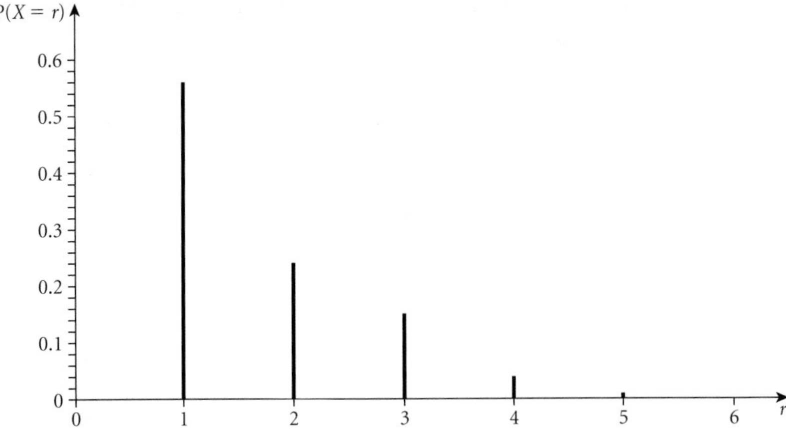

Figure 4.2

EXAMPLE 4.1

Two tetrahedral dice, each with faces labelled 1, 2, 3 and 4, are thrown and the random variable X represents the sum of the numbers shown on the dice.

(i) Find the probability distribution of X.

(ii) Illustrate the distribution and describe the shape of the distribution.

(iii) What is the probability that any throw of the dice results in a value of X which is an odd number?

SOLUTION

(i) The table shows all the possible totals when the two dice are thrown.

		First die			
	+	1	2	3	4
Second die	1	2	3	4	5
	2	3	4	5	6
	3	4	5	6	7
	4	5	6	7	8

You can use a table to write down the probability distribution for X.

r	2	3	4	5	6	7	8
$P(X = r)$	$\frac{1}{16}$	$\frac{2}{16}$	$\frac{3}{16}$	$\frac{4}{16}$	$\frac{3}{16}$	$\frac{2}{16}$	$\frac{1}{16}$

(ii) The vertical line chart in figure 4.3 illustrates this distribution, which is symmetrical.

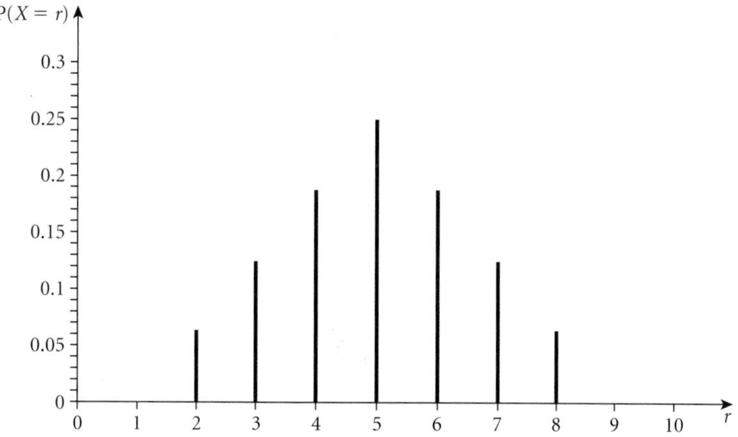

Figure 4.3

(iii) The probability that X is an odd number

$$= P(X = 3) + P(X = 5) + P(X = 7)$$
$$= \frac{2}{16} + \frac{4}{16} + \frac{2}{16}$$
$$= \frac{1}{2}$$

As well as defining a discrete random variable by tabulating the probability distribution, another effective way is to use an algebraic definition of the form $P(X = r) = f(r)$ for given values of r.

The following example illustrates how this may be used.

EXAMPLE 4.1

The probability distribution of a random variable X is given by

$P(X = r) = kr$ for $r = 1, 2, 3, 4$

$P(X = r) = 0$ otherwise.

(i) Find the value of the constant k.

(ii) Illustrate the distribution and describe the shape of the distribution.

(iii) Two successive values of X are generated independently of each other. Find the probability that

(a) both values of X are the same

(b) the total of the two values of X is greater than 6.

SOLUTION

(i) Tabulating the probability distribution for X gives:

r	1	2	3	4
$P(X = r)$	k	$2k$	$3k$	$4k$

Since X is a random variable, $\sum P(X = r) = 1$

$\Rightarrow \quad k + 2k + 3k + 4k = 1$

$\Rightarrow \quad 10k = 1$

$\Rightarrow \quad k = 0.1$

Hence $P(X = r) = 0.1r$, for $r = 1, 2, 3, 4$, which gives the following probability distribution.

r	1	2	3	4
$P(X = r)$	0.1	0.2	0.3	0.4

(ii) The vertical line chart in figure 4.4 illustrates this distribution. It has negative skew.

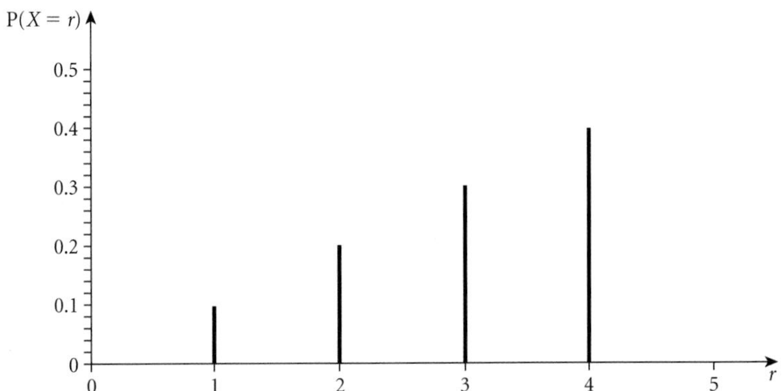

Figure 4.4

(iii) Let X_1 represent the first value generated and X_2 the second value generated.

(a) P(both values of X are the same)

$= P(X_1 = X_2 = 1 \text{ or } X_1 = X_2 = 2 \text{ or } X_1 = X_2 = 3 \text{ or } X_1 = X_2 = 4)$

$= P(X_1 = X_2 = 1) + P(X_1 = X_2 = 2) + P(X_1 = X_2 = 3) + P(X_1 = X_2 = 4)$

$= P(X_1 = 1) \times P(X_2 = 1) + P(X_1 = 2) \times P(X_2 = 2)$

$\quad + P(X_1 = 3) \times P(X_2 = 3) + P(X_1 = 4) \times P(X_2 = 4)$

$= (0.1)^2 + (0.2)^2 + (0.3)^2 + (0.4)^2$

$= 0.01 + 0.04 + 0.09 + 0.16$

$= 0.3$

(b) P(total of the two values is greater than 6)

$= P(X_1 + X_2 > 6)$

$= P(X_1 + X_2 = 7 \text{ or } 8)$

$= P(X_1 + X_2 = 7) + P(X_1 + X_2 = 8)$

$= P(X_1 = 3) \times P(X_2 = 4) + P(X_1 = 4) \times P(X_2 = 3)$
$\quad + P(X_1 = 4) \times P(X_2 = 4)$

$= 0.3 \times 0.4 + 0.4 \times 0.3 + 0.4 \times 0.4$

$= 0.12 + 0.12 + 0.16$

$= 0.4$

EXERCISE 4A

1 Two footballers are practising kicking into a goal. They give themselves points if they score, as follows. If they are in front of the goal they score one point, if they are to the side of the goal they get two points and if they score when the other one tackles them they score four points. The footballers are of equal ability and the probability distribution of X, the number of points for any kick, is as follows.

r	0	1	2	4
$P(X = r)$	c	0.4	0.3	0.2

(i) Calculate the value of c.

(ii) They have two kicks at the goal each and their scores are independent. What are the possible total scores for one of the footballers?

(iii) Explain why it is not possible for one footballer to score 7 points with the two kicks.

(iv) What is the probability of one footballer scoring 8 points and the other one scoring no points?

2 The probability distribution of X, the number of babies born to a small African mammal, can be modelled by

$$P(X = r) = \frac{kr}{6} \qquad \text{for } r = 0, 1, 2, 3, 4.$$

(i) Find the value of k and tabulate the probability distribution (i.e. write it out as a table).

(ii) According to the model, what is the most likely number of babies born?

3 A geologist measures the lengths of a large number of pebbles on a beach. He records the results to the nearest 10 mm. He finds that a good model for the probability distribution is

$$P(X = r) = k(50r - r^2) \qquad \text{for } r = 10, 20, 30, 40, 50.$$

(i) Find the value of k and tabulate the probability distribution.

(ii) What is the probability of a randomly selected pebble being greater than 30 mm in length?

4 The probability distribution of Y, the number of live cubs born to mature females of a type of wolf, is modelled by

$$P(Y = 0) = 0.32$$

$$P(Y = r) = \frac{kr}{10} \qquad \text{for } r = 1, 2, 3, 4, 5, 6, 7$$

$$P(Y \geqslant 8) = 0.12$$

(i) Find the value of k and tabulate the probability distribution.

(ii) There are two wolf packs in a wolf sanctuary and the dominant female in each pack has cubs. Find the probability that

(a) both have eight or more cubs

(b) the total number of cubs in their litters is three.

(iii) Comment on the algebraic model used above.

5 A magician has five cards. She says she can predict a card drawn at random. She claims to know which card someone in the audience has picked and after it is chosen she writes it down. The card is replaced and the procedure is repeated for a second time. Long experience shows the probability distribution of X, the total number of cards the magician gets correct, to be

$$P(X = r) = (3 + r)k \qquad \text{for all possible values of } r.$$

(i) What values can r take?

(ii) Find the value of k and tabulate the probability distribution.

(iii) What would the probabilities be by chance?

(iv) How can she do better than chance?

6 Some students are given 5 minutes to solve some anagrams. The number of anagrams solved is recorded. The probability distribution of N, the number of anagrams solved, can be modelled by

$$P(N = r) = 2(8 - r)k \qquad \text{for } r = 0, 1, 2, 3, 4, 5.$$

(i) Find the value of k and tabulate the probability distribution.

(ii) What is the probability of a randomly selected student solving three or more anagrams?

(iii) What is the probability of two randomly selected students solving exactly three anagrams?

7 Some psychology students are planning an experiment. They will ask a large number of people to chose a number from the digits 0, 1, 2 or 3. They want to find a discrete random variable to model their choices. One possible model is given by

$$P(X = r) = k(r + 1)! \qquad \text{for } r = 0, 1, 2, 3$$

$$P(X = r) = 0 \qquad \text{otherwise}$$

where k is a constant and $r! = r \times (r - 1) \times (r - 2) \times \ldots \times 2 \times 1$.

(i) Show that $k = \frac{1}{33}$ and construct a table to show the distribution.

(ii) Illustrate the distribution of X using a vertical line chart.

(iii) Do you think this is a realistic model?

8 A student studying operational research is modelling the punctuality of the 0805 train from Glasgow from Monday to Friday inclusive. The number of days, N, the train is on time can be modelled by a discrete random variable with a probability distribution given by

$$P(N = r) = (r(r - 5) + 7)k \qquad \text{for } r = 0, 1, 2, 3, 4, 5.$$

(i) Find the value of the constant, k, and tabulate the probability distribution.

(ii) Illustrate the distribution of N using a vertical line chart.

(iii) Comment on the distribution and whether calculating the expected value for N is useful.

9 An archaeology student finds an old Roman coin. Her friend says that the design of the coin means it will be biased when it is tossed. They discuss the probability of a fair coin being tossed three times and decide that a probability distribution for tossing a fair coin could be

$$P(X = r) = \frac{(r + 1)(4 - r) - 3}{8} \qquad \text{for } r = 0, 1, 2, 3,$$

where X is the number of heads shown when the coin is tossed three times.

(i) Using the probability distribution above, show that it does give the probabilities of zero, one, two and three heads being shown when a fair coin is tossed three times. These probabilities are $\frac{1}{8}, \frac{3}{8}, \frac{3}{8}$ and $\frac{1}{8}$.

They then decide to experiment with the old coin found. After many repeats of the experiment of tossing the Roman coin three times, they decide that the probability distribution is approximately as given in the table.

r	0	1	2	3
$P(X = r)$	0.0	0.1	0.4	0.5

(ii) How does this table suggest the coin is biased?

(iii) Show that this is consistent, to 1 decimal place, with the probability of a head being 0.8.

10 A type of bird found in Asia lays up to five eggs. The probability distribution of the number of eggs, X, can be modelled by

$$P(X = r) = kr(6 - r) \qquad \text{for } 0 \leqslant r \leqslant 5$$
$$P(X = r) = 0 \qquad \text{otherwise.}$$

(i) Find the value of k and tabulate the probability distribution.

(ii) Find the modal number of eggs laid by this bird.

(iii) Assuming the probability of an egg hatching is 0.6, find the probability of a bird having five eggs all of which hatch.

(iv) Make one criticism of the model.

Expectation and variance

AVONFORD STAR

Car-share scheme a success – claims Council

The car-share scheme *Travel Wise* has just completed its first half-year of operation. Figures just released show that the reduction in the number of cars travelling through the town centre at peak times is almost entirely due to the success of *Travel Wise*.

Council spokesman, Andrew Siantonas, told the *Star*, 'Not only has the volume of traffic in Avonford at peak times fallen, but we believe that a significant factor is the success of the car-share scheme.

The most recent figures we have indicate that the proportion of cars with only one driver in the car has fallen significantly.'

? What statistical evidence do you think the Council's claim is based on?

A second traffic survey, at critical points around the town centre, was conducted at peak travelling times over a period of a working week. This time the survey involved 800 cars. The number of people in each car is shown in the table.

Number of people per car	1	2	3	4	5	>5
Frequency	280	300	164	52	4	0

? How would you compare the results in the two traffic surveys?

The survey involved 800 cars. This is a fairly large sample and so, once again, it is reasonable to use the results to estimate the probabilities of the various possible outcomes: 1, 2, 3, 4, 5 people per car, as before.

Outcome (Number of people)	1	2	3	4	5	>5
Probability (Relative frequency)	0.35	0.375	0.205	0.065	0.005	0

One way to compare the two probability distributions, before and after the car sharing campaign, is to calculate a measure of central tendency and a measure of spread.

The most useful measure of central tendency is the *mean* or *expectation* of the random variable and the most useful measure of spread is the *variance*. To a large extent the calculation of these statistics mirrors the corresponding statistics for a frequency distribution, $\bar{x}$ and s^2.

ACTIVITY

Find the mean and variance of the frequency distribution for the people-per-car survey following the introduction of the car-sharing scheme.

Using relative frequencies generates an alternative approach which gives the *expectation* $\mathrm{E}(X) = \mu$ and *variance* $\mathrm{Var}(X) = \sigma^2$ for a discrete random variable.

We define Expectation, $\mathrm{E}(X)$ as $\sum r\mathrm{P}(X = r)$

and Variance, $\mathrm{Var}(X)$ as

$$\mathrm{E}(X - \mu)^2 = \sum(r - \mu)^2\mathrm{P}(X = r)$$

or $$\mathrm{E}(X^2) - \mu^2 = \sum r^2\mathrm{P}(X = r) - \left[\sum r\mathrm{P}(X = r)\right]^2.$$

The second version of the variance is often written as $\mathrm{E}(X^2) - [\mathrm{E}(X)]^2$, which can be remembered as

the expectation of the squares minus the square of the expectation.

To see how expectation and variance is calculated we use the probability distribution we have just developed. We will use these statistics to compare the distribution of numbers of people per car before and after the introduction of the car-sharing scheme.

When calculating the expectation and variance of a discrete probability distribution, you will find it helpful to set your work out systematically in a table.

			(a)	**(b)**
r	$\mathrm{P}(X = r)$	$r\mathrm{P}(X = r)$	$r^2\mathrm{P}(X = r)$	$(r - \mu)^2\mathrm{P}(X = r)$
1	0.35	0.35	0.35	0.35
2	0.375	0.75	1.5	0
3	0.205	0.615	1.845	0.205
4	0.065	0.26	1.04	0.26
5	0.005	0.025	0.125	0.045
Totals	1	2	4.86	0.86

In this case:

$$\begin{aligned}\mathrm{E}(X) = \mu &= \sum r\mathrm{P}(X = r)\\ &= 1 \times 0.35 + 2 \times 0.375 + 3 \times 0.205 + 4 \times 0.065 + 5 \times 0.005\\ &= 2\end{aligned}$$

and $\text{Var}(X) = \sigma^2 =$ **(a)** $\sum r^2\text{P}(X = r) - \left[\sum r\text{P}(X = r)\right]^2$

$$= 1^2 \times 0.35 + 2^2 \times 0.375 + 3^2 \times 0.205 + 4^2 \times 0.065 + 5^2 \times 0.005 - 2^2$$

$$= 4.86 - 4 = 0.86$$

or **(b)** $\sum (r - \mu)^2\text{P}(X = r)$

$$= (1-2)^2 \times 0.35 + (2-2)^2 \times 0.375 + (3-2)^2 \times 0.205 + (4-2)^2 \times 0.065 + (5-2)^2 \times 0.005$$

$$= 0.86$$

The equivalence of the two methods is proved in the appendix.

In practice, method **(a)** is to be preferred since the computation is usually easier, especially when the expectation is other than a whole number.

ACTIVITY

Carry out similar calculations for the expectation and variance of the probability distribution *before* the car-sharing experiment (see page 126).
Using these two statistics, judge the success or otherwise of the scheme.

EXAMPLE 4.3

The discrete random variable X has the following probability distribution.

r	0	1	2	3
$\text{P}(X = r)$	0.2	0.3	0.4	0.1

(i) Find $\text{E}(X)$ and $\text{E}(X^2)$.
(ii) Find $\text{Var}(X)$ using **(a)** $\text{E}(X^2) - \mu^2$ **(b)** $\text{E}([X - \mu]^2)$.

SOLUTION

r	$\text{P}(X = r)$	$r\text{P}(X = r)$	**(a)** $r^2\text{P}(X = r)$	**(b)** $(r - \mu)^2\text{P}(X = r)$
0	0.2	0	0	0.392
1	0.3	0.3	0.3	0.048
2	0.4	0.8	1.6	0.144
3	0.1	0.3	0.9	0.256
Totals	1	1.4	2.8	0.84

(i) $\text{E}(X) = \mu = \sum r\text{P}(X = r)$

$$= 0 \times 0.2 + 1 \times 0.3 + 2 \times 0.4 + 3 \times 0.1$$

$$= 1.4$$

$\text{E}(X^2) = \sum r^2\text{P}(X = r)$

$$= 0 \times 0.2 + 1 \times 0.3 + 4 \times 0.4 + 9 \times 0.1$$

$$= 2.8$$

(ii) **(a)** $\text{Var}(X) = \text{E}(X^2) - \mu^2$
$= 2.8 - 1.4^2$
$= 0.84$

(b) $\text{Var}(X) = \text{E}([X - \mu]^2) = \sum(r - \mu)^2\text{P}(X = r)$
$= (0 - 1.4)^2 \times 0.2 + (1 - 1.4)^2 \times 0.3 + (2 - 1.4)^2 \times 0.4 + (3 - 1.4)^2 \times 0.1$
$= 0.392 + 0.048 + 0.144 + 0.256$
$= 0.84$

Notice that the two methods of calculating the variance in part **(ii)** give the same result, since one formula is just an algebraic rearrangement of the other.

? Look carefully at both methods for calculating the variance.
Are there any situations where one method might be preferred to the other?

As well as being able to carry out calculations for the expectation and variance you are often required to solve problems in context. The following example illustrates this idea.

EXAMPLE 4.4

Laura has one pint of milk on three days out of every four and none on the fourth day. A pint of milk costs 40p. Let X represent her weekly milk bill.

(i) Find the probability distribution of her weekly milk bill.
(ii) Find the mean (μ) and standard deviation (σ) of her weekly milk bill.
(iii) Find **(a)** $\text{P}(x > \mu + \sigma)$ **(b)** $\text{P}(x < \mu - \sigma)$.

SOLUTION

(i) The delivery pattern repeats every four weeks.

M	Tu	W	Th	F	Sa	Su	Number of pints	Milk bill
✓	✓	✓	✗	✓	✓	✓	6	£2.40
✗	✓	✓	✓	✗	✓	✓	5	£2.00
✓	✗	✓	✓	✓	✗	✓	5	£2.00
✓	✓	✗	✓	✓	✓	✗	5	£2.00

Tabulating the probability distribution for X gives the following.

r (£)	2.00	2.40
$\text{P}(X = r)$	0.75	0.25

(ii) $\mathrm{E}(X) = \mu = \sum r\mathrm{P}(X = r)$
$= 2 \times 0.75 + 2.4 \times 0.25$
$= 2.1$

$\mathrm{Var}(X) = \sigma^2 = \mathrm{E}(X^2) - \mu^2$
$= 4 \times 0.75 + 5.76 \times 0.25 - 2.1^2$
$= 0.03$
$\Rightarrow \quad \sigma = \sqrt{0.03} = 0.17$ (correct to 2 s.f.)

Hence her mean weekly milk bill is £2.10, with a standard deviation of about 17 pence.

(iii) (a) $\mathrm{P}(X > \mu + \sigma) = \mathrm{P}(X > 2.27) = 0.25$
(b) $\mathrm{P}(X < \mu - \sigma) = \mathrm{P}(X < 1.93) = 0$

EXERCISE 4B

1 Some history students are studying games played by the Greeks. They are interested in *astragalos*, a dice-type game using the knuckle bones of sheep or goats. They wonder how easy it is to cheat. They decide to investigate two different *astragaloi* both with the numbers 1, 2, 3, 4, 5 and 6 on them. The students suspect the bones are not equally likely to generate all six numbers fairly so they throw the first *astragalos* a large number of times, record the results and calculate the probabilities of all the scores.

Score	1	2	3	4	5	6
Probability	0.1	0.2	0.2	0.1	0.3	0.1

(i) Calculate the mean score for this *astragalos.*

(ii) Another student, who studies mathematics, says that the mean for a fair *astragalos* is 3.5. Show the calculation that gives the mean as 3.5.

(iii) The second *astragalos* is thrown and the following results obtained. Calculate the mean score.

Score	1	2	3	4	5	6
Probability	0.1	0.2	0.3	0.1	0.1	0.2

(iv) The student throwing this *astragalos* says it must be fair. Comment on his result.

2 A biologist is carrying out research into eel numbers. Over a long period, she sets an eel trap every day; 24 hours later she records the number of eels in the trap, releases them and then re-sets it. She finds the probability distribution of the number of eels, X, to be as follows.

r	$\leqslant 4$	5	6	7	8	9	10	$\geqslant 11$
$\mathrm{P}(X = r)$	0	0.3	0.2	0.2	0.1	0.1	0.1	0

(i) Find the mean number of eels caught per day.

(ii) Find the variance of the number of eels caught per day.

(iii) What is the probability that, on a randomly selected day, the biologist traps more than seven eels?

The biologist had done exactly the same experiment 5 years ago. At that time the probability distribution was as follows.

r	$\leqslant 6$	7	8	9	10	11	12	$\geqslant 13$
$P(X = r)$	0	0.2	0.1	0.2	0.1	0.3	0.1	0

(iv) How has the distribution changed?

3 A corner shop is planning a sales campaign for a set of ten plastic dinosaurs. They give one away to every child who uses the shop. Their model for the projected sales per child, X, of the remaining dinosaurs is

$P(X = 0) = P(X = 9) = 0.3$

$P(X = r) = kr(9 - r)$ for $1 \leqslant r \leqslant 8$.

(i) Find the value of k and tabulate the probability distribution.

(ii) What is the probability of a child buying more than three dinosaurs?

(iii) What is the mean number of dinosaurs bought?

(iv) About 600 children visit the shop. How many dinosaurs should the shop buy?

4 A company which hires out equipment by the day has three mowers. The number, X, of mowers which are hired on any one day has the following probability distribution.

$$P(X = r) = k\left(\tfrac{1}{2}\right)^r \quad \text{for } r = 0, 1, 2 \text{ and } 3.$$

(i) Show that $k = \frac{8}{15}$.

(ii) Sketch the probability distribution of X.

(iii) Calculate the expectation and variance of X.

(iv) The income from hiring a mower is £25 per day. Deduce the mean and variance of the daily income from hiring out mowers.

[MEI, *part*]

5 In a statistical survey of cars coming into a city centre during the morning rush hour, the number of occupants, X, is modelled by the probability distribution

$$P(X = r) = \frac{k}{r} \quad \text{for } r = 1, 2, 3, 4.$$

(i) Tabulate the probability distribution and determine the value of k.

(ii) Illustrate the distribution using a suitable diagram.

(iii) Calculate $E(X)$ and $Var(X)$.

During a campaign by the city council to reduce the volume of traffic, pairs of single occupant drivers are put in touch with each other and encouraged to share their journeys.

(iv) Without further calculations, state, with reasons, the effect on each of E(X) and Var(X).

[MEI, *part*]

6 A set of five cards, bearing the numbers 1 to 5 respectively, is shuffled. Two cards are chosen at random. Let X represent the absolute difference between the numbers on the two cards.

(i) Show that the possible values of X are 1, 2, 3, 4.

(ii) Show that $\mathrm{P}(X = 1) = 0.4$, and give the probabilities of the other values of X. Draw a sketch to illustrate the probability distribution of X.

(iii) Find E(X) and Var(X).

In a fund-raising game, two sets of five cards are placed face down on a table. A player chooses two cards at random from one set. If the value of X is the same for both sets, the player wins £X. Otherwise the player wins nothing.

(iv) Find the probability that the player wins a prize.

(v) The organisers wish to make an average profit of 10 pence per game. How much should they charge per game?

[MEI]

7 A baker receives an order for three fruit cakes and five sponge cakes. She places each cake in a box but does not label the boxes. Later she discovers that the decoration of the fruit cakes had not been completed properly, and she asks her assistant to find the fruit cakes and complete the decoration. Let X represent the number of boxes the assistant has to open so as to find all three fruit cakes. You are given that the probability distribution for X is

$$\mathrm{P}(X = r) = \tfrac{1}{112}(r - 1)(r - 2) \qquad \text{for } r = 3, 4, 5, 6, 7, 8.$$

(i) Tabulate the distribution.

(ii) Find the mean and variance of X.

(iii) Tabulate the cumulative distribution function of X. State the least integer m such that $\mathrm{P}(X \leqslant m) \geqslant 0.5$.

[MEI, *part*]

8 A team of five, the *Ambridge Archers*, takes part in an archery competition, where the objective is to hit the 'bull' on the target. Each member of the team, independently, has a probability of 0.4 of hitting the 'bull'. A single round consists of each archer shooting once at the target. Let X represent the number of hits obtained by the team in one round.
The probability distribution of X is given in the following table.

r	0	1	2	3	4	5
$\mathrm{P}(X = r)$	0.0778	0.2592	0.3456	0.2304	0.0768	0.0102

The number of points, Y, scored by the team in the round is given by the formula $Y = \frac{1}{2}X(X + 1)$. (For example, if $X = 5$ then $Y = 15$.)

(i) Obtain the probability distribution of Y and illustrate it in a sketch.

(ii) Find $E(Y)$ and $Var(Y)$.

(iii) Find the probability that after three rounds the team has scored exactly 1 point.

The *Ambridge Archers* are competing against the five *Borset Bowmen*, each of whom also has probability 0.4 of hitting the 'bull'.

(iv) Find the probability that after the first round the team scores are equal.

[MEI, *adapted*]

9 In a lucky dip, there are ten bags of sweets, of which four are *Saturn Selection* and the rest *Venus Variety*. Three friends each take a bag at random. Let X represent the number of bags of *Saturn Selection* which the friends have between them.

The probability distribution for X is given in the following table.

r	0	1	2	3
$P(X = r)$	$\frac{1}{6}$	$\frac{1}{2}$	$\frac{3}{10}$	$\frac{1}{30}$

(i) Illustrate the distribution with a sketch.

(ii) Calculate the expectation and variance of X.

Each *Saturn Selection* costs 40 pence and each *Venus Variety* costs 30 pence.

(iii) Show that the total cost of the three bags of sweets is $(90 + 10X)$ pence.

(iv) Deduce the mean of this total cost.

[MEI, *part*]

EXERCISE 4C MIXED EXERCISE

1 In an exploration to find oil a company drills three boreholes. The probability of each borehole finding oil is 0.2.

(i) Draw a tree diagram to show the possible outcomes from the three boreholes.

(ii) Copy and complete this table giving the probability distribution for different numbers of successful boreholes.

Number of successful boreholes	0	1	2	3
Probability				

The cost of each borehole is £3 million. If oil is found it will produce a subsequent profit of £40 million.

(iii) Find the expected profit from the exploration.

2 Dan's hobby is archery. When shooting at a target, he scores 1, 2 or 3 points when he hits the target, depending on how close he is to the centre. If he misses the target completely he scores 0 points. From past experience, the distribution of X, his score for each shot, is as follows.

r	0	1	2	3
$P(X = r)$	0.1	0.4	0.3	0.2

(i) Tabulate the cumulative distribution function for X, i.e. $P(X \leqslant r)$ for $r = 0, 1, 2, 3$.

Dan has three shots at the target and his scores are independent. Let L be the discrete random variable which represents the largest of the three scores.

(ii) Explain why $P(L \leqslant 2) = [P(X \leqslant 2)]^3 = 0.512$.
Find similarly $P(L \leqslant 1)$.
Write down $P(L = 0)$ and $P(L \leqslant 3)$.

(iii) Use the probabilities calculated in **(ii)** to write down the probability distribution for L.

(iv) Find the mean and variance of L. [MEI]

3 I was asked recently to analyse the number of goals scored per game by our local ladies hockey team. Having studied the results for the whole of last season, I proposed the following model, where the discrete random variable X represents the number of goals scored per game by the team.

$$P(X = r) = k(r + 1)(5 - r)^2 \qquad \text{for } r = 0, 1, 2, 3.$$

(i) Show that k is 0.01 and illustrate the probability distribution with a sketch.

(ii) Find the expectation and variance of X.

(iii) Assuming that the model is valid for the forthcoming season, find the probability that

(a) the team will fail to score in the first two games

(b) the team will score a total of four goals in the first two games.

What other assumption is necessary to obtain these answers?

(iv) Give two distinct reasons why the model might not be valid for the forthcoming season. [MEI]

4 Contestants taking part in a quiz show are asked at most five questions. A contestant who answers a question wrongly is asked no further questions. The five questions are of increasing difficulty.

For each individual question, the probability of a randomly chosen contestant answering correctly is given in the table below.

Question number	1	2	3	4	5
Probability that this question is answered correctly	0.75	0.5	0.4	0.3	0.25

Let X represent the number of questions that a randomly chosen contestant answers correctly. The probability distribution for X is given in the table below.

r	0	1	2	3	4	5
$P(X = r)$	0.25	0.375	0.225	0.105	0.033 75	0.011 25

(i) Use information from the first table to show how $P(X = 0)$ and $P(X = 5)$ in the second table can be derived.

(ii) Find $E(X)$ and $Var(X)$.

A prize of £(1000×2^r) is awarded to a contestant who answers r successive questions correctly. In one particular show there are three contestants.

(iii) Find the probability that

(a) the first contestant wins at least £8000

(b) at least one of the three contestants leaves with the top prize.

(iv) People who apply to take part in the quiz have to pay £1 to the quiz organisers. How many applications are required in order to provide the expected prize money to be given out in this show?

[MEI]

5 A model of a candidate's mark in an examination is as follows. The mark scored is modelled as $t + X$, where t is the mark which the candidate's true ability warrants and X is a random integer in the range -5 to 5. The distribution for X is taken to be

$$P(X = r) = P(X = -r) = k(6 - r) \qquad r = 0, 1, 2, 3, 4, 5.$$

(i) Tabulate the distribution, and show that $k = \frac{1}{36}$, and sketch the distribution.

(ii) Write down the expectation of X and find the variance of X.

(iii) Find the probability of a candidate scoring a mark which is higher than his true ability warrants.

Now suppose that candidates may take the examination on two or more occasions, with the highest mark being counted. Assume the candidate's true ability does not change.

(iv) Find the probability that the mark which counts is higher than the candidate's true ability warrants if he takes the examination

(a) twice

(b) four times.

(v) Explain, in the light of your answers to part **(iv)**, what the model implies for candidates who take the examination repeatedly. Identify one weakness in the modelling assumptions.

[MEI]

6 An arcade game takes one token per game. The possible outcomes of a game are as follows.

The player loses the game and loses the token: probability 0.75
The player draws the game and the token is returned: probability 0.20
The player wins the game and receives 10 tokens: probability 0.05

(i) Show that this situation can be modelled by a random variable, X, which takes values $-1, 0, 9$. Explain what X represents.

(ii) Find $\mathrm{E}(X)$ and explain what its sign indicates.

(iii) Find $\mathrm{Var}(X)$.

George decides he will buy nine tokens and play exactly nine games.

(iv) Find the expected number of tokens that George will have at the end of the nine games.

Find the probability that after nine games he has

(v) no tokens left

(vi) more than nine tokens left.

[MEI]

7 A survey is taken of a random sample of drivers to determine how many motoring offences, if any, they have committed. A model is proposed in which the discrete random variable X represents the number of motoring offences. The distribution of X is as follows.

$$\mathrm{P}(X = 0) = 0.66$$

$$\mathrm{P}(X = r) = k(0.4)^{r-1} \qquad r = 1, 2, 3, 4.$$

(i) Show that k is approximately 0.21.

(ii) Sketch this discrete probability distribution. Describe in words what the model indicates about the number of offences committed by motorists.

(iii) Obtain the mean and variance for the number of motoring offences per driver according to this model.

(iv) Obtain the mean for the number of motoring offences per driver *excluding those drivers who have committed no offences.*

[MEI]

KEY POINTS

1 For a discrete random variable, X, which can take only the values $r_1, r_2, \ldots, r_n$, with probabilities $p_1, p_2, \ldots, p_n$ respectively:

- $p_1 + p_2 + \ldots + p_n = \sum_{k=1}^{n} p_k = \sum_{k=1}^{n} \mathrm{P}(X = r_k) = 1; p_i > 0$

2 A discrete probability distribution is best illustrated by a vertical line chart.

- The expectation $= \mathrm{E}(X) = \mu = \sum r\mathrm{P}(X = r)$.
- The variance $= \mathrm{Var}(X) = \sigma^2$

$$= \mathrm{E}(X - \mu)^2 = \sum (r - \mu)^2 \mathrm{P}(X = r)$$

or $$\mathrm{E}(X^2) - [\mathrm{E}(X)]^2 = \sum r^2\mathrm{P}(X = r) - \left[\sum r\mathrm{P}(X = r)\right]^2$$

5 Further probability

An estate had seven houses;
Each house had seven cats;
Each cat ate seven mice;
Each mouse ate seven grains of wheat.
Wheat grains, mice, cats and houses,
How many were there on the estate?

Ancient Egyptian problem

AVONFORD STAR

Child Prodigy

Little Gary Forest looks like any other toddler but all the evidence points to him being a budding genius.

Recently Gary's mother gave him five bricks to play with, each showing one of the numbers **1**, **2**, **3**, **4** and **5**. Without hesitation Gary sat down and placed them in the correct order.

Little Gary Forest looks like being a budding genius!

What is the probability that Gary chose the bricks at random and just happened by chance to get them in the right order?

There are two ways of looking at the situation. You can think of Gary selecting the five bricks as five events, one after another. Alternatively, you can think of 1, 2, 3, 4, 5 as one outcome out of several possible outcomes and work out the probability that way.

Five events

Look at the diagram.

1	2	3	4	5

Figure 5.1

If Gary had actually chosen them at random:

the probability of first selecting **1** is $\frac{1}{5}$
the probability of next selecting **2** is $\frac{1}{4}$
the probability of next selecting **3** is $\frac{1}{3}$
the probability of next selecting **4** is $\frac{1}{2}$
then only **5** remains so the probability of selecting it is 1.

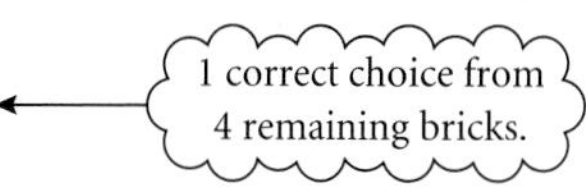

So the probability of getting the correct numerical sequence at random is

$\frac{1}{5} \times \frac{1}{4} \times \frac{1}{3} \times \frac{1}{2} \times 1 = \frac{1}{120}.$

Outcomes

How many ways are there of putting five bricks in a line?

To start with there are five bricks to choose from, so there are five ways of choosing brick 1. Then there are four bricks left and so there are four ways of choosing brick 2. And so on.

The total number of ways is

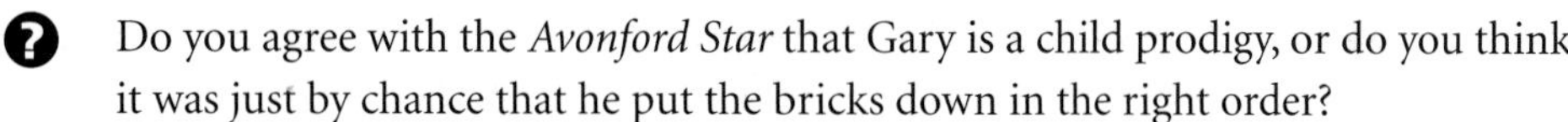

5	×	4	×	3	×	2	×	1	= 120
Brick 1		Brick 2		Brick 3		Brick 4		Brick 5	

Only one of these is the order 1, 2, 3, 4, 5, so the probability of Gary selecting it at random is $\frac{1}{120}$.

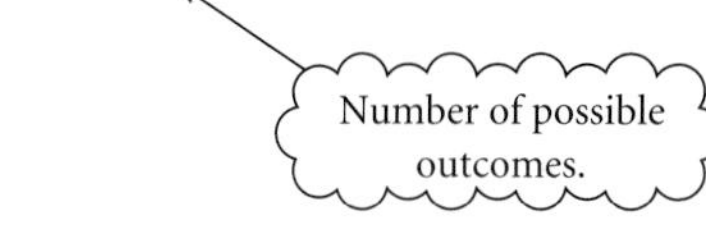

? Do you agree with the *Avonford Star* that Gary is a child prodigy, or do you think it was just by chance that he put the bricks down in the right order?

What further information would you want to be convinced that he is a budding genius?

Factorials

In the last example you saw that the number of ways of placing five different bricks in a line is $5 \times 4 \times 3 \times 2 \times 1$. This number is called 5 *factorial* and is written 5!. You will often meet expressions of this form.

In general the number of ways of placing n different objects in a line is $n!$, where $n! = n \times (n-1) \times (n-2) \times \ldots \times 3 \times 2 \times 1$.

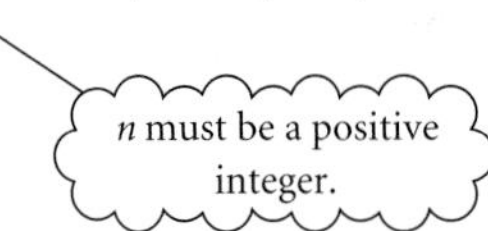
n must be a positive integer.

EXAMPLE 5.1

Calculate 7!

SOLUTION

$$7! = 7 \times 6 \times 5 \times 4 \times 3 \times 2 \times 1 = 5040$$

Some typical relationships between factorial numbers are illustrated below:

$10! = 10 \times 9!$ or in general $n! = n \times [(n-1)!]$
$10! = 10 \times 9 \times 8 \times 7!$ or in general $n! = n \times (n-1) \times (n-2) \times [(n-3)!]$

These are useful when simplifying expressions involving factorials.

EXAMPLE 5.2

Calculate $\dfrac{5!}{3!}$

SOLUTION

$$\frac{5!}{3!} = \frac{5 \times 4 \times 3!}{3!} = 5 \times 4 = 20$$

EXAMPLE 5.3

Calculate $\dfrac{7! \times 5!}{3! \times 4!}$

SOLUTION

$$\frac{7! \times 5!}{3! \times 4!} = \frac{7 \times 6 \times 5 \times 4 \times 3! \times 5 \times 4!}{3! \times 4!} = 7 \times 6 \times 5 \times 4 \times 5 = 4200$$

EXAMPLE 5.4

Write $37 \times 36 \times 35$ in terms of factorials only.

SOLUTION

$$37 \times 36 \times 35 = \frac{37 \times 36 \times 35 \times 34!}{34!} = \frac{37!}{34!}$$

EXERCISE 5A

1 Calculate these.

(i) $6!$ (ii) $\frac{6!}{3!}$ (iii) $\frac{5! \times 4!}{3! \times 2!}$

2 Simplify these.

(i) $\frac{5!}{2!}$ (ii) $\frac{5!}{3!}$

3 Write these in factorial notation.

(i) $5 \times 4 \times 3 \times 2 \times 1$ (ii) $\frac{6 \times 5 \times 4}{3 \times 2}$

4 How many different three-letter arrangements can be formed from the letters DNA if letters cannot be repeated?

5 Ten rugby teams have to play each other once in a league. How many matches will there be?

6 In how many ways can a gymnast arrange five pieces of equipment if
(i) they have to be in a row
(ii) the trampette has to be the last in the line?

7 (i) How many ways can the letters NEWTON be arranged?
(ii) How many three-letter arrangements can be made from the six letters?

8 A home alarm system uses a four-digit number as the security code. Digits may be repeated. How many different ways are there of choosing a code in the following cases?
(i) Any digit from 0 to 9 can be used
(ii) No code consisting of consecutive numbers in ascending order can be used
(iii) No code can begin or end with zero

9 A pig farmer has a code for each breeding sow. The code is a four-digit number.
(i) If the first digit has to be 2, how many different numbers are available for the farmer to use?
(ii) The farmer then decides instead to use a letter at the beginning of the code and three digits after it.
(a) How many codes can he now choose from?
(b) The letters O and I are now excluded. How many codes can he now choose?
(iii) In a later development, all farms are given a code. This is made up from three letters (excluding O and I) followed by three digits. How many possible codes are there if
(a) repeats of letters and digits are allowed
(b) repeats are not allowed?

10 Horses can be 'freeze marked' with a code so they can be identified if they are stolen. One stable uses a letter followed by a single digit then another letter then another single digit, for example, P5D8.

(i) How many possible codes can the stable use?

(ii) A horse from this stable has been stolen. The owner knows the code starts with P5 but cannot remember the rest of it. She hears that a horse is being sold at a horse fair with a code beginning with P5. What is the probability of it being her horse?

(iii) The stable decides to add another digit or letter to increase the number of codes available. Which should they choose and why?

11 A company offering microchip implants for domestic pets uses eight-digit codes but the digit 0 is not allowed. After some years they run out of new numbers.

(i) How many animals have been chipped by then?

(ii) The company then uses fifteen-digit codes instead. The digit 0 is still not allowed. There are now other companies offering microchipping too so the company decides to start all their codes with the digits 55. What is the maximum number of codes they can now use?

12 An internet bank requires customers to login using various passwords. After typing in their account number and branch sort code they are asked for a four-digit PIN number. PIN means Personal Identifier Number. Customers may choose any set of four digits.

(i) **(a)** How many four-digit numbers can customers choose from?

(b) If the bank decided to make the PIN number have five digits, how many numbers could customers then choose from?

(ii) The bank then asks for a combination of four letters.

(a) How many possible combinations could the customers choose if they can use lower case letters only?

(b) If they have to choose one upper case letter and three lower case letters in any order, how many combinations are there now?

(c) The bank now decides to let the customers have a mixture of upper and lower case letters. How many ways can a customer choose a combination of letters now?

1 Solve the inequality $n! > 10^m$ for each of the cases $m = 3, 4, 5$.

2 In how many ways can you write 42 using factorials only?

3 **(i)** There are 4! ways of placing the four letters S, T, A, R in a line, if each of them must appear exactly once. How many ways are there if each letter may appear any number of times (i.e. between 0 and 4)?

(ii) There are 4! ways of placing the letters S, T, A, R in line. How many ways are there of placing in line the letters

(a) S, T, A, A **(b)** S, T, T, T?

Permutations

AVONFORD STAR

Beginner's Luck for Joyeeta

It was Joyeeta Ganguly's first ever visit to the racecourse and she left staggering under the weight of her winnings.

It all happened on the 3.15, a 16-horse race, when Joyeeta picked the first, second and third placed horses in the correct order for a special 500-1 bet.

'I just chose the horses with pretty names' said Joyeeta.

What is the probability of Joyeeta's result?

The winner can be chosen in 16 ways.
The second horse can be chosen in 15 ways.
The third horse can be chosen in 14 ways.

Thus the total number of ways of placing three horses in the first three positions is $16 \times 15 \times 14 = 3360$. So the probability that Joyeeta's random selection is correct is $\frac{1}{3360}$.

In this example attention is given to the order in which the horses finish. The solution required a *permutation* of three objects from sixteen.

In general the number of permutations, ${}^n\mathrm{P}_r$, of r objects from n is given by ${}^n\mathrm{P}_r = n \times (n-1) \times (n-2) \times \ldots \times (n-r+1)$.

This can be written more compactly as

$$ {}^n\mathrm{P}_r = \frac{n!}{(n-r)!} $$

Combinations

It is often the case that you are not concerned with the order in which items are chosen, only with which ones are picked.

To take part in the National Lottery you fill in a ticket by selecting 6 numbers out of a possible 49 (numbers 1, 2, ..., 49). When the draw is made a machine selects six numbers at random. If they are the same as the six on your ticket, you win the jackpot.

? You have the six winning numbers. Does it matter in which order the machine picked them?

The probability of a single ticket winning the jackpot is often said to be 1 in 14million. How can you work out this figure?

The key question is, how many ways are there of choosing 6 numbers out of 49?

If the order mattered, the answer would be ${}^{49}P_6$, or $49 \times 48 \times 47 \times 46 \times 45 \times 44$.

However, the order does not matter. 1, 3, 15, 19, 31 and 48 is the same as 15, 48, 31, 1, 19, 3 and 3, 19, 48, 1, 15, 31 and lots more. For each set of six numbers there are 6! arrangements that all count as being the same.

So, the number of ways of selecting six balls, given that the order does not matter, is $\dfrac{49 \times 48 \times 47 \times 46 \times 45 \times 44}{6!}$

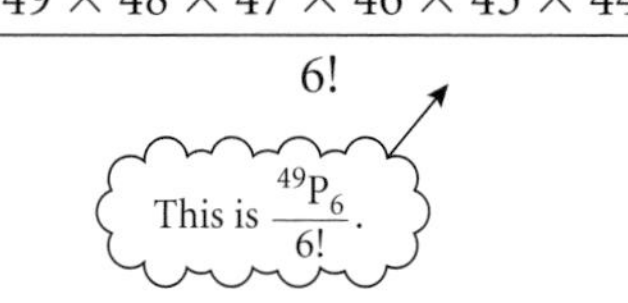

This is called the number of *combinations* of 6 objects from 49 and is denoted by ${}^{49}C_6$.

? Show that ${}^{49}C_6$ can be written as $\dfrac{49!}{6! \times 43!}$.

Returning to the National Lottery, it follows that the probability of your one ticket winning the jackpot is $\dfrac{1}{{}^{49}C_6}$.

? Check that this is about 1 in 14 million.

This example shows a general result, that the number of ways of selecting r objects from n, when the order does not matter, is given by

$$^nC_r = \frac{n!}{r!(n-r)!} = \frac{^nP_r}{r!}$$

How can you prove this general result?

Another notation for ^nC_r is $\binom{n}{r}$.

The notation $\binom{n}{r}$ looks exactly like a column vector and so there is the possibility of confusing the two. However, the context should usually make the meaning clear.

EXAMPLE 5.5

A School Governors' committee of five people is to be chosen from eight applicants. How many different selections are possible?

SOLUTION

$$\text{Number of selections} = {^8C_5} = \frac{8!}{5! \times 3!} = \frac{8 \times 7 \times 6}{3 \times 2 \times 1} = 56$$

EXAMPLE 5.6

In how many ways can a committee of four people be selected from four applicants?

SOLUTION

Common sense tells us that there is only one way to make the committee, that is by appointing all applicants. However, if we work from the formula

$$^4C_4 = \frac{4!}{4! \times 0!} = \frac{1}{0!} \text{ and this must} = 1.$$

To achieve the answer 1 requires the convention that 0! is taken to be 1.

Use the convention $0! = 1$ to show that $^nC_0 = {^nC_n} = 1$ for all values of n.

The binomial coefficients, ^nC_r

In the last section you met numbers of the form ^nC_r. These are called the binomial coefficients; the reason for this is explained in the appendix on page 444 and in the next chapter.

ACTIVITY

Use the formula $^nC_r = \dfrac{n!}{r!(n-r)!}$ and the results $\binom{n}{0} = \binom{n}{n} = 1$ to check that the entries in this table, for $n = 6$ and 7, are correct.

r	0	1	2	3	4	5	6	7
$n = 6$	1	6	15	20	15	6	1	–
$n = 7$	1	7	21	35	35	21	7	1

It is very common to present values of ^nC_r in a table shaped like an isosceles triangle, known as Pascal's triangle.

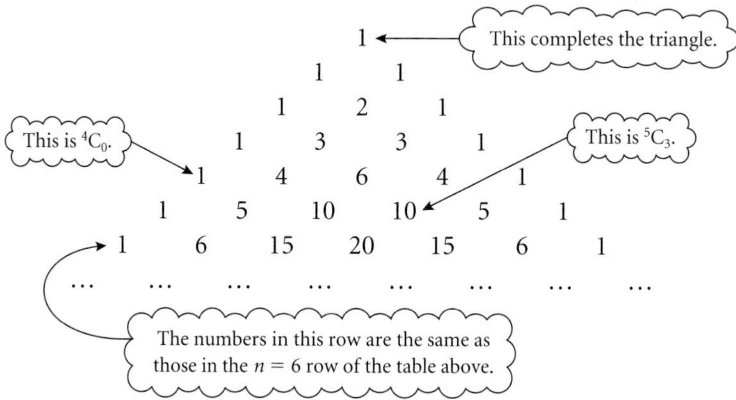

Pascal's triangle makes it easy to see two important properties of binomial coefficients.

1 Symmetry: $^nC_r = {}^nC_{n-r}$

If you are choosing 11 players from a pool of 15 possible players you can either name the 11 you have selected or name the 4 you have rejected. Similarly, every choice of r objects included in a selection from n distinct objects corresponds to a choice of $(n - r)$ objects which are excluded. Therefore $^nC_r = {}^nC_{n-r}$.

This provides a short cut in calculations when r is large. For example

$$^{100}C_{96} = {}^{100}C_4 = \frac{100 \times 99 \times 98 \times 97}{1 \times 2 \times 3 \times 4} = 3\,921\,225.$$

It also shows that the list of values of ^nC_r for any particular value of n is unchanged by being reversed. For example, when $n = 6$ the list is the seven numbers 1, 6, 15, 20, 15, 6, 1.

2 Addition: $^{n+1}C_{r+1} = {^nC_r} + {^nC_{r+1}}$

Look at the entry 15 in the bottom row of Pascal's triangle, towards the right. The two entries above and either side of it are 10 and 5,

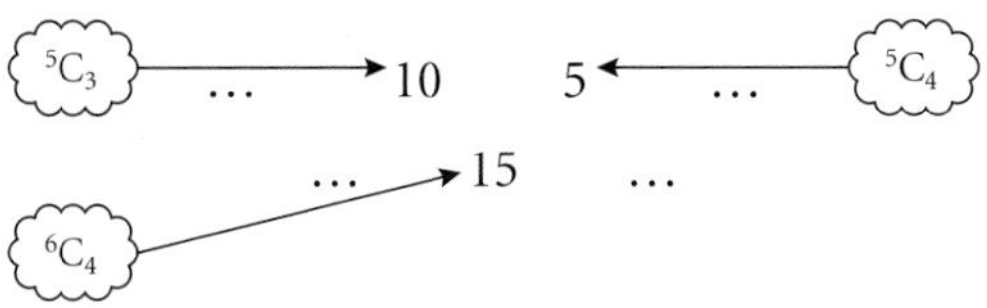

and $15 = 10 + 5$. In this case $^6C_4 = {^5C_3} + {^5C_4}$. This is an example of the general result that $^{n+1}C_{r+1} = {^nC_r} + {^nC_{r+1}}$. Check that all the entries in Pascal's triangle (except the 1s) are found in this way.

This can be used to build up a table of values of ^nC_r without much calculation. If you know all the values of ^nC_r for any particular value of n you can add pairs of values to obtain all the values of $^{n+1}C_r$, i.e. the next row, except the first and last, which always equal 1.

Why is this so? Suppose you are choosing $r + 1$ objects from $n + 1$ distinct objects. You can do this in $^{n+1}C_{r+1}$ ways. Now give any one particular object a label, X say. The selections now split into two categories, those which contain X and those which do not. If X is included you have to choose r more objects from the other n objects; this can be done in ^nC_r ways. If X is not included you have to choose all $r + 1$ objects from the other n objects; this can be done in $^nC_{r+1}$ ways. Between them these two cases cover all the possibilities, and therefore $^{n+1}C_{r+1} = {^nC_r} + {^nC_{r+1}}$.

ACTIVITY

Use a computer spreadsheet to produce several rows of Pascal's triangle.

Use the relationship

$$^{n+1}C_{r+1} = {^nC_r} + {^nC_{r+1}}$$

in your spreadsheet to generate the terms of the triangle that are not 1.

How can you prove $^{n+1}C_{r+1} = {^nC_r} + {^nC_{r+1}}$ using algebra?

Calculating probabilities in less simple cases

EXAMPLE 5.7

A committee of 5 is to be chosen from a list of 14 people, 6 of whom are men and 8 women. Their names are to be put in a hat and then 5 drawn out.

What is the probability that this procedure produces a committee with no women?

SOLUTION

The probability of an all-male committee of 5 people is given by

$$\frac{\text{The number of ways of choosing 5 people out of 6}}{\text{The number of ways of choosing 5 people out of 14}}$$

There are 6 men.

There are 14 people.

$$= \frac{{}^{6}C_5}{{}^{14}C_5} = \frac{6}{2002} \approx 0.003.$$

AVONFORD STAR

Where will the bus go?

John Crawler, Operations Director for Avonford Transport, has announced that the public will be consulted about the exact route of the new bus service due to start in April. Mr Crawler said 'The new route will run from Avonford to Chandford via Brantwood and will be extended to Digby when new buses arrive in September. As local people know, there are several roads connecting these towns, so we need to find out from our future passengers which one of the many possible routes will be the most useful.'

Local resident Agnes Philpott is not happy. 'The chances of their getting the route that suits me are less than one in a hundred' she complained.

Is Agnes right? How many routes are there from Avonford to Digby? Start by looking at the first two legs, Avonford to Brantwood and Brantwood to Chandford.

There are three roads from Avonford to Brantwood and two roads from Brantwood to Chandford. How many routes are there from Avonford to Chandford passing through Brantwood on the way?

Look at figure 5.2.

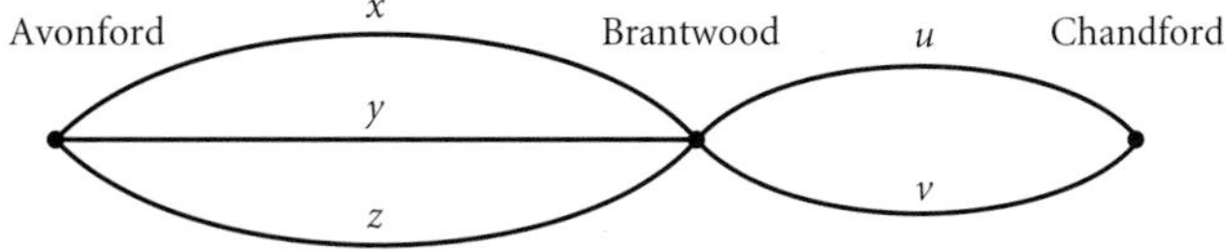

Figure 5.2

The answer is $3 \times 2 = 6$ because there are three ways of doing the first leg, followed by two for the second leg. The six routes are

$x - u \quad y - u \quad z - u$

$x - v \quad y - v \quad z - v.$

There are also four roads from Chandford to Digby. So each of the six routes from Avonford to Chandford has four possible ways of going on to Digby. There are now $6 \times 4 = 24$ routes. See figure 5.3.

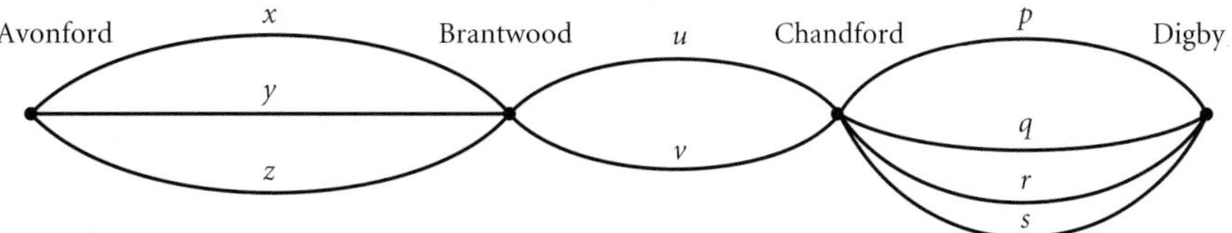

Figure 5.3

They can be listed systematically as follows:

$x-u-p$	$y-u-p$	$z-u-p$	$x-v-p$	$y-v-p$	$z-v-p$
$x-u-q$	....	....	....	....	....
$x-u-r$	....	....	....	....	....
$x-u-s$	....	....	....	....	$z-v-s$

In general, if there are a outcomes from experiment A, b outcomes from experiment B and c outcomes from experiment C then there are $a \times b \times c$ different possible combined outcomes from the three experiments.

?

1 If Avonford Transport chooses its route at random, what is the probability that it will be the one Agnes Philpott wants?
Is her comment in the newspaper justified?

2 In this example the probability was worked out by finding the number of possible routes. How else could it have been worked out?

EXAMPLE 5.8

A cricket team consisting of 6 batsmen, 4 bowlers and 1 wicket-keeper is to be selected from a group of 18 cricketers comprising 9 batsmen, 7 bowlers and 2 wicket-keepers. How many different teams can be selected?

SOLUTION

The batsmen can be selected in ${}^9C_6$ ways.
The bowlers can be selected in ${}^7C_4$ ways.
The wicket-keepers can be selected in ${}^2C_1$ ways.
Therefore total number of teams

$$\begin{aligned} &= {}^9C_6 \times {}^7C_4 \times {}^2C_1 \\ &= \frac{9!}{3!\,6!} \times \frac{7!}{3!\,4!} \times \frac{2!}{1!\,1!} \\ &= \frac{9 \times 8 \times 7}{3 \times 2 \times 1} \times \frac{7 \times 6 \times 5}{3 \times 2 \times 1} \times 2 \\ &= 5880 \text{ ways.} \end{aligned}$$

EXERCISE 5B

1 **(i)** In how many different ways can 6 models be picked from the 20 available models for a fashion show?

(ii) In another show 40 models are taking part. In how many different ways may 8 winners, numbered 1, 2, 3, …, 8, be chosen?

2 A shuttle team of astronauts has 7 members. How many ways can the team be selected if they are to be chosen from

(i) 10 people **(ii)** 15 people?

There are 9 women and 27 men from whom the team will be chosen. NASA has selected one of the women as commander and she insists that one other member of the team should be a woman and the others men.

(iii) In how many ways can the team now be chosen?

3 Ravin has a new iPod mini and sets up a list with 30 tracks on it. He has 40 tracks to choose from.

(i) How many ways can he set up his list?

He now decides to make two lists of different types of music. He has 20 'garage' tracks and 20 'dance' tracks. He wants 12 'garage' tracks and 18 'dance' tracks in his two lists.

(ii) How many ways can he choose the 'garage' tracks he wants?

(iii) How many ways can he chose all the tracks he wants? Give your answer in standard form to 3 significant figures.

4 I have a box of chocolates with ten different chocolates left in it. Of these, there are six which I particularly like. However, I intend to offer my three friends one chocolate each before I eat the rest. How many different selections of chocolates can I be left with after my friends have chosen?

Show that 36 of these selections leave me with exactly five chocolates which I particularly like.

How many selections leave me with

(i) all six **(ii)** exactly 4 **(iii)** exactly 3

of the chocolates which I particularly like.

Assuming that my friends choose at random, what is the most likely outcome and what is the probability of that outcome? [MEI]

5 At a small branch of the MidWest bank the manager has a staff of 12, consisting of five men and seven women including a Mr Brown and a Mrs Green. The manager receives a letter from head office saying that four of his staff are to be made redundant. In the interests of fairness the manager selects the four staff at random.

(i) How many different selections are possible?

(ii) How many of these selections include both Mr Brown and Mrs Green?

(iii) Write down the probability that both Mr Brown and Mrs Green will be made redundant.

Before the redundancies are announced, a further letter arrives from head office saying that, in accordance with the company's equal opportunities policy, two men and two women must be made redundant. The manager scraps the original redundancy list and now chooses two men at random and two women at random.

(iv) How many different selections are possible now?

(v) Find the probability that both Mr Brown and Mrs Green are made redundant now. [MEI]

6 *Product 2000* is a scratchcard game. Each scratchcard has 12 squares. Five of these squares contain numbers and the other seven are blank. The five squares which contain numbers are selected at random in the printing process. The diagram shows the layout on a typical card.

		10	
5		50	
	8		40

Initially all 12 squares are covered; the players have to scratch the cover off exactly three squares. The order in which squares are scratched is unimportant.

(i) In how many ways can a player choose three squares to scratch?

(ii) How many of these ways reveal two numbers and one blank?

(iii) What is the probability that all three squares reveal numbers?

All the scratchcards are printed with the same set of five numbers. A player wins £10 if all three of the squares scratched off reveal numbers, and the prize is increased to £25 if the product of all three numbers is 2000.

(iv) Show that the probability of the player winning exactly £10 with one scratchcard is $\frac{2}{55}$.

(v) A player buys two scratchcards. Find the probability that the player wins

(a) exactly £10 **(b)** at least £25. [MEI]

7 The European Union is about to set up three new regulatory bodies: the Avocado Authority, the Broccoli Board and the Courgette Commission. The European Union has 15 member countries. Each of the three new bodies to be set up will have one member from each of six different countries. Some countries may be represented on more than one body, and some may be represented on none.

(i) In how many ways can the six countries to be represented on the Avocado Authority be chosen?

Find the number of ways in which the three bodies can be made up in each of the following cases. Give your answers in scientific notation correct to 3 significant figures (e.g. 1.23×10^4). Note that the order in which countries are allocated to the bodies does not matter.

(ii) The six countries for each body are chosen freely from the 15 member countries.

(iii) France insists on being represented on each body and Britain insists on *not* being represented on any of them, but otherwise the countries are chosen freely.

(iv) No country may be on both the Avocado Authority and the Broccoli Board, but otherwise the countries are chosen freely.

[MEI]

8 A draw is being made for the quarter-finals of a knock-out table tennis tournament. Eight counters, alike in every respect except that they are numbered from 1 to 8 inclusive, are placed in a bag and drawn one by one, without replacement. A typical draw might produce the numbers in the order 3, 5, 7, 2, 1, 8, 6, 4, resulting in the matches:

Match *A*	3	plays	5
Match *B*	7	plays	2
Match *C*	1	plays	8
Match *D*	6	plays	4

(i) In how many different orders can the counters be drawn from the bag?

(ii) In how many ways can the counters be drawn such that

(a) players 1 and 2 play each other in match *A*

(b) players 1 and 2 play each other?

(iii) Find the probability that

(a) players 1 and 2 play each other

(b) players 1 and 2 do not play each other.

In fact, players 1, 2, 3 and 4 are girls and the rest are boys.

(iv) In how many ways can the counters be drawn such that the girls play each other in matches *A* and *B* and the boys play each other in matches *C* and *D*?

(v) What is the probability that no girl plays a boy in the quarter-finals?

[MEI]

9 A squad of 16 cricketers has been chosen to represent England on a foreign tour. The squad contains 8 batsmen, 6 bowlers and 2 wicket-keepers. A team of 11 players is to be chosen from the squad. A team must contain 6 batsmen, 4 bowlers and 1 wicket-keeper.

(i) In how many ways can the 6 batsmen be chosen?

Find the number of ways of selecting the team in each of the following cases.

(ii) All 16 squad members are available to play.

(iii) The tour captain, who is a batsman, must play and one of the bowlers is unable to play because of injury.

Once the team has been selected, a batting order has to be decided. All eleven players are included in the order, with the batsmen occupying positions 1 to 6 inclusive.

Find the number of different batting orders if

(iv) there are no other restrictions

(v) two particular batsmen must occupy the first two positions (either way round) and the wicket-keeper bats at position 7.

Now suppose that 11 of the 16 players are chosen at random.

(vi) Find the probability that they consist of the correct numbers of batsmen, bowlers and wicket-keepers to form a team. [MEI]

10 The diagram shows a security lock with ten buttons.

0	1	2	3	4
5	6	7	8	9

To open the lock the correct four buttons have to be pressed simultaneously.

(i) How many different combinations of four buttons are there?

I have forgotten the correct combination, but I recall that exactly two of the four digits are odd.

(ii) Show that the probability that I get the combination correct at the first attempt is 0.01.

(iii) What is the probability that I need more than two attempts to find the correct combination?

The manufacturers want to make the ten-button lock more secure by reducing the probability that it can be opened by chance.

(iv) Could the lock be made more secure by redesigning it so that some other number of buttons has to be pressed simultaneously? Justify your answer.

A different type of security lock also has ten buttons, numbered 0 to 9. To open this lock four *different* buttons have to be pressed, one at a time, in a specific order. Once again I recall that exactly two of the four digits are odd.

(v) Find the probability that I open the lock at the first attempt. [MEI]

11 My computer has 16 memory chips in it and there is a problem which indicates that exactly two of these chips are faulty. To locate the faulty chips I have to remove them one by one for testing.

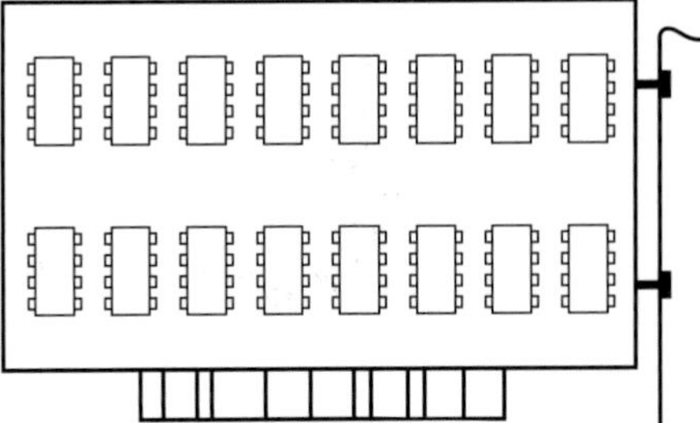

(i) How many different ways are there of choosing two chips from 16, irrespective of order?

(ii) Write down the probability that

(a) the first chip I test is faulty

(b) the first and second chips I test are both faulty.

(iii) Find the probability that the faulty chips are the first and eighth that I test.

(iv) Write down the probability that the faulty chips are the second and eighth that I test.

(v) Obtain the probability that I need *exactly* eight tests to find the two faulty chips.

(vi) Find the probability that I need *at most* eight tests to find the two faulty chips.

[MEI]

12 Next September I intend to buy a new car. Its registration plate will be of the form

HW53 MSD

where HW is the local area code for the Isle of Wight, 53 represents the second half of the year 2003, and the last three letters are chosen at random.

The five parts of the question refer to the last three letters of the registration plate. You may assume that all 26 letters in the alphabet, of which 5 are vowels and 21 are consonants, are used for each of the random choices.

(i) Find the probability that the random letters on the plate are MSD, appearing in that order.

(ii) Find the probability that the letters are M, S, D in any order.

(iii) Find the probability that just two of the letters are the same.

(iv) Find the probability that just one of the letters is a vowel.

(v) Given that just one of the three letters is a vowel, find the probability that the first and last letters are the same.

[MEI]

KEY POINTS

1. The number of ways of arranging n unlike objects in a line is $n!$
2. $n! = n \times (n-1) \times (n-2) \times (n-3) \times \ldots \times 3 \times 2 \times 1$.
3. The number of permutations of r objects from n is

$$^{n}\mathrm{P}_r = \frac{n!}{(n-r)!}.$$

4. The number of combinations of r objects from n is

$$^{n}\mathrm{C}_r = \frac{n!}{(n-r)!\,r!}.$$

5. For permutations the order matters. For combinations it does not.
6. By convention $0! = 1$.

6 The binomial distribution

To be or not to be, that is the question.

Shakespeare (Hamlet)

AVONFORD STAR

Samantha's great invention

Mother of three, Samantha Weeks, has done more than her bit to protect the environment. She has invented the first cheap energy-saving light bulb.

Now Samantha is out to prove that she is not only a clever scientist but a smart business women as well. For Samantha is setting up her own factory to make and sell her SUPERSAVER bulbs.

Samantha admits there are still some technical problems ...

Samantha Weeks hopes to make a big success of her light industry

Samantha's production process is indeed not very good and there is a probability of 0.1 that any bulb will be substandard and so not last as long as it should.

She decides to sell her bulbs in packs of three and believes that if one bulb in a pack is substandard the customers will not complain but that if two or more are substandard they will do so. She also believes that complaints should be kept down to no more than 2.5% of customers. Does she meet her target?

Imagine a pack of Samantha's bulbs. There are eight different ways that good (G) and substandard (S) bulbs can be arranged in Samantha's packs, each with its associated probability.

Arrangement	Probability	Good	Substandard
G G G	$0.9 \times 0.9 \times 0.9 = 0.729$	3	0
G G S	$0.9 \times 0.9 \times 0.1 = 0.081$	2	1
G S G	$0.9 \times 0.1 \times 0.9 = 0.081$	2	1
S G G	$0.1 \times 0.9 \times 0.9 = 0.081$	2	1
G S S	$0.9 \times 0.1 \times 0.1 = 0.009$	1	2
S G S	$0.1 \times 0.9 \times 0.1 = 0.009$	1	2
S S G	$0.1 \times 0.1 \times 0.9 = 0.009$	1	2
S S S	$0.1 \times 0.1 \times 0.1 = 0.001$	0	3

Putting these results together gives this table.

Good	Substandard	Probability
3	0	0.729
2	1	0.243
1	2	0.027
0	3	0.001

So the probability of more than one substandard bulb in a pack is

$$0.027 + 0.001 = 0.028 \text{ or } 2.8\%$$

This is slightly more than the 2.5% that Samantha regards as acceptable.

What business advice would you give Samantha?

In this example we wrote down all the possible outcomes and found their probabilities one at a time, as you do in a tree diagram. Even with just three bulbs this was repetitive. If Samantha had packed her bulbs in boxes of six it would have taken 64 lines to list them all. Clearly we need to find a less cumbersome approach.

You will have noticed that in the case of two good bulbs and one substandard, the probability is the same for each of the three arrangements in the box.

Arrangement	Probability	Good	Substandard
G G S	$0.9 \times 0.9 \times 0.1 = 0.081$	2	1
G S G	$0.9 \times 0.1 \times 0.9 = 0.081$	2	1
S G G	$0.1 \times 0.9 \times 0.9 = 0.081$	2	1

So the probability of this outcome is $3 \times 0.081 = 0.243$. The number 3 arises because there are three ways of arranging two good and one substandard bulb in the box. This is a result you have already met in the previous chapter but written slightly differently.

EXAMPLE 6.1

How many different ways are there of arranging the letters *GGS*?

SOLUTION

Since all the letters are either *G* or *S*, all you need to do is to count the number of ways of choosing the letter *G* two times out of three letters. This is

$$^3C_2 = \frac{3!}{2! \times 1!} = \frac{6}{2} = 3.$$

So what does this tell you? There was no need to list all the possibilities for Samantha's boxes of bulbs. The information could have been written down like this.

Good	Substandard	Expression	Probability
3	0	${}^3C_3\,(0.9)^3$	0.729
2	1	${}^3C_2\,(0.9)^2(0.1)^1$	0.243
1	2	${}^3C_1\,(0.9)^1(0.1)^2$	0.027
0	3	${}^3C_0\,(0.1)^3$	0.001

The binomial distribution

Samantha's light bulbs are an example of a common type of situation which is modelled by the binomial distribution. In describing such situations in this book, we emphasise the fact by using the word trial rather than the more general term experiment.

- You are conducting trials on random samples of a certain size, denoted by n.
- There are just two possible outcomes (in this case substandard and good). These are often referred to as *success* and *failure*.
- Both outcomes have fixed probabilities, the two adding to 1. The probability of success is usually called p, that of failure q, so $p + q = 1$.
- The probability of success in any trial is constant and is independent of the outcomes of previous trials.

You can then list the probabilities of the different possible outcomes as in the table above.

The method of the previous section can be applied more generally. You can call the probability of a substandard bulb p (instead of 0.1), the probability of a good bulb q (instead of 0.9) and the number of substandard bulbs in a packet of three, X.

Then the possible values of X and their probabilities are as shown in the table below.

r	0	1	2	3
$\mathrm{P}(X = r)$	q^3	$3pq^2$	$3p^2q$	p^3

This package of values of X with their associated probabilities is called a *binomial probability distribution*, a special case of a discrete random variable.

If Samantha decided to put five bulbs in a packet the probability distribution would be

r	0	1	2	3	4	5
$P(X = r)$	q^3	$5pq^4$	$10p^2q^3$	$10p^3q^2$	$5p^4q$	p^5

10 is ${}^5C_2$.

The entry for $X = 2$, for example, arises because there are two 'successes' (substandard bulbs), giving probability p^2, and three 'failures' (good bulbs), giving probability q^3, and these can happen in ${}^5C_2 = 10$ ways. This can be written as $P(X = 2) = 10p^2q^3$.

If you are already familiar with the binomial theorem, you will notice that the probabilities in the table are the terms of the binomial expansion of $(q + p)^5$. This is why this is called a binomial distribution. Notice also that the sum of these probabilities is $(q + p)^5 = 1^5 = 1$, since $q + p = 1$, which is to be expected since the distribution covers all possible outcomes.

Note

More detailed information about the binomial theorem is given in the appendix on page 444.

The general case

The general binomial distribution deals with the possible numbers of successes when there are n trials, each of which may be a success (with probability p) or a failure (with probability q); p and q are fixed positive numbers and $p + q = 1$. This distribution is denoted by $B(n, p)$. So, the original probability distribution for the number of substandard bulbs in Samantha's boxes of three is $B(3, 0.1)$.

For $B(n, p)$, the probability of r successes in n trials is found by the same argument as before. Each success has probability p and each failure has probability q, so the probability of r successes and $(n - r)$ failures in a particular order is $p^r q^{n-r}$. The positions in the sequence of n trials which the successes occupy can be chosen in ${}^nC_r$ ways. Therefore

$$P(X = r) = {}^nC_r p^r q^{n-r} \quad \text{for } 0 \leqslant r \leqslant n.$$

The successive probabilities for $X = 0, 1, 2, \ldots, n$ are the terms of the binomial expansion of $(q + p)^n$.

Notes

1 The number of successes, X, is a variable which takes a restricted set of values ($X = 0, 1, 2, \ldots, n$) each of which has a known probability of occurring. This is an example of a *random variable*. Random variables are usually denoted by upper case letters, such as X, but the particular values they may take are written in lower case, such as r. To state that X has the binomial distribution $B(n, p)$ you can use the abbreviation $X \sim B(n, p)$, where the symbol $\sim$ means 'has the distribution'.

2 It is often the case that you use a theoretical distribution, such as the binomial, to describe a random variable that occurs in real life. This process is called modelling and it enables you to carry out relevant calculations. If the theoretical distribution matches the real-life variable perfectly, then the model is perfect. Usually, however, the match is quite good but not perfect. In this case the results of any calculations will not necessarily give a completely accurate description of the real-life situation. They may, nonetheless, be very useful.

EXERCISE 6A

1 Five coins drop out of a man's pocket.

(i) Find the probability that the number landing showing heads is

(a) 0 **(b)** 1 **(c)** 2 **(d)** 3 **(e)** 4 **(f)** 5.

(ii) Add the six probabilities that you found in part **(i)** together and explain your answer.

2 The probability that a typist makes at least one mistake on a page is $\frac{4}{10}$.

(i) A random sample of five of the typist's pages is to be taken. Find the probability that the number containing at least one mistake is

(a) 0 **(b)** 1 **(c)** 2 **(d)** 3 **(e)** 4 **(f)** 5.

Give your answers correct to 4 decimal places.

(ii) Explain how you can check your answers to part **(i)** by finding the total of the six probabilities.

3 An old computer crashes on 25% of the occasions that it is used.

(i) It is to be used three times in one day. Find the probability that the number of times it will crash is

(a) 0 **(b)** 1 **(c)** 2 **(d)** 3.

(ii) Which is the more likely, that it crashes once in three uses or twice in six uses?

4 The probability that a seed from a rare cactus germinates is 0.05. A botanist collects 20 seeds and plants them.

(i) Find the probability that the number of seeds germinating is

(a) 0 **(b)** 1 **(c)** 2 **(d)** more than 2.

(ii) What is the most likely number of the 20 seeds to germinate?

5 In an experiment, needles are thrown in a random manner on to a large board covered in squares. The probability that a needle will land fully inside a square is 0.15.

(i) On one occasion eight needles are thrown. Find the probability that the number of needles landing fully inside a square is

(a) 0 **(b)** 1 **(c)** 2 **(d)** less than 3.

(ii) What is the most likely number of the eight needles to land fully inside a square?

6 A particular type of cuckoo is endangered. Research shows that 1 in 8 of newly hatched chicks of this type of cuckoo is female. As part of a conservation exercise ten chicks are hatched.

(i) Estimate the probability that the number of females among the chicks is

(a) 0 **(b)** at least 1.

(ii) Later in the year, a further batch of 20 eggs is to be hatched. Which is the more likely, that none of them is a female or that at least one of them is a female?

7 Research shows that the probability of a professional footballer breaking a metatarsal bone during the course of a season is 0.1.

(i) Write down the probability that a professional footballer goes through a season without breaking a metatarsal bone.

(ii) A professional footballer plays for seven seasons. Find the probability that he does not break a metatarsal bone.

(iii) A team starts a season with a squad of 25 players. Find the probability that by the end of the season

(a) none of them will have broken a metatarsal bone

(b) exactly one of them will have broken a metatarsal bone

(c) at least two of them will have broken a metatarsal bone.

8 Experiments have shown that if a particular type of drawing pin is thrown in the air then it will, on average, land point up on 35% of occasions. 20 such pins are thrown.

(i) Find the probability that the number landing point up is exactly

(a) 1 **(b)** 3 **(c)** 5.

(ii) Find the most likely number of the 20 to land point up.

9 A coin is tossed six times.

(i) Find the probability that it shows heads on exactly four occasions if

(a) it is unbiased

(b) it is biased, with a probability of $\frac{3}{5}$ of showing heads

(c) it is biased, with a probability of $\frac{2}{3}$ of showing heads.

(ii) In which case in part **(i)**, **(a)**, **(b)** or **(c)**, is the probability largest? Could you have predicted this answer without doing any calculations?

10 70% of people are older than Joe Smith. He meets ten people one morning.

(i) Estimate the probability that exactly seven of the ten are older than Joe.

(ii) What is the most likely number, out of the ten people, to be older than Joe? Give evidence for your answer.

(iii) What assumption did you need to make to answer these questions? Why might this assumption be incorrect?

The expectation of B(n, p)

EXAMPLE 6.2

The number of substandard bulbs in a packet of three of Samantha's bulbs is modelled by the random variable X. $X \sim B(3, 0.1)$.

(i) Find the expected frequencies of obtaining 0, 1, 2 and 3 substandard bulbs in 2000 packets.

(ii) Find the mean number of substandard bulbs per packet.

SOLUTION

(i) $P(X = 0) = 0.729$ (as on page 166), so the expected frequency of packets with no substandard bulbs is $2000 \times 0.729 = 1458$.

Similarly, the other expected frequencies are

for 1 substandard bulb: $2000 \times 0.243 = 486$

for 2 substandard bulbs: $2000 \times 0.027 = 54$

for 3 substandard bulbs: $2000 \times 0.001 = 2$.

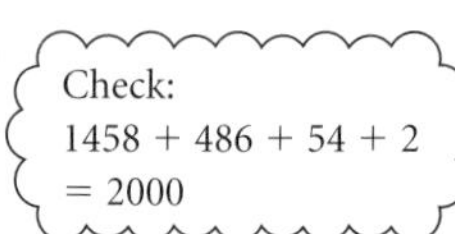

(ii) The expected total of substandard bulbs in 2000 packets is

$$0 \times 1458 + 1 \times 486 + 2 \times 54 + 3 \times 2 = 600.$$

Therefore the mean number of substandard bulbs per packet is $\frac{600}{2000} = 0.3$.

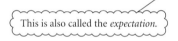

This is also called the *expectation*.

Notice in this example that to calculate the mean we have multiplied each probability by 2000 to get the frequency, multiplied each frequency by the number of faulty bulbs, added these numbers together and finally divided by 2000. Of course we could have obtained the mean with less calculation by just multiplying each number of faulty bulbs by its probability and then summing, i.e. by finding $\sum_{r=0}^{3} rP(X = r)$. This is the standard method for finding an expectation, as you saw in Chapter 4.

Notice also that the mean or expectation of X is $0.3 = 3 \times 0.1 = np$. The result for the general binomial distribution is the same.

If $X \sim B(n, p)$ then the expectation of X is np.

This seems obvious: if the probability of success in each single trial is p, then the expected numbers of successes in n independent trials is np. However, since what seems obvious is not always true, a proper proof is required.

Take the case when $n = 5$. The distribution table for $\mathrm{B}(5, p)$ is as on page 167, and the expectation of X

$$= 0 \times q^5 + 1 \times 5pq^4 + 2 \times 10p^2q^3 + 3 \times 10p^3q^2 + 4 \times 5p^4q + 5 \times p^5$$
$$= 5pq^4 + 20p^2q^3 + 30p^3q^2 + 20p^4q + 5p^5$$
$$= 5p(q^4 + 4pq^3 + 6p^2q^2 + 4p^3q + p^4)$$
$$= 5p(q + p)^4$$

Take out the common factor $5p$.

$$= 5p$$

Since $q + p = 1$.

The proof in the general case follows the same pattern: the common factor is now np, and the expectation simplifies to $np(q + p)^{n-1} = np$. The details are more fiddly because of the manipulations of the binomial coefficients.

ACTIVITY

If you want a challenge write out the details of the proof that if $X \sim \mathrm{B}(n, p)$ then the expectation of X is np.

Using the binomial distribution

AVONFORD STAR

Calvin's Tips

If you are to be successful at the tables you must develop an insight into probability. Nobody makes money playing against the odds in the long term. Try to argue your way round this problem.

Which is more likely: that you get at least one 6 when you throw a die six times, or that you get at least two 6s when you throw it twelve times?

On a single throw of a die the probability of getting a 6 is $\frac{1}{6}$ and that of not getting a 6 is $\frac{5}{6}$.

So the probability distributions for the two situations in Calvin's problem are $\mathrm{B}\left(6, \frac{1}{6}\right)$ and $\mathrm{B}\left(12, \frac{1}{6}\right)$ giving probabilities of:

$$1 - {}^6\mathrm{C}_0\left(\tfrac{5}{6}\right)^6 = 1 - 0.335 = 0.665 \text{ (at least one 6 in six throws)}$$

and

$$1 - \left[{}^{12}\mathrm{C}_0\left(\tfrac{5}{6}\right)^{12} + {}^{12}\mathrm{C}_1\left(\tfrac{5}{6}\right)^{11}\left(\tfrac{1}{6}\right)\right] = 1 - (0.112 + 0.269)$$
$$= 0.619 \text{ (at least two 6s in 12 throws)}$$

So at least one 6 in six throws is somewhat more likely.

EXAMPLE 6.3

Extensive research has shown that one person out of every four is allergic to a particular grass seed. A group of 20 university students volunteer to try out a new treatment.

(i) What is the expectation of the number of allergic people in the group?

(ii) What is the probability that

(a) exactly two

(b) no more than two of the group are allergic?

(iii) How large a sample would be needed for the probability of it containing at least one allergic person to be greater than 99.9%?

(iv) What assumptions have you made in your answer?

SOLUTION

This situation is modelled by the binomial distribution with $n = 20$, $p = 0.25$ and $q = 0.75$. The number of allergic people is denoted by X.

(i) Expectation $= np = 20 \times 0.25 = 5$ people.

(ii) $X \sim \text{B}(20, 0.25)$

(a) $\text{P}(X = 2) = {}^{20}\text{C}_2(0.75)^{18}(0.25)^2 = 0.067$

(b)
$$\begin{aligned}\text{P}(X \leqslant 2) &= \text{P}(X = 0) + \text{P}(X = 1) + \text{P}(X = 2)\\ &= (0.75)^{20} + {}^{20}\text{C}_1(0.75)^{19}(0.25) + {}^{20}\text{C}_2(0.75)^{18}(0.25)^2\\ &= 0.003 + 0.021 + 0.067\\ &= 0.091\end{aligned}$$

(iii) Let the sample size be n (people), so that $X \sim \text{B}(n, 0.25)$.

The probability that none of them is allergic is

$$\text{P}(X = 0) = (0.75)^n$$

and so the probability that at least one is allergic is

$$\begin{aligned}\text{P}(X \geqslant 1) &= 1 - \text{P}(X = 0)\\ &= 1 - (0.75)^n\end{aligned}$$

So we need $\quad 1 - (0.75)^n > 0.999$

$$(0.75)^n < 0.001$$

Solving gives

$$\begin{aligned}(0.75)^n &= 0.001\\ n \log 0.75 &= \log 0.001\\ n &= \log 0.001 \div \log 0.75\\ &= 24.01\end{aligned}$$

So 25 people are required.

Notes

1 Although 24.01 is very close to 24 it would be incorrect to round down. $1 - (0.75)^{24} = 0.998\,996\,6$ which is just less than 99.9%.

2 You can also use trial and improvement on a calculator to solve for n.

(iv) The assumptions made are:

(a) That the sample is random. This is almost certainly untrue. University students are nearly all in the 18–25 age range and so a sample of them cannot be a random sample of the whole population. They may well also be unrepresentative of the whole population in other ways. Volunteers are seldom truly random.

(b) That the outcome for one person is independent of that for another. This is probably true unless they are a group of friends from, say, an athletics team, where those with allergies are less likely to be members.

Does the binomial distribution really work?

EXPERIMENT

In Calvin's first case you threw a die six times (or six dice once each).

$X \sim \mathrm{B}\left(6, \frac{1}{6}\right)$ and this gives the probabilities in the table.

So if you carry out the experiment of throwing six dice 1000 times and record the number of 6s each time, you should get none about 335 times, one about 402 times and so on. What does 'about' mean? How close an agreement can you expect between experimental and theoretical results?

Number of 6s	Probability
0	0.335
1	0.402
2	0.201
3	0.054
4	0.008
5	0.001
6	0.000

You could carry out the experiment with dice, but it would be very time-consuming even if several people shared the work. Alternatively you could simulate the experiment on a spreadsheet using a random number generator.

INVESTIGATION

This is a true story. During voting at a by-election, an exit poll of 1700 voters indicated that 50% of people had voted for the Labour Party candidate. When the real votes were counted it was found that he had in fact received 57% support.

Carry out a computer simulation of the situation and use it to decide whether the difference was likely to have occurred because of the random nature of the sample, faulty sampling techniques or other possible reasons you can think of.

EXERCISE 6B

1 Long-term studies have shown that, in a certain country, 51% of newborn babies are boys and 49% are girls.

(i) Write down the expected number of boys in a family of five.

(ii) A family with five children is selected at random. Calculate the probability that the number of boys is

(a) 0 **(b)** 1 **(c)** 2 **(d)** 3 **(e)** 4 **(f)** 5.

2 It is known that, in a particular country, 10% of people have red hair. A group of 18 people from this country go on a holiday tour.

(i) What is the expected number of people with red hair in the group?

(ii) Calculate the probability that exactly two people in the group have red hair.

(iii) Predict the most likely number of red-haired people in the group and then do appropriate calculations to see if you are right.

3 A wind-powered supply of electricity operates one day in four. The binomial distribution is used as a model for the number of days it operates in any given period.

(i) Write down the expected number of days that the supply operates

(a) in a single week

(b) in a four-week period.

(ii) Calculate the probability that the supply operates for exactly the expected number of days in a four-week period.

(iii) State the assumptions underlying the use of the binomial distribution. Comment on whether these assumptions are likely to hold in this situation.

4 **(i)** In a manufacturing process, 5% of articles are defective. A large batch of articles is examined. Calculate the probability that the number of defectives in a sample of ten articles from the batch is

(a) 0 **(b)** 1 **(c)** at least 2.

(ii) The process is changed and, as a result, the overall percentage of defectives may have changed. It is decided that if at least two in a sample of ten from a future large batch are defective, then the whole batch is rejected. Calculate the probability that

(a) a batch in which 3% are defective is rejected

(b) a batch in which 15% are defective is accepted.

5 Charles manufactures biased 'coins' and sells them to a casino. He sells red coins with a probability of $\frac{2}{3}$ of showing heads, and blue coins with a probability of $\frac{1}{3}$ of showing heads.

(i) Calculate the probability that when

(a) four red coins are tossed, exactly three show heads

(b) four blue coins are tossed, exactly three show heads

(c) eight coins are tossed, four of each colour, exactly three of each colour show heads.

(ii) Write down the expected number of heads when

(a) a red coin is tossed four times

(b) a blue coin is tossed four times.

6 Gregor Mendel, who invented the science of genetics, used symbols like AA, Aa and aa to represent the three possible *genotypes* for a given characteristic in a plant. His notation is still used.
In a particular population, the proportions of *genotypes* AA, Aa and aa are 0.16, 0.48 and 0.36 respectively.

(i) Eight plants are selected at random. Find the probability that
  (a) one is of type AA
  (b) four are of type Aa
  (c) three are of type aa.

(ii) Find the expected numbers of the various genotypes in 5000 plants.

(iii) What do the figures 0.16, 0.48 and 0.36 tell you about the proportions of the genes A and a in the population?

7 A mega-tsunami struck Scotland 7000 years ago. It is conjectured that mega-tsunamis occur at random somewhere in the world once every 10 000 years so that the probability, p, of a mega-tsunami occurring in any given year is $\frac{1}{10\,000}$.

(i) Calculate the probability that there will be no mega-tsunami
  (a) next year
  (b) in the next 50 years
  (c) in the next 100 years.

A geologist claims that mega-tsunamis are more common than originally thought and that the correct value of p is actually $\frac{1}{7000}$.

(ii) What is the probability now that there will be no mega-tsunami
  (a) next year
  (b) in the next 50 years
  (c) in the next 100 years?

(iii) Calculate the expected number of occurrences in the next 80 years using each value of p in turn.

8 Before the Three Gorges Project on the Yangtze River, major flooding occurred on average once every 10 years. It is anticipated that, after the completion of the project (in 2009), major flooding will be reduced to once every 100 years.

(i) Taking $p = \frac{1}{10}$ for the probability that there will be flooding in any given year, calculate the probability that there will be
  (a) at least one flood in a 25-year period
  (b) floods in at least two years in a 25-year period.

(ii) Now taking $p = \frac{1}{100}$ for the probability that there will be flooding in any given year, calculate the probability that there will be
  (a) at least one flood in a 25-year period
  (b) floods in at least two years in a 25-year period.

(iii) Compare your answers for the two probabilities and comment.

9 The data below summarises the outbreaks of war in the 432 years from 1500 AD to 1931 AD inclusive over the whole world.

Number of outbreaks of war per year	0	1	2	3	4
Frequency	223	142	48	15	4

Source: *The World of Mathematics*

(i) Find the mean number of outbreaks of war per year.

(ii) Deduce that the mean number of outbreaks *per day*, p, is about 0.0019.

(iii) Use your answer to part **(ii)** to show that the probability of at least one war breaking out in one year of 365 days is almost exactly 0.5.

(iv) Find the probability that in a five-year period there will be

(a) no war

(b) three or more years in which at least one war breaks out.

(v) How many wars are to be expected in a ten-year period? Round your answer to the nearest whole number.

10 The probability, p, that a particular type of light bulb which has already had 40 hours of use will fail before it has had 60 hours of use is taken to be 0.05.

(i) Find the probability that, of 12 such light bulbs,

(a) at least one will fail before it has had 60 hours of use

(b) exactly two will fail before they have had 60 hours of use.

The probability, p, that a particular type of light bulb which has already had 40 hours of use will fail before it has had 75 hours of use is taken to be 0.45.

(ii) Find the probability that, of 12 such light bulbs,

(a) at least one will fail before it has had 75 hours of use

(b) exactly two will fail before they have had 75 hours of use.

(iii) What is the most likely number, out of 12, to fail in each case?

11 Records show that, on average, 25 tornadoes occur in the British Isles in a year.

(i) Assuming that only one tornado occurs per day, write down the probability of a tornado occurring on a particular day, assuming there are 365 days in a year.

(ii) Find the probability there is no tornado in a particular three-month period of 90 days.

(iii) What assumption have you made in finding the answer to part **(ii)**? Why might it not be so surprising if no tornado occurred in a three-month period?

12 A class of 30 students is given homework to do in which they each have to toss a coin ten times. Assume that all the coins used are fair.

(i) Find the probability that a coin tossed ten times shows a head exactly five times.

(ii) Write down the expected number of students in the class who report a result of five heads.

(iii) Find the probability that a coin tossed ten times will show either all heads or all tails.

(iv) Find the probability that *at least* one student in the class will report all heads or all tails.

(v) Find the probability that *exactly* one student in the class will report all heads or all tails.

[MEI]

13 A market researcher has been commissioned to interview left-handed people. She approaches people, chosen at random, in a busy shopping centre. You may assume that 12% of the population are left-handed.

(i) Find the probability that the first 5 people she approaches are right-handed.

(ii) How many people does she need to approach so that the probability of there being at least one left-handed person is greater than 0.5?

(iii) Find the probability that exactly 4 out of the first 14 people she approaches are left-handed.

(iv) Hence find the probability that she has to approach 15 people so as to find 5 left-handed people.

(v) Given that the first 5 people she approaches are right-handed, find the probability that she has to approach a total of 15 people so as to find 5 left-handed people.

[MEI]

INVESTIGATION

(i) Some unbiased coins are tossed. Find the probability that when

(a) there are 10 coins, 5 land heads uppermost

(b) there are 20 coins, 10 land heads uppermost

(c) there are 40 coins, 20 land heads uppermost.

(ii) Continue the sequence. Search for an approximate pattern and check it with further calculation. You may find it helpful to tabulate your results using a graphic calculator or a computer.

KEY POINTS

1 The binomial distribution may be used to model situations in which:

- you are conducting trials on random samples of a certain size, n
- there are two possible outcomes, often referred to as success and failure
- both outcomes have fixed probabilities, p and q, and $p + q = 1$
- the probability of success in any trial is constant and is independent of the outcomes of previous trials

2 The probability that the number of successes, X, has the value r, is given by

$$P(X = r) = {}^{n}\mathrm{C}_r q^{n-r} p^r.$$

3 For $\mathrm{B}(n, p)$ the expectation of the number of successes is np.

To be and not to be, that is the answer. *Piet Hein*

7 Hypothesis testing using the binomial distribution

You may prove anything by figures.

An anonymous salesman

AVONFORD STAR

Machoman Dan

Beer drinking Dan Ellis has just become a father for the eighth time, and they are ALL BOYS.

Find Dan at his local and he will tell you that having no girls among the eight shows that he is a real man.

'When I was just a lad at school I said I had macho chromosomes,' Dan claims.

'Now I have been proved right.'

Cheers! Dan Ellis reckons his all-boy offspring prove he's a real man

What do you think?

There are two quite different points here.

The first is that you have probably decided that Dan is a male chauvinist, preferring boys to girls. However, you should not let your views on that influence your judgement on the second point, his claim to be biologically different from other people, with special chromosomes.

There are two ways this claim could be investigated, to look at his chromosomes under a high magnification microscope or to consider the statistical evidence. Since you have neither Dan Ellis nor a suitable microscope to hand, you must resort to the latter.

If you have eight children you would expect them to be divided about evenly between the sexes, 4 − 4, 5 − 3 or perhaps 6 − 2. When you realised that a baby was on its way you would think it equally likely to be a boy or a girl until it were born, or a scan were carried out, when you would know for certain one way or the other.

In other words you would say that the probability of its being a boy was 0.5 and that of its being a girl 0.5. So you can model the number of boys among eight children by the binomial distribution B(8, 0.5).

This gives these probabilities, shown in figure 7.1.

Boys	Girls	Probability
0	8	$\frac{1}{256}$
1	7	$\frac{8}{256}$
2	6	$\frac{28}{256}$
3	5	$\frac{56}{256}$
4	4	$\frac{70}{256}$
5	3	$\frac{56}{256}$
6	2	$\frac{28}{256}$
7	1	$\frac{8}{256}$
8	0	$\frac{1}{256}$

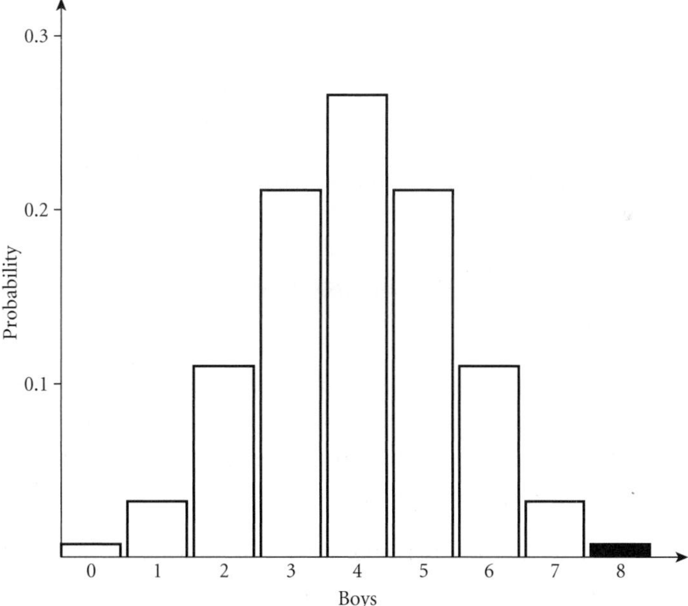

Figure 7.1

So you can say that, if a biologically normal man fathers eight children, the probability that they will all be boys is $\frac{1}{256}$ (shaded in figure 7.1).

This is unlikely but by no means impossible.

Note

The probability of a baby being a boy is not in fact 0.5 but about 0.503. Boys are less tough than girls and so more likely to die in infancy and this seems to be nature's way of compensating. In most societies men have a markedly lower life expectancy as well.

? You may think Dan Ellis a thoroughly objectionable character but in some countries large sections of society value boys more highly than girls. Medical advances mean that it will soon be possible to decide in advance the sex of your next baby. What would be the effect of this on a country's population if, say, half the parents decided to have only boys and the other half to let nature take its course?

(This is a real problem. The social consequences could be devastating.)

Defining terms

In the last example we investigated Dan Ellis's claim by comparing it to the usual situation, the unexceptional. If we use p for the probability that a child is a boy then the normal state of affairs can be stated as

$$p = 0.5.$$

This is called the *null hypothesis*, denoted by H_0.

Dan's claim (made, he says, before he had any children) was that

$$p > 0.5$$

and this is called the *alternative hypothesis*, H_1.

The word hypothesis (plural *hypotheses*) means a theory which is put forward either for the sake of argument or because it is believed or suspected to be true. An investigation like this is usually conducted in the form of a test, called a *hypothesis test*. There are many different sorts of hypothesis tests used in statistics; in this chapter you meet only one of them.

It is never possible to prove something statistically in the sense that, for example, you can prove that the angle sum of a triangle is 180°. Even if you tossed a coin a million times and it came down heads every single time, it is still possible that the coin is unbiased and just happened to land that way. What you can say is that it is very unlikely; the probability of it happening that way is $(0.5)^{1\,000\,000}$ which is a decimal that starts with over 300 000 zeros. This is so tiny that you would feel quite confident in declaring the coin biased.

There comes a point when the probability is so small that you say 'That's good enough for me. I am satisfied that it hasn't happened that way by chance.'

The probability at which you make that decision is called the *significance level* of the test. Significance levels are usually given as percentages; 0.05 is written as 5%, 0.01 as 1% and so on.

So in the case of Dan Ellis, the question could have been worded

Test, at the 1% significance level, Dan Ellis's boyhood claim that his children are more likely to be boys than girls.

The answer would then look like this:

Setting up the hypothesis test

Null hypothesis, H_0:	$p = 0.5$	(Boys and girls are equally likely)
Alternative hypothesis, H_1:	$p > 0.5$	(Boys are more likely)
Significance level:	1%	

Calculating the probability

Probability of 8 boys from 8 children $= \frac{1}{256} = 0.0039 = 0.39\%$.

Interpreting the probability

Since $0.39\% < 1\%$ we reject the null hypothesis and accept the alternative hypothesis. We accept Dan Ellis's claim.

This example also illustrates some of the problems associated with hypothesis testing. Here is a list of points you should be considering.

Hypothesis testing checklist

1 Was the test set up before or after the data were known?

The test consists of a null hypothesis, an alternative hypothesis and a significance level.

In this case, the null hypothesis is the natural state of affairs and so does not really need to be stated in advance. Dan's claim 'When I was just a lad at school I said I had macho chromosomes' could be interpreted as the alternative hypothesis, $p > 0.5$.

The problem is that one suspects that whatever children Dan had he would find an excuse to boast. If they had all been girls, he might have been talking about 'my irresistible attraction for the opposite sex' and if they had been a mixture of girls and boys he would have been claiming 'super-virility' just because he had eight children.

Any test carried out retrospectively must be treated with suspicion.

2 Was the sample involved chosen at random and are the data independent?

The sample was not random and that may have been inevitable. If Dan had lots of children around the country with different mothers, a random sample of eight could have been selected. However, we have no knowledge that this is the case.

The data are the sexes of Dan's children. If there are no multiple births (for example, identical twins), then they are independent.

3 Is the statistical procedure actually testing the original claim?

Dan Ellis claims to have 'macho chromosomes' whereas the statistical test is of the alternative hypothesis that $p > 0.5$. The two are not necessarily the same. Even if this alternative hypothesis is true, it does not necessarily follow that Dan has macho chromosomes.

The ideal hypothesis test

In the ideal hypothesis test you take the following steps, in this order.

1 Establish the null and alternative hypotheses.
2 Decide on the significance level.
3 Collect suitable data using a random sampling procedure that ensures the items are independent.
4 Conduct the test, doing the necessary calculations.
5 Interpret the result in terms of the original claim, theory or problem.

There are times, however, when you need to carry out a test but it is just not possible to do so as rigorously as this.

In the case of Dan Ellis, you would require him to go away and father eight more children, this time with randomly selected mothers, which is clearly impossible. Had Dan been a laboratory rat and not a human, however, you probably could have organised it.

Choosing the significance level

If, instead of 1%, we had set the significance level at 0.1%, then we would have rejected Dan's claim, since $0.39\% > 0.1\%$. The lower the percentage in the significance level, the more stringent is the test.

The significance level you choose for a test involves a balanced judgement.

Imagine that you are testing the rivets on an aeroplane's wing to see if they have lost their strength. Setting a small significance level, say 0.1%, means that you will only declare the rivets weak if you are very confident of your finding. The trouble with requiring such a high level of evidence is that even when they are weak you may well fail to register the fact, with the possible consequence that the aeroplane crashes. On the other hand if you set a high significance level, such as 10%, you run the risk of declaring the rivets faulty when they are all right, involving the company in expensive and unnecessary maintenance work.

The question of how you choose the best significance level is, however, beyond the scope of this introductory chapter.

EXAMPLE 7.1

Here is another example, from 'Calvin's Tips' in the Avonford Star. Cover up the solution and then, as you work your way through it, see if you can predict the next step at each stage.

Does the procedure follow the steps of the ideal hypothesis test?

AVONFORD STAR

Calvin's Tips

I was at a casino the other evening. After several hours' play, a lady whom I shall call Leonora had lost a lot of money. She complained to the management that one of the dice was biased, with a tendency to show the number 1.

The management agreed to test the die at the 5% significance level, throwing it 20 times. If the test supported Leonora's view she would get her money refunded, otherwise she would be asked to leave the premises and never return.

The results were as follows.

1	6	6	5	5
1	2	3	2	3
4	4	4	1	4
1	1	4	1	3

What happened to my friend Leonora?

SOLUTION

Setting up the hypothesis test

Let p be the probability of getting 1 on any throw of the die.

Null hypothesis, H_0: $p = \frac{1}{6}$ (The die is unbiased)
Alternative hypothesis, H_1: $p > \frac{1}{6}$ (The die is biased towards 1)
Significance level: 5%

Calculating the probability

The results may be summarised as follows.

Score	1	2	3	4	5	6
Frequency	6	2	3	5	2	2

Under the null hypothesis, the number of 1s obtained is modelled by the binomial distribution, $B(20, \frac{1}{6})$, which gives the following probabilities.

Number of 1s	Expression	Probability
0	$\left(\frac{5}{6}\right)^{20}$	0.0261
1	$^{20}C_1 \left(\frac{5}{6}\right)^{19}\left(\frac{1}{6}\right)$	0.1043
2	$^{20}C_2 \left(\frac{5}{6}\right)^{18}\left(\frac{1}{6}\right)^2$	0.1982
3	$^{20}C_3 \left(\frac{5}{6}\right)^{17}\left(\frac{1}{6}\right)^3$	0.2379
4	$^{20}C_4 \left(\frac{5}{6}\right)^{16}\left(\frac{1}{6}\right)^4$	0.2022
5	$^{20}C_5 \left(\frac{5}{6}\right)^{15}\left(\frac{1}{6}\right)^5$	0.1294
6	$^{20}C_6 \left(\frac{5}{6}\right)^{14}\left(\frac{1}{6}\right)^6$	0.0647
7	$^{20}C_7 \left(\frac{5}{6}\right)^{13}\left(\frac{1}{6}\right)^7$	0.0259
8	$^{20}C_8 \left(\frac{5}{6}\right)^{12}\left(\frac{1}{6}\right)^8$	0.0084
⋮	⋮	⋮
20	$\left(\frac{1}{6}\right)^{20}$	0.0000

The probability of 1 coming up between 0 and 5 times is found by adding these probabilities to get 0.8981.

If you worked out all these and added them you would get the probability that the number of 1s is 6 or more (up to a possible 20). It is much quicker, however, to find this as 1 − 0.8981 (the answer above) = 0.1019.

Calling X the number of 1s occurring when a die is rolled 20 times, the probability of six or more 1s is given by

$$P(X \geqslant 6) = 1 - P(X \leqslant 5) = 1 - 0.8981 = 0.1019,$$

about 10%.

Interpreting the probability

Since 10% > 5%, the null hypothesis (the die is unbiased) is accepted.

The probability of a result at least as extreme as that observed is greater than the 5% cut off that was set in advance, that is, greater than the chosen significance level.

The alternative hypothesis (the die is biased in favour of the number 1) is rejected, even though the number 1 did come up more often than the other numbers.

AVONFORD STAR

Leonara did not get her money back but the management relented and did not ban her from the Casino.

Note

Notice that this is a test not of the particular result (six 1s) but of a result at least as extreme as this (at least six 1s), the area shaded in figure 7.2. A hypothesis test deals with the probability of an event 'as unusual as or more unusual than' what has occurred.

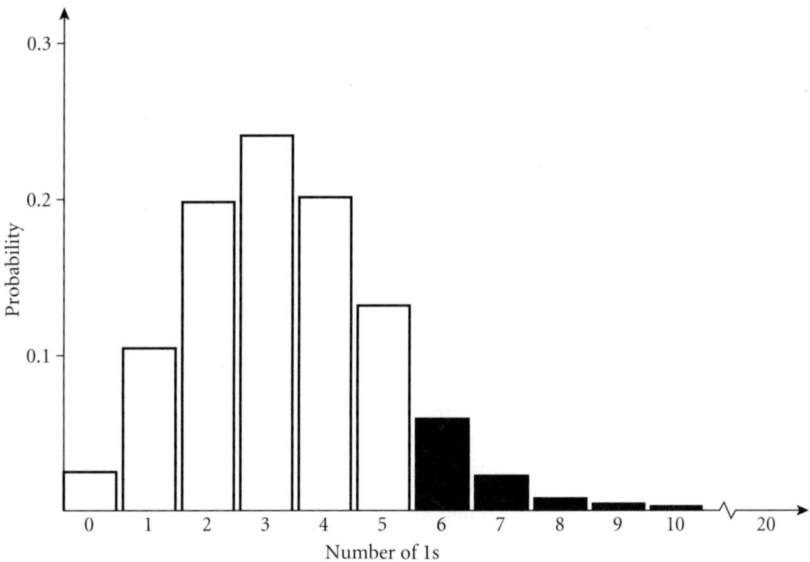

Figure 7.2

Another method

You could have found the probability of up to five scores of 1 using *cumulative binomial probability* tables. These give $P(X \leqslant x)$ when $X \sim B(n, p)$ for $x = 0, 1, 2, \ldots, n$ and values of p from 0.05 to 0.95 at intervals of 0.05 plus $\frac{1}{6}, \frac{1}{3}, \frac{2}{3}, \frac{5}{6}$. There is a separate table for each value of n from 1 to 20. Look up under $n = 20$.

n	x \ p	0.050	0.100	0.150	$\frac{1}{6}$	0.200	0.250	0.300	$\frac{1}{3}$	0.350
20	0	0.3585	0.1216	0.0388	0.0261	0.0115	0.0032	0.0008	0.0003	0.0002
	1	0.7358	0.3917	0.1756	0.1304	0.0692	0.0243	0.0076	0.0033	0.0021
	2	0.9245	0.6769	0.4049	0.3287	0.2061	0.0913	0.0355	0.0176	0.0121
	3	0.9841	0.8670	0.6477	0.5665	0.4114	0.2252	0.1071	0.0604	0.0444
	4	0.9974	0.9568	0.8298	0.7687	0.6296	0.4148	0.2375	0.1515	0.1182
	5	0.9997	0.9887	0.9327	0.8982	0.8042	0.6172	0.4164	0.2972	0.2454
	6	1.0000	0.9976	0.9781	0.9629	0.9133	0.7858	0.6080	0.4973	0.4166
	7		0.9996	0.9941	0.9887	0.9679	0.8982	0.7723	0.6615	0.6010
	8		0.9999	0.9987	0.9972	0.9900	0.9591	0.8867	0.8095	0.7624
	9		1.0000	0.9998	0.9994	0.9974	0.9861	0.9520	0.9081	0.8782
	10			1.0000	0.9999	0.9994	0.9961	0.9829	0.9624	0.9468
	11				1.0000	0.9999	0.9991	0.9949	0.9870	0.9804

In this case $p = \frac{1}{6}$ so the probability of up to five scores of 1 is 0.8982, the same result as before apart from the last figure where there is a difference of 1 from rounding.

Look in the table. Just below 0.8982 is 0.9629. What information is given by $0.9629 - 0.8982 = 0.0647$?

EXERCISE 7A

In all these questions you should apply this checklist to the hypothesis test.

1 Was the test set up before or after the data were known?
2 Was the sample used for the test chosen at random and are the data independent?
3 Is the statistical procedure actually testing the original claim?

You should also comment critically on whether these steps have been followed.

1 Establish the null and alternative hypotheses.
2 Decide on the significance level.
3 Collect suitable data using a random sampling procedure that ensures the items are independent.
4 Conduct the test, doing the necessary calculations.
5 Interpret the result in terms of the original claim, theory or problem.

1 Alvin is a league football referee. The captain of one of the teams complains that the coin Alvin uses at the start of matches is biased towards heads. Alvin conducts an experiment to test whether this is the case. He tosses the coin 20 times and it lands heads on 15 occasions.

(i) Write down the null and alternative hypotheses for the test.
(ii) Complete the test, using a 5% significance level.
(iii) Should Alvin get a new coin?

2 Research shows that on 35% of occasions when a standard drawing pin is thrown in the air, it will land point down.
Salome has a box of a new type of drawing pins. She conducts an experiment to test whether this type of drawing pin is less likely than others to land point down. She selects eight drawing pins at random and throws them up in the air. None of them lands point down.

(i) Write down null and alternative hypotheses for Salome's test.
(ii) Complete the test, using a 5% significance level.
(iii) What features of the design of a drawing pin do you think would make it less likely to land point down?

3 Just before a general election, opinion polls show that 30% of the population in general support the Democratic Party. A random sample of 20 active boxers are asked which party they support; only two say the Democratic Party.

(i) What is probability that a randomly selected member of the population in general does not support the Democratic Party?

(ii) State suitable null and alternative hypotheses to test whether active boxers were less likely to vote for the Democratic Party than the population in general.

(iii) Complete the test, using a 5% significance level.

(iv) On reading about this finding, a sports commentator writes 'The boxing community have abandoned the Democratic Party.' Comment.

4 A survey shows that in one region of the UK, 75% of secondary school students never walk to school.

(i) What is the probability that a randomly selected secondary school student in this region sometimes walks to school?

(ii) 20 secondary school students in this region are selected at random. Use cumulative binomial probability tables to find the probability that at least 10 sometimes walk to school.

(iii) At a particular secondary school in this region, it is found that 10 of a random sample of 20 secondary school students sometimes walk to school. State suitable null and alternative hypotheses to test the hypothesis that the proportion who sometimes walk to this school is larger than is usual.

(iv) Complete the test, using a 5% significance level.

(v) Give one reason why a particular school might have a higher than average proportion of its students who sometimes walk to school.

5 At a particular date it is estimated from a carefully constructed survey that 60% of the public in a country are in general agreement with their President's foreign policy.
Three years later a randomly selected group of 16 people are asked their opinion on their President's foreign policy. Seven are in general agreement.

(i) State null and alternative hypotheses for a test of whether there has been a decline in support for the President's foreign policy.

(ii) Complete the test, at the 10% significance level.

6 I have taken part in weekly General Knowledge quizzes at the Fox and Hounds for many years and kept a record of my performance. Overall, I get 40% of the questions right.
On a particular evening there is a new quiz master. It is suggested that the questions will be easier than usual. In fact I get 10 questions out of 16 right.

(i) State null and alternative hypotheses for a test of whether the questions have become easier.

(ii) Complete the test, at the 10% significance level.

(iii) Repeat the test, this time at the 5% significance level.

7 Last year 35% of trains on the Eastern Line arrived more than 10 minutes late. The train-operating company claim there will be an improvement in performance this year. From a random sample of 10 trains in the first week of this year, all but one arrived within the 10-minute margin.

(i) State null and alternative hypotheses for a test of whether there has been an improvement in performance.

(ii) Complete the test, at the 10% significance level.

(iii) Give one reason to be sceptical about the result of the test.

8 Sonya is a basket ball player. She claims that she can score a basket from 5 metres on 70% of her attempts.

(i) One day, at practice, Sonya has ten attempts from 5 metres and scores on four of them. Her rival, Carol, says 'This proves statistically that you are over-stating your success rate.' Carry out a suitable hypothesis test to demonstrate Carol's claim.

(ii) The next day Sonya succeeds on eight attempts out of ten. Use the evidence from all 20 attempts to perform another test at the 5% significance level.

(iii) Comment on whether the conditions for a binomial model apply in this example. What does this tell you about the validity of Carol's test?

9 An anthropologist claims that in a particular tribe more pairs of *dizygotic* (non-identical) twins are of the same sex than the usual 50% proportion one would expect.

(i) Two people are selected at random. Assuming that they are chosen from a population with equal numbers of males and females, show that the probability that they are both the same sex is 0.5.

(ii) In a particular village the anthropologist finds 12 pairs of dizygotic twins; 5 pairs are both male, 3 are both female and 4 are one male and one female. He tests his claim, at the 10% significance level.

(a) State his null and alternative hypotheses.

(b) Complete the test.

(c) Comment on the validity of this test.

In a second village there are 7 pairs of dizygotic twins, of which 3 are both male and 3 both female.

(iii) Using the data for both villages together, test the anthropologist's claim. Comment on the validity of your result.

10 The customer's quality requirements from the manufacturer of some 6 mm bore bolts is satisfied if 95% of a batch are within the tolerance of 0.05 mm. A random sample of 100 bolts is selected from a large batch which just meets this quality requirement.

(i) Find the probabilities that out of this sample the number of bolts that are within the tolerance is

(a) exactly 98

(b) at least 98.

(ii) A sample of 100 from a large batch contains 98 of an acceptable standard. Is this evidence, at the 5% significance level, that the batch is better than the customer's requirement? Give your reasons.

Critical values and critical regions

In Example 7.1 the number 1 came up six times and this was not enough to get poor Leonora a refund. What was the least number of times 1 would have had to come up for the test to give the opposite result?

We again use X to denote the number of times 1 comes up in the 20 throws and so $X = 6$ means that the number 1 comes up six times.

We know from our earlier work that the probability that $X \leqslant 5$ is 0.8982 and we can use the binomial distribution to work out the probabilities that $X = 6$, $X = 7$, etc.

$$P(X = 6) = {}^{20}C_6\left(\tfrac{5}{6}\right)^{14}\left(\tfrac{1}{6}\right)^6 = 0.0647$$
$$P(X = 7) = {}^{20}C_7\left(\tfrac{5}{6}\right)^{13}\left(\tfrac{1}{6}\right)^7 = 0.0259$$

We know $P(X \geqslant 6) = 1 - P(X \leqslant 5) = 1 - 0.8982 = 0.1018$.

0.1018 is a little over 10% and so greater than the significance level of 5%. There is no reason to reject H_0.

What about the case when the number 1 comes up seven times, that is $X = 7$?

$$\text{Since } P(X \leqslant 6) = P(X \leqslant 5) + P(X = 6)$$
$$P(X \leqslant 6) = 0.8982 + 0.0647 = 0.9629$$

$$\text{So } P(X \geqslant 7) = 1 - P(X \leqslant 6)$$
$$= 1 - 0.9629 = 0.0371 = 3.71\%$$

Since $3.7\% < 5\%$ H_0 is now rejected in favour of H_1.

You can see that Leonora needed the 1 to come up seven or more times if her case was to be upheld. She missed by just one. You might think Leonora's 'all or nothing' test was a bit harsh. Sometimes tests are designed so that if the result falls within a certain region further trials are recommended.

In this example the number 7 is the *critical value* (at the 5% significance level), the value at which you change from accepting the null hypothesis to rejecting it. The range of values for which you reject the null hypothesis, in this case $X \geqslant 7$, is called the *critical region.*

It is sometimes easier in hypothesis testing to find the critical region and see if your value lies in it, rather than working out the probability of a value at least as extreme as the one you have, the procedure used so far.

The quality control department of a factory tests a random sample of 20 items from each batch produced. A batch is rejected (or perhaps subject to further tests) if the number of faulty items in the sample, X, is more than 2.

This means that the critical region is $X \geqslant 3$.

It is much simpler for the operator carrying out the test to be told the critical region (determined in advance by the person designing the procedure) than to have to work out a probability for each test result.

Test procedure

Take 20 pistons

If 3 or more are faulty REJECT the batch

EXAMPLE 7.2

World-wide 25% of men are colour-blind but it is believed that the condition is less widespread among a group of remote hill tribes. An anthropologist plans to test this by sending field workers to visit villages in that area. In each village 30 men are to be tested for colour-blindness. Find the critical region for the test at the 5% level of significance.

SOLUTION

Setting up the hypothesis test

Let p be the probability that a man in that area is colour-blind.

Null hypothesis, H_0: $p = 0.25$
Alternative hypothesis, H_1: $p < 0.25$ (Less colour-blindness in this area)
Significance level: 5%

Calculating the critical region

With the hypothesis H_0, if the number of colour-blind men in a sample of 30 is X, then $X \sim B(30, 0.25)$.

The critical region is the region $X \leqslant k$, where

$$P(X \leqslant k) \leqslant 0.05 \quad \text{and} \quad P(X \leqslant k + 1) > 0.05$$

Since $n = 30$ is too large for the available tables you have to calculate the probabilities:

$$P(X = 0) = (0.75)^{30} = 0.00018$$
$$P(X = 1) = {}^{30}C_1(0.75)^{29}(0.25) = 0.00179$$
$$P(X = 2) = {}^{30}C_2(0.75)^{28}(0.25)^2 = 0.00863$$
$$P(X = 3) = {}^{30}C_3(0.75)^{27}(0.25)^3 = 0.02685$$
$$P(X = 4) = {}^{30}C_4(0.75)^{26}(0.25)^4 = 0.06042.$$

So $P(X \leqslant 3) = 0.00018 + 0.00179 + 0.00863 + 0.02685 \approx 0.0375 \leqslant 0.05$

but $P(X \leqslant 4) \approx 0.0979 > 0.05$.

Therefore the critical region is $X \leqslant 3$.

What is the critical region at the 10% significance level?

In many other hypothesis tests it is usual to find the critical values from tables. Later books in this series cover several such tests.

EXPERIMENTS

Mind reading

Here is a simple experiment to see if you can read the mind of a friend whom you know well. The two of you face each other across a table on which is placed a coin. Your friend takes the coin and puts it in one or other hand under the table. You have to guess which one.

Play this game at least 20 times and test at the 10% significance level whether you can read your friend's mind.

Smarties

Get a large box of Smarties and taste the different colours. Choose the colour, C, which you think has the most distinctive flavour.

Now close your eyes and get a friend to feed you Smarties. Taste each one and say if it is your chosen colour or not. Do this for at least 20 Smarties and test at the 10% significance level whether you can pick out those with colour C by taste.

Left and right

It is said that if people are following a route which brings them to a T-junction where they have a free choice between turning left and right the majority will turn right.

Design and carry out an experiment to test this hypothesis.

Note

This is taken very seriously by companies choosing stands at exhibitions. It is considered worth paying extra for a location immediately to the right of one of the entrances.

EXERCISE 7B

1 A new drug is being developed for post-natal depression. The manufacturers believe it will be successful in at least 70% of cases. An investigation is carried out on a sample of 16 women and the drug proves successful for 7.

(i) State null and alternative hypotheses for testing the manufacturers' belief.

(ii) State the critical region for the test for a 5% significance level.

(iii) Complete the test.

2 Over a long period of time, on 75% of Saturdays Sunil successfully completes the Sudoku puzzle in the paper within 30 minutes. Following a serious accident, he completes only 6 of the next 14 puzzles within 30 minutes.

(i) Give null and alternative hypotheses for testing whether Sunil's speed in solving the puzzle has decreased.

(ii) Find the critical region for the test at the 10% significance level.

(iii) Complete the test.

(iv) Show that, if the number of puzzles had been 13 instead of 14, then the critical region would be unchanged.

(v) Is the critical region altered in either situation if the significance level is changed to 5%? Explain why.

3 A country is at war and expecting to be invaded. As a precaution all road signs have been removed but, as a result, people frequently get lost. When Mr Jones is lost he follows the car in front when he comes to a T-junction. He believes that, more often than not, this will result in his taking the correct road. He uses the next ten occasions when he has lost his way as a sample to test his belief.

(i) Write down null and alternative hypotheses for the test.

(ii) Find the critical region for the test at the 10% significance level.

(iii) Mr Jones takes the correct road on eight out of the ten occasions. Complete the hypothesis test to decide whether Mr Jones' belief is justified.

4 It is known that the probability of the standard variety of a plant reaching maturity in a given type of soil is 0.35. A new variety is introduced and a sample of 17 are planted in that type of soil. Ten of them reach maturity. This sample is used for a hypothesis test, at the 5% significance level, of whether the new variety is more likely to reach maturity.

(i) State the null and alternative hypotheses.

(ii) Find the critical region for the test.

(iii) Complete the test.

Another new variety of the plant produces only one maturing plant out of 17 planted in the same kind of soil.

(iv) Test whether this gives sufficient evidence, at the 5% level, that this variety has less chance of maturation than the standard variety.

5 The politicians in a country are considering changing its currency to the euro. An economist claims that the cost of living will go up if they do so. He claims that this is about to happen in another country which will shortly join the euro. To test the economist's theory, the politicians select, at random, 15 commonly sold items and compare their prices in the other country before and after it joins the euro. The 5% significance level is chosen for the test.

(i) Write down suitable null and alternative hypotheses for the test.

In fact the price of exactly ten items increases.

(ii) Find the minimum number of items whose price would have to increase for the alternative hypothesis to be accepted at the 5% significance level. Deduce the critical region for the test.

(iii) Complete the test.

(iv) Give one criticism of this as a test for determining whether the cost of living will go up if their currency is changed to the euro.

6 A company is planning a new training scheme to replace the existing one, which is very unpopular. The company will introduce the new scheme if they believe that more than half their employees are in favour of it.
As a pilot study they test the new scheme on a random sample of 20 employees who are asked to rate it 'positive' or 'negative'. 14 say 'positive' and only 6 say 'negative'. They use these data to carry out a hypothesis test at the 10% significance level.

(i) State null and alternative hypotheses for this test.

(ii) Find the critical region for the test.

(iii) Complete the test.

(iv) Should the company introduce the new scheme?

1-tailed and 2-tailed tests

Think back to the two examples in the first part of this chapter.

What would Dan have said if his eight children had all been girls?
What would Leonora have said if the number 1 had not come up at all?

In both our examples the claim was not only that something was unusual but that it was so in a particular direction. So we looked only at one side of the distributions when working out the probabilities, as you can see in figure 7.1 on page 179 and figure 7.2 on page 185. In both cases we applied 1-tailed tests. (The word tail refers to the shaded part at the end of the distribution.)

If Dan had just claimed that there was something odd about his chromosomes, then you would have had to work out the probability of a result as extreme on either side of the distribution, in this case eight girls or eight boys, and you would then apply a 2-tailed test.

Here is an example of a 2-tailed test.

EXAMPLE 7.3

The producer of a television programme claims that it is politically unbiased. 'If you take somebody off the street it is 50:50 whether he or she will say the programme favours the government or the opposition', she says.

However, when ten people, selected at random, are asked the question 'Does the programme support the government or the opposition?', nine say it supports the government.

Does this constitute evidence, at the 5% significance level, that the producer's claim is inaccurate?

SOLUTION

Setting up the hypothesis test

Read the last sentence carefully and you will see that it does not say in which direction the bias must be. It does not ask if the programme is favouring the government or the opposition, only if the producer's claim is inaccurate. So you must consider both ends of the distribution, working out the probability of such an extreme result either way; 9 or 10 saying it favours the government, or 9 or 10 the opposition. This is a 2-tailed test.

If p is the probability that somebody believes the programme supports the government, you have

Null hypothesis, H_0:	$p = 0.5$	(Claim accurate)
Alternative hypothesis, H_1:	$p \neq 0.5$	(Claim inaccurate)
Significance level:	5%	
	2-tailed test	

Calculating the probability

The situation is modelled by the binomial distribution B(10, 0.5) and is shown in figure 7.3.

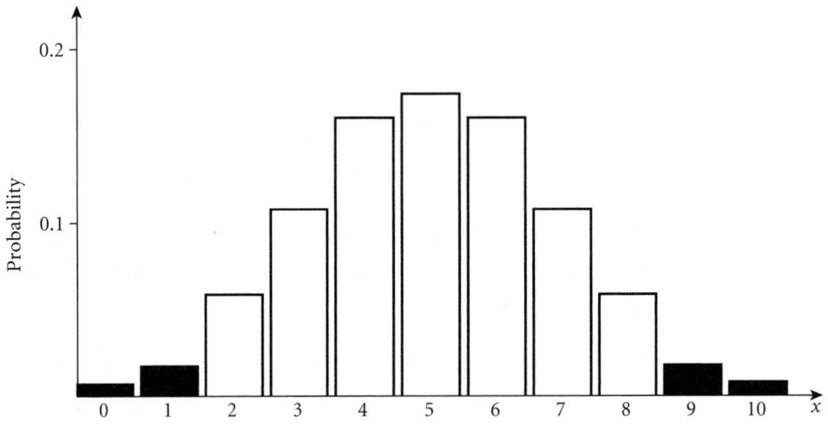

Figure 7.3

This gives

$$P(X=0) = \frac{1}{1024} \qquad P(X=1) = \frac{10}{1024}$$

$$P(X=10) = \frac{1}{1024} \qquad P(X=9) = \frac{10}{1024}$$

where X is the number of people saying the programme favours the government. Thus the total probability for the two tails is $\frac{22}{1024}$ or 2.15%.

Interpreting the probability

Since $2.15\% < 5\%$ the null hypothesis is rejected in favour of the alternative, *that the producer's claim is inaccurate.*

Note

You have to look carefully at the way a test is worded to decide if it should be 1-tailed or 2-tailed.

Dan Ellis claimed his chromosomes made him more likely to father boys than girls. That requires a 1-tailed test.

In Calvin's story, Leonora claimed the die was biased in the direction of too many 1s. Again a 1-tailed test.

The test of the television producer's claim was for inaccuracy in either direction and so a 2-tailed test was needed.

Asymmetrical cases

In the example above the distribution was symmetrical and so the 2-tailed test was quite simple to apply. In the next case the distribution is not symmetrical and the test has to be carried out by finding out the critical regions at each tail.

EXAMPLE 7.4

Pepper moths occur in two varieties, light and dark. The proportion of dark moths increases with certain types of atmospheric pollution.

In a particular village, 25% of the moths are dark, the rest light. A biologist wants to use them as a pollution indicator. She traps samples of 15 moths and counts how many of them are dark.

For what numbers of dark moths among the 15 can she say, at the 10% significance level, that the pollution level is changing?

SOLUTION

Setting up the hypothesis test

In this question you are asked to find the critical region for the test:

H_0: $p = 0.25$ (The proportion of dark moths is 25%)
H_1: $p \neq 0.25$ (The proportion is no longer 25%)
Significance level 10%
2-tailed test

where p is the probability that a moth selected at random is dark.

Finding the critical region

You want to find each tail to be as nearly as possible 5% but both must be less than 5%, something that is easiest done using cumulative binomial distribution tables.

Look under $n = 15$, for $p = 0.25$.

n	x \ p	0.050	0.100	0.150	$\frac{1}{6}$	0.200	0.250	0.300	$\frac{1}{3}$	0.350	0.400
15	0	0.4633	0.2059	0.0874	0.0649	0.0352	0.0134	0.0047	0.0023	0.0016	0.0005
	1	0.8290	0.5490	0.3186	0.2596	0.1671	0.0802	0.0353	0.0194	0.0142	0.0052
	2	0.9638	0.8159	0.6042	0.5322	0.3980	0.2361	0.1268	0.0794	0.0617	0.0271
	3	0.9945	0.9444	0.8227	0.7685	0.6482	0.4613	0.2969	0.2092	0.1727	0.0905
	4	0.9994	0.9873	0.9383	0.9102	0.8358	0.6865	0.5155	0.4041	0.3519	0.2173
	5	0.9999	0.9978	0.9832	0.9726	0.9389	0.8516	0.7216	0.6184	0.5643	0.4032
	6	1.0000	0.9997	0.9964	0.9934	0.9819	0.9434	0.8689	0.7970	0.7548	0.6098
	7		1.0000	0.9994	0.9987	0.9958	0.9827	0.9500	0.9118	0.8868	0.7869
	8			0.9999	0.9998	0.9992	0.9958	0.9848	0.9692	0.9578	0.9050
	9			1.0000	1.0000	0.9999	0.9992	0.9963	0.9915	0.9876	0.9662
	10					1.0000	0.9999	0.9993	0.9982	0.9972	0.9907
	11						1.0000	0.9999	0.9997	0.9995	0.9981
	12							1.0000	1.0000	0.9999	0.9997
	13									1.0000	1.0000
	14										
	15										

From this you can see that the left-hand tail includes 0 but not 1 or more; the right-hand tail is 8 and above but not 7.

Interpreting the critical region

So the critical regions are less than 1 and more than 7 dark moths in the 15. For these values she would claim the pollution level is changing.

Note

This is really quite a crude test. The left-hand tail is 1.34%, the right-hand (1 – 0.9827) or 1.73%. Neither is close to 5%. This situation would be improved if you were to increase the sample size; 15 is a small number of moths on which to base your findings. However, for large samples you would expect to use either the Normal or the Poisson approximation to the binomial distribution; these are covered in Unit 2.

EXERCISE 7C

Most of the questions in this exercise ask you to carry out a test. This involves

- *stating the null and alternative hypotheses*
- *finding the test statistic or the relevant probability*
- *interpreting the test statistic or probability.*

1 A particular wild animal lives in isolated colonies at various locations around the world. Studies have shown that, worldwide, 40% of the offspring survive beyond their first birthday. Scientists in Siberia believe that the colony living there has an unusual survival rate. They track a sample of 17 newly born offspring; only 3 survive.

(i) Carry out a test, at the 10% significance level, of whether the Siberian colony has an unusual survival rate.

(ii) Comment on the difficulty of finding a truly random sample. Could this affect the outcome of the experiment?

2 The probability of success in a gambling game based on chance is known to be 0.1. Calvin plays the game regularly at a casino and believes that he is not winning often enough. He thinks about accusing the casino of cheating but decides that first he will conduct an experiment. He plays a sample of 20 games and has no successes.

(i) Carry out a hypothesis test to determine whether, at the 5% significance level, his probability of success is different from 0.1.

(ii) Design a better experiment for Calvin.

3 Overall, 15% of the earth in a particular city is known to be contaminated by toxic chemicals and so to be useless for vegetable gardens. A particular area of the city is surveyed by testing the earth in 15 randomly selected places. It is found that the earth is not contaminated in any of them.

(i) Carry out a test of whether the earth in this area has a different contamination level from the city as a whole, using a 5% significance level.

Another area is tested in 17 places and the earth is found to be toxic in 5 of them.

(ii) Carry out a test at the 5% significance level of whether the contamination level in this area is greater than that in the city as a whole.

4 A newspaper claims that 20% of athletes in a large meeting are taking a particular banned substance. The organisers decide to carry out an experiment to investigate if this claim is correct, knowing that it could be an over-estimate or an under-estimate. They select a random sample of 18 athletes and test them for the substance.

(i) Find the critical region for a suitable hypothesis test at the 5% significance level.

(ii) Carry out the hypothesis test in the cases when the number of positive results is

(a) 0 **(b)** 6.

(iii) The newspaper claims that a 1-tailed test should have been used. Comment.

5 Drivers should stop at amber lights! A motoring magazine claims that 60% of female drivers stop at amber traffic lights.
A safety organisation decides to investigate whether this figure is correct. They make observations, starting at 5 pm, of the first 20 female drivers to arrive at a particular set of traffic lights when they are at amber. Eight of them stop.

(i) Carry out a suitable hypothesis test, at the 5% significance level.

The safety organisation is criticised on the grounds that the sample is not random.

(ii) Explain why this criticism is justified.

A more nearly random sample is taken, this time of both male and female drivers, with the following results.

	Number stopping	**Number not stopping**
Male	2	8
Female	3	7

(iii) Test the following three hypotheses at the 5% significance level.

(a) 60% of female drivers stop at amber lights.

(b) 40% of male drivers stop at amber lights.

(c) 50% of all drivers stop at amber traffic lights.

6 There is soon to be a referendum on a proposed new constitution for the Lesch Republic. The President appears on television in an attempt to persuade people to vote 'Yes'. Before the speech it is known that 45% will vote 'Yes', 25% are undecided and 30% will vote 'No'. It is unclear what effect the television appearance will have. Some people will be convinced by the President and decide to vote 'Yes'; however, others, who were going to vote 'Yes' but dislike the President, may now change their minds.
After the programme, a random sample of 20 people are interviewed; three say they will vote 'Yes', nine say they will vote 'No' and the remainder are undecided.

(i) Carry out a test, at the 5% significance level, of whether there has been a change in the proportion intending to vote 'Yes'.

(ii) Carry out another test, also at the 5% significance level, this time of whether the proportion of undecided voters has increased.

7 A distributor of flower bulbs has a large stock of daffodil and tulip bulbs mixed in the ratio 2:1 respectively. A machine packs bulbs, chosen at random, in boxes of 15.

(i) What is the probability that a bulb chosen at random from the stock is a daffodil?

(ii) Find the probability that a box of bulbs contains

(a) exactly ten daffodils

(b) six or more tulips.

(iii) Five boxes are chosen at random. Find the probability that they do not all contain six or more tulips.

The distributor receives a new delivery of bulbs. She wishes to investigate whether or not the ratio of daffodil to tulip bulbs is 2:1. She carries out a hypothesis test based on a random sample of 15 bulbs. The proportion of daffodils in this delivery is denoted by p.

(iv) State, in terms of p, the null and alternative hypotheses being tested.

(v) Find the critical region for the test, conducted at the 10% significance level, explaining carefully how you obtained your answer. Draw a diagram, in the form of a number line, on which is indicated what numbers of daffodils in the sample are acceptable and what numbers are not acceptable.

[MEI]

8 Ingrid claims that weather patterns have changed over the years in the northern hemisphere country where she lives. She has records covering many years, which show that the rainfall exceeded 60 cm in 5% of months in the past. However, it exceeded 60 cm in exactly 3 of the 12 months in 2006. Ingrid claims that a hypothesis test based on these data is significant at the 5% level.

(i) Carry out Ingrid's hypothesis test.

Ingrid writes about her results in a national newspaper. Several people write in with criticisms.

(ii) A statistician says, 'You claim it is a 2-tailed test but the sample is so small that there is no lower critical region'.

(a) Show that this is indeed the case.

(b) Find the smallest sample size for which a result of no months with rainfall exceeding 60 cm would lie in the critical region for the test.

(iii) A meteorologist says, 'We all know there are wet years and dry years. If one month is very wet, the next one is likely to be wet too.' If this is true, how does it undermine the assumptions needed for a binomial test?

(iv) A philosopher says, 'This is unscientific. All you have done is to form a theory around past data and then use the data to support your theory.' Design a new experiment that will take this objection into account, and also those from the statistician and the meteorologist.

KEY POINTS

1 Hypothesis testing checklist

- Was the test set up before or after the data were known?
- Was the sample involved chosen at random and are the data independent?
- Is the statistical procedure actually testing the original claim?

2 Steps for conducting a hypothesis test

- Establish the null and alternative hypotheses.
- Decide on the significance level.
- Collect suitable data using a random sampling procedure that ensures the items are independent.
- Conduct the test, doing the necessary calculations.
- Interpret the result in terms of the original claim, theory or problem.

Unit 2

8 The Poisson distribution

There is a special department of hell for students of probability. In this department are many typewriters and many monkeys. Every time that a monkey walks on a typewriter, it types by chance one of Shakespeare's sonnets.

Bertrand Russell

AVONFORD STAR

Full moon madness hits Avonford bypass

Since opening two years ago, Avonford bypass has seen more than its fair share of accidents but last night was way beyond that ever experienced before. There were no less than four separate accidents during the hours of darkness. And it was full moon!

Was it, we wonder, full moon madness? Or was it just one of those statistical quirks that happens from time to time?

Our astrology expert, Jessie Manning, told us that this was only to be expected when the moon dominates Saturn.

However, the local scientist Ali Ahmed took a different view. 'We must be careful of jumping to the wrong conclusions' he said when we telephoned him this morning. 'This is a load of dangerous rubbish that will lead more vulnerable people to believe dangerous things. I am not a statistician so I cannot tell you what the chances are of there being four accidents in one evening, but I reckon that it is a statistical possibility.'

How would you decide whether four accidents in a night are reasonably likely? The first thing is to look at past data, and so learn about the distribution of accidents.

The bypass was opened nearly two years ago and the figures, not including the evening described in the article, are shown in the table.

(A day is taken to run from one midday to the next.)

Number of accidents per day, x	0	1	2	3	>3
Frequency, f	395	235	73	17	0

These figures look as though the data could be drawn from a particular distribution called the Poisson distribution. This distribution gives the probability of the different possible number of occurrences of an event in a given time interval under certain conditions. The checklist below gives the conditions necessary for a situation to be described using a Poisson distribution.

- The events occur independently.
- The events occur at random.
- The probability of an event occurring in a given time interval does not vary with time.

In this case, the given time interval is one day, or 24 hours. An event is an accident.

The total number of accidents has been

$$0 \times 395 + 1 \times 235 + 2 \times 73 + 3 \times 17 = 432.$$

The number of days has been

$$395 + 235 + 73 + 17 = 720.$$

So the mean number of accidents per day has been $\dfrac{432}{720} = 0.6$

The Poisson distribution is an example of a probability model. It is usually defined by the mean number of occurrences in a time interval and this is denoted by λ.

The probability that there are r occurrences in a given interval is given by $\dfrac{\lambda^r}{r!}e^{-\lambda}$.

The value of e is 2.718 281 828 459.... There is a button for it on your calculator.

So, the probability of

0 occurrences is $e^{-\lambda}$
1 occurrence is $\lambda e^{-\lambda}$
2 occurrences is $\dfrac{\lambda^2}{2!}e^{-\lambda}$
3 occurrences is $\dfrac{\lambda^3}{3!}e^{-\lambda}$
and so on.

In this example, $\lambda = 0.6$. The probabilities and expected frequencies in 720 days are shown in the table.

Number of accidents per day	0	1	2	3	4	5	>5
Probability (to 4 d.p.)	0.5488	0.3293	0.0988	0.0197	0.0030	0.0004	0
Expected frequency (to 1.d.p.)	395.1	237.1	71.1	14.2	2.1	0.3	0

? Explain where the various figures in this table have come from.

? Compare the expected frequencies with those observed.
Is the Poisson distribution a good model?

The table shows that with this model you would expect 2.4 days in 720, or just over one day per year, on which there would be four or more accidents. It would seem as though the local scientist Ali Ahmed was right; the seemingly high number of accidents last night could be just what the statistical model would lead you to expect. There is no need to jump to the conclusion that another factor, such as the full moon, influenced the data.

ACTIVITY Use your calculator to find the probability of 0, 1, 2 and 3 occurrences of an event which has a Poisson distribution with a mean, λ, of 2.5.

Use of tables

Another way to find probabilities in a Poisson distribution is to use tables of *cumulative Poisson probabilities*, such as those given in the MEI Students' Handbook.

In these tables you are not given $P(X = r)$ but $P(X \leq r)$. This means that it gives the sum of the probabilities of 0 up to r events.

In the example of the accidents on Avonford bypass the mean, $\bar{x}$, was 0.6 and probabilities of $X = 0$ and $X = 1$ were calculated to be 0.5488 and 0.3293.

To find these values in the tables, look at the column for $\lambda = 0.6$. The first entry in this column is 0.5488, representing the probability that there are no accidents.

x \ λ	0.10	0.20	0.30	0.40	0.50	0.60	0.70	0.80	0.90
0	0.9048	0.8187	0.7408	0.6703	0.6065	0.5488	0.4966	0.4493	0.4066
1	0.9953	0.9825	0.9631	0.9384	0.9098	0.8781	0.8442	0.8088	0.7725
2	0.9998	0.9989	0.9964	0.9921	0.9856	0.9769	0.9659	0.9526	0.9371
3	1.0000	0.9999	0.9997	0.9992	0.9982	0.9966	0.9942	0.9909	0.9865
4		1.0000	1.0000	0.9999	0.9998	0.9996	0.9992	0.9986	0.9977
5				1.0000	1.0000	1.0000	0.9999	0.9998	0.9997
6							1.0000	1.0000	1.0000
7									

The second entry in the column is 0.8781. This is the probability that there will be 0 or 1 accidents.

To find the probability that there is one accident, subtract these two values giving $0.8781 - 0.5488 = 0.3293$.

In the same way, the probability that there are 2 accidents is found by taking the second entry from the third.

Continuing the process gives the following.

Number of accidents	Probability	Number of accidents	Probability
0	0.5488	0	0.5488
0 or 1	0.8781	1	$0.8781 - 0.5488 = 0.3293$
0, 1 or 2	0.9769	2	$0.9769 - 0.8781 = 0.0988$
0, 1, 2 or 3	0.9966	3	$0.9966 - 0.9769 = 0.0197$
0, 1, 2, 3 or 4	0.9996	4	$0.9996 - 0.9966 = 0.0030$

How can you use the tables to find the probability of exactly 5 accidents in any night? Check that you get the same answer by entering $\frac{0.6^5}{5!}e^{-0.6}$ into your calculator.

You can see that the probability of having four accidents in one night is 0.0030. The probability of having four *or more* accidents in one night is 1 – probability of having three or fewer accidents, which is 0.9966. So the probability of having four or more accidents is $1 - 0.9966 = 0.0034$.

In other words, 34 in every 10 000 days or roughly 2.5 days in 720. This confirms that it is not necessary to look for other explanations for the four accidents in the same night.

You will see that the tables in the Students' Handbook cover values of λ from 0.01 to 10.90. You will clearly have a problem if you are trying to calculate probabilities with a value of λ that is not given in the tables. In such cases you will need to use the formula.

ACTIVITY

You were asked to find the probabilities of 0, 1, 2 and 3 occurrences of an event with a mean, λ, of 2.5 in the previous activity.

Now use the cumulative Poisson probability tables to find these probabilities.

EXAMPLE 8.1

The mean number of typing errors in a document is 1.5 per page. Find the probability that on a page chosen at random there are

(i) no mistakes

(ii) more than two mistakes.

SOLUTION

If you assume that spelling mistakes occur independently and at random then the Poisson distribution is a reasonable model to use.

(i) For $\lambda = 1.5$ the tables give P(0 mistakes) $= 0.2231$.

x \ λ	1.00	1.10	1.20	1.30	1.40	1.50	1.60	1.70	1.80	1.90
0	0.3679	0.3329	0.3012	0.2725	0.2466	0.2231	0.2019	0.1827	0.1653	0.1496
1	0.7358	0.6990	0.6626	0.6268	0.5918	0.5578	0.5249	0.4932	0.4628	0.4337
2	0.9197	0.9004	0.8795	0.8571	0.8335	0.8088	0.7834	0.7572	0.7306	0.7037
3	0.9810	0.9743	0.9662	0.9569	0.9463	0.9344	0.9212	0.9068	0.8913	0.8747
4	0.9963	0.9946	0.9923	0.9893	0.9857	0.9814	0.9763	0.9704	0.9636	0.9559
5	0.9994	0.9990	0.9985	0.9978	0.9968	0.9955	0.9940	0.9920	0.9896	0.9868
6	0.9999	0.9999	0.9997	0.9996	0.9994	0.9991	0.9987	0.9981	0.9974	0.9966
7	1.0000	1.0000	1.0000	0.9999	0.9999	0.9998	0.9997	0.9996	0.9994	0.9992
8				1.0000	1.0000	1.0000	1.0000	0.9999	0.9999	0.9998
9								1.0000	1.0000	1.0000

(ii) P(more than 2 mistakes) $= 1 - $ P(up to 2 mistakes)
$= 1 - 0.8088$
$= 0.1912$

How would you answer this question using the Poisson formula? Check that you get the same answers.

Historical note

Simeon Poisson was born in France in 1781. He worked as a mathematician in Paris for most of his life after giving up the study of medicine. His contribution to mathematics embraced electricity, magnetism and planetary orbits and ideas in integration as well as in statistics. He wrote over 300 papers and articles.

The modelling distribution that takes his name was originally derived as an approximation to the binomial distribution.

EXERCISE 8A

1 The number of cars passing a point on a country lane has a mean of 1.8 per minute.

Using the Poisson distribution, find the probability that in any one minute there are

(i) no cars **(ii)** one car **(iii)** two cars
(iv) three cars **(v)** more than three cars.

2 A fire station experiences an average call-out rate of 2.2 every period of three hours.

Using the Poisson distribution, find the probability that in any period of three hours there will be

(i) no call outs **(ii)** one call out
(iii) two call outs **(iv)** three call outs
(v) four call outs **(vi)** more than four call outs.

3 The number of radioactive particles emitted in a minute from a meteorite is recorded on a Geiger counter. The mean number is found to be 3.5 per minute.

Using the Poisson distribution, find the probability that in any one minute there are

(i) no particles **(ii)** two particles **(iii)** at least five particles.

4 Bacteria are distributed independently of each other in a solution and it is known that the number of bacteria per millilitre follows a Poisson distribution with a mean of 2.9.

Find the probability that a sample of 1 ml of solution contains

(i) no bacteria **(ii)** one bacterium **(iii)** two bacteria

(iv) three bacteria **(v)** more than three bacteria.

5 The demand for cars from a car hire firm may be modelled by a Poisson distribution with a mean of 4 per day.

(i) Find the probability that in a randomly chosen day the demand is for

(a) no cars **(b)** one car **(c)** two cars **(d)** three cars.

(ii) The firm has five cars available for hire.
Find the probability that demand exceeds the number of cars available.

6 A book of 500 pages has 500 misprints. Using the Poisson distribution, find the probability that a given page contains

(i) exactly three misprints

(ii) more than three misprints.

7 190 raisins are put into a mixture which is well stirred and made into 100 small buns.
What is the most likely number of raisins found in a bun?

8 Small hard particles are found in the molten glass from which glass bottles are made. On average 20 particles are found in 100 kg of molten glass. If a bottle made of this glass contains one or more such particles it has to be discarded.

Bottles of mass 1 kg are made using this glass.

(i) Criticise the following argument.
Since the material for 100 bottles contains 20 particles, approximately 20% will have to be discarded.

(ii) Making suitable assumptions, which should be stated, develop a correct argument using a Poisson model and find the percentage of faulty 1 kg bottles to 3 significant figures.

9 A hire company has two lawnmowers which it hires out by the day. The number of demands per day may be modelled by a Poisson distribution with mean 1.5. In a period of 100 working days, how many times do you expect

(i) neither lawnmower to be used

(ii) some requests for a lawnmower to have to be refused?

Conditions for modelling data with a Poisson distribution

You met the idea of a probability model in Unit 1. The binomial distribution is one example. The Poisson distribution is another model. A model in this context means a theoretical distribution that fits your data reasonably well.

You have already seen that the Poisson distribution provides a good model for the data for the *Avonford Star* article on accidents on the bypass.

Here are the data again.

Number of accidents per day, x	0	1	2	3	>3
Frequency, f	395	235	73	17	0

For these data, $n = 720$, $\sum xf = 432$ and $\sum x^2f = 680$.

So the mean, $\bar{x} = \dfrac{432}{720}$
$= 0.6$

$S_{xx} = \sum x^2f - n\bar{x}^2$
$= 680 - 720 \times 0.6^2$
$= 420.8$

So the variance, $s^2 = \dfrac{S_{xx}}{n-1}$
$= \dfrac{420.8}{719}$
$= 0.585$

You will notice that the mean, 0.6, and the variance, 0.585, are very close in value. This is a characteristic of the Poisson distribution and provides a check on whether it is likely to provide a good model for a particular data set.

In the theoretical Poisson distribution, the mean and the variance are equal. It is usual to call λ the *parameter* of a Poisson distribution, rather than either the mean or the variance. The common notation for describing a Poisson distribution is Poisson(λ); so Poisson(2.4) means the Poisson distribution with parameter 2.4.

You should check that the conditions on page 203 apply; the events should occur at random, independently and with fixed probability.

EXAMPLE 8.2

A mail order company receives a steady supply of orders by telephone. The manager wants to investigate the pattern of calls received so he records the number of calls received per day over a period of 40 days as follows.

Number of calls per day	0	1	2	3	4	5	>5
Frequency of calls	8	13	10	6	2	1	0

(i) Calculate the mean and variance of the data. Comment on your answers.
(ii) State whether the conditions for using the Poisson distribution as a model apply.
(iii) Use the Poisson distribution to predict the frequencies of 0, 1, 2, 3, … calls per day.
(iv) Comment on the fit.

SOLUTION

(i) These are the summary statistics for the data.

$n = 40, \sum xf = 64$ and $\sum x^2 f = 164$.

$$\text{So the mean, } \bar{x} = \frac{\sum xf}{n} = \frac{64}{40} = 1.6$$

$$S_{xx} = \sum x^2 f - n\bar{x}^2 = 164 - 40 \times 1.6^2 = 61.6$$

$$\text{So the variance, } s^2 = \frac{S_{xx}}{n-1} = \frac{61.6}{39} = 1.5795$$

The mean is close to the variance, so it may well be appropriate to use the Poisson distribution as a model.

(ii) It is reasonable to assume that

- the calls occur independently
- the calls occur at random
- the probability of a call being made on any day of the week does not vary with time, given that there is a steady supply of orders.

(iii) The cumulative Poisson probability tables with $\lambda = 1.6$ give the following.

Number of calls	Probability	Number of calls	Probability	Expected frequency (probability × 40)
0	0.2019	0	0.2019	8.1
0 or 1	0.5249	1	0.5249 − 0.2019 = 0.3230	12.9
0, 1 or 2	0.7834	2	0.7834 − 0.5249 = 0.2585	10.3
0, 1, 2 or 3	0.9212	3	0.9212 − 0.7834 = 0.1378	5.5
0, 1, 2, 3 or 4	0.9763	4	0.9763 − 0.9212 = 0.0551	2.2
0, 1, 2, 3, 4 or 5	0.9940	5	0.9940 − 0.9763 = 0.0177	0.7
0, 1, 2, 3, 4, 5, 6 or more	1	>5	1 − 0.9940 = 0.0060	0.2

(iv) The table shows the actual and theoretical frequencies.

Number of calls per day	0	1	2	3	4	5	>5
Actual frequency of calls	8	13	10	6	2	1	0
Theoretical frequency of calls (1 d.p.)	8.1	12.9	10.3	5.5	2.2	0.7	0.2

The fit is very good, as might be expected with the mean and variance so close together.

EXAMPLE 8.3

Avonford Town Football Club recorded the number of goals scored in each of their 30 matches in one season.

Number of goals, x	0	1	2	3	4	>4
Frequency, f	12	12	4	1	1	0

(i) Calculate the mean and variance for this set of data.

(ii) State whether the conditions for using the Poisson distribution apply.

(iii) Calculate the expected frequencies for a Poisson distribution having the same mean number of goals per match.

(iv) Comment on the fit.

SOLUTION

(i) For this set of data

$n = 30, \sum xf = 27$ and $\sum x^2 f = 53$.

$$\text{So the mean, } \bar{x} = \frac{\sum xf}{n} = \frac{27}{30} = 0.9$$

$$S_{xx} = \sum x^2 f - n\bar{x}^2 = 53 - 30 \times 0.9^2 = 28.7$$

$$\text{So the variance, } s^2 = \frac{S_{xx}}{n-1} = \frac{28.7}{29} = 0.9897$$

(ii) It is reasonable to assume that

- the goals are scored independently
- the goals are scored at random
- the probability of scoring a goal is constant from one match to the next.

In addition, the value of the mean is close to the value of the variance. Hence, the Poisson distribution can be expected to provide a reasonably good model.

(iii) Using the cumulative Poisson probability tables for $\lambda = 0.9$ gives the following.

Number of goals	Probability	Number of goals	Probability	Expected frequency (probability × 30)
0	0.4066	0	0.4066	12.2
0 or 1	0.7725	1	$0.7725 - 0.4066 = 0.3659$	11.0
0, 1 or 2	0.9371	2	$0.9371 - 0.7725 = 0.1646$	4.9
0, 1, 2 or 3	0.9865	3	$0.9865 - 0.9371 = 0.0494$	1.5
0, 1, 2, 3 or 4	0.9977	4	$0.9977 - 0.9865 = 0.0112$	0.3
0, 1, 2, 3, 4, 5 or more	1	>4	$1 - 0.9977 = 0.0023$	0.1

(iv) The table shows the actual and theoretical frequencies.

Number of goals, x	0	1	2	3	4	>4
Actual frequency, f	12	12	4	1	1	0
Theoretical frequency	12.2	11.0	4.9	1.5	0.3	0

As expected from the closeness of the values for the mean and the variance, the fit is very good.

? In Example 8.3 it was claimed that the numbers of goals scored in a match were independent of each other. To what extent do you think this is true?

EXERCISE 8B

1 The number of bacteria in fifty 100 cc samples of water are given in the following table.

Number of bacteria per sample	0	1	2	3	4 or more
Number of samples	23	16	9	2	0

(i) Find the mean and the variance of the number of bacteria in a 100 cc sample.

(ii) State whether the conditions for using the Poisson distribution as a model apply.

(iii) Using the Poisson distribution with the mean found in part **(i)**, estimate the probability that another 100 cc sample will contain

(a) no bacteria

(b) more than four bacteria.

2 Avonford Town Council agree to install a pedestrian crossing near to the library on Prince Street if it can be shown that the probability that there are more than four accidents per month exceeds 0.1.

The number of accidents recorded in the last 10 months are as follows.

3 2 2 1 0 2 5 4 3 1

(i) Calculate the mean and variance for this set of data.

(ii) Is the Poisson distribution a reasonable model in this case?

(iii) Using the Poisson distribution with the mean found in part **(i)**, find the probability that, in any month taken at random, there are more than four accidents.

Hence say whether Avonford Town Council should install the pedestrian crossing.

3 The numbers of customers entering a shop in 40 consecutive periods of one minute are given below.

3 0 0 1 0 2 1 0 1 1
0 3 4 1 2 0 2 0 3 1
1 0 1 2 0 2 1 0 1 2
3 1 0 0 2 1 0 3 1 2

(i) Draw up a frequency table and illustrate it by means of a vertical line graph.

(ii) Calculate values of the mean and variance of the number of customers entering the shop in a one-minute period.

(iii) Fit a Poisson distribution to the data and comment on the degree of agreement between the calculated and observed values.

[MEI, *part*]

4 A machine in a factory produces components continuously. Each day a sample of 20 components are selected and tested. Over a period of 30 days the number of defective components in the sample is recorded as follows.

Number of defectives per sample	0	1	2	3	4	>4
Number of samples	8	9	8	3	2	0

The quality control inspector says that he will stop production if any sample contains five or more defective components.

(i) Find the mean and variance of the number of defectives per sample.

(ii) State whether the data can be modelled by the Poisson distribution.

(iii) Using the Poisson distribution with the mean found in part **(i)**, find the probability that on any one day the quality control inspector will stop production.

5 In a college, the number of accidents to students requiring hospitalisation in one year of 30 weeks is recorded as follows.

Number of accidents requiring hospitalisation each week	0	1	2	3 or more
Frequency	25	4	1	0

The Principal uses these data to assess the risk of such accidents.

(i) Is the Poisson distribution a suitable model for this assessment? State the assumptions that need to be made about the data provided for this to be so.

(ii) Assuming that the Poisson distribution is a suitable model, calculate the probability that

(a) in any one week there will be three accidents requiring hospitalisation

(b) in a term of eight weeks there will be no accidents.

6 A count was made of the red blood corpuscles in each of the 64 compartments of a haemocytometer with the following results.

Number of corpuscles	2	3	4	5	6	7	8	9	10	11	12	13	14
Frequency	1	5	4	9	10	10	8	6	4	3	2	1	1

Estimate the mean and variance of the number of red blood corpuscles in each compartment.

Explain how the values you have obtained support the view that these data are a sample from a Poisson population.

Using the Poisson distribution as a model, estimate the expected number of compartments containing 2, 3, 4 and 5 red corpuscles.

[MEI, *adapted*]

7 The coach arriving into Avonford coach station each morning at 0800 has a capacity of 54 passengers. (On this route standing passengers are not allowed.) Over a period of time the number of passengers alighting at the coach station on 20 days was recorded as follows.

50	50	50	50	50	51	51	51	51	51
51	51	52	52	52	52	52	52	53	54

(i) Show that in this case the Poisson distribution is not a suitable distribution to model the number of passengers arriving each day.

In fact, 50 of the passengers were regular commuters. The random variable, X, is the number of passengers arriving at Avonford on this coach other than the 50 regulars.

(ii) Show that the Poisson distribution is a reasonable fit for these data.

(iii) Use this distribution with your mean for the data above to estimate the probability that on any given day someone had to be left behind because the coach was full.

The sum of two or more Poisson distributions

If two independent Poisson distributions have means of λ and μ, then the sum of the distributions is also a Poisson distribution and has a mean of $\lambda + \mu$.

EXAMPLE 8.4

A company accepts orders for their product either online or by telephone.

Special Offer exclusive to *Avonford Star* readers

A case of the finest wines specially selected from France

Buy online at our website **www.avonfordstar.co.uk** or telephone 0123 456789 during office hours.

The mean number of sales per day by telephone order is 1.5.
The mean number of online purchases is 2.5.

What is the probability of the company receiving exactly two orders on one day?

SOLUTION

You can model the number of telephone orders per day as Poisson distribution with a mean of 1.5 and the number of orders received online as an independent Poisson distribution with a mean of 2.5.

In this example you are interested in the total number of orders per day. The sum of two independent Poisson distributions with means of λ and μ is a Poisson distribution with a mean of $\lambda + \mu$.
So in this case the mean is $1.5 + 2.5 = 4$.
The distribution of the total number of orders per day is Poisson with a parameter of 4.

From the cumulative Poisson probability tables, the probability of obtaining exactly two orders is $0.2381 - 0.0916 = 0.1465$.

The conditions for adding two Poisson distributions together are that the random variables are independent of each other.

(e) ***Alternative solution***

An alternative solution involves listing the ways in which two orders in one day could be obtained by the two methods.

The two orders could be as follows.

Telephone order	Probability ($\lambda = 1.5$)	Online order	Probability ($\mu = 2.5$)	Total probability
0	0.2231	2	0.2565	$0.2231 \times 0.2565 = 0.0572$
1	0.3347	1	0.2052	$0.3347 \times 0.2052 = 0.0687$
2	0.2510	0	0.0821	$0.2510 \times 0.0821 = 0.0206$
				Total = 0.1465

Explain where the figures in this table come from.

You can imagine that doing such problems this way can rapidly become far too cumbersome. For example, to find the probability of receiving eight orders would involve a great deal of work!

EXAMPLE 8.5

A family categorises the mail received each day into three types: financial (such as bills and communications from the bank), circulars (including all kinds of junk mail) and personal (letters from friends, etc.).

The three types may each be modelled by independent Poisson distributions with means 1.1, 1.8 and 1.3 items of mail per day, respectively.

Find the probability that in any one day

(i) the number of items of mail that are personal or financial exceeds three

(ii) the total number of items of mail is less than five.

SOLUTION

You are given that the delivery of the different types of mail may be modelled by Poisson distributions and it is reasonable to assume that

- they are independent
- they occur randomly
- the probability of a delivery does not vary with time.

(i) For financial or personal mail the parameter is $1.1 + 1.3 = 2.4$.
From cumulative Poisson probability tables with $\lambda = 2.4$:

$$\begin{aligned}\text{P(number exceeds 3)} &= 1 - \text{P(number is 3 or less)}\\ &= 1 - 0.7787\\ &= 0.2213\end{aligned}$$

(ii) For all mail the parameter is $1.1 + 1.8 + 1.3 = 4.2$.
From tables, with $\lambda = 4.2$:

$$\begin{aligned}\text{P(total number is less than 5)} &= \text{P(total number is less than } \textit{or equal to } 4)\\ &= 0.5898\end{aligned}$$

EXERCISE 8C

1 The lost property office at a mainline station records items left on trains handed in in two categories. Category A is clothing (including umbrellas, coats, gloves, etc.) and category B is paperwork (including briefcases, papers, books, etc.).
Over a period of time the mean number of items in category A handed in per day is 2 and the mean number in category B per day is 3.
These distributions may be assumed to be independent of each other and each may be modelled by the Poisson distribution.
Find the probability that

(i) in one day there are no items handed in

(ii) in one day there is exactly one item handed in

(iii) in one day there are exactly two items handed in.

2 On a particular stretch of road one morning the number of cars travelling into town past a particular point per 10-second interval has a mean of 3.0 and the number of cars travelling out of town past the same point has a mean of 1.3 per 10-second interval.
Assuming that both may be modelled by independent Poisson distributions, find the probability that in any interval of 10 seconds

(i) no cars pass in either direction

(ii) a total of five cars pass.

3 A certain condition affecting the blood is caused by the presence of two types of deformed corpuscles, *A* and *B*. It is known that if, on average, the total number of deformed corpuscles exceeds 6 per 0.001 cm^3 of blood then a person will show symptoms of the condition.
A newly married couple undergo a test and are told that, for each child they have, the number of type *A* corpuscles per 0.001 cm^3 of blood can be modelled by a Poisson distribution with mean 1.3 and the number of type *B* corpuscles per 0.001 cm^3 of blood can be modelled by a Poisson distribution with mean 1.6.

(i) Find the probability that a particular child will show symptoms of the condition.

(ii) State any assumptions you have made.

4 In the refectory of a college both coffee and tea are sold. During the 'non-teaching' parts of the day the number of cups of coffee and of tea sold per five-minute interval may be considered to be independent Poisson distributions with means of 2.7 and 1.5 respectively.
Calculate the probabilities that, in a given five-minute interval,

(i) exactly one cup of coffee and one cup of tea are sold

(ii) exactly two drinks are sold

(iii) more than five drinks are sold.

5 The water in a tank is contaminated with bacteria. The bacteria are located at random and independently and the mean number per millilitre of liquid is known to be 1.1.

(i) Find the probability that a sample of 1 ml of liquid contains more than two bacteria.

Five samples, each of 1 ml of liquid, are taken.

(ii) Find the mean number of bacteria for the five samples, taken together.

(iii) Find the probability that, in the five samples, there are in total

(a) no bacteria

(b) less than three bacteria.

6 A businessman receives an average of two emails per hour related to his business and 1.5 emails per hour on personal matters.

Find the probability that in any randomly chosen hour

(i) he receives no emails

(ii) he receives more than five emails.

7 To justify the building of the Avonford bypass, a research company carried out an investigation into the number of lorries passing through the centre of the town on the north–south road.
They found that the mean number of lorries per five-minute interval were 5.0 travelling north and 3.0 travelling south.

Find the probability that in any given interval of 5 minutes

(i) no lorries passed through travelling north
(ii) a total of fewer than six lorries passed through
(iii) a total of at least six lorries passed through
(iv) a total of exactly six lorries passed through.

8 An insurance company has 40 000 clients covered for 'severe industrial accident'. Such accidents are estimated to affect 1 in 200 000 of the population in any year, and they are assumed to occur independently of each other.
Let X be the number of claims for severe industrial accident received by the company in any one year.

(i) The variable X is modelled by a Poisson distribution with parameter λ. Write down the value of λ.
(ii) Find the probability that the number of claims received by the company in a year is
(a) zero **(b)** one **(c)** two or more.

A second insurance company offers cover on the same terms for severe industrial accident, and it receives an average of 1.2 claims per year.

(iii) Estimate the number of clients insured for severe industrial accident with the second company.
(iv) The two companies merge. Find the probability that the number of claims received by the merged company in a year is
(a) zero **(b)** two.

The Poisson approximation to the binomial distribution

You met the binomial distribution in Chapter 6. Look at this example of its use.

EXAMPLE 8.6

In a certain part of the country 1 in 50 children have accidentally broken a bone in their body by the age of five.
If 100 five-year-old children are chosen at random, what is the probability that exactly four of the children have suffered a broken bone?

SOLUTION

This distribution is a binomial distribution with $n = 100$, $p = \frac{1}{50}$ and $q = \frac{49}{50}$.

The probability of four children having had broken bones is
${}^{100}C_4\left(\frac{1}{50}\right)^4\left(\frac{49}{50}\right)^{96} = 0.0902.$

A calculation like this can be rather cumbersome. In some cases the cumulative binomial probability table can be used, but this is not always so.

Sometimes the Poisson distribution can provide a good approximation to the binomial distribution. For this to be the case you require

- n to be large
- p to be small (indicating that the event is rare)
- np not to be too large (typically less than 10).

In Example 8.6, the mean of the binomial distribution is given by $np = 100 \times \frac{1}{50} = 2$ so, for the Poisson approximation, take $\lambda = 2$.

Using the tables gives the probability of four children having suffered a broken bone as $0.9473 - 0.8571 = 0.0902$.

You can see that the answer is the same as the exact answer from the binomial distribution correct to 4 decimal places.

ACTIVITY

e *Accuracy*

Working out the equivalent Poisson distribution terms can be very much simpler than the binomial terms, but they are only approximations. How accurate are they?

An important question is how accurate do they need to be? In most cases you are only modelling a distribution based on a few values so this approximation is often good enough.

This table gives the figures for the situation in Example 8.6.

Number of cases	Probability by binomial	Probability by Poisson
0	0.1326	0.1353
1	0.2707	0.2707
2	0.2734	0.2707

In this table the first 2 decimal places of the corresponding values are the same (although one of them is not accurate to 2 decimal places).

Consider now the situation where the distribution is B(1000, 0.002). The mean value is still $np = 1000 \times 0.002 = 2$. So if you redraw the table the right-hand column remains the same, but the binomial probabilities are much closer.

$$P(X = 0) = \left(\frac{499}{500}\right)^{1000} = 0.1351$$

$$P(X = 1) = 1000\left(\frac{1}{500}\right)\left(\frac{499}{500}\right)^{999} = 0.2707$$

$$P(X = 2) = 1000 \times \frac{999}{2}\left(\frac{1}{500}\right)^{2}\left(\frac{499}{500}\right)^{998} = 0.2709$$

These results can be shown in a table.

Number of cases	Probability by binomial	Probability by Poisson
0	0.1351	0.1353
1	0.2707	0.2707
2	0.2709	0.2707

Construct similar tables for B(10 000, 0.0002) and for B(100 000, 0.000 02).

EXAMPLE 8.7

The probability that a component produced in a factory is defective is 0.005.

(i) A sample of 500 components are tested. Find the probability that

(a) exactly two components are defective

(b) more than two components are defective.

(ii) Find the number of components that need to be tested to be 99% sure of obtaining at least one defective.

SOLUTION

The distribution is binomial with $n = 500$ and $p = 0.005$.
This gives the mean as $np = 500 \times 0.005 = 2.5$

The conditions for using the Poisson distribution have been met since

- p is small
- n is large
- $np = 2.5$, which is not large.

So the Poisson approximation to the binomial is appropriate with $\lambda = np = 2.5$ and the cumulative Poisson probability tables can be used.

(i) (a) Probability of two defectives $= 0.5438 - 0.2873$
$= 0.2565$

(b) Probability of more than two defectives $= 1 - \text{P}(0, 1 \text{ or } 2 \text{ defectives})$
$= 1 - 0.5438$
$= 0.4562$

(ii) Call the number of components tested n.
Then the distribution of the number of defectives in samples of this size is approximately Poisson with parameter $\lambda = 0.005 \times n$.

The probability that the number of defectives in this sample is zero is $1 - 0.99 = 0.01$.

Looking for 0.01 in the tables with $x = 0$ gives $\lambda = 4.59$.

$0.005n = 4.59$
$n = 918.$

The value of 4.59 for λ is found by interpolation between the values for 4.50 and 4.60 given in the tables.

EXERCISE 8D

1 It is known that, on a production line, the probability that an item is faulty is 0.1. A sample of 50 items is chosen at random and checked for faults.
  (i) Find the probability that there will be no faulty items and also the probability that there will be three faulty items using
    (a) the binomial distribution
    (b) a Poisson distribution.
  (ii) Comment on your answers to part **(i)**.

  After an improvement in the production line the probability that an item is faulty is now 0.01. A sample of 500 items is chosen at random and checked for faults.
  (iii) Find the probability that there will be no faulty items and also the probability that there will be three faulty items using
    (a) the binomial distribution
    (b) a Poisson distribution.
  (iv) Comment on your answers to part **(iii)**.

2 A chemical firm produces bottles of shampoo. It is found over a long period of time that 1 in 50 bottles contains enough impurity to render the shampoo unusable.
  A random sample of 100 bottles is taken. What is the probability that more than five of them will be unusable?

3 The mean number of accidents in a factory is known to be 2.8 per month. Records of recorded accidents are scrutinised for a random sample of ten months.
  (i) Justify the use of the Poisson distribution to model this distribution.
  (ii) Find the probability that
    (a) each of the ten months had at least one accident
    (b) in exactly eight of the months there was at least one accident.
  (iii) If the first three months of a year are chosen, show that it is rather improbable that in this time interval there will be fewer than 3 accidents or more than 15.

4 It is found that 1 in 200 patients who stay more than three days in a hospital develop an illness that is unrelated to the cause of their admission.
  During one year, 1000 people are in the hospital for more than three days. Estimate the probability that more than five of them develop another disease.

5 A sociologist claims that only 2.5% of all students from inner-city schools go on to university.
  A group of 300 students are randomly chosen from inner-city schools from around the country.
  (i) Show why the Poisson distribution may be used as an approximation to the binomial distribution to model this situation.
  (ii) Calculate the probability that, if the sociologists' claim is true, from this group of 300 students more than six go to university.

6 (i) State the conditions under which it is permissible to use the Poisson distribution as an approximation to the binomial distribution.

It is known that 0.5% of components produced by a factory are defective. Each day a random sample of 200 components is inspected.

(ii) Find the probability that there are no defectives in the daily sample.

(iii) Find the probability that there is at least one defective on any day.

(iv) How many components are inspected in three days?

(v) Find the probability that there are at least three defective components in a period of three days.

(vi) Explain why you would expect the answer to part **(v)** to be greater than the answer to part **(iii)**.

7 A car has a part that lasts, in safari conditions, on average, 1000 miles before failing. A driver is setting out on a safari of 3000 miles. She wants to know how many spare parts to take with her. She fits a new part before she starts.

(i) The Poisson distribution is used to model this situation. State the value of λ.

(ii) Find the probability that

(a) the fitted part does not fail

(b) 0 or 1 parts fail

(c) 0, 1 or 2 parts fail

(d) 0, 1, 2 or 3 parts fail.

(iii) Find the number of spare items the driver should carry to be 95% sure of having enough parts to be able to complete the safari.

8 Among the population of a large city, the proportion of people with blue eyes is 0.2. A random group of ten people are selected.

(i) Find the probability that there will be

(a) no person with blue eyes

(b) at least two people with blue eyes.

In the same population the proportion of people with a randomly occurring medical condition is 0.002. A random group of 1000 people is selected.

(ii) Find the probability that there will be

(a) no person with the condition

(b) at least two people with the condition.

9 A man is trying to persuade people to join an organisation. He knows that the probability of being successful in persuading a person at random to join is 0.02.

(i) One day he tries 100 people. What is the probability of recruiting at least one person?

(ii) On another day he tries 200 people. What is the probability of recruiting at least one person?

(iii) How many people should he try in order to be 99% sure of recruiting at least one person?

KEY POINTS

1 The Poisson probability distribution

- The Poisson distribution is used to model the probability distribution of the numbers of occurrences of an event in a given interval when
  - occurrences are independent
  - occurrences are random
  - the probability of an occurrence is constant over time.
- The Poisson distribution is defined by a parameter, λ.
- The probability of r occurrences is $\frac{\lambda^r}{r!}e^{-\lambda}$
- The value of the mean is often taken to be the parameter λ. The value of the variance of the distribution is close to λ.
- The Poisson distribution is often an appropriate model for the probability distribution of the number of occurrences of a *rare* event.

2 The sum of two Poisson distributions

If two independent random variables both have Poisson distributions with parameters of λ and μ, then their sum also has a Poisson distribution and its parameter is $\lambda + \mu$.

3 Approximating the binomial distribution by a Poisson distribution

- The Poisson distribution may be used to model a binomial distribution, $B(n, p)$, provided that
  - n is large
  - p is small
  - np is not too large.

9 The Normal distribution

We look forward to the day when everyone will receive more than the average wage.

Australian Minister of Labour

AVONFORD STAR

Baby boom this Christmas

It was a very busy Christmas Day in the Maternity Wing of Avonford Hospital. Twelve 'Christmas Day' babies were born this year – a record for the hospital. One of the babies, Alex, baby son of Julia and Michael Pritchard of Central Way, Avonford weighed in at 11.1 lbs – the heaviest baby to be born at the hospital for at least five years.

Was Alex exceptionally heavy? Is he one in a hundred, or a thousand or even a million? In order to be able to answer this question you need to know the distribution of the birth weights of babies born in this country.

It is known from national records that the mean and standard deviation of birth weights are 7.18 lb and 1.21 lb respectively.

Like many other naturally occurring measurements, the birth weights of babies may be modelled by a *Normal distribution*, as shown in figure 9.1.

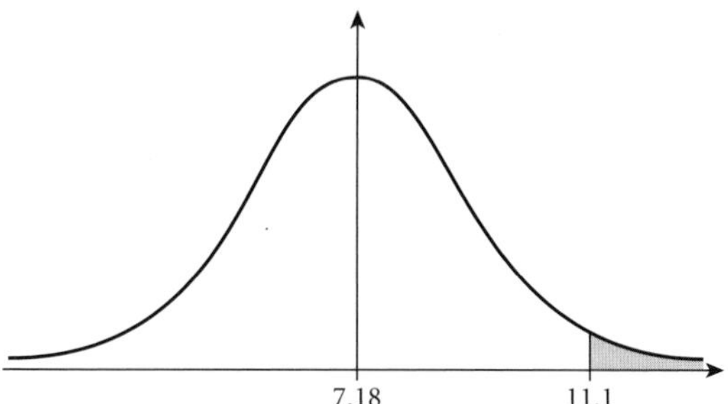

Figure 9.1

 How many standard deviations was Alex's birth weight above the mean?

The Normal distribution is one of the most important distributions in statistics for two main reasons.

1 Many physical, biological, economic and social measurements can be modelled by a Normal distribution. These are just a few examples.
   - The heights of adult females in this country
   - The blood pressure of 30-year-old males
   - The yield of barley from plots of a given size
   - Test scores, e.g. IQ scores
   - The length of life of electrical components
   - The errors in astronomical measurements
   - The mass of hen's eggs
   - The rainfall in a particular area over a number of years

2 The Normal distribution is fundamental in the analysis of the results from a sample and in the drawing of conclusions from these results. This is explored more fully in Chapter 11.

The key features of a Normal distribution

Look at the curves in figure 9.2.

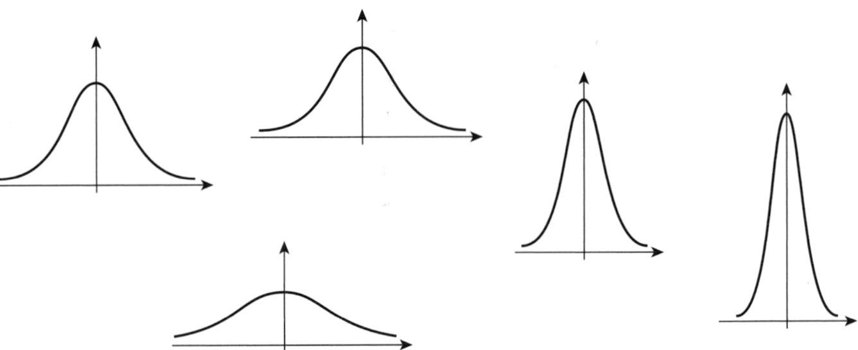

Figure 9.2

They all illustrate Normal distributions, with the following key features.

- They are continuous.
- They are symmetrical about the mean (also mode = median = mean).
- They are 'bell-shaped'.
- The curves get closer to the axis with increasing distance from the mean.
- The area under the curve is always 1 (they are probability distributions).

There is one further feature shared by *all* Normal distributions. Although they may appear to differ in how spread out they are, in each case the same area lies within a given number of standard deviations of the mean. Thus, for example

- 68.3% of the area lies within one standard deviation of the mean
- 95.4% of the area lies within two standard deviations of the mean
- 99.7% of the area lies within three standard deviations of the mean.

So *all* Normal distributions have exactly the same shape, provided the same scale is used on the horizontal axis for the number of standard deviations. The number of standard deviations is denoted by z.

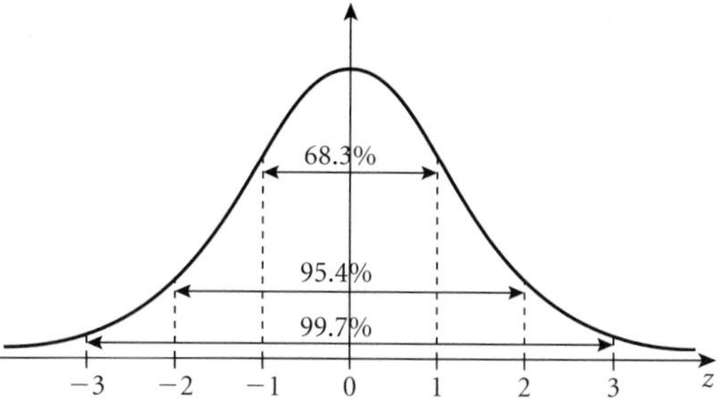

Figure 9.3

The important implication of this fact is that one Normal distribution table of probability values can be used for *all* Normal probability situations.

Using the Normal distribution table

Figure 9.4 shows a Normal distribution with part of the area under it shaded. This area is given in the Normal distribution table and is denoted by $\Phi(z)$ where z is the number of standard deviations.

Φ is the upper case Greek letter phi'. It sounds like '*fie*'.

In figure 9.4, $z = 1.75$ and so the shaded area is $\Phi(1.75)$.

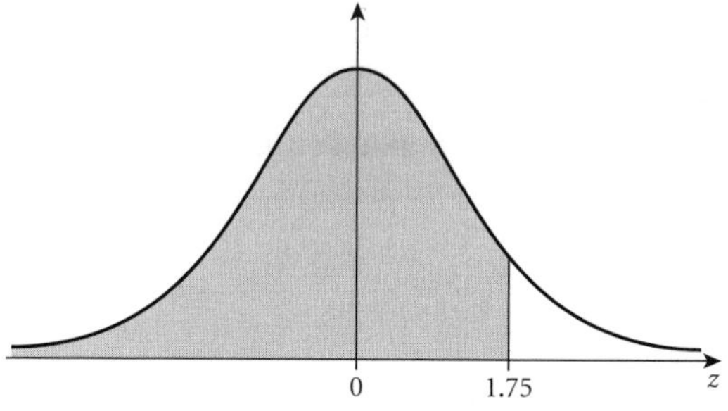

Figure 9.4

Note that $\Phi(z)$ is always the area to the left of z and represents $P(Z \leqslant z)$.

The values of $\Phi(z)$ are given in the Normal distribution table, an extract of which is printed below.

z	.00	.01	.02	.03	.04	.05	.06	.07	.08	.09	1	2	3	4	5	6	7	8	9
											(add)								
0.0	.5000	5040	5080	5120	5160	5199	5239	5279	5319	5359	4	8	12	16	20	24	28	32	36
0.1	.5398	5438	5478	5517	5557	5596	5636	5675	5714	5753	4	8	12	16	20	24	28	32	35
0.2	.5793	5832	5871	5910	5948	5987	6026	6064	6103	6141	4	8	12	15	19	23	27	31	35
0.3	.6179	6217	6255	6293	6331	6368	6406	6443	6480	6517	4	8	11	15	19	23	26	30	34
0.4	.6554	6591	6628	6664	6700	6736	6772	6808	6844	6879	4	7	11	14	18	22	25	29	32
0.5	.6915	6950	6985	7019	7054	7088	7123	7157	7190	7224	3	7	10	14	17	21	24	27	31
0.6	.7257	7291	7324	7357	7389	7422	7454	7486	7517	7549	3	6	10	13	16	19	23	26	29
0.7	.7580	7611	7642	7673	7704	7734	7764	7794	7823	7852	3	6	9	12	15	18	21	24	27
0.8	.7881	7910	7939	7967	7995	8023	8051	8078	8106	8133	3	6	8	11	14	17	19	22	25
0.9	.8159	8186	8212	8238	8264	8289	8315	8340	8365	8389	3	5	8	10	13	15	18	20	23
1.0	.8413	8438	8461	8485	8508	8531	8554	8577	8599	8621	2	5	7	9	12	14	16	18	21
1.1	.8643	8665	8686	8708	8729	8749	8770	8790	8810	8830	2	4	6	8	10	12	14	16	19
1.2	.8849	8869	8888	8907	8925	8944	8962	8980	8997	9015	2	4	6	7	9	11	13	15	16
1.3	.9032	9049	9066	9082	9099	9115	9131	9147	9162	9177	2	3	5	6	8	10	11	13	14
1.4	.9192	9207	9222	9236	9251	9265	9279	9292	9306	9319	1	3	4	6	7	8	10	11	13
1.5	.9332	9345	9357	9370	9382	9394	9406	9418	9429	9441	1	2	4	5	6	7	8	10	11
1.6	.9452	9463	9474	9484	9495	9505	9515	9525	9535	9545	1	2	3	4	5	6	7	8	9
1.7	.9554	9564	9573	9582	9591	9599	9608	9616	9625	9633	1	2	3	3	4	5	6	7	8
1.8	.9641	9649	9656	9664	9671	9678	9686	9693	9699	9706	1	1	2	3	4	4	5	6	6
1.9	.9713	9719	9726	9732	9738	9744	9750	9756	9761	9767	1	1	2	2	3	4	4	5	5

To find the value of $\Phi(1.75)$ go to row 1.7 and column 0.05 and read the value at the intersection.

$$\Phi(1.75) = 0.9599.$$

How would you find the value of $\Phi(1.756)$?

What is **(i)** $\Phi(2.3)$ **(ii)** $\Phi(2.17)$ **(iii)** $\Phi(1.925)$?

Some books of tables also give values of $\phi(z)$. These are the points you would use to draw the Normal distribution curve accurately. Be careful not to confuse ϕ, which is the lower case 'phi', with the upper case Φ. In this book the table used will always be that for $\Phi(z)$.

Standardising the variable

The question 'Was Alex exceptionally heavy?' was asked immediately after the *Avonford Star* article. You are now in a position to answer this question.

The mean birth weight of babies is 7.18 lb, with standard deviation 1.21 lb, so at 11.1 lb, Alex was $\frac{11.1 - 7.18}{1.21} = 3.240$ standard deviations above the mean.

This process is called 'standardising the variable'.

In order to discover whether Alex was exceptionally heavy you want to know the probability that a baby is 11.1 lb or more at birth. This is the shaded area in figure 9.5.

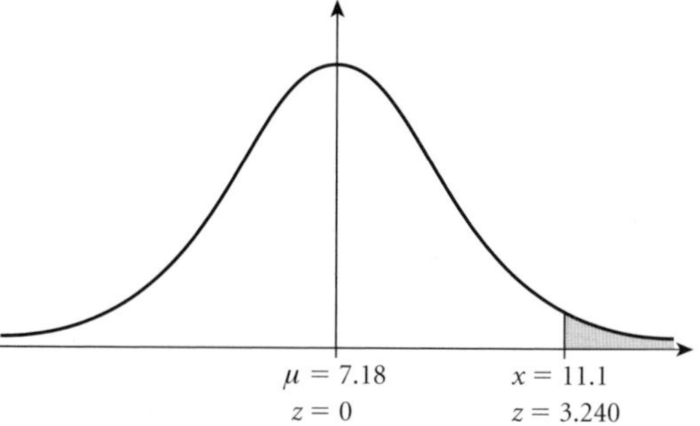

Figure 9.5

To find this area start by finding the area to the left of it, as shown in figure 9.6.

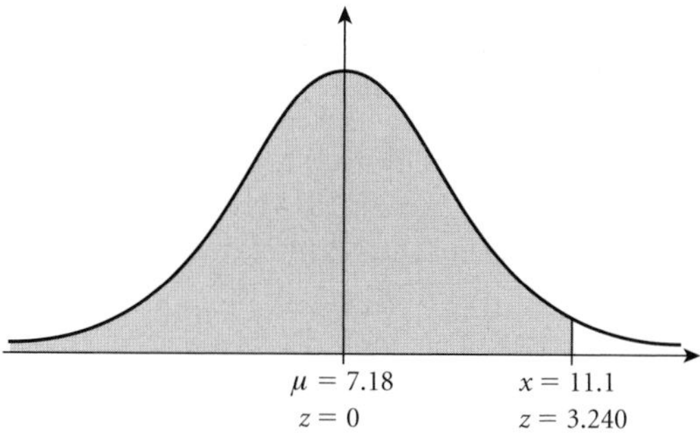

Figure 9.6

From the Normal distribution table, this is $\Phi(3.240) = 0.9994$.

Since the total area is 1, the required area to the right is $1 - 0.9994 = 0.0006$.

So you would expect only 6 babies out of 10 000 to weigh 11.1 lb or more at birth. This is not very likely. It would be fair to say that Alex was 'exceptionally heavy'.

Notation

Figure 9.6 has already introduced you to some of the notation which is used with Normal distributions. In the *Avonford Star* example, the upper case letter, X, would be used to describe the birth weight of babies and the lower case letter, x, to indicate a particular value. ($x = 11.1$ in figure 9.6.) The upper case letter, Z, would be used for the standardised variable and the lower case letter, z, to indicate a particular value. ($z = 3.240$ corresponds to $x = 11.1$ in figure 9.6.) The Greek letters, μ (pronounced '*mu*') and σ (pronounced '*sigma*') are used for the mean and the standard deviation of the distribution X so, in this example, $\mu = 7.18$ and $\sigma = 1.21$. This information is summarised in the following table.

	Actual distribution, X	Standardised distribution, Z
Mean	μ	0
Standard deviation	σ	1
Particular value	x	$z = \dfrac{x - \mu}{\sigma}$

In Z1 you met the notation $X \sim \mathrm{B}(n, p)$ to indicate that the random variable X has the binomial distribution with parameters n and p, where n represents the number of trials and p the probability of success. The corresponding notation for the Normal distribution with mean μ and variance σ^2 (so the standard deviation is σ) is $X \sim \mathrm{N}(\mu, \sigma^2)$. This is a standard notation and widely used so you must be familiar with it.

Modelling using the Normal distribution

The next example shows you how to use the Normal distribution table in a variety of situations. There are three key steps.

- Standardise the variable.
- Draw a sketch diagram.
- Find the area required using the Normal distribution table.

EXAMPLE 9.1

Assuming that the distribution of heights of girls at a particular age is Normal with a mean of 147.2 cm and a standard deviation of 5.0 cm, find the probability that a girl selected at random is

(i) under 150 cm
(ii) over 155 cm
(iii) under 142 cm
(iv) at least 140 cm
(v) between 149 cm and 152 cm
(vi) between 143 cm and 153 cm
(vii) between 141 cm and 146 cm.

SOLUTION

Call X the random variable 'the heights, in cm, of the girls at a particular age', where the mean = 147.2 cm and the standard deviation = 5.0 cm, so that $X \sim \mathrm{N}(147.2, 5.0^2)$.

To standardise X use $Z = \dfrac{X - 147.2}{5.0}$.

(i) In this case the standardised variable is $\dfrac{150 - 147.2}{5.0} = 0.56$.

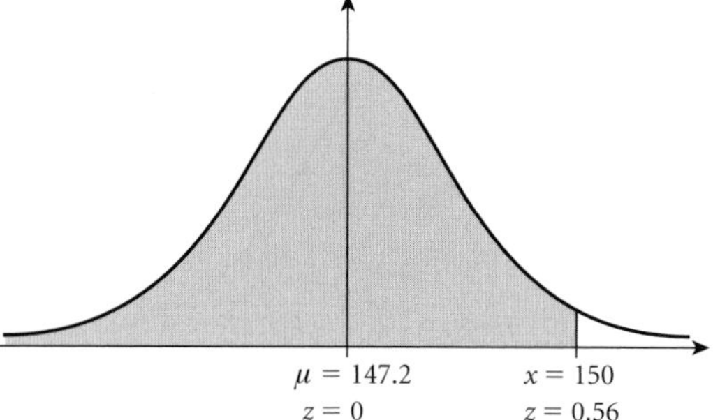

Figure 9.7

So the area required is $\Phi(0.56) = 0.7123$.

The probability that a girl selected at random is under 150 cm is 0.7123.

(ii) For 155 cm the standardised variable is $\dfrac{155 - 147.2}{5.0} = 1.56$.

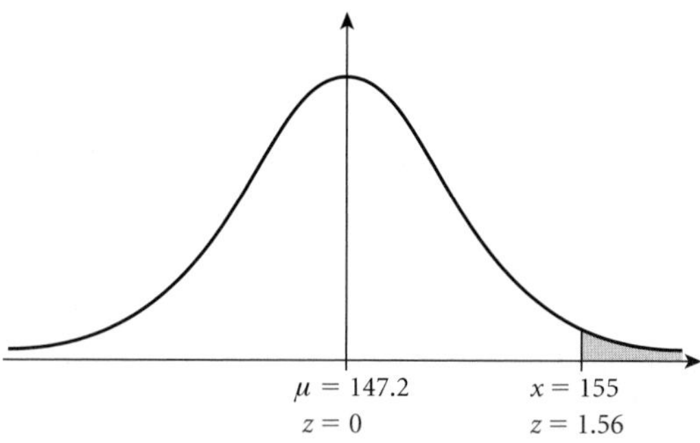

Figure 9.8

So the area required is $1 - \Phi(1.56)$
$= 1 - 0.9406$
$= 0.0594$

The probability that a girl selected at random is over 155 cm is 0.0594.

(iii) For 142 cm the standardised variable is $\dfrac{142 - 147.2}{5.0} = -1.04$.

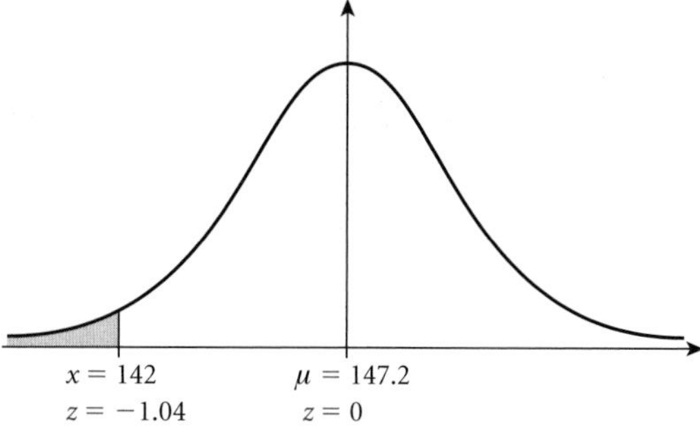

Figure 9.9

By symmetry, the area to the left of -1.04 is the same as the area to the right of 1.04.

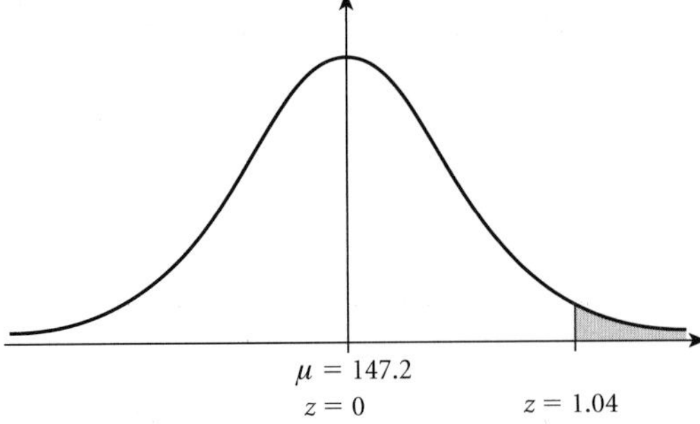

Figure 9.10

So the area required is $1 - \Phi(1.04)$
$= 1 - 0.8508$
$= 0.1492$

The probability that a girl selected at random is under 142 cm is 0.1492.

(iv) For 140 cm the standardised variable is $\dfrac{140 - 147.2}{5.0} = -1.44.$

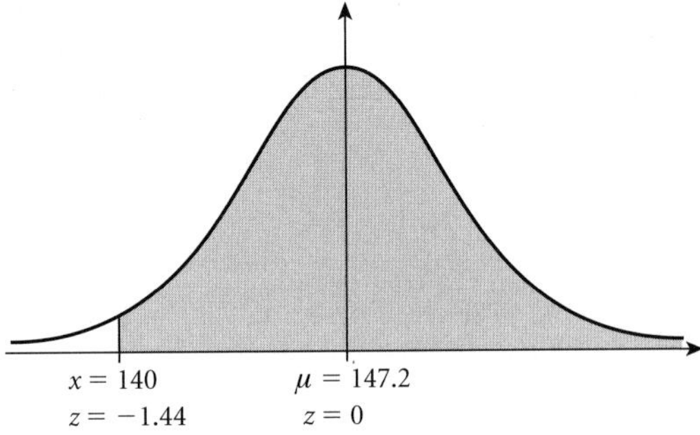

Figure 9.11

By symmetry, the area to the right of -1.44 is the same as the area to the left of 1.44.

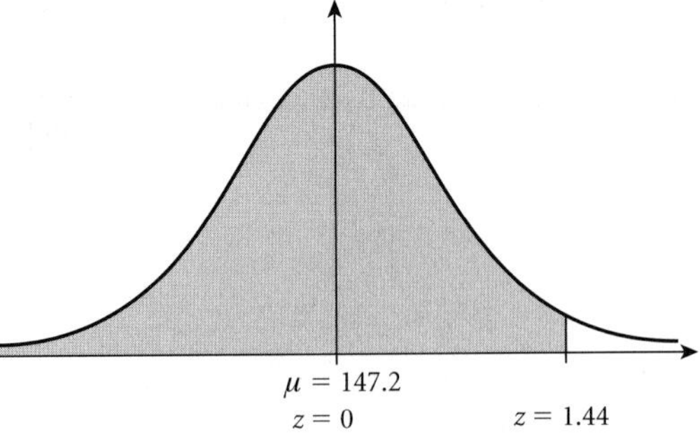

Figure 9.12

So the area required is $\Phi(1.44) = 0.9251$.

The probability that a girl selected at random is over 140 cm is 0.9251.

(v) For 149 cm the standardised variable is $\dfrac{149 - 147.2}{5.0} = 0.36.$

For 152 cm, the standardised variable is $\dfrac{152 - 147.2}{5.0} = 0.96.$

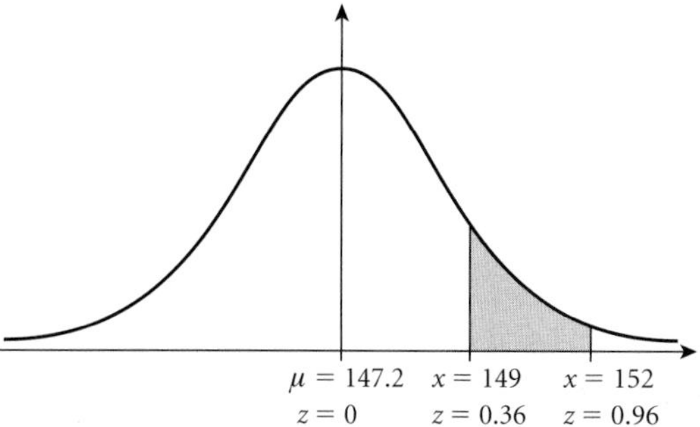

Figure 9.13

This can be thought of as the difference between the two areas.

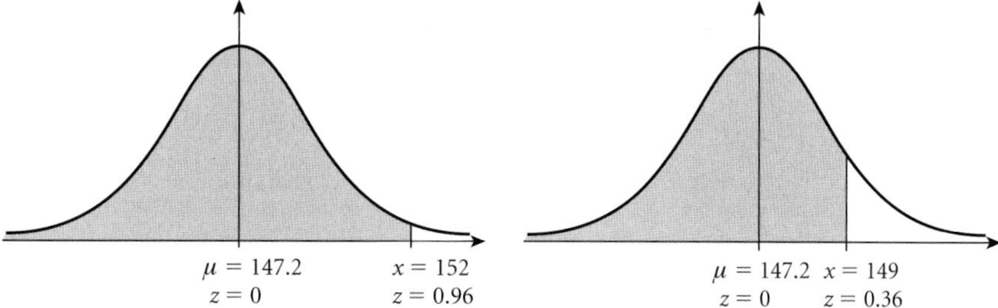

Figure 9.14

So the area required is $\Phi(0.96) - \Phi(0.36)$
$= 0.8315 - 0.6406$
$= 0.1909$

The probability that a girl selected at random is between 149 cm and 152 cm is 0.1909.

(vi) For 143 cm the standardised variable is $\dfrac{143 - 147.2}{5.0} = -0.84.$

For 153 cm, the standardised variable is $\dfrac{153 - 147.2}{5.0} = 1.16.$

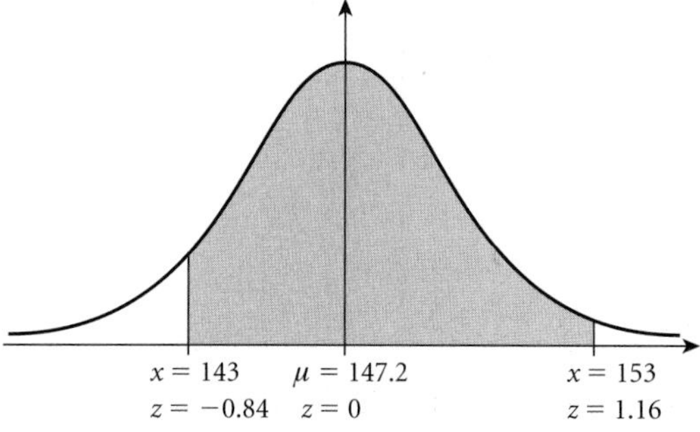

Figure 9.15

This can be thought of as the difference between the two areas.

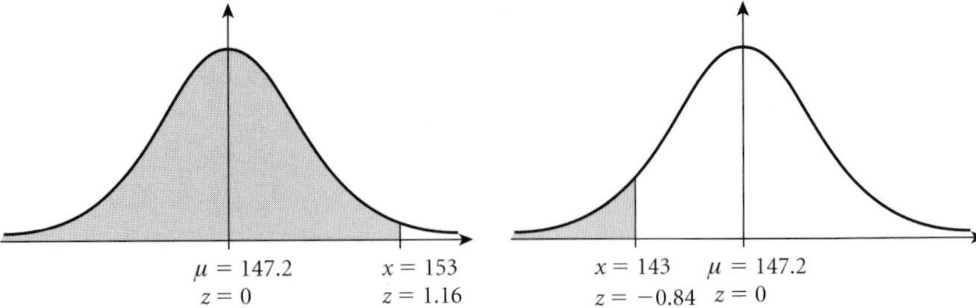

Figure 9.16

In the right-hand diagram, by symmetry, the area to the left of -0.84 is the same as the area to the right of 0.84, which is $1 - \Phi(0.84)$.

So the area required is $\Phi(1.16) - (1 - \Phi(0.84))$
$= 0.8770 - (1 - 0.7995)$
$= 0.8770 - 0.2005$
$= 0.6765$

The probability that a girl selected at random is between 143 cm and 153 cm is 0.6765.

(vii) For 141 cm the standardised variable is $\dfrac{141 - 147.2}{5.0} = -1.24$.

For 146 cm the standardised variable is $\dfrac{146 - 147.2}{5.0} = -0.24$.

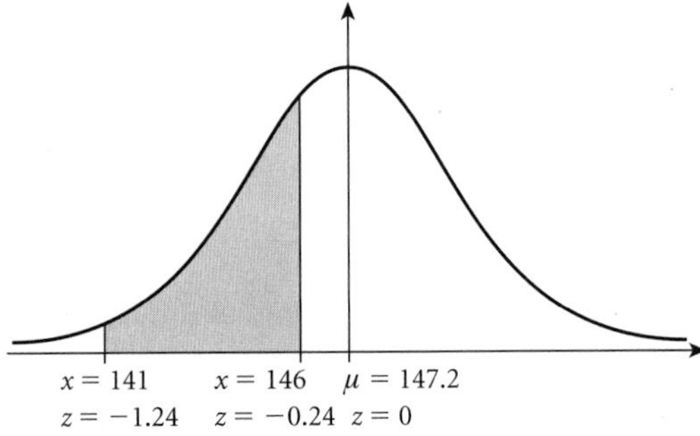

Figure 9.17

By symmetry the shaded area in figure 9.17 is the same as the shaded area in figure 9.18.

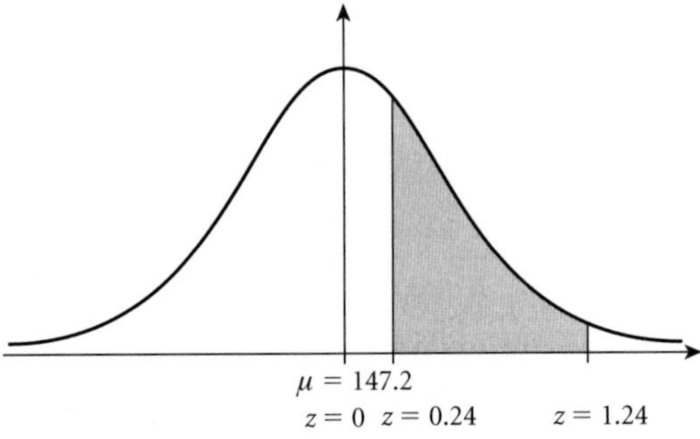

Figure 9.18

So the required area is $\Phi(1.24) - \Phi(0.24)$
$= 0.8925 - 0.5948$
$= 0.2977$

The probability that a girl selected at random is between 141 cm and 146 cm is 0.2977.

The work in parts **(ii)** and **(iii)** of Example 9.1 can be generalised to give these results.

$$P(Z > z) = 1 - \Phi(z) \text{ and } \Phi(-z) = 1 - \Phi(z)$$

? How would you illustrate these results on sketches of the Normal distribution?

Percentiles

If the mean and standard deviation of a Normal distribution are known, you can calculate the *percentile* corresponding to a particular result. This is shown in the next example.

EXAMPLE 9.2

In monitoring a child's growth, paediatricians often quote physical measurements in two ways: as the readings taken and as percentiles.
Assume that the weights of 30-month-old boys are Normally distributed with a mean of 30 lb and a standard deviation of 3 lb.

(i) What is the percentile corresponding to a weight of 33 lb?
(ii) What is the percentile corresponding to a weight of 25.2 lb?

SOLUTION

(i) For a weight of 33 lb the standardised score is $\dfrac{33 - 30}{3} = 1.0$.

So the percentile is given by $100 \times \Phi(1.0) = 84.13\%$.

This means that a 30-month-old boy who weighs 33 lb is on the 84.13th percentile and so will be in the top quarter of the population (that is, greater than the 75th percentile).
Only 15.87% of boys at that age will be 33 lb or heavier.

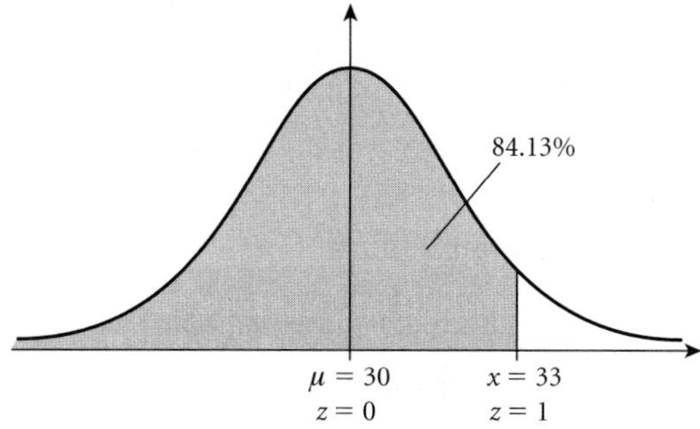

Figure 9.19

(ii) For a weight of 25.2 lb the standardised score is $\frac{25.2 - 30.0}{3} = -1.6$.

So the percentile is given by $100 \times \Phi(-1.6)$
$= 100 \times (1 - \Phi(1.6))$
$= 5.48\%$

This means that only 5.48% of boys of that age will be 25.2 lb or lighter.

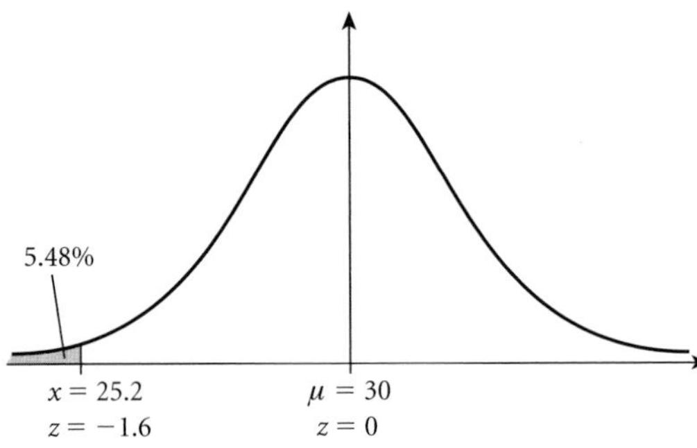

Figure 9.20

Sometimes you will want to ask the reverse question and find the score corresponding to a particular percentile.

EXAMPLE 9.3

Diastolic blood pressure is Normally distributed with a mean of 80 mmHg and a standard deviation of 12 mmHg.

(i) What is the blood pressure at the 75th percentile?
(ii) What is the blood pressure at the 40th percentile?

SOLUTION

The answers are found by reversing the steps in Example 9.2.

(i) If z is the standardised score for the 75th percentile then $100 \times \Phi(z) = 75$. Therefore $\Phi(z) = 0.75$.

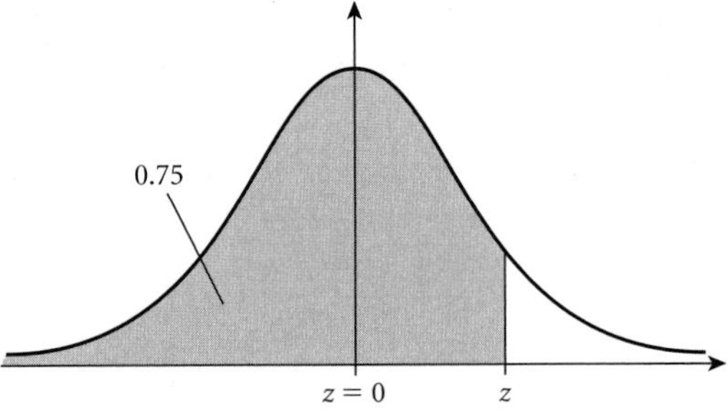

Figure 9.21

The *inverse Normal table* can be used to find the value of z corresponding to $p = 0.75$.

Here is an extract of the table.

p	.000	.001	.002	.003	.004	.005	.006	.007	.008	.009
.50	.0000	.0025	.0050	.0075	.0100	.0125	.0150	.0175	.0201	.0226
.51	.0251	.0276	.0301	.0326	.0351	.0376	.0401	.0426	.0451	.0476
.52	.0502	.0527	.0552	.0577	.0602	.0627	.0652	.0677	.0702	.0728
.53	.0753	.0778	.0803	.0828	.0853	.0878	.0904	.0929	.0954	.0979
.54	.1004	.1030	.1055	.1080	.1105	.1130	.1156	.1181	.1206	.1231
.70	.5244	.5273	.5302	.5330	.5359	.5388	.5417	.5446	.5476	.5505
.71	.5534	.5563	.5592	.5622	.5651	.5681	.5710	.5740	.5769	.5799
.72	.5828	.5858	.5888	.5918	.5948	.5978	.6008	.6038	.6068	.6098
.73	.6128	.6158	.6189	.6219	.6250	.6280	.6311	.6341	.6372	.6403
.74	.6433	.6464	.6495	.6526	.6557	.6588	.6620	.6651	.6682	.6713
.75	.6745	.6776	.6808	.6840	.6871	.6903	.6935	.6967	.6999	.7031
.76	.7063	.7095	.7128	.7160	.7192	.7225	.7257	.7290	.7323	.7356
.77	.7388	.7421	.7454	.7488	.7521	.7554	.7588	.7621	.7655	.7688
.78	.7722	.7756	.7790	.7824	.7858	.7892	.7926	.7961	.7995	.8030
.79	.8064	.8099	.8134	.8169	.8204	.8239	.8274	.8310	.8345	.8381

The z value corresponding to $p = 0.75$ is 0.6745.

In order to find the actual blood pressure, you reverse the steps you took when finding the standardised score.

Multiply the z value by the standard deviation: $0.6745 \times 12 = 8.094$
Then add the mean: $80 + 8.094 = 88.094$

This gives the blood pressure at the 75th percentile as 88 mmHg (to the nearest whole number).

(ii) If z is the standardised score for the 40th percentile then $100 \times \Phi(z) = 40$. Therefore $\Phi(z) = 0.40$.

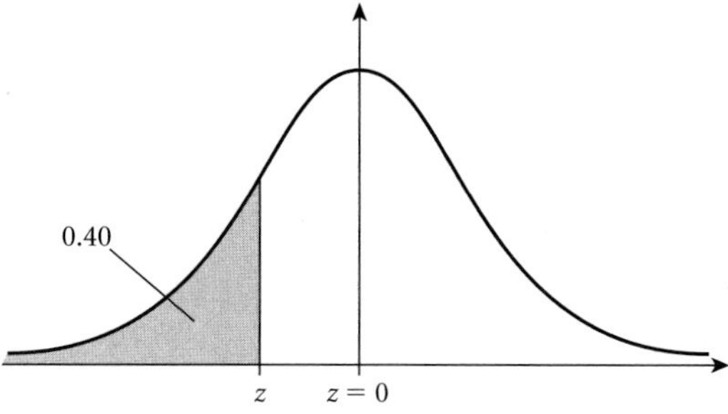

Figure 9.22

By symmetry, the shaded area in figure 9.22 is the same as the shaded area in figure 9.23.

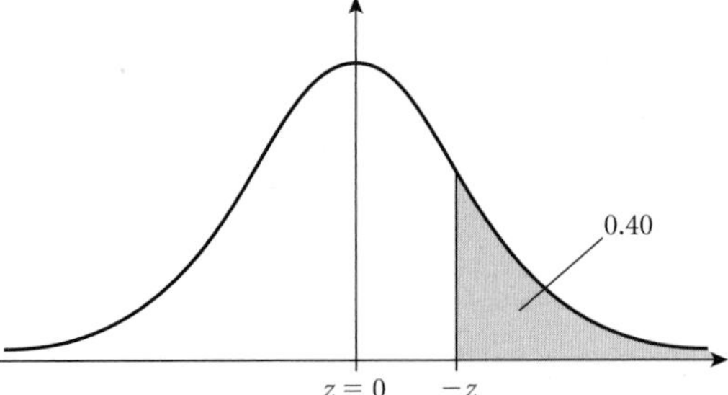

Figure 9.23

So $\Phi(-z) = 1 - 0.40 = 0.60$.

From the inverse Normal table $-z = 0.2533$.
Therefore $z = -0.2533$.

In order to find the actual blood pressure, you reverse the steps you took when finding the standardised score.

Multiply the z value by the standard deviation: $12 \times (-0.2533) = -3.0396$
Then add the mean: $80 - 3.0396 = 76.9604$

This gives the blood pressure at the 40th percentile as 77 mmHg (to the nearest whole number).

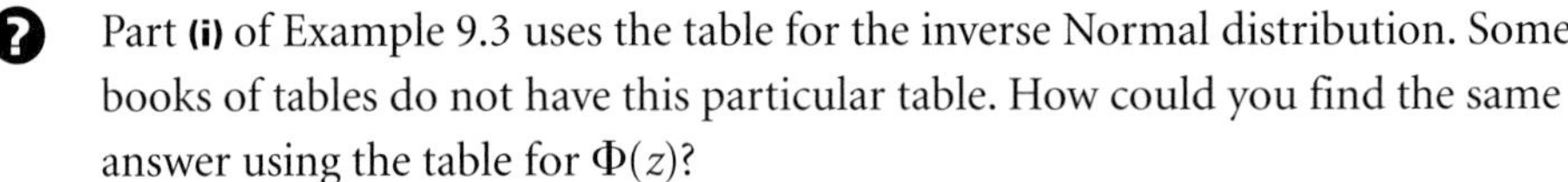

Part **(i)** of Example 9.3 uses the table for the inverse Normal distribution. Some books of tables do not have this particular table. How could you find the same answer using the table for $\Phi(z)$?

Sometimes you can use the inverse Normal table to find the mean and standard deviation of a population. This is illustrated in the next example.

EXAMPLE 9.4

The lifetimes of electric light bulbs can be modelled by the Normal distribution with mean μ hours and standard deviation σ hours. It is found that

- 5% of the bulbs last for at least 1150 hours
- 10% fail within the first 950 hours.

Find μ and σ.

SOLUTION

Begin by representing the information given in the question in a diagram. Denote the z values corresponding to 950 and 1150 by z_1 and z_2 respectively. (As 950 is to the left of the mean, z_1 will be negative.)

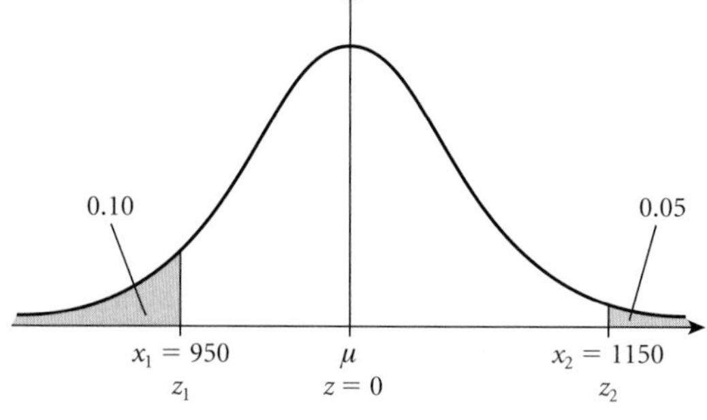

Figure 9.24

As 95% of the area is to the left of the z_2 line, $\Phi(z_2) = 0.95$.
From the inverse Normal table, $z_2 = 1.645$.

From figure 9.24 you can deduce the equation $\mu + 1.645\sigma = 1150$.

As 10% of the area is to the left of the z_1 line, $\Phi(z_1) = 0.1$.
So, by symmetry, $\Phi(-z_1) = 0.9$.
From the inverse Normal table, $-z_1 = 1.282$.
Therefore $z_1 = -1.282$.

From figure 9.24 you can deduce a second equation, $\mu - 1.282\sigma = 950$.

This gives two simultaneous equations for μ and σ.

$$\mu + 1.645\sigma = 1150 \qquad ①$$
$$\mu - 1.282\sigma = 950 \qquad ②$$

Subtracting equation ② from equation ① gives

$$2.927\sigma = 200$$
$$\sigma = 68.3$$

Substituting for σ in equation ① gives

$$\mu + 1.645 \times 68.3 = 1150$$
$$\mu = 1037.6$$

The mean, μ, is 1037.6 hours and the standard deviation, σ, is 68.3 hours.

ACTIVITY

Find out how you would use a graphic calculator, rather than tables, to solve the problems in this chapter. Experiment with a few examples. Remember, it is important that you understand the ideas behind the calculations and that you can describe your method.

Historical note

The Normal distribution is sometimes referred to as the Gaussian distribution in honour of the German mathematician Karl Fredrick Gauss (1777–1855). Known as 'the prince of mathematicians', Gauss had a profound influence in many fields of mathematics and science and is often ranked besides Euler, Newton and Archimedes as one of history's greatest mathematicians.

EXERCISE 9A

1 Assuming that the distribution of heights of boys at a particular age is Normal with a mean of 152.0 cm and a standard deviation of 5.0 cm, find the probability that a boy selected at random is

(i) under 155 cm
(ii) over 158 cm
(iii) under 147 cm
(iv) at least 145 cm
(v) between 154 cm and 159 cm
(vi) between 144 cm and 154 cm
(vii) between 143 cm and 150 cm.

2 Packets of raisins are nominally 250 g in weight. The actual weights have a Normal distribution with a mean of 255.2 g and a standard deviation of 2.6 g.

(i) What is the probability that a packet is underweight?
(ii) What is the weight exceeded by 20% of the packets?
(iii) What is the weight exceeded by 70% of the packets?
(iv) What proportion of the packets have a weight within one standard deviation of the mean?

3 The weights of babies at birth can be assumed to be Normally distributed with a mean of 7.18 lb and a standard deviation of 1.21 lb.

(i) What is the percentile corresponding to a weight of 8.65 lb?
(ii) What is the percentile corresponding to a weight of 6.75 lb?
(iii) What is the weight at the 80th percentile?
(iv) What is the weight at the 20th percentile?
(v) What is the interquartile range (that is, between the 25th and 75th percentiles)?

4 The lengths of a machined component are distributed Normally with a mean of 8.6 cm and a standard deviation of 0.85 cm.
Find

(i) the proportion that are shorter than 9 cm
(ii) the proportion that are longer than 9.2 cm
(iii) the proportion that are no further than 0.3 cm from the mean
(iv) the value of L if the probability that the length of the component is greater than L cm is 0.115.

5 Assume that the masses of adult men can be modelled by the Normal distribution with mean 75 kg and standard deviation 5 kg.

(i) What is the probability than an adult man will have a mass greater than 77.55 kg?
(ii) What is the probability that an adult man will have a mass less than 68.4 kg?
(iii) What is the probability that an adult man will have a mass between 76.6 kg and 83.5 kg?
(iv) What is the probability that an adult man will have a mass between 67.4 kg and 79.6 kg?
(v) 62% of adult men have a mass greater than M kg. What is the value of M?
(vi) What is the interquartile range for the masses of adult men?

6 The lifetime of an electrical component is distributed Normally with a mean of 2000 hours and a standard deviation of 120 hours.

(i) Find the probability that a component lasts

(a) more than 2080 hours

(b) less than 1960 hours

(c) between 1948 and 2012 hours.

(ii) For how long would you expect

(a) 95% of the components to last

(b) 50% of the components to last

(c) 40% of the components to last?

7 The length of a component is Normally distributed with a standard deviation of 2 cm. 12% of the components are longer than 14 cm.

(i) Calculate the mean length of the components.

(ii) Find the percentage of components that are longer than 13 cm.

8 The times taken by a train to travel between two stations are Normally distributed with a standard deviation of 3 minutes. It is found that 10% of times are less than 13 minutes.

(i) Find the mean time taken.

(ii) Calculate the percentage of times that are longer than 18 minutes.

9 The weight of the contents of a jar is known to be Normally distributed. 12% weigh more than 508 g and 20% weigh more than 502 g. Find the mean and standard deviation of the weights.

10 Assume that the lifetime of a certain type of light bulb can be modelled by the Normal distribution. It is found that 6% of the bulbs last for more than 1100 hours and 14% for less than 970 hours. What are the mean and standard deviation of the lifetime of this type of bulb?

11 A high jumper estimates that he can clear 1.70 m nine times out of ten but can only clear 1.90 m three times out of ten. You can assume that the heights he jumps are Normally distributed.

(i) What is the mean height?

(ii) What height can he expect to clear only once in ten attempts?

12 The quartiles of a Normal distribution are known to be 11 and 19. Find the mean and variance of the distribution.

13 The heights of men are known to be Normally distributed with a standard deviation of 3 cm. The top 20%, with heights over 190 cm, are eligible for the police force.

(i) Find the mean height of men.

(ii) For those who are eligible for the police force, find the proportion whose height is over 195 cm.

14 In a distant country an examination board pre-ordained that 20% of the entry should be given a Distinction, 40% a Merit, 30% a Pass and 10% Fail. In the actual examination the results were Normally distributed with a mean of 75 and a standard deviation of 10. Where should the boundary marks for the different grades be set?

15 My journey time to school each morning is Normally distributed with a mean of 25 minutes and a standard deviation of 4 minutes.

(i) I leave home at 8.00 am, and consider myself late if I arrive after 8.30 am. Calculate the probability of my being late.

(ii) By what time should I leave so that I am late on at most one day in 50? Give your answer to the nearest minute.

[MEI, *adapted*]

16 From a large sample of bars of soap produced by a machine it is found that the mean weight of the bars is 425.1 grams with a standard deviation of 1.6 grams. Assuming that the weights are distributed Normally, calculate the percentage of bars of soap produced by the same machine that will weigh

(i) less than 424 grams

(ii) not more than 425.5 grams

(ii) between 426 grams and 428 grams.

If an adjustment can be made to the machine which alters the mean but leaves the standard deviation unchanged, what should be the new mean weight if it is required that 95% of the bars of soap weigh less that 427 grams?

[MEI]

17 A factory produces a very large number of steel bars. The lengths of these bars are Normally distributed with 33% of them measuring 20.06 cm or more and 12% of them measuring 20.02 cm or less.

Write down two simultaneous equations for the mean and standard deviation of the distribution and solve to find values to 4 decimal places. Hence estimate the proportion of steel bars which measure 20.03 cm or more.

The bars are acceptable if they measure between 20.02 cm and 20.08 cm. What percentage are rejected as being outside the acceptable range?

[MEI]

18 A farmer finds that his hens lay eggs which have a mean weight of 48 grams with a standard deviation of 4 grams. Eggs are specified as 'small' if they weigh less than 45 grams, 'medium' if they weigh between 45 grams and 52 grams, and 'large' if they weigh more than 52 grams. Assuming that the weights are distributed Normally, find the expected number of small, medium and large eggs in a batch of 1000 eggs.

After changing his chicken feed the farmer notices that there is a decrease of 10% in the number of large eggs produced by his chickens. Assuming that the standard deviation of the weights of the eggs has remained unchanged, calculate the new mean weight of the eggs and the percentage increase in the number of small eggs.

[MEI]

The sum and difference of Normal variables

AVONFORD STAR

Try your hand at rowing

The Avonford Rowing Club is running a fun event next Saturday, 17th June in order to encourage more people to take up rowing. They are looking for students who will take part in a 'mixed pairs' competition. There are three categories based on the combined weight of the two rowers.

(i) Heavyweight – combined weight greater than 130 kg
(ii) Lightweight – combined weight less than 115 kg
(iii) Middleweight – combined weight between 115 kg and 130 kg

For further information please contact the secretary, Adam Float on floata@arc.com by Wednesday, 14th June at the latest.

It is known that the weights of male and female students are both Normally distributed.
The male students have a mean weight of 66.5 kg and a standard deviation of 5.0 kg.
The female students have a mean weight of 55.5 kg and a standard deviation of 4.0 kg.
A 'mixed pair' is formed by randomly pairing a male student and a female student.

So far the problems in this chapter have involved a single Normal variable. How then do you cope with the combined weight of two students?

It is common sense that the mean of the combined weight is 66.5 kg + 55.5 kg = 122 kg.

What about the standard deviation of the combined weight?

As the standard deviation of the weights for the male and female students are 5.0 kg and 4.0 kg respectively, you might expect that you would also add the standard deviations to find the standard deviation of the combined weight, but you would be wrong. It is not the standard deviations that you have to add but the variances.

The variance of the combined weight is $5.0^2 + 4.0^2 = 41.0$.
So the standard deviation of the combined weight is $\sqrt{41.0} = 6.403$ kg.

This important result is summarised below.

If X and Y are two independent Normal random variables, where $X \sim \mathrm{N}(\mu_1, \sigma_1{}^2)$ and $Y \sim \mathrm{N}(\mu_2, \sigma_2{}^2)$, the resultant distribution is also a Normal distribution with

$$X + Y \sim \mathrm{N}(\mu_1 + \mu_2, \sigma_1{}^2 + \sigma_2{}^2).$$

In words, this is saying that the distribution for the sum of two Normal distributions is also a Normal distribution, with the mean being the sum of the means and the variance being the sum of the variances.

So, if the weights, in kilograms, of the male and female students are called X and Y respectively, then their combined weight, $X + Y$, will be Normally distributed with a mean of 122.0 kg and a standard deviation of 6.403 kg. That is, $X + Y \sim \text{N}(122.0, 6.403^2)$.

EXAMPLE 9.5

For the situation in the *Avonford Star* article, find the probability that a mixed pair will be in

(i) the heavyweight category
(ii) the lightweight category
(iii) the middleweight category.

SOLUTION

(i) For the heavyweight category the combined weight has to be greater than 130 kg.

For 130 kg, the standardised variable is $\dfrac{130 - 122}{6.403} = 1.249$.

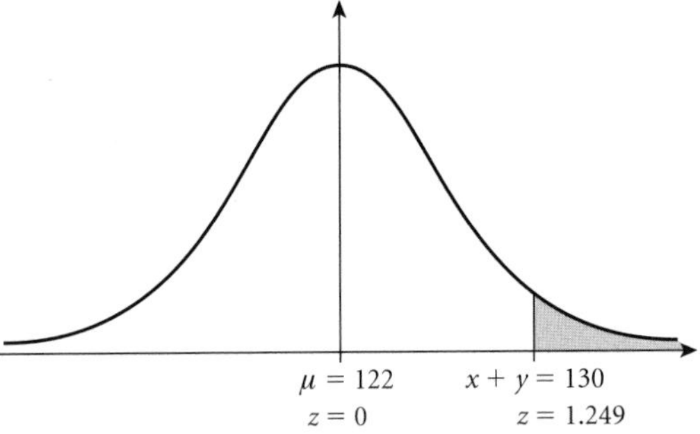

Figure 9.25

So the area required is $1 - \Phi(1.249)$
$= 1 - 0.8941$
$= 0.1059$

The probability that a mixed pair is in the heavyweight category is 0.1059.

(ii) For the lightweight category the combined weight has to be less than 115 kg.

For 115 kg the standardised variable is $\dfrac{115 - 122}{6.403} = -1.093$.

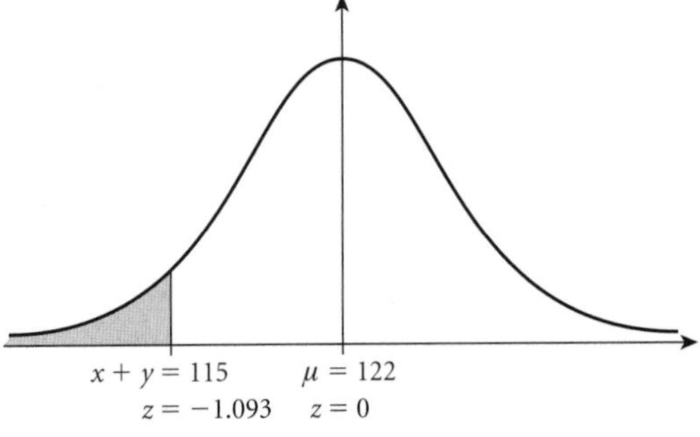

Figure 9.26

By symmetry, the area to the left of -1.093 is the same as the area to the right of 1.093.

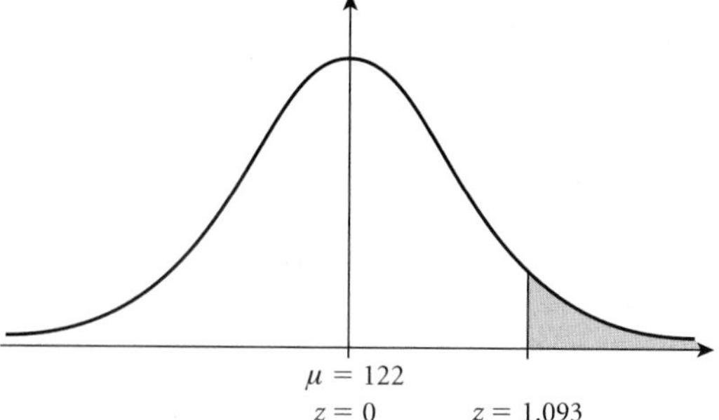

Figure 9.27

So the area required is $1 - \Phi(1.093)$

$= 1 - 0.8628$

$= 0.1372$

The probability that a mixed pair is in the lightweight category is 0.1372.

(iii) In order to find the probability that a mixed pair is in the middleweight category, think of the graph and use your previous results.

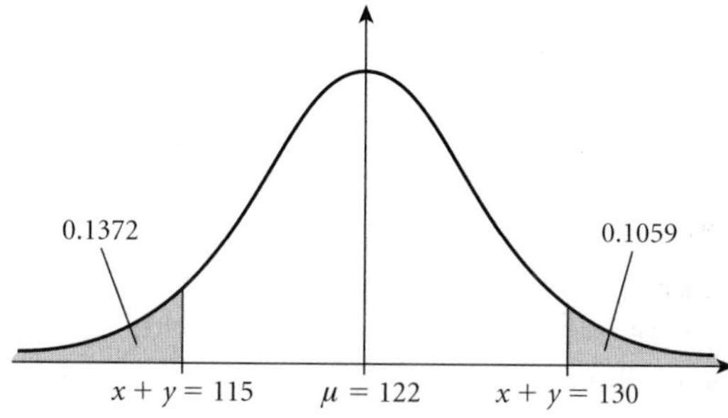

Figure 9.28

So the probability that the combined mass lies between 115 kg and 130 kg is $1 - 0.1372 - 0.1059 = 0.7569$.

? This is not a very satisfactory division into the three categories. A more even division would be to have 30% lightweight, 40% middleweight and 30% heavyweight. What boundary masses should you have in order to achieve this?

In the first part of this section you learned how to deal with the sum of two Normal variables. Now you will see what to do when you have the difference of two Normal variables.

It is common sense that the mean of the difference of two Normal variables is the difference of the means of the two distributions. Then, as with the sum of two Normal variables, you must add the variances of the two distributions.

When you had the sum of two Normal variables you added the variances, so you might expect that when you are dealing with the difference of two Normal variables you would subtract the variances. This cannot be correct as it may lead to a negative value for the variance, which is not possible.

This result is summarised below.

If X and Y are two independent Normal random variables, where $X \sim \mathrm{N}(\mu_1, \sigma_1^2)$ and $Y \sim \mathrm{N}(\mu_2, \sigma_2^2)$, the resultant distribution is also a Normal distribution with

$$X - Y \sim \mathrm{N}(\mu_1 - \mu_2, \sigma_1^2 + \sigma_2^2).$$

In words, this is saying that the distribution for the difference of two Normal distributions is also a Normal distribution, with the mean being the difference of the means and the variance being the *sum* of the variances.

EXAMPLE 9.6

A joiner buys pieces of timber. The lengths are Normally distributed with a mean of 200 cm and a standard deviation of 3 cm. The pieces he cuts from them have a mean length of 160 cm and a standard deviation of 4 cm. These lengths are also Normally distributed. The discarded pieces are called 'off cuts'.

(i) What are the mean and standard deviation of the off cuts?
(ii) What is the probability that an off cut will be at least 45 cm long?
(iii) What is the probability that an off cut will have a length between 37 cm and 43 cm?

SOLUTION

(i) The mean length of the off cuts is $200 - 160 = 40$ cm.
The variance of the length of the off cuts is $3^2 + 4^2 = 25$.
So the standard deviation of the length of the off cuts is $\sqrt{25} = 5$ cm

(ii) For 45 cm the standardised variable is $\dfrac{45 - 40}{5} = 1$.

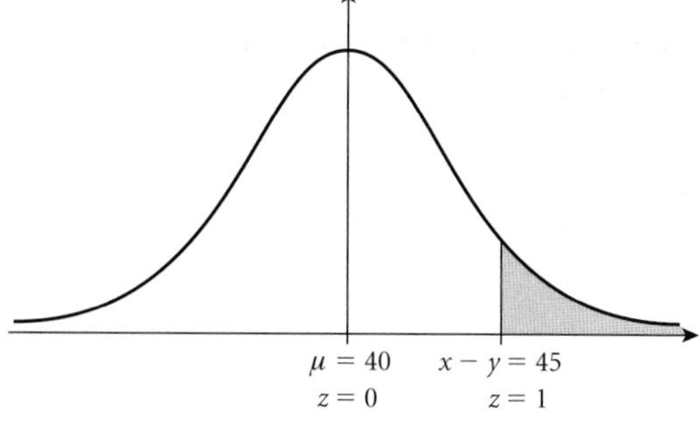

Figure 9.29

So the area required is $1 - \Phi(1)$
$= 1 - 0.8413$
$= 0.1587$

The probability that the length of an off cut is greater than 45 cm is 0.1587.

(iii) For 37 cm the standardised variable is $\dfrac{37 - 40}{5} = -0.6$.

For 43 cm the standardised variable is $\dfrac{43 - 40}{5} = 0.6$.

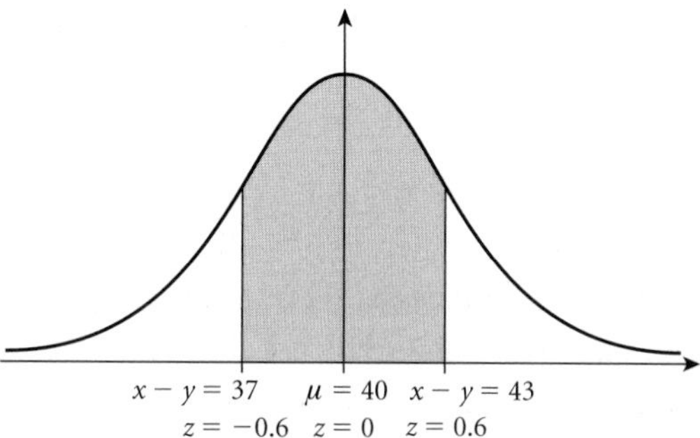

Figure 9.30

The required area is symmetrical about the mean and is twice the area between 0 and 0.6.
This is

$2 \times (\Phi(0.6) - 0.5)$
$= 2 \times (0.7257 - 0.5)$
$= 2 \times 0.2257$
$= 0.4514$

The probability that an off cut will have a length between 37 cm and 43 cm is 0.4514.

EXAMPLE 9.7

Bananas are transported in wooden boxes but, under health and safety regulations, there is a maximum permitted combined weight for bananas and box of 54 kg. The weight of the bananas is Normally distributed with a mean of 40 kg and a standard deviation of 4 kg and the weight of the boxes is Normally distributed with a mean of 5 kg and a standard deviation of 1.5 kg. What proportion of consignments are overweight?

SOLUTION

The mean weight of a consignment is $40 + 5 = 45$ kg.
The variance of the weight of a consignment is $4^2 + 1.5^2 = 18.25$.
So the standard deviation is $\sqrt{18.25} = 4.272$ kg.

The consignment will be overweight if the total weight of bananas and box is greater than 54 kg.

For 54 kg the standardised variable is $\dfrac{54 - 45}{4.272} = 2.107$

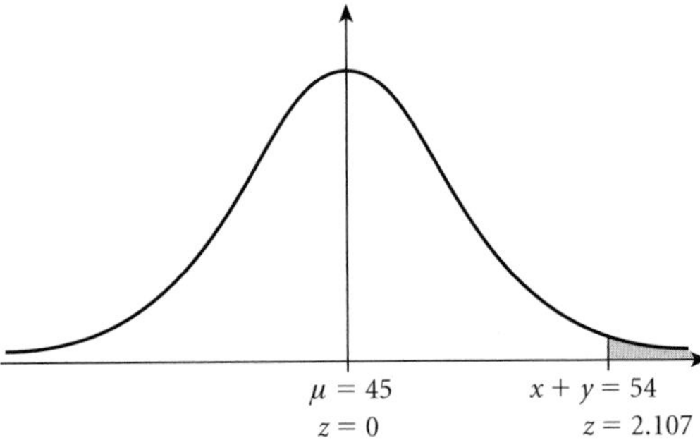

Figure 9.31

So the area required is
$1 - \Phi(2.107)$
$= 1 - 0.9824$
$= 0.0176$

1.76% of consignments will be overweight.

EXAMPLE 9.8

For my journey to work I can either use public transport or go by car. The times for the journey to work, T minutes for public transport and C minutes for car, have the following distributions: $T \sim \text{N}(26, 5^2)$ and $C \sim \text{N}(20, 3^2)$. What is the probability that public transport will be quicker?

SOLUTION

Public transport will be quicker when the difference in the times taken by public transport and car is negative.

The mean of the difference in the times of the journeys is $26 - 20 = 6$ minutes.
The variance of the difference in the times of the journeys is $5^2 + 3^2 = 34$.

So the standard deviation is $\sqrt{34} = 5.831$ minutes.

For 0 minutes the standardised variable is $\dfrac{0-6}{5.831} = -1.029$.

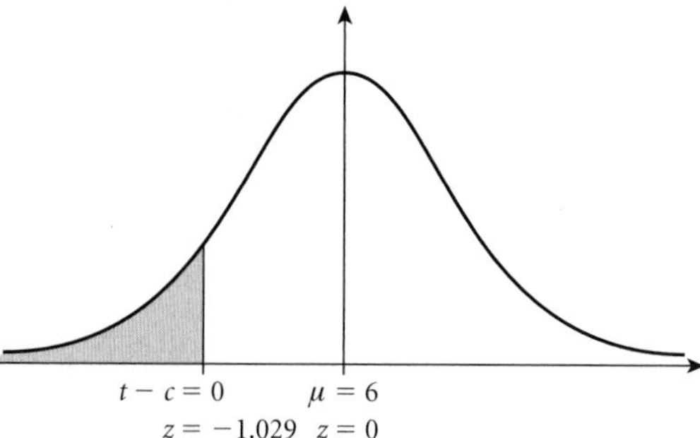

Figure 9.32

By symmetry, the area to the left of -1.029 is the same as the area to the right of 1.029.

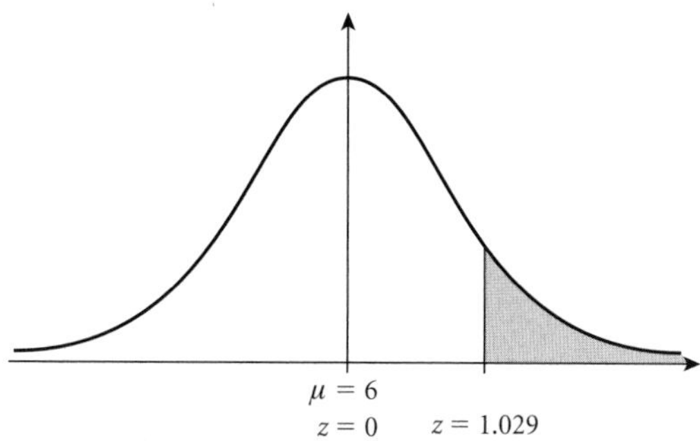

Figure 9.33

So the required area is $1 - \Phi(1.029)$
$= 1 - 0.8482$
$= 0.1518$

15.18% of the time it would be quicker to go to work by public transport.

e Using the Normal distribution for discrete variables

In Chapter 1 examples were given of *discrete variables*, such as the number of goals a football team scores, British shoe sizes, IQ scores and marks in a test, and *continuous variables*, such as distance, mass, weight and temperature. In this chapter on the Normal distribution all the examples and questions have involved variables that are continuous. The question arises 'Can the Normal distribution be used for questions involving discrete variables?'

The secret is to divide the continuous axis into discrete units as shown in figure 9.34.

Discrete		118		119		120		121		122		123		124	
Continuous	$117\frac{1}{2}$		$118\frac{1}{2}$		$119\frac{1}{2}$		$120\frac{1}{2}$		$121\frac{1}{2}$		$122\frac{1}{2}$		$123\frac{1}{2}$		$124\frac{1}{2}$

Figure 9.34

So, for example, a value of 120 is represented by $119.5 \leqslant x < 120.5$.

This is known as *using a continuity correction.*

EXAMPLE 9.9

The results of an intelligence test are Normally distributed with a mean of 100 and a standard deviation of 15.

(i) What is the probability that an IQ score is 120 or greater?
(ii) What is the probability that an IQ score is less than 84?

SOLUTION

(i) If an IQ score is 120 or greater, then $x \geqslant 119.5$.

For 119.5 the standardised variable is $\dfrac{119.5 - 100}{15} = 1.3$.

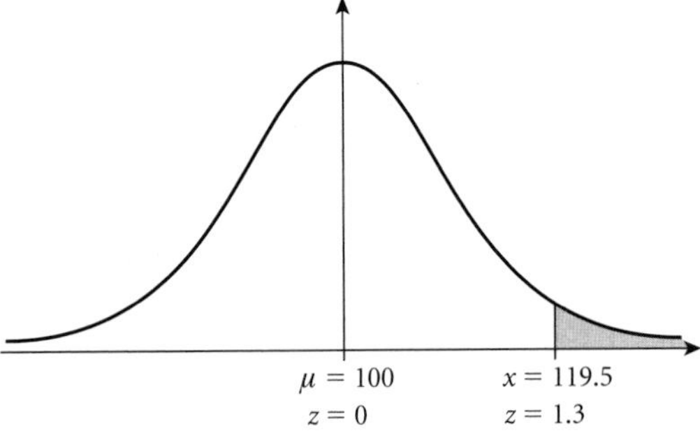

Figure 9.35

So the area required is $1 - \Phi(1.3)$
$= 1 - 0.9032$
$= 0.0968$

The probability that an IQ score is 120 or greater is 0.0968.

(ii) If an IQ score is less than 84, then, since 84 is *not* included, $x < 83.5$.

For 83.5 the standardised variable is $\dfrac{83.5 - 100}{15} = -1.1$.

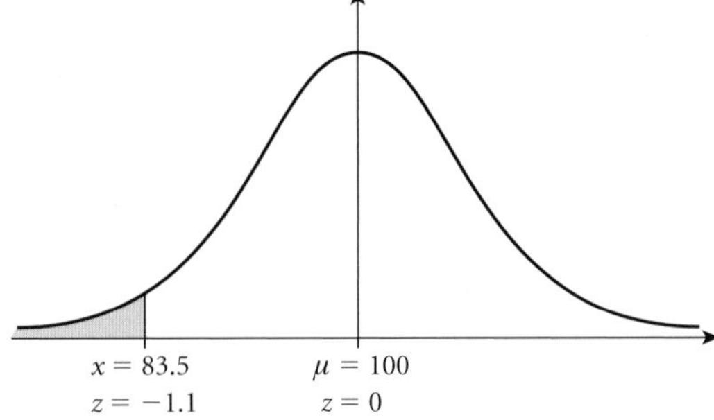

Figure 9.36

So the area required is $\Phi(-1.1)$
$= 1 - \Phi(1.1)$
$= 1 - 0.8643$
$= 0.1357$

The probability that an IQ score is less than 84 is 0.1357.

EXERCISE 9B

1 M and F represent the masses of male and female yellow-pine chipmunks. Both M and F are Normally distributed such that $M \sim \text{N}(54, 14)$ and $F \sim \text{N}(58, 10)$, where all masses are given in grams. One male chipmunk and one female chipmunk are chosen at random.

(i) Find the probability that the male chipmunk has a mass exceeding 56 g.
(ii) Find the probability that the female chipmunk has a mass exceeding 56 g.
(iii) Find the probability that their total mass is greater than 115 g.
(iv) Find the probability that the mass of the male chipmunk is greater than that of the female chipmunk.

2 At one stage in the manufacture of an article, a cylindrical rod with a circular cross-section has to fit into a circular socket. Quality control measurements show that the distribution of rod diameters is Normal with a mean of 5.01 cm and a standard deviation of 0.03 cm, while that of socket diameters is independently Normal with a mean of 5.11 cm and a standard deviation of 0.04 cm. If components are selected at random for assembly, what proportion of rods will not fit?

[MEI, *adapted*]

3 The mass of a camera and its case are both Normally distributed, the camera with a mean of 460 g and a standard deviation of 10 g and the case with a mean of 80 g and a standard deviation of 4 g. Find the probability that

(i) the total mass of the camera and case lies between 525 g and 550 g
(ii) the total mass of two cameras and their cases is under 1100 g.

4 The mass of a full can of drink may be taken to be Normally distributed with a mean of 250 g and a standard deviation of 8 g. The mass of the empty can may be taken to be Normally distributed with a mean of 35 g and a standard deviation of 3 g.

(i) What is the mean and standard deviation of the mass of the drink in the can?

(ii) What is the probability that two cans will provide you with at least 450 g of drink?

5 A machine is used to fill cans of soup with a nominal volume of 0.450 litres. Suppose that the machine delivers a quantity of soup which is Normally distributed with mean μ litres and standard deviation σ litres. Given that $\mu = 0.457$ and $\sigma = 0.004$, find the probability that a randomly chosen can will contain less than the nominal volume.

It is required by law that no more than 1% of cans contain less than the nominal volume.

Find

(i) the least value of μ which will comply with the law if $\sigma = 0.004$

(ii) the greatest value of σ which will comply with the law if $\mu = 0.457$.

[MEI]

6 Electronic sensors of a certain type fail when they become too hot. The temperature at which a randomly chosen sensor fails is T°C, where T is modelled as a Normal random variable with mean μ and standard deviation σ.

In a laboratory test, 98% of a random sample of sensors continued working at a temperature of 80°C, but only 4% continued working at 104°C.

(i) Show the given information on a sketch of the distribution of T.

(ii) Determine estimates of the values of μ and σ.

More extensive tests confirm that T is Normally distributed, but with $\mu = 94.5$ and $\sigma = 5.7$. Use these figures in the rest of the question.

(iii) Determine what proportion of sensors will operate in boiling water (i.e. at 100°C).

(iv) The manufacturers wish to quote a safe operating temperature at which 99% of the sensors will work. What temperature should they quote?

[MEI]

7 At a play centre parents pay a fixed fee and may leave their children for as long as they wish. The management's records show that the most common length of stay is 80 minutes, and that 25% of children stay longer than 90 minutes. The length of time a child stays appears to be reasonably well modelled by a Normal distribution.

(i) Show the information given on a sketch of the Normal distribution. Determine the mean and standard deviation of the distribution.

In the rest of the question assume that the mean length of stay is 80 minutes and the standard deviation is 15 minutes.

(ii) Calculate the probability that a child stays for more than 2 hours.

The management decide to introduce a closing time of 5.00 pm.

(iii) Explain why the proposed model could not now apply to children arriving at 4.00 pm.

(iv) Give the latest time of arrival for which you consider the model still to be reasonable. Justify your answer.

[MEI, *adapted*]

KEY POINTS

1 The notation used for a Normal random variable, X, with mean μ and standard deviation σ is $X \sim \mathrm{N}(\mu, \sigma^2)$.

2 The particular value, x, drawn from a Normal distribution with mean μ and standard deviation σ can be standardised to give the value z by using the transformation $z = \dfrac{x - \mu}{\sigma}$.

3 The area to the left of the value z in the diagram below, representing the probability of a value less than z, is denoted by $\Phi(z)$ and is read from the Normal distribution table.

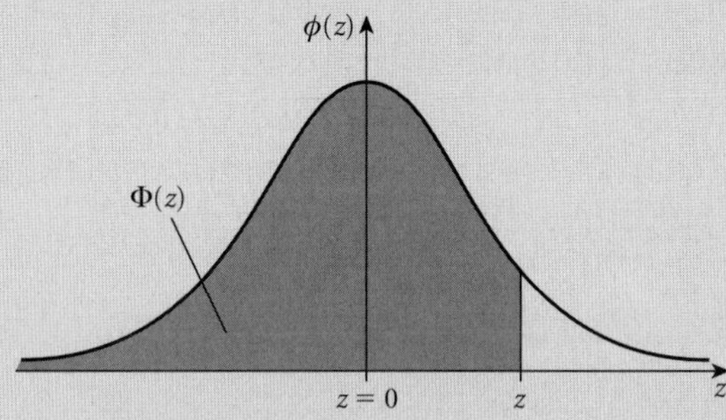

4 If X and Y are two independent Normal random variables, where $X \sim \mathrm{N}(\mu_1, \sigma_1^2)$ and $Y \sim \mathrm{N}(\mu_2, \sigma_2^2)$, then

- $X + Y \sim \mathrm{N}(\mu_1 + \mu_2, \sigma_1^2 + \sigma_2^2)$
- $X - Y \sim \mathrm{N}(\mu_1 - \mu_2, \sigma_1^2 + \sigma_2^2)$

that is, add or subtract the means as appropriate but add the variances in both cases.

10 The chi-squared test

Forty for you, sixty for me
And equal partners we will be.

Gerald Barzan

AVONFORD STAR

Choose your hospital ward carefully!

Statistics released today as part of the new government 'Clean Hospitals' initiative show that at Avonford Hospital your ward has a major effect on your chance of post-operative infection. If you are on the Lennon ward of Avonford's hospital, you are about four times as likely to suffer an infection within three months of being in hospital than if you are on the Starr ward. The McCartney and Harrison wards come in between these two.

	Ward			
	Lennon	**Harrison**	**McCartney**	**Starr**
Infection	14	8	7	4
No infection	217	175	153	245

Look at the figures. They speak for themselves. The percentage of patients getting an infection is a massive 6.1% for the Lennon ward compared to a mere 1.6% for the Starr ward.

Our advice to our readers: Don't let them put you in Lennon!

Do you think this is a responsible article?

To give a full answer to that question you will need to judge whether the differences between the figures are large enough to show likely underlying differences between the wards or whether they are just the sort of random fluctuations you expect in any statistical data.

You can investigate situations like this using the χ^2 test for association. (χ is the Greek letter '*chi*'; it is equivalent to our '*ch*' and you pronounce it '*ky*' as in '*Kylie*'.)

This example involved a sample of 823 of all the Avonford Hospital patients. The use of the χ^2 test depends on the assumption that the data have come from a random sample and this is taken to be the case in the work that follows.

The χ^2 test for association

The table in the article is called a *contingency table*. Two variables are recorded for each item of data, in this case the ward in which a person is placed and whether or not the person gets an infection. The contingency table in this example has 2 *rows* and 4 *columns* so it is a 2×4 table. It has 8 *cells*.

The null hypothesis for this test is that there is no association between the variables represented in the contingency table. The alternative hypothesis is that there is an association.

Setting up the hypothesis test

H_0: There is no association between the ward a patient is in and whether the patient gets an infection.

H_1: There is an association between the ward a patient is in and whether the patient gets an infection.

1-sided test

The χ^2 goodness of fit test is a 1-sided test.

Significance level: 5%

5% is a suitable significance level in this situation.

e In this book, the χ^2 test is described as 1-sided rather than 1-tailed. An explanation for this is given on page 480 in the answers.

Calculating the test statistic

The first step in calculating the test statistic is to work out the totals for each row and column in the contingency table. Make an extra row and column to record your answers.

	Lennon	Harrison	McCartney	Starr	Total
Infection	14	8	7	4	33
No infection	217	175	153	245	790
Total	231	183	160	249	823

This shows you that the overall proportion with an infection is $\frac{33}{823}$ and the overall proportion without an infection is $\frac{790}{823}$.

Since the number of patients who were in Lennon ward was 231, if the null hypothesis is true you would expect the numbers with and without infections to be as follows.

With infections: $\frac{33}{823} \times 231 = 9.26$ (to 2 decimal places)

Without infections: $\frac{790}{823} \times 231 = 221.74$ (to 2 decimal places)

These are called the expected frequencies and are denoted by f_e.

By contrast the observed frequencies, f_o, were 14 and 217.

It may seem strange, but do *not* round your expected frequencies to the nearest whole number. The observed frequencies will, however, naturally be whole numbers.

Now work out the expected frequencies for all the entries in the contingency table in the same way.

f_e	Lennon	Harrison	McCartney	Starr	Total
Infection	$\frac{33 \times 231}{823} = 9.26$	$\frac{33 \times 183}{823} = 7.34$	$\frac{33 \times 160}{823} = 6.42$	$\frac{33 \times 249}{823} = 9.98$	33
No infection	$\frac{790 \times 231}{823} = 221.74$	$\frac{790 \times 183}{823} = 175.66$	$\frac{790 \times 160}{823} = 153.58$	$\frac{790 \times 249}{823} = 239.02$	790
Total	231	183	160	249	823

The corresponding table for the observed frequencies was given in the article.

f_o	Lennon	Harrison	McCartney	Starr	Total
Infection	14	8	7	4	33
No infection	217	175	153	245	790
Total	231	183	160	249	823

The next stage is to work out $\frac{(f_o - f_e)^2}{f_e}$ for each cell in the contingency table.

$\frac{(f_o - f_e)^2}{f_e}$	Lennon	Harrison	McCartney	Starr
Infection	$\frac{(14 - 9.26)^2}{9.26} = 2.43$	$\frac{(8 - 7.34)^2}{7.34} = 0.06$	$\frac{(7 - 6.42)^2}{6.42} = 0.05$	$\frac{(4 - 9.98)^2}{9.98} = 3.58$
No infection	$\frac{(217 - 221.74)^2}{221.74} = 0.10$	$\frac{(175 - 175.66)^2}{175.66} = 0.00$	$\frac{(153 - 153.58)^2}{153.58} = 0.00$	$\frac{(245 - 239.02)^2}{239.02} = 0.15$

The test statistic, denoted by X^2, is the sum of the entries in all these cells.

$$X^2 = \sum_{\text{All groups}} \frac{(f_o - f_e)^2}{f_e}$$

$$= 2.43 + 0.06 + 0.05 + 3.58 + 0.10 + 0.00 + 0.00 + 0.15$$

$$= 6.37$$

Interpreting the test statistic

As with any other hypothesis test, the test statistic is compared with the critical value. Before you can find the critical value you need to find the *degrees of freedom*, denoted by ν, for the situation.

ν is the symbol for '*nu*', the Greek letter equivalent to our '*n*'; it is pronounced 'new'. Degrees of freedom are described in more detail in the next section of this chapter. For this type of test, ν is given by

$$\nu = (m - 1) \times (n - 1)$$

where m is the number of rows in the contingency table and n is the number of columns.

In this case $m = 2$ and $n = 4$, so

$$\nu = (2 - 1) \times (4 - 1)$$
$$= 3.$$

Tables for the χ^2 test show that, for 3 degrees of freedom and a 5% significance level, the critical value is 7.815. An extract from the χ^2 tables is shown below.

$p\%$ / ν	99	97.5	95	90	10	5.0	2.5	1.0	0.5
1	.0001	.0010	.0039	.0158	2.706	3.841	5.024	6.635	7.879
2	.0201	0.506	0.103	0.211	4.605	5.991	7.378	9.210	10.60
3	0.115	0.216	0.352	0.584	6.251	7.815	9.348	11.34	12.84
4	0.297	0.484	0.711	1.064	7.779	9.488	11.14	13.28	14.86
5	0.554	0.831	1.145	1.610	9.236	11.07	12.83	15.09	16.75

The χ^2 tables are given in columns with headings of values of $p\%$ of 99, 97.5, 95, 90 and then 10, 5.0, 2.5, 1.0, 0.5. You use one of the later columns, in this case the one headed 5.0, to find the critical value. The early columns are used in some other applications of the χ^2 distribution, including that described later in this chapter, on page 274.

If the test statistic is less than the critical value, the null hypothesis is accepted at that significance level. On the other hand, if the test statistic is greater than the critical value, the null hypothesis is rejected and the alternative hypothesis is accepted at that significance level.

In this example, since $6.37 < 7.815$, the null hypothesis is accepted.

The test suggests that there is no association between the ward a patient is in and whether the patient gets an infection. So a proper statistical analysis shows that the claims in the *Avonford Star* article are not justified.

? Which cell made the biggest contribution to the value of X^2 in this example? What does this tell you about the incidence of infections at Avonford Hospital?

The p value

An alternative way of interpreting this result is as a *p value.* As you can see in figure 10.1, the test statistic of 6.37 lies between the 10% critical value of 6.251 and the 5% critical value of 7.815. So the *p* value lies between 10% and 5%.

p value

$p\%$ / ν	99	97.5	95	90	10	5.0	2.5	1.0	0.5
1	.0001	.0010	.0039	.0158	2.706	3.841	5.024	6.635	7.879
2	.0201	0.506	0.103	0.211	4.605	5.991	7.378	9.210	10.60
3	0.115	0.216	0.352	0.584	6.251	7.815	9.348	11.34	12.84

6.37

Figure 10.1

The *p* value is the probability that the result, or one more extreme, would be obtained by chance if the null hypothesis is true. So the larger the *p* value, the more willing you are to accept the null hypothesis. In this case the *p* value is greater than the significance level set for the test and so the null hypothesis is accepted. Many statistics computer packages give you the actual *p* value. In this case it is 9.5%.

Cells with small expected frequencies

The χ^2 test can be unreliable in cases where the expected frequency, f_e, for one or more cells is small. A common rule-of-thumb is to say that the value of f_e for all cells should be at least 5. In tests for goodness of fit, which are covered later in this chapter, it is common to combine a cell for which f_e is less than 5 with a neighbouring cell so that their combined value of f_e is greater than 5. This, however, is not good practice for contingency tables; it may be possible to combine two categories or it may be that a larger sample is required.

e *Yates' correction*

The approximations that are always present in χ^2 tests begin to break down for contingency tables that are only of size 2×2. To help overcome this, some people suggest that, for 2×2 contingency tables the values of $f_o - f_e$ should be made less extreme by 0.5 when working out the test statistic.

So, 0.5 is subtracted from the positive values of $(f_o - f_e)$ and added to the negative values when working out the test statistic $X^2 = \sum_{\text{All groups}} \frac{(f_o - f_e)^2}{f_e}$. This is known as Yates' correction. It was first suggested by Frank Yates, a great statistician, in the 1930s. Yates' correction is never used for contingency tables that are bigger than 2×2.

Ideas underlying the χ^2 test

In the χ^2 test you compare expected frequencies, f_e, with observed frequencies, f_o. The differences are given by $(f_o - f_e)$. For theoretical reasons it is appropriate to consider the squares of these differences, $(f_o - f_e)^2$.

A problem arises with this measure in that it is not standardised; the larger the sample the larger the sum of these squared differences. This is overcome by dividing each value of $(f_o - f_e)^2$ by f_e. Summing the resultant quantities for all the cells, or groups, gives the test statistic

$$X^2 = \sum_{\text{All groups}} \frac{(f_o - f_e)^2}{f_e}.$$

The test statistic X^2 has a χ^2 distribution. The exact shape of the χ^2 distribution depends on the degrees of freedom but, for $\nu \geqslant 2$, the general shape is that illustrated in figure 10.2. The less well theory and observations match, the greater is the value of X^2 and the further to the right on the graph its location. In the diagram the value of X^2 is greater than the critical value, and so to the right of it, and the null hypothesis is rejected.

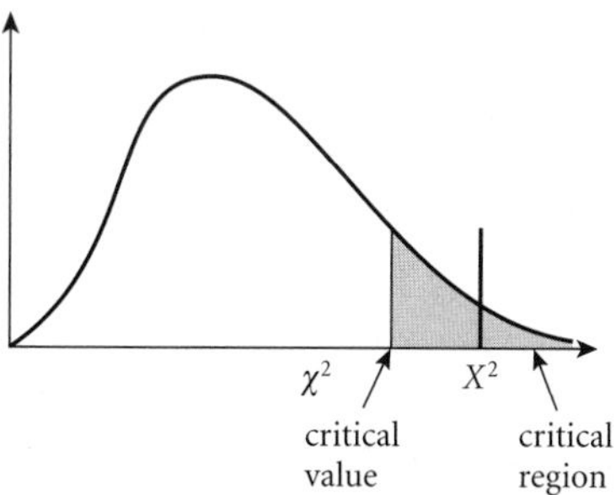

Figure 10.2 *The χ^2 distribution*

EXERCISE 10A

1 Two students investigate whether people are more likely to be helpful in a busy street or a quiet street. One of them drops a bag of apples at randomly selected times during the day and the other watches to see whether anyone helps by picking them up and returning them to their owner.

The results are as follows.

	Busy	Quiet
Helped	14	20
Not helped	10	6

Use a χ^2 test at the 5% significance level to see whether there appears to be any difference between the response of people in a busy street and in a quiet street.

2 A previously unknown species of bat is discovered in a remote cave. A random sample of 50 of the bats are collected for observation and then released. Some of them have stripes on their wings and others do not. The numbers of each sex with and without stripes are given in the table below.

	Stripes	No stripes
Male	16	4
Female	9	21

Test at the 1% significance level whether there is any association between a bat's sex and its having stripes.

3 A poultry breeder is concerned that many of her chickens' eggs are infertile. A friend suggests that their fertility rate will be improved if the chickens are given different living conditions instead of being confined to a small run. She carries out an experiment in which some of her birds are kept as before, others are allowed to roam free and a third group are put in a field full of cows. She keeps random samples of the eggs from the three groups separately and then places them in incubators for hatching. The results are as follows.

	In run	Roaming	With cows
Fertile	25	45	27
Infertile	29	10	6

Use a χ^2 test at the 0.5% significance level to investigate whether there is any association between the birds' living conditions and the fertility of their eggs.

4 Two drugs, A and B, can be used as treatment for a disease. In a trial, 80 patients were treated with one or other of the drugs and then reviewed one year later. The selection of the patients for the different treatments was made at random. The results are shown in the table below.

	Better	No change	Worse
Drug A	32	12	6
Drug B	7	10	13

Is there evidence, at the 5% significance level, of a difference in the effectiveness of the two drugs?

5 A group of parents claim that living close to electricity pylons increases the likelihood of asthma in children under 4 years of age. An investigation is carried out on a random sample of children, with the following results.

	Distance of home from pylons		
	Less than 1 km	**1–2 km**	**More than 2 km**
Asthma	9	16	8
No asthma	24	50	40

Does the study show evidence of association, at the 10% significance level, between childhood asthma and living near electricity pylons?

6 Avonford Council are discussing whether to introduce speed cameras on the roads leading into the town. Councillor Jones says 'It is a waste of time. Cars slow down for the camera and speed up again as soon as they have passed it.' Councillor Smith says 'They may speed up a little but not very much so overall people are safer.'

They agree to an experiment. Suitable locations for speed cameras are chosen on two similar roads into the town; a speed camera is put on one but not the other. Randomly selected cars are then observed 500 metres into town from the two locations. They are classified as 'Not speeding', 'Speeding mildly' or 'Speeding seriously'. The results are as follows.

	Not speeding	**Speeding mildly**	**Speeding seriously**
Speed camera	35	55	10
No speed camera	32	22	46

(i) Use the data to carry out a test, at the 0.5% significance level, of whether speed cameras do influence drivers' subsequent speed.

(ii) Which cells make the largest contribution to the test statistic? Comment.

7 Newspaper articles with the headline 'Too posh to push' have suggested that professional women are choosing to have their first baby by Caesarean section rather than have a natural birth. In a recent survey of attitudes of women pregnant with their first child, the following responses were given when a random sample of women were asked whether they would choose a Caesarean section rather than a natural birth.

	Caesarean	Don't mind	Natural birth
Non-professional	42	13	39
Professional	59	4	33

Is there evidence, at the 5% significance level, of association between the attitudes of women and their professional status?

8 The following results were obtained from a survey of attitudes to smoking in restaurants. The respondents were selected at random.

	Against	Don't mind	For
Current smoker	12	21	27
Ex-smoker	32	27	10
Never smoked	19	30	22

(i) Carry out a χ^2 test at the 5% significance level of whether there is association between the smoking habits of individuals and their attitude to smoking in restaurants.

(ii) Which category, current smoker, ex-smoker or never smoked, contributes the least to the value of X^2?

(iii) Which three cells contribute the most to the value of X^2?

(iv) What conclusions can you draw from the survey?

9 A survey is carried out into the lion populations in five different regions of Africa, designated A, B, C, D and E. The lions are classified as male, female or juvenile. Observations are carried out on random samples from these lion populations with the following results.

	A	B	C	D	E
Male	22	12	35	12	38
Female	56	15	60	29	92
Juvenile	35	24	40	15	81

Test whether the survey provides evidence, at the 10% significance level, of association between the composition of the lion populations and their locations.

Degrees of freedom

Jasmine is a psychology student. She is carrying out an experiment in which she asks a number of young men to choose ten adults at random and get them to fill in a questionnaire. Jasmine is not actually interested in the questionnaire. What she wants to know is whether her interviewers are more likely to select women than men. Here are some of her results. (Notice that this is not a contingency table.)

Experiment on young men
(Each one chooses 10 people to interview)

Interviewer	Female	Male
Andrew	6	4
Charles	3	7
Hanif	5	5
Sunny	7	3
Leroy	10	0
Edward	8	2
Kwame	7	3
Sanjay	6	4

? How many numbers has Jasmine written down?
Did she really need to write all of these numbers down?

The first interviewer on the list was Andrew and he chose six women. Since he interviewed ten people in all, you know that he must have chosen four men. Similarly for all the others; in fact Jasmine did not really need her right-hand column at all.

In this table the number of groups, k, is 16. However, only 8 of them are actually free because when you know them, you know the rest. This is described by saying that there are 8 *free variables in the system* or that there are 8 *degrees of freedom.*

ACTIVITY

Here is a 3 × 5 contingency table. The Total row and the Total column are also given.

	A	B	C	D	E	Total
P						100
Q						150
R						250
Total	80	120	140	100	60	500

Start putting numbers in the empty cells. How many numbers are you free to choose? How many do you not get a choice over?

What would the answers be for a contingency table with m rows and n columns?

The χ^2 test is used in a variety of situations, not just as a test for association in contingency tables. You always need to know the degrees of freedom. It is often helpful to use the equation

$$\text{degrees of freedom } (\nu) = \text{number of groups } (k) - \text{number of restrictions } (r).$$

In the example of Jasmine's students, each interviewer was required to carry out exactly ten interviews and in each case this placed a restriction on the numbers in the table. So there were eight restrictions, one for each interviewer. So in that case the equation

$$\nu = k - r$$

is $\quad 8 = 16 - 8.$

? In the Activity above you worked with a 3 × 5 contingency table. You should have found that there were 8 degrees of freedom. How many restrictions were there? How can you explain that number?

So far you have used the χ^2 test on contingency tables. The restrictions are the row and column totals. In the next section of this chapter the χ^2 test is used to test how well particular distributions fit observed data. This is called *testing for goodness of fit.* In some goodness of fit tests you need to use the data to estimate parameters, such as the mean, of those distributions. Each parameter that you estimate gives another restriction when you are working out the appropriate degrees of freedom. A table of degrees of freedom for different χ^2 tests is given later in this chapter, on page 274.

EXERCISE 10B

1 You are meeting a friend on a train and you know she has definitely got on it. The train has eight carriages.

(i) How many carriages must you be prepared to search to be certain of finding your friend?

(ii) How many carriages must you be prepared to search before you are certain which carriage your friend is in?

2 Sam is doing a probability experiment in his mathematics class. Here are the instructions.

> Take three coins and toss them together. Record how many heads you get. The answer will be 0, 1, 2 or 3. Do this 50 times and record your results.
>
> Then fill in a table like this one.

Number of heads	0	1	2	3
Frequency				

How many degrees of freedom are there when Sam fills in the table? Explain your answer.

3 Ruth, Serena and Tamara are told to roll a die 60 times each as part of a probability experiment. They have to fill in the frequencies in this table of results.

Number on die / **Frequency**	1	2	3	4	5	6	**Total**
Ruth							60
Serena							60
Tamara							60
Total							

They decide to talk instead and to invent some numbers to complete the table.

(i) How many empty cells are there in the table as shown?

(ii) How many numbers are they free to invent when they fill the cells?

(iii) How many numbers are they not free to invent when they fill the cells?

4 In a questionnaire, students are asked to rate a lecturer on a scale of 1 to 4.

Poor	1
Fair	2
Good	3
Excellent	4

The results are recorded in the frequency row in a table like this.

Score	1	2	3	4
Frequency				

In each of situations **(i)** and **(ii)**

(a) state how many of the cells can be filled in freely

(b) state how many restrictions there are

(c) describe the restrictions.

(i) 100 students fill in the questionnaire.

(ii) 100 students fill in the questionnaire and the average is 2.4.

INVESTIGATION

Look at this sudoku puzzle. When it is completed, each row, each column and each of the nine square blocks contains each of the digits 1, 2, 3, 4, 5, 6, 7, 8 and 9 exactly once. You can state this as three rules.

1 The same number may not appear twice in any row.

2 The same number may not appear twice in any column.

3 The same number may not appear twice in any of the square blocks.

	7	5	6					
9	8	2	4			5		
				5				
1								
5	9	3			6	2		1
	6		3				4	
3		8	5	2	9	7		
				8				4
7			1			3		

Source: *The Independent on Sunday*, 19/3/06

Use **only** these three rules to answer the following questions. (Experts at solving sudoku puzzles use other techniques as well as these rules.)

(i) How many numbers can you place in the following squares at the start of the puzzle?

(a) The top left square

(b) The middle square

(c) The bottom right square

(ii) How many degrees of freedom do you have for filling in each of the three squares in part **(i)**?

(iii) Find a square for which there are 7 degrees of freedom at the start of the puzzle.

(iv) A good sudoku player only fills in a square for which there is 1 degree of freedom. How many such squares are there at the start of this puzzle?

AVONFORD STAR

Snakes galore

Yesterday afternoon Jimmy Rawlings had to be rushed to Avonford Hospital after he inadvertently trod on a snake. A hospital spokesperson said this is the fourth case this year; 'There seems to be a spate of them and all from different parts of the region'.

Is this evidence, the Star asks, of global warming in the Avonford area?

Do you think it is a bit far fetched to use snake bites as evidence of global warming?

You would expect some random variation in the number of cases treated per year by a hospital and this year may just be one of those years that has more than usual. Before you can decide whether this is the case, you need a model for the probability distribution of different numbers of cases, and suitable data. A snake bite is a rare event in Britain and so you might well expect the number of cases to be modelled by a Poisson distribution.

Following the article in the *Avonford Star*, a doctor who has been carrying out research into the frequency with which different types of accidents are treated, writes in with the following data, covering the last 100 years.

Number of snake bites	0	1	2	3	4	5	6+
Observed frequency, f_o	31	34	20	9	4	2	0

The question then arises 'Is the Poisson distribution a reasonable model for these data?'. You can answer this by carrying out a χ^2 goodness of fit test, as follows.

Setting up the hypothesis test

H_0: The Poisson distribution is a good model.

H_1: The Poisson distribution is not a good model.

1-sided test

The χ^2 goodness of fit test is a 1-sided test.

Significance level: 5%

5% is a suitable significance level in this situation.

Calculating the test statistic

Since the parameter that defines the Poisson distribution is equal to its mean, the first step is to find the mean of the sample data.

$$\text{Mean} = \frac{(31 \times 0) + (34 \times 1) + (20 \times 2) + (9 \times 3) + (4 \times 4) + (2 \times 5)}{100}$$

$$= 1.27$$

For the Poisson distribution with parameter 1.27, the probabilities and expected frequencies for 100 years are as follows.

Number of snake bites	Probability	Expected frequency, f_e
0	$e^{-1.27} = 0.281$	28.1
1	$e^{-1.27} \times 1.27 = 0.357$	35.7
2	$e^{-1.27} \times \frac{1.27^2}{2!} = 0.226$	22.6
3	$e^{-1.27} \times \frac{1.27^3}{3!} = 0.096$	9.6
4	$e^{-1.27} \times \frac{1.27^4}{4!} = 0.030$	3.0
5+	$1 - (0.281 + 0.357 + 0.226 + 0.096 + 0.030)$ $= 0.010$	1.0

? The probabilities in this table have been worked out on a calculator and then rounded to 3 decimal places. What is the accuracy of the expected frequencies?

Cells with small expected frequencies

Notice that the expected frequencies for four snake bites and for five or more snake bites are both less than 5 and indeed come to less than 5 in total. When you are carrying out a χ^2 goodness of fit test, it is usual to combine cells to ensure that in each case the expected frequency is greater than 5. So the 3, 4 and 5+ groups are combined into one group; this is described as 3+ in the table below. The expected frequency of this group is 9.6 + 3.0 + 1.0 = 13.6 and the observed frequency is 9 + 4 + 2 = 15.

Number of snake bites	0	1	2	3+
Observed frequency, f_o	31	34	20	15
Expected frequency, f_e	28.1	35.7	22.6	13.6

You are now in a position to work out the test statistic $X^2 = \sum_{\text{All groups}} \frac{(f_o - f_e)^2}{f_e}$, as shown below.

Number of snake bites	0	1	2	3+
$\frac{(f_o - f_e)^2}{f_e}$	$\frac{(31 - 28.1)^2}{28.1}$ $= 0.299$	$\frac{(34 - 35.7)^2}{35.7}$ $= 0.0810$	$\frac{(20 - 22.6)^2}{22.6}$ $= 0.299$	$\frac{(15 - 13.6)^2}{13.6}$ $= 0.144$

So,

$$X^2 = \sum_{\text{All groups}} \frac{(f_o - f_e)^2}{f_e} = 0.299 + 0.081 + 0.299 + 0.144$$

$$= 0.823$$

Interpreting the test statistic

The next step is to compare the test statistic, $X^2 = 0.823$, with the critical χ^2 value.

To find the critical value, you first need to know the degrees of freedom. You know that

degrees of freedom (ν) = number of groups (k) − number of restrictions (r).

In this case, there are two restrictions.

- The total of the frequencies (100)
- The Poisson parameter (1.27)

There are four groups, so $\nu = 4 - 2 = 2$. There are 2 degrees of freedom.

The critical value for 2 degrees of freedom at the 5% significance level is found from the χ^2 tables. It is 5.991.

Since the test statistic, 0.823, is less than the critical value, 5.991, the null hypothesis is accepted. The Poisson distribution is indeed a good model for the incidence of snake bites in the Avonford area.

This example began with the *Avonford Star* article. In one year four people had suffered snake bites. The hypothesis test has shown that is reasonable to assume a Poisson distribution so you are now in a position to estimate the probability of the observed result, or a more extreme case, happening by chance. It is

1 − Probability of 0, 1, 2 or 3 snake bites

and so

$$1 - (0.281 + 0.357 + 0.226 + 0.096) = 0.040.$$

This is a probability of about $\frac{1}{25}$, so it is unusual but by no means impossible.

? Where did the figures, 0.281, 0.357, 0.226 and 0.096, in the calculation above come from?

? How could this analysis be set up as a hypothesis test? What would you conclude from such a test at the 5% significance level and at the 1% significance level?

In the situation described above the χ^2 test was used to investigate the goodness of fit of a Poisson distribution to a given data set. Similar χ^2 tests can be used for other distributions. In the next example the test is carried out to investigate the goodness of fit of a model in which the outcomes are in a given proportion and in Example 10.2 a binomial distribution is used.

EXAMPLE 10.1

Frequencies in a given proportion

A botanist is investigating a particular type of plant which can have red, pink or white flowers. She collects data from a random sample of 160 plants.

Flower colour	Red	Pink	White	Total
Frequency	20	69	71	160

She has a theory that the different colour flowers should occur in the ratio,

Red : Pink : White = 1 : 6 : 9.

Test, at the 5% significance level, whether her theory is consistent with the data.

SOLUTION

Setting up the hypothesis test

H_0: The different colour flowers occur in the ratio,
Red : Pink : White = 1 : 6 : 9.

H_1: The different colour flowers do not occur in this ratio.

1-sided test

Significance level: 5%

Calculating the test statistic

Since $1 + 6 + 9 = 16$, the fractions of the different colour flowers should, according to the null hypothesis, be $\frac{1}{16}$, $\frac{6}{16}$ and $\frac{9}{16}$. So the expected frequencies are calculated as follows.

Flower colour	Red	Pink	White
Expected frequency, f_e	$\frac{1}{16} \times 160 = 10$	$\frac{6}{16} \times 160 = 60$	$\frac{9}{16} \times 160 = 90$

The observed frequencies, f_o, are those given in the question.

Flower colour	Red	Pink	White
Observed frequency, f_o	20	69	71

So the test statistic is given by

$$X^2 = \sum_{\text{All groups}} \frac{(f_o - f_e)^2}{f_e}$$
$$= \frac{(20-10)^2}{10} + \frac{(69-60)^2}{60} + \frac{(71-90)^2}{90}$$
$$= 10 + 1.35 + 4.011$$
$$= 15.361$$

Interpreting the test statistic

In this situation there are three groups and one restriction (the total frequency of 160) so the degrees of freedom are given by

$$\nu = 3 - 1 = 2.$$

Notice that in this case you did not use the data to estimate any population parameter, as you did in the example about snake bites, so there are no further restrictions.

The critical value for the χ^2 test at the 5% significance level for $\nu = 2$ is 5.991.

Since the test statistic, 15.361, is greater than the critical value of 5.991, the null hypothesis is rejected. The evidence does not support the botanist's theory.

EXAMPLE 10.2

A binomial distribution

A medical researcher wants to decide whether a common medical condition runs in families (and so might have a genetic cause), or whether it occurs independently and with a fixed probability, p. He selects 200 sets of 6 closely related people at random and determines how many people in each set have the condition. The results are as follows.

Number in set with the condition	0	1	2	3	4	5	6	**Total**
Frequency	15	40	68	47	24	5	1	200

The researcher says that if the condition occurs independently and with a fixed probability, this distribution should be well modelled by a binomial distribution, and so he wishes to check whether this is indeed the case.

SOLUTION

Setting up the hypothesis test

H_0: The underlying distribution is binomial.
(The probability, p, has yet to be determined.)
H_1: The underlying distribution is not binomial.
1-sided test
Significance level: 5%

Calculating the test statistic

In order to work out the expected frequencies, you need to use the experimental data to calculate the probability, p.

The total number of people with the condition in the sample is

$$(15 \times 0) + (40 \times 1) + (68 \times 2) + (47 \times 3) + (24 \times 4) + (5 \times 5) + (1 \times 6) = 444.$$

The total number of people in the sample is $200 \times 6 = 1200$.

So the probability, p, is given by $p = \frac{444}{1200} = 0.37$.

Now you can work out the probabilities of the various outcomes, as follows.

Number with the condition	Probability, p
0	${}^6C_0 \times 0.63^6 = 0.0625$
1	${}^6C_1 \times 0.63^5 \times 0.37 = 0.220$
2	${}^6C_2 \times 0.63^4 \times 0.37^2 = 0.323$
3	${}^6C_3 \times 0.63^3 \times 0.37^3 = 0.253$
4	${}^6C_4 \times 0.63^2 \times 0.37^4 = 0.112$
5	${}^6C_5 \times 0.63 \times 0.37^5 = 0.026$
6	${}^6C_6 \times 0.37^6 = 0.003$

To find the expected frequencies, f_e, you multiply the probabilities by the total number of sets (each of six people), in this case 200.

Number with the condition	0	1	2	3	4	5 or 6
Expected frequency, f_e	12.5	44.1	64.7	50.7	22.3	5.8

? Why have the columns for 5 and 6 been combined?

The corresponding table of observed frequencies is

Number with the condition	0	1	2	3	4	5 or 6
Observed frequency, f_o	15	40	68	47	24	6

and so the test statistic, X^2, can now be calculated.

$$X^2 = \sum_{\text{All groups}} \frac{(f_o - f_e)^2}{f_e}$$

$$= \frac{(15 - 12.5)^2}{12.5} + \frac{(40 - 44.1)^2}{44.1} + \frac{(68 - 64.7)^2}{64.7} + \frac{(47 - 50.7)^2}{50.7}$$

$$+ \frac{(24 - 22.3)^2}{22.3} + \frac{(6 - 5.8)^2}{5.8}$$

$$= 1.456$$

Interpreting the test statistic

In this situation there are six groups and two restrictions: the total frequency of 200 and the estimated probability. So the degrees of freedom are given by

$$\nu = 6 - 2 = 4.$$

Notice that in this case you used the data to estimate one population parameter (the probability) and this provided the second restriction.

The critical value for $\nu = 4$ at the 5% significance level is 9.488.

Since 1.456 is less than 9.488 the null hypothesis, that the underlying distribution is binomial, is accepted.

In the binomial distribution the value of p is constant and so, in this case, does not vary from one family to another. The evidence does not support the hypothesis that the disease runs in families. Consequently a genetic link would not be expected.

? This example was about a medical researcher wanting to establish whether a particular condition ran in families and so had a possible genetic link. Describe the shape of distribution you would expect from this experiment if this were the case.

Goodness of fit tests for other distributions

The same general method is used for goodness of fit tests for other distributions. The main difference from one distribution to another is in terms of what population parameters you need to estimate and the effect on the degrees of freedom.

Thus, if you are testing for a Normal distribution, you need to estimate both the mean and standard deviation from the data, making two restrictions. A third restriction comes from the total number, so in that case $\nu = k - 3$.

The table below summarises the degrees of freedom appropriate to commonly used χ^2 tests.

Distribution	**Groups**	**Totals**	**Parameters needed**		**Total number of restrictions**	**Degrees of freedom, ν**
Specified proportion	k	1	0	–	1	$k - 1$
Binomial	k	1	1	p	2	$k - 2$
Poisson	k	1	1	λ	2	$k - 2$
Normal	k	1	2	μ, σ	3	$k - 3$
Contingency table, $m \times n$	$m \times n$	$m + n - 1$	0	–	$m + n - 1$	$(m - 1) \times (n - 1)$

Remember that the χ^2 test is an upper tail 1-sided test. Thus, if a test is at the 5% significance level, the critical region is on the right and represents the full 5%. Quite a common mistake is to make the 5% into two tails, each of $2\frac{1}{2}$%.

e Figures that match too well

AVONFORD STAR

Is Jemmy a fraud?

Over recent years, local man Jemmy 'Diceman' Turpin has often claimed to be able to throw dice with wonderful accuracy. Only last week, in the privacy of his own house, he threw a die 60 times. Jemmy says 'The perfect result would have been for each number to come up 10 times. I was off form; 1, 2, 5 and 6 all came up 10 times but 3 only came up 8 times and 4 came up 12 times.'

Now Avonford College student Angela Ghosh has challenged Jemmy to repeat his performance in public. 'Statistics don't work like that,' she says 'You expect more random variation.' The *Star* joins Angela in asking 'Is Jemmy a fraud?'

Suppose you apply a χ^2 test to Jemmy's results. The expected and observed results are as follows.

Score	1	2	3	4	5	6
Expected frequency, f_e	10	10	10	10	10	10
Observed frequency, f_o	10	10	8	12	10	10

The value of X^2 is given by

$$X^2 = \sum_{\text{All groups}} \frac{(f_o - f_e)^2}{f_e}$$

$$= \frac{(10-10)^2}{10} + \frac{(10-10)^2}{10} + \frac{(8-10)^2}{10} + \frac{(12-10)^2}{10} + \frac{(10-10)^2}{10} + \frac{(10-10)^2}{10}$$

$$= 0.8$$

There are six groups and only one restriction so there are 5 degrees of freedom. (In this case the frequencies are in a given proportion.)

Look at the line in the tables for $\nu = 5$. You can see that the value of 0.8 for X^2 lies in the left-hand part of the table, between 99% and 97.5%.

ν \ p%	99	97.5	95	90	10	5.0	2.5	1.0	0.5
1	.0001	.0010	.0039	.0158	2.706	3.841	5.024	6.635	7.879
2	.0201	0.506	0.103	0.211	4.605	5.991	7.378	9.210	10.60
3	0.115	0.216	0.352	0.584	6.251	7.815	9.348	11.34	12.84
4	0.297	0.484	0.711	1.064	7.779	9.488	11.14	13.28	14.86
5	0.554	0.831	1.145	1.610	9.236	11.07	12.83	15.09	16.75

0.8

Figure 10.3

While it does not prove that the data have been collected dishonestly, a value of X^2 in this part of the table should arouse suspicion. There are four possible explanations.

- The data have been invented.
- Data which do not fit well have been rejected.
- The data have been used to construct the theory and are then being used to confirm it.
- The data have been honestly obtained and just happen to fit very well.

Even if the data have been collected honestly, people will be disinclined to believe them if they fit so well. Repeating the experiment should remove such doubt. So Angela Ghosh, the Avonford student, is quite right to call for Jemmy to repeat his performance, and in public.

When a small value of X^2 arises, it does not mean that you can, or should, suddenly change from a goodness of fit test into one of whether the data were honestly collected. There is no such test. All it tells you is that it might be wise to check that the data collection was carried out satisfactorily.

EXERCISE 10C

1 A plant has two colours of flowers, blue and white. A botanist has a theory that the two colours should occur in the ratio 1 : 3. She collects data from a random sample of 80 flowers. 66 of them are white and the rest blue. She plans to carry out a χ^2 test to determine whether the data support her theory.

(i) Explain why there is 1 degree of freedom in this case.

(ii) Carry out the test at the 5% significance level, stating the null and alternative hypotheses and the conclusion.

2 A geneticist is studying a situation where there are three types of offspring, T_1, T_2 and T_3. In a random sample of size 70, there are 8 of type T_1, 26 of type T_2 and 36 of type T_3.

A simple model for this situation is that T_1 occurs with probability $\frac{1}{4}$, T_2 with probability $\frac{1}{2}$ and T_3 with probability $\frac{1}{4}$. Write down the appropriate expected frequencies. Test at the 5% level of significance the hypothesis that this model applies.

[MEI, *part*]

3 Peter and Jane are playing the well-known game 'Paper, Scissors, Stone'. Each player chooses one of them at random and they both reveal their choice at the same time. The rules are:

- Paper beats stone; stone beats scissors; scissors beat paper.
- If both players make the same choice, that round is a draw.

(i) Find the probabilities of the possible outcomes (Peter wins, Jane wins, there is a draw) in any round, if Peter and Jane both choose at random.

In a game of 30 rounds Peter wins 5 times, Jane wins 16 times and there are 9 draws. Jane claims that she can read Peter's mind and that is why she is so successful.

(ii) State null and alternative hypotheses relating to Jane's claim and carry out a suitable χ^2 test at the 5% significance level.

4 The numbers of emissions from a radioactive source in 1000 intervals, each of 10 seconds, are recorded using a Geiger counter.

Number of emissions	0	1	2	3	4	5	6	7	8	9	**Total**
Observed frequency, f_o	47	177	228	211	165	104	36	23	6	3	1000

(i) Find the mean and variance of these data. Comment on your answers.

(ii) Test at the 5% significance level whether the Poisson distribution, with the mean you found in part **(i)** as parameter, provides a suitable model for the data.

5 At the last general election, the Green Party candidate for the constituency of Avonford received 37% of the vote. An opinion poll is taken to determine whether there has been any change in the level of support for the Green Party in Avonford since the election. 400 people are selected at random for the poll and the results are as follows.

Number expressing support for the Green Party	166
Number expressing support for other parties	234

(i) Calculate the expected frequencies corresponding to the observed frequencies above on the assumption that that support for the Green Party has not changed.

(ii) Carry out an appropriate χ^2 test at the 5% significance level, stating clearly the null and alternative hypotheses under test and the conclusion reached.

6 A fruit farmer's apples are graded on a scale from A to D before sale. Lengthy past experience shows that the percentages of apples in the four grades are as follows.

Grade	A	B	C	D
Percentage	29%	38%	27%	6%

The farmer introduces a new treatment and applies it to a small number of trees to see if it affects the distribution of grades. The apples produced by these trees are graded as follows.

Grade	A	B	C	D
Number of apples	79	94	58	19

(i) Write down suitable null and alternative hypotheses for a χ^2 test.

(ii) Calculate the expected number of apples in each grade under the null hypothesis.

(iii) Carry out the χ^2 test at the 5% level of significance. State the conclusions of the test clearly.

[MEI]

7 A train-operating company collects data on the number of its trains that arrived at their final destinations more than one hour late. The monthly figures for each month in one calendar year are as follows.

J	F	M	A	M	J	J	A	S	O	N	D
6	10	8	4	6	9	13	16	11	23	17	9

(i) Carry out a χ^2 test at the 5% significance level to determine whether or not late running is more likely to occur in some months than others. (You may take all months to be of the same length.)

(ii) Which one of the following is likely to have been a major contributory cause to your answer to part **(i)**: overheating, frozen points, leaves on the rails?

8 The NRS social grade definitions are used to describe social class. A random sample of 400 residents of Avonford is taken and each person in the sample is assigned to one of the classes. The table below gives the numbers from the Avonford sample in the various classes together with the national percentages of people in the various classes.

Band	Number of people in sample, f_o	National percentage
A	23	3.4%
B	95	21.6%
C1	95	29.1%
C2	60	21.0%
D	65	16.2%
E	62	8.7%
Total	400	100.0%

(i) Find the expected frequency within each band in Avonford based on the national proportions.

(ii) Carry out a χ^2 test, at the 0.5% significance level, to investigate whether the class distribution in Avonford differs from the national one.

(iii) Comment on the Avonford distribution in the light of your conclusions.

9 It is said that the Poisson distribution provides a good model for the number of goals scored in football matches. The data below refer to the total numbers of goals in one season's matches of a football league.

Number	0	1	2	3	4	5	6	7	>7
Frequency	82	139	89	41	20	6	1	2	0

(i) Find the mean and variance of these data.

(ii) Test whether the Poisson distribution provides a suitable model for the data at the 5% significance level. (Use the mean that you found in part **(i)** as the parameter.)

A football enthusiast claims that it is well known that in the long term the mean number of goals per league game is 1.7.

(iii) Use the Poisson distribution with parameter 1.7 to draw up a frequency table for the expected number of goals.

(iv) Explain why the degrees of freedom are given by $\nu = k - 1$ and not $\nu = k - 2$ in this case.

(v) Carry out the test and comment on your conclusion.

10 A local council has records of the number of children and the number of households in its area. It is therefore known that the average number of children per household is 1.40. It is suggested that the number of children per household can be modelled by the Poisson distribution with parameter 1.40. In order to test this, a random sample of 1000 households is taken, giving the following data.

Number of children	0	1	2	3	4	5+
Number of households	273	361	263	78	21	4

(i) Find the corresponding expected frequencies obtained from the Poisson distribution with parameter 1.40.

(ii) Carry out a χ^2 test, at the 5% level of significance, to determine whether or not the proposed model should be accepted. State clearly the null and alternative hypotheses being tested and the conclusion which is reached.

[MEI]

11 A psychology researcher has a theory that men prefer to work in groups with other men and women prefer to work with other women. He conducts an experiment at a GCSE revision course attended by 180 students aged 15 or 16; most of them did not previously know anyone else attending. At one stage the students are asked to form into 36 groups each of 5 people to work together on a project. The psychologist counts the numbers of boys and girls in each group.

Group	5G 0B	4G 1B	3G 2B	2G 3B	1G 4B	0G 5B
Frequency	10	1	6	9	4	6

(i) Find the numbers of girls and boys on the course, and state the probability, p, that a randomly selected student is a girl.

(ii) Use the binomial distribution to find the frequencies you would expect in these groups if boys and girls joined groups at random.

The researcher is going to carry out a χ^2 test to see how well the binomial distribution models these data. He uses 2 degrees of freedom.

(iii) Explain how he comes up with this number.

(iv) Carry out the χ^2 test at the 1% significance level, stating the null and alternative hypotheses and the conclusion.

(v) The researcher claims that this shows that men and women really do not like working together. Explain why his claim may not be justified.

12 *Chiptech* produce computer chips for use in microprocessors. The quality control department regularly takes random samples of size 10 and notes the value of X, the number of faulty chips. The results for 100 such samples were as follows.

X	0	1	2	3	4	5	6	$\geqslant 7$
f	11	18	23	21	14	11	2	0

(i) Explain why X could reasonably be modelled by a binomial distribution.

(ii) Use the data to estimate p, the probability that a chip chosen at random will be faulty. Hence calculate the expected frequencies for the binomial model.

(iii) Carry out a suitable test, at the 5% significance level, to determine whether or not the model fits the data well.

(iv) Comment on the principal points of difference between the data and the model.

[MEI]

KEY POINTS

1. The χ^2 test can be used as a test for association and a test for goodness of fit.
2. The data are grouped.
3. In a goodness of fit test, if the expected frequency for a group is small, typically less than 5, it is usually combined with another group.
4. In the test for association, the groups are the cells of a contingency table.
5. In the test for association, the null hypothesis is that the variables are not associated; the alternative hypothesis is that they are associated.
6. In goodness of fit tests, the null hypothesis is that the distribution in question is the underlying distribution for the data, or provides a good model; the alternative hypothesis is that this is not the case.
7. The χ^2 test is a 1-tailed test.
8. The expected frequency, f_e, and the observed frequency, f_o, for each group are compared.
9. The test statistic is $X^2 = \sum_{\text{All groups}} \frac{(f_o - f_e)^2}{f_e}$.
10. Critical values are obtained from tables, for the appropriate significance level and degrees of freedom.
11. If the test statistic is less than the critical value, the null hypothesis is accepted.
12. The degrees of freedom for different situations are given in the table below.

Distribution	Groups	Totals	Parameters needed		Total number of restrictions	Degrees of freedom, ν
Specified proportion	k	1	0	–	1	$k-1$
Binomial	k	1	1	p	2	$k-2$
Poisson	k	1	1	λ	2	$k-2$
Normal	k	1	2	μ, σ	3	$k-3$
Contingency table, $m \times n$	$m \times n$	$m+n-1$	0	–	$m+n-1$	$(m-1)\times(n-1)$

11 Using the Normal distribution to interpret sample data

The proof of the pudding is in the eating.
By a small sample we may judge the whole piece.

Don Quixote

AVONFORD STAR

The Proposed Ring Road

Sir,

I was very surprised and rather annoyed at the report in last Thursday's *Avonford Star* which stated that in a recent survey '58% of the people in Avonford are in favour of the proposal to build a ring road to the north of the town'. Where did your reporter get these figures? Who was asked? I wasn't asked. Those of us who have businesses in the centre of town are dead against the proposal as it is bound to affect our trade. Let us have a proper debate about this proposal in which everyone has the opportunity to put their point of view and let us not be influenced by biased headlines such as last week's 'Majority favour ring road'.

Philip Butcher
Chair of Avonford Council of Trade

This letter raises a number of important questions.

- What was the question asked in the survey?
- How was the sample of people chosen?
- Was it a random sample?
- How large was the sample?
- How valid is it to make a statement about the views of the people of Avonford on the basis of a sample from the population?

This chapter takes up the last point and considers some of the conclusions that can be drawn from a random sample about the population itself.

In order to get a feel of what actually happens when you take a sample you should conduct the following experiment, preferably in a small group so that the work can be shared. It is a computer simulation of the throws of a fair six-sided die.

ACTIVITY

In this computer simulation you will need to generate the random numbers 1, 2, 3, 4, 5, 6. In EXCEL you can do this using the instruction INT(RAND()*6 + 1).

Here is the procedure for the simulation.

(i) Generate a random sample of size 5 and calculate the sample mean, $\bar{x}$. For example, if the sample generated is 4, 1, 5, 6, 2, the sample mean
$$\bar{x} = \frac{4+1+5+6+2}{5} = 3.6.$$

(ii) Repeat step **(i)** a further 999 times.

(iii) For the 1000 sample means you now have, find
- **(a)** the minimum value of the sample means
- **(b)** the maximum value of the sample means
- **(c)** the mean of the sample means
- **(d)** the variance of the sample means.

(iv) In order to investigate how the size of the sample affects the results, repeat steps **(i)** to **(iii)** with samples of size 10, 20 and 40. Present your results in the table like the one below.

Size of the sample (n)	**5**	**10**	**20**	**40**
Minimum value of the sample means				
Maximum value of the sample means				
Mean of the sample means				
Variance of the sample means				

? What do you notice about the mean and the variance of the sample means?

For an unbiased six-sided die $P(X = r) = \frac{1}{6}$ for $r = 1, 2, 3, 4, 5, 6$.

Using the results from Chapter 4,

$$\begin{aligned}\text{Mean: } E(X) &= \mu \\ &= \sum rP(X = r) \\ &= 1 \times \tfrac{1}{6} + 2 \times \tfrac{1}{6} + 3 \times \tfrac{1}{6} + 4 \times \tfrac{1}{6} + 5 \times \tfrac{1}{6} + 6 \times \tfrac{1}{6} \\ &= 3.5\end{aligned}$$

$$\begin{aligned}\text{Variance: } \text{Var}(X) &= \sigma^2 \\ &= E(X^2) - \mu^2 \\ &= \sum r^2P(X = r) - \mu^2 \\ &= 1^2 \times \tfrac{1}{6} + 2^2 \times \tfrac{1}{6} + 3^2 \times \tfrac{1}{6} + 4^2 \times \tfrac{1}{6} + 5^2 \times \tfrac{1}{6} + 6^2 \times \tfrac{1}{6} - (3.5)^2 \\ &= 2.917\end{aligned}$$

So, when an unbiased six-sided die is thrown, the mean of the population is 3.5 and the variance of the population is 2.917.

Before you continue, think about the conjectures you can make about the distribution of sample means from the following.

(i) Your tabulated results from the activity on page 283 (if you have not managed to complete the activity you will find a typical set of results in the answers at the back of the book)

(ii) The theoretical results for the mean and variance when an unbiased six-sided die is thrown

---

Here are some conjectures you may have suggested.

1 The larger the sample size (n), the smaller the range.

2 The means of the sample means are the same regardless of the size of the sample (so are independent of n).

3 The mean of the sample means is equal to the mean of the population.

4 The variance of the sample means is inversely proportional to n (so, for example, doubling the sample size halves the variance).

5 The variance of the sample means is approximately $\frac{1}{n}$ times the variance of the population.

You may find point **3** confusing as it involves three different 'means': the mean of the population which is usually denoted by μ, the sample mean which is often denoted by $\bar{x}$ and the mean of the sample means.
It is worth spending time sorting out in your own mind what each of these three means represents.

These five conjectures identify two of the three key elements of a very important theorem in statistics, called the *Central Limit Theorem*.

> The Central Limit Theorem states that, when a random sample of size n is drawn from a population with mean μ and variance σ^2, the distribution of sample means is approximately Normal with mean μ and variance $\frac{\sigma^2}{n}$.
>
> The larger the sample size, the more closely the distribution of sample means tends to the Normal distribution.

This is a surprising result, which is immensely powerful. It is fundamental to much of statistics. It is saying that for sufficiently large samples, the distribution of sample means is approximately Normal, *even if the distribution from which the sample has been drawn is **not** Normal.* The larger the sample size, the closer is the distribution to the Normal.

In the activity on page 283 your sample was drawn from a uniform distribution.

If you had drawn a graph of the sample means in your experiment you would have found that it was approximately Normal in shape – a remarkable result!

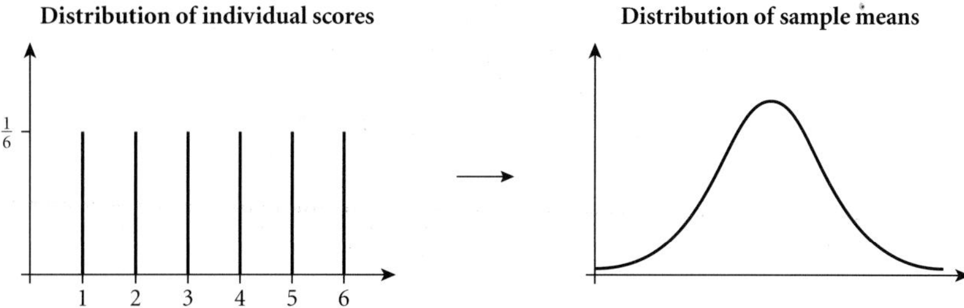

Figure 11.1

There are two important further points to note.

- When the parent population from which the sample is drawn has a Normal distribution, then the distribution of sample means is also a Normal distribution, even for small samples.
- As a rule of thumb, a sample of size 30 or more is considered a large sample and the distribution of sample means can be taken to be a Normal distribution.

Figure 11.2 shows the relationship between the parent population that is a Normal distribution with mean μ and variance σ^2, and the distribution of sample means for samples of size n. The standard deviation of the distribution of sample means, $\frac{\sigma}{\sqrt{n}}$, is known as the *standard error of the sample mean.*

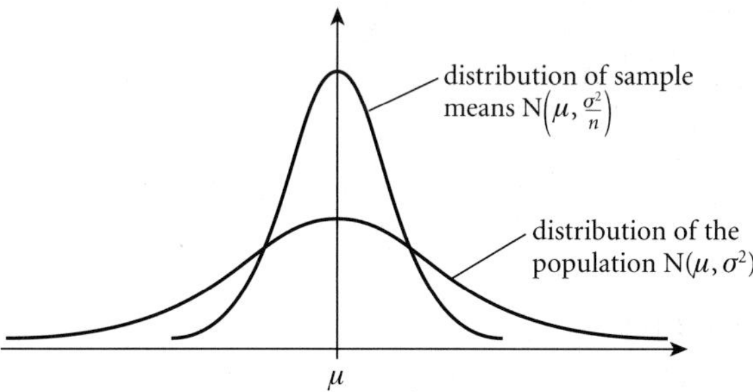

Figure 11.2

The distribution of the sample mean

EXAMPLE 11.1

The heights of 8-year-old girls are Normally distributed with a mean of 115 cm and a standard deviation of 5 cm, that is $N(115, 5^2)$.

(i) An 8-year-old girl is chosen at random. What is the probability that she is taller than 117 cm?

(ii) A random sample of 25 girls is chosen. What is the probability that the sample mean is greater than 117 cm?

SOLUTION

(i) For 117 cm, the standardised variable is $z = \dfrac{117 - 115}{5} = 0.4$.

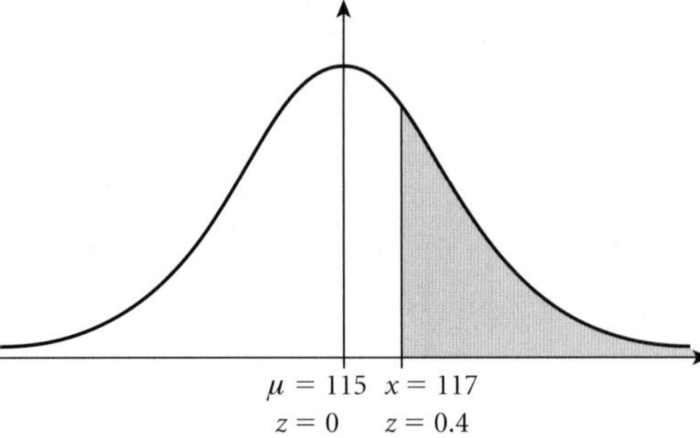

Figure 11.3

So the area required is $1 - \Phi(0.4)$

$= 1 - 0.6554$

$= 0.3446$

The probability that a girl selected at random is taller than 117 cm is 0.3446.

(ii) Since the parent population is Normal, the distribution of sample means for a sample of size 25 will be Normal with a mean of 115 cm and a variance of $\dfrac{5^2}{25} = 1$, so the standard deviation is 1.

For 117 cm, the standardised variable is $\dfrac{117 - 115}{1} = 2$.

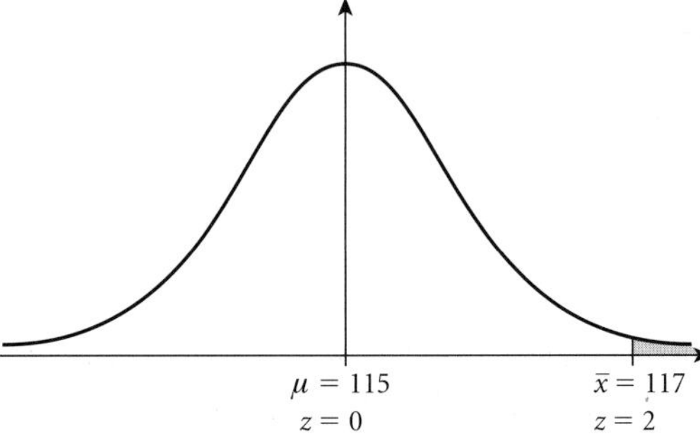

Figure 11.4

So the area required is $1 - \Phi(2)$

$= 1 - 0.9772$

$= 0.0228$

The probability that the sample mean is greater than 117 cm is 0.0228.

? Why are the answers to parts **(i)** and **(ii)** not the same?

EXAMPLE 11.2

The mean height, in inches, of adult men is 70 and the standard deviation is 4. What is the probability that the average height of a random group of 64 men will lie between 69 inches and 71 inches?

SOLUTION

You are not told anything about the distribution of the parent population in this question but, as a sample size of 64 is a large sample, the distribution of sample means is Normal with mean 70 and variance $\frac{4^2}{64} = 0.25$, so the standard deviation is 0.5.

For 69 inches the standardised variable is $\frac{69 - 70}{0.5} = -2$.

For 71 inches the standardised variable is $\frac{71 - 70}{0.5} = 2$.

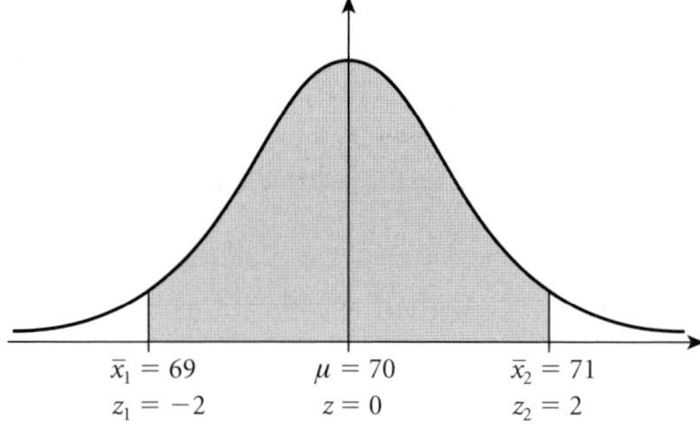

Figure 11.5

So the area required is $\Phi(2) - \Phi(-2)$
$= 2 \times \Phi(2) - 1$
$= 2 \times 0.9772 - 1$
$= 0.9544$

The probability that the average height of a random group of 64 men will lie between 69 inches and 71 inches is 0.9544.

A hypothesis test for the mean using the Normal distribution

One of the main applications of the Central Limit Theorem is in testing whether a given value for a population mean is consistent with the result obtained from a sample. This is known as a 'hypothesis test for the mean'. However it cannot be applied in every case. Certain conditions must hold if it is to be used. These are the key questions to consider.

- Is the sample large?
- Is the underlying population Normally distributed?
- Is the population variance known?

You can use this decision tree to decide which test to use.

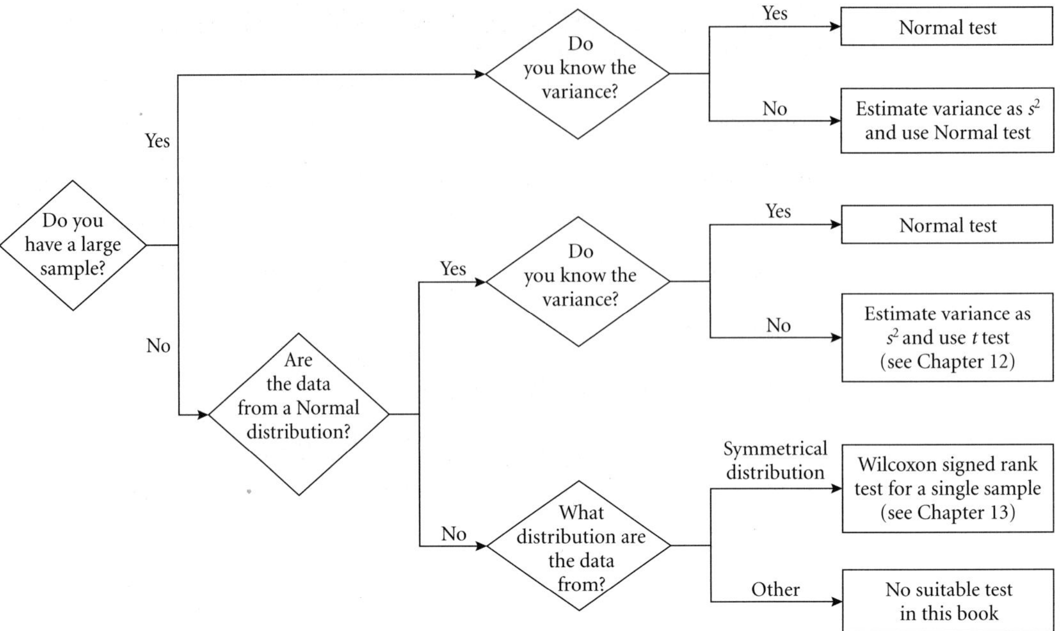

Figure 11.6

Note

As a rule of thumb, a sample may be considered as large if n is 30 or more. For a large sample the distribution of sample means can be taken as Normal, and the standard deviation of the sample as a good estimate of the standard deviation of the population.

EXAMPLE 11.3

A machine is set to produce rods of length L cm, with a mean of 10.6 cm and a variance of 0.8 cm^2. A quality control check on 50 rods produced a mean of 10.41 cm. Test, at the 5% significance level, if the machine setting is too low.

SOLUTION

Setting up the hypothesis test

H_0: $\mu = 10.6$ cm, the machine setting is correct.

H_1: $\mu < 10.6$ cm, the machine setting is too low.

Significance level: 5%

This is given in the question.

This is a 1-tailed test as you are investigating whether the setting is 'too low'.

Calculating the test statistic

50 items have been collected and the sample mean is 10.41 cm.

The population variance is known and the sample size is large, so the distribution of sample means, if the null hypothesis is true, is Normal with mean 10.6 and standard deviation $\sqrt{\frac{0.8}{50}}$, that is, $\overline{X} \sim \mathrm{N}\left(10.6, \frac{0.8}{50}\right)$.

For 10.41 cm the standardised value is $\dfrac{10.41 - 10.6}{\sqrt{\frac{0.8}{50}}} = -1.502$,

so the test statistic is -1.502.

Interpreting the test statistic

The significance level is 5% and it is a 1-tailed test, so the *critical value* is -1.645 since $\Phi(1.645) = 0.95$. This is shown in figure 11.7. The shaded region is called the *critical region.*

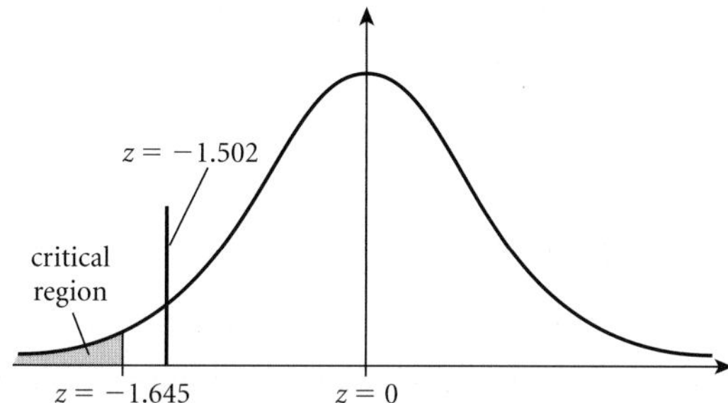

Figure 11.7

As -1.502 is greater than -1.645, the test statistic does not lie in the critical region, so the result is not significant. Therefore H_0 is accepted; the data indicate that the machine setting is correct.

In general

- If the value of the test statistic lies in the critical region, reject H_0.
- If the value of the test statistic does not lie in the critical region, accept H_0.

An alternative approach is to use *probabilities* instead of *critical values*, and so find the *p value.*

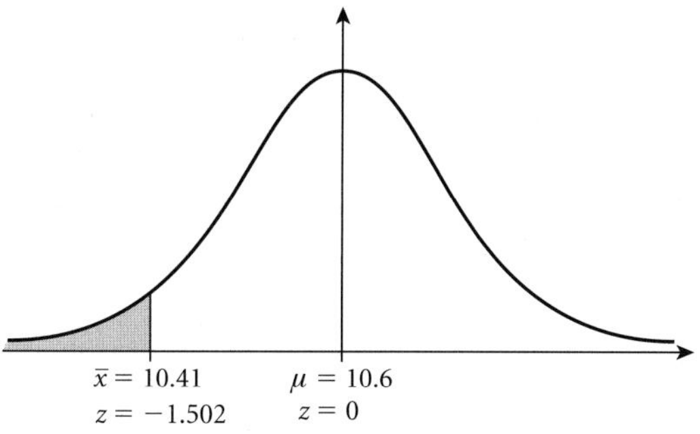

Figure 11.8

$$P(\bar{x} < 10.41) = \Phi(-1.502)$$
$$= 1 - \Phi(1.502)$$
$$= 1 - 0.9334$$
$$= 0.0666$$

This is the *p value.*

As 0.0666 is greater than 0.05, the result is not significant at the 5% level, so H_0 is accepted; the data indicate that the machine setting is correct.

EXAMPLE 11.4

Over a long period a long jumper has found that the lengths of his jumps have been Normally distributed with a mean of 5.76 m and a standard deviation of 0.36 m. After adopting a new technique the lengths of his next six jumps in competition were as follows.

5.66 m	5.86 m	6.09 m
5.55 m	6.15 m	5.97 m

Does this suggest, at the 10% significance level, that the new technique has made a difference to his performance?

SOLUTION

Setting up the hypothesis test

H_0: $\mu = 5.76$ m, there is no difference in his performance.
H_1: $\mu \neq 5.76$ m, the new technique 'has made a difference'.
Significance level: 10%

This is a 2-tailed test as the question asks whether the new technique 'has made a difference', so the athlete could either have improved or got worse.

Calculating the test statistic

Six jumps were recorded and the sample mean is 5.88 m.

As the sample has been drawn from a parent population which is Normally distributed with a known variance, the size of the sample does not matter. The distribution of sample means, if the null hypothesis is true, is Normal with a mean of 5.76 and a standard deviation of $\frac{0.36}{\sqrt{6}}$, that is, $\bar{X} \sim N\left(5.76, \frac{0.36^2}{6}\right)$.

For 5.88 m the standardised value is $\dfrac{5.88 - 5.76}{\frac{0.36}{\sqrt{6}}} = 0.816$,

so the test statistic is 0.816.

Interpreting the test statistic

The significance level is 10% and it is a 2-tailed test (5% at each end), the critical values are ± 1.645 since $\Phi(1.645) = 0.95$.

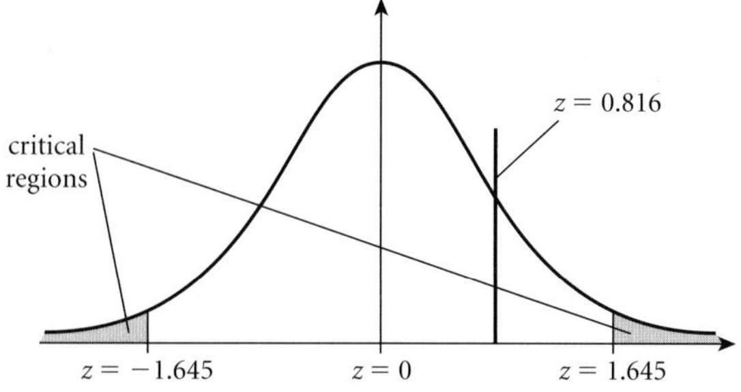

Figure 11.9

As 0.816 is less than 1.645, the result is not significant at the 10% level, so H_0 is accepted; the data indicate that there is no difference in performance.

Again, you can use the alternative approach of finding the *p value*.

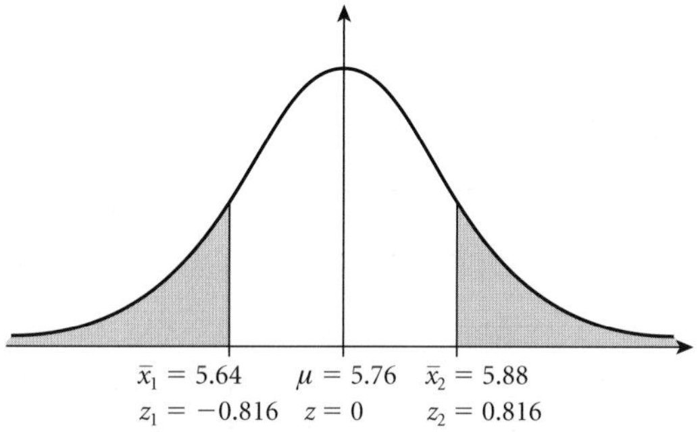

Figure 11.10

$$
\begin{aligned}
P(\bar{x} < 5.64 \text{ or } \bar{x} > 5.88) &= 2(1 - \Phi(0.816)) \\
&= 2(1 - 0.7927) \\
&= 0.4146
\end{aligned}
$$

So the *p value* is 0.4146.

As 0.4146 is greater than 0.10, the result is not significant at the 10% level, so H_0 is accepted; the data indicate that there is no difference in performance.

EXAMPLE 11.5

An intelligence test was designed to have a mean score of 100. A researcher put forward a theory that people are becoming more intelligent (as measured by this particular test). A random sample of 120 people was selected and given the test. The following is a summary of the results.

$$n = 120 \qquad \sum x = 12\,420 \qquad \sum x^2 = 1\,320\,675$$

Do these results support the researcher's assertion at the 5% significance level?

SOLUTION

Setting up the hypothesis test

H_0: $\mu = 100$, there is no change in the level of intelligence.
H_1: $\mu > 100$, people are becoming more intelligent.
Significance level: 5%

This is a 1-tailed test as you are investigating whether people are becoming more intelligent.

Calculating the test statistic

From the results given above you can calculate the mean and variance of the sample.

$$\bar{x} = \frac{\sum x}{n} = \frac{12\,420}{120} = 103.5$$

$$s^2 = \frac{\sum x^2 - n\bar{x}^2}{n-1} = \frac{1\,320\,675 - (120 \times 103.5^2)}{119} = 295.84$$

In this example you are not given any information about the distribution or the variance of the parent population. However, as the sample size is large you can

1 use the standard deviation of the sample as an estimate of the population standard deviation
2 use the Normal for the distribution of sample means.

So, the distribution of sample means, if the null hypothesis is true, is Normal with mean 100 and variance $\frac{295.84}{120}$, that is, $\bar{X} \sim \mathrm{N}(100, \frac{295.84}{120})$.

As the mean of the sample is 103.5, its standardised value is $\dfrac{103.5 - 100}{\sqrt{\dfrac{295.84}{120}}} = 2.229$, so the test statistic is 2.229.

Interpreting the test statistic

The significance level is 5% and it is a 1-tailed test, so the critical value is 1.645 since $\Phi(1.645) = 0.95$.

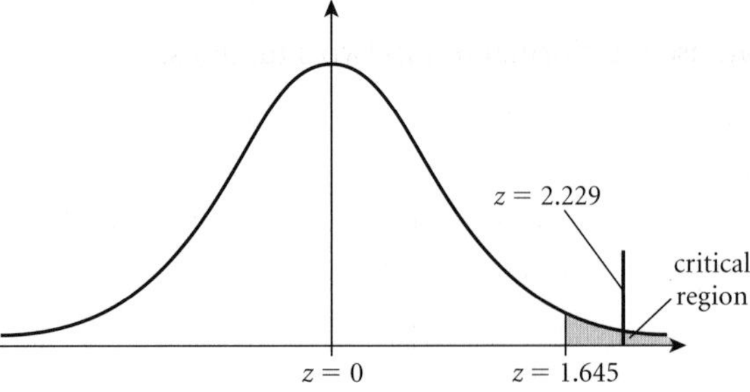

Figure 11.11

As 2.229 is greater than 1.645, the result is significant at the 5% level, so H_0 is rejected; the data suggests that people are becoming more intelligent.

The alternative approach based on finding the *p value* gives

$$\begin{aligned}P(\bar{x} > 103.5) &= 1 - \Phi(2.229)\\ &= 1 - 0.9871\\ &= 0.0129\end{aligned}$$

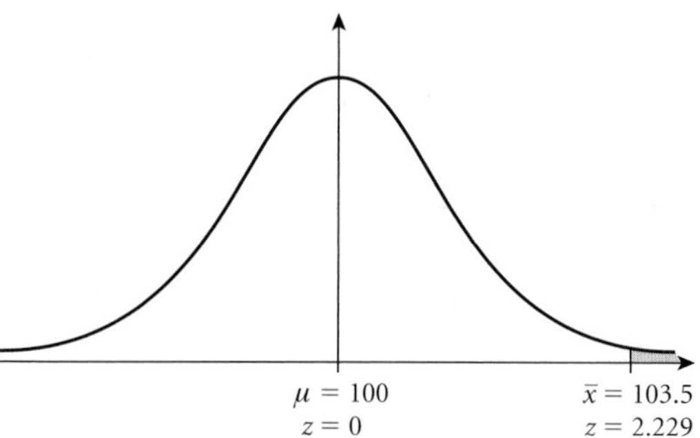

Figure 11.12

As 0.0129 is less than 0.05, the result is significant at the 5% level, so H_0 is rejected; the data suggests that people are becoming more intelligent.

Normal hypothesis test for the mean: summary

Firstly, a reminder that, as with other hypothesis tests, you take these steps.

1. Set up the hypothesis test.
2. Calculate the test statistic.
3. Interpret the test statistic.

Examples 11.3, 11.4 and 11.5 highlight several of the key features you need to consider when conducting a hypothesis test for the mean using the Normal distribution.

- The null hypothesis is H_0: μ = a given value.
- There are three possible choices for the alternative hypothesis, H_1.
  $\mu \neq$ the given value (2-tailed test)
  $\mu <$ the given value (1-tailed test)
  $\mu >$ the given value (1-tailed test)
- You can use the Normal test in two situations.
  1. When the sample size is large (n is 30 or more). If you do not know the population variance, you can estimate it as s^2.
  2. When the sample size is small *but* you know that the parent population has a Normal distribution *and* you know the population variance.

Note

In some books, hypothesis tests for the mean using the Normal distribution are referred to as '*z* tests'.

ACTIVITY

It is fairly easy to set up a graphic calculator to carry out a Normal test, displaying both the results and associated area under the Normal curve.

Use a graphic calculator to solve Examples 11.3, 11.4 and 11.5.

EXERCISE 11A

1 Over a long period it has been found that the lengths of metal rods produced by a particular machine are Normally distributed with a mean of 98 cm and a standard deviation of 6 cm.

(i) Find the probability that a single rod chosen at random will have a length

(a) greater than 96 cm

(b) less than 101 cm

(c) between 95 cm and 100 cm.

(ii) Find the probability that the sample mean from a sample of size 16 will have a length

(a) greater than 96 cm

(b) less than 101 cm

(c) between 95 cm and 100 cm.

2 A machine makes electrical resistors having a mean resistance of 50 ohms and a standard deviation of 4 ohms. Assume that the distribution of the resistances is Normal.

(i) Find the probability that a single resistor chosen at random will have a resistance

(a) less than 48.3 ohms

(b) greater than 51.2 ohms

(c) between 48.7 ohms and 49.7 ohms.

(ii) Find the probability that the sample mean from a sample of size 16 will have a resistance

(a) less than 48.3 ohms

(b) greater than 51.2 ohms

(c) between 48.7 ohms and 49.7 ohms.

3 The masses of individual chocolates are Normally distributed with a mean of 10 g and a standard deviation of 2 g. They are packed in boxes of 25.

(i) Find the probability that the mass of a particular chocolate lies between 9.5 g and 10.5 g.

(ii) Find the probability that the average mass of a chocolate in a box lies between 9.9 g and 10.1 g.

(iii) Find the probability that the total contents of a box have a mass between 247 g and 253 g.

4 The contents of bottles of Avonford Cream sherry are Normally distributed with a mean of 76 cl and a standard deviation of 2 cl. A sample of six bottles is taken. What is the probability that the average content of these bottles will be less than 75 cl?

5 For each of the following, a random sample of size n is taken from a Normal population with known standard deviation. The sample mean, $\bar{x}$, is calculated. Carry out hypotheses tests, given H_0 and H_1, at the significance level indicated.

	σ	n	$\bar{x}$	H_0	H_1	Significance level
(i)	7	20	117	$\mu = 120$	$\mu \neq 120$	2%
(ii)	5	10	57.8	$\mu = 55$	$\mu > 55$	5%
(iii)	6	15	56.5	$\mu = 60$	$\mu < 60$	1%
(iv)	9	25	204.2	$\mu = 200$	$\mu \neq 200$	1%

6 It has been found from experience that a particular type of thread has a mean breaking strength of 11.6 N and a standard deviation of 2.1 N. In a random sample of 36 threads, taken from a large batch of recently produced threads, the mean breaking strength was found to be 10.9 N. Test, at the 5% significance level, whether there has been a change in the breaking strength of this type of thread.

7 The masses of a group of adult students are known to be Normally distributed with a standard deviation of 3.6 kg. A sample of size 20 is taken and the mean found to be 65.4 kg. Test, at the 1% significance level, the null hypothesis that the population mean is 67.2 kg against the alternative hypothesis that the mean is less than 67.2 kg.

8 Over a number of years the mean mark in a standard test has been 70% with a standard deviation of 10%. This year 78 students took the examination and had an average of 68%. Does this suggest that these students are worse than expected?

9 The scores on an IQ test are known to be Normally distributed with a mean of 100 and a standard deviation of 15. A random sample of eight patients who are suffering from a particular disease had IQ scores of 119, 131, 95, 107, 125, 90, 123 and 89. Test, at the 5% significance level, whether the disease has affected their IQ scores.

10 A random sample of 100 ball bearings had a sample mean for the diameter of 14.66 mm and a standard deviation of 1.31 mm. Test, at the 2% level of significance, whether the mean diameter of the population of ball bearings is 15 mm.

11 The heights of adult women in England are Normally distributed with a mean of 63.2 inches and a standard deviation of 3.9 inches. A random sample of ten women from Lancashire has a mean height of 61.4 inches. The investigator wants to know whether, at the 5% level of significance, this provides sufficient evidence to say that the mean height of women in Lancashire is less than that for England overall.

(i) State the null and alternative hypotheses.
(ii) Calculate the test statistic.
(iii) Find the critical value for this test.
(iv) State whether the result is significant.

12 A manufacturer claims that the light bulbs he sells last for more than 900 hours. In order to test this claim, at the 5% significance level, the retailer takes a random sample of 40 bulbs and finds that the lifetime of the sample has a mean of 917 hours and a standard deviation of 65 hours.
(i) State the null and alternative hypotheses.
(ii) Calculate the test statistic.
(iii) Find the critical value for this test.
(iv) State whether the manufacturer's claim is justified.

13 Over a number of years the mean score in a statistics aptitude test given to first year biology undergraduates has been 65. In order to get some early information as to whether this year's intake was another average group, a keen lecturer gave the test to a random sample of 45 new students. These are the test scores.

84	59	79	39	78	79	75	85	45	83	76	52	73	86	38
41	59	64	73	61	79	48	79	71	69	42	63	65	81	58
90	53	71	65	72	59	61	70	73	62	57	55	66	80	50

(i) Calculate the mean and standard deviation of the data.
(ii) State suitable null and alternative hypotheses.
(iii) Carry out a hypothesis test, at the 5% significance level, stating your conclusion carefully.

14 The weights of steaks sold by a supermarket are distributed Normally with mean μ and standard deviation 0.02 lb. A quality control inspector tests the hypothesis that $\mu = 1$ lb at the 5% level of significance. He takes a random sample of five steaks whose weights (in lb) are:

0.977 1.014 0.989 0.972 0.968

His null hypothesis is that $\mu = 1$ lb and he performs a two-tailed test. State the alternative hypothesis and perform the test.

Another inspector is employed to check that customers are not (on average) sold underweight steaks. If he had conducted a 1-tailed test using the same random sample, the same level of significance and the same null hypothesis, what would have been his alternative hypothesis and his conclusion? [MEI]

15 A chemical is packed into bags by a machine. The mean weight of the bags is controlled by the machine operator, but the standard deviation is fixed at 0.96 kg. The mean weight should be 50 kg, but it is expected that the machine has been set to give underweight bags. If a random sample of 36 bags has a total weight of 1789.20 kg, is there evidence to support the suspicion?

(You must state the null and alternative hypotheses and you may assume that the weights of the bags are Normally distributed.) [MEI]

16 In a clinical trial a newly developed drug is administered to a random sample of 50 suitable patients. Give a reason why neither the patients nor the doctors should be told that the treatment is a new one.

The times to recovery, x days, are recorded and the results are summarised by $\sum x = 257, \sum x^2 = 1729$. It is known that the standard treatment gives a mean recovery time of 6.1 days. Stating clearly your null and alternative hypotheses, carry out a significance test at the 5% level to determine whether or not the new drug represents an improvement.

[MEI, *part*]

17 When watching games of men's basketball, I have noticed that the players are often tall. I am interested to find out whether or not men who play basketball really are taller than men in general.

I know that the heights, in metres, of men in general have the distribution $N(1.73, 0.08^2)$. I make the assumption that the heights, X metres, of male basketball players are also Normally distributed, with the same variance as the heights of men in general, but possibly with a larger mean.

(i) Write down the null and alternative hypotheses under test.

I propose to base my test on the heights of eight male basketball players who recently appeared for our local team, and I shall use a 5% level of significance.

(ii) Write down the distribution for the sample mean, $\overline{X}$, for samples of size 8 drawn from the distribution of X, assuming that the null hypothesis is true.

(iii) Determine the critical region for my test, illustrating your answer with a sketch.

(iv) Carry out the test, given that the mean height of the 8 players is 1.765 m. You should present your conclusions carefully, stating any additional assumption you need to make.

[MEI, *part*]

Confidence intervals for a population mean

For her sociology project Anna decided to investigate the number of television sets her fellow students have in their homes. She asked 40 students from the 1076 homes represented in her school to answer the question 'How many TVs do you have in your household?'. These are her results.

3	2	2	1	4	2	3	5	1	0	2	1	2	1	2	3	4	3	5	2
3	2	1	0	2	3	4	3	1	4	3	2	2	1	2	3	1	2	2	3

Nothing has been said about the sampling procedures. If these were not suitable then the data may be worthless and any resulting calculations and conclusions may be misleading.

The population in this investigation is the households represented by the students in the school.

Assuming that the data are valid

the sample mean, $\bar{x} = 2.3$
and the standard deviation, $s = 1.203$.

? Would you expect 2.3 be an accurate estimate for the mean number of TVs per household for the parent population?

? What would you expect to be the outcome if another student, Richard, also took a sample of 40?
What if there were a team of interviewers all taking samples of 40?

It was stated earlier in this chapter that for large samples, the distribution of sample means is Normal so you would expect that the distribution of sample means found by the interviewers might look like figure 11.13.

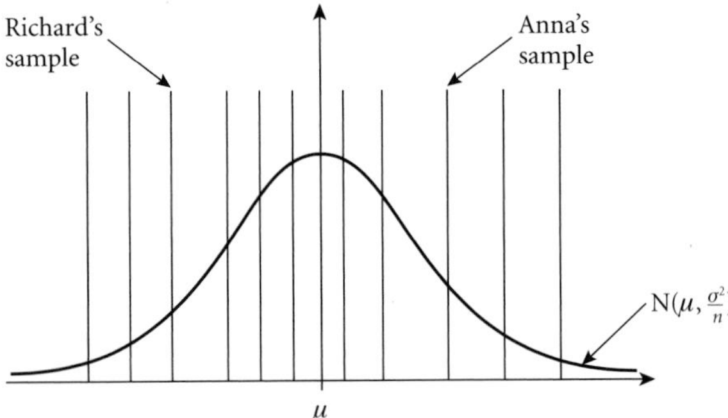

Figure 11.13

Probably the most common approach for estimating the mean of a population is to use the mean calculated from a sample. So Anna's estimate for the mean number of TVs per household would be 2.3. This is known as a *point estimate* for the mean of the population.

As different samples give different means and therefore different point estimates for the mean of the population, an alternative approach would be to try to find an *interval estimate* that hopefully would include the population mean. In Anna's project the sample mean is 2.3 so a starting point would be to use an *interval estimate* for the population mean centred on 2.3. The population mean, μ, would lie between (2.3 − 'a bit') and (2.3 + 'a bit'). This can be written as

$$2.3 - \text{'a bit'} < \mu < 2.3 + \text{'a bit'}.$$

Such an interval is called a *confidence interval.*

The size of the 'bit' part depends on how confident you want to be that your interval does include the true population mean, μ. If you want your interval to include the true population mean 95% of the time then you would need a wider interval than if you were happy with 90% confidence. For 95% confidence the 'bit' part would be bigger.

As standard deviation is a measure of spread, it would be natural for the 'bit' part to be a multiple of the standard deviation of the distribution of sample means $\frac{\sigma}{\sqrt{n}}$, so you can write the confidence interval as

$$\bar{x} - k\frac{\sigma}{\sqrt{n}} < \mu < \bar{x} + k\frac{\sigma}{\sqrt{n}}.$$

For the 95% confidence interval the value of k is 1.960 because $\Phi(1.960) = 0.975$.

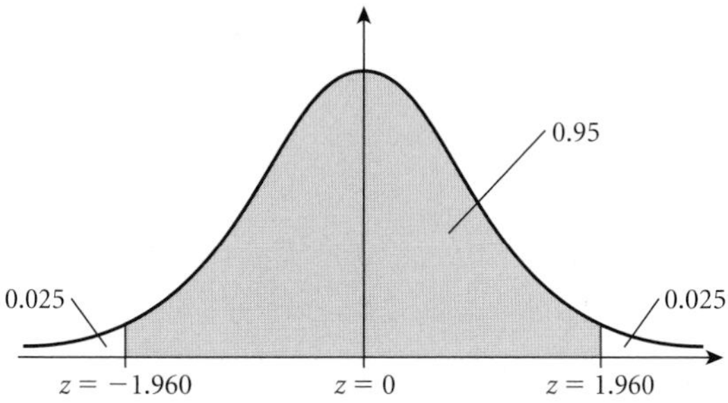

Figure 11.14

A 95% confidence interval is sometimes written using the set notation.

$$\left[\bar{x} - 1.960\frac{\sigma}{\sqrt{n}},\ \bar{x} + 1.960\frac{\sigma}{\sqrt{n}}\right]$$

The end-points of this interval are called the *confidence limits.*

You can state that, for 95% of samples, the interval $\left[\bar{x} - 1.960\frac{\sigma}{\sqrt{n}},\ \bar{x} + 1.960\frac{\sigma}{\sqrt{n}}\right]$ will contain the mean of the population, μ.

The statement above has been worded carefully and it is incorrect to express it as '95% of the time the population mean μ lies in the interval $\left[\bar{x} - 1.960\frac{\sigma}{\sqrt{n}},\ \bar{x} + 1.960\frac{\sigma}{\sqrt{n}}\right]$'.

If you took a number of samples of size n from the parent population and calculated the 95% confidence interval in each case you would end up with a diagram similar to figure 11.15. Notice that the population mean μ is a fixed but unknown value. Different samples will give rise to different confidence intervals.

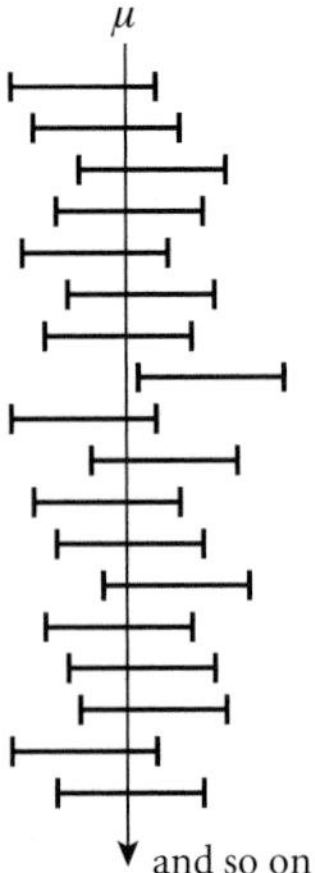

Figure 11.15

On average, 95% of the confidence intervals in figure 11.15 would include the true mean μ.

Similarly, confidence intervals for other percentages can be calculated using the appropriate value of k in the interval $\left[\bar{x} - k\frac{\sigma}{\sqrt{n}},\ \bar{x} + k\frac{\sigma}{\sqrt{n}}\right]$.

You have seen that k is 1.960 for the 95% confidence interval. Here are some other common values for k.

$k = 1.645$ for the 90% confidence interval
$k = 2.326$ for the 98% confidence interval
$k = 2.576$ for the 99% confidence interval

You will notice that the higher the percentage, the wider the interval.

You can give a confidence interval in the same two situations in which you can use a hypothesis test for a sample mean.

1 When the sample size is large (n is 30 or more). If you do not know the population variance, you can estimate it as s^2.

2 When the sample size is small *but* you know that the parent population has a Normal distribution *and* you know the population variance.

This chapter deals only with two-sided symmetrical confidence intervals, which are referred to simply as 'confidence intervals'. Confidence intervals do not need to be symmetrical and can be one-sided.

EXAMPLE 11.6

Use Anna's data on page 297 to calculate a 95% confidence interval for the number of television sets per household.

SOLUTION

The sample mean for the number of TVs per household, $\bar{x}$, is 2.3 and the standard deviation, s, is 1.203.

As the sample was large you can estimate the standard deviation of the population, σ, by using the standard deviation of the sample, s, that is, use $\sigma = 1.203$.

A confidence interval can be calculated as $\left[\bar{x} - k\frac{\sigma}{\sqrt{n}}, \ \bar{x} + k\frac{\sigma}{\sqrt{n}}\right]$.

In this case the sample mean, $\bar{x} = 2.3$.

The standard error of the mean, $\frac{\sigma}{\sqrt{n}} = \frac{1.203}{\sqrt{40}}$.

For the 95% confidence interval k is 1.960 because $\Phi(1.960) = 0.975$.

So the 95% confidence interval is from $2.3 - 1.960 \times \frac{1.203}{\sqrt{40}}$ to $2.3 + 1.960 \times \frac{1.203}{\sqrt{40}}$,

that is, from 1.93 to 2.67.

So, instead of giving a point estimate of 2.3 for the mean number of TVs per household, Anna would be better to give the 95% confidence interval [1.93, 2.67]. While she can have no confidence that 2.3 is correct for the population mean (though it may be close) she can know that the probability is 0.95 that the interval [1.93, 2.67] does include the true mean for the number of TVs per household.

EXAMPLE 11.7

A random sample of ten rods was taken from a Normal population with a standard deviation of 0.39 cm. These were the lengths of the rods.

12.6 cm	13.6 cm	12.3 cm	13.1 cm	12.9 cm
13.2 cm	12.6 cm	12.9 cm	13.4 cm	12.4 cm

Calculate the 98% confidence interval for the mean length of the population of rods.

SOLUTION

As the parent population has a Normal distribution the confidence interval is given by $\left[\bar{x} - k\frac{\sigma}{\sqrt{n}}, \ \bar{x} + k\frac{\sigma}{\sqrt{n}}\right]$.

In this case the sample mean, $\bar{x} = 12.9$ cm.

The standard error of the mean $\frac{\sigma}{\sqrt{n}} = \frac{0.39}{\sqrt{10}}$.

For the 98% confidence interval k is 2.326 because $\Phi(2.326) = 0.99$.

So the 98% confidence interval is from $12.9 - 2.326 \times \frac{0.39}{\sqrt{10}}$ to $12.9 + 2.326 \times \frac{0.39}{\sqrt{10}}$, that is, from 12.61 to 13.19.

EXAMPLE 11.8

The mean mass of a random sample of 50 bags of sugar was found to be 496 g with a standard deviation of 5.4 g. Find the 90% confidence interval for the mean mass of bags of sugar.

SOLUTION

You are not told anything about the distribution or variance of the parent population.

However, as the sample size is large you may use $\left[\bar{x} - k\frac{\sigma}{\sqrt{n}}, \bar{x} + k\frac{\sigma}{\sqrt{n}}\right]$ for the confidence interval, taking the standard deviation of the sample as an approximation for the standard deviation of the population, and so may use $\sigma = 5.4$ g and find k from the Normal distribution.

In this case the sample mean, $\bar{x} = 496$.

The standard error of the mean, $\frac{\sigma}{\sqrt{n}} = \frac{5.4}{\sqrt{50}}$.

For the 90% confidence interval k is 1.645 because $\Phi(1.645) = 0.95$.

So the 90% confidence interval is from $496 - 1.645 \times \frac{5.4}{\sqrt{50}}$ to

$496 + 1.645 \times \frac{5.4}{\sqrt{50}}$, that is, from 494.74 to 497.26.

Hypothesis testing and confidence intervals

There is a very close connection between hypothesis tests and confidence intervals. This is illustrated in the following example.

EXAMPLE 11.9

Assume that the masses of locusts are Normally distributed. The results from a random sample of 40 locusts gave a mean mass of 12.19 g and a standard deviation of 0.65 g.

(i) Find a 95% confidence interval for the mean mass of locusts.

(ii) Use your answer to part **(i)** to test, at the 5% significance level, that the mean mass of locusts is 12.0 g.

SOLUTION

(i) A confidence interval is given by $\left[\bar{x} - k\frac{\sigma}{\sqrt{n}}, \bar{x} + k\frac{\sigma}{\sqrt{n}}\right]$.

In this case the sample mean, $\bar{x} = 12.19$.

As the standard deviation of the population is not known but the sample is large, σ is approximated by s, so using $\sigma = 0.65$ the standard error of the mean, $\frac{\sigma}{\sqrt{n}}$ is $\frac{0.65}{\sqrt{40}}$.

For the 95% confidence interval, k is 1.960 because $\Phi(1.960) = 0.975$.

So the 95% confidence interval is from $12.19 - 1.960 \times \frac{0.65}{\sqrt{40}}$ to $12.19 + 1.960 \times \frac{0.65}{\sqrt{40}}$, that is, from 11.99 to 12.39.

(ii) H_0: $\mu = 12.0$, the mean mass of locusts is 12.0 g.
H_1: $\mu \neq 12.0$, the mean mass of locusts is not 12.0 g.

As 12.0 lies within the 95% confidence interval the result is not significant at the 5% level, so H_0 is accepted; the data indicates that the mean mass of locusts is 12.0 g.

Why does this work?

In the hypothesis test, the standardised value for 12.19 is $\dfrac{12.19 - 12.0}{\frac{0.65}{\sqrt{40}}} = 1.849.$

Since the significance level is 5%, the critical values are ± 1.960.

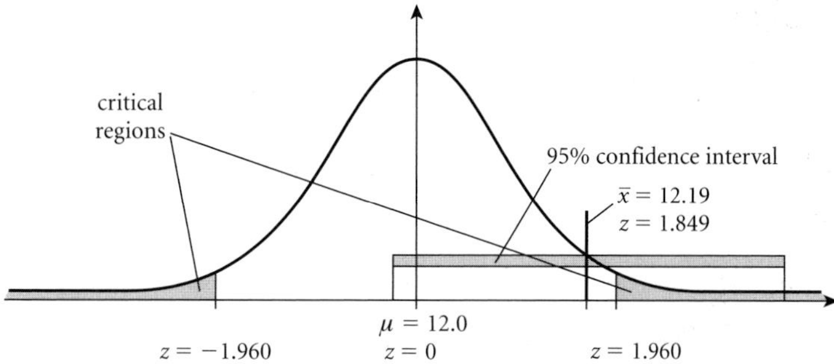

Figure 11.16

As 1.849 is less than 1.960, the result is not significant at the 5% level, so H_0 is accepted.

Alternatively you can express the 95% confidence interval in terms of the *z values.*

The confidence interval for *actual values* is

$$\left[12.19 - 1.960 \times \frac{0.65}{\sqrt{40}}, 12.19 + 1.960 \times \frac{0.65}{\sqrt{40}}\right]$$, that is [11.99, 12.39].

So the confidence interval for z values is $[1.849 - 1.960, 1.849 + 1.960]$, that is $[-0.111, 3.809]$.

You can see that $z = 0$ (which corresponds to $\mu = 12.0$) lies within this confidence interval.

In general,

- if the value being tested under H_0 lies *within* the 95% confidence interval then H_0 is accepted at the 5% significance level
- if it lies *outside* the 95% confidence interval then H_0 is rejected at the 5% significance level.

Notes

1 As this chapter is only dealing with two-sided symmetrical confidence intervals, the corresponding hypothesis tests have to be two-tailed.

2 The percentage level for the confidence interval and the percentage significance level for the associated hypothesis test always add to 100. For example, with a 90% confidence interval, the significance level for the hypothesis test is 10%.

EXERCISE 11B

1 A machine produces ball bearings whose masses are known to be Normally distributed with a standard deviation of 0.04 g. A random sample of ten ball bearings had a mean mass of 0.82 g.

Find these confidence intervals for the mean mass of the ball bearings.

(i) 95% **(ii)** 99%

2 Frozen peas are sold in bags, the weights of which are Normally distributed with a standard deviation of 4.8 g. These are the weights of seven bags chosen randomly.

283 g 279 g 282 g 297 g 289 g 273 g 301 g

Obtain these confidence intervals for the mean weight of a bag of frozen peas.

(i) 95% **(ii)** 97% **(iii)** 98%

3 The reaction times of international sprinters in athletics are known to be distributed Normally with a standard deviation of 0.044 seconds. When a random sample of 16 of these top athletes was tested, the mean reaction time was found to be 0.153 seconds. What are these confidence intervals for the mean reaction time for international sprinters?

(i) 80% **(ii)** 90%

4 The mean and standard deviation of the diameters of a sample of 80 rods manufactured by a company are 8.62 mm and 0.13 mm respectively. Find these confidence limits for the mean diameter of all the rods manufactured by the company.

(i) 90% **(ii)** 95% **(iii)** 99%

5 The times, in minutes, for a group of 50 eight-year-old children to perform a simple task are summarised as follows.

$$\sum x = 415 \qquad \sum x^2 = 3723$$

(i) Calculate the mean and standard deviation of the data.

(ii) Find a 95% confidence interval for the mean time to perform the task.

6 100 bags of dried fruit of a particular brand are weighed and the mean mass is found to be 523 g with a standard deviation of 8.5 g. Find these confidence intervals for the mean mass of bags of dried fruit of this brand.

(i) 90% **(ii)** 95% **(iii)** 97%

7 The 95% confidence interval for the mean mass of male first year university students is [66.9 kg, 68.1 kg], based on a sample of size 60.

(i) Find the value of $\bar{x}$, the mean of the sample.

(ii) Find the standard deviation, σ, of the population, assuming that the masses of the students are Normally distributed.

(iii) What is the 99% confidence interval for the mean mass?

8 A company makes fishing weights of a certain size with a standard deviation of 0.8 g. A random sample of 30 such weights has a mean of 12.6 g.

(i) Write down the 95% confidence interval for the true mean weight.

(ii) Is it likely that the true mean weight is 12.4 g? Justify your answer.

9 The label on a particular size of milk bottle states that it holds 1.136 litres of milk. In an investigation at the bottling plant, the contents, x litres, of 100 such bottles are carefully measured. The data are summarised by

$$\sum x = 112.4 \qquad \sum x^2 = 126.80$$

(i) Estimate the variance of the underlying population.

(ii) Provide a 90% confidence interval for the mean of the underlying population, stating the assumptions you have made.

(iii) A manager states that 'the probability that the population mean lies in the calculated interval is 90%'. Explain why this interpretation is wrong. Give the correct interpretation of the interval.

(iv) Use the calculated interval to explain whether it appears that the target of 1.136 litres in a bottle is being met.

[MEI]

10 The weights of coffee in tins used by the catering trade are distributed Normally with standard deviation 0.071 kg.

A random sample of n tins is taken in order to determine a symmetrical 99% confidence interval for the mean weight μ kg of coffee in a tin. How large should n be for the total width of this interval to be less than 0.05 kg?

In a separate investigation a random sample of 36 tins has a mean weight of 0.981 kg. Test at the 1% significance level the null hypothesis H_0 that $\mu = 1$, the alternative hypothesis H_1 being $\mu < 1$.

[MEI, *part*]

11 In an investigation concerning acid rain, a large number of specimens of rain water were collected at different times over a wide area. These may be considered as a large random sample. They were analysed for acidity and the readings for a standard measure of acidity are summarised by

$$\text{number of specimens} = 75, \qquad \sum x = 282.6, \qquad \sum x^2 = 1096.42$$

(i) Estimate the variance of the underlying population.

(ii) Provide a 90% two-sided confidence interval for the population mean acidity of the rain water.

[MEI, *part*]

12 Trials are being made of a simple device to reduce the amount of water used in each flush of a particular type of domestic lavatory. At an early stage of the investigation, the volumes x of water used in 200 flushes were measured (in litres); the data are summarised by

$$\sum x = 1964.0 \qquad \sum x^2 = 19\,311.60.$$

(i) Calculate an estimate of the variance of the underlying population.

(ii) Provide a 95% confidence interval for the mean of the underlying population, stating the assumptions you have made.

(iii) Give a clear interpretation of a 95% confidence interval.

(iv) Use your interval to discuss whether it is reasonable to suppose that the mean of the underlying population is

(a) 10 litres

(b) 9.8 litres.

[MEI]

13 The errors in the readings made on a measuring instrument can be modelled by the continuous random variable X which has a mean μ and standard deviation σ. If the instrument is correctly calibrated then $\mu = 0$.

In order to check the calibration of the instrument, the errors in a random sample of 40 readings were determined. These data are summarised by

$$\sum x = 120, \qquad \sum x^2 = 3285.$$

(i) Estimate σ^2.

(ii) Carry out a hypothesis test, at the 5% level of significance, to test whether the machine is, or is not, correctly calibrated. You should state your hypotheses and conclusions carefully.

(iii) Obtain a 95% confidence limit for μ.

[MEI, *part*]

1 The distribution of sample means

- The Central Limit Theorem states that when a random sample of size n is drawn from a population with mean μ and variance σ^2, the distribution of sample means has mean μ and variance $\frac{\sigma^2}{n}$. For large values of n, the distribution of sample means is close to the Normal distribution, $\bar{X} \sim N\left(\mu, \frac{\sigma^2}{n}\right)$.
- The standard deviation of the distribution of sample means, $\frac{\sigma}{\sqrt{n}}$, is known as the standard error of the mean.

2 Hypothesis testing

The key features of the hypothesis test for the mean using the Normal distribution, also known as the z test, are as follows.

- The null hypothesis is H_0: μ = a given value.
- There are three possible choices for the alternative hypothesis, H_1.
  $\mu \neq$ the given value (2-tailed test)
  $\mu <$ the given value (1-tailed test)
  $\mu >$ the given value (1-tailed test)
- You can use the Normal test in two situations.
  - When the sample size is large (n is 30 or more). If you do not know the population variance, you can estimate it as s^2.
  - When the sample size is small *but* you know that the parent population has a Normal distribution *and* you know the population variance.

3 Confidence intervals

- A confidence interval is calculated from sample data.
- The confidence interval for μ is $\left[\bar{x} - k\frac{\sigma}{\sqrt{n}}, \bar{x} + k\frac{\sigma}{\sqrt{n}}\right]$.
- You can give a confidence interval in the same situations in which you can use a hypothesis test for a sample mean (see above).
- The value of k for any confidence level can be found by using the Normal distribution tables.
- Commonly used values of k are
  1.645 for a 90% confidence interval
  1.960 for a 95% confidence interval
  2.326 for a 98% confidence interval
  2.576 for a 99% confidence interval.

12 Small samples and the t distribution

Small is beautiful. *E.F. Shumacher*

AVONFORD STAR

Local Butcher Charged

From our crime correspondent:
Local butcher, Adam Plunkett, 42, appeared before Avonford Court charged with selling pies which did not contain sufficient meat. The pies were advertised as containing at least 150 grams of meat each, but there have been complaints recently that his pies have been short of meat. The local trading standards inspector had visited the butcher's shop and made a detailed analysis of a random sample of ten pies. The inspector stated that the average weight of meat in the pies that he had inspected was 143 grams, which is under the advertised 150 grams. Mr Plunkett was heard to say, 'I don't know what all the fuss is about. Some are bound to be a bit over and some a bit under. Half the ones the inspector analysed were at least the right weight.' The case was adjourned for a week.

These were the weights, in grams, of the pies in the sample referred to in the article.

151 138 130 153 150 129 134 142 151 152

On the basis of this sample, do you think that there is enough evidence to convict Mr Plunkett?

Ideally you would like to be able to test the hypothesis, H_0, that 'the mean weight of meat is 150 grams' but the sample is small, just ten pieces of information.

What do you know?

- The sample mean, $\bar{x}$, is 143 g.
- The sample standard deviation, s, is 9.603 g.

*What do you **not** know?*

- The mean of the population, μ. (This is what is being investigated.)
- The standard deviation of the *population*, σ.
- The underlying distribution of the population.

Since this is a small sample you cannot assume that the standard deviation calculated from the sample will be close in value to the standard deviation of the population. You cannot, therefore, standardise the Normal variable using

$z = \dfrac{\bar{x} - \mu}{\dfrac{\sigma}{\sqrt{n}}}$ as you did in Chapter 11.

The *t* distribution

In 1908, W.S. Gosset discovered that when a *random* sample of size n (even when n is small), with standard deviation s, is drawn from a Normal population, then the statistic

$$t = \frac{\bar{x} - \mu}{\frac{s}{\sqrt{n}}}$$

has a symmetrical, bell-shaped distribution, like the Normal distribution but with a greater spread.

It is called the *t distribution with* $n - 1$ *degrees of freedom.* You met the idea of degrees of freedom in Chapter 10. The symbol for degrees of freedom is ν so, for the t distribution, $\nu = n - 1$.

Unlike the Normal distribution, there is a different t distribution curve for each sample size, so there is a family of t distribution curves. A couple of members of the family of t distribution curves are illustrated in figure 12.1, together with the Normal curve.

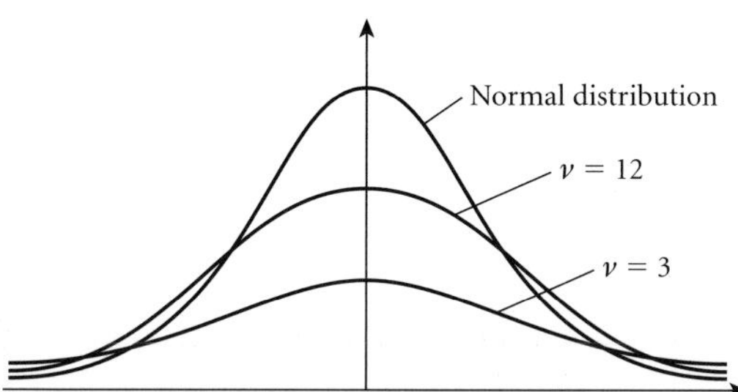

Figure 12.1

You should notice two features of the curves.

- The fewer the degrees of freedom, the flatter the shape of the curve, resulting in greater area in the tails of the distribution.
- The greater the degrees of freedom, the closer the curve is to the Normal distribution curve.

Two important conditions underlie the use of the t distribution.

- The sample is drawn from a Normal population. If this is not the case, the use of the t distribution is not valid.
- The sample is a random sample.

Historical note

William S. Gosset (1876–1937) studied both Mathematics and Chemistry at Oxford before working in Dublin for Guinness as a scientist. He had a particular interest in statistical techniques and through his work in the breweries had access to a large amount of statistical data. Gosset developed techniques to handle the data he had, including the discovery of the *t* distribution. Gosset published his work under the pseudonym 'Student' and so the *t* test is often called Student's *t* test.

Hypothesis tests and confidence intervals using the *t* distribution are constructed in much the same way as those using the Normal distribution.

Figure 12.2 shows the critical regions at the *p*% level of significance.

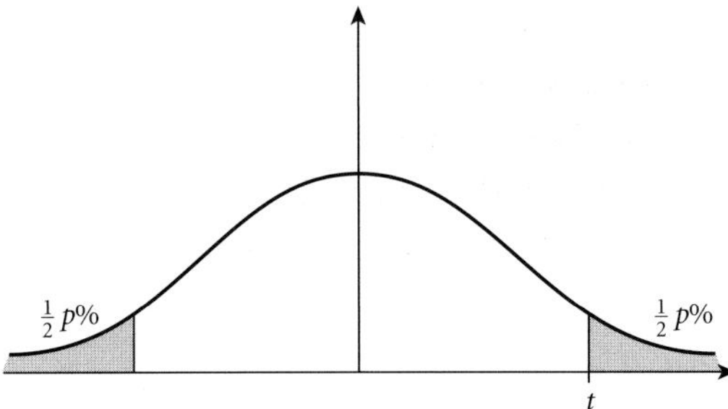

Figure 12.2

The table gives the percentage points of the *t* distribution for various degrees of freedom.

ν \ $p\%$	10	5	2	1
1	6.314	12.71	31.82	63.66
2	2.920	4.303	6.965	9.925
3	2.353	3.182	4.541	5.841
4	2.132	2.776	3.747	4.604
5	2.015	2.571	3.365	4.032
6	1.943	2.447	3.143	3.707
7	1.895	2.365	2.998	3.499
8	1.860	2.306	2.896	3.355
9	1.833	2.262	2.821	3.250
10	1.812	2.228	2.764	3.169
11	1.796	2.201	2.718	3.106
12	1.782	2.179	2.681	3.055
13	1.771	2.160	2.650	3.012
14	1.761	2.145	2.624	2.977
15	1.753	2.131	2.602	2.947
20	1.725	2.086	2.528	2.845
30	1.697	2.042	2.457	2.750
50	1.676	2.009	2.403	2.678
100	1.660	1.984	2.364	2.626
∞	1.645	1.960	2.326	2.576

= percentage points of the Normal distribution N(0, 1)

EXAMPLE 12.1

Figure 12.3 shows the graph of a *t* distribution.

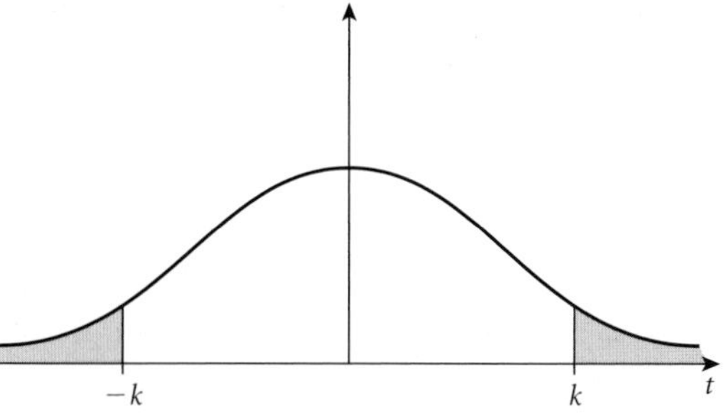

Figure 12.3

What is the value of k when

(i) $\nu = 12$ and the shaded area to the left is 0.01

(ii) $\nu = 7$ and the total shaded area is 0.10

(iii) $\nu = 15$ and the total unshaded area is 0.95

(iv) $\nu = 10$ and the area to the left of k is 0.95?

SOLUTION

(i) If the shaded area to the left is 0.01 then the total shaded area is 0.02.
From the tables under $p = 2\%$ and $\nu = 12$ you find that $k = 2.681$.

(ii) Directly from the tables under $p = 10\%$ and $\nu = 7$ you find that $k = 1.895$.

(iii) If the unshaded area is 0.95, the shaded area is 0.05.
From the tables under $p = 5\%$ and $\nu = 15$ you find that $k = 2.131$.

(iv) If the area to the left of k is 0.95, the shaded area to the right is 0.05.
This means that the total shaded area is 0.10.
From the tables under $p = 10\%$ and $\nu = 10$ you find that $k = 1.812$.

Comparing the tables for the Normal and *t* distributions

You will have noticed that the *t* distribution table is presented in a different way from the Normal distribution table. The main reason is that *all* Normal distributions have exactly the same shape, provided the same scale is used on the horizontal axis for 'number of standard deviations'. The important implication of this fact is that one Normal distribution table of probability values can be used for *all* Normal probability situations.

However, the *t* distribution

- has a different shape for different numbers of degrees of freedom
- is used mainly for hypothesis tests and constructing confidence intervals, so only the critical values are needed.

The *t* distribution table combines degrees of freedom, probabilities and critical values.

In the last line of the t distribution table, where the degrees of freedom is written as ∞, there is the note: 'Percentage points of the Normal distribution N(0, 1)'. Why does the value 2.326 appear in the inverse Normal table opposite $p = 0.99$, but in the t distribution under 2%?

Because of the way the t distribution tables are given you cannot use them to find an exact p value, only limits between which it must lie, for example, between 0.01 and 0.005. This is in contrast to the Normal distribution where you can find the p value. However, standard computer packages will give you the p value for a t distribution.

With knowledge of the t distribution for small samples, you are now in a position to carry out an appropriate test for the situation in the *Avonford Star* article, concerning Mr Plunkett's pies.

EXAMPLE 12.2

These are the weights, in grams, of the ten pies in the sample taken by the Trading Standards Inspector from Mr Plunkett's shop.

151 138 130 153 150 129 134 142 151 152

Is there evidence to suggest that the pies contain less than the stated 150 g of meat?

SOLUTION

Setting up the hypothesis test

H_0: $\mu = 150$, the mean population weight is 150 g.
H_1: $\mu < 150$, the mean population weight is less than 150 g.

You are investigating whether Mr Plunkett's pies contain *less* than 150 g of meat, so it is a 1-tailed test.

No significance level has been stated but 5% is a suitable level to choose in this situation.

While it has not been stated explicitly that the weights of the pies are Normally distributed, it is reasonable to assume that this is the case so it is appropriate to use the t distribution.

Calculating the test statistic

The test statistic is given by $t = \dfrac{\bar{x} - \mu}{\dfrac{s}{\sqrt{n}}}$.

Sample size, $n = 10$

Sample mean, $\bar{x} = 143$

Standard deviation, $s = 9.603$

$$t = \frac{143 - 150}{\dfrac{9.603}{\sqrt{10}}}$$

$$= -2.305$$

Interpreting the test statistic

From the t distribution table for $\nu = 9$ and a 1-tailed test at the 5% significance level, the critical value is -1.833.

ν \ p%	(10)	5	2	1
1	6.314	12.71	31.82	63.66
2	2.920	4.303	6.965	9.925
3	2.353	3.182	4.541	5.841
4	2.132	2.776	3.747	4.604
5	2.015	2.571	3.365	4.032
6	1.943	2.447	3.143	3.707
7	1.895	2.365	2.998	3.499
8	1.860	2.306	2.896	3.355
(9) →	(1.833)	2.262	2.821	3.250

? Explain why you look in the tables under $p = 10\%$ and $\nu = 9$ and then take the negative value. Illustrate the critical region on a diagram. Where is -2.305 on the diagram?

As -2.305 is less than -1.833 the test statistic lies in the critical region, so the result is significant. That means that the null hypothesis, H_0, is rejected and the alternative hypothesis, H_1, is accepted.

The data support the view that, at the 5% significance level, the mean weight of meat in a pie is less than 150 g, so it appears that Mr Plunkett does have a case to answer.

An alternative approach is to find the *p value* corresponding to $t = -2.305$. You can do this in two ways.

Either, you can determine from the tables that p lies between 5% and 2% because 2.305 is between 2.262 and 2.821, so the probability you want lies between 2.5% and 1% (since the test is 1-tailed). As this probability is less than 5%, the null hypothesis, H_0, is rejected.

ν \ $p\%$	10	5	2	1
1	6.314	12.71	31.82	63.66
2	2.920	4.303	6.965	9.925
3	2.353	3.182	4.541	5.841
4	2.132	2.776	3.747	4.604
5	2.015	2.571	3.365	4.032
6	1.943	2.447	3.143	3.707
7	1.895	2.365	2.998	3.499
8	1.860	2.306	2.896	3.355
9	1.833	2.262	2.821	3.250

↑
2.305

Or, if you have the appropriate calculator or use a statistics package you can find that $p = 4.66\%$, so the probability you want is 2.33%. As 2.33% is less than 5%, the null hypothesis, H_0, is rejected.

Here is another example of a hypothesis test on a sample mean of a small sample.

EXAMPLE 12.3

When a machine is in proper working order, it cuts rods with a mean length of 75.6 cm. To determine whether the machine is performing properly, a random sample of 15 rods is taken and each one is measured precisely. The 15 rods have a mean length of 75.94 cm with a standard deviation of 0.64 cm. Test, at the 5% significance level, the hypothesis that the machine is in proper working order. Assume that the lengths of the rods are Normally distributed.

SOLUTION

Setting up the hypothesis test

H_0: $\mu = 75.6$, the mean length of the rods is 75.6 cm.
H_1: $\mu \neq 75.6$, the mean length of the rods is not 75.6 cm.
2-tailed test: The rods may be either too long or too short.
Significance level: 5%

Calculating the test statistic

The t test is appropriate here as the sample is small and you are told that the lengths of the rods are Normally distributed.

Sample size, $n = 15$

Sample mean, $\bar{x} = 75.94$

Standard deviation, $s = 0.64$

$$\text{The test statistic, } t = \frac{\bar{x} - \mu}{\frac{s}{\sqrt{n}}}$$

$$= \frac{75.94 - 75.6}{\frac{0.64}{\sqrt{15}}}$$

$$= 2.058$$

Interpreting the test statistic

From the t distribution tables for $\nu = 14$ and a 2-tailed test at the 5% significance level, the critical values are ± 2.145.

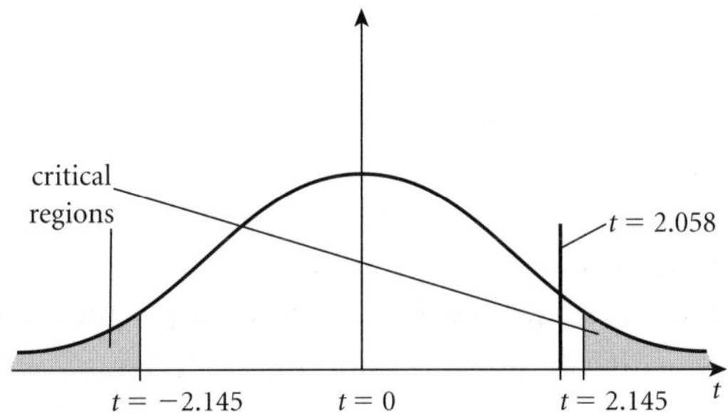

Figure 12.4

Since 2.058 is less than 2.145 the test statistic does not lie within the critical region, so the null hypothesis, H_0, is accepted.

The test shows that, at the 5% significance level, the machine is in proper working order.

? How would you calculate the p value in this case? Its value is, in fact, 5.88. What does this tell you?

EXERCISE 12A

1 A sample of size 10 was chosen randomly from a Normal population. These are the results.

1.46	−0.52	1.51	0.66	0.92
−0.13	0.46	−0.33	1.15	−0.09

(i) Find the mean and the variance of the data.

(ii) Test, at the 10% level of significance, the hypothesis that the mean of the population is zero.

2 Eight observations were taken at random from a Normal population. The data are summarised by $\sum x = 101.6$ and $\sum x^2 = 1290.56$.

(i) Find the mean and the variance of the data.

(ii) Test, at the 5% level of significance, the hypothesis that the mean of the population is 12.55.

3 A machine produces washers. When the machine is in proper working order, their thickness is Normally distributed with a mean of 0.60 mm. To determine whether the machine is in proper working order one day, a sample of 15 washers is chosen randomly. The mean thickness of the washers in the sample is 0.57 mm and the standard deviation is 0.04 mm. Test if the machine is in proper working order at

(i) the 5% significance level

(ii) the 1% significance level.

4 A printing machine is known to turn out an average of 35 copies a minute. A modification is made to the machine in order to increase its output. In a random sample of five test runs the number of copies produced in a minute are 37, 36, 38, 36 and 39.

(i) Is this increase statistically significant at the 1% level?

(ii) State the distributional assumption underlying your analysis in part **(i)**.

5 The lifetimes of electric light bulbs produced by a company may be modelled by a Normal distribution. In the past the mean lifetime has been 1200 hours. A random sample of 12 electric light bulbs was chosen from a recently produced batch. The mean lifetime was 1185 hours and the standard deviation was 15.0 hours. Test, at the 5% level of significance, the hypothesis that the mean lifetime of the bulbs has decreased.

6 The setting on a lathe is 45.0 cm. The mean and standard deviation of a random sample of size 12 were 45.51 cm and 0.61 cm respectively. Test, at the 5% significance level, whether the machine needs to be adjusted. State any assumptions you have had to make.

7 A machine produces rods with diameters that are Normally distributed with a mean of 8.00 mm. After modification of the machine, the diameters of a random sample of 10 rods produced were found to have a mean of 8.05 mm with a variance of 0.0025 mm^2. At the 1% level of significance, would you conclude that the mean diameter has increased after the modification?

8 A trial is being made of a new diet for feeding pigs. Ten pigs are selected and their increases in weight, in kilograms, are measured, over a certain period using the new diet. The data are as follows.

15.2 13.8 14.6 15.8 13.1 14.9 17.2 15.1 14.9 15.2

The underlying population can be assumed to be Normally distributed.

Using an established diet, the mean increase in weight of pigs over the period is known to be 14.0 kg. Test at the 5% level of significance whether the new diet is an improvement, stating carefully your null and alternative hypotheses and your conclusion.

[MEI, *part*]

9 A machine is in use for packing sugar into bags of nominal weight 1000 g. It is assumed that the distribution of the weights for this machine is Normal. A random sample of 9 bags packed by this machine is found to have the following weights (in grams).

1012 996 984 1005 1008 994 1003 1017 1002

Test at the 5% level of significance whether it may be assumed that the mean weight for this machine is 1000 g.

[MEI, *part*]

10 A commuter's train journey to work is scheduled to take 52 minutes. Having noticed that he is *always* late, even when the trains are running normally, he decided to keep records for a random sample of 10 journeys. On two of these occasions, there were major signal failures leading to severe disruption and complete suspension of services. He therefore decided to eliminate these two occasions from his records. On the other eight occasions, his journey times in minutes were as follows.

65 61 62 60 59 62 61 57

Carry out a two-sided 5% test of the hypothesis that his overall mean lateness is 10 minutes. State the required distributional assumption underlying your analysis.

[MEI, *part*]

11 The senior technician of a university science department is considering using a new supplier of chemicals for student laboratory experiments. These chemicals do not need to be of a very high grade of purity, but must be sufficiently pure that the experiments can be conducted efficiently and safely. The new supplier states that the average level of impurity in the chemicals it supplies is no more than 4%. The senior technician carefully measures the impurity in a random sample of eight of these chemicals and finds the percentages to be as follows.

3.9 4.5 4.7 4.3 4.9 3.4 4.5 5.0

(i) State the appropriate null and alternative hypotheses for the usual t test for examining whether the supplier is meeting the stated standard.

(ii) Explain why the corresponding test based on the Normal distribution cannot be used.

(iii) What condition is necessary for the correct use of the *t* test?

(iv) Carry out the test, using a 5% significance level.

[MEI, *part*]

Confidence intervals from small samples

In Chapter 11, the 95% confidence interval for the mean of a population was shown to be the interval

$$\left[\bar{x} - 1.96\frac{\sigma}{\sqrt{n}},\ \bar{x} + 1.96\frac{\sigma}{\sqrt{n}}\right]$$

where $\bar{x}$ is the mean of a *large* sample of size n and σ is the standard deviation of the population.

What do you do if the sample is small and the standard deviation of the population is not known? The following example shows how the *t* distribution can be used.

EXAMPLE 12.4

In the *Avonford Star* story at the start of this chapter, a random sample was taken of Mr Plunkett's pies. These were their weights, in grams.

151 138 130 153 150 129 134 142 151 152

What is a 95% confidence interval for the weight of Mr Plunkett's pies?

SOLUTION

Earlier in this chapter it was noted that nothing has been stated explicitly about the distribution of the weights of the pies, but that it is reasonable to assume that they are Normally distributed.

The 95% confidence interval for the mean of the population if the sample is small and drawn from a Normal population is given by the interval

$$\left[\bar{x} - k\frac{s}{\sqrt{n}},\ \bar{x} + k\frac{s}{\sqrt{n}}\right]$$

where $\bar{x}$ is the mean of the sample
n is the sample size
s is the standard deviation of the sample
k is the relevant value in the 5% column of the *t* distribution table.

For this example you already know that $n = 10$, $\bar{x} = 143$ and $s = 9.603$.

For a 95% confidence interval for the mean weight of Mr Plunkett's pies, you look under $p = 5\%$ and $\nu = 9$ (since $\nu = 10 - 1$) to get $k = 2.262$.

This gives a 95% confidence interval of

$$\left[143 - 2.262 \times \frac{9.603}{\sqrt{10}},\ 143 + 2.262 \times \frac{9.603}{\sqrt{10}}\right]$$

$$= [136.1, 149.9]$$

For a 95% confidence interval, what is the value of k when

(i) $n = 5$ **(ii)** $n = 15$ **(iii)** $n = 30$?

Note

When $n = 30$ you should have found that k is about 2.04 (the nearest value in the tables to $\nu = 29$), which is quite close to the 1.96 used in the Normal distribution. This is consistent with the rule of thumb that samples of size 30 or more are considered large.

Confidence intervals for other percentages can be calculated using the appropriate value of k in the interval $\left[\bar{x} - k\frac{s}{\sqrt{n}},\ \bar{x} + k\frac{s}{\sqrt{n}}\right]$.

What value of k would you use for

(i) a 98% confidence interval when $n = 12$

(ii) a 90% confidence interval when $n = 50$?

With a 95% confidence interval, you would expect that 95% of the time the interval $\left[\bar{x} - k\frac{s}{\sqrt{n}},\ \bar{x} + k\frac{s}{\sqrt{n}}\right]$ (with the relevant value of k) will include the mean of the population, μ. If you want to be more certain that the interval you calculate does include the mean of the population, μ, then you should choose a higher percentage. But the disadvantage is that for a given sample size you end up with a wider interval, which may not be of much help to you.

EXAMPLE 12.5

A random sample of six ropes have the following breaking strengths.

6250 N 7010 N 6830 N 6570 N 6940 N 6780 N

Give 90% confidence limits for the mean breaking strength. What important assumption did you have to make?

SOLUTION

From the data $\sum x = 40\,380$ and $\sum x^2 = 272\,148\,400$.

So $\bar{x} = \dfrac{40\,380}{6} = 6730$

and $s = \sqrt{\dfrac{272\,148\,400 - 6 \times 6730^2}{6 - 1}} = 279.64$

For a 90% confidence interval you look up the tables under $p = 10\%$ and $\nu = 5$ to get $k = 2.015$.

So the 90% confidence interval is

$$\left[6730 - 2.015 \times \frac{279.64}{\sqrt{6}}, 6730 + 2.015 \times \frac{279.64}{\sqrt{6}}\right] = [6500, 6960]$$

The confidence limits are therefore 6500 N and 6960 N.

Assumption: For the use of the *t* distribution to be valid, the sample has to be drawn from a Normal population. This is probably a realistic assumption to make in this example.

Note

You were told in the question that it was a random sample, the other important condition.

Hypothesis testing and confidence intervals

There is a very close relationship between hypothesis tests and confidence intervals. This is illustrated in the following example.

EXAMPLE 12.6

A random sample of fifteen observations are taken from a Normal population. These are the results.

5.83	4.33	5.35	4.88	5.37	4.59	5.72	5.28
5.34	4.83	5.19	4.74	5.39	5.47	4.79	

(i) Test, at the 5% significance level, the hypothesis that the mean of the population is 4.90.

(ii) Construct a 95% confidence interval for the mean.

SOLUTION

(i) From the data you can calculate that $n = 15$, $\sum x = 77.1$ and $\sum x^2 = 398.8418$

so, $\bar{x} = \dfrac{77.1}{15} = 5.14$

and $s = \sqrt{\dfrac{398.8418 - 15 \times 5.14^2}{15 - 1}} = 0.4266.$

Setting up the hypothesis test

H_0: $\mu = 4.90$, the mean of the population is 4.90.
H_1: $\mu \neq 4.90$, the mean of the population is not 4.90.
Significance level: 5%

? Why is this a 2-tailed test?

Calculating the test statistic

The t distribution is appropriate here as the question says that the sample is random and taken from a Normal population.

Sample size, $n = 15$

Sample mean, $\bar{x} = 5.14$

Standard deviation, $s = 0.4266$

$$\text{The test statistic, } t = \frac{\bar{x} - \mu}{\frac{s}{\sqrt{n}}}$$

$$= \frac{5.14 - 4.90}{\frac{0.4266}{\sqrt{15}}}$$

$$= 2.179$$

Interpreting the test statistic

From the t distribution tables for $\nu = 14$ and a 2-tailed test at the 5% significance level, the critical values are ± 2.145.

As 2.179 is greater than 2.145, the null hypothesis, H_0, is rejected and the alternative hypothesis, H_1, is accepted.

So the test shows that, at the 5% significance level, the mean is not 4.90.

Alternatively, the p value in this case is 4.7%. As the p value is less than 5%, H_0 is rejected.

(ii) The 95% confidence interval is given by $\left[\bar{x} - k\frac{s}{\sqrt{n}},\ \bar{x} + k\frac{s}{\sqrt{n}}\right]$.

$n = 15$, $\bar{x} = 5.14$, $s = 0.4266$ and $k = 2.145$ (under $p = 5\%$ and $\nu = 14$ in the t distribution table).

So the 95% confidence interval is

$$\left[5.14 - 2.145 \times \frac{0.4266}{\sqrt{15}},\ 5.14 + 2.145 \times \frac{0.4266}{\sqrt{15}}\right] = [4.904, 5.376]$$

Note that the value of 4.90, being tested for the mean, is outside the confidence interval.

Example 12.6 links the ideas of hypothesis testing and confidence intervals.

- If the value being tested under H_0 lies *within* the 95% confidence interval then H_0 is accepted at the 5% significance level.
- If it lies *outside* the 95% confidence interval then H_0 is rejected at the 5% significance level.

In Example 12.6 the value being tested is 4.90 (which is the proposed mean of the population). This lies *outside* the 95% confidence interval [4.904, 5.376], so H_0 is rejected at the 5% significance level. This agrees with the conclusion in part **(i)** that the mean is not 4.90.

EXERCISE 12B

1 A sample of size 10 was chosen randomly from a Normal population. These are the results.

7.34 7.15 7.42 7.43 7.26 7.38 7.48 7.27 7.35 7.42

(i) Find the mean and variance of the data.

(ii) Give 95% confidence limits for the mean.

2 A random sample of size eight was chosen from a Normal population. The data are summarised by

$\sum x = 288, \qquad \sum x^2 = 10\,388.$

(i) Find the mean and variance of the data.

(ii) Give 90% confidence limits for the mean.

3 It is known that the breaking strengths of nylon threads are Normally distributed. A sample of 14 nylon threads is chosen. Their breaking strengths have a mean of 85.6 Newtons and a standard deviation of 1.63 Newtons. Give 90% and 98% confidence limits for the mean breaking strength. State any assumption you need to make.

4 A machine is set to produce rods of length 14.25 cm. The lengths, in centimetres, of a random sample of seven rods were found to be as follows.

14.37 14.42 14.63 14.21 14.38 14.41 14.29

(i) Give 95% confidence limits for the mean length of the rods. State any assumptions on which your method is based.

(ii) Is the result consistent with the nominal length of the rods?

5 A Statistics class carries out an experiment to estimate the mean length, μ cm, of the left feet of ten-year-old children. The lengths, x cm, of the left feet of 15 such children were measured. The data are summarised by

$\sum x = 288, \qquad \sum x^2 = 5553.$

(i) Calculate the mean and variance of the data, and use them to find a 95% confidence interval for μ. State clearly two important assumptions which you need to make.

(ii) Give a clear interpretation of a 95% confidence interval.

[MEI, *adapted*]

6 A Youth Club has a large number of members (referred to as the *population* in the remainder of the question). In order to find the distribution of weekly allowances of the members, a random sample of 10 is questioned.

(i) Describe a method of producing a random sample.

Such a random sample produced the following weekly allowances.

£5.20	£4.40	£3.00	£2.00	£3.30
£7.50	£5.00	£6.50	£4.80	£5.70

(ii) Estimate the population mean and variance.

(iii) Find a 95% confidence interval for the population mean. State any assumptions on which your method is based.

(iv) Explain how the width of the confidence interval may be reduced. Assuming the same variance as in part **(ii)**, what must the sample size be to reduce the width to £2?

[MEI]

7 A rail commuter suspects that the train he travels to work by arrives late regularly. On five such journeys he noted the times, T minutes, by which the train was late. The data were summarised by

$$\sum t = 11.8, \qquad \sum t^2 = 65.3.$$

(i) Find the mean and standard deviation of the data, and use them to find a and b, the lower and upper limits for the 90% confidence interval for μ, the mean time by which the train is late. State clearly two important assumptions you need to make.

(ii) The commuter interprets the results in part **(i)** as 'the probability that μ lies between a and b is 0.9'. Comment on this interpretation.

(iii) Use your result in part **(i)** to test whether the commuter's suspicions are justified. State the significance level at which the test is carried out.

(iv) The railway management notes the value of T on a further 40 occasions. State, with reasons, how you might expect its confidence interval for μ to differ from the one calculated in part **(i)**.

[MEI]

8 A notional allowance of 9 minutes has been given for the completion of a routine task on a production line. The operatives have complained that it appears usually to take slightly longer.

An inspector took a sample of 12 measurements of the time required to undertake this task. The results (in minutes) were as follows.

9.4	8.8	9.3	9.1	9.4	8.9
9.3	9.2	9.6	9.3	9.3	9.1

(i) Stating carefully your null and alternative hypotheses and the assumptions underlying your analysis, test at the 1% level of significance whether the task is indeed taking on average longer than 9 minutes.

(ii) Provide a two-sided 95% confidence interval for the mean time required to undertake the task.

[MEI]

9 A tax inspector is carrying out an audit survey of firms located in a certain city. From a list of all N such firms, a random sample of size n is selected for detailed study.

For a random sample of size $n = 14$, the values of a particular financial indicator are found to be

8.6	9.1	9.3	8.2	8.9	9.2	9.9
9.2	9.4	8.7	9.1	10.2	9.2	9.1

Obtain a two-sided 99% confidence interval for the mean value of this indicator in the underlying population. State any required assumption and explain carefully the interpretation of the interval.

[MEI, *part*]

10 A pharmaceutical company manufactures a pill which initially contains 30 milligrams of a certain vitamin. It is known that, over time, this content gradually decreases. A health and safety inspector is examining these pills six months after manufacture. An average content of the vitamin in the pills of 23.8 milligrams or more will be regarded as satisfactory but if it is less than 23.8 milligrams then this is unsatisfactory.

(i) State carefully the null and alternative hypotheses the inspector is testing.

Six months after manufacture, a sample of 10 pills is carefully tested and their vitamin contents, in milligrams, are found to be

24.0 23.7 23.6 23.6 23.9 23.5 23.6 23.8 23.8 23.6

(ii) Carry out the inspector's test, stating carefully the assumptions underlying your analysis, using a 5% significance level.

(iii) Provide a two-sided 95% confidence interval for the mean content.

[MEI]

11 Experiments with a new variety of tomato are being conducted at an agricultural research station. The crop is grown under carefully controlled conditions on ten experimental plots and the yields, in kg per plot, are found to be as follows.

60.2 63.4 58.8 63.6 64.7 62.5 66.0 59.1 65.1 62.0

It is known that an established variety of tomato would have a mean yield of 60.0 kg per plot on the experimental plots. Test, at the 5% level of significance, whether the new variety has an increased mean yield, stating clearly your null and alternative hypotheses. State also the assumptions underlying your analysis.

Provide a two-sided 95% confidence interval for the mean yield of the new variety.

[MEI, *part*]

12 The 95% confidence interval for the mean length of rods is calculated from a sample of ten rods, chosen randomly from a Normal population. The interval is [27.6, 29.8].

(i) Find the mean and variance of the lengths of the rods in the sample.

(ii) What is the 99% confidence interval for the mean length of the rods?

KEY POINTS

1 The means of small random samples, drawn from a Normal population where the mean, μ, and standard deviation, σ, are not known, have a t distribution.

2 Sample data may be used to carry out a hypothesis test on the null hypothesis that the population mean has some particular value, μ.

The test statistic to use is $t = \dfrac{\bar{x} - \mu}{\dfrac{s}{\sqrt{n}}}$ and the critical values are read from the t distribution table.

3 The degrees of freedom, ν, are given by $\nu = n - 1$.

4 The confidence interval for μ is given by $\left[\bar{x} - k\dfrac{s}{\sqrt{n}},\ \bar{x} + k\dfrac{s}{\sqrt{n}}\right]$.

5 The value of k for any confidence level can be found by using the t distribution table.

13 The Wilcoxon signed rank test

If a man will begin with certainties, he shall end in doubts; but if he will be content to begin with doubts, he shall end in certainties.

Sir Francis Bacon

AVONFORD STAR

Public votes new shopping centre the tops – at last!

It's official – the public have voted the newly opened Regent Shopping Centre a definite asset to the town, despite the considerable and prolonged disruption the building works have caused. Town Centre Manager, Paul Clay, expressed relief at the outcome, which further showed that 25% of those asked voted it 'the tops'.

Details of the survey may be found on the *Avonford Star* website.

Up to now the statistical tests you have used require the assumption that the underlying population is Normally distributed, or that you had large samples. Life is not always quite so simple and there are many situations where data simply do not behave like that.

Take the poll on the shopping centre as an example. The data here are a collection of opinions. In fact the journalist asked a question that required more than just a 'Yes' or 'No' answer. People were asked to comment on the statement 'The new Regent Shopping Centre is an asset to the town' and given a choice of answers from 'Definitely an asset, it's the tops' to 'No definitely not an asset, it's awful'.

While it is undoubtedly impressive that 25% of those asked went so far as to say it was the tops, you should be asking yourself 'I wonder what percentage thought it awful?' Darell Huff, who wrote a famous and humorous book called *How to Lie with Statistics*, might well have said of the newspaper report, 'It's the figures that aren't there that are important.'

Here are all the responses, recorded on a data collection sheet.

Person number	Definitely an asset, it's the tops.	Yes, it's a good asset.	Yes, it's an asset, it's OK.	I have no opinion.	Not really an asset.	I don't think it's an asset at all, it's not very good.	No, definitely not an asset, it's awful.
1					✗		
2		✗					
3	✗						
4				✗			
5					✗		
6		✗					
7				✗			
8	✗						
9						✗	
10			✗				
11		✗					
12	✗						

A statistical hypothesis test would help here. It would tell you how likely it is that the result has arisen purely by chance. If it is not very likely you can sit up and take notice of the outcome.

The hypothesis you would want to test would be: 'The public considers the new shopping centre an asset.'

The first problem is what figures to use in this situation? The responses are words not numbers, but you can solve this by allocating a number to each response, with 1 for 'Definitely an asset, it's the tops' to 7 for 'No, definitely not an asset, it's awful'. This gives you a *rating scale* of responses, which substitutes a number for each opinion.

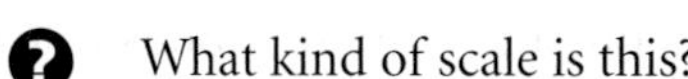

What kind of scale is this?

Always be cautious with rating scales as people are not like rulers, watches or thermometers. The difference between opinions cannot be neatly measured in the same way as the differences between two lengths, times or temperatures. Is the difference between 'Yes, it's a good asset' (2) and 'Yes it's an asset, it's OK' (3) the same amount of difference of opinion as between 'I have no opinion' (4) and 'Not really as asset' (5)? Is it sensible to measure the difference between two opinions numerically?

Is the opinion 'Yes it's an asset, it's OK', rated as 3, three times weaker than the opinion rated as 1, 'Definitely an asset, it's the tops'? There is, nevertheless, an order to the different opinions. Think of other situations where there is an order, but doing arithmetic with the numbering does not make sense.

The journalist chose 12 people, at random, and these were their responses given on the data sheet.

5 2 1 4 5 2 4 1 6 3 2 1

At first glance, as you have a small sample, this looks like a candidate for a *t* test, which you met in Chapter 12, where you might find whether or not the mean is 4, representing the 'no opinion' response.

What assumption underlies the *t* test?
Why would the *t* test not be appropriate here?

In this situation an alternative test is the Wilcoxon signed rank test. This is an example of a non-parametric test. It requires no assumption about an underlying Normal distribution.

⚠ The term non-parametric tests has generally come to mean tests where there is no assumption that the underlying population has a Normal distribution.

A common mistake is to think such tests require no assumptions, but this is not true. The assumption made for the Wilcoxon test is that the variable being tested is symmetrically distributed about the median, which would also be the mean. Remember too that it is still vitally important that your sample has been randomly chosen from the population.

Frank Wilcoxon's revolutionary idea was to use the ranks rather than the data themselves for a test. There are several Wilcoxon tests.

- The Wilcoxon signed rank test can be used for a single sample, such as you have with the shopping centre survey.
- The Wilcoxon signed rank test can also be used for paired data samples (see Chapter 15).
- Where you have two unrelated samples which you wish to compare, the Wilcoxon rank sum test is used (see Chapter 16); this test is very similar to the Mann–Whitney test.

Do you think that asking 12 people about the new shopping centre is too small a sample?

The Wilcoxon signed rank test for a single sample

The responses people gave about the shopping centre are represented by these numerical ratings.

5 2 1 4 5 2 4 1 6 3 2 1

where having no opinion equates to 4, the median value. A quick 'eyeball' test shows that none of those questioned thought it was awful and only one person thought it not very good, so a first impression is that people generally approve.

If you start by assuming that in the population there is no opinion one way or the other, and that people's responses are symmetrically distributed about 'no opinion', you can test the hypothesis that people think the shopping centre is an asset, with the null hypothesis that people have no opinion about it so that their response is the median value, 4.

Setting up the hypothesis test

As people who think the shopping centre is an asset will give a rating of less than 4, the null and alternative hypotheses can be stated as follows.

H_0: The median response is 4.
H_1: The median response is less than 4.
1-tailed test
Significance level: 5%

Why is this a 1-tailed test?

Calculating the test statistic

There are 4 steps to the test. Some people find the mnemonic DRASTIC helps them to remember it.

It's not so **DRAStiC** after all: **D**ifference **RA**nk **S**um **C**ompare.

1 Find the difference between each value and the median.
Using a table is the easiest way to organise the figures.

Rating	Rating − median (4)
5	$5 - 4 = 1$
2	$2 - 4 = -2$
1	$1 - 4 = -3$
4	$4 - 4 = 0$
5	$5 - 4 = 1$
2	$2 - 4 = -2$
4	$4 - 4 = 0$
1	$1 - 4 = -3$
6	$6 - 4 = 2$
3	$3 - 4 = -1$
2	$2 - 4 = -2$
1	$1 - 4 = -3$

2 Ignore the zeros and rank the remaining scores.
Ignore the signs and start with the *smallest* difference, give it rank 1.
Where two or more differences have the same value, find their mean rank and use this.

Ignoring the zeros leaves you with ten values.
In calculating the ranks, you have three values of 1, four of 2, and three of 3.
The three values of 1 occupy the ranks 1, 2 and 3, which have a mean of 2, so they are all given the rank of 2.
The four values of 2 occupy the ranks 4, 5, 6 and 7, which have a mean of 5.5, so they are ranked 5.5.
The three values of 3 have ranks 8, 9 and 10 which have a mean of 9, so they are all ranked 9.

Again, it is easiest to summarise your working in a table.

Rating	Rating − 4	Absolute value	Ranking	+	−
5	1	1	2	2	
2	−2	2	5.5		5.5
1	−3	3	9		9
4	0	0	Ignore		
5	1	1	2	2	
2	−2	2	5.5		5.5
4	0	0	Ignore		
1	−3	3	9		9
6	2	2	5.5	5.5	
3	−1	1	2		2
2	−2	2	5.5		5.5
1	−3	3	9		9
			Total	9.5	45.5

3 Sum the ranks of the positive differences, W_+, and sum the ranks of the negative differences W_-.

W_+, the sum of the ranks of the positive differences is

$$2 + 2 + 5.5 = 9.5.$$

W_-, the sum of the ranks of the negative differences is

$$5.5 + 9 + 5.5 + 9 + 2 + 5.5 + 9 = 45.5.$$

Now check that $W_+ + W_-$ is the same as $\frac{1}{2}n(n+1)$, where n is the number in the sample (having ignored the zeros). In this case $n = 10$.

$$\frac{1}{2}n(n+1) = \frac{1}{2} \times 10 \times 11 = 55$$

$$W_+ + W_- = 9.5 + 45.5 = 55$$

Interpreting the test statistic

4 Compare the test statistic with the critical value in the tables.

For a 1-tailed test where the alternative hypothesis is that the median is less than a given value, the test statistic is W_+. In this case the alternative hypothesis is that the median is less than 4 so the test statistic is W_+.

If the null hypothesis is true, and the median is 4, you would expect W_- and W_+ to have roughly the same value.

You are interested in W_+, the sum of the ranks of ratings greater than 4. W_+ is much less than W_-, which suggests that more people felt the shopping centre was an asset. It could also suggest that those who were in favour of the shopping centre expressed a strong view, with lots of high numbers in the ranks.

Now you need to compare the value of W_+, the test statistic, with the critical value from the table of critical values for the Wilcoxon single sample and paired sample tests.

1-tailed	5%	$2\frac{1}{2}$%	1%	$\frac{1}{2}$%
2-tailed	10%	5%	2%	1%
n				
2				
3				
4				
5	0			
6	2	0		
7	3	2	0	
8	5	3	1	0
9	8	5	3	1
10	10	8	5	3
11	13	10	7	5
12	17	13	9	7
13	21	17	12	9
14	25	21	15	12
15	30	25	19	15

The key question is 'Is W_+ significantly smaller than would happen by chance?' The table helps you decide this by supplying the critical value. For a sample of 10 at the 5% significance level for a 1-tailed test, the value is 10.

The test statistic, W_+, is 9.5.
The critical value is 10.
As 9.5 is less than 10, the evidence suggests that you can reject the null hypothesis.

Your conclusion is that the evidence shows, at the 5% significance level, that the public thinks the new shopping centre is an asset to the town.

Choosing the test statistic

You need to be careful to choose the appropriate test statistic for the problem you are tackling.

For a 2-tailed test the test statistic is the smaller of W_+ and W_-.

For a 1-tailed test where the alternative hypothesis is that the median is *greater* than a given value, the test statistic is W_-.

For a 1-tailed test where the alternative hypothesis is that the median is *less* than a given value, the test statistic is W_+.

Historical note

Frank Wilcoxon (1892–1965) was an outstanding chemist whose interest in statistics first started while studying fungicides, when he and his colleagues studied Fisher's newly published *Statistical Methods for Research Workers*. In 1945 he published his paper setting out the rank sum and signed rank tests, which are still named after him.

His background was colourful. A keen cyclist and motorcyclist, he and his twin sister were born in an Irish castle to wealthy American parents. He grew up in the States, ran away to sea, worked as an oil worker and as a tree surgeon, and attended a military academy before finally entering college, aged 26, to read chemistry.

e The sign test

A very simple test of opinion about the shopping centre would assume that people are equally likely to approve or not, with probability 0.5. You could count up the number of responses greater than 4 and work out, using the binomial distribution, how likely you are to have this number. This is known as the sign test. It is very useful but it does not make full use of all the information you have available as it ignores the magnitudes of the differences from the median. The Wilcoxon test, on the other hand, makes use of this information and, as a result, is more powerful.

EXAMPLE 13.1

Student satisfaction surveys ask students to rate a particular course, on a scale of 1 (poor) to 10 (excellent). In previous years the replies have been symmetrically distributed about a median of 4. This year there has been a much greater online element to the course, and staff want to know how the rating of this version of the course compares with the previous one.

14 students, randomly selected, were asked to rate the new version of the course. These are their ratings.

1	3	6	4	7	2	3
6	5	2	3	4	1	2

Is there any evidence at the 5% level of significance that students rate this version of the course differently?

SOLUTION

Setting up the hypothesis test

The null hypothesis is that there is no change in the rating given by the students, and so the median is still 4. The alternative hypothesis is that the median is not 4. The alternative hypothesis is not that the median is greater than 4, nor is it that it is less than 4, just that it is not 4, so it is a 2-tailed test.

H_0: The median is 4.
H_1: The median is not 4.
2-tailed test
Significance level: 5%

Assumption: The ratings are still symmetrically distributed.

Calculating the test statistic

Taking your '**DRAS**ti**C** steps', you find the difference, rank, sum and compare the test statistic with the critical value. Much of the working is best done in a table.

Rating	Frequency	Rating − 4	Absolute value	Ranking	+	−
1	2	$1 - 4 = -3$	3	11		$2 \times 11 = 22$
2	3	$2 - 4 = -2$	2	7		$3 \times 7 = 21$
3	3	$3 - 4 = -1$	1	2.5		$3 \times 2.5 = 7.5$
4	2	$4 - 4 = 0$	Ignore			
5	1	$5 - 4 = 1$	1	2.5	2.5	
6	2	$6 - 4 = 2$	2	7	$2 \times 7 = 14$	
7	1	$7 - 4 = 3$	3	11	11	
				Total	27.5	50.5

To find the ranks:
Notice there are four absolute values of 1 so these have the ranks 1, 2, 3 and 4, with a mean of 2.5.
The five with value 2, have ranks 5, 6, 7, 8 and 9, with a mean of 7.
The three 3s have ranks 10, 11 and 12, with a mean of 11.

$$\begin{aligned} W_- &= (2 \times 11) + (3 \times 7) + (3 \times 2.5) \\ &= 22 + 21 + 7.5 \\ &= 50.5 \end{aligned}$$

$$\begin{aligned} W_+ &= 2.5 + (2 \times 7) + 11 \\ &= 2.5 + 14 + 11 \\ &= 27.5 \end{aligned}$$

Check that $W_+ + W_- = \frac{1}{2}n(n + 1)$.

$n = 12$ since we have ignored the two zeros.

$W_+ + W_- = 27.5 + 50.5 = 78$

$\frac{1}{2}n(n + 1) = \frac{1}{2} \times 12 \times 13 = 78$

Do not be tempted to omit this check. It will tell you whether or not you have calculated W_+ and W_- correctly.

Interpreting the test statistic

Now you need to choose your test statistic.
For a 2-tailed test it is the smaller of W_+ and W_-.
Here this is $W_+ = 27.5$.

From the tables, the critical value for a 2-tailed test at the 5% significance level for a sample of 12 is 13.

As 27.5 is greater than 13, you accept the null hypothesis at the 5% significance level.
You can conclude that the evidence shows that the introduction of a greater online element to the course has had no significant effect on the ratings, at the 5% level.

? When you write 'accept the null hypothesis at the 5% significance level' what do you mean by 'at the 5% significance level'? What does it tell you?

EXERCISE 13A

1 New recruits to a call centre are given initial training in answering customer calls. Following this training they are independently assessed on their competence and are rated on a score of 1 to 10, 1 representing 'totally incompetent' to 10 'totally competent'. It is usual for the trainees' scores to be symmetrically distributed about a median of 6. A new trainer has been appointed. These are the scores of her first 19 trainees.

6	5	6	9	7	3	4	6	7	2
9	8	7	4	5	6	9	5	7	

Is there evidence at the 5% level that the new trainer has made any difference?

2 It is recommended that women should not consume more than 70 g of fat per day. A random sample of 12 student nurses at St Clare's were asked to estimate as carefully as possible how much fat they ate on one particular day. These are the results, measured in grams.

85	120	45	95	100	50
65	85	105	125	65	49

Is there evidence at the 5% level that student nurses at St Clare's are consuming more fat than they should?

3 The numbers of waders feeding in Sampford creek is being logged. At the same time last year, the median number seen each day at a certain time was 8. Records for the last 16 days show the following numbers of birds.

7	9	12	14	7	7	15	12
10	7	7	12	9	7	15	15

Is there evidence at the 5% level that the number of waders feeding at the creek at this time of year has increased?

4 A dental nurse has carried out a large survey of patient stress levels, asking patients to rate their stress level while having treatment on a score of 1 to 10; 1 being 'stress free' to 10 being 'unbearably stressful'. The responses were symmetrically distributed with a median of 4.

The dentist plays Radio 1 while treating patients as he thinks this relaxes them. The dental nurse now suggests changing to Classic FM for a week, and asks 17 patients at random to rate their stress levels. These are the results.

9	1	5	3	4	2	8	3	6
6	4	4	3	1	10	7	2	

Is there evidence at the 1% level that listening to Classic FM has reduced patients' stress levels?

5 It has been suggested that British office workers are not taking their full lunch breaks but spend part of them working at their desks. The median lunch 'hour' is now 34 minutes. An office supervisor in a large purchasing department, intrigued by this, noted the time spent away from their desks at lunchtime by ten randomly chosen staff members, without their knowledge. These are data, in minutes, that she collected.

55 20 31 12 18 35 28 16 14 32

She was shocked when she looked at the data. Does it suggest, at the 5% level, that her staff are taking even less than 34 minutes away from their desks at lunchtime?

6 The local paper reckons the rate of pay for babysitters is now £6 an hour. Teenagers dispute this. A random sample of teenagers who babysit are asked what their pay rates are per hour. This required some calculation as most were paid per night. These are the results, in £ per hour.

5 5 4 3 7 3 5 3 8 2

Is there any evidence at the 5% level that the median is not £6?
Is there any evidence at the 5% level that the median rate of pay of the teenagers is less than £6 an hour?

KEY POINTS

1 The Wilcoxon signed rank test (single sample) is used for testing the null hypothesis that the population median of a random variable is equal to a given value M. It is assumed that the variable is symmetrically distributed about its median.

2 This is the procedure for the test.

- Find the difference between each value and the median.
- Ignore the zeros. Rank the remaining scores by ignoring the signs and giving the lowest rank to the smallest difference. Where two or more differences have the same value, find their mean rank and use this.
- Sum the ranks of the positive differences, W_+, and sum the ranks of the negative differences W_-. Check that $W_+ + W_- = \frac{1}{2}n(n + 1)$, where n is the number in the sample having ignored the zeros.
- For a 2-tailed test the test statistic is the smaller of W_+ and W_-.
  For a 1-tailed test where the alternative hypothesis is that the median is greater than a given value, the test statistic is W_-.
  For a 1-tailed test where the alternative hypothesis is that the median is less than a given value, the test statistic is W_+.
- Compare the test statistic, W, with the critical value in the tables. The null hypothesis is rejected if W is less than or equal to the critical value.

Unit 3

14 Sampling and experimental design

You don't have to eat the whole ox to know that it is tough.

Anon but frequently misattributed to Dr Samuel Johnson

AVONFORD STAR

£1m a year lost locally through work-related illness. Typists beware!

Local industry could be losing over £1m each year through work-related illness according to a report published this week by Saferty, a local Health and Safety consultancy. This staggering figure was based on replies from six local companies sampled by Saferty.

Andy Syson, of Saferty, added 'We know that nationally there are over 20 000 new cases each year, and that typists, as well as road workers, are 15 times more likely than others to acquire musculoskeletal disorders through their work.'

Sampling

Sampling is everywhere these days: market research, statistical process control, clinical trials and predicting election outcomes. Understanding the processes and practicalities involved helps not only when you need to gather data through sampling but also, equally importantly, it helps you evaluate information from others: always look critically at the sample used.

? In the article above, is it realistic of Saferty to draw the conclusion that £1m is lost locally based on a sample of only six local companies?

? If you had to choose six companies to represent local industry, what might you want to know about all the local companies first?

Reasons for sampling

Why sample? In a nutshell: cost and time! When conducting a survey it is usually far too expensive and too time-consuming to collect data from every member of the *population* you are interested in, exceptions being the General Election and the Census. Instead we collect it from a *sample*, or subset, of the population. The process is described as *sampling*.

The two reasons for collecting data are

- to estimate values of characteristics of the parent population
- to conduct a hypothesis test.

Keep in mind that, although you are collecting data from a sample, it is the much larger population that you are really interested in.

A population need not be human. In statistics a population is the collection of all the items about which you want to know something, be it customers, computers, chip shops or Cornishmen. This is also referred to as the *parent population*, or *target population*, as it is the one you are interested in and targeting. This population can be finite, such as footballers playing in the UK, or infinite such as water in the oceans sampled to study the effects of pollution.

List five other finite populations and five other infinite populations you, or others, might be interested in sampling.

What type of data will you collect?

There are two different types of data you are likely to collect: qualitative data such as opinions, and quantitative data such as measurements. Qualitative data include verbal or narrative pieces of data; quantitative data are anything that can be measured and expressed in numbers.

Qualitative data will result in conclusions such as: 'Most people are in favour of having the new bypass, but some think the existing road should simply be made a dual carriageway.' Quantitative data will lead to statements such as 'The effect of taking medication for a month is a mean weight loss of 1.52 kg with standard deviation 0.44 kg.'

Data is the raw material. Information is what you get when you organise and analyse your data.

The difference between statistics and parameters

Although data from your sample will be of immediate interest, the point of collecting them is usually to deduce information about the entire population. In statistics this is called making inferences. Moreover, using statistics, you can calculate how accurate your predictions about the whole population are likely to be; you can provide a measure of reliability, a confidence interval, which will depend on the size of your sample. It is important to realise, however, that you can only calculate a confidence interval if your sample is a random sample and therefore free from bias.

The values you derive from samples are called *sample statistics* or just *statistics*; the mean is written as $\bar{x}$ and the variance as s^2. We use them to estimate the characteristics of the population, its *parameters*, such as the mean, μ, and variance, σ^2.

How large should a sample be?

If it is to be of any use, the sample must be representative of the whole of the population you are interested in and not be biased in any way. This is where the skill in sampling lies: in choosing a sample that is as representative as possible. Market research companies spend much time, money and effort in trying to do just that.

As a general rule the larger the sample, the better it is for estimating characteristics of the population: its parameters such as the mean, μ, and variance, σ^2. You will get a more accurate estimate of the mean height of men by measuring 50 of them rather than just 2. If you collect too much data, however, it will take you too long to process it.

Historical note

An extreme case of data taking a long time to process occurred with the 1880 Census in the USA. (A Census is a 100% sample.) It took no less than 7 years to tabulate the results.

Take a look at the picture below, and imagine it cut into pieces as a jigsaw. As a rough analogy, taking a sample is like picking jigsaw pieces out of a box and trying to guess what the picture is like from the few pieces you have chosen. If you took very few pieces they might all be sky and rock face and you might miss out the fact that the picture contained a steam train running along the shoreline. Ideally you will take a large sample, and somehow ensure that you have pieces from all the different areas of the picture to get as good an idea as possible of what it contains. The more complex the picture, the more pieces you need to get a good idea of the overall picture. The same is true of populations – the greater the variability in a population, the larger the sample you need.

In practice, the size of your sample is constrained by time and cost and there is a balancing act between the constraints and the requirement to collect as good data as possible.

With qualitative outcomes you often do not need a large sample; you get to a point where you know what people think and the range of their opinions and it is really just a waste of time and money asking yet more respondents.

The one exception is opinion polls, especially where there is little difference between the level of support for the outcomes. Distinguishing between a 49% vote and 51% vote is difficult. Professional pollsters trying to predict the outcome of the General Election take a sample of about 1600, expecting 1200 responses.

By contrast, when trying to estimate population parameters your sample size should be at least 30 and should be as large as time and cost permit. Many government surveys sample in excess of 20 000 people.

There is no one right answer to the question of the best sample size. Choosing the right size of sample for your survey or experiment depends on the answers to three important questions.

1 How much variability is there in the population? The more variability, the larger the sample needed.

2 What proportion of the population has the attribute you are interested in? If approximately 49% of the population are going to vote for Paul Main in an election and 51% for Joy Perkins, you will need a large sample size to be confident of predicting the winner.

3 How large a margin of error will you tolerate and what confidence level will you be using? 95%? Smaller margins of error require larger samples.

Having said that, a sample size of between 50 and 100 is sensible for most purposes. If you are expecting a lot of non-responses you will need to start with a much larger sample size. In the trickiest case of an almost equal proportion of the population divided between two opinions, or characteristics, a sample of 100 will give a 10% margin of error either way; but to reduce this to 5% you will need a sample of 400.

A census

In statistical terminology a census is where we collect information about every member of the parent population. One particular example of a census is the Census, which is carried out every 10 years, of all people and households in the United Kingdom. This provides data at a local level, as well as a national level, for both local and national government, for commerce and for the public.

Historical note

Censuses have been taken for centuries as rulers realised that they needed to know how much wealth everybody had, for tax purposes, and how many men were available to fight. The Chinese, the Babylonians, the Egyptians and the Romans all held censuses. It was a 5-yearly Census of Caesar Augustus that is recorded in the Bible at the time of the birth of Christ.

In England, it was William the Conqueror who conducted the first census of property in 1086. He compiled the Domesday Book, again it was for taxation purposes. Quebec held its first official Census in 1666, Iceland in 1703 and Sweden in 1749, but in Britain the first Census was not held until 10 March 1801, after much debate and considerable opposition to the idea.

The Census of 1841 is regarded as the first truly modern census, when for the first time the head of each household was given a form to fill in on behalf of everyone in the household on a certain day. The most recent Census was on 29 April 2001 and the next is being planned for 2011.

ACTIVITY

Visit Neighbourhood statistics on the National Statistics website www.neighbourhood.statistics.gov.uk.

- Use the information there to find some Census data for your own area, such as the population.
- Follow the links to 'Census', 'What is a census?' and 'Census history' to find out in which UK Census computers were used for the first time.
- Read the Census return of Queen Victoria or Charles Dickens.

Many other countries have fascinating Census websites, particularly the United States, the Census Bureau at www.census.gov, and Canada, the Census of Canada at www12.statcan.ca/english/census01/home/index. Visit those to see what information there is, and in particular how it is displayed and made available.

Experiments and surveys

When you require data, you will either use data collected by somebody else (secondary data), or collect it yourself (primary data). How the data are collected is of crucial importance since no amount of statistical technique can change bad data into good, and bad data are often useless or even misleading.

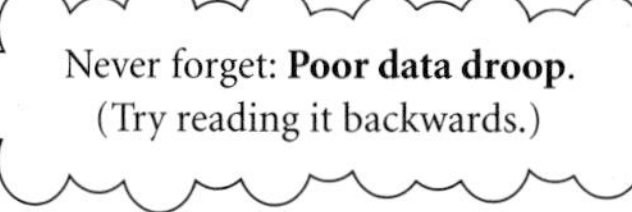

Never forget: **Poor data droop**.
(Try reading it backwards.)

How can a randomly selected sample of only about 1200 people indicate the outcome of a General Election?

How can a well-designed experiment give clear evidence of the effectiveness of a new medical treatment?

These two examples illustrate the difference between a *survey*, the first example, and an *experiment*, the second. In a survey you take a *snapshot* of what is happening without influencing the situation in any way. In an *experiment* you do something to things or people in order to observe what happens. *Experimental design* is covered later in the chapter.

Planning

The use of probability in both experiments and sampling is one of the fundamental concepts of statistics, but you need plenty of practical common sense as well. Whether it is an experiment or a survey that you are conducting, you need a plan of action, of which choosing the sample is an integral part. Statisticians will tell you that time spent planning is worth at least quadruple the time saved later. They will also tell you of the number of times they are consulted about the analysis of a survey and discover that the researchers never collected the one bit of data they really needed.

The first thing to decide, and often the hardest, is *exactly what* it is you are trying to find out. It is also helpful to ask yourself these questions.

- *Who* needs the information?
- By *when*?
- For *what purpose*?
- Will any *action* be taken as a result of your findings?

The answers to these questions will help you to decide how much trouble, in terms of time and money, you need to take to obtain a reasonable enough answer and, in turn, influence your choice of sampling method.

Research students and others often look up similar surveys or experiments as part of the planning process. They conduct a literature search first to make sure that 'their' data do not already exist, or that the problem has not been well researched already. In general looking at what others have done also helps to sharpen up your ideas about exactly what it is you are after.

Having decided what you want to find out, you need to decide on

- the variables you are going to measure
- how you will measure them
- to what degree of accuracy.

Avoid the temptation to collect too much data; collecting data that you are not going to use just wastes time, particularly when it comes to data input.

Carry out a small pilot survey first and pilot the analysis as well. The sample need not be very representative and can be very small, but it will help you identify which questions need improving, and whether you are collecting the data you really need. Statisticians will tell you that a pilot is worth its weight in gold.

You are asked to conduct a survey of thumb sizes of students. How will you measure these? What problems will be involved?

Bias

When you are designing your sampling method, you aim to pick a representative sample free from bias. It is no good, however, having a representative, bias-free, sample of people (or things), if you then introduce bias at the data collection stage. This is a particular danger when conducting surveys using questionnaires.

Bias may be introduced not only by whom you ask, but also by who does the asking, and their understanding of what the survey is about.

A survey is being carried out into aspects of relationships between teenage boys and girls. Who do you think would get the most accurate responses?
- The mother of one of the sample
- A teacher
- One of the students
- A policeman
- An adult who they do not know

In general people want to please you and want to give what they think you think is the 'right' answer.

- Beware of leading questions, 'Do you agree that …' as this may distort people's true opinions.
- Avoid memory questions such as 'What is the mileage of your car?' if you want accuracy.
- Personal and controversial questions need to be approached with care. 'How old are you?' or 'How much do you earn?' or 'Do you take drugs?' may not evoke an accurate response.
- Can personal questions be avoided? Do you need to know a person's exact age, or just which age range they fall into?
- As a general rule leave personal questions to the end of any questionnaire so that, by the time you ask them, people have already given you much useful information even if at that point they walk off.

What problems would arise if you tried to use a questionnaire to find out the extent of drug taking among 40 to 50-year-olds?

ACTIVITY

The Centre for Applied Social Surveys (CASS), run jointly by The National Centre for Social Research, the University of Southampton and the University of Surrey, has an online question bank, at http://qb.soc.surrey.ac.uk, in which you can read all the questions asked in a wide variety of government surveys, as well as details of the sampling methodology and the final reports.

- At the entry page click on 'Questionnaires' and you will be presented with a long list of surveys. Select 'Census of Population 2001' to see the questionnaire used.

It is often useful, when designing questionnaires, to see how someone else has phrased a question.

- Write two questions designed to enquire about a person's general health and the amount of exercise they do, as if these questions were part of a questionnaire about health and fitness.
- From the CASS website select 'Topics' and the 'Leisure and lifestyles' topic and pick one of the questionnaires listed there to discover how someone else wrote similar questions, which were used for real. How did yours compare?

ACTIVITY

Ipsos MORI, www.ipsos-mori.com, is famous for its surveys, as is Gallup in the United States, www.gallup.com. Have a look at their websites and select one of their most recent surveys. Particularly notice

- what the purpose of the poll was
- what questions were asked
- the sample size
- how the sample was selected
- how the findings were presented.

INVESTIGATION

e Randomised response technique

There are ways round asking sensitive questions, provided that you have a reasonable sample size. 80 university students are given this exercise.

Toss a coin twice. If it comes up heads the first time, answer question H; if it comes up tails the first time, answer question T.

H: Have you ever smoked cannabis?
T: Did the *second* toss of the coin come up tails?

28 answer Yes and 52 answer No. Estimate the proportion of students who have smoked cannabis. How does this provide an estimate of the numbers who have smoked cannabis?

EXERCISE 14A

For each of the scenarios below, identify the *population* and the *sample*. Identify possible sources of bias in the sample and comment on the sample size.

1 A national newspaper runs an article suggesting that the hours worked by junior hospital doctors are now well within the European Working Time Directive. The paper receives 250 letters from junior hospital doctors complaining that their hours are still well over 50 per week.

2 A town-centre shopping complex wants to know more about the characteristics of its customers and, in particular, how far they have travelled. The centre manager decides to employ staff to interview a random sample of 20 people entering the car park between 09:00 and 16:00 one Wednesday.

3 A researcher wishes to undertake a study of the amount of exercise undertaken by young people in a particular town and plans to interview a random sample of 2500 young people using the local leisure centre.

4 A charity wishes to assess the impact of its recent national advertising campaign by using a telephone survey, phoning a random sample of 200 people whose names appear in the London telephone directories.

Sampling methods

Understanding exactly what you want and why you want it is the best safeguard against choosing an inappropriate sample.

There are a variety of sampling methods, which are each described below. It is assumed that the sampling is done without replacement so that, for example, the same person will not be asked for their opinion twice or the same building surveyed twice for structural faults.

The basis for selecting any sample is the list of all the subjects from which the sample is to be chosen; this is called the *sampling frame*. Examples are the Postcode Address File (PAF), the Electoral register, telephone directories and maps. A problem, of course, is that the list may not be up to date.

The Postcode Address File (PAF), marketed by Royal Mail, deserves special mention, as it is one of the most commonly used sampling frames, particularly for Government surveys. It lists all postal delivery points in the country and distinguishes between 'small users' (usually households) and 'large users' who have their own postcodes. It represents the fullest and most up-to-date register of household addresses, as almost all correspond to one delivery point, or letterbox.

An even greater problem than not being up to date is that the sampling frame simply may not exist in the first place, nor would it be possible to construct one. For example, what sampling frame is there for all the butterflies on heathland in southern England? As you will see, it is still possible to take a sample but it is more difficult to ensure that it is representative.

With most forms of sampling there is always the problem of those who do not, or will not, respond. This can cause a particular problem if many of the non-respondents have similar characteristics as that section of the population will end up under-represented. There are no easy answers.

Random sampling

A random sample is not a haphazard sample as some people think. Random means lack of predictability, or lack of pattern, without bias. The selection of any member of the population is independent of the selection of any other member of the same population.

The most rigorous form of sampling is called *simple random sampling*; in this, every sample of a given size has an equal, non-zero, probability of being selected. By contrast, the term *random sampling* is applied to situations where each individual has a known non-zero probability of being selected. These probabilities may or may not be equal, but they can be calculated.

? *A simple random sample*

Every Wednesday and Saturday a sample of size 6 is taken from the numbers 1, 2, 3, …, 49. It is the National Lottery. Which of these samples is more likely to be chosen?

(i) 3, 12, 15, 28, 39, 45

(ii) 1, 2, 3, 4, 5, 6

(iii) The same six numbers as were chosen last week

With simple random sampling every possible sample of a given size is equally likely to be selected from a population. As a consequence of this, every member of the population has an equal chance of being chosen. You may sometimes see this referred to as an *epsem* sample: Equal Probability of SElection Method.

The converse is not true. It is possible to have a sample in which each member of the population has an equal chance of being chosen, but it is not a simple random sample, because not all samples are possible.

One such example is an estate agents with 15 branches each with 12 staff. A sample is taken by choosing one member of staff at random from each branch, giving a sample size of 12. Although each member of staff has an equal chance of being chosen the sample cannot contain two members of staff from the same branch, so it is not a simple random sample of all staff.

Simple random samples are the samples beloved by statisticians because, from them, you can calculate how accurate your predictions about the whole population are likely to be. Alas the drawback is that simple random samples are much easier to talk about than to take.

For simple random sampling it is essential that you have an accurate sampling frame and this is frequently the most difficult thing to find for your parent population. Imagine trying to find the sampling frame of cat owners or of owners of wireless connectable laptops. Using a simple random sample is also expensive as the respondents may be scattered over a wide area.

Once you have a list of names, or items, you could write them on a piece of paper, put them in a hat, shake it well and draw out a sample. This would be a simple random sample, but be sure to shake well.

Historical note

In the Vietnam War eligible young men in the United States were drafted to fill vacancies in the armed forces that could not be filled through voluntary means. A large glass container held 366 blue plastic balls containing every possible day of the year and the order in which they were pulled out determined the order in which men would be called up. After the first draw it was noticed that those with birthdays later in the year were more likely to be drafted. The capsules containing the dates had been put in the container month by month, with January first, at the bottom and December on top. Subsequent mixing efforts were insufficient to overcome this sequencing and so there was not randomisation.

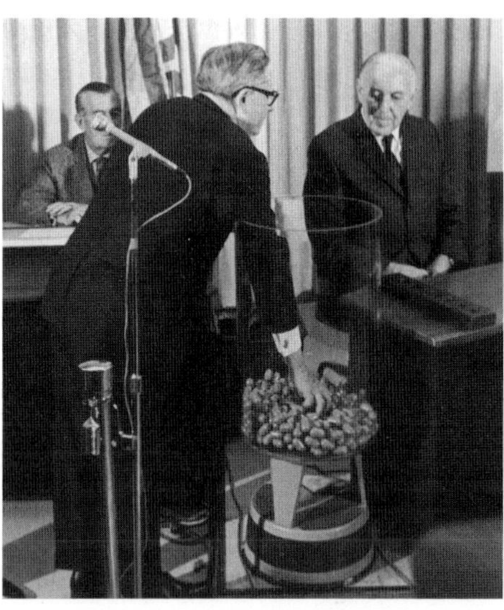

On 4 January 1970, the *New York Times* ran a long article, 'Statisticians Charge Draft Lottery Was Not Random', illustrated with a bar chart of the monthly averages.

An alternative method to the hat is to allocate a number to each member of the parent population and then use random number tables to select the required size of sample.

Random numbers can be generated using a calculator or computer program. Most electronic calculators have a RAN# function that produces a random decimal number between 0 and 1. The formula =RAND( ) in Excel achieves the same result, but to more decimal places.

There are also printed tables of random numbers. An extract from one is printed on the next page.

68236	35335	71329	96803	24413
62385	36545	59305	59948	17232
64058	80195	30914	16664	50818
64822	68554	90952	64984	92295
17716	22164	05161	04412	59002
03928	22379	92325	79920	99070
11021	08533	83855	37723	77339
01830	68554	86787	90447	54796
36782	73208	93548	77405	58355
58158	45059	83980	40176	40737

To make the tables easy to read there is a line between every fifth number and between every fifth row. The sequence of numbers, however, has no gaps. When reading from random number tables you can begin anywhere (chose a number at random) but having started you must continue to read across the line or down a column and not jump about.

The following examples illustrate some of the variety of ways in which random number tables may be used.

EXAMPLE 14.1

A market researcher wants to take a random sample of two houses from a street containing houses numbered 1 to 48. Use the following extract from a table of random sampling numbers to choose the two houses.

68236 35335 71329 96803 24413

SOLUTION

Houses in a road usually have numbers attached, which is convenient as the items in the parent population are ready numbered. The houses are numbered up to 48, so read off the random numbers in pairs.

68 <u>23</u> 63 53 <u>35</u> 71 32 99 68 03 24 41

Take the first two pairs that are less than or equal to 48. These give house numbers 23 and 35.

If by any chance when choosing your sample in this way you choose the same item twice, simply ignore the second one and continue until you have filled your quota with different items.

EXAMPLE 14.2

Use the random number function on a calculator to do the same exercise.

SOLUTION

You would use RAN# and with successive entries might come up with 0.866, 0.928, 0.350, 0.055.

There are now two approaches. You could use the random numbers as a series of random numbers and read them off in pairs: 86 69 28 35 00 55, in which case you would choose houses 28 and 35.

Alternatively you could multiply 0.866 by 48, the number of houses, and round the answer.

$0.866 \times 48 = 41.568$ so choose house number 42.
$0.928 \times 48 = 44.544$ so choose house number 45 as the second one.

EXAMPLE 14.3

The market researcher now wishes to choose a random sample of two houses from a much longer road, with 200 houses. Use the extract from the table of random sampling numbers to choose the two houses.

68236	35335	71329	96803	24413
62385	36545	59305	59948	17232
64058	80195	30914	16664	50818
64822	68554	90952	64984	92295
17716	22164	05161	04412	59002

SOLUTION

The houses are numbered up to 200 so read off the random numbers in threes. Notice how the last number in the first row is read with the first two numbers in the second row.

682 363 533 571 329 968 <u>032</u> 441 362
385 365 455 930 559 948 <u>172</u> 326

The two houses are 32 and 172.

EXAMPLE 14.4

Investors in People wish to interview a random sample of three members of staff from the ten people employed by *Lanchester's*. Choose the members of staff using the extract from the random number tables given in Example 14.3.

SOLUTION

There are ten members of staff, each of whom is given a number. Because there are only ten you can use all ten digits, 0 to 9, and still identify each member of staff uniquely.

0 Braithwaite	1 Lennon	2 Johnston	3 Morgan	4 Reeves
5 Slaich	6 Emrouznejad	7 Mashhoudy	8 Barnes	9 Baker

The first row in the table of random numbers is:

68236 35335 71329 96803 24413.

Read off the first three individual digits: 6 8 2.
So Emrouznejad, Barnes and Johnston are selected.

Notice also that 100 items can be numbered with the 100 pairs of digits 00 to 99.

Using random numbers to sample from maps

You can use random numbers to provide grid references for sampling points on maps or other grids. You can use pre-existing grids, such as those on Ordnance Survey maps or construct your own. In figure 14.1, the two pairs of random numbers 86 and 69 would select the point marked.

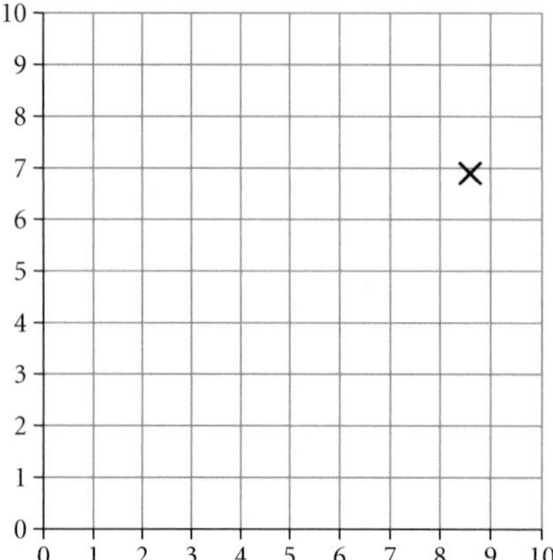

Figure 14.1

EXAMPLE 14.5

A botanist uses a 10×10 grid to survey an area of moorland to determine the prevalence of a particular plant. At each point she determines the presence, or absence, of the plant.

Use the extract from the table of random numbers to select ten points.

68236	35335	71329	96803	24413
62385	36545	59305	59948	17232
64058	80195	30914	16664	50818
64822	68554	90952	64984	92295
17716	22164	05161	04412	59002

SOLUTION

Reading off the numbers in pairs, these are the grid references of the selected points.

68 23	63 53	35 71	32 99	68 03
24 41	36 23	85 36	54 55	93 05

These are illustrated in figure 14.2.

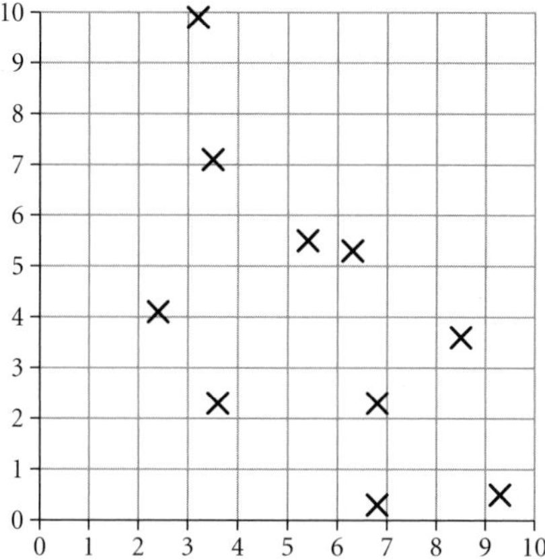

Figure 14.2

When you plot a random sample on a grid, the pattern often looks patchy rather than uniform. On a practical point, when the botanist is out on the moor it may be difficult for her to locate all the points randomly selected, particularly if some are in the middle of a bog.

An alternative method, if you just wanted to identify the squares as complete squares, would be to number them from 1 to 100 and take a simple random sample of numbers from 1 to 100. Sitting and observing butterflies in one such square might be one way of sampling the butterflies on heathland in southern England referred to earlier in the chapter.

Systematic sampling

A business consultant wants to investigate the pattern of takings at a garage and decides to select 20 days at random from a year. She chooses a day at random by sticking a pin in the calendar, and then looks at the till receipts for that day and every 18th day thereafter. This is an example of systematic sampling, which can be described as random sampling with a system!

From the sampling frame, a starting point is chosen at random and thereafter every nth member is chosen. The value of n depends on the size of the sample required. If the business consultant wants a sample of 20 days; there are 365 days in a year. $n = \frac{365}{20} = 18.25$ so she needs to look at every 18th day. The danger with systematic sampling is that it may interact with some hidden pattern in the population.

? The business consultant decides that 20 days are not enough and that she needs 52. What problem would arise if she used the method described above?

? A cavity wall insulation salesman has been told to start at the second house and visit every third. Why might his sample of customers be biased?

Systematic sampling is much easier to carry out than random sampling, offering great savings in time and effort. It also has the advantage of spreading the sample more evenly throughout the parent population.

Stratified sampling

Sometimes the target population can be naturally split up into non-overlapping groups and you would want to sample from each of them. In such a case you might well use a stratified sample.

? A large school catering for Years 7 to 14 is proposing a new school uniform. They decide to investigate the views of the students by asking a sample of 24 students what they think about it. How could they select the sample so as to be representative of the school as a whole?

The different groups are called *strata* (singular: *stratum*). You would try to ensure that the proportions of individuals from the various strata in the sample match the proportions in the whole population. This is illustrated in the next example.

EXAMPLE 14.6

The staff in a company are classified as follows.

Male, full-time	90
Male, part-time	18
Female, full-time	9
Female, part-time	63

A researcher wishes to take a proportionally stratified sample of 40 staff, stratified according to the above categories. Find the number of staff to be chosen from each stratum.

SOLUTION

The first step is to find the total number of staff.

$$90 + 18 + 9 + 63 = 180$$

Then calculate the percentage in each group.

Male, full-time: $\frac{90}{180} \times 100 = 0.5 \times 100 = 50\%$

Male, part-time: $\frac{18}{180} \times 100 = 0.1 \times 100 = 10\%$

Female, full-time: $\frac{9}{180} \times 100 = 0.05 \times 100 = 5\%$

Female, part-time: $\frac{63}{180} \times 100 = 0.35 \times 100 = 35\%$

So, in a sample of 40,

50% should be male, full-time: 50% of 40 = 20
10% should be male, part-time: 10% of 40 = 4
5% should be female, full-time: 5% of 40 = 2
35% should be female, part-time: 35% of 40 = 14.

Stratification can help you make your estimates of population parameters more precise, particularly where the population falls into natural groups, such as age ranges, income bands or ethnic groups. If 60% of the population are male you may want to ensure that men answer exactly 60 out of 100 questionnaires, though this does mean you need to know the proportion of men in the first place.

Interviewers can be trained for particular strata, for example, collecting information from a particular age group or ethnic group, and results from each stratum may be of interest taken separately. If the strata are geographical areas, taking a sample from each seems an obvious exercise and saves money.

? In a study of smoking habits, what factors would you use to stratify the population? Would you use the same factors for a study of mobile phone usage? If not what factors would you use?

The downside to stratified sampling is that it might be difficult to identify appropriate strata. It is also true that the analysis of the results is more complex.

Cluster sampling

? A health worker from the World Health Organisation wants to investigate the incidence of diabetes among the inhabitants of the Brazilian rainforest. How would she go about it?

In cluster sampling the sample consists of groups or clusters of whatever it is you are sampling. For example, if you are sampling households, your sample will consist of several clusters of households, each cluster being a number of households from the same area.

Clusters could be, for example, groups of streets, schools, companies on a business park or shops in an out-of-town retail centre. To ensure a representative spread across the population of interest, each cluster chosen should be as dissimilar as possible. If groups of streets were taken as clusters, you would probably choose some with detached houses, some with terraced houses and some with flats. Once you have chosen the clusters you can then take a simple random sample, or use some other sampling method, to identify the shops, households, etc. you wish to survey.

Cluster sampling is easier to organise, quicker and cheaper than other forms of random sampling. Visiting clusters of respondents saves travelling time, which in turn saves money. In addition you will not need complete information about the population in the first place. The drawback is that the sampling error is likely to be larger than with a simple random sample, so a larger sample size may be needed to compensate, which increases the cost.

Quota sampling

A supermarket wants to find out about their customers' food preferences. Ten sixth form students are employed as interviewers one Saturday morning. Each student is told to ask ten adult men, ten adult women, five teenagers and five children to complete a short questionnaire.

Why is this not a random sample? What advantages does it have?

This is an example of quota sampling, which is a non-random sampling method. The selection of the sample is made by the interviewer, who has been given quotas to fill from each specified sub-group, defined by, for example, gender and age range.

Although it is usually not as representative of the population as a whole as other sampling methods, this type of sample is quick and cheap to organise, which has many advantages. It also eliminates the problem of non-response as the interviewers simply go on asking people until their quotas are filled.

The Census data give us lots of information about population characteristics and can be matched to a particular area. This means that, if you want, you can choose your quotas to match the local population characteristics, so that your sample is reasonably representative.

Because this is not a random sample, it is not possible to estimate the sampling error and you cannot use the data to calculate confidence intervals. It is, nevertheless, extremely useful, particularly when someone requires non-precise information in a hurry.

One national market research organisation conducts a regular omnibus survey in which the questions are bought by a number of clients to meet their individual needs. Each month, in 210 representative parliamentary constituencies, they interview ten respondents chosen by their interviewers to match a given quota based on gender, household tenure, age and working status. Overall, the quotas ensure that the demographic profile of the sample matches the actual profile of the country.

Other samples: the opportunity sample and panel sampling

The opportunity sample, sometimes called the fortuitous sample, is simply one that happens to come your way, and would be silly to ignore. A delegate at a medical conference might want to ask other delegates about their views on the latest Government proposals for health. A doctor, interested in a particular illness, might begin her research with her own patients.

In some medical situations, or where sample measurements are expensive or usually impossible to make, the opportunity sample may be too good to miss.

What useful data might have been collected at the time of the Buncefield oil depot fire, when a large oil storage depot went up in flames?

Panel sampling is the name given to selecting a panel of people who are then surveyed again and again over a period of time, which may be a matter of years. Usually the initial sample is chosen very carefully to be as representative of the population as possible. The British Household Panel Survey, a multipurpose study which interviews all members of a household, is a panel survey.

Multistage sampling

Multistage sampling is where the items to be sampled are chosen in more than one stage and it can involve more than one sampling method.

An example is the Expenditure and Food Survey, a continuous survey of household expenditure, food consumption and income, in which 12 000 households are surveyed.

The sample is a multistage stratified random sample with clustering, drawn from the Small Users file of the Postcode Address File. 672 postal sectors are randomly selected after being arranged in strata defined by Government Office Regions and two 1991 Census variables, socio-economic group and ownership of cars. At the next stage, clusters of address are drawn from each postal sector.

ACTIVITY

- Visit the Centre for Applied Social Surveys (CASS) at http://qb.soc.surrey.ac.uk.
- Select the questionnaires section.
- Choose three different surveys and look at the description of the sampling method for each.

EXERCISE 14B

In questions **1** to **4**

(i) identify the population, the variable being measured and the sample.

(ii) Each situation contains a source of probable bias. Identify why you think bias might occur and state how the sample conclusions will probably differ from the truth about the population.

(iii) Suggest a better method of sampling.

1 In a survey to obtain views on unemployment from the adults of Avonford, people were stopped by an interviewer as they came out of

(a) a travel agent **(b)** a supermarket **(c)** a job centre.

2 A survey of the price of overnight accommodation was undertaken in a town with 40 three-star hotels, 50 two-star hotels and 10 one-star hotels. A sample of ten hotels was obtained by numbering the hotels from 00 to 99 and using random number tables.

3 In the run up to a General Election, a party worker wished to carry out an opinion poll, so selected a random sample of 60 from the electoral register for the constituency and phoned up those whose phone numbers she could find.

4 A young couple asked an advice columnist if having children was worth the problems involved. She asked her readers 'If you had your chance again, would you have children?' 70% of those who replied said they would not.

5 What is the difference between a random sample and a simple random sample?

6 Using the random numbers

35335 71329 96803 24413 62385
36545 59305 59948 17232

(i) select a simple random sample of two letters of the alphabet

(ii) select two students from a list of 650.

7 A simple random sample of 200 adults from Earlsdon is required.

(i) Suggest a method for obtaining such a sample.

(ii) One suggested method was to take a simple random sample of 200 households, and select one adult at random from each household. Why will this not produce a simple random sample of 200 adults from Earlsdon?

8 You wish to interview the head of households in a simple random sample of four houses in a road with 224 houses in it, numbered 1 to 224 including a number 13. Explain how you would select the four houses using the following extract from a table of random numbers and write down the house numbers of those you will be interviewing.

68236	35335	71329	96803	24413
62385	36545	59305	59948	17232
64058	80195	30914	16664	50818
64822	68554	90952	64984	92295
17716	22164	05161	04412	59002

9 A crude model of a large city is given by a circle of radius 10 cm inside which is a concentric circle of radius 5 cm representing the area of high population density. This map was divided into square sampling units of side 0.2 cm.

(i) Describe a possible method for selecting a random sample of ten of the squares.

(ii) A random sample of ten squares was chosen, as shown on the map. Interviewers counted the number of overcrowded families in each of the squares.

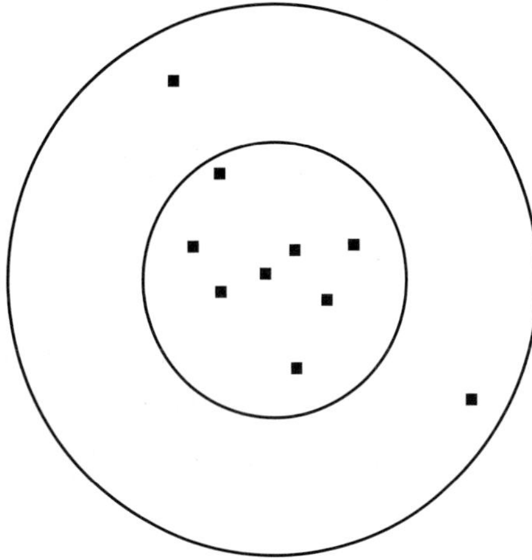

The eight inner units had 10, 16, 8, 11, 12, 10, 7 and 14 overcrowded families. The two outer units had 5 and 9 overcrowded families. Obtain an estimate of the total number of overcrowded families in the city.

10 You wish to carry out a survey in your school, college or university to see which pop group is the most popular at the moment. You decide to sample 10% of the students.

(i) Describe two ways in which a random sample of 10% of the students may be chosen.

(ii) Give two reasons why the random samples chosen in the ways you have described might not be representative.

11 The director of a firm wishes to carry out a survey to see what level of satisfaction there is with the works canteen. He decides to sample 120 workers. The work force is made up of 500 factory workers, 70 clerical staff and 30 managerial staff. Describe how he could sample the whole workforce in such a way that each group of workers is fairly represented in the sample.

12 An opinion poll is being taken in a constituency and a simple random sample of 100 electors is required from one area. The electoral roll for that area has 5000 names on it. Three methods are suggested for selecting the sample. For each of these methods of selection, state, with reasons, whether the sample is a simple random sample. Where a sample is not a simple random sample, explain to what extent, if any, this is likely to invalidate the opinion poll.

(i) Generate 100 random numbers in the range 1 to 5000 and select the corresponding people on the electoral roll.

(ii) Find a road with 100 houses in it and select one elector from each house.

(iii) Select people in positions 1, 51, 101, 151, ..., 4951 on the electoral roll.

Experimental design

AVONFORD STAR

High street vouchers drastically reduce absenteeism!

Health service boss Helen Alston is delighted with the latest scheme at Avonford Hospital that aims to cut the number of days lost through absenteeism. Cleaning, catering and some care staff who have six months' unbroken attendance record are being given £25 in high street vouchers to spend on whatever they like as a reward for simply turning up to work. Alston says 'This may sound a crazy and expensive idea, but I have seen it work in other sectors so wanted to give it a try here – and it is actually saving us money, as well as reducing the hassle of having to find cover at the last minute.'

Helen Alston has conducted an experiment. She has done something, by introducing vouchers for good attendance, observed what happened, compared the outcome with what happened before the voucher scheme was introduced, and evaluated the result.

The reason for conducting an experiment is to test a hypothesis. In the *Avonford Star* article the hypothesis was that introducing high street vouchers as a reward for good attendance would reduce absenteeism. The tricky bit is ensuring that your experiment is actually testing your hypothesis. There could be other factors at work that actually cause the outcome you observe, but of which you may be unaware. What Helen Alston forgot to tell the *Avonford Star* was that, along with the voucher scheme, she introduced a new system of rotas which enabled staff to have time off when they needed it most and to know their shifts for the whole of the month in advance.

Designing good experiments is not easy. You need to be aware of every possible factor that might affect the outcome. You also need to be aware that human behaviour is a very complex thing, so any experiments involving humans need to be designed extremely carefully and, in addition, must take into account ethical considerations.

It is important to understand that in an experiment you *do* something, which affects the outcome. This may be giving out high street vouchers, improving the infrastructure in an area, sending staff on a training course, or planting seeds in different types of soil.

- An *experiment* involves doing something to things, or people, in order to observe what happens.
- The things are called *experimental units* or, in the case of people, *subjects*.
- What you 'do' is called a *treatment*.

Doing, observing, comparing and evaluating are the essence of carrying out an experiment but the most important part is planning the initial design. At the outset of the experiment you need to the following.

- Identify the question.
- Identify all the variables and, in particular, the ones you are interested in.
- Control the variables you are not interested in so that they do not contribute to the outcome of the experiment.
- Decide which variables are likely to depend on others and which are likely to be independent.
- The *independent variables*, or *explanatory variables*, are the ones that cause something to happen. Explanatory variables are also called *factors*.
- Each treatment is a combination of one or more explanatory variables.
- The value of the explanatory variable is called its *level*. This might be a number, such as the cash value of the high street vouchers, or a qualitative description, such as the variety of seed planted.
- *Dependent variables*, or *response variables*, are the ones you measure to determine the effect. They are the variables whose values you expect to change as a result of applying different treatments.

The key principles in designing an experiment are *control*, *randomisation* and *replication*. Finally beware of a lack of realism. Experimental conditions, particularly those involving people, may not realistically represent the conditions you are really interested in studying.

Control

Experiments allow you to study the effects of treatments of interest and allow you to control the environment of the experimental units so that other factors, which are of no interest, can be held constant.

The simplest form of control is where experiments compare treatments. This includes treatment being compared with non-treatment.

There are two ways of doing this. In the first you have two or more groups of experimental units, or subjects, and treat each differently to compare the outcome; a *between-subjects design.* These are two independent samples and any statistical tests you apply will be two-sample tests. The groups should be matched as closely as possible in all respects, except for the treatment they receive. One group will be the non-treated group, which is called a *control group.*

The second way is to use a paired sample, where you use the same experimental units, or people, throughout the experiment and give all the treatments to each. This is called a *within-subjects* design.

The choice of method depends on the experiment, as well as the time and money available. If you are comparing the efficiency of a new teaching method of algebra you cannot teach the same students using both the old and the new methods. Students are likely to gain some understanding of algebra using the first method and this effect would carry over and influence the results from the second method.

In a *blind test* the subject is unaware which treatment they are receiving, though the evaluator knows whether or not the subject is in the control group.

In a *double-blind test* neither the evaluator nor the subject knows which items or people are in the control group. Double-blind tests are particularly useful in medicine as they help eliminate self-deception and wishful thinking.

Historical note

In 1998, an American National Security laboratory tested a mechanical 'Lifeguard' which claimed to be able to detect a living human being by receiving a signal from the heartbeat at distances of up to 20 metres through any material.

For the test, five large plastic packing crates were set up in a line at 30-foot intervals and the test operator, using the 'Lifeguard' tried to detect the only crate containing a human. Whether a crate would be empty or contain a person for each trial was determined by random assignment.

To check that the 'Lifeguard' was working, ten trials were carried out. In these the test operator, who was a senior person from the manufacturers of the device, was allowed to see which crate the human entered and then used the 'Lifeguard' to detect his presence. In those ten trials the 'Lifeguard' performed well: 10 out of 10 crates were correctly identified.

The trial was then repeated 25 times but this time neither the test operator nor the investigators knew which case the human was in. This time only 6 out of 25 cases were correctly identified, a result that is no better than random chance.

Randomisation

You can only be confident in the results of comparing the effects of several treatments if all the treatments are applied to similar groups of experimental units. The simplest way is to use chance to allocate the treatments to experimental units, or subjects. This is called *randomisation.*

Remember that allocating experimental units, or subjects, randomly does not mean haphazardly. In particular, nobody should make the allocation based on his or her own judgement of randomness. People are experts at introducing bias, even if it is subconsciously. Stick to an objective method using random numbers.

Replication

An experiment on one thing, or one person, does not provide sufficient evidence of anything so there is a need to repeat, or *replicate*, the experiment several times. You need to apply each treatment to a large enough number of experimental units, or subjects, to be able to draw conclusions.

Lurking and confounding variables

In a well-controlled experiment the results only depend on the variables, or combination of variables, you are testing. Your aim is to ensure that every other variable, which is not of interest, remains unchanged throughout the experiment. Unfortunately, despite your best efforts, you will frequently not succeed in achieving this ideal level of control.

There are two reasons. Firstly there may be variables that have an important effect on the results, but you are totally unaware of them; or, even if you know of these variables, you may consider them completely irrelevant. They lurk in the background and are called *lurking variables.* A lurking variable is one that has an important effect but is not included in the variables being studied.

At Avonford Hospital the introduction of new rotas was a lurking variable. In experiments where you ask each subject to do a large number of tests, or do anything for a long time, fatigue may become a lurking variable.

The second reason why your experiment may not be as well controlled as you hoped are the *confounding variables*, which sound confusing and that is just what they are. If you have two variables, which you may or may not know about, and their effects cannot be distinguished from each other, they confuse the issue. You do not know which is responsible for what. These variables are called confounding variables.

Notice that a lurking variable may also be a confounding variable. Look back to the article about Avonford Hospital on page 341; the rotas are an example of a lurking variable. Was the improvement in absenteeism due to the vouchers or the rotas? How could Helen Alston tell?

There may be other variables that change in any groups you are studying but, if they affect each group in the same way, they are just a nuisance, *nuisance variables.*

Design of experiments

Now that you have reviewed the principles of experimental design, you have arrived at the crunch: actually designing one. This is not easy, particularly as you are likely to encounter unforeseen snags. For this reason it is very useful, if at all possible, to conduct a pilot experiment first.

Here are two situations where an experiment needs to be designed. Think how you might design each one and what the possible problems might be. Then read the rest of this chapter, which describes some common designs.

The strawberries

Helley's Nurseries has just developed a new variety of strawberry, Spangella, which it hopes will be very popular because of its increased yield. Before marketing it the nursery wants to compare the yield with that of its standard variety. It has ten fields available for the experiment.

The clinical experiment

A clinician wishes to investigate whether or not a new drug, used as part of a programme of diet, exercise and drug treatment, could assist obese individuals to lose weight. There are 37 otherwise healthy patients available for the study.

Completely randomised design

In the experiments above you need to decide which field, or part of a field, has which strawberry and which patients are to receive the new drug and which the placebo. (Hopefully you did think about using a look-alike placebo in the drug trial.) The simplest way of doing this is to allocate strawberry plants or drug at random. This way avoids any characteristics of fields or people influencing the choice and any differences between the groups will have arisen by chance. Where the variability in your experimental units, plots or people, is unknown, this might be the best you can do.

An experiment where the treatments are allocated to the experimental units, or subjects, completely at random, is said to be a *completely randomised design.*

If the fields are too small to be divided into more than two plots, why might this not be the best way of doing it?

Matched pairs design

If the ten strawberry fields are so small that each one can only be divided into two plots the variability between even these 20 plots might mask the differences in yield with a completely randomised design. Matching each pair of plots in one field and growing one variety on one and the other on the other, then comparing yields could obtain more precise results.

In the weight loss experiment it might also be possible to match the patients by such characteristics as age, gender, height, initial weight, family history of obesity, motivation and number of previous attempts to lose weight. Matching the pairs as closely as possible can be difficult, which is why identical twins are the ideal matched pair for many psychology experiments. If it is not possible to match the patients a completely randomised design would be preferable.

A design where experimental units or subjects are matched as closely as possible and one is given one treatment while the other is given another, or none, is called a *matched pairs design*. You will need to use a paired-sample procedure (see Chapter 15) to analyse the results.

Depending on the experiment, it is sometimes possible to use subjects as their own control. They get both treatments, the order in which they receive them being randomly determined, for example by tossing a coin. This is a special case of a matched pairs design and is called a *repeated measures design* or *cross over trial.*

Randomised block design

In the weight loss experiment it might not be possible to match pairs of patients but it might be considered that a family history of obesity is an important factor, in which case two groups of patients might be identified: those with and those without a family history of obesity. Within each group patients would be randomly allocated to the drug.

Next year the nursery might want to compare the yields of four existing varieties of runner beans in their ten fields, so that they can decide on which two to continue selling. They know that in general their ten fields differ in fertility but cannot quantify this in any way. If the ten fields were large enough they could be subdivided into several plots and all four varieties allocated at random within each field.

This type of design is called a *randomised block design.* A block is simply a group of experimental units, or subjects, which are known to be similar in some way and where the similarity is likely to affect the outcome of the experiment. Once the blocks have been determined the treatments are randomly allocated within each block.

In a matched pairs design each pair is a block. In our examples the two groups of patients and the ten fields are blocks. If the fields are divided into 8, 12, 16 or any multiple of four blocks so that the same number of the four different varieties of runner bean plants is planted in each, it will be what is known as a *balanced design.* This is preferable from an analysis point of view.

Although the analysis of the results of a randomised block design can get complicated, always start with the production of simple tables and charts of the data as these may make the conclusion obvious.

ACTIVITY

The weight loss case study scenario is similar to the Case Studies in Medicine material provided by the Royal Statistical Society Centre for Statistical Education. Visit their site at www.rsscse.org.uk/resources/schools.asp to download data relating to a real-life study to see what conclusions you would draw from the experiment. Full explanatory notes are provided.

e Latin squares

A bakery wants to buy a new packaging machine. There are three possible machines and the manufacturer will let the bakery have the use of all three for a week. The bakery uses three different types of packaging: for large cakes, for small cakes and for specialist cakes. The rate at which items can be packaged depends not only on the nature of the packaging but also on the operator.

The treatments are the three different machines. The response variable is the number of packages produced. If there were only one operator you could use a randomised block design with the blocks being each of the three types of packaging. This does not make the best use of the time available since with three operators you could use all three machines during the week and gather far more data. What you need is a different experimental design: a *Latin square design.*

A Latin square has n columns and n rows in which n symbols are written such that each symbol occurs just once in each column and row. The concept in a Latin square design is that each machine is used once by each operator and once on each type of packaging.

For

- three machines called 1, 2 and 3
- three operators called Angela, Barbara and Chris
- three different types of packages for large cakes, small cakes and specials

this would be a possible design.

		Operator		
		Angela	**Barbara**	**Chris**
Package type	**Large cakes**	3	2	1
	Small cakes	2	1	3
	Specials	1	3	2

An analysis of the results will provide information about differences between the machines, the operators and the effects of the different packages. We have assumed, however, that any interaction between machines, operators and types of packaging are negligible.

A Latin square design enables you to look at situations where there are three variables. A *Greco-Latin square* combines two Latin squares so that you can study the effects of four variables (rows, columns, letters and numbers) each with three levels, using only nine runs of an experiment.

3	2	1
2	1	3
1	3	2

a	b	c
c	a	b
b	c	a

a3	b2	c1
c2	a1	b3
b1	c3	a2

A case study: the Salk vaccine trial

In the early 1950s polio was a frightening disease and one with the most inexplicable behaviour. It appeared in epidemic waves in one community one year and in another the next, hitting hardest at young children and, surprisingly, usually affecting those who were best off in terms of nutrition, housing and hygiene. Although it was responsible for relatively few deaths (about 6% of all deaths in the 5 to 9 age group) it left many children paralysed or crippled and some who could only survive in respirators. In 1952 there were over 60 000 cases in the United States.

These factors, together with the earlier involvement of President Franklin D Roosevelt, led to a very great concern about the nature of polio, with the result that money and effort were spent on research into the disease. The cause of polio was found to be a virus and the search was on for an effective vaccine.

Smallpox and influenza (flu) illustrate two different approaches to the preparation of vaccines. For smallpox a closely-related live virus is used, cowpox, which is ordinarily incapable of causing serious disease in humans but which nevertheless gives rise to antibodies which protect against smallpox. In the case of flu, instead of using a closely-related live virus, the vaccine is a solution of the dead flu virus, which still has enough antigenic activity to produce the required antibodies.

Both these methods were explored for polio. Vaccines were produced but at least one actually caused cases of paralytic polio so all were withdrawn! In the early 1950s Jonas Salk at the University of Pittsburgh developed a killed-virus vaccine, which was shown to be safe and to induce high levels of antibodies in children on whom it had been tested. However, it was thought unsafe to release the vaccine for general use without convincing proof of its effectiveness; hence the decision to undertake a large-scale field trial.

Polio is not easy to diagnose in its early stages, but its effects range from mild fever and weakness to paralysis and death. The virus turns out to be quite common and it is thought that most adults had actually experienced a polio infection sometime in their lives without being aware of it. The rate of occurrence of polio at this time was about 50 per 100 000.

? How might you have conducted this experiment, bearing in mind that your subjects are children, what you do to them will affect their health, maybe their lives, and that the outcome of your experiment will dramatically affect the lives of millions.

There are three important things to consider.

1 How will you set up a control group, especially bearing in mind that it was difficult to predict where the next outbreak might be?

2 How large will your sample be?

3 What are the ethical issues involved?

What happened

The first surprise may be the numbers involved: 1 829 916 children. Such an experiment does pose some ethical problems as well as the practical ones of persuading parents to allow their children to be vaccinated with something that might be totally ineffective, a placebo, or might be the real thing, which of course might also be totally ineffective. In the end there were two experiments conducted in different areas. In both there were control groups but the difference lay in how these groups were chosen.

In the *placebo control* experiment every child was vaccinated, but some of them only received salt solution instead of the vaccine. Each vial of the fluid was identified by a code number so that nobody involved in the vaccination or in subsequently diagnosing a suspected case of polio knew which child had received the vaccine and which child had received salt solution. Only after a final diagnosis had been made in each case was the code broken to identify whether or not that child had received the vaccine.

In the *observed control* experiment vaccination was offered to all children in the second grade of participating schools, the treated group. Children in the first and third grades of these schools were the control group, who were also followed up for the incidence of polio.

The results of the experiment showed the effectiveness of the vaccine and it was released for general use.

EXERCISE 14C

1 Criticise the following statement: 'A study of the benefits of vitamin C showed that 90% of people suffering from a cold when given vitamin C recovered within a week.'

2 A researcher wanted to give two different groups of students (mathematicians and computer scientists) an aptitude test. The students sat the test in different rooms, one of which was extremely hot as it was a sunny day.

(i) The differences in performance could have be caused by at least three different factors. What are these?

(ii) How could the test have been better carried out?

3 A manufacturer of dishwasher powder wanted to test a new formulation that would be particularly suitable for fine china with gold leaf. A researcher has suggested that they wash two identical sets of china 1000 times, one with the standard powder and the other with the new. After the 1000 washes the two sets would be compared. Write a set of simple instructions so that a completely randomised design may be used.

4 A bank wishes to improve the mathematical ability of its employees and is keen to evaluate a CD with interactive training material. The Personnel Officer has arranged for 20 employees to take a mathematics test. They are given back their marked scripts together with the CD and told that they will be given the same test again next week. The next week the same employees retake the test and their scores show a remarkable improvement. The Personnel Officer is convinced of the value of the CD. Criticise the design of this experiment. How might you improve on it?

5 A doctor wishes to carry out a trial of a drug which is thought to reduce the incidence of migraines. He has ten willing volunteers amongst his patients who are all severe migraine sufferers. Suggest a design for his experiment. What ethical issues does an experiment like this raise?

KEY POINTS

1 A sample is a subset of a population.

2 The reasons for sampling are
- to estimate values of the parameter in the parent population
- to conduct a hypothesis test
- to acquire qualitative data.

3 A census is a 100% sample in which data are collected from every member of a population.

4 A sample should be as representative of the population as possible and large enough for the purpose.

5 Different sampling methods include
- simple random sampling
- stratified sampling
- cluster sampling
- systematic sampling
- quota sampling
- opportunity sampling.

6 A survey is a process for collecting data about people or things.

7 An experiment involves doing something to things, or people, in order to observe what happens.

8 The key principles to bear in mind in experimental design are
- control
- randomisation
- replication.

9 The 'things' are called experimental units or, in the case of people, subjects.

10 What you 'do' is called a treatment.

11 Each treatment is a combination of one or more explanatory variables called factors.

12 The value of the explanatory variable is called its level.

13 The response variables, which are the ones you measure, are the variables whose value you expect to change as a result of applying different treatments or factors.

14 The aim of the experiment is to compare treatments or to compare a treatment with no treatment.

15 A control is no treatment.

16 In a completely randomised design, treatments are allocated randomly to the experimental units.

17 A matched pairs design compares two treatments. Experimental units or subjects are matched as closely as possible and one is given one treatment while the other is given the other treatment (or none).

18 In a randomised block design, the experimental units, or subjects, are divided into blocks and the treatments are randomly allocated to the experimental units within the blocks.

15 Hypothesis tests on paired samples

Love means never having to say you are sorry.

Erich Seagal

Statistics means never having to say you are certain.

Myles Hollander

AVONFORD STAR

Our athletes can't run at night!

Following a very disappointing performance by Avonford Harriers athletes at the recent County Athletics Championships, local statistician Sandie Green has come up with an explanation. Our athletes can't run at night!

Although many of our athletes got through the first-round heats in the morning session, most of them failed to get through the semi-final stage in the evening. It was initially thought that our athletes were not good enough but Sandie came up with an alternative explanation.

'It is clear that Avonford runners perform better in the morning. This is probably because they do more of their training early in the morning before going to work' Sadie told us. 'Before the next County Championships we must look in more detail at the training of these athletes'.

Paired and unpaired experiments

Is this a valid explanation or just a feeble excuse for poor performances? In order to test this, the coach conducts a simple experiment. He takes a random sample of seven Avonford Harriers athletes, who run 400 metres in both a morning and an evening session.

The results are shown in the table.

Athlete	Evening time	Morning time
SD	47.2	46.2
SC	47.6	47.1
MM	46.8	46.7
OC	47.4	47.4
SR	48.3	48.5
MW	50.3	49.3
NF	52.1	50.1

In this experiment the same seven athletes were timed for the morning and evening sessions. This is an example of a *paired design*. On other occasions you may not be able to use the same subjects in the two conditions; for example, some of the athletes may not be available or they may be injured. If you had chosen marathon runners you would have got very odd results if you had insisted that they ran a race in the morning and then in the afternoon.

In many experiments it is not possible to use the same subjects for both conditions and in such cases an unpaired test has to be used. Unpaired design is covered in the next chapter.

However, attempts are often made to match subjects so that a paired test can be used.

For example in many social science research projects pairs of identical twins are used.

Terminology

- In this example, the random sample consists of seven Avonford Harriers athletes, who run 400 metres in both a morning and an evening session.
- Population 1 is the times, X, of all Avonford Harriers athletes over 400 metres in the morning; it has mean $\overline{X}$. A sample of size 7 has been taken from this, $x_1, x_2, x_3, \ldots, x_7$.
- Population 2 is the times, Y, of all Avonford Harriers athletes over 400 metres in the evening; it has mean $\overline{Y}$. The equivalent sample of size 7 has been taken from this, $y_1, y_2, y_3, \ldots, y_7$.
- The paired sample has differences $d_1, d_2, d_3, \ldots, d_7$, where $d_1 = y_1 - x_1$, $d_2 = y_2 - x_2, \ldots, d_7 = y_7 - x_7$, drawn from a population of differences, D, with mean $\overline{D}$.

So the Avonford Harriers data can be reduced to the set of values, $d_1, d_2, \ldots, d_7$ of the differences in the morning and evening times, as shown in the table.

Athlete	Evening time, y_i	Morning time, x_i	Difference, $d_i = y_i - x_i$
SD	47.2	46.2	1
SC	47.6	47.1	0.5
MM	46.8	46.7	0.1
OC	47.4	47.4	0
SR	48.3	48.5	−0.2
MW	50.3	49.3	1
NF	52.1	50.1	2

If these figures come from a population with mean zero, then you would expect to see approximately equal numbers and sizes of positive and negative differences in the sample. What you want to decide is whether the seven differences listed above are, on the whole, so obviously positive that it is unlikely that they came from a population with a mean of zero.

To do this you use a paired-sample test. In this chapter two such tests are covered, the paired-sample *t* test and the Wilcoxon signed rank test for paired samples.

The paired-sample *t* test

Setting up the hypothesis test

H_0: $\overline{D} = 0$, there is, on average, no difference between the performance of Avonford athletes in the morning and the evening.

H_1: $\overline{D} > 0$, on average, Avonford athletes are faster in the morning than in the evening (hence the times for the mornings are smaller).

1-tailed test

Significance level: 5% ← 5% is a suitable level in this situation.

The form of the alternative hypothesis, which claims that Avonford athletes are faster in the morning rather than just being different, indicates that a 1-tailed test is appropriate.

Calculating the test statistic

The sample values are 1, 0.5, 0.1, 0, −0.2, 1 and 2. (These are the differences, *d*.)

Start by calculating the sample mean and standard deviation of the differences.

$$\bar{d} = 0.6286$$
$$s = 0.7675$$

← Use your calculator to check these values for yourself.

The test statistic, *t*, is given by

$$t = \frac{\bar{d}}{\frac{s}{\sqrt{n}}}$$

$$= \frac{0.6286}{\frac{0.7675}{\sqrt{7}}}$$

$$= 2.167$$

Interpreting the test statistic

In this case $n = 7$ and, as before with a t test, $\nu = n - 1 = 7 - 1 = 6$.

The critical value, at the 5% significance level, for a one-tailed t test with 6 degrees of freedom, is found in the t tables under $\nu = 6$ and $p = 10\%$.

ν \ $p\%$	10	5	2	1
1	6.314	12.71	31.82	63.66
2	2.920	4.303	6.965	9.925
3	2.353	3.182	4.541	5.841
4	2.132	2.776	3.747	4.604
5	2.015	2.571	3.365	4.032
6	1.943	2.447	3.143	3.707
7	1.895	2.365	2.998	3.499
8	1.860	2.306	2.896	3.355
9	1.833	2.262	2.821	3.250
10	1.812	2.228	2.764	3.169
11	1.796	2.201	2.718	3.106
12	1.782	2.179	2.681	3.055

Remember the tables are constructed to give each tail a probability of $\frac{1}{2}p\%$.

This gives a critical value of 1.943.

Since 2.167 is greater than 1.943, the null hypothesis is rejected and the alternative hypothesis is accepted.

The evidence supports, at the 5% significance level, the statement in the *Avonford Star* that the athletes are faster in the morning.

Rationale

It is useful at this stage to think more clearly about what is happening when you apply this test.

The values $d_1, d_2, , \ldots , d_7$, where $d_1 = y_1 - x_1$, $d_2 = y_2 - x_2$, …, are a sample of size 7. In this test, D is assumed to be Normally distributed. The standard deviation of the parent population is unknown so the standard deviation, s, of the sample is used as an estimate for it. That is why you use a t test. The null hypothesis is that the mean of D is zero.

? If the mean of D is zero, what does this tell you about populations 1 and 2, the morning times and the afternoon times?

The test statistic, t, is given by

$$t = \frac{\bar{d}}{\frac{s}{\sqrt{n}}}.$$

It has a t distribution with $n - 1$ degrees of freedom.

In the case where $n = 7$, the test statistic has 6 degrees of freedom and the test statistic is given by

$$t = \frac{\bar{d}}{\frac{s}{\sqrt{7}}}.$$

? Compare this with the approach to the t test for a single sample. What do you notice?

Testing for a non-zero value of the difference of two means

In the example above the null hypothesis, H_0, was that the mean value, $\bar{D}$, of the population difference, D, is zero. Sometimes, as in the next example, you will need to test that the population difference has some other value, denoted by k.

EXAMPLE 15.1

Do people tend to marry other people of the same age? A student investigates the statement that women on average marry men 4 years older than themselves. She takes a random sample of ten married couples in England and records the age, to the nearest $\frac{1}{10}$ of a year, at which they married. These are her results.

Age of husband, x_i	36.3	42.3	37.4	26.5	21.5	30.8	32.9	56.3	25.2	30.9
Age of wife, y_i	33.6	35.7	29.8	27.1	20.2	25.2	27.4	45.7	23.6	25.7

Carry out the appropriate hypothesis test.

SOLUTION

Define population 1 as the ages, X, at which men marry in England.
It has mean $\bar{X}$.
A sample of size 10 has been taken from this, $x_1, x_2, x_3, \ldots, x_{10}$.

Define population 2 as the ages, Y, at which women marry in England.
It has mean $\bar{Y}$.
The equivalent sample of size 10 has been taken from this, $y_1, y_2, y_3, \ldots, y_{10}$.

? Why is this a paired sample?

The paired sample has differences $d_1, d_2, \ldots, d_{10}$, where $d_1 = x_1 - y_1$, $d_2 = x_2 - y_2, \ldots, d_{10} = x_{10} - y_{10}$, drawn from a population of differences, D, with mean $\bar{D}$.

So the data are reduced to the set of values, $d_1, d_2, \ldots, d_{10}$, of the differences in ages, shown in the table.

Husband, x_i	36.3	42.3	37.4	26.5	21.5	30.8	32.9	56.3	25.2	30.9
Wife, y_i	33.6	35.7	29.8	27.1	20.2	25.2	27.4	45.7	23.6	25.7
Difference, $d_i = x_i - y_i$	2.7	6.6	7.6	−0.6	1.3	5.6	5.5	10.6	1.6	5.2

Setting up the hypothesis test

H_0: $\overline{D} = 4$, there is a 4-year difference between the ages of husbands and wives when they marry.

H_1: $\overline{D} \neq 4$, the difference between the ages of husbands and wives when they marry is not 4 years.

2-tailed test

Significance level: 5%

 Why is this a 2-tailed test?

Calculating the test statistic

Start by calculating the sample mean and standard deviation of the differences, $d_1, d_2, \ldots, d_{10}$.

$$\bar{d} = 4.61$$
$$s = 3.3617$$

The test statistic, t, is given by $t = \dfrac{\bar{d} - k}{\dfrac{s}{\sqrt{n}}}$ where $k = 4$.

$$t = \frac{4.61 - 4}{\dfrac{3.3617}{\sqrt{10}}}$$
$$= 0.5738$$

Interpreting the test statistic

In this case $n = 10$ so $\nu = n - 1 = 10 - 1 = 9$.

The critical value, at the 5% significance level, for a 2-tailed t test with 9 degrees of freedom is 2.262.

Since 0.5738 is less than 2.262, the null hypothesis is accepted.

The evidence supports the statement that there is a 4-year difference between the mean ages of husbands and wives when they marry, at the 5% significance level.

? What would you have concluded if this test had been significant?

Assumptions for the *t* test

There are two assumptions when carrying out a t test.

1 The sample taken is random.

2 The variable is Normally distributed.

? In the first example a random sample of Avonford Harriers athletes was taken. Are the differences between morning and evening times Normally distributed? How could you check whether the model of a Normal distribution fits the differences?

EXERCISE 15A

1 'It is clear that Avonford runners perform better in June than in July when the main competitions are' moaned the Avonford athletics coach. This conclusion was based on the following results. A random sample of ten athletes was selected for one distance, the 400 metres. The results are shown in the table.

Runner	A	P	C	T	E	F	W	D	J	B
June time	45.2	47.5	46.5	46.4	48.5	49.6	50.1	51.2	49.8	50.3
July time	47.8	47.4	46.9	46.4	49.3	50.1	51.1	52.3	49.2	48.6

Use an appropriate t test, at the 5% significance level, to examine whether the mean difference between the times is zero. Also state the required distributional assumption.

2 A company purchases a chemical from a supplier. It is specified that the chemical should contain no more than 7.5% of impurity. To investigate this, the company arranges that a random sample of deliveries is checked by the supplier and by the company itself. The percentages of impurity as found by the supplier and the company are as follows.

Delivery	A	B	C	D	E	F	G	H	I	J
Supplier's determination	7.7	9.4	6.6	5.5	8.1	4.9	5.9	6.9	9.0	7.4
Company's determination	7.5	9.1	6.8	5.4	8.0	4.7	5.6	6.9	9.3	7.7

Use an appropriate t test, at the 5% level of significance, to examine whether the mean determinations of percentage of impurity by the company and supplier may be assumed to be equal, stating clearly your null and alternate hypotheses and the required distributional assumption. [MEI, *part*]

3 A psychologist is studying the possible effect of hypnosis on dieting and weight loss. Nine people (who may be considered as a random sample from the population under study) volunteer to take part in the experiment. Their weights are measured. Then, under hypnosis, they are told that they will seldom feel hungry and will eat less than usual. After a month, their weights are measured again. The results in kilograms are as follows.

Person	Initial weight	Weight after one month
A	83.7	81.5
B	83.9	80.0
C	68.2	68.8
D	74.9	74.1
E	81.0	82.6
F	72.8	69.2
G	61.3	63.4
H	77.9	74.7
I	69.6	66.2

(i) Use an appropriate t test to examine whether, overall, the mean weight has been reduced over the month, at the 5% level of significance.

(ii) What distributional assumption is needed?

[MEI, *part*]

4 In a steelworks, several skilled technicians are testing two machines that can be used to cut rods of steel to, approximately, the required lengths. The machines always cut to slightly above the specified length, so that the rod may be ground down to the required length. However, this causes a waste of time and material. The purpose of the test is to find which machine, if either, is better on the whole at cutting very near to the specified length and thus minimising wastage.

Each technician uses each machine to cut rods to a particular specified length. The excess length is then carefully measured, and the results, in centimetres, are as follows.

Technician	Machine A	Machine B
1	2.9	1.9
2	1.8	1.4
3	4.7	3.4
4	2.7	3.3
5	2.9	2.0
6	2.4	2.4
7	5.2	3.2
8	2.9	2.1

Use an appropriate t test to examine at the 5% level of significance, whether either machine is better, stating carefully your null and alternative hypotheses.

[MEI, *part*]

5 A taxi fleet manager thinks that fuel consumption might be improved by adopting a new design of tyre. An experiment is conducted to compare fuel consumption using this new design and using standard tyres. Ten taxis are selected at random from the fleet, fitted with the new tyres, and driven for a month in normal service, each keeping its own driver throughout the trial. The average fuel consumption over this period is measured for each taxi, and compared with the average fuel consumption for a previous similar period with the standard tyres. The results for average fuel consumption, in litres per 100 kilometres, are as follows.

Taxi	1	2	3	4	5	6	7	8	9	10
New tyres	18.2	17.6	19.4	17.9	18.9	17.4	18.5	19.0	18.9	17.2
Standard tyres	19.0	17.1	19.6	19.0	18.8	18.9	18.8	19.7	18.3	18.4

It is desired to examine the null hypothesis that, on the whole, the fuel consumption is the same with new and standard tyres against the alternative that it is better (i.e. the result, in litres per 100 km, is smaller) with the new tyres. Making an appropriate assumption, which should be carefully stated, use a t test to examine the above hypothesis at the 5% level of significance.

[MEI, *part*]

6 A therapist is studying the effect of a particular type of therapy on a phobic reaction. A random sample of ten patients is available. For each patient, the intensity of the phobic reaction is measured, on a suitable scale, before and after therapy. The results are as follows.

Patient	**Intensity before therapy**	**Intensity after therapy**
A	72	66
B	59	40
C	45	58
D	87	56
E	37	15
F	64	66
G	7	15
H	75	31
I	14	3
J	50	36

Use an appropriate t procedure to test, at the 5% level of significance, whether the therapy on the whole reduces the intensity of the reaction, stating clearly your null and alternative hypotheses and the required distributional assumption.

[MEI, *part*]

7 A fermentation process causes the production of an enzyme. The amount of the enzyme present in the mixture after a certain number of hours needs to be measured accurately. An inspector is comparing two procedures for doing this, there being a suspicion that the procedures are leading to different results. Eight samples are therefore taken and each is divided into two sub-samples of which one is randomly assigned for analysis by the first procedure and the other by the second. The data (in a convenient unit of concentration) are as follows.

Sample	1	2	3	4	5	6	7	8
Result (procedure 1)	214.6	226.2	219.6	208.4	215.1	220.8	218.4	212.3
Result (procedure 2)	211.8	224.7	219.8	205.2	212.6	218.0	219.2	209.7

It is understood that the underlying populations are satisfactorily modelled by Normal distributions. Use an appropriate t test to examine these data, stating clearly the null and alternative hypotheses you are testing. Use a 1% significance level.

[MEI, *part*]

The Wilcoxon signed rank test for paired samples

In the previous section you met the paired-sample t test. However, to use this test, the differences must be Normally distributed. What happens if the differences are not Normally distributed? An alternative test is the Wilcoxon signed rank test for paired samples.

Sometimes the Wilcoxon signed rank test for single samples is known simply as the Wilcoxon single sample test. Similarly the Wilcoxon signed rank test for paired samples may be referred to as the Wilcoxon paired samples test.

You have already met the Wilcoxon signed rank test for single samples and know that it is a non-parametric or distribution-free test. No assumption of underlying Normality is needed. It is used to test the null hypothesis that the median of the distribution is equal to some value. It can also be used for data where a numerical scale is inappropriate but where it is possible to rank the observations.

Look again at the example of the 400 metre runners. Using the t test depended on the assumption that the distribution of the differences is Normal. If you do not believe this assumption is valid, you need to conduct a different test. The data are shown again in the table.

Athlete	Evening time	Morning time
SD	47.2	46.2
SC	47.6	47.1
MM	46.8	46.7
OC	47.4	47.4
SR	48.3	48.5
MW	50.3	49.3
NF	52.1	50.1

EXAMPLE 15.2

Carry out the Wilcoxon signed rank test on the data in the table above.

SOLUTION

Setting up the hypothesis test

H_0: There is no difference between the median of the times of Avonford athletes in the evening and in the morning.

H_1: There is a positive difference between the median of the times of Avonford athletes in the evening and in the morning.

1-tailed test

Significance level: 5%

The form of the alternative hypothesis, which claims that the times of the Avonford athletes are greater in the evening, rather than just being different, indicates that a 1-tailed test is appropriate.

Calculating the test statistic

The Avonford data can be reduced to a set of values, $d_1, d_2, \ldots, d_7$, of the differences in the morning and the evening times, as shown in the table.

Athlete	Evening time, y_i	Morning time, x_i	Difference, $d_i = y_i - x_i$
SD	47.2	46.2	1
SC	47.6	47.1	0.5
MM	46.8	46.7	0.1
OC	47.4	47.4	0
SR	48.3	48.5	−0.2
MW	50.3	49.3	1
NF	52.1	50.1	2

The athlete OC has a difference of 0 so this value is ignored and the value of n is reduced to 6.

Athlete	y_i	x_i	$d_i = y_i - x_i$	Rank	+	−
SD	47.2	46.2	1	4.5	4.5	
SC	47.6	47.1	0.5	3	3	
MM	46.8	46.7	0.1	1	1	
SR	48.3	48.5	−0.2	2		2
MW	50.3	49.3	1	4.5	4.5	
NF	52.1	50.1	2	6	6	
				Total	19	2

W_+, the sum of the ranks of the positive differences is

$$4.5 + 3 + 1 + 4.5 + 6 = 19.$$

W_-, the sum of the ranks of the negative differences is 2.

Check that $W_+ + W_-$ is the same as $\frac{1}{2}n(n+1)$.

$$W_+ + W_- = 19 + 2 = 21$$
$$\tfrac{1}{2}n(n+1) = \tfrac{1}{2} \times 6 \times 7 = 21$$

For a 1-tailed test where the alternative hypothesis is that there is a positive difference, the test statistic is W_-, so the test statistic is W_-, which is 2.

If you are testing for a negative difference you would use W_+ as the statistic.

Interpreting the test statistic

From the tables, the critical value at the 5% significance level for $n = 6$ is $W = 2$.

You reject the null hypothesis if the test statistic is less than or equal to the critical value.

Since 2 is equal to 2 you reject the null hypothesis.

There is evidence of a difference between the median of the differences between the performance of Avonford athletes in the morning and in the evening. At the 5% significance level, the data support the claim that the athletes perform better in the morning.

Which test to use: Wilcoxon or *t*?

Notice that the conclusion using the Wilcoxon test is the same as for that using the t test but that there has been no assumption that the distribution of the differences is Normal. The Wilcoxon signed rank test is therefore very useful when there is doubt over whether this assumption is true.

You may find this decision tree useful to decide which test to use.

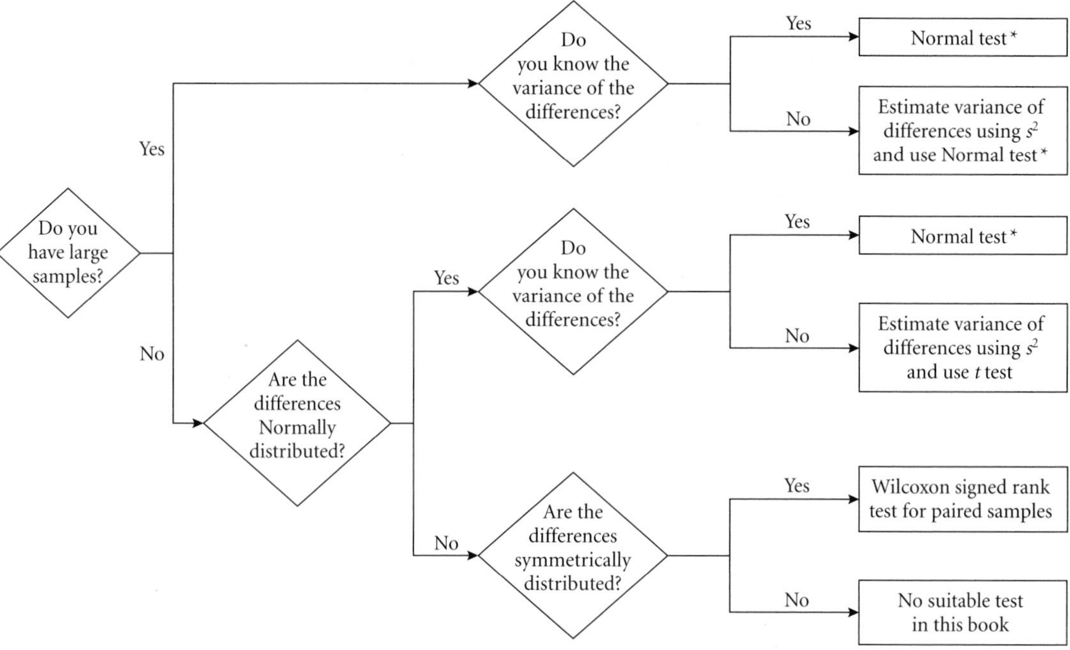

Figure 15.1

AVONFORD STAR

Letters to the editor

Dear Sir or Madam

I am a student at Avonford College. When I am studying I like to listen to music. I find I remember things better if there is something playing in the background. However, my parents are always complaining that I'm not concentrating if there is music on. What do other people find?

Yours sincerely,
Anita Barford

EXAMPLE 15.3

A psychologist saw Anita's letter and decided to do a survey to discover whether background music has any effect on the recall of students. A sample of eight students is given a memory test with and without music. The results are shown in the following table. A high score indicates good recall.

Student	Recall (no music)	Recall (with music)
AB	12	8
CT	10	8
GR	8	3
SH	10	10
JT	13	7
GW	8	6
MB	11	12
KY	15	12

Carry out a Wilcoxon signed rank test to determine whether background music has any effect on the recall of the students.

SOLUTION

Setting up the hypothesis test

H_0: There is no difference between the median of the recall of students with or without music.

H_1: There is a difference between the median of the recall of students with or without music.

2-tailed test

Significance level: 5%

Calculating the test statistic

First calculate the differences and rank them.

Student	Recall (no music)	Recall (with music)	Differences	Rank	+	−
AB	12	8	4	5	5	
CT	10	8	2	2.5	2.5	
GR	8	3	5	6	6	
SH	10	10	0	Ignore		
JT	13	7	6	7	7	
GW	8	6	2	2.5	2.5	
MB	11	12	−1	1		1
KY	15	12	3	4	4	
				Total	27	1

Summing the + and – columns gives $W_+ = 27$ and $W_- = 1$.

Carrying out the check, $W_+ + W_- = 28$ and, with $n = 7$, $\frac{n(n+1)}{2} = 28$.

For a 2-tailed test the test statistic is the smaller of W_+ and W_-, so the test statistic is $W = 1$.

Interpreting the test statistic

From tables, for a 5% significance level for a 2-tailed test, the critical value for $n = 7$ is $W = 2$.

Since 1 is smaller than 2, the null hypothesis is rejected.

At the 5% significance level, the evidence supports the alternative hypothesis that there is a difference between the median of the differences between the recall of students with or without music.

Does this experiment suggest that Anita or her parents are correct?

Sometimes the data are presented in rows rather than columns. Although you can work in rows using the same headings, differences, + and −, you may find it easier to work in columns, as in the above examples.

EXERCISE 15B

1 Anita asked the psychologist what sort of music he played during the experiment. When he answered easy listening music she said she always played classical music. He conducts another experiment on ten students. The results are shown in the table below.

Student	Recall (no music)	Recall (classical music)
ER	36	38
HG	37	39
JE	28	32
WB	20	15
PT	43	47
BG	28	19
KH	31	23
TR	25	32
LK	44	46
WR	25	28

Use an appropriate Wilcoxon procedure to test whether recall improves with the use of classical music. Carry out the test at the 5% significance level.

2 Avonford council is concerned about the amount of lead in the air in its town centre. In order to reduce this it is decided to do some traffic calming in some of the streets with the aim of cutting down the number of vehicles. Opponents of the scheme feel that this has added to the problem, as cars spend a longer time queuing in these streets and hence increase the pollution. The council samples the amount of lead in the air at 11 sites around the town centre. Here are their results.

Amount of lead (in parts per million)

Site	1	2	3	4	5	6	7	8	9	10	11
Before	210	89	56	167	46	67	98	121	144	67	34
After	243	76	53	187	38	63	87	132	160	67	28

Do the data show that the council measures have changed the amount of lead in the air? Carry out the test at the 5% significance level.

3 Records have been kept, during a large number of working days, of the numbers of heavy lorries per hour travelling eastbound and westbound on a certain stretch of main road. It is anticipated that there will be some variation from hour to hour, and it is thought that these variations might not be modelled by a Normal distribution. Therefore, the Wilcoxon paired sample test is to be used to examine whether, overall, the distributions of eastbound and westbound numbers can be assumed to have the same location parameter. The data for a random sample of 12 hours are as follows.

Time	1	2	3	4	5	6	7	8	9	10	11	12
East	89	94	79	70	86	68	73	76	85	75	57	66
West	71	90	58	46	94	55	51	92	84	77	71	73

Carry out the test, at the 5% significance level.

[MEI, *part*]

4 A psychologist is studying the possible effect of hypnosis on dieting and weight loss. Nine people (who may be considered as a random sample from the population under study) volunteer to take part in the experiment. Their weights are measured. Then, under hypnosis, they are told that they will seldom feel hungry and will eat less than usual. After a month, their weights are measured again. The results in kilograms are as follows.

Person	Initial weight	Weight after one month
A	83.7	81.5
B	83.9	80.0
C	68.2	68.8
D	74.9	74.1
E	81.0	82.6
F	72.8	69.2
G	61.3	63.4
H	77.9	74.7
I	69.6	66.2

(i) Use an appropriate Wilcoxon test to examine whether, overall, the mean weight has been reduced over the month, at the 5% level of significance.

(ii) Using only the information given in the question, explain why the Wilcoxon test may be a more appropriate test than the t test.

[MEI, *adapted*]

5 A therapist is studying the effect of a particular type of therapy on a phobic reaction. A random sample of ten patients is available. For each patient, the intensity of the phobic reaction is measured, on a suitable scale, before and after therapy. The results are as follows.

Patient	Intensity before therapy	Intensity after therapy
A	72	66
B	59	40
C	45	58
D	87	56
E	37	15
F	64	66
G	7	15
H	75	31
I	14	3
J	50	36

Use an appropriate Wilcoxon procedure to test, at the 5% level of significance, whether the therapy on the whole reduces the intensity of the reaction, stating clearly your null and alternative hypotheses.

[MEI, *adapted*]

6 An inspector is examining the lengths of time to complete various routine tasks taken by employees who have been trained in two different ways. He wants to examine whether the two methods lead, overall, to the same times. Ten different tasks have been prepared. Each task is undertaken by a randomly selected employee who has been trained by method A and by a randomly selected employee who has been trained by method B. The times to completion, in minutes, are shown in the table.

Task	1	2	3	4	5	6	7	8	9	10
Time taken by method A employee	18.2	17.6	19.4	17.9	18.9	17.4	18.5	19.0	18.9	17.2
Time taken by method B employee	19.0	17.1	19.6	19.0	18.8	18.9	18.8	19.7	18.3	18.4

(i) Explain why these data should be analysed by a paired-sample test.

(ii) Use an appropriate Wilcoxon test to examine these data, stating clearly the null and alternative hypotheses you are testing. Use a 5% significance level.

[MEI, *part*]

KEY POINTS

1 Paired (or matched) data arise when the same two measurements are taken for the same or equivalent individuals.

2 A paired-sample test is carried out on the difference, D, between the two measurements. For the measurements $x_1, x_2, x_3, \ldots, x_n$ and $y_1, y_2, y_3, \ldots, y_n$ the differences are $d_1 = x_1 - y_1, d_2 = x_2 - y_2, \ldots, d_n = y_n - x_n$.

3 For a t test of the null hypothesis that there is no difference in the means of the two populations, i.e. $\overline{D} = 0$, the test statistic, t, is given by $\dfrac{\overline{d}}{\frac{s}{\sqrt{n}}}$.

4 For the null hypothesis $\overline{D} = k$, where there is a suspected difference between the two populations, the test statistic, t, is given by $\dfrac{\overline{d} - k}{\frac{s}{\sqrt{n}}}$.

5 The t test may be used if the differences are Normally distributed and the sample has been selected at random.

6 If the differences are not Normally distributed, the Wilcoxon signed rank test is a possible alternative to the t test.

7 Use this procedure to calculate the test statistic for the Wilcoxon signed rank test.
- Calculate each paired difference, $d_1, d_2, \ldots, d_n$.
- Ignore any items where the difference is zero, and reduce the sample size accordingly.
- Rank the differences, ignoring the signs.
- Label each rank with its sign, according to the sign of the associated difference.
- Calculate W_+, the sum of the ranks of the positive differences, and W_-, the sum of the ranks of the negative differences.
- Check that $W_+ + W_- = \dfrac{n(n+1)}{2}$.
- For a 2-tailed test the test statistic is the smaller of W_+ and W_-.
  For a 1-tailed test where the alternative hypothesis is that there is a positive difference the test statistic is W_-.
  For a 1-tailed test where the alternative hypothesis is that there is a negative difference the test statistic is W_+.
- Look up in tables the critical value for the appropriate value of ν and make a comparison and conclusion.
- The null hypothesis is rejected if the test statistic, W, is less than or equal to the appropriate critical value.

16 Hypothesis tests on unpaired samples

In earlier times they had no statistics and so they had to fall back on lies.

Stephen Leacock

AVONFORD STAR

Grumpy driving test examiners

It has come to the notice of our reporters that not all driving tests are examined at the same standard in our town. Our reporter, Peter Burrow, interviewed several people who had taken their driving test recently. Nicola said that she found one of the examiners, we shall call him Mr A, very harsh, he seemed to record every fault. Jamie passed at his second attempt and felt that the second examiner, we shall call her Ms B, was much more sympathetic.

We questioned the test centre who told us that in Avonford testers are continuously monitored on a special scale measuring how severe they are. The two testers in question had been with the centre for many years, and the centre told us their average scores for the last month and their long-term variability. These figures showed that Mr A is indeed harsher than Ms B.

Here is a summary of the data the *Avonford Star* reporter collected.

Mr A:	Sample	Mean 48.0, sample size 120
	Population	Standard deviation 12
Ms B:	Sample	Mean 46.0, sample size 100
	Population	Standard deviation 15

Does this data support the *Avonford Star* reporter's conclusion that Mr A is harsher than Ms B?

Before you can decide this you need to select an appropriate test.

Selecting the appropriate test for unpaired samples

This chapter covers several possible two-sample tests on the means or medians of unpaired samples and you need to take considerable care to make sure you choose the one that is most appropriate. As when you decided which test to use on a single sample in Chapter 11, there are three key questions to consider.

- Are the samples large?
- Are the underlying populations Normally distributed?
- Are the population variances known?

The first question separates out large sample and small sample situations.

Large samples

If the answer to the first question is 'Yes, the samples are large', then the situation is straightforward. You use a Normal test, whatever the answers to the other two questions. In fact you do not need the second question at all. The answer to the third question, however, tells you the test statistic to use.

If you know the variances, σ_1^2 and σ_2^2, of the underlying populations, the test statistic is

$$z = \frac{(\bar{x}_1 - \bar{x}_2) - (\mu_1 - \mu_2)}{\sqrt{\dfrac{\sigma_1^2}{n_1} + \dfrac{\sigma_2^2}{n_2}}}.$$

This test statistic covers the general case where the null hypothesis is that there is some fixed value, say k, for the value of $\mu_1 - \mu_2$, the difference between the means of the two populations from which the samples are drawn. However, you will often be testing the null hypothesis that the populations from which the two samples are drawn have the same means and so $\mu_1 = \mu_2$. In such cases the test statistic is just

$$z = \frac{(\bar{x}_1 - \bar{x}_2)}{\sqrt{\dfrac{\sigma_1^2}{n_1} + \dfrac{\sigma_2^2}{n_2}}}.$$

If you do not know the population variances and so have to estimate them from the sample data, as s_1^2 and s_2^2, the appropriate test statistic is

$$z = \frac{(\bar{x}_1 - \bar{x}_2) - (\mu_1 - \mu_2)}{\sqrt{\dfrac{s_1^2}{n_1} + \dfrac{s_2^2}{n_2}}}.$$

This formula, too, looks rather simpler in the case when $\mu_1 = \mu_2$.

Why would you not use the t test with large samples when the variances are estimated?

Small samples

If your answer to the first question is 'No, the samples are small', the situation is rather more complicated.

The second question 'Are the underlying populations Normally distributed?' is important for small samples. If the answer to the second question is 'Yes, the underlying populations are (or may be assumed to be) Normally distributed', the third question is also important. It asks if you know the population variances; if the answer is 'Yes', you use the Normal test. If the answer is 'No' you use the t test;

however, before you can do this you must estimate the variances from the samples and then combine them using the formula for a pooled estimate,

$$s^2 = \frac{(n_1 - 1)s_1^2 + (n_2 - 1)s_2^2}{n_1 + n_2 - 2}.$$

The pooled estimate method should only be used in cases where it is known that the two population variances, σ_1^2 and σ_2^2, are equal, or it is reasonable to assume that they are. Otherwise there is no simple test for this case, except possibly the Wilcoxon rank sum test.

If the answer is 'No, you do not know the population variances', then you can use neither a Normal test nor a *t* test. You may, however, be able to use the Wilcoxon rank sum test and this is covered later in this chapter. This information in this section is summarised in figure 16.1.

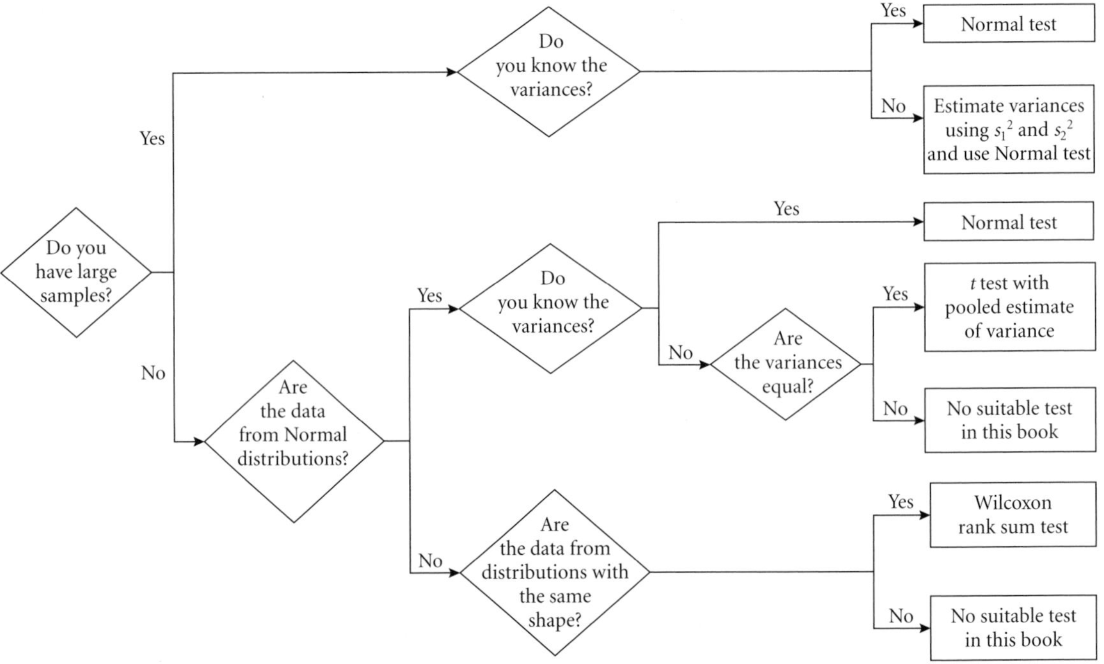

Figure 16.1

The Normal test for unpaired samples

As you can see from figure 16.1, there are three situations in which you would use the Normal distribution to test the differences between means. These are illustrated in the next three examples.

You are now in a position to decide whether the data that the *Avonford Star* reporter collected support the conclusion that Mr A is harsher than Ms B.

EXAMPLE 16.1

Here is the summary of the data the *Avonford Star* reporter collected again.

Mr A:	Sample	Mean number of faults recorded 48.0
		Sample size 120
	Population	Standard deviation 12
Ms B:	Sample	Mean number of faults recorded 46.0
		Sample size 100
	Population	Standard deviation 15

Test, at the 5% significance level, whether there is a difference between the mean number of faults recorded by the two testers, as claimed by the *Avonford Star*.

SOLUTION

Notation

Call Mr A's data sample 1 and Ms B's data sample 2.

Then the data are summarised as follows.

Mr A:	Sample 1:	$\bar{x}_1 = 48.0$, $n_1 = 120$
	Population 1:	mean $= \mu_1$, $\sigma_1 = 12$
Ms B	Sample 2:	$\bar{x}_2 = 46.0$, $n_2 = 100$
	Population 2:	mean $= \mu_2$, $\sigma_2 = 15$

These figures were given in the question.

Choosing which test

Think about the key questions and look at the decision tree in figure 16.1.

- Are the samples large? Answer Yes.
- Are the underlying populations Normally distributed? Answer No.
- Are the population variances known? Answer Yes.

You cannot assume this as no information is given in the question.

You have a large sample so you can use a Normal test, even though you do not know how the underlying population is distributed. You are told the population standard deviations so you do not have to estimate these.

Setting up the hypothesis test

H$_0$: $\mu_1 = \mu_2$, the two instructors recorded the same number of faults.

H$_1$: $\mu_1 > \mu_2$, Mr A recorded more faults.

1-tailed test

Significance level: 5%

Calculating the test statistic

In this case the standard deviations, σ_1 and σ_2, of the two populations are known so the test statistic is given by

$$z = \frac{(\bar{x}_1 - \bar{x}_2) - (\mu_1 - \mu_2)}{\sqrt{\dfrac{\sigma_1^2}{n_1} + \dfrac{\sigma_2^2}{n_2}}}$$

and in this case $\mu_1 - \mu_2 = 0$.

As these are large sample sizes, by the Central Limit Theorem, the distribution of $\bar{X}_1 - \bar{X}_2$ will be approximately Normal with mean $\mu_1 - \mu_2$ and variance $\dfrac{\sigma_1^2}{n_1} + \dfrac{\sigma_2^2}{n_2}$ so

$$z = \frac{48.0 - 46.0}{\sqrt{\dfrac{144}{120} + \dfrac{225}{100}}} = 1.077 \text{ to 3 decimal places.}$$

Interpreting the test statistic

For a 1-tailed test at the 5% significance level the tables give the critical value to be $z = 1.645$.

Since 1.077 is less than 1.645 the null hypothesis is accepted at the 5% significance level.

The *Avonford Star* reporter was not justified in claiming that Mr A is harsher than Ms B.

What would have happened if the distributions of test scores for the two testers were known to be approximately Normal?

EXAMPLE 16.2

After this year's examinations there is thought to be a difference between the performance of students on two Psychology modules, A and B. Many of this year's students commented that they thought that module B was much harder. A random sample of scripts for modules A and B produces the following results.

Module A: Mean score 52.0
Sample standard deviation 20
Sample size 100

Module B: Mean score 48.0
Sample standard deviation 20
Sample size 150

Test, at the 5% significance level, whether there is a difference between the performances of students on the two modules.

SOLUTION

Notation

Call the data for module A sample 1 and those for module B sample 2.

Then the data are summarised as follows.

Module A:	Sample 1:	$\bar{x}_1 = 52.0$, $s_1 = 20$, $n_1 = 100$
	Population 1:	mean $= \mu_1$
Module B:	Sample 2:	$\bar{x}_2 = 48.0$, $s_2 = 20$, $n_2 = 150$
	Population 2:	mean $= \mu_2$

Choosing which test

Think about the key questions and look at the decision tree in figure 16.1.

- Are the samples large? Answer Yes.
- Are the underlying populations Normally distributed? Answer No.
- Are the population variances known? Answer No.

You cannot assume this as no information is given in the question.

You have a large sample so you can use a Normal test, even though you do not know how the underlying population is distributed. As you do not know the population variances, you have to estimate these from the samples.

Setting up the hypothesis test

H_0: $\mu_1 = \mu_2$, the modules have the same mean score.
H_1: $\mu_1 > \mu_2$, module A has a higher mean score.
1-tailed test
Significance level: 5%

Calculating the test statistic

In this case the standard deviations, σ_1 and σ_2, of the two populations are not known, however, you can estimate them as s_1 and s_2, so the test statistic, in its simplified form, is given by

$$z = \frac{\bar{x}_1 - \bar{x}_2}{\sqrt{\frac{s_1^2}{n_1} + \frac{s_2^2}{n_2}}}.$$

Substituting the values of $\bar{x}_1$, $\bar{x}_2$, n_1, n_2, s_1 and s_2 gives

$$z = \frac{52.0 - 48.0}{\sqrt{\frac{20^2}{100} + \frac{20^2}{150}}} = 1.549 \text{ to 3 decimal places.}$$

Interpreting the test statistic

For a 1-tailed test at the 5% significance level the tables give the critical value to be $z = 1.645$.

Since 1.549 is less than 1.645, the null hypothesis is accepted at the 5% significance level.

The evidence does not support that the mean score for module A was higher.

EXAMPLE 16.3

Scientists are carrying out a study into a particular species of snake. Among other things this involves investigating the lengths of adult specimens. It is known that the lengths are Normally distributed with a standard deviation of 7.0 cm for males and 8.5 cm for females. The scientists have a theory that, on average, the male snakes are 3 cm longer than the females. They trap 9 adult male snakes and 11 adult females.

These were their lengths, in centimetres.

Males: 65.2 76.4 55.0 58.9 67.2 70.8 65.5 66.0 75.3

Females: 45.2 67.1 47.4 55.9 62.1 66.0 68.3 49.2 56.7 59.3 52.0

Test the scientists' theory at the 10% significance level.

SOLUTION

Notation

Call data for the male snakes sample 1 and for the female snakes sample 2.

The data are summarised as follows.

Males:	Sample 1:	$\bar{x}_1 = 66.7$, $n_1 = 9$
	Population 1:	mean $= \mu_1$, $\sigma_1 = 7.0$
Females:	Sample 2:	$\bar{x}_2 = 57.2$, $n_2 = 11$
	Population 2:	mean $= \mu_2$, $\sigma_2 = 8.5$

Choosing which test

Think about the key questions and look at the decision tree in figure 16.1.

- Are the samples large? Answer No.
- Are the underlying populations Normally distributed? Answer Yes.
- Are the population variances known? Answer Yes.

You have a small sample but, as you are told that the underlying population is Normally distributed and you know the population variances, you can use a Normal test.

Setting up the hypothesis test

H_0: $\mu_1 - \mu_2 = 3$, the mean length of males is 3 cm greater than that of females.

H_1: $\mu_1 - \mu_2 \neq 3$, the mean length of males is not 3 cm greater than that of females.

2-tailed test

Significance level: 10% ← (This was specified in the question.)

 Why is this a 2-tailed test?

Calculating the test statistic

The test statistic is given by

$$z = \frac{(\bar{x}_1 - \bar{x}_2) - (\mu_1 - \mu_2)}{\sqrt{\dfrac{\sigma_1^{\,2}}{n_1} + \dfrac{\sigma_2^{\,2}}{n_2}}}$$

Substituting the values of $\bar{x}_1$, $\bar{x}_2$, n_1, n_2, σ_1 and σ_2 gives

$$z = \frac{(66.7 - 57.2) - (3)}{\sqrt{\dfrac{7^2}{9} + \dfrac{8.5^2}{11}}} = 1.875 \text{ to 3 decimal places.}$$

Interpreting the test statistic

For a 2-tailed test at the 10% significance level the critical value is 1.645.

Since 1.875 is greater than 1.645, the null hypothesis is rejected at the 10% significance level.

The evidence does support the scientists' hypothesis that, on average, the male snakes are 3 cm longer than the females.

The *t* test for unpaired samples

AVONFORD STAR

New one-way system causing traffic chaos

Once again traffic chaos descended on Avonford as the schools returned after the summer holidays. The new one-way system, introduced in July so that commuters could get to work on time, has been an absolute disaster. We thought the situation was bad in June, but it is far worse now! There were major hold-ups at the Town Hall roundabout, caused by the new one-way system in Corporation Street. Long queues occurred in New Street, leading up to the college. The *Star* has always opposed this hair-brained scheme and today we reveal the results of our own statistical survey. Far from shortening journey times, the average time has increased by over 4 minutes. For full details of the survey visit our website. Put a stop to this chaotic system now!

The website reveals that two random samples were taken. In June, before the new one-way system came in, a sample of eight drivers were timed from leaving the Carpenter Estate to arriving at the Town Hall. A second sample of nine different drivers were timed over the same journey in August, the day after the new system was introduced.

These are unpaired samples since the *Avonford Star* did not choose the same drivers. This could be because the drivers did not do the same journey in June and August. The data were as follows.

June

23 minutes 56 seconds	24 minutes 32 seconds	24 minutes 21 seconds
25 minutes 28 seconds	22 minutes 34 seconds	23 minutes 32 seconds
22 minutes 5 seconds	23 minutes 48 seconds	

Sample size 8
Summary (in minutes): mean = 23.78, standard deviation = 1.08

August

27 minutes 52 seconds	29 minutes 22 seconds	27 minutes 51 seconds
30 minutes 45 seconds	27 minutes 15 seconds	26 minutes 56 seconds
27 minutes 48 seconds	25 minutes 59 seconds	31 minutes 48 seconds

Sample size 9
Summary (in minutes): mean = 28.40, standard deviation = 1.88

Do these data confirm the *Avonford Star's* conclusion that the traffic system has got worse?

Notation

Call the June data sample 1, and those for August sample 2.
Then the data are summarised as follows.

Sample 1 (June):
$\overline{x_1} = 23.78, s_1 = 1.08, n_1 = 8$

Sample 2 (August):
$\overline{x_2} = 28.40, s_2 = 1.88, n_2 = 9$

Call the population mean for journeys in June, μ_1, and for journeys in August, μ_2.

It is reasonable to assume that the populations of journey times in both June and August are Normally distributed.

Choosing which test

Think about the key questions and look at the decision tree in figure 16.1.

- Are the samples large? Answer No.
- Are the underlying populations Normally distributed? Answer Yes.
- Are the population variances known? Answer No.

You have a small sample but the underlying populations are Normally distributed. As you don't know the population variances, you use a pooled estimate for the variance and carry out a t test.

Setting up the hypothesis test

H_0: $\mu_1 = \mu_2$, the mean journey time is unchanged.
H_1: $\mu_1 < \mu_2$, the mean journey time has increased.
1-tailed test
Significance level: 5%

5% is a suitable level in this situation.

? Why is this a 1-tailed test?

Calculating the test statistic

According to the null hypothesis the two samples are drawn from a common population. In a situation like this it is usual to use both of the sample variances to estimate the population variance, s^2, and standard deviation, s, in the pooled variance formula.

$$s^2 = \frac{(n_1 - 1)s_1^2 + (n_2 - 1)s_2^2}{n_1 + n_2 - 2}$$

In this case

$$s^2 = \frac{(8 - 1) \times 1.08^2 + (9 - 1) \times 1.88^2}{8 + 9 - 2}$$

$$= 2.4293 \text{ to 4 decimal places.}$$

So $s = 1.5586$ to 4 decimal places.

The test statistic is

$$t = \frac{(\overline{x_1} - \overline{x_2}) - (\mu_1 - \mu_2)}{s\sqrt{\dfrac{1}{n_1} + \dfrac{1}{n_2}}}$$

and, since the null hypothesis is $\mu_1 = \mu_2$, this simplifies to

$$t = \frac{\overline{x_1} - \overline{x_2}}{s\sqrt{\dfrac{1}{n_1} + \dfrac{1}{n_2}}},$$

giving

$$t = \frac{23.78 - 28.40}{1.5586\sqrt{\left(\frac{1}{8}\right) + \left(\frac{1}{9}\right)}}$$

$$= -6.100 \text{ to 3 decimal places.}$$

Interpreting the test statistic

For this test the degrees of freedom are given by $\nu = n_1 + n_2 - 2$.
In this case $\nu = 8 + 9 - 2 = 15$.

For a 1-tailed test at the 5% significance level and $\nu = 15$ the tables give the critical value to be -1.753.

Since -6.100 is less than -1.753, the null hypothesis is rejected.

The evidence supports a difference between the means of the two sets of journeys, at the 5% significance level. The *Avonford Star* was justified in publishing its concerns that journey times have got longer.

Assumptions for the unpaired *t* test

The assumptions needed for the unpaired *t* test are quite severe.

- The two samples must be independent random samples of the populations involved.
- The random variables measured must be Normally distributed and have equal variances in the two conditions.

? Was it reasonable to make these assumptions about the two samples of journey times above?

EXERCISE 16A

1 A factory receives deliveries of an electrical component from two suppliers, A and B. The resistances of these components are critical. Inspectors are checking whether, on average, resistances of components from supplier A are the same as those from supplier B. The resistances are measured from two random samples. The results, in ohms, are as follows.

Supplier A: 18.62 18.44 18.47 18.45 18.29 18.65 18.41 18.50 18.44

Supplier B: 18.53 18.64 18.58 18.62 18.72 18.65 18.45 18.69

(i) State the null and alternative hypotheses and the required assumptions for the use of a *t* test.

(ii) Carry out the test at the 5% level of significance.

[MEI, *part*]

2 A company has two factories, A and B. 47 people are employed at factory A and 73 people are employed at factory B. The mean number of days' absence per month for factory A is calculated as 3.12 days, with a variance of 2.86. Factory B has a mean of 2.73 days and a variance of 2.34. The company wishes to investigate whether factory B has a lower mean absence rate than factory A.

(i) State the null and alternative hypotheses.

(ii) Complete the test at the 5% level of significance.

3 A pharmaceutical company is investigating whether a new drug for patients with heart disease successfully reduces blood cholesterol levels. Nine such patients receive the drug while, as a control, eight other patients receive a placebo (a treatment that should have no effect). Each of these groups of patients can be considered as a random sample from the relevant population. At the end of the trial period, the blood cholesterol levels of the patients are found to be as follows, measured in a suitable unit. For convenience the observations in each group have been arranged in ascending order.

Drug:	243	246	250	257	260	262	267	287	295
Placebo:	249	266	273	280	284	285	288	293	

It is desired to examine whether patients treated with the drug in this way may be assumed to have lower blood cholesterol levels than patients who receive the placebo.

(i) State the null and alternative hypotheses and the required assumptions for the use of a t test.

(ii) Carry out the test at the 5% level of significance.

[MEI, *adapted*]

4 Investigations are being carried out on the time taken to cook a ready meal using two different ovens, P and Q. It is known that this time varies and that the variations can be accounted for by taking the cooking time to be Normally distributed. Information from the manufacturers states the true standard deviation to be 0.9 minutes for each oven. A random sample was taken for each oven.

These were the cooking times, in minutes, for oven P.

17.8 23.6 21.1 19.4 19.6 20.9 20.0 18.9 20.3

The mean of 20 cooking times for oven Q was 19.33 minutes.

Examine, at the 5% significance level, whether the true mean cooking times for the two ovens differ.

5 A liquid product is sold in containers. The containers are filled by a machine. The volumes of liquid, in millilitres, in a random sample of 6 containers were found to be

497.8 501.4 500.2 500.8 498.3 500.0

After overhaul the volumes of liquid, in millilitres, in a random sample of 11 containers were found to be

501.1 499.6 500.3 500.9 498.7 502.1
500.4 499.7 501.0 500.1 499.3

It is desired to examine whether the average volume of liquid delivered to a container by the machine is the same after overhaul as it was before.

(i) State the assumptions that are necessary for the use of the customary t test.

(ii) State the null and alternative hypotheses that are to be tested.

(iii) Carry out the test, using a 5% level of significance.

[MEI, *part*]

6 The customers of a local branch of a bank are invited to comment on various aspects of the service. Their comments are translated into an overall 'satisfaction score'. This score can be taken to be Normally distributed over the whole population of customers. A staff-training programme has recently been completed.

A random sample of scores before the programme was

126 93 114 107 98 112

A separate random sample of scores after the programme was

124 107 117 136 120 122

Test at the 5% level of significance the null hypothesis that the mean score is the same after training against the alternative that the mean is higher, assuming that the underlying variances are equal.

[MEI, *part*]

7 Two different designs for a large open-plan office are being compared in respect of the amount of light available at locations where employees will be working. The amount of light is measured by photoelectric cells at 12 randomly selected locations for one design and, independently, at 10 randomly selected locations for the other design. It is desired to examine whether, overall, the mean amount of light delivered is the same in the two designs. The data, in a standard unit, are summarised as follows.

First design: $n_1 = 12$, $\bar{x} = 9.85$, $\sum_{i=1}^{n} (x_i - \bar{x})^2 = 23.410$

Second design: $n_2 = 10$, $\bar{y} = 8.76$, $\sum_{i=1}^{n} (x_i - \bar{x})^2 = 23.058$

(i) State the null and alternative hypotheses and the required assumptions for the use of a t test.

(ii) Carry out the test at the 10% level of significance.

[MEI, *part*]

8 A country has two seasons, known locally as 'Hot' and 'Cold'. It is known that the noon temperatures within any season are Normally distributed, and that the standard deviation for the Hot season is 3.6 °C and for the Cold season it is 6.4°. A meteorologist wishes to test her theory that the mean noon temperature in the Hot season is 8 °C higher than that in the Cold season.

She measures the noon temperature, in degrees Celsius, on a random sample of days in both seasons.

Cold season:

22.4 14.7 19.8 10.4 11.3 18.4 2.2 10.6 12.2

Hot season:

22.6 24.4 19.4 18.4 28.4 25.4 26.4

Carry out a suitable test of the meteorologist's theory at the 5% significance level.

The Wilcoxon rank sum test

Earlier in this chapter you used unpaired Normal and *t* tests. However, these tests rely on conditions relating to the sample sizes, whether the underlying distributions are Normal and whether the population variances are known or have to be estimated from the samples. An alternative test that does not require these conditions is the Wilcoxon rank sum test for unpaired samples. As with the Wilcoxon signed rank test, this is a test on the median rather than the mean.

Assumption

Although you do not have to be able to assume that the two variables are Normally distributed, as is required for the *t* and Normal tests on small samples, the Wilcoxon rank sum test does require the two distributions to have the same shape, even though they may be differently located with one having larger values than the other.

The procedure for the Wilcoxon rank sum test is illustrated in the following example.

EXAMPLE 16.4

The psychologist conducts another experiment to test the memory of students. He wants to test whether playing pop music has a detrimental effect on the recall of students compared with when there is no music playing in the background. The results are shown in the table.

Recall (pop music)	Recall (no music)
8	13
8	9
3	9
10	10
7	11
9	7
12	11
12	15
	14
	16
	12
	9

Carry out a Wilcoxon rank sum test at the 5% significance level.

SOLUTION

Setting up the hypothesis test

H_0: The median difference between the performance of students with pop music and with no music is zero.

H_1: The median difference between the performance of students with pop music and with no music is not zero, with students performing worse with pop music.

1-tailed test

Significance level: 5%

Calculating the test statistic

There are 8 + 12 = 20 measurements.

Start by ranking them, ignoring their signs. Assign 1 to the smallest value, 2 to the next, etc. If you get tied ranks, i.e. two or more equal sample values, average the ranks across the tied observations. In this example you have two values that are 7, which are equal second in size. These are given the rank of $\frac{2 + 3}{2} = 2.5$.

Recall (pop music), X	Rank	Recall (no music), Y	Rank
8	4.5	13	17
8	4.5	9	7.5
3	1	9	7.5
10	10.5	10	10.5
7	2.5	11	12.5
9	7.5	7	2.5
12	15	11	12.5
12	15	15	19
		14	18
		16	20
		12	15
		9	7.5
Total	60.5	**Total**	149.5

It is conventional to call the size of the smaller sample m and that of the larger sample n. It is also conventional to call the variable of the smaller sample X and that of the larger sample Y.

So in this example

X represents the scores for pop music: $m = 8$.
Y represents the scores for no music: $n = 12$.
The sum of the X ranks is denoted by $W_X = 60.5$.
The sum of the Y ranks is denoted by $W_Y = 149.5$.

The test statistic, W, is the value for the smaller sample so, in this case,

$$W = W_X = 60.5.$$

At this point, always check that the total of W_X and W_Y is $\dfrac{(m+n)(m+n+1)}{2}$.

In this case,

$$W_X + W_Y = 60.5 + 149.5 = 210,$$

and with $m = 8$ and $n = 12$,

$$\frac{(m+n)(m+n+1)}{2} = \frac{(8+12)(8+12+1)}{2} = 210.$$

Interpreting the test statistic

Critical values for this test are given in tables of critical values for the Wilcoxon rank sum 2-sample test.

For a 5% significance level, the critical value for $m = 8$ and $n = 12$ is $W = 62$.

1-tailed		5%	$2\frac{1}{2}$%	1%	$\frac{1}{2}$%
2-tailed		10%	5%	2%	1%
m	n				
8	8	51	49	45	43
8	9	54	51	47	45
8	10	56	53	49	47
8	11	59	55	51	49
8	12	62	58	53	51
8	13	64	60	56	53
8	14	67	62	58	54
8	15	69	65	60	56
8	16	72	67	62	58
8	17	75	70	64	60
	18	77	72	66	

Since 60.5 is less than 62, the null hypothesis is rejected at the 5% significance level.

There is evidence of a difference between the performances of students with pop music and with no music, with students performing worse with pop music.

e The Mann–Whitney test

An equivalent test to the Wilcoxon rank sum test is provided by the Mann–Whitney test. The two tests always produce the same result.

The same notation is used for both the Wilcoxon rank sum test and the Mann–Whitney test. X denotes the random variable for the smaller sample and this sample has size m. The random variable for the larger sample is denoted by Y and the sample size is n.

This is the procedure for the Mann–Whitney test.

- For each value in the X sample, count the number of values in the Y sample that are smaller than it.
- Add to this half the number of values in sample Y that are equal to it.
- Add up the numbers obtained in this way for each value in sample X to obtain the test statistic, T_X.

This method is illustrated using the data from Example 16.4. You will find it helpful to place the data in the two columns in order and this has been done.

Recall (pop music), X	Recall (no music), Y	Number of values in Y smaller than X	Number of values in Y equal to X
3	7	0	0
7	9	0	1
8	9	1	0
8	9	1	0
9	10	1	3
10	11	4	1
12	11	7	1
12	12	7	1
	13		
	14		
	15		
	16		
	Total	21	7

So the test statistic is given by

$$T_X = 21 + \tfrac{1}{2} \times 7 = 24.5.$$

The critical value from the tables is 26.

Since 24.5 is less than 26, the null hypothesis is rejected at the 5% significance level.

There is evidence of a difference between the performances of students with pop music and with no music, with students performing worse with pop music.

1 A psychologist wants to investigate whether there is any connection between stress and gender. From earlier research the psychologist suspects that men will display more symptoms of stress than females. A questionnaire is designed to establish an index of stress. These are the results.

Male stress	41	59	36	42	46	54	36	45	60	72
Female stress	43	34	43	33	59	60	32	47		

(i) State the null and alternative hypotheses.

(ii) Carry out an appropriate non-parametric test at the 5% level to investigate whether there is evidence to support the psychologist's suspicions.

2 An experiment is conducted to test whether factory workers produce fewer finished items in cool conditions than they do when it is warmer. The number of finished items produced in shifts when it is warm and when it is cool are recorded.

Cool conditions:	141	341	244	176	208	
Warm conditions:	359	190	442	466	419	313

(i) State the null and alternative hypotheses.

(ii) Carry out an appropriate non-parametric test at the 5% level.

3 A mobile phone company is analysing calls made by customers on two different tariffs, C and D. The company records the lengths of random samples of eight calls by customers on tariff C and seven calls made by customers on tariff D. The lengths, in minutes, are as follows.

Tariff C:	0.84	3.92	4.74	0.39	5.18	4.36	1.79	3.94
Tariff D:	0.65	1.36	2.83	0.26	0.34	3.65	1.67	

Use an appropriate non-parametric test, at the 10% level of significance, to examine whether there are, on the whole, any differences between lengths of calls on these two tariffs. [MEI, *part*]

4 Using the Wilcoxon rank sum test, is there a significant difference, at a 5% significance level, between the scores achieved by students in these two statistics AS tests?

Test 1:	17	15	9	11	8	16	12	11	12	18
Test 2:	15	9	11	15	9	15	12			

5 Managers at Peterborough airport are studying the times taken by arriving passengers to pass through customs.

These are the times, in minutes, for a random sample of seven passengers arriving in the morning.

12 15 18 21 25 22 11

These are the times, in minutes, for a random sample of six passengers arriving in the evening.

22 25 16 24 28 22

Use a Wilcoxon test to examine, at the 5% level of significance, whether there is a difference in the times.

6 In a research experiment students are given cards containing ten facts and then asked to recall these when tested by male or female questioners. The researcher suspects there is a difference in responses, with higher scores when questioned by a female. These are the data.

Male questioner:	3	4	5	6	8	9
Female questioner:	5	6	7	8	10	10

Use a Wilcoxon test to examine, at the 5% level of significance, whether there is a difference in the responses.

KEY POINTS

1 There are a number of different two-sample hypothesis tests for the mean.

2 To decide which test to use, consider the following questions and use the decision tree in figure 16.1 on page 394.
- Are the samples large?
- Are the underlying populations Normally distributed?
- Are the population variances known?

3 For the Normal and t tests, the null and alternative hypotheses take the form

H_0: $\mu_1 - \mu_2 = k$ where k is some fixed value.
H_1: $\mu_1 - \mu_2 < k$ or $\mu_1 - \mu_2 > k$ or $\mu_1 - \mu_2 \neq k$.

However it is often the case that you are testing for equal population means and in that case, the null and alternative hypotheses take the form

H_0: $\mu_1 = \mu_2$.
H_1: $\mu_1 < \mu_2$ or $\mu_1 > \mu_2$ or $\mu_1 \neq \mu_2$.

4 When you know the population variances, the test statistic for the Normal test is given by $z = \dfrac{(\bar{x}_1 - \bar{x}_2) - (\mu_1 - \mu_2)}{\sqrt{\dfrac{\sigma_1^2}{n_1} + \dfrac{\sigma_2^2}{n_2}}}$.

This simplifies to $z = \dfrac{(\bar{x}_1 - \bar{x}_2)}{\sqrt{\dfrac{\sigma_1^2}{n_1} + \dfrac{\sigma_2^2}{n_2}}}$ when $\mu_1 = \mu_2$.

5 For the Normal test when you do not know the population variances, you estimate the population variances as s_1 and s_2 and the test statistic is given by $z = \dfrac{(\bar{x}_1 - \bar{x}_2) - (\mu_1 - \mu_2)}{\sqrt{\dfrac{s_1^2}{n_1} + \dfrac{s_2^2}{n_2}}}$.

This simplifies to $z = \dfrac{(\bar{x}_1 - \bar{x}_2)}{\sqrt{\dfrac{s_1^2}{n_1} + \dfrac{s_2^2}{n_2}}}$ when $\mu_1 = \mu_2$.

6 To use a t test you need to make a pooled estimate of the population variance using $s^2 = \dfrac{(n_1 - 1)s_1^2 + (n_2 - 1)s_2^2}{n_1 + n_2 - 2}$.

7 The test statistic for the t test is given by $t = \dfrac{(\overline{x}_1 - \overline{x}_2) - (\mu_1 - \mu_2)}{s\sqrt{\dfrac{1}{n_1} + \dfrac{1}{n_2}}}$.

This simplifies to $t = \dfrac{(\overline{x}_1 - \overline{x}_2)}{s\sqrt{\dfrac{1}{n_1} + \dfrac{1}{n_2}}}$ when $\mu_1 = \mu_2$.

8 For the Wilcoxon rank sum test the null and alternative hypotheses are

H_0: The random variables X and Y have the same median.

H_1: The median of X is different from that of Y (2-tailed) or larger than that of Y (1-tailed) or smaller than that of Y (1-tailed).

9 This is the procedure to calculate the test statistic for the Wilcoxon rank sum test.

- By convention, call the random variable in the smaller sample X and that of the larger sample Y and call the size of the smaller sample m and that of the larger sample n.
- Rank the $m + n$ sample values, ignoring the signs.
- If two or more sample values are equal, each is assigned the mean of their tied ranks.
- Calculate W_X, the sum of the ranks of the x values and W_Y, the sum of the ranks of the y values.
- Check that the total of $W_X + W_Y = \dfrac{(m + n)(m + n + 1)}{2}$.
- Select the value of W corresponding to the smaller sample size. Using the usual convention this is W_X.
- The null hypothesis is rejected if the test statistic, W, is less than or equal to the appropriate critical value found in the tables.

17 Correlation

It is a capital mistake to theorise before one has data.

Bishop Butler

AVONFORD STAR

Avonford's love affair with the car

Did you know that you are giving away the secret of your salary every time you drive into town to shop? New evidence has been produced to indicate that the more you earn the more money you spend on your car.

Sociology student, Monica Jones, has just presented her report on a survey carried out locally. Her conclusions point to the fact that the higher earners in the town drive around in more expensive cars. She even claims that she can deduce the salary of the driver of a car given its make and age!

Monica is studying Sociology at Avonford Community College. Part of the A level course includes carrying out a survey. She told our roving reporter that she was interested in cars and thought that the idea of comparing people's salaries with their cars was interesting. 'I thought before I started that there might be a connection' she said, 'and, from the evidence I have collected, I was clearly right. I know I only asked a small number of people but since they were a random selection I think you can conclude that the same would be true for the whole population of Avonford.'

So you six-figure salary earners out there – if you don't want to reveal too much then the *Star's* advice is to buy an old banger!

Bivariate data

Here are the data for the sample of 20 people.

Income (thousands of pounds per annum)	15	18	22	23	28	30	33	33	38	39
Value of car (thousands of pounds)	1.0	0.7	2.6	0.6	3.0	7.8	3.8	4.8	4.9	6.1

Income (thousands of pounds per annum)	40	42	44	47	49	50	55	57	57	60
Value of car (thousands of pounds)	7.9	7.3	7.1	10.3	12.1	9.8	13.1	15.6	14.3	18.2

These are *bivariate data.* In each case there is a pair of values representing two properties or characteristics of the item. The two properties for this set of data are income and the value of the car.

You can plot bivariate data on a scatter diagram. In this case we can conveniently write the annual income (in thousands of pounds) as the x value and the value of the car (in thousands of pounds) as the y value.

Thus Mr Ames earns £60 000 and owns a car worth £18 200. The data pair for Mr Ames can be written as (60, 18.2).

The scatter diagram for these data is shown in figure 17.1.

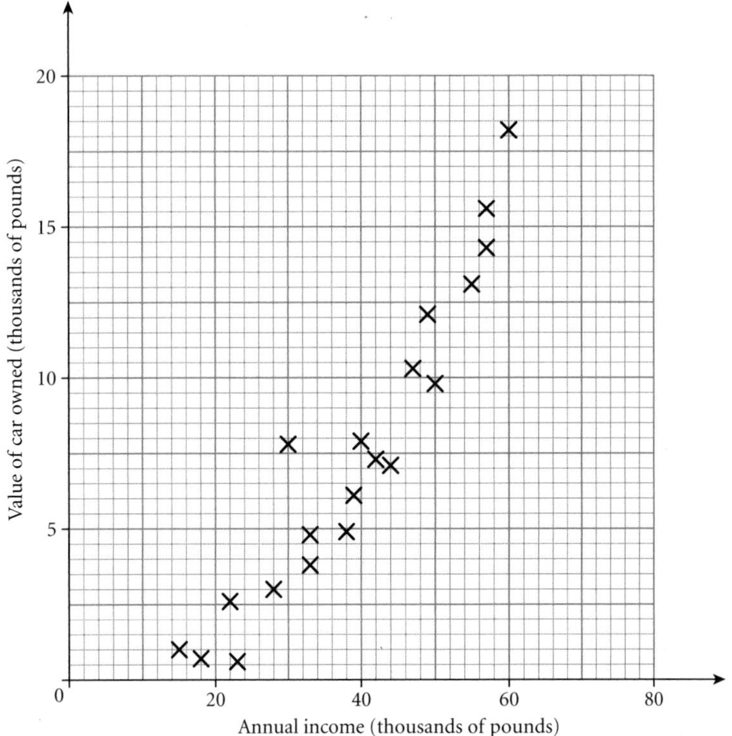

Figure 17.1

? Look at the pattern of the data points in the scatter diagram. Does it indicate what Monica claims?

In this case the population is the population of Avonford car owners. For her survey, Monica can only take a sample from this population: asking everybody (i.e. doing a census) is not a possibility. If it is a randomly selected sample then it should be reasonably representative of the population.

A scatter diagram will illustrate association between the variables. If you can draw a straight line that fits the data reasonably well, the association is described as *linear*. The level of linear association is described as *correlation*. This chapter is about ways of calculating and interpreting measures of correlation.

Look at the two scatter diagrams on the next page.

In figure 17.2 the data are truly scattered. There is no correlation.

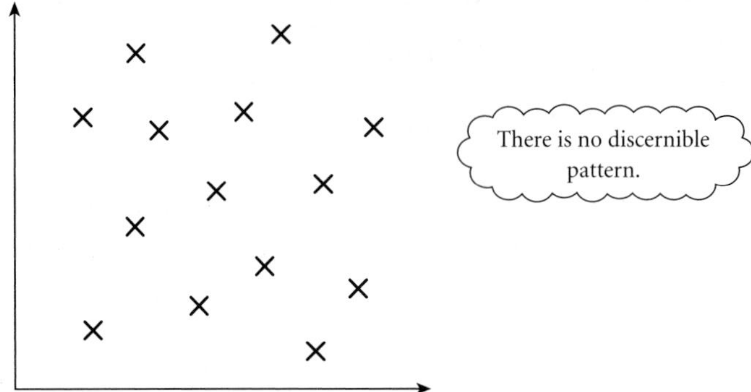

Figure 17.2

In figure 17.3, as one variable increases the other decreases. There is correlation and in this case it is negative.

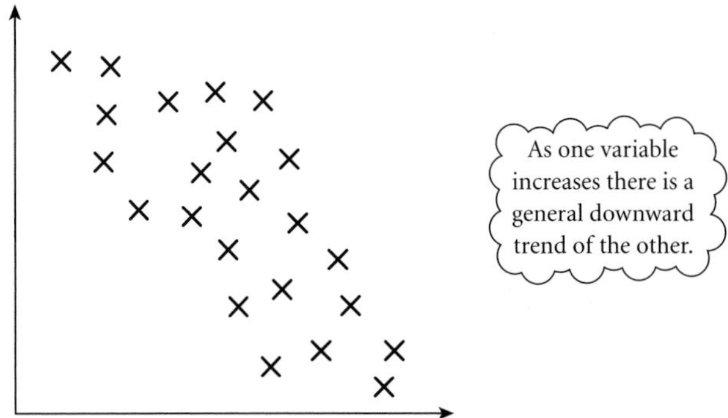

Figure 17.3

In the example from the *Avonford Star* article, illustrated in figure 17.1, there appears to be positive correlation between income and the value of the car driven.

Rogue values and outliers

A scatter diagram will sometimes include one or two *outliers*, points that are far away from the others. They do not fit the pattern. Should such data be rejected from the sample as being untypical of the population? Outliers that appear in a sample should be questioned but not automatically rejected.

Here are three data pairs that Monica might have collected in her sample. Should she have accepted or rejected them?

(i) (60, 0.3)
Ms Smith has a good managerial job in an industrial company and earns a good wage.
However, she is firmly convinced that it is cheaper to use older cars which are cheaper to run and to maintain. Consequently, at the time when Monica did her survey Ms Smith was running an old Ford which was worth just £300.

(ii) (12, 20)
Mr Townsend has a disability. Because of his condition he is jobless and so receives only state benefits but the car he uses has been specially constructed for him and so is worth more than ordinary cars.

(iii) (300, 0.5)
Mr Uncliffe has a semi-skilled job in a local factory and he lives in a part of the town where the housing is not the most expensive.

Take care here. Some software packages automatically reject outliers. Computers cannot, of course, make decisions about whether an outlier is an error or not.

Describing variables

A bivariate distribution involves two variables. You need to be clear about their nature.

Dependent and independent variables

The scatter diagram in figure 17.1 was drawn with the value of the car on the y axis and the income on the x axis.

In this example, earning more allows you to buy and run a more expensive car so that the value of the car is dependent on your income. You do not, however, earn more money by driving a more valuable car; your income is not dependent on the value of your car.

So, in this case, income is the independent variable and, by convention, shown on the x axis. The value of the car is the dependent variable and so goes on the y axis.

Random and non-random variables

In this case the sample was chosen at random and so the data pairs have unpredictable values. It is important for all that follows on correlation that both values are random. That is, that the member of the population is chosen at random without prior conditions upon either variable. In addition, there should be no formula connecting the two variables.

The methods that follow quantify linear correlation but, for the methods to be valid, the variables must be random on random. Two examples are described below: neither of them is suitable for such analysis because the variables are not random on random.

Controlled variables

You want to compare shoe sizes with height and you select someone with shoe size 1, someone with shoe size 2, etc, up to someone with shoe size 12, and you measure their heights. Your sample would not be random because people have been chosen according to their shoe size. The shoe size variable is said to be *controlled.*

Formulae

You want to compare temperatures in degrees Celsius and degrees Fahrenheit. You measure a random sample of temperatures in both Celsius and Fahrenheit. Then, however random the choice of temperatures, the measurements in degrees Fahrenheit are exactly determined by that in degrees Celsius (and vice versa) because their relationship is fixed by a formula.

? Other members of Monica's sociology group collected the following bivariate data.

Identify the independent and dependent variables and decide in each case whether one of the variables is controlled or connected by a formula.

(i) Height and weight of students in the college

(ii) The height of a plant against its age in days, with measurements made daily at midday

(iii) The time of swing of a pendulum against its length

Interpreting scatter diagrams

A scatter diagram provides you with a lot of useful information, including whether it is safe to carry out correlation calculations on the data.

Look at figure 17.4. The scatter diagram seems to indicate that the points all roughly lie on a straight line. However, this in itself is not as much as you need. In addition, almost all of the points form a roughly elliptical cloud of points. This shape usually arises when both variables are Normally distributed and random. Before proceeding further with the analysis described below you should draw a scatter diagram and check that you can fit an ellipse round the data.

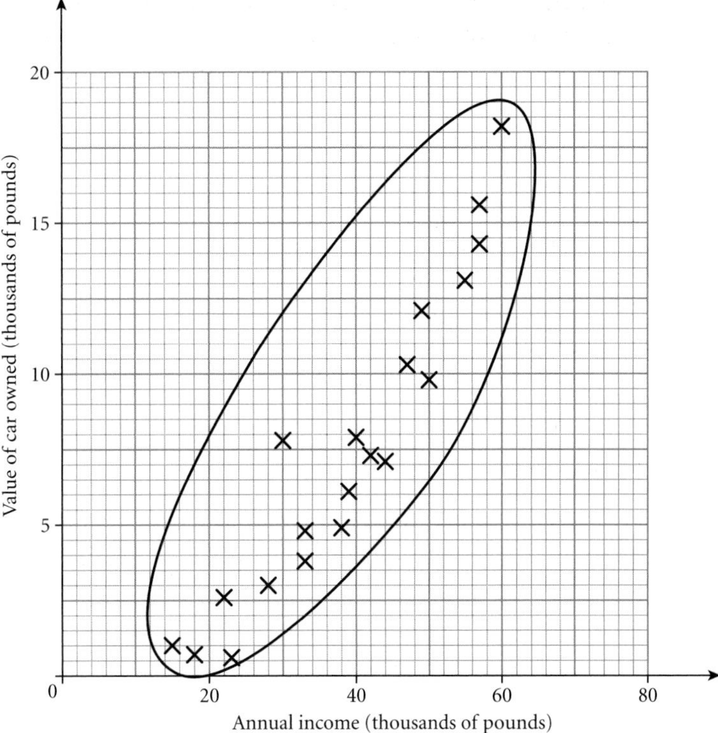

Figure 17.4

If a reasonably compact ellipse can be drawn around the data points, then it is safe to proceed. If such an ellipse cannot be drawn without excluding some of the points, then you should question either those points or even the whole data set.

Some common cases are illustrated in figures 17.5, 17.6 and 17.7.

The scatter diagram in figure 17.5 shows two outliers.

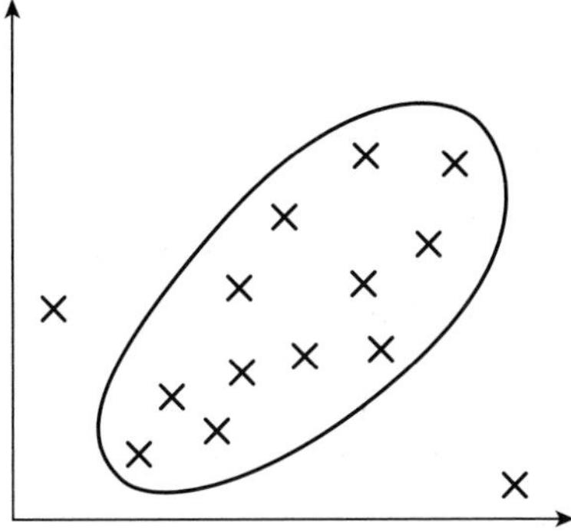

Figure 17.5

The scatter diagram in figure 17.6 shows the data to be in two islands. You should ask if you really have one population or two.

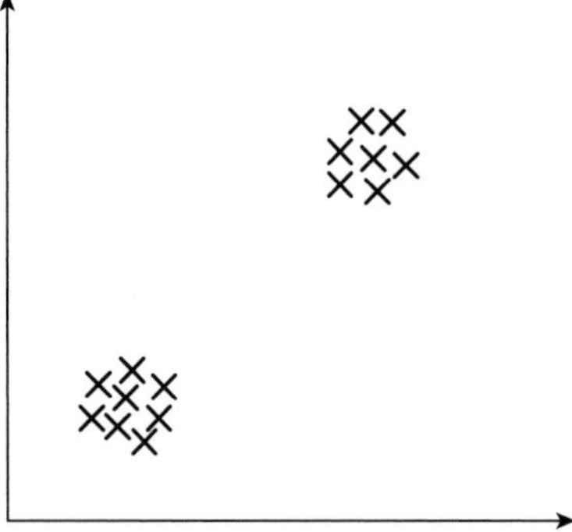

Figure 17.6

The scatter diagram in figure 17.7 shows a non-linear relationship.

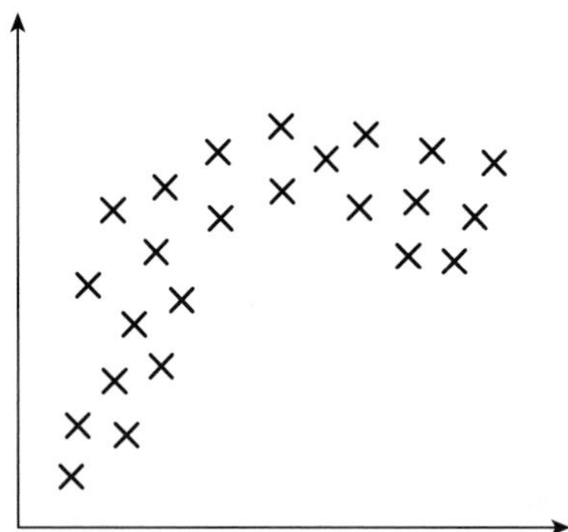

Figure 17.7

The analysis that follows assumes that there is a level of linear association.

Pearson's product moment correlation coefficient

The scatter diagram in figure 17.4 indicates that there may well be an association between people's income and the value of the car that they own, so it is reasonable to calculate a correlation coefficient.

To measure the level of association, start by calculating the arithmetic mean of the x and y variables.

Here are the data that gave rise to the *Avonford Star* article again.

Income (thousands of pounds per annum)	15	18	22	23	28	30	33	33	38	39
Value of car (thousands of pounds)	1.0	0.7	2.6	0.6	3.0	7.8	3.8	4.8	4.9	6.1

Income (thousands of pounds per annum)	40	42	44	47	49	50	55	57	57	60
Value of car (thousands of pounds)	7.9	7.3	7.1	10.3	12.1	9.8	13.1	15.6	14.3	18.2

The mean values of the variables are given by

$$\begin{aligned}\bar{x} &= \frac{1}{n}\sum x \\ &= \frac{1}{20} \times 780 \\ &= 39\end{aligned}$$

$$\begin{aligned}\bar{y} &= \frac{1}{n}\sum y \\ &= \frac{1}{20} \times 151 \\ &= 7.55\end{aligned}$$

And so the mean point, $(\bar{x}, \bar{y})$, is (39, 7.55).

Plotting the mean point on the scatter diagram and drawing vertical and horizontal lines through the point divides the diagram into four regions.

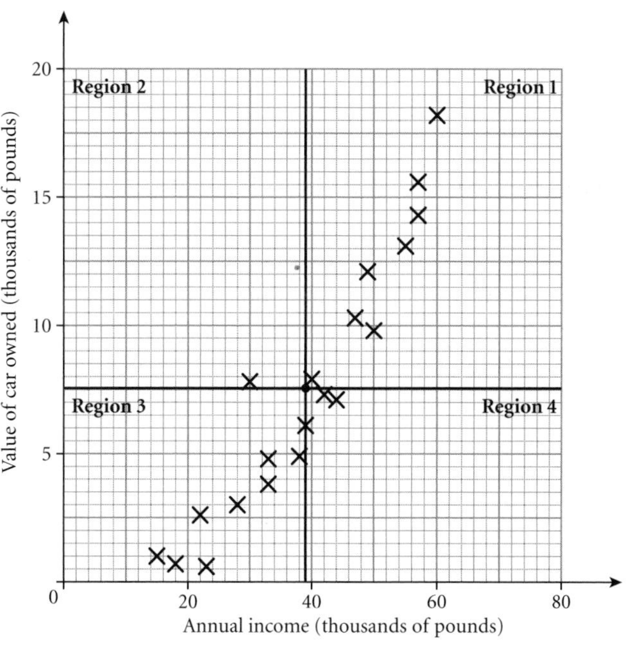

Figure 17.8

You can think of the mean point, $(\bar{x}, \bar{y})$, as the middle of the scatter diagram and so you can treat it as the origin. Relative to this point, the co-ordinates of the point (x, y) become $(x - \bar{x}, y - \bar{y})$.

Now look at the product $(x - \bar{x}) \times (y - \bar{y})$ for the points.

In regions 1 and 3 the product $(x - \bar{x}) \times (y - \bar{y})$ is positive for every point.

? Explain why the product $(x - \bar{x}) \times (y - \bar{y})$ is negative for every point in regions 2 and 4.

The sum for all the points is $\sum(x - \bar{x}) \times (y - \bar{y})$, and this is denoted by S_{xy}.

An alternative and often more convenient formula for S_{xy} is $S_{xy} = \sum xy - n\bar{x}\bar{y}$.

In this case,
$$\begin{aligned} S_{xy} &= \sum xy - n\bar{x}\bar{y} \\ &= 15 \times 1 + 18 \times 0.7 + \ldots + 60 \times 18.2 - 20 \times 39 \times 7.55 \\ &= 7143.3 - 5889 \\ &= 1254.3 \end{aligned}$$

Where there is positive correlation most of the points will lie in regions 1 and 3 and so the sum of the products, S_{xy}, will be positive.

Where there is negative correlation most of the points will lie in regions 2 and 4 and so the sum of products, S_{xy}, will be negative.

Where there is no correlation the points will be scattered throughout all four regions so the sum of the products, S_{xy}, could be anything. You would expect that since some will be positive and some negative the sum will be small.

Note that in calculating the value of S_{xy}

- no allowance has been made for the number of items of data
- no allowance has been made for the spread within the data
- no allowance has been made of the units of x and y.

To allow for both the number of items and the spread within the data, together with the units of x and y, the value of S_{xy} is divided by the square root of the product of S_{xx} and S_{yy}.

This gives the formula $r = \dfrac{S_{xy}}{\sqrt{S_{xx}S_{yy}}}$

The value r is called *Pearson's product moment correlation coefficient.*

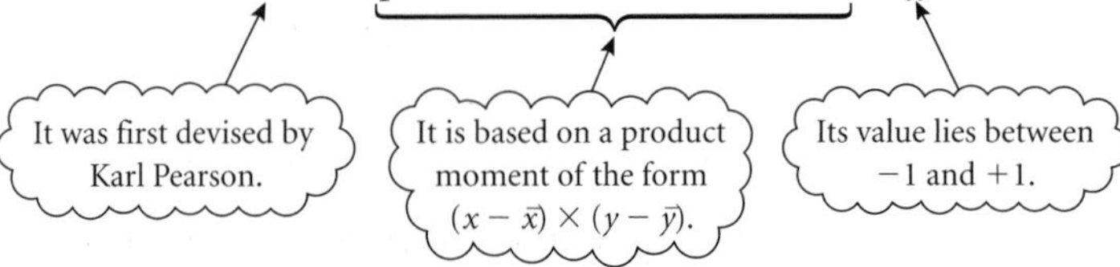

It was first devised by Karl Pearson.
It is based on a product moment of the form $(x - \bar{x}) \times (y - \bar{y})$.
Its value lies between −1 and +1.

It is sometimes referred to simply as pmcc.

As with the formula for the sum of the products, S_{xy}, there are two ways of writing the formulae for S_{xx} and S_{yy}.

$$S_{xy} = \sum(x - \bar{x})(y - \bar{y}) \quad \text{or} \quad S_{xy} = \sum xy - n\bar{x}\bar{y}$$

$$S_{xx} = \sum(x - \bar{x})^2 \quad \text{or} \quad S_{xx} = \sum x^2 - n\bar{x}^2$$

$$S_{yy} = \sum(y - \bar{y})^2 \quad \text{or} \quad S_{yy} = \sum y^2 - n\bar{y}^2$$

For the *Avonford Star* data,

$$S_{xx} = 3502$$

$$S_{yy} = 502.45$$

$$S_{xy} = 1254.3$$

and so
$$r = \frac{S_{xy}}{\sqrt{S_{xx} \times S_{yy}}} = \frac{1254.3}{\sqrt{3502 \times 502.45}} = 0.9456$$

You will usually use the statistics functions of your calculator to work out these values and so you need to become familiar with the facilities for doing so.

ACTIVITY

Here is a set of five bivariate data points.

(1, 5) (2, 7) (2, 9) (4, 9) (6, 10)

(i) Without using a calculator, find the following.

$\sum x$, $\sum y$, $\bar{x}$, $\bar{y}$, $\sum x^2$, $\sum y^2$, $\sum xy$, $\sum(x - \bar{x})^2$, $\sum(y - \bar{y})^2$ and $\sum(x - \bar{x})(y - \bar{y})$

(ii) Show that for these data the two alternative formulae for S_{xx} give the same answers. Do the same for S_{yy} and S_{xy}.

(iii) Now find the value of r.

(iv) Now use your calculator to find the value of r, checking that you get the same answer.

This value of r provides a standardised measure of correlation. Its value lies in the range -1 to $+1$. For perfect negative correlation the value is -1 and for perfect positive correlation the value is $+1$.

In cases of little or no correlation the value of r will be close to 0. It follows that the nearer the value is to $+1$ or -1, the stronger the correlation.

If you get a value for r that is greater than $+1$ or less than -1, then you have made a mistake!

You will learn how to interpret the value of r later in the chapter.

EXAMPLE 17.1

A small random sample of broad beans was examined and, for each bean, the mass and the length were measured and recorded.

Mass (g)	0.8	0.9	0.9	1.1	1.1	1.3	1.5	1.7	1.8	1.9
Length (cm)	1.5	1.6	1.9	2.0	2.1	2.3	2.2	2.4	2.4	2.6

(i) Illustrate the data on a scatter diagram and comment on whether it is appropriate to calculate a correlation coefficient.

(ii) Calculate Pearson's product moment correlation coefficient, r.

SOLUTION

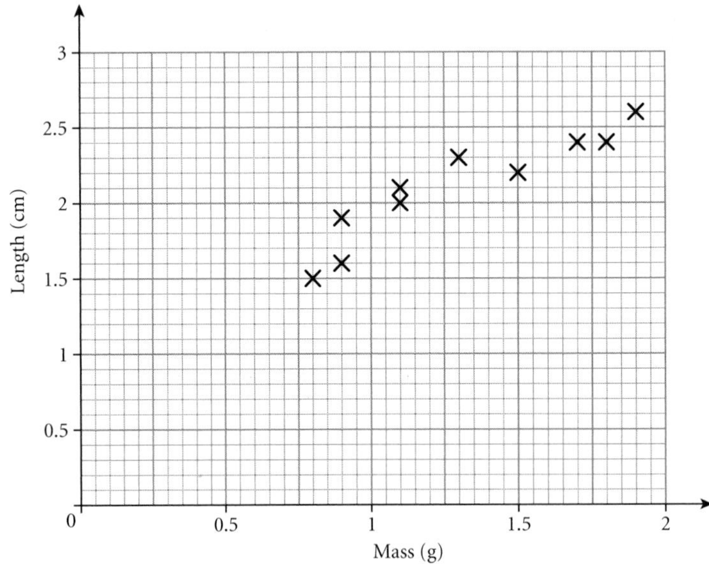

Figure 17.9

These data appear to fit approximately to a straight line. Both variables are random and it is possible to fit an ellipse round the points. So the set is suitable for calculating a correlation coefficient.

(ii) For these data,

$$\sum x = 13, \quad \sum y = 21, \quad \sum x^2 = 18.36, \quad \sum y^2 = 45.24, \quad \sum xy = 28.49$$

So $\bar{x} = \frac{13}{10} = 1.3, \quad \bar{y} = \frac{21}{10} = 2.1$

It follows that $S_{xx} = \sum x^2 - n\bar{x}^2 = 18.36 - 10 \times 1.3^2 = 1.46$

$$S_{yy} = \sum y^2 - n\bar{y}^2 = 45.24 - 10 \times 2.1^2 = 1.14$$

$$S_{xy} = \sum xy - n\bar{x}\bar{y} = 28.49 - 10 \times 1.3 \times 2.1 = 1.19$$

So $r = \dfrac{S_{xy}}{\sqrt{S_{xx} \times S_{yy}}} = \dfrac{1.19}{\sqrt{1.46 \times 1.14}} = 0.9224$

There is strong correlation for this set of data.

ACTIVITY

Using a spreadsheet

In the previous activity you worked out Pearson's product moment correlation coefficient by hand. However, it is much easier if you use a suitable calculator or a spreadsheet package.

The following shows how to use Excel to do the calculations in Example 17.1.

(i) Enter the x values in cells A1 to A10 and the y values in cells B1 to B10.

(ii) In any other cell, enter this formula: =PEARSON(A1:A10,B1:B10).

(iii) Highlight the data, then use the 'Scatter' option in the Chartwizard to generate the scatter diagram which you can customise and label as you wish.

	A	B	C	D	E	F	G	H	I
1	0.8	1.5							
2	0.9	1.6							
3	0.9	1.9							
4	1.1	2.0							
5	1.1	2.1							
6	1.3	2.3							
7	1.5	2.2							
8	1.7	2.4							
9	1.8	2.4							
10	1.9	2.6							
11									
12	PMCC	0.922397							
13									
14									
15									
16									
17									
18									
19									
20									

ACTIVITY

Using a graphic calculator

The facility to calculate Pearson's product moment correlation coefficient is standard on graphic calculators.

Using your graphic calculator, find the pmcc for the data in Example 17.1. (You may find it helpful to consult your instruction manual.)

Historical note

Karl Pearson was one of the founders of modern statistics. Born in 1857, he was a man of varied interests and he practised law for three years before being appointed Professor of Applied Mathematics and Mechanics at University College, London in 1884. Pearson made contributions to various branches of mathematics but is particularly remembered for his work on the applications of statistics to biological problems in heredity and evolution. He died in 1936.

EXERCISE 17A

The questions in this exercise cover the calculation of Pearsons product moment correlation coefficient. You should complete the calculations in a variety of ways, using the different formulae and also using a spreadsheet and your graphic calculator. The interpretation of the correlation coefficient is covered in the next section of this chapter.

1 Samples of large bivariate populations produce the following summary statistics.

In each case calculate the product moment correlation coefficient between x and y.

(i) $\sum x = 25.2$, $\sum y = 17.8$, $\sum x^2 = 72.0$, $\sum y^2 = 40.5$, $\sum xy = 49.3$, $n = 10$

(ii) $\sum x = 48.1$, $\sum y = 320$, $\sum x^2 = 138.63$, $\sum y^2 = 5454$, $\sum xy = 772.4$, $n = 20$

(iii) $\sum x = 179$, $\sum y = 173$, $\sum x^2 = 2889$, $\sum y^2 = 2495$, $\sum xy = 1610$, $n = 15$

2 A sample of a large bivariate population produces the following data pairs.

x	52	47	40	37	35	29
y	13	15	18	19	21	20

(i) Draw a scatter diagram for these data.
(ii) Calculate Pearson's product moment correlation coefficient.

3 A sample of ten students was chosen from Year 12 in a college. They were asked how far they had to travel to college (to the nearest 0.5 kilometre) and the average number of minutes spent in study at home in the evening. The results are shown in the table.

Distance from college, x km	6	2	2.5	4	8.5	7.5	0.5	4	6	9
Time spent studying, y minutes	90	80	80	75	65	60	90	65	55	40

(i) Draw a scatter diagram for these data.
(ii) Explain why it is appropriate to use Pearson's product moment correlation coefficient with these data.
(iii) Calculate the product moment correlation coefficient.

4 A sample of eight mackerel were taken and the mass of the heart and the mass of the liver were recorded. The results are shown in the table.

Mass of heart, x g	3.2	2.3	3.9	4.5	2.1	3.7	4.1	2.9
Mass of liver, y g	5.2	5.6	6.8	6.3	5.4	6.7	6.6	5.8

(i) Draw a scatter diagram for these data.
(ii) Explain why it is appropriate to use Pearson's product moment correlation coefficient with these data.
(iii) Calculate the product moment correlation coefficient.

5 The ages in years (in which the months have been converted to decimals to one decimal place) and heights (to the nearest centimetre) of ten children are shown in the table.

Age, x years	5.5	6.6	7.1	7.5	8.3	8.3	9.7	10.1	11.3	12.5
Height, y cm	120	117	121	123	121	127	125	130	131	135

(i) Plot a scatter diagram of these data.

(ii) Explain why it is appropriate to use Pearson's product moment correlation coefficient with these data.

(iii) Calculate the product moment correlation coefficient.

The meaning of a sample correlation coefficient

You have now seen how to calculate Pearson's product moment correlation coefficient. If this value is close to $+1$ or -1 then this is an indication of strong positive or negative correlation; if it is close to 0 then it is an indication of little or no correlation.

The value you obtain is for the data from your sample. The sample is taken from a parent population. The sample correlation coefficient is used to provide evidence about the level of correlation in the whole parent population.

In Example 17.1 a sample was taken from a population of broad beans. If the sample chosen was truly representative of the population, then you can use it to make inferences about the population.

The correlation coefficient of the population is denoted by ρ (the Greek letter '*rho*', pronounced 'row' as in 'row a boat').

The calculated value of r can be used as an estimate for ρ. However, it can also be used as a test statistic for a hypothesis test on the value of ρ.

In the simplest test, the null hypothesis is that there is no correlation within the population.

H_0: $\rho = 0$ There is no correlation between the two variables.

There are three forms for the alternative hypothesis, depending on the situation you are investigating.

H_1: $\rho \neq 0$ There is correlation between the two variables (2-tailed test).
H_1: $\rho > 0$ There is positive correlation between the two variables (1-tailed test).
H_1: $\rho < 0$ There is negative correlation between the two variables (1-tailed test).

The value of r that you calculate from the sample is the test statistic. You find the critical value from tables; it will depend on the sample size, the significance level at which you are testing and whether you are carrying out a 1-tailed or a 2-tailed test.

The following examples show how this hypothesis test is carried out.

EXAMPLE 17.2

It is thought that students who are good at weightlifting are not good at ice-skating. Philip decides to test, at the 5% level of significance, whether this could be so. He collects data on the maximum weight lifted and the maximum score in an ice-skating competition for a random sample of ten students at Avonford College and calculates the value of r to be -0.6753. Set up the hypothesis test and decide whether Philip can claim negative correlation between the weights lifted and the ice-skating scores.

SOLUTION

Setting up the hypothesis test

H_0: $\rho = 0$, there is no correlation between the weights lifted and the ice-skating scores.

H_1: $\rho < 0$, there is negative correlation between the weights lifted and the ice-skating scores.

1-tailed test

Significance level: 5%

Notice that this test is for negative correlation.

Calculating the test statistic

You are given that $n = 10$ and $r = -0.6753$.

Interpreting the test statistic

You now need to find the *critical value*. You use tables of critical values for the product moment correlation coefficient, r.

Look for $n = 10$ and a 5% significance level for a 1-tailed test.

1-tailed	5%	$2\frac{1}{2}$%	1%	$\frac{1}{2}$%
2-tailed	10%	5%	2%	1%
n				
1				
2				
3	0.9877	0.9969	0.9995	0.9999
4	0.9000	0.9500	0.9800	0.9900
5	0.8054	0.8783	0.9343	0.9587
6	0.7293	0.8114	0.8822	0.9172
7	0.6694	0.7545	0.8329	0.8745
8	0.6215	0.7067	0.7887	0.8343
9	0.5822	0.6664	0.7498	0.7977
10	0.5494	0.6319	0.7155	0.7646
11	0.5214	0.6021	0.6851	0.7348
12	0.4973	0.5760	0.6581	0.7079

The critical value is -0.5494.

Notice how the negative value is used in this case since the test is for negative correlation.

Since −0.6753 is more extreme than −0.5494, the null hypothesis is rejected. The claim that there is negative correlation between the weights lifted and the ice-skating scores is accepted at the 5% significance level.

If Philip had found that the value of r was −0.3494, what conclusion would he have reached?

EXAMPLE 17.3

Megan wants to test whether there is any connection between the reaction time of students and their ability to perform well at sprinting in athletics. She selects 12 students at random and carries out a reaction test with each, recording the time to react. She also records their time to run a 100 metre race. The results are shown in the table.

Student	A	B	C	D	E	F	G	H	I	J	K	L
Reaction time (seconds)	5.4	6.4	4.2	7.0	5.7	4.6	8.7	5.6	4.7	4.3	5.1	6.5
Time to run 100 m (seconds)	12.3	14.2	12.9	14.9	13.6	11.9	15.1	12.9	13.6	12.7	12.8	14.3

Test, using the 5% significance level, whether there is any correlation between the variables.

SOLUTION

Setting up the hypothesis test

H_0: $\rho = 0$, there is no correlation between the reaction time and the time to run 100 m.

H_1: $\rho \neq 0$, there is correlation between the reaction time and the time to run 100 m.

2-tailed test ← You are investigating whether there is any correlation, positive or negative.

Significance level: 5%

Calculating the test statistic

For these data,

$$\sum x = 68.2, \quad \sum y = 161.2, \quad \sum x^2 = 406.3, \quad \sum y^2 = 2176.92, \quad \sum xy = 928.41$$

So $\bar{x} = \frac{1}{n}\sum x = \frac{1}{12} \times 68.2 = 5.6833$

$\bar{y} = \frac{1}{n}\sum y = \frac{1}{12} \times 161.2 = 13.4333$

Note that the intermediate figures have been rounded but the calculations have been carried out using the unrounded values.

$$S_{xx} = \sum x^2 - n\bar{x}^2 = 406.3 - 12 \times 5.6833^2 = 18.6967$$

$$S_{yy} = \sum y^2 - n\bar{y}^2 = 2176.92 - 12 \times 13.4333^2 = 11.4667$$

$$S_{xy} = \sum xy - n\bar{x}\bar{y} = 928.41 - 12 \times 5.6833 \times 13.4333 = 12.2567$$

So $r = \dfrac{S_{xy}}{\sqrt{S_{xx} \times S_{yy}}} = \dfrac{12.2567}{\sqrt{18.6967 \times 11.4667}} = 0.8371.$

Interpreting the test statistic

For $n = 12$ and a 2-tailed test at the 5% significance level, the critical value is 0.5760.

Since 0.8371 is greater than 0.5760 the null hypothesis is rejected. At the 5% significance level the evidence supports the alternative hypothesis that there is correlation between the variables. Reaction times and sprint times do seem to be connected.

EXAMPLE 17.4

AVONFORD STAR

Letters to the Editor

Dear Sir,

We have received news today of the national crime rate. The Home Secretary claims that over the whole country, the crime rate has fallen. What is of more interest to individuals like me is the crime rate in our town of Avonford. The Home Secretary thinks that the larger the town or city the greater the crime rate. So, as we all know, manpower is siphoned off to work in the cities, leaving the smaller places like Avonford without adequate protection. Avonford surely shows that the Home Secretary is wrong. Crime rate is not related to the size of the town so it solves nothing to police the bigger cities leaving us prone to petty criminals. Let's mount a campaign to get our police force back!

Yours sincerely,

Harry Peel

A student reads the article and decides to carry out a survey of towns and cities by collecting information about the size of the population and the crime rate for a random sample of towns and cities off the internet. The results are given in the following table.

Population, x (in 100 000)	0.4	0.5	0.7	0.8	1.1	1.7	2.1	2.6	2.9	3.3	4.0
Crime rate, y (per 1000 population)	2.7	5.1	4.9	3.6	4.3	4.1	5.1	4.8	5.5	4.7	5.8

Test, using the 5% significance level, the hypothesis that the larger the town the greater the crime rate.

SOLUTION

Setting up the hypothesis test

H_0: $\rho = 0$, there is no correlation between the population size and the crime rate.

H_1: $\rho > 0$, there is positive correlation between the population size and the crime rate.

1-tailed test

Significance level: 5%

Calculating the test statistic

For these data, $S_{xx} = 15.3818$, $S_{yy} = 7.84$ and $S_{xy} = 7.03$

giving $r = \dfrac{S_{xy}}{\sqrt{S_{xx} \times S_{yy}}} = \dfrac{7.03}{\sqrt{15.3818 \times 7.84}} = 0.6402$

Interpreting the test statistic

For $n = 11$ and a 1-tailed test at the 5% significance level, the critical value is 0.5214.

Since 0.6402 is greater than 0.5214, the null hypothesis is rejected. The evidence supports the suggestion, at the 5% significance level, that the crime rate is higher in large towns.

Interpreting correlation

You need to be careful when trying to draw conclusions from significant correlation coefficients.

Correlation does not imply causation

There is, for example, a high level of correlation between children's reading ability and their height. You might be tempted to conclude that being taller makes children better readers. Such a conclusion would be seriously misleading. As children get older their reading ability gets better and they get taller. It is not true to say that being taller makes you better at reading, or that being better at reading makes you taller! Both are caused by something else: the child's age.

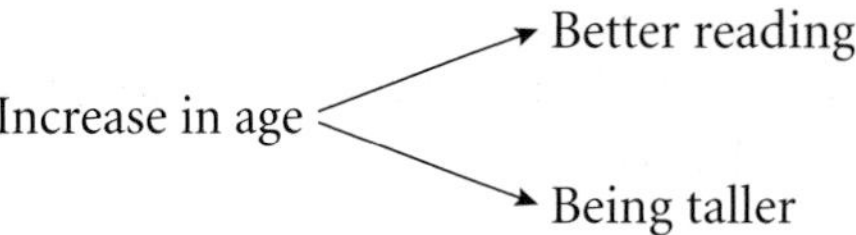

Non-linear association

A low value of r indicates that there is little or no correlation. There are, however, other forms of association which are non-linear. Two of these are illustrated in figure 17.10.

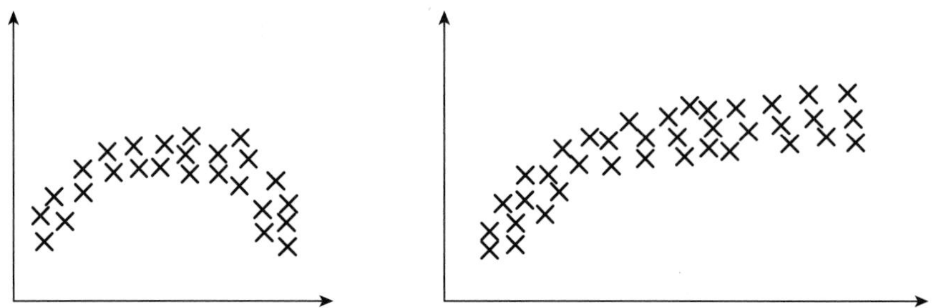

Figure 17.10 *Scatter diagrams showing non-linear correlation*

Extrapolation

As a result of taking a bivariate sample, you may establish a linear relationship between the two variables. However, you can only be confident in applying it within the range of values covered by the sample.

For example, on the basis of sample data you might establish a linear relationship between children's age and the pocket money they are given by their parents. However, you would not be justified in trying to make predictions beyond the age covered by the sample.

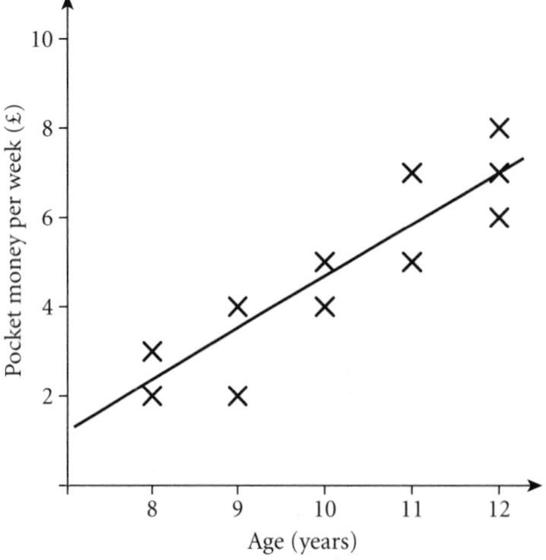

Figure 17.11

? The scatter diagram in figure 17.11 illustrates a relationship for the ages 8 to 12. How do you think this relationship might continue?

e Degrees of freedom

Look at the scatter diagram in figure 17.12. There are just two points (1, 1) and (3, 2).

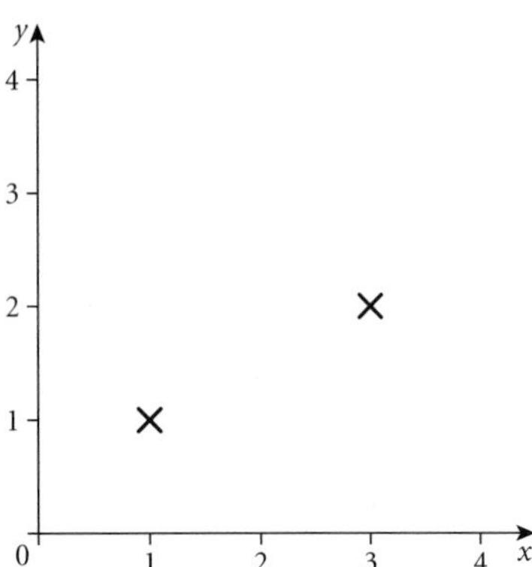

Figure 17.12

? Show by calculation that, for these two points, the value of r is 1.

? Do you get the same value for r for any two points when the one to the right is higher than the one on the left?

Now look at the scatter diagram in figure 17.13.

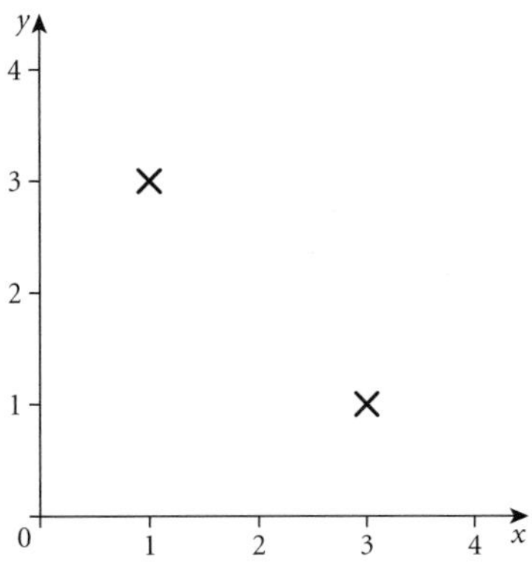

Figure 17.13

? What is the value of r in this case?

You might be tempted to conclude that with a sample of size 2 you always have perfect correlation. That would be misleading. It is actually the case that you can say nothing about the level of correlation if $n = 2$. It is only when you have three or more points that you can start to make any meaningful statement about their correlation; in effect the first two points do not count.

Another way of saying this is that the degrees of freedom, ν, are given by $\nu = n - 2$.

These days most tables of critical values are given for n but be careful because some are given for ν instead.

EXERCISE 17B

1 A sample of 12 items is chosen and two characteristics, x and y are measured. A scatter diagram indicates a linear association between the values. You are given the following information.

$$\sum x = 156, \quad \sum y = 264, \quad \sum x^2 = 2496, \quad \sum y^2 = 7016, \quad \sum xy = 3819$$

(i) Calculate Pearson's product moment correlation coefficient.

(ii) Perform the following hypothesis tests using the 5% significance level, stating carefully your conclusions.

(a) H_0: $\rho = 0$, H_1: $\rho > 0$.

(b) H_0: $\rho = 0$, H_1: $\rho \neq 0$.

2 A sample of 40 items is chosen and two characteristics, x and y, are measured. Perform the following hypothesis tests, stating carefully your conclusions.

(i) H_0: $\rho = 0$, H_1: $\rho > 0$, $r = 0.3333$, using the 5% significance level.

(ii) H_0: $\rho = 0$, H_1: $\rho < 0$, $r = -0.3333$, using the 1% significance level.

(iii) H_0: $\rho = 0$, H_1: $\rho \neq 0$, $r = 0.3333$, using the 5% significance level.

3 In a factory where hand-made goods are produced a quality score is assigned to the production of each craftsman for each day. (The better the quality, the higher the score.) The craftsmen work at their own pace, but the manager thinks that the faster they work (and therefore the greater the number of items made) the lower the quality of the finished product. The manager takes a random sample of craftsmen one day and records the number of items they finish in the day and the quality score given to them.

No. of items finished	16	23	17	27	20	18	19	26	29	21	25	19
Quality score	20	8	16	8	10	11	10	9	5	10	8	0

(i) Plot a scatter diagram for these data. Is it reasonable to use correlation?

(ii) State suitable null and alternative hypotheses to test the manager's theory.

(iii) Calculate Pearson's product moment correlation coefficient.

(iv) Complete the hypothesis test using the 5% significance level and comment on the result.

4 It is a widely held view that mathematicians are also good at music. John decided to test this theory on a small sample of students who had recently completed an AS level in mathematics and who played an instrument. The uniform marks (out of 300) gained by ten students are given in the table together with the grade attained on their best instrument at the time of the mathematics examinations.

Student	A	B	C	D	E	F	G	H	I	J
Maths mark	265	234	280	221	190	171	139	143	206	97
Music grade	7	6	8	5	5	6	4	5	7	3

(i) Plot a scatter diagram for these data. Is it reasonable to use correlation?

(ii) State suitable null and alternative hypotheses to test the theory.

(iii) Complete the hypothesis test at the 5% significance level and comment on the result.

5 A researcher has a theory that body mass and metabolic rate are linearly related with positive association. She took a sample of ten students and recorded the following results.

Student	A	B	C	D	E	F	G	H	I	J
Mass (kg)	57	59	64	65	66	67	71	72	73	81
Metabolic rate	1200	1340	1356	1459	1465	1501	1534	1586	1589	1601

(i) Plot a scatter diagram for these data. Is it reasonable to use correlation?

(ii) State suitable null and alternative hypotheses to test the theory.

(iii) Complete the hypothesis test at the 1% significance level and comment on the result.

6 A university currently assesses the ability of students who apply to enrol on a degree course in sociology by setting two tests. One is a general knowledge test and the other is an IQ test. The Admissions Tutor believes that the tests assess different aptitudes and so does not expect any correlation between the scores. A statistics lecturer claims that there will be a positive association between the scores and that the assessment of the second test does not add to any information given by the first test. He decides to test this theory by looking at the scores of 15 applicants chosen at random.

General knowledge score	27	25	26	25	33	30	35	27	38	27	15	19	22	23	34
IQ score	123	124	122	123	130	128	120	119	132	121	119	110	112	113	117

(i) Plot a scatter diagram for these data. Is it reasonable to use correlation?

(ii) State suitable null and alternative hypotheses to test the theory.

(iii) Complete the hypothesis test at the 5% significance level and comment on the result.

7 Are people who are good at crossword puzzles also good at Suduko puzzles? A researcher carries out an investigation by asking for volunteers of people who regularly do both types of puzzle. He gives a random sample of ten people a crossword puzzle and a Sudoku puzzle and records the times (to the nearest minute) that they take to complete the puzzles.

Crossword	22	23	25	19	20	15	20	29	30	19
Sudoku	8	9	11	7	9	8	10	11	15	9

(i) Plot a scatter diagram for these data. Is it reasonable to use correlation?
(ii) State suitable null and alternative hypotheses to test the theory.
(iii) Complete the hypothesis test at the 5% significance level and comment on the result.

8 A games teacher thinks that the taller you are the better you are at long distance running. He tests the theory by taking a random sample of ten students from his school and recording their height (in centimetres, correct to the nearest centimetre) and the time taken to complete the school cross-country race (in minutes, correct to the nearest minute). The results are shown in the table.

Height (cm)	160	162	165	170	171	173	175	177	179	182
Time (minutes)	24	25	20	21	22	23	19	18	21	18

(i) Plot a scatter diagram for these data. Is it reasonable to use correlation?
(ii) State suitable null and alternative hypotheses to test the theory.
(iii) Complete the hypothesis test at the 5% significance level and comment on the result.

9 A scientist carries out an experiment in which he takes random samples of water and nets fish from a particular stretch of river over a period of years. He wishes to test the theory that there is an association between the levels of pollutant and the number of fish in the river. His data are shown in the table, in appropriate units.

Level of pollutant	20	30	32	55	40	72	68	60	48	54
Number of fish	30	22	15	23	10	13	15	18	20	22

(i) Plot a scatter diagram for these data.
(ii) Identify the outlier in the data. Explain how this might have arisen.
(iii) State suitable null and alternative hypotheses to test the theory using all ten items of data.
(iv) Complete the hypothesis test at the 5% significance level and comment on the result.
(v) Repeat the test on the nine pairs of data after removing the outlier and comment on your result.

10 An estate agent thinks that large houses have large gardens and vice versa. He chooses a random sample of the houses that his company are offering for sale.

Number of rooms	6	7	8	8	9	9	10	12	13	13
Size of garden (in square metres)	80	75	90	120	60	90	120	80	100	150

(i) Plot a scatter diagram for these data. Is it reasonable to use correlation?

(ii) State suitable null and alternative hypotheses to test the theory.

(iii) Complete the hypothesis test at the 5% significance level and comment on the result.

Rank correlation

AVONFORD STAR

Ill feeling at piano competition

The annual Avonford piano competition took place last weekend. The main interest was in the children's section where there was a large entry covering all ages. They did their parents and teachers proud.

But Maria Pockon was not happy with her third place in the adult section and protested to the organisers. She said 'In the summing up, the first judge praised my Beethoven. He said that if this was the last day of his life he would die a happy man having heard me play. So how can the other judge give me such a low rating? They have clearly been working to different criteria and this is not fair for anyone and cannot be right for the competition.'

The organisers held firm over the decisions, however. Their spokesperson, Jane Briggs, said 'We have used these judges for many years and no one has ever complained before. The whole issue is ridiculous. They use the same criteria and agree closely with each other. But they are human beings and you cannot expect them to agree exactly on every ranking. The way we choose the winner is the fairest for all.'

For full details, see the *Avonford Star* website.

In this competition the two judges rank the competitors in position rather than giving them marks. The competitor who the judge thinks is the best is given 1 and the worst is given 6. The winner of the competition is decided by adding the ranks, with the lowest total being the winner.

Here are the rankings for the six competitors. (Maria Pockon was competitor F.)

Competitor	A	B	C	D	E	F
Judge 1 (x)	6	5	4	3	2	1
Judge 2 (y)	4	6	3	2	1	5
Sum of ranks	10	11	7	5	3	6
Final position	5	6	4	2	1	3

So competitor E was the winner, even though judge 1 ranked her second to Maria.

The data are bivariate, but the values are ranks rather than scores. In such cases you would use rank correlation.

Spearman's rank correlation coefficient

? Is it reasonable in the piano competition to calculate the winner by adding the ranks?

? What were the grounds of Maria's complaint?

? Is it reasonable to assume that the judges were marking according to the same criteria, in which case there would be a high level of association?

To test whether Maria has any grounds for her complaint, you need a test of whether or not the rankings given by the judges are associated. Such a test is provided by Spearman's rank correlation test.

The test statistic, Spearman's rank correlation coefficient, is denoted r_s and is given by

$$r_s = 1 - \frac{6\sum d^2}{n(n^2 - 1)}$$

where $d = x - y$ for each pair of ranks and n is the number of data pairs.

The test for the music competition is set up as follows.

Setting up the hypothesis test

H_0: There is no association between the underlying judgements.
H_1: There is positive association between the underlying judgements.
1-tailed test
Significance level: 5%

Calculating the test statistic

The first part of the calculation of the test statistic, r_s for this set of data is shown in the table below.

Competitor	A	B	C	D	E	F
Judge 1 (x)	6	5	4	3	2	1
Judge 2 (y)	4	6	3	2	1	5
$d = x - y$	2	−1	1	1	1	−4
d^2	4	1	1	1	1	16

d is the difference between the rankings of the two judges.

This tells you that

$$\sum d^2 = 4 + 1 + 1 + 1 + 1 + 16 = 24$$

The sample size is $n = 6$.

So
$$\begin{aligned} r_s &= 1 - \frac{6\sum d^2}{n(n^2 - 1)} \\ &= 1 - \frac{6 \times 24}{6 \times (6^2 - 1)} \\ &= 1 - 0.6857 \\ &= 0.3143 \end{aligned}$$

Interpreting the test statistic

The critical values for Spearman's rank correlation coefficient are different from those for Pearson's product moment correlation coefficient. In books of tables they often appear close together.

The significance level is 5% and it is a 1-tailed test with $n = 6$. Look up the critical value in the table.

1-tailed	5%	$2\frac{1}{2}$%	1%	$\frac{1}{2}$%
2-tailed	10%	5%	2%	1%
n				
1				
2				
3				
4	1.0000			
5	0.9000	1.0000	1.0000	
6	0.8286	0.8857	0.9429	1.0000
7	0.7143	0.7857	0.8929	0.9286
8	0.6429	0.7381	0.8333	0.8810
9	0.6000	0.7000	0.7833	0.8333
10	0.5636	0.6485	0.7455	0.7939
11	0.5364	0.6182	0.7091	0.7545

The critical value is 0.8286.

Since 0.3143 is less than 0.8286 the test statistic does not lie in the critical region and so at the 5% significance level you would accept the null hypothesis. Maria does seem to have some grounds for complaint.

You can see that the closer the ranks, the smaller the value of d for each pair and so the smaller the value of the sum of d^2, and so the nearer to 1 is the coefficient.

 If you place these values into a spreadsheet and calculate the value of the Pearson's product moment correlation coefficient, what value do you get?

As with other examples in this chapter, the sample size is rather too small for a robust test. However, the value of n was chosen to be small so as to keep the example simple and easy to read. The principles remain the same for large samples.

Tied ranks

If two or more items are ranked equally then you give them the mean of the ranks that they would have had if they had not been tied.

For example, six people enter a driving competition. Their scores are 8, 8, 7, 4, 4, 4.

In everyday life you would rank them 1st = , 1st = , 3rd, 4th = , 4th = , 4th = .

For rank correlation you would rank them 1.5, 1.5, 3, 5, 5, 5.

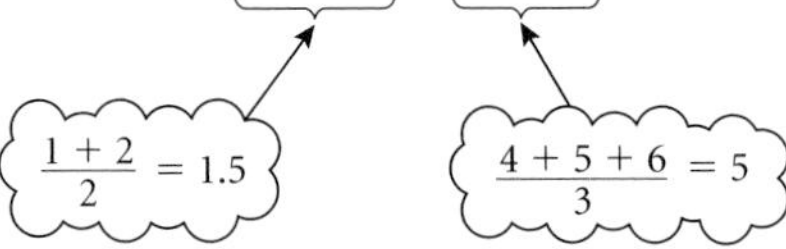

Historical note

Charles Spearman was born in London in 1893. He studied psychology in Leipzig after a number of years in the army. He obtained a doctorate before moving to University College, London, first as a lecturer then a professor. He pioneered the application of statistical techniques within psychology and developed the technique known as factor analysis in order to analyse different aspects of human ability. He died in 1945. He was the first to derive this coefficient and so it is known as Spearman's rank correlation coefficient.

EXAMPLE 17.5

In a physical training course, ten participants had to undergo two different tests, one being a long-distance run and the other a rock-climbing test. They were ranked as shown in the table.

Participants	A	B	C	D	E	F	G	H	I	J
Test 1	5	4	8	7	1	2	3	10	6	9
Test 2	5	6	7	9	3	2	1	8	4	10

Use Spearman's rank correlation coefficient to test whether there is evidence, at the 1% significance level, of positive association between the test results in the underlying population.

SOLUTION

Setting up the hypothesis test

H_0: There is no association between the test results in the underlying population

H_1: There is positive association between the test results in the underlying population.

1-tailed test

Significance level: 1%

Calculating the test statistic

The calculation to find r_s is as follows.

Participants	A	B	C	D	E	F	G	H	I	J
Test 1, x	5	4	8	7	1	2	3	10	6	9
Test 2, y	5	6	7	9	3	2	1	8	4	10
$d = x - y$	0	−2	1	−2	−2	0	2	2	2	−1
d^2	0	4	1	4	4	0	4	4	4	1

$$\sum d^2 = 0 + 4 + 1 + 4 + 4 + 0 + 4 + 4 + 4 + 1 = 26$$

The sample size is $n = 10$.

So
$$r_s = 1 - \frac{6\sum d^2}{n(n^2 - 1)}$$
$$= 1 - \frac{6 \times 26}{10 \times 99}$$
$$= 1 - 0.1576$$
$$= 0.8424$$

Interpreting the test statistic

The tables give the critical value of r for a 1-tailed test at the 1% level of significance, when $n = 10$, as 0.7455.

Since 0.8424 is greater than 0.7455, the null hypothesis is rejected. There is evidence at the 1% significance level of positive association implying that the better the participant is at running the better he or she is at rock-climbing.

When to use rank correlation

Rank correlation should be used in the following situations.

- When variable values have been obtained and a scatter diagram indicates that there is association but it is not linear.
- When variable values are available but it might be too costly or time consuming to measure them.
- When only ranks are available; this might be when ranks are given but not according to a numerical scale.

EXERCISE 17C

1 A test is being carried out, at the 5% significance level, of whether there is any association between two rankings. Find the critical value for r_s in each of these two cases.

(i) $n = 30$

(ii) $n = 60$

2 A rank correlation of 0.60 is calculated from ten pairs of data. Is this significant at the 5% level

(i) in a 1-tailed test

(ii) in a 2-tailed test?

3 Two racegoers predict the result in a horse race as follows.

Prediction 1	6	2	5	1	4	3
Prediction 2	5	1	6	4	3	2
Result	5	2	3	1	6	4

(i) Find Spearman's rank correlation coefficient between

(a) prediction 1 and the result

(b) prediction 2 and the result.

(ii) Which was the closer match?

4 Two judges at a Mr Universe competition produced the following rankings.

Contestant	A	B	C	D	E	F	G	H	I
Judge 1	6	3	1	9	2	5	4	7	8
Judge 2	5	2	4	7	1	8	3	6	9

(i) State suitable null and alternative hypotheses to test the level of agreement between the two judges.

(ii) Calculate Spearman's rank correlation coefficient.

(iii) Complete the hypothesis test using the 5% significance level.

5 Elira and Beth were asked to judge the quality of ten drinks and place them in rank order. Their ranks are given in the table.

Drink	A	B	C	D	E	F	G	H	I	J
Elira's ranks	10	9	4	1	2	6	7	5	3	8
Beth's ranks	9	6	1	2	3	8	7	5	4	10

Use Spearman's rank correlation coefficient to test, at the 5% level of significance, whether Elira and Beth are in agreement over the drinks.

6 Ten students each take two aptitude tests. Their marks are as follows.

Student	A	B	C	D	E	F	G	H	I	J
Test X	15	6	9	4	18	17	13	19	8	7
Test Y	13	3	12	6	8	16	15	20	11	9

(i) Plot a scatter diagram of these marks.

(ii) Which student scored marks which seem to be inconsistent with the rest? Do you know of any reason to justify excluding them?

(iii) Explain why, for these data, the product moment correlation coefficient may be a less suitable coefficient than Spearman's rank correlation coefficient.

(iv) State suitable null and alternative hypotheses to test the level of agreement between the two marks.

(v) Calculate Spearman's rank correlation coefficient.

(vi) Carry out the hypothesis test at the 5% significance level and comment on the result.

7 A firm which produces garden fertilisers believes that it has found a new compound that will increase the yield from tomato plants. A large number of tomato seedlings are treated with different amounts of fertiliser, x grams, at regular intervals. The yield, y kg, of tomatoes is measured for each plant.

From the large number of plants a random selection of 12 plants are chosen and the results are summarised in the table below.

Fertiliser, x grams	1	3	4	6	7	10	12	15	16	18	19	21
Yield, y kg	3.2	4.0	5.7	6.2	8.3	8.5	8.6	8.4	7.9	7.6	7.5	7.2

(i) Illustrate these data on a scatter diagram. What does it show?

(ii) Rank the data.

(iii) Carry out the hypothesis test at the 5% significance level and comment on the result.

(iv) Calculate Spearman's rank correlation coefficient for the 8 plants with the lowest amounts of fertiliser.

(v) Comment on the rank correlation coefficients for all 12 plants and for the 8 in part **(iv)**.

8 A competition, in which there are ten contestants, is judged by three judges, X, Y and Z, who rank the contestants. The winner is decided as follows.

- Spearman's rank correlation coefficient is calculated for each pair of judges X and Y; Y and Z; Z and X.
- The pair whose rank correlation coefficient is nearest to 1 are used to judge the winner; the ranks of the third judge are discarded.
- The final positions are determined by adding the ranks of the two judges and the lowest score is the winner.

The rank orders given by each judge were as follows.

Contestant	A	B	C	D	E	F	G	H	I	J
Judge X	2	7	4	8	9	3	10	1	6	5
Judge Y	4	7	3	6	8	2	10	1	9	5
Judge Z	2	10	5	9	7	4	8	1	6	3

Determine the final positions in the competition.

9 At the end of a word-processing course the trainees are given a document to type. They are assessed on the time taken and on the quality of their work. For a random sample of 12 trainees the following results were obtained.

Trainee	A	B	C	D	E	F	G	H	I	J	K	L
Quality (%)	97	96	94	91	90	87	86	83	82	80	77	71
Time (seconds)	210	230	198	204	213	206	200	186	192	202	191	199

(i) Calculate Spearman's coefficient of rank correlation for the data. Explain what the sign of your correlation coefficient indicates about the data.

(ii) Carry out a test, at the 5% level of significance, of whether or not there is any association between the time taken and the quality of work for trainees who have attended this word-processing course. State clearly the null and alternative hypotheses under test and the conclusion reached.

[MEI]

10 A fertiliser additive is claimed to enhance the growth of marrows. To test the claim statistically, a random sample of ten marrows is treated with varying levels of additive. The amounts of additive and the eventual weights of the marrows are given in the table.

Amount of additive (oz)	8.2	3.5	8.8	1.6	1.9	9.9	5.8	5.5	4.4	3.9
Weight of marrow (lbs)	6.6	7.2	8.4	4.7	7.4	8.7	7.5	7.3	5.9	7.0

(i) Rank the data and calculate Spearman's coefficient of rank correlation.

(ii) State appropriate null and alternative hypotheses for the test. Justify the alternative hypothesis you have given.

(iii) Carry out the test using a 5% level of significance. State clearly the conclusion reached.

(iv) Suppose it was discovered that the figures for the amounts of additive shown in the table were weights in grams rather than ounces. State, with reasons, whether this does or does not invalidate your answer.

[MEI]

KEY POINTS

1 A scatter diagram is a graph to illustrate bivariate data. If you can draw a straight line that fits the data reasonably well, the association between the variables is described as linear. The level of linear association is known as correlation.

2 When investigating the level of correlation by taking a sample, both variables must be random.

3 This is the notation for n pairs of observations, (x, y).

$$\bar{x} = \frac{1}{n}\sum x \qquad \bar{y} = \frac{1}{n}\sum y$$

$$S_{xx} = \sum(x - \bar{x})^2 = \sum x^2 - n\bar{x}^2$$

$$S_{yy} = \sum(y - \bar{y})^2 = \sum y^2 - n\bar{y}^2$$

$$S_{xy} = \sum(x - \bar{x})(y - \bar{y}) = \sum xy - n\bar{x}\bar{y}$$

4 Pearson's product moment correlation coefficient (the pmcc) may be used when a scatter diagram indicates a level of linear association.

Pearson's product moment correlation coefficient is given by

$$r = \frac{S_{xy}}{\sqrt{S_{xx} \times S_{yy}}}$$

The value of r always lies between -1 and 1. r is the test statistic for a hypothesis test on the population correlation coefficient.

5 When conducting a hypothesis test, the null hypothesis is that there is no correlation between the two variables.

H_0: $\rho = 0$ There is no correlation between the two variables.

There are three possible forms for the alternative hypothesis, depending on the situation you are investigating.

H_1: $\rho \neq 0$ There is correlation between the two variables (2-tailed test).
H_1: $\rho > 0$ There is positive correlation between the two variables (1-tailed test).
H_1: $\rho < 0$ There is negative correlation between the two variables (1-tailed test).

6 Spearman's rank correlation coefficient, r_s, may be used when association is not necessarily linear or when only ranks are available.

Spearman's rank correlation coefficient is given by

$$r_s = 1 - \frac{6\sum d_i^2}{n(n^2 - 1)}$$

where $d_i = x_i - y_i$.

The value of r_s always lies between -1 and 1.
r_s is the test statistic for a hypothesis test of association.
The hypothesis test is set up in a similar way to that using Pearson's product moment correlation coefficient as the test statistic.

Appendices

1 The derivation of the alternative form of the sum of squares, S_{xx}

$$S_{xx} = \sum(x - \bar{x})^2$$

$$= \sum(x^2 - 2x\bar{x} + \bar{x}^2)$$

$$= \sum x^2 - \sum 2x\bar{x} + \sum \bar{x}^2$$

$$= \sum x^2 - 2\bar{x}\sum x + n\bar{x}^2$$ ← because $\bar{x}$ is a constant

$$= \sum x^2 - 2n\bar{x}^2 + n\bar{x}^2$$ ← $\bar{x} = \frac{\sum x}{n} \Rightarrow \sum x = n\bar{x}$

$$= \sum x^2 - n\bar{x}^2$$

2 The binomial theorem

A typical binomial expression may be written $(x + y)^n$.

'Binomial' means 'two numbers' and these are x and y. When the binomial expression is used to find a probability distribution, n is a positive whole number and x and y represent probabilities adding up to 1.

There are two common ways of expanding, or multiplying out, a binomial expression: by using Pascal's triangle or the formula for ${}^nC_r$.

Pascal's triangle

If you multiply out $(x + y)^4$, you get $1x^4 + 4x^3y + 6x^2y^2 + 4xy^3 + 1y^4$. You can find the various coefficients in this expression (1, 4, 6, 4, 1) by looking along row 4 of Pascal's triangle.

Row	
0	1
1	1 1
2	1 2 1
3	1 3 3 1
4	1 4 6 4 1
5	1 5 10 10 5 1

and so on

To find the next row of Pascal's triangle you put 1 in both of the outside positions, and then find the number to go in each place by adding the two diagonally above it.

The reason for doing this can be seen by considering the process of obtaining the expansion of $(x + y)^5$ from the known expansion of $(x + y)^4$. This involves multiplying $x^4 + 4x^3y + 6x^2y^2 + 4xy^3 + y^4$ by $x + y$ and then collecting like terms.

For example, the term in x^3y^2 is the sum of the two products $y \times 4x^3y$ and $x \times 6x^2y^2$, giving the coefficient $4 + 6 = 10$, and the 4 and 6 are the entries in row 4 diagonally above the first entry 10 in row 5.

The numbers in row 5 are

1 5 10 10 5 1

so row 6 is

1 6 15 20 15 6 1

Pascal's triangle is a quick and easy way of working out the binomial coefficients if n is not too large. However, it soon becomes cumbersome, particularly if you only want to work out a single coefficient.

You will probably have noticed that Pascal's triangle has strong connections with the table values of ${}^nC_r$ given on page 154. The values agree up to $n = 6$. Moreover, Pascal's triangle and the table have the same 'law of growth': the addition of values diagonally above for Pascal's triangle and the property ${}^{n+1}C_{r+1} = {}^nC_r + {}^nC_{r+1}$ for the table (you should convince yourself that these amount to the same thing by looking at some particular cases, e.g. $n = 4$, $r = 1$). Therefore the initial agreement must continue and so Pascal's triangle and the table of values of ${}^nC_r$ give the same information (which, of course, is why the ${}^nC_r$ are called binomial coefficients).

Values of ${}^nC_r$ can also be found from your calculator, or from the Table of binomial coefficients in your student's handbook. Rows which are cut short in this table can be completed by symmetry using ${}^nC_r = {}^nC_{n-r}$.

EXAMPLE A

Find the first four terms of the expansions of **(i)** $(x+y)^{17}$ **(ii)** $(x+y)^{25}$.

SOLUTION

(i) From the $n = 17$ row of the table of binomial coefficients

$$(x+y)^{17} = x^{17} + 17x^{16}y + 136x^{15}y^2 + 680x^{14}y^3 + \ldots$$

(ii) The table stops before $n = 25$, so you use ${}^nC_r = \dfrac{n!}{r!(n-r)!}$ to find the coefficients:

$$\begin{aligned}(x+y)^{25} &= {}^{25}C_0x^{25} + {}^{25}C_1x^{24}y + {}^{25}C_2x^{23}y^2 + {}^{25}C_3x^{22}y^3 + \ldots \\ &= x^{25} + 25x^{24}y + 300x^{23}y^2 + 2300x^{22}y^3 + \ldots\end{aligned}$$

EXERCISE A

1 Write out these binomial expansions in full.

(i) $(a+b)^2$ **(ii)** $(c+d)^3$ **(iii)** $(e+f)^4$ **(iv)** $(l+m)^5$

(v) $(p+q)^6$ **(vi)** $(s+t)^8$

2 Find the terms requested in these binomial expansions.

(i) The term in n^2y^3 in $(n+y)^5$

(ii) The term in q^6p^4 in $(q+p)^{10}$

(iii) The first four terms of $(h+k)^{18}$

(iv) The first three and last three terms of $(q+pt)^{27}$

3 (i) Work out the sum of the coefficients in each of the first six rows of the table of binomial coefficients.

(ii) Make a conjecture about the value of $\sum_{r=0}^{n} {}^nC_r$. Prove your conjecture.

[Hint: put $x = y = 1$ in a suitable binomial expansion.]

Answers

Chapter 1

(page 4)

The editor has explained clearly why the investigation is worth doing: there is growing concern about cycling accidents involving children.

Good quality data is data that best represents the research topic: in this case it is to establish whether or not the number of accidents is significant.

(page 5)

The reporter is focusing on two aspects of the investigation: he is looking at cycling accidents in the area over a period of time and he is considering the distribution of ages of accident victims.

Another thing he might consider is to investigate accidents in a similar community in order to be able to make comparisons.

(page 8)

Not all the branches have leaves. However, all the branches must be shown in order to show correctly the shape of the distribution.

(page 10)

If the basic stem-and-leaf diagram has too many lines, you may *squeeze* it as shown below. In doing this you lose some of the information but you should get a better idea of the shape of the distribution.

Unsqueezed

30 | 2 represents 3.02

30	2 6
31	4
32	0 5
33	3
34	3 6 7
35	0 3 4 4 8
36	0 0 4 4 4
37	0 1 1 3 3 4 8
38	3 3 3 5
39	0 0 4
40	2
41	0 0 1 1 4 4
42	
43	0 2 4

Squeezed

The data is rounded to one decimal place, so 3.02 becomes 3.0 etc.

3* | 0 represents 3.0

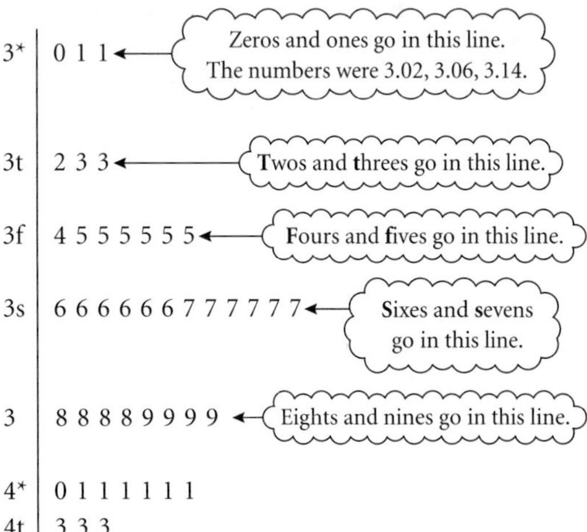

❓ (page 10)

Positive and negative data can be represented on a stem-and-leaf diagram in the following way.

Data set:

−36 −32 −28 −25 −24 −20 −18
−15 −12 −6 5 8 12 13 18 26

$n = 16$

−3 | 2 represents −32

Stem	Leaves
−3	6 2
−2	8 5 4 0
−1	8 5 2
−0	6
0	5 8
1	2 3 8
2	6

Exercise 1A (page 11)

1 (i) $n = 12$

9 | 9 represents £99 000

Stem	Leaves
9	9
10	3 8
11	0 9
12	0 5 9
13	0 0
14	0
15	
16	
17	5

(ii) The distribution is fairly symmetrical but has one outlier, a house costing £175 000.

2 (i) $n = 15$

4 | 5 represents £45

Stem	Leaves
0	0 4
1	5 8
2	0 2 8 8 8
3	0 1 4
4	2
5	
6	
7	
8	0
9	0

(ii) Most students earn £30 or less but two earn considerably more, £80 and £90.

3 (i) $n = 14$

5 | 9 represents 59 million people

Stem	Leaves
0	4 5 5 8 9
1	0 0 1 6
2	
3	9
4	
5	8 9 9
6	
7	
8	2

(ii) Most countries have populations of under 16 million people but there are five countries with larger populations and one with 82 million (Germany), which is very large.

4 (i) $n = 20$

| 7 | 1 represents 7.1 mm

Set 1	Stem	Set 2
	4	0
5	5	2 3 5
2 0	6	0 6
6 3	7	1 3 5
8	8	8
0	9	
6 3	10	
6	11	

(ii) The crustaceans in set 2 are shorter, possibly because the parasites have impeded their growth.

5 (i) $n = 20$

| 16 | 1 represents 1.61 kg

Feed with additives	Stem	Ordinary feed
	16	1
9 2	17	0 2 2 3 4 8
7 6 6 5 5 2	18	1 3 3
1 0	19	

(ii) The poultry that have been fed on feed with additives have put on more weight.

6 (i) $n = 14$

26 | 5 represents 26 500 feet

Stem	Leaves
26*	4 4 4
26	5 5 7 8 9
27*	
27	8 8 9
28*	2 3
28	
29*	0

(ii) All of the mountains are lower than 28 300 feet except Everest.

(iii) **(a)** 2.5% **(b)** 2.8%

7 **(i)** $n = 14$

2 | 9 | represents 29 moths

Colder temperature		Normal temperature
9	0	
7 6 4 2	1	8
3 1	2	1 3 5 8 9
	3	0

(ii) There are fewer moths on nights when the temperature is colder than usual.

8 **(i)** $n = 24$

| 1 | 2 represents 12 correct spellings

Without music		With music
9 9 8 8 8 7 3	0	
2 1 0 0 0	1	1 1 1 2 3 3 4 4 5 8 9
	2	2

(ii) $n = 24$

Without music		With music
3	0*	
9 9 8 8 8 7	0	
2 1 0 0 0	1*	1 1 1 2 3 3 4 4
	1	5 8 9
	2*	2

(iii) Yes

(iv) The students listening to music remembered more spellings.

(v) Listening to music helps the students to remember spellings better.

? (page 18)

The median as it is not affected by the extreme values.

Exercise 1B (page 19)

1 **(i)** Mean = 3.1, mode = 3, median = 3, mid-range = 3.5

(ii) Mean = 33.8125 minutes, mode = 29 minutes, median = 28.5 minutes, mid-range = 66.5 minutes

(iii) Mean = 32.2, no mode, median = 31, mid-range = 31

2 **(i)** **(a)** Mean = 2.89, mode = 0, median = 3, mid-range = 3

(b) The mode is most appropriate since it represents a typical night's drinking. However, the manager would not want to run out so would also consider the mean.

(ii) **(a)** Mean = 5.54 m, mode = 1.9 m, median = 5.7 m, mid-range = 5 m

(b) The mode is of no use. The mid-range and mean are affected by extreme values (1.9 m and 8.1 m), so the median is the most appropriate. The scientist can compare the medians from different samples collected elsewhere.

(iii) **(a)** Mean = 19.4, mode = 0, median = 4, mid-range = 60.5

(b) The mode is the most appropriate since it shows the player is not reliable. The mean and mid-range are affected by outliers but the median is also useful.

(iv) **(a)** Mean = 9.6 lb, no mode, median = 8.5 lb, mid-range = 12.5 lb

(b) The median is the most appropriate as all those above it can have their names published.

(v) **(a)** Mean = 23.4, mode = 24, median = 25, mid-range = 22.5

(b) The mode is most appropriate as an indication of likely take-up.

(vi) **(a)** Mean = 13.8 kg, mode = 14.8 kg, median = 13.85 kg, mid-range = 13.55 kg

(b) The mean is the most appropriate; this allows you to work out the average per chimpanzee.

Exercise 1C (page 22)

1 **(i)** 7 **(ii)** 7 **(iii)** 7 **(iv)** 7

2 **(i)** £1.50 **(ii)** £2.00 **(iii)** £3.00 **(iv)** £2.10

(v) It is a small sample so the mode is not appropriate. The mean and mid-range are affected by outliers so the median is best.

3 **(i)** 38 hours **(ii)** 37 hours **(iii)** 36.9 hours

(iv) The mean since it allows him to work out the total wage bill.

4 **(i)** 5 **(ii)** 5 **(iii)** 5.5 **(iv)** 5.52

(v) Schools quote the mean number of GCSEs but the mode is useful too.

5 **(i)** 9 mm **(ii)** 10 mm

(iii) 10 mm **(iv)** 9.86 mm

(v) The garden centre is likely to require seedlings of uniform height so the mode probably gives the seedsman the most useful information as the height to which the seedlings grew after 5 days is likely to give a good indication of future height.

6 **(i)** Mode = 5, median = 4, mid-range = 2.5

(ii) 3.1

(iii) The ornithologist would find the mode helpful as she needs to know if the typical number of eggs is changing. She would also find the mean helpful as this is related to the total number of eggs.

? (page 26)

The upper boundaries are not stated. 0– could mean 0–9 or it could mean at least 0.

? (page 28)

The mode can be estimated as in this example for a unimodal histogram.

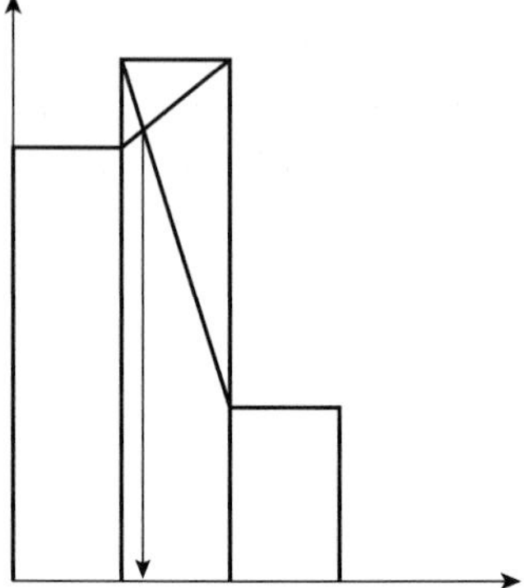

The median can be estimated by interpolation of the interval containing the median or by use of a cumulative frequency curve.

The mid-range can be estimated if you know the least *possible* value in the first interval and the maximum *possible* value in the last interval.

The mean of the original data is 39.73. The estimate is reasonably close at 39.855.

? (page 29)

The median, as it is least affected by extreme values.

? (page 30)

The fairest answer is there is not enough information. Ignoring the journalistic prose, '...our town council rate somewhere between savages and barbarians...', the facts given are correct. However, to say whether or not the council is negligent one would need to compare accident statistics with other *similar* communities. Also, one would need to ask who is responsible for a cyclist's risk of having or not having an accident? Perhaps parents should ensure there is adequate training given to their children, and so on.

? (page 31)

Robert needs to increase his estimate by 0.5 cm (162.32 cm becomes 162.82 cm). The mean of the raw data is 162.86 cm. The estimated value is very close.

Exercise 1D (page 32)

1 176.1 mm

2 **(i)** The spread is symmetrical. **(ii)** 27.1 mm

3 **(i)**

Age, A (years)	% children who have just learned to conserve	Total % of children who can conserve
$A \leqslant 6$	0	0
$6 < A \leqslant 6\frac{1}{2}$	3	3
$6\frac{1}{2} < A \leqslant 7$	7	10
$7 < A \leqslant 7\frac{1}{2}$	28	38
$7\frac{1}{2} < A \leqslant 8$	42	80
$8 < A \leqslant 8\frac{1}{2}$	15	95
$8\frac{1}{2} < A \leqslant 9$	5	100

(ii) 7.62 years

4 **(i)** Branch A: £1156, branch B: £984
(ii) Employees at branch B earn less.

5 **(i)** London: £307 000, Scotland: £144 000
Houses in Scotland are much cheaper than those in London.
(ii) London: £338 000, Scotland: £150 000

6 **(i)** 226.4 g
(ii) 11 out of the 66 packets, 17%, are underweight and this is unacceptable.
(iii) The mean weight is above 225 g, the weight printed on the packet, and so overall the company is not cheating its customers. However, they should try to reduce the variability in the weights of the packets.

? (page 36)

With the item £90 removed the mean = £15.79, compared to £19.50. The extreme value 'dragged' the value of the mean towards it.

? (page 37)

Each deviation is by definition the data value–the mean. As the mean is *central* to the data, some deviations will be negative (below the mean) and some will be positive (above the mean). The total above the mean cancels out the total below the mean.

❓ (page 38)

If the mean, $\bar{x}$, is not exact in decimal form, then calculations by hand using the definition of S_{xx} may be tedious and/or prone to arithmetic errors by premature approximation of $\bar{x}$. The alternative formulation of S_{xx} may be more appropriate in such cases.

❓ (page 38)

Working for either method of finding S_{xx} could be set out in a table as follows.

x	$(x - x)^2$	x^2
0	$(0-1)^2 = 1$	0
1	$(1-1)^2 = 0$	1
0	$(0-1)^2 = 1$	0
...	...	...
4	$(4-1)^2 = 9$	16
Totals	20	30

❓ (page 40)

The situation is identical to that of calculating the *msd*, where the formulation used to calculate S_{xx} may depend on the value of the mean.

❓ (page 43)

Using 656 instead of the accurate value of 655.71 ... results in

$$msd = 430\,041.14\ldots - 430\,336$$
$$= -294.85\ldots$$

which, being negative, is impossible.

❓ (page 44)

With the value 96 omitted the mean = 54.2, standard deviation = 8.3. The value 96 is more than five standard deviations above the new mean value.

Exercise 1E (page 45)

1 Sheltered position: mean = 10.3 mm, standard deviation = 2.11 mm
Exposed position: mean = 2.05 mm, standard deviation = 0.986 mm
In the exposed position, the mean and standard deviation are smaller than for the seaweed in the sheltered position.

2 **(i)** Mean = 57.6% bad sectors, standard deviation = 23.10% bad sectors
(ii) The quality is more consistent in the second batch of disks. This makes it easier for the company's sales people to make accurate claims about the number of good sectors.

3 Speedometer A: mean = 40.85 mph, root mean square deviation = 0.93 mph
Speedometer B: mean 41.1 mph, root mean square deviation = 1.54 mph
Speedometer A reads closer to 40 mph than speedometer B and the root mean square deviation is smaller, showing that the readings are closer together. Speedometer A is the better speedometer.

4 **(i)** Wine 1: mean = 3.5, standard deviation = 0.837
Wine 2: mean = 3.5, standard deviation = 1.643
(ii) Both wines have the same mean but the standard deviation for wine 1 is much lower than that for wine 2. People's reactions to wine 2 are more varied.

5 **(i)** Mean = 9 hours, standard deviation = 2.72 hours
(ii) **(a)** 187.02 hours
(b) 8.13 hours
(c) 2.67 hours

6 **(i)**

Weight of potato, w (g)	Mid-interval value	King Edward	Desiree
$0 < w \leqslant 100$	50	6	5
$100 < w \leqslant 200$	150	8	8
$200 < w \leqslant 300$	250	13	12
$300 < w \leqslant 400$	350	15	5
$400 < w \leqslant 500$	450	9	7
$500 < w \leqslant 600$	550	5	5

(ii) King Edward: mean = 300 g, standard deviation = 143.97 g
Desiree: mean = 288.1 g, standard deviation = 156.10 g
(iii) King Edward better, larger mean and smaller standard deviation. Supermarkets prefer to buy vegetables that are similar in size.

7 '*Look and say*': mean = 11.3, standard deviation = 2.07
'*Phonic*': mean = 13.8, standard deviation = 1.60
The '*phonic*' method is better as the mean is higher and the standard deviation is smaller.

8 (i) Median = 6, mode = 5

(ii) A value can be considered to be an outlier if it is more than two standard deviations from the mean.
$5.95 + 2 \times 2.58 = 11.11$ and $15 > 11.11$ so 15 can be regarded as an outlier.

(iii) (a) Could be older child looking after younger ones so valid or could all be children with learning problems so valid or could be a party for young children so a 15-year-old should not be there so invalid.

(b) The scores on two dice cannot add up to 15 so invalid.

(iv) Median = 5.5, mode = 5

(v) The mean and standard deviation would be reduced.

(vi) The diagram is positively skewed. Removing outlier reduces the skewness and the diagram becomes more symmetrical.

9 (i) Mean = £208.42, standard deviation = £19.11

(ii) $\sum y = £4644.40$

Standard deviation $= \sqrt{\frac{S_{yy}}{n-1}} = £23.16$

So $S_{yy} = 8582.1696$

$S_{yy} = \sum y^2 - n\bar{y}^2$

So $\sum y^2 = S_{yy} + n\bar{y}^2$

$= 8582.1696 + 17 \times 273.20^2$

$= 1\,277\,432.25$

(iii) Mean = £246.39, standard deviation = £38.79

? (page 50)

Yes but the coded data would have been different: −2, −1, 0, 1, 2, 3.

Exercise 1F (page 51)

1 (i) Mean = 35.5 °C, standard deviation = 46.1 °C

(ii) 308.5° Kelvin

(iii) 46.1° Kelvin

2 (i) Mean = £8938, standard deviation = £2897

(ii) $a = 1.49$ euros

(iii) Mean = 13 318 euros, standard deviation = 4317 euros

3 Mean = 54, standard deviation = 6.6

4 (i) Rule is new score = 2 × old score − 20
So adjusted mean = 2 × 35 − 20 = 50 and adjusted standard deviation = 2 × 3 = 6
The rule gives results with too low a mean so it is not fair.
However, the standard deviation is acceptable.

(ii) A better rule is new score = 2 × old score − 10
Gives the same mean and standard deviation as for teenage players so is fair.

5 (i) Class width = 10 and frequency density = 0.5
Frequency = 10 × 0.5 = 5

Time (seconds)	Frequency	Time	Cumulative frequency
0–10	5	<10	5
10–20	11	<20	16
20–30	17	<30	33
30–40	10	<40	43
40–50	5	<50	48
50–60	2	<60	50

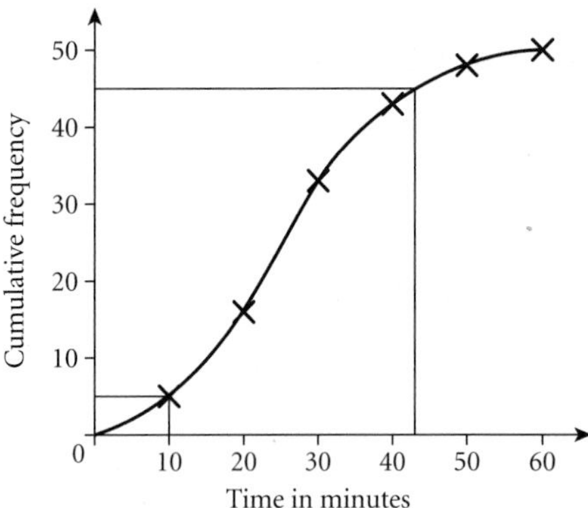

(ii) 10th percentile = 10 seconds,
90th percentile = 43 seconds
80% of the data lies between these percentiles.

(iii) Mean = 26 seconds,
standard deviation = 12.66 ($S_{xx} = 7850$)

(iv) The mid-interval values were used to calculate the mean in part **(iii)** so using the upper class boundary will increase all the times by 5 seconds. The mean would increase by 5 seconds but the standard deviation would not be affected.

6 (i)

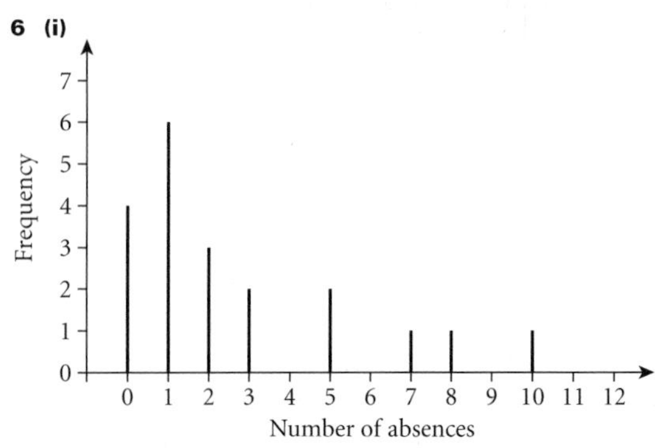

(ii) Mode = 1, median = 1.5

(iii) Mean = 2.65,
standard deviation = 2.89 (S_{xx} = 158.55)

(iv) Let p be the number of times each student was present and a be the number of times each student was absent then use coding.
$p = 30 - a$ so $\bar{p} = 30 - \bar{a} = 30 - 2.65 = 27.35$
The standard deviation is the same, 2.89.
The new distribution will have a negative skew.

(v) There were 53 absences in total.
The number of times boys were absent
$= 3 \times 12 = 36$.
So the number of times girls were absent
$= 53 - 36 = 17$
Mean number of times girls were absent
$= 17 \div 8 = 2.125$

(vi) 2.83

Exercise 1G (page 53)

1 (i) Stimulating environment:
mean = 2.3 g, median = 2.2 g,
mode = 2.2 g and 2.4 g
Unstimulating environment: mean = 1.78 g,
median = 1.75 g, mode = 1.7 g

(ii) The cortexes of the rats in the stimulating environment have a larger mean, median and modal weight.

(iii) Stimulating environment: 0.346 g
Unstimulating environment: 0.129 g

(iv) The standard deviation of the rats who lived in the stimulating environment is bigger than those in the other group.

(v) The researcher will conclude that the brains of rats in a stimulating environment grow larger and also show more variation in size.

2 (i) $n = 21$
3 | 2 represents 32 minutes

0	0 0 0 5
1	0 2 3 5 6 6 7 8
2	1 4 6 6
3	2 5
4	2
5	
6	1
7	3

The distribution has positive skewness.

(ii) Mode = 0 minutes, median = 17 minutes,
mean = 22 minutes
The mode is not representative. The mean is affected by the extreme values, 61 and 73. The median is the most representative measure.

(iii) Standard deviation = 18.78 minutes (S_{xx} = 7056)
Mean + 2 × standard deviation = 59.56 so 61 and 73 are outliers.

(iv) Reduction of current mean by 20% gives 17.6 minutes.
Maximum time for rest of May
= 545.6 − 462 = 83.6 minutes
(8.36 minutes per day)

3 (i) 21.54 seconds

(ii) The median and the mode are close and the mean is quite close so the distribution is fairly symmetrical.
A lap time of 29 seconds would not affect mode. The median would be slightly affected as there are now 25 laps so median will be 13th lap and not 12.5th value. The mean will increase slightly.

4 (i) David: 17.77 seconds, Ravin: 17.03 seconds, Stephen: 18.10 seconds, Henry: 18.07 seconds, Ahmed: 17.07 seconds, Mark: 18.13 seconds

(ii) David, Ravin and Ahmed

(iii) Sally: 18.6 seconds, Heidi: 20.4 seconds, Comfort: 17.2 seconds, Angela: 19.2 seconds,
Ketaki: 17.9 seconds, Lois: 18.4 seconds

5 (i) Sheltered shore: mean = 1.863
Exposed shore: mean = 1.624
The mean height to aperture ratio for the exposed dog whelks is smaller than the mean height to aperture ratio for the sheltered dog whelks. The dog whelks in the exposed position need to have a larger foot area, and hence a larger aperture, in relation to their height so they can cling more firmly to rocks in rough seas. Their shells do not need to be large as the smaller surface area means less damage. The larger aperture measurement gives a smaller ratio value.

(ii) Sheltered shore: standard deviation = 0.159
Exposed shore: standard deviation = 0.258
The standard deviation for the height to aperture ratio of the exposed dog whelks is larger than that for the sheltered dog whelks. A possible reason for this is that the exposed dog whelks grow more erratically.

6 (i) 17.5, 19.5, 23, 27, 31, 37, 46 years, respectively

(ii) WW1: 24 years, WW2: 27 years

(iii) WW1: 32 → 32.5 years, WW2: 33 → 33.5 years

(iv) Both distributions are positively skewed and, as a consequence, the mid-ranges do not provide typical values.

(v) Those who died in WW1 were younger than those who died in WW2.

7 $n = 30$

4	4 represents 44 years
2*	6 7 9 9
3	0 1 1 2 2 2 3 3 3 4
3*	5 6 7 8 8 8 8 9
4	0 2 2 4
4*	5 9
5	2
5*	
6	1

The distribution is positively skewed with a modal group of 30–34 years.

Mean age = 36.86 years ≈ 37 years

Mean age of women = 35.6 years ≈ 36 years

8 (i)

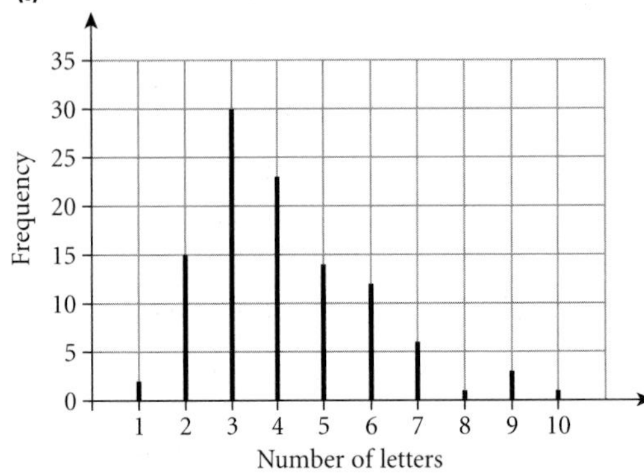

(ii) Mode = 3, median = 4, mid-range = 5.5

The distribution shows positive skewness.

(iii) Mean = 4.14,

standard deviation = 1.81 ($S_{xx} = 349.06$)

Mean − 2 × standard deviation = 0.52

Mean + 2 × standard deviation = 7.76

Words with 8, 9 or 10 letters are outliers.

Do not exclude since occasional long words do occur in such passages.

(iv) The mean number of letters per word is greater in the second passage and there is much greater variation in the number of letters per word. You would expect a greater proportion of longer words in adult fiction.

Chapter 2

❓ (page 59)

209 people in Downlee have their own e-mail address (29% of 720). 240 people in Avonford use the Web for at least eight hours per week (50% of 480).

❓ (page 63)

The ratio of the areas reflects the ratio of the total turnover, that is 3:4, so the radii are in the ratio $\sqrt{3} : \sqrt{4}$.

The angle subtended at the centre by the sector representing wages is greater in the circle for the year 2007. The actual amount has increased because the total turnover in 2007 is greater.

Bar charts are better as it is easier to read the actual values. Using a pie chart only gives relative values and then only approximately.

Exercise 2A (page 63)

1 (i) **(a)** Numerical data/discrete
(b) Vertical line chart

(ii) **(a)** Categorical data
(b) Bar chart or pie chart

(iii) **(a)** Numerical data/continuous
(b) Histogram or stem-and-leaf diagram

(iv) **(a)** Numerical data/discrete
(b) Vertical line chart

(v) **(a)** Numerical data/discrete
(b) Vertical line chart

(vi) **(a)** Numerical data/discrete
(b) Vertical line chart

(vii) **(a)** Numerical data/continuous
(b) Histogram or stem-and-leaf diagram

(viii) **(a)** Numerical data/discrete
(b) Vertical line chart

(ix) **(a)** Numerical data/discrete
(b) Vertical line chart

(x) **(a)** Numerical data/continuous
(b) Histogram or stem-and-leaf diagram

2 (i) 8 cm

(ii) The diagrams shown here are quarter-size.

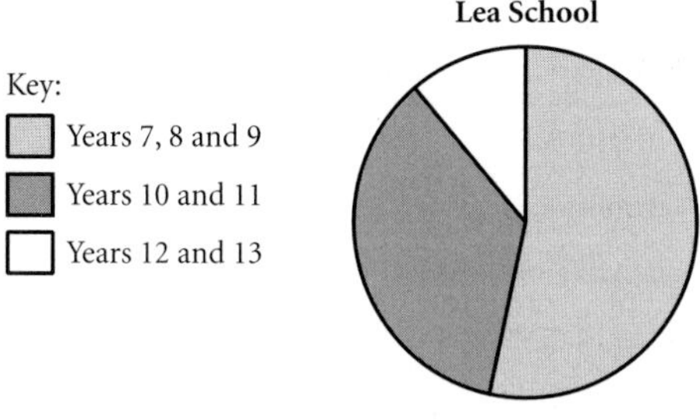

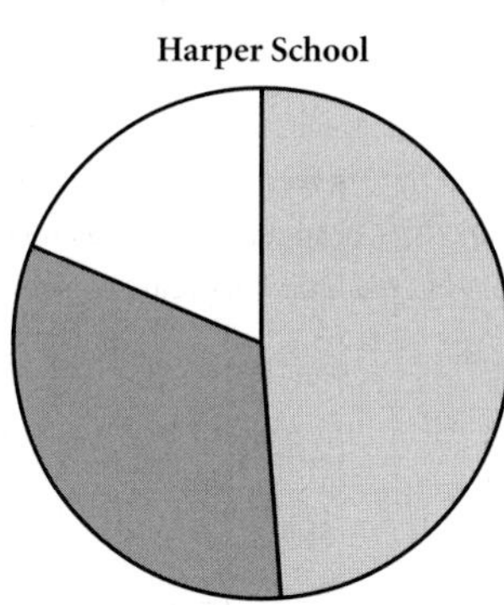

3 (i) Key: Working Leisure With family

Number of hours

90, 80, 70, 60, 50, 40, 30, 20, 10, 0

Teacher Postman Sky TV technician Doctors receptionist

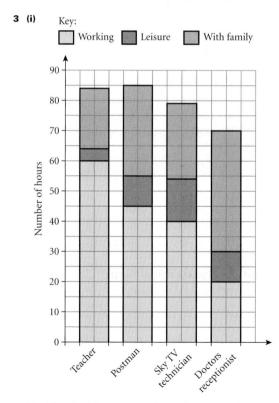

(ii) The chart because you do not have to analyse the figures.

(iii) The teacher works more hours than the other three people in this survey but if the chart were drawn for the school holidays then it would be very different. The survey should be done over a whole year to make the comparisons fair.
The survey could also be improved by having more than three categories so all of the 168 hours in a week are accounted for.

4 (i) Ratio of areas = 900 : 2500 = 9 : 25
Ratio of radii = 3 : 5

(ii)

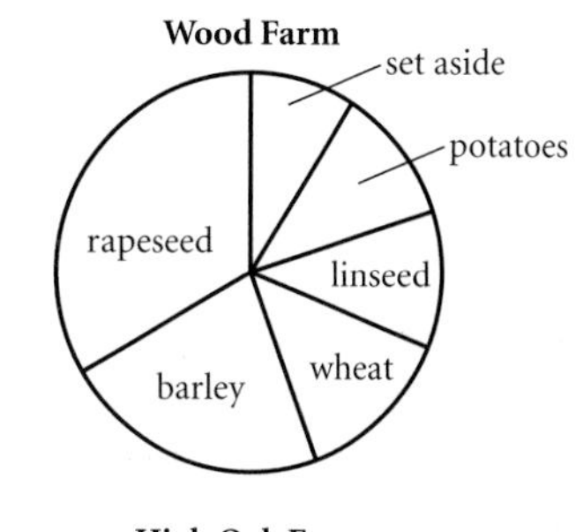

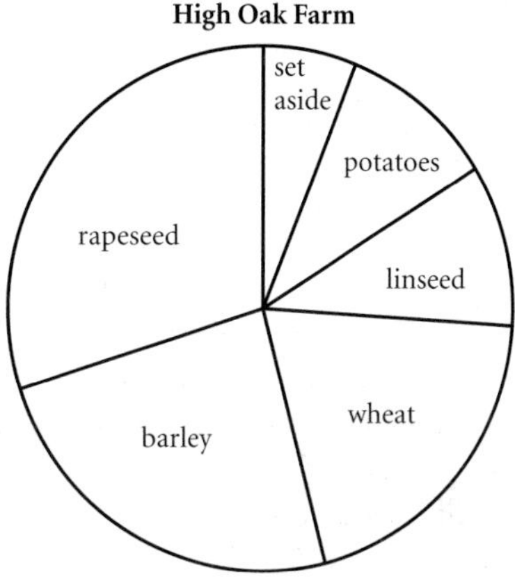

5 (i) Radius of smaller (2004) pie chart should be 4.5 cm. The diagrams shown here are half-size.

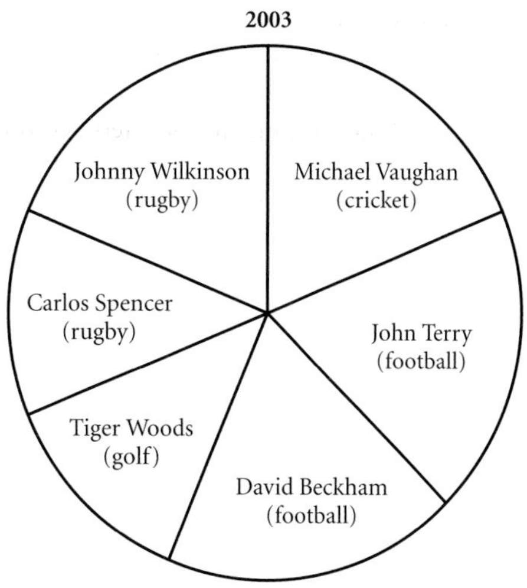

2004

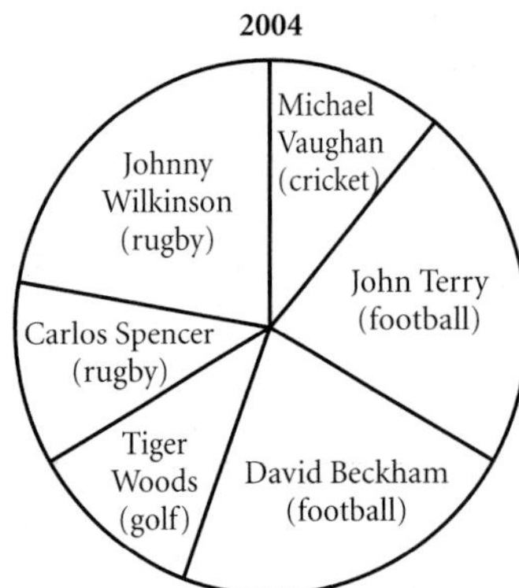

(ii)

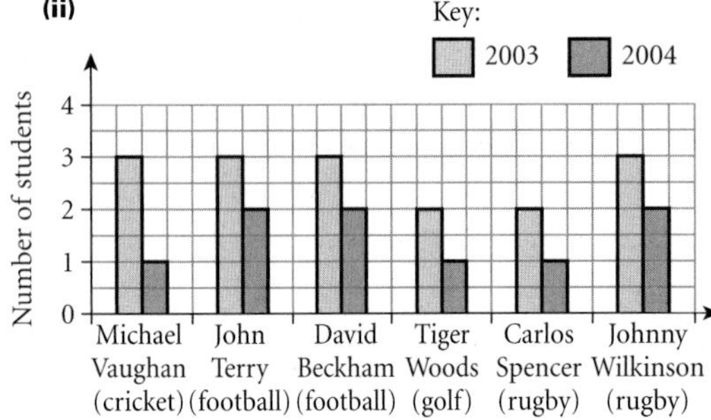

6 (i) Bar chart or pie chart

(ii) The gender of the student together with the mathematician named, to answer questions such as 'Did more girls than boys write Jane O'Hara?'

❓ (page 67)

You must compare the *area* of each of the columns and choose the one with the greatest area.

❓ (page 70)

The first interval has width 9.5, the last 10.5. All the others are 10. The reason for this is that the data can neither be negative nor exceed 70. So even if part marks were given, and so a mark such as 22.6 was possible, a student still could not obtain less than 0 or more than the maximum of 70.

Exercise 2B (page 72)

1 (i)

Height (inches)	Class width	Frequency	Frequency density
$73 < \text{height} \leqslant 75$	2	5	2.5
$75 < \text{height} \leqslant 77$	2	1	0.5
$77 < \text{height} \leqslant 78$	1	0	0
$78 < \text{height} \leqslant 79$	1	2	2
$79 < \text{height} \leqslant 81$	2	4	2
$81 < \text{height} \leqslant 85$	4	3	0.75

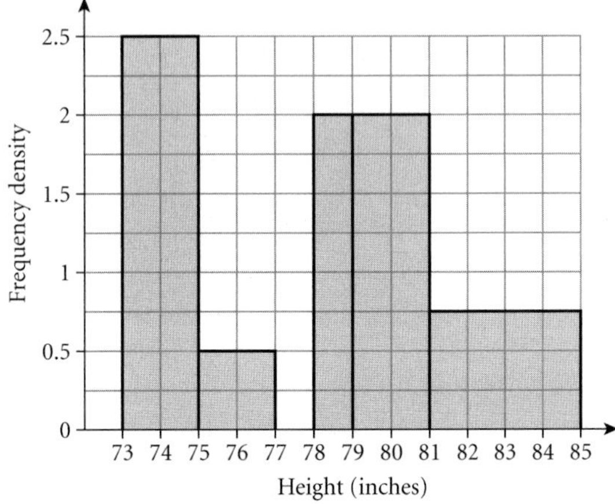

(ii) All the players are at least 73 inches (6 ft 1 inch). Three are over 81 inches (6 ft 9 inches), which is very tall.
The modal group is $73 < \text{height} \leqslant 75$ inches.

(iii) 78 inches

2 (i)

Height (cm)	Class boundaries	Class width	Frequency	Frequency density
10–19	$9.5 \leqslant h < 19.5$	10	1	0.1
20–29	$19.5 \leqslant h < 29.5$	10	2	0.2
30–39	$29.5 \leqslant h < 39.5$	10	5	0.5
40–49	$39.5 \leqslant h < 49.5$	10	10	1
50–69	$49.5 \leqslant h < 69.5$	20	10	0.5

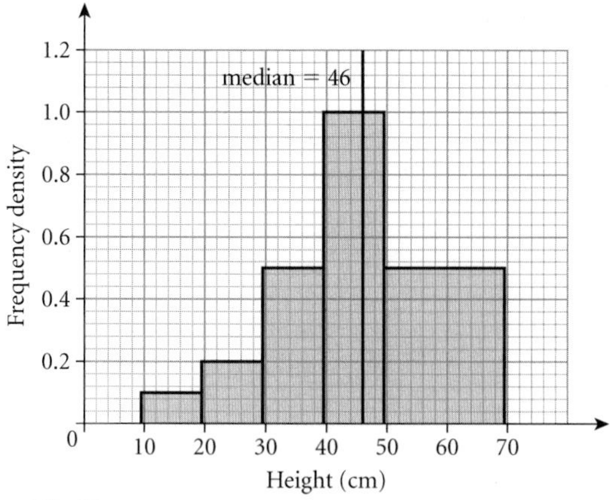

(ii) 28

(iii) 46 cm; The areas on either side of the line are equal.

3 (i)

Length (mm)	Class boundaries	Mid-value, x	Frequency	fx
$80 \leqslant$ length < 99	$79.5 <$ length $\leqslant 99.5$	89.5	8	716
$100 \leqslant$ length < 119	$99.5 <$ length $\leqslant 119.5$	109.5	2	219
$120 \leqslant$ length < 129	$119.5 <$ length $\leqslant 129.5$	124.5	2	249
$130 \leqslant$ length < 159	$129.5 <$ length $\leqslant 159.5$	144.5	6	867
$160 \leqslant$ length < 169	$159.5 <$ length $\leqslant 169.5$	164.5	2	329
Totals			20	2380

Estimated mean length of a pencil = 119 mm

(ii) 119.85 mm **(iii)** 0.71%

(iv) No, the actual mean and the estimated mean are very close.

4 (i)

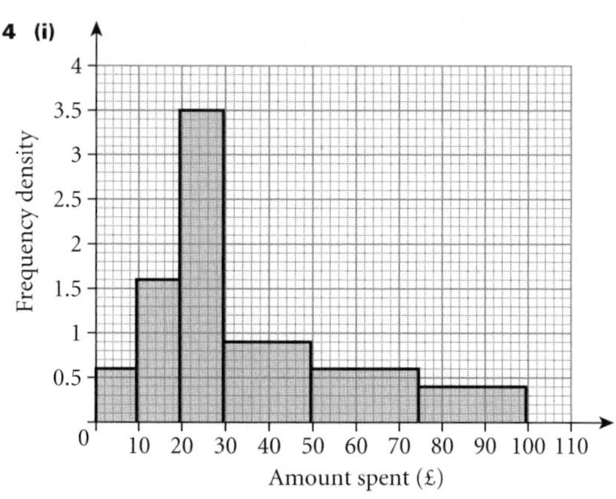

(ii) Mean = £36.78,
standard deviation = £23.43 ($S_{xx} = 54\,341.19$)

5 (i)

Distance (miles)	Class boundaries	Class width	Frequency	Frequency density
20–59	19.5–59.5	40	160	4
60–79	59.5–79.5	20	20	1
80–99	79.5–99.5	20	100	5
100–119	99.5–119.5	20	200	10
120+	119.5–		0	0

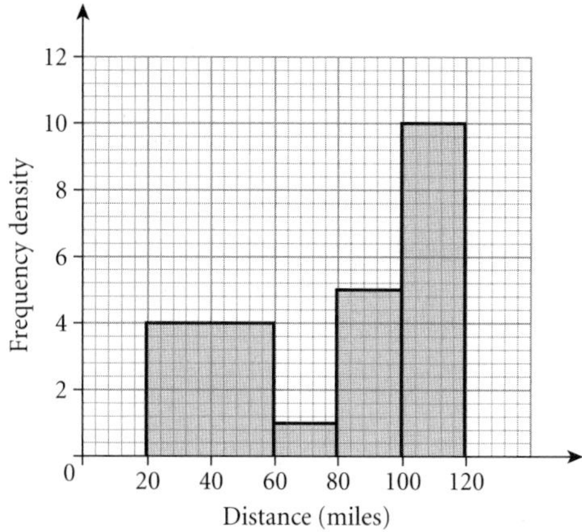

(ii) Most of the sales representatives drove between 100 and 119 miles on that day.
Mean = 80.3 miles, median = 91.5 miles
The histogram shows that the distribution is not symmetrical, which is supported by the mean and the median not being close.

6 (i) Time is continuous and the bars should be joined together and have no gaps.
The vertical scales are different for the different graphs and do not have a title.

(ii) 23 June 2005: There is a peak in the number of hits at lunchtime and very few hits during the early hours of the morning.
26 June 2005: There are peaks in the number of hits at lunchtime and late in the evening.
14 July 2005: From about 11:00 until 00:00, there is a fairly constant number of hits, although there are peaks at 17:00 and 23:00. There are also more hits during the early hours of the morning than on the other days.

Activity (Page 76)

For a list of n items of data, an *Excel* spreadsheet uses the 'method of hinges'. It places the median, Q_2, at position $\frac{n+1}{2}$, the lower quartile, Q_1, at position $\frac{1}{2}\left(1 + \frac{n+1}{2}\right) = \frac{1}{2} + \frac{n+1}{4}$ and the upper quartile, Q_3, at position $\frac{1}{2}\left(\frac{n+1}{2} + n\right) = \frac{3(n+1)}{4} - \frac{1}{2}$.

Whilst the quartiles Q_1 and Q_3 differ from those obtained with a graphic calculator, either method is acceptable.

? (page 77)

The data are a sample from a parent population. The true values for the quartiles are those of the parent population, but these are unknown.

Exercise 2C (page 83)

1 (i) 3.5

(ii) $Q_1 = 1$, $Q_3 = 6$, $IQR = 5$

(iii) Using $Q_1 - 1.5 \times IQR$ gives -6.5 and $Q_3 + 1.5 \times IQR$ gives 13.5 so there are no outliers.

2 (i) The Year 11 results are higher overall, the interquartile range of the Year 11 results is less than that of the Year 10 results, the median of the Year 11 results is higher than that of the Year 10 results.

(ii) The students are working harder in Year 11, their examination year.

3 (i) **(a)** Breeder 1: median = 6, Breeder 2: median = 7

(b) Breeder 1: $Q_1 = 5$, $Q_3 = 7$, $IQR = 2$
Breeder 2: $Q_1 = 5$, $Q_3 = 8$, $IQR = 3$

(c) Breeder 1: $Q_1 - 1.5 \times IQR = 2$
so one outlier, 0
$Q_3 + 1.5 \times IQR = 10$ so no outliers
Breeder 2: $Q_1 - 1.5 \times IQR = 0.5$ so no outliers
$Q_3 + 1.5 \times IQR = 12.5$ so no outliers

(ii) Breeder 2 is more successful because there are no outliers and the median is higher.

4 (i)

Age (years)	Frequency	Age	Cumulative frequency
0–9	0	<10	0
10–19	8	<20	8
20–29	18	<30	26
30–39	7	<40	33
40–49	3	<50	36
50–59	3	<60	39

(ii)

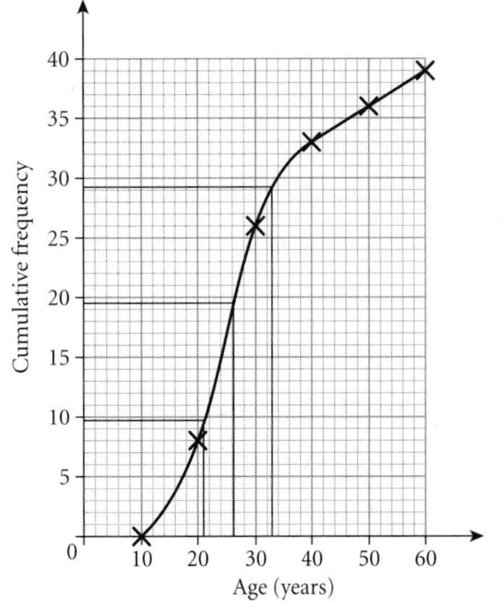

(iii) Median ≈ 26 years, $Q_1 \approx 21$ years, $Q_3 \approx 33$ years, $IQR \approx 12$ years

(iv) Most members are under 40 years old.

5 (i)

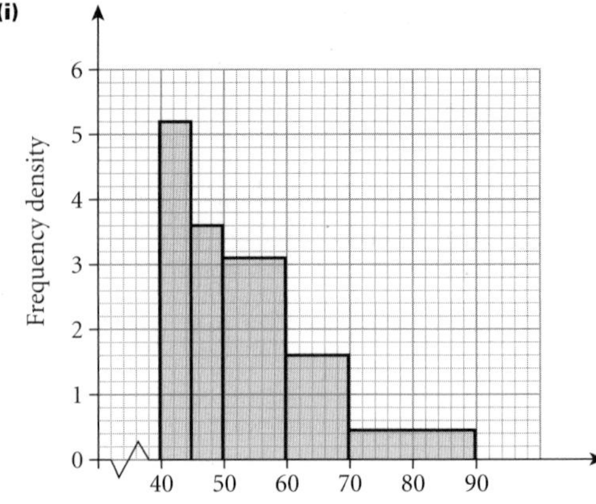

(ii) The distribution is positively skewed. The mode is at the extreme left of the distribution. Other possible answers are the range is 50 and the median is 52.

Exercise 2D (page 85)

1 By January 2005 there are no corporate investors.
By April 2005 the shares owned by employees of the club have been bought.
By June 2005 almost 100% of the shares are owned by one person.

2 (i) Mean = 299.923 °C,
standard deviation = 1.43 °C ($S_{xx} = 157.5385$)

(ii), (iii)

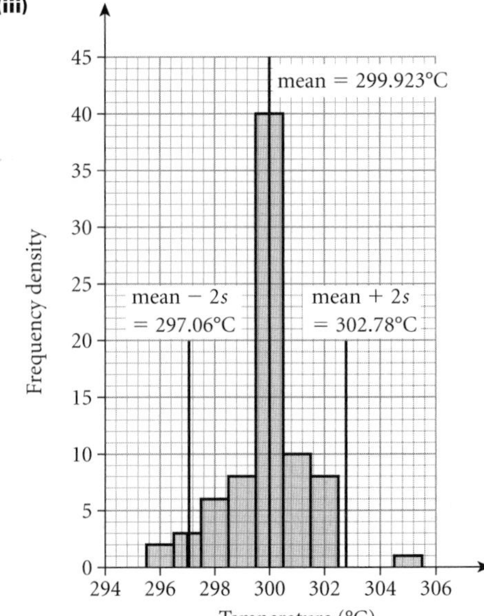

(iv) 6 ovens (7.7%) in the sample are more than the specified 2° away from 300°. The company clearly needs to improve its temperature control mechanism. Most of the faulty ovens are too cool but the one at 305° is too hot and is also an outlier within the data; this oven may have a different fault from the others.

3 (i) Median = 3.50 to 3.51 kg
Q_1 = 3.10 to 3.15 kg, Q_3 = 3.80 to 3.85 kg
IQR = 0.65 to 0.75 kg

(ii)

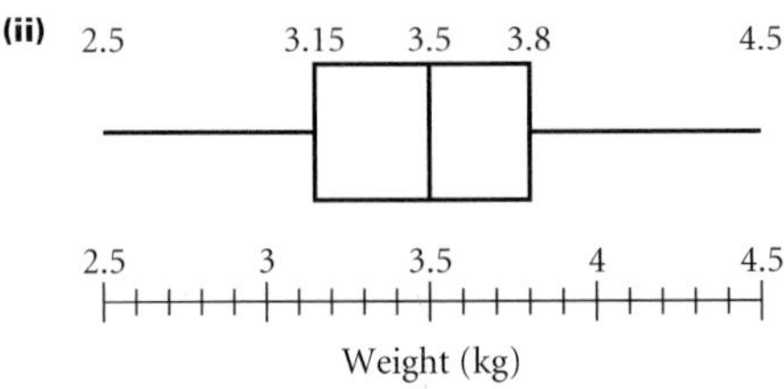

(iii)

Weight of baby	Mid-value	Frequency
$2.50 < x \leqslant 2.75$	2.625	7
$2.75 < x \leqslant 3.00$	2.875	15
$3.00 < x \leqslant 3.25$	3.125	30
$3.25 < x \leqslant 3.50$	3.375	22
$3.50 < x \leqslant 3.75$	3.625	33
$3.75 < x \leqslant 4.00$	3.875	23
$4.00 < x \leqslant 4.25$	4.125	12
$4.25 < x \leqslant 4.50$	4.375	8

Mean = 3.49 kg

(iv) 2.23 kg

(v) The median will decrease and the interquartile range will increase because the additional data are at the lower end of the range.

4 (i) Mode = 7, median = 6
The distribution shows negative skewness *or* is unimodal.

(ii)

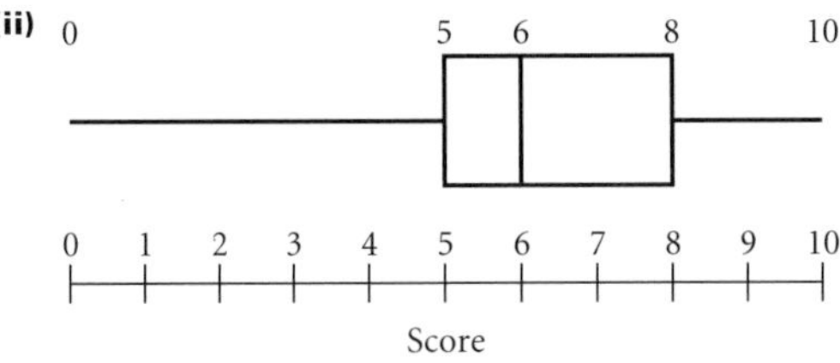

(iii) Mean = 6.1,
standard deviation = 2.248 (S_{xx} = 5050)

(iv) Number of points = $3x - (10 - x) = 4x - 10$

(v) Mean number of points = $4\bar{x} - 10$
$= 4 \times 6.1 - 10 = 14.4$
Standard deviation = $4 \times 2.248 = 8.992$

5 (i)

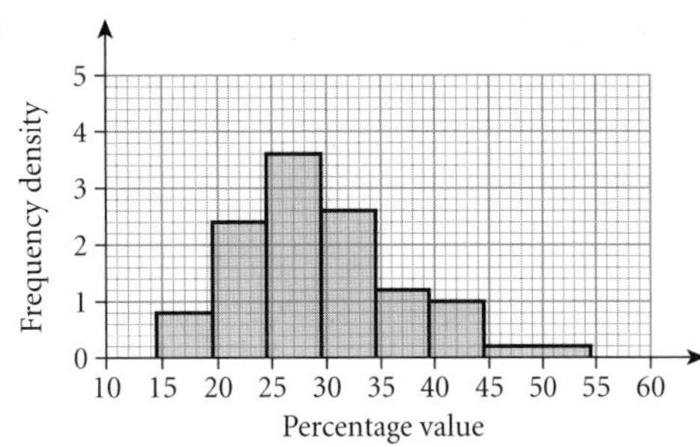

(ii) 29%

(iii) Mean = 29.92%,
standard deviation = 7.60% (S_{xx} = 57 112.5)
Mean + 2 × standard deviation = 45.12
Mean − 2 × standard deviation = 14.72
So there are 2 possible outliers, the values in the $45 \leqslant x < 55$ class.

(iv) Diesel cars have a higher mean indicating that they hold their value better than cars with petrol engines.

6 (i) Median = 8 to 8.5 minutes
Q_1 = 5 minutes, Q_3 = 13.5 minutes
IQR = 8.5 minutes

(ii)

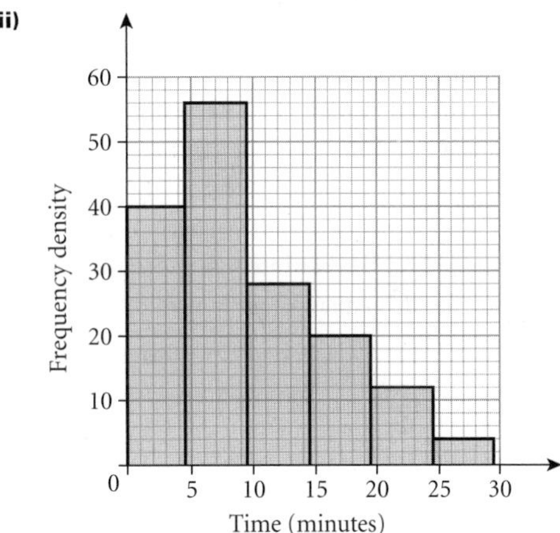

(iii) 10 minutes

(iv) **(a)** False
(b) True
(c) False
(d) True

7 (i) 25

(ii) Total area = $0.2 \times 10 + 0.8 \times 5 + 1.8 \times 5$
$+ 2.8 \times 5 + 3.8 \times 5 + 5 \times 5 + 3.4 \times 5 + 1 \times 10$
$= 2 + 4 + 9 + 14 + 19 + 25 + 17 + 10$
= 100 apples

(iii) 69.55 mm
The answer is only an estimate because the data has been grouped.

(iv) 70.4 mm

(v) The distribution has a negative skew and the modal group is 70–75 mm. The distribution is unimodal.

(vi) An outlier is greater/less than mean $\pm\ 2 \times$ standard deviation
$= 69.55 \pm 18 = 51.55$ and 87.55.
There are approximately 6 apples that are outliers.

8 (i) It is not clear whether a value such as 1 should be included in the 0 to 1 class or the 1 to 2 class. A clear classification is $0 < x\ 1, 1 < x \leqslant 2$, etc.

(ii)

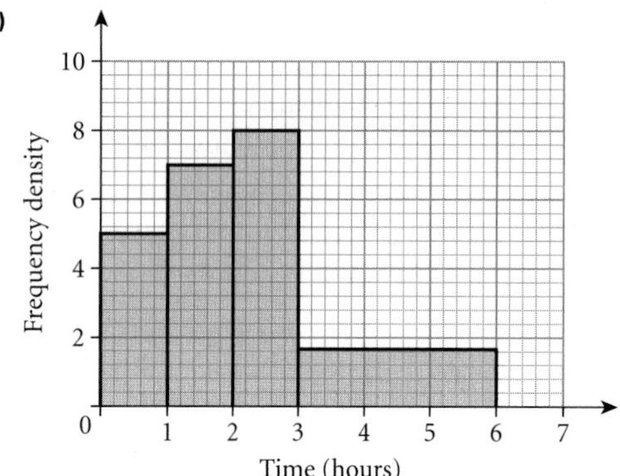

(iii) Mean = 1.91 hours,
standard deviation = 1.49 hours ($S_{xx} = 62.034\,48$)

(iv) Using mid-interval values and zero:
$8.3 \times 0 + 19.4 \times 0.5 + 29.2 \times 1.5 + 23.6 \times 2.5 + 19.5 \times m = 2.1 \times 100$ where m is the mid-interval for the last interval, more than 3 hours.
Solving this equation gives $m = 5$.

Chapter 3

Exercise 3A (page 102)

1 (i)

	Married	Unmarried	Total
Men	18	2	20
Women	45	15	60
Total	63	17	80

(ii) To know what types of people work for the company.
To help the company advertise for new staff.

(iii) (a) $\frac{9}{40}$ or 0.225 **(b)** $\frac{3}{16}$ or 0.1875
(c) $\frac{1}{40}$ or 0.025 **(d)** $\frac{63}{80}$ or 0.7875

2 (i)

	Cow	Goat	Total
Brown	4	16	20
White	6	10	16
Total	10	26	36

(ii) (a) $\frac{4}{9}$ **(b)** $\frac{5}{18}$ **(c)** $\frac{4}{9}$

3 (i) $\frac{1}{2}$ **(ii)** $\frac{19}{62}$ or 0.306
(iii) $\frac{40}{62} = \frac{20}{31}$ or 0.645 **(iv)** $\frac{42}{62} = \frac{21}{31}$ or 0.677

4 (i) 120 **(ii)** 120
(iii) $\frac{49}{54}$ or 0.907 **(iv)** $\frac{2}{27}$ or 0.074
(v) $\frac{8}{53}$ or 0.151 **(vi)** $\frac{1}{53}$ or 0.0189

5 (i) 9

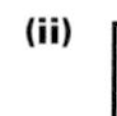

(ii)

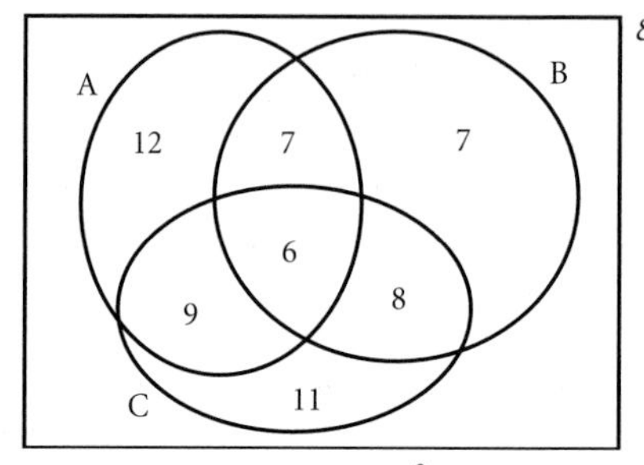

(iii) 34 **(iv)** $\frac{2}{5}$

6 (i)

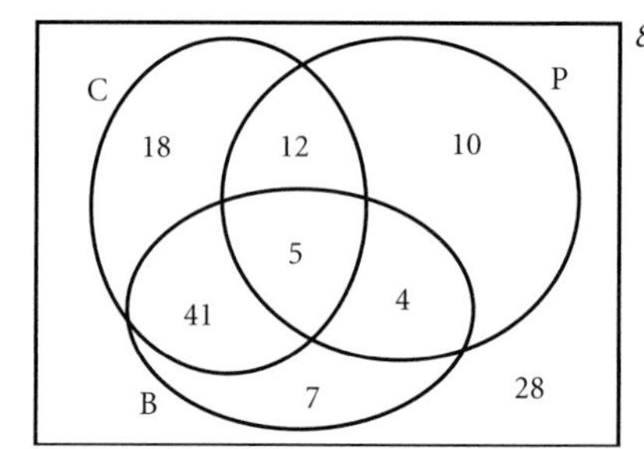

(ii) 28 **(iii)** $\frac{57}{125}$ or 0.456 **(iv)** $\frac{7}{25}$ or 0.28

7 (i) 196 **(ii)** 13
(iii) $\frac{16}{77}$ or 0.208 **(iv)** $\frac{57}{385}$ or 0.148

8 (i) $\frac{1}{1000}$ **(ii)** $\frac{999}{1000}$
(iii) £2825 **(iv)** 176 or more
(v) £4650
(vi) Option A: £4500, option B: £5350
Option B is better.
(vii) Option A: £2000, option B: £2350
Option B is still better.
(viii) P(winning a prize with option A) $= \frac{1}{5000}$
P(winning a prize with option B) $= \frac{1}{1000}$
so a ticket holder with a ticket from option B is more likely to win a prize.

Exercise 3B (page 110)

1 (i)

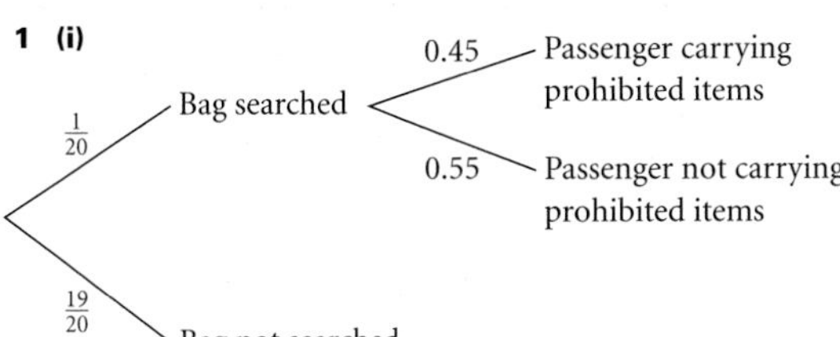

(ii) 0.0225 **(iii)** 0.0275 **(iv)** 880

2 (i)

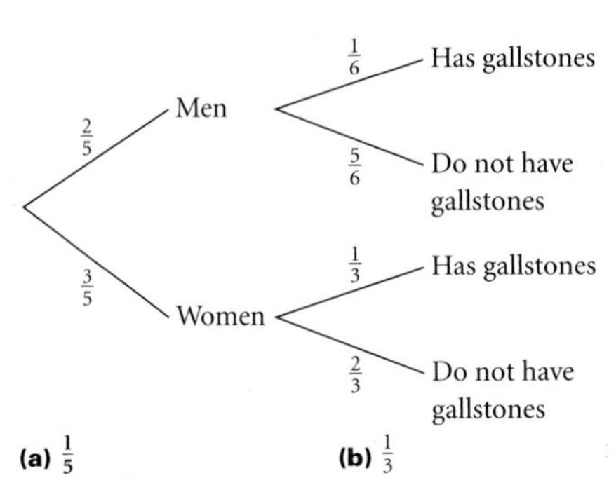

(ii) (a) $\frac{1}{5}$ **(b)** $\frac{1}{3}$

(iii) 0.08 or $\frac{2}{25}$

3 (i)

Time of train	Probability of catching train	Probability of being on time for work
7.00 am	0.8	0.95
7.10 am	0.15	0.8
7.20 am	0.05	0.5

Time of train

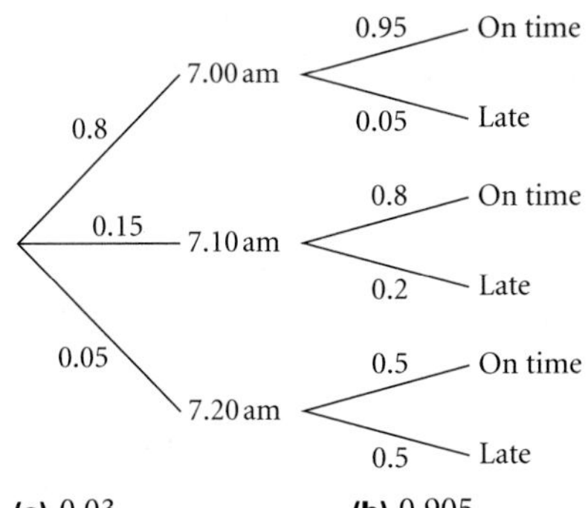

(ii) (a) 0.03 **(b)** 0.905

(iii) 0.095

(iv) The probability of Mr Brown being late is 0.095 which is approximately 1 day out of 10 or 2 working days a month. This would not be acceptable and he would be likely to face disciplinary action.

4 (i)

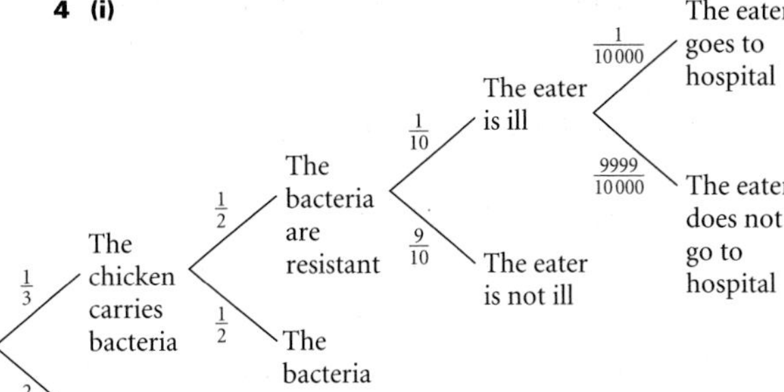

(ii) $\frac{59}{60}$ or 0.983

(iii) $\frac{1}{600\,000}$ or 0.000 001 667

(iv) (a) 16 667 **(b)** 1.667

(v) The sample of 150 is not small but it has not been described as random. The sampling method should be looked at critically.

5 (i)

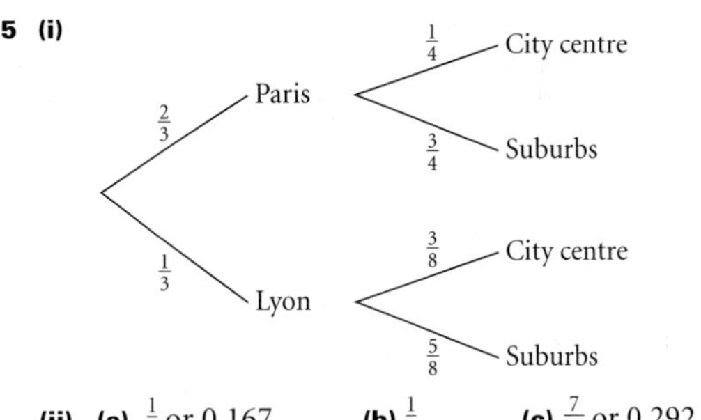

(ii) (a) $\frac{1}{6}$ or 0.167 **(b)** $\frac{1}{2}$ **(c)** $\frac{7}{24}$ or 0.292

(iii) The suburbs

6 (i) (a) $\frac{19\,999}{20\,000}$ or 0.999 95

(b) $\frac{1}{4\,000\,000}$ or 0.000 000 25

(ii) (a) $\frac{149\,999}{150\,000}$ or 0.999 993 333…

(b) $\frac{1}{50\,000\,000}$ or 2×10^{-8}

7 (i)

$\frac{15}{20}$ B
$\frac{14}{19}$ B: $\frac{13}{18}$ B, $\frac{5}{18}$ G
$\frac{5}{19}$ G: $\frac{14}{18}$ B, $\frac{4}{18}$ G
$\frac{5}{20}$ G
$\frac{15}{19}$ B: $\frac{14}{18}$ B, $\frac{4}{18}$ G
$\frac{4}{19}$ G: $\frac{15}{18}$ B, $\frac{3}{18}$ G

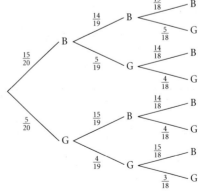

(ii) (a) $\frac{91}{228}$ or 0.399 **(b)** $\frac{35}{76}$ or 0.46

(iii) (a) $\frac{3185}{8664}$ or 0.3676

(b) $\frac{3185}{8664} + \left(\frac{91}{228}\right)^2 = 0.53$ (to 2 s.f.)

8 (i)

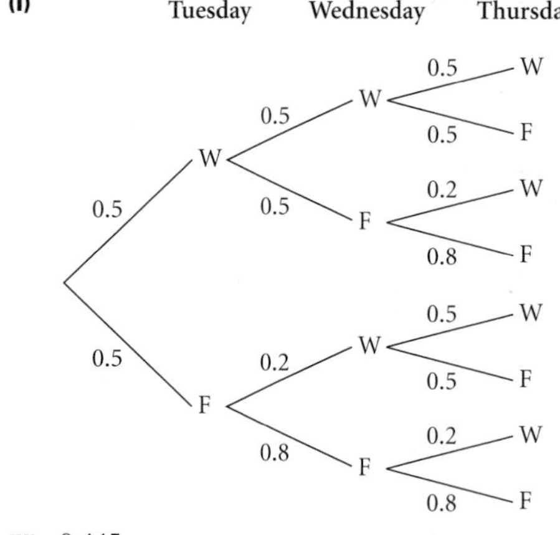

(ii) 0.445

9 (i) 0.07 **(ii)** 0.33 **(iii)** 0.93

❓ (page 118)

$P(T|S) = \frac{109}{169} = 0.645$

$P(T|S') = \frac{43}{87} = 0.494$

So $P(T|S) \neq P(T|S')$

❓ (page (118)

T those who had training; *T'* those with no training; *S* those who stayed in the company; $\mathcal{E}$ all employees. *S'* is inside the $\mathcal{E}$ box but not in the *S* region.

For example, in part **(i)**, the answer is $\frac{152}{256}$. 152 is in *T* (but not in *T'*), 256 is everyone.

❓ (page 120)

The first result was used in answering part **(i)** and the second result in answering part **(iii)**.

Exercise 3C (page 120)

1 (i)

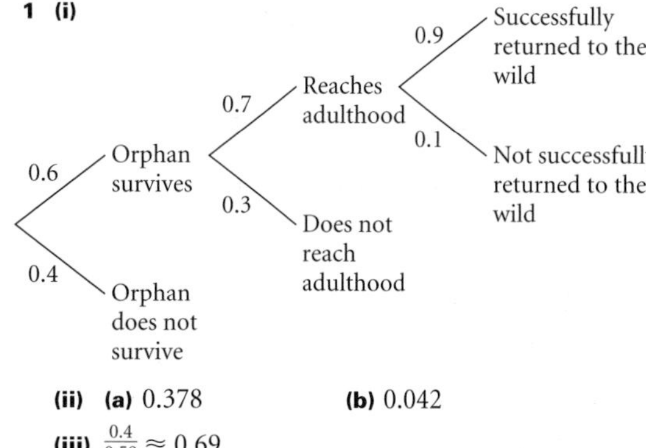

(ii) (a) 0.378 **(b)** 0.042

(iii) $\frac{0.4}{0.58} \approx 0.69$

2 (i)

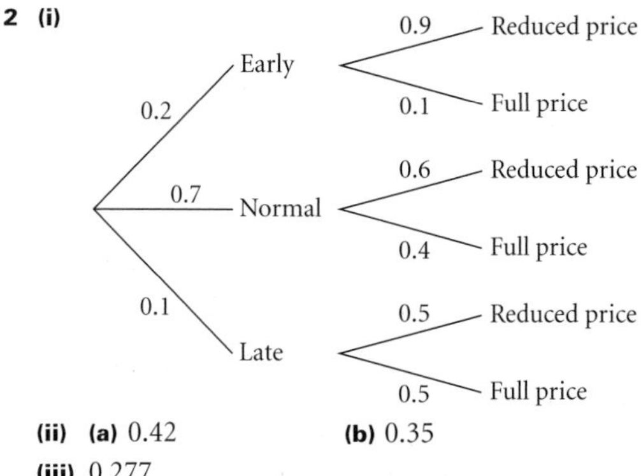

(ii) (a) 0.42 **(b)** 0.35

(iii) 0.277

3 (i)

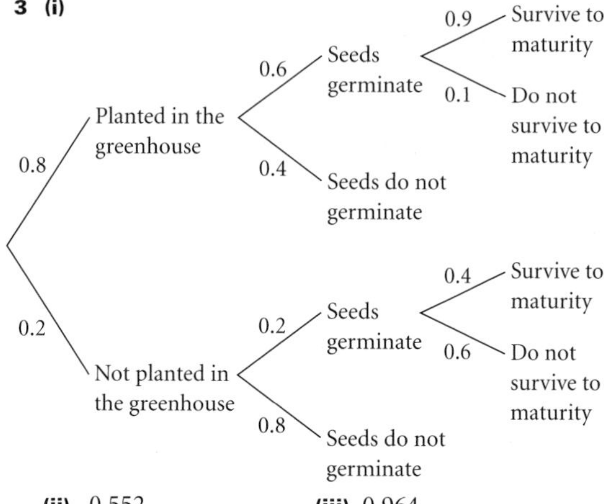

(ii) 0.552 **(iii)** 0.964

4 (i) (a) $\frac{65}{503}$ or 0.129

(b) $\frac{55}{503}$ or 0.109

(c) $\frac{28}{503} = 0.0557$

(ii) $\frac{133}{178} = 0.747$

5 (i) (a) 0.001 **(b)** 0.024 **(c)** 0.144

(ii) 0.198

(iii) 0.9

(iv) £20

6 (i) $\frac{10}{143}$ or 0.699 **(ii)** $\frac{21}{26}$ or 0.808

(iii) $\frac{216}{2197}$ or 0.098 **(iv)** $\frac{1}{169}$ or 0.005 92

(v) $\frac{36}{169}$ or 0.2130

7 (i) (a) $\frac{3}{40}$ or 0.075 **(b)** $\frac{37}{40}$ or 0.925

(ii) 0.286

(iii) (a) 0.315 **(b)** 0.24

8 (i)

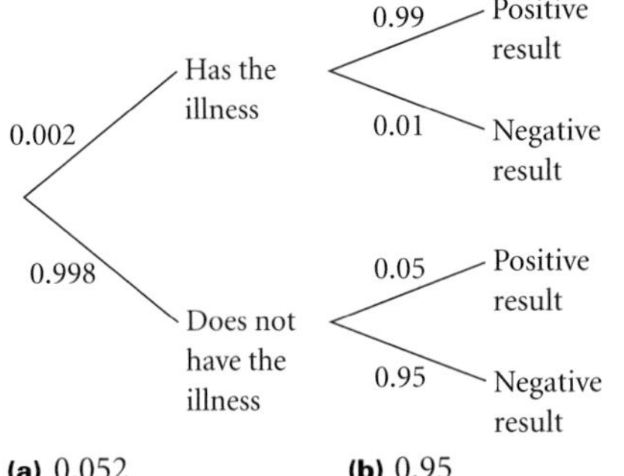

(ii) (a) 0.052 **(b)** 0.95

(iii) P(baby has illness given test result is positive)

$= \dfrac{\text{P(baby has illness} \cap \text{test is positive)}}{\text{P(test is positive)}}$

$= \dfrac{0.002 \times 0.99}{0.052}$

$= 0.038$

The low value means the test is not effective.

(iv) 0.998

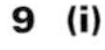

9 (i)

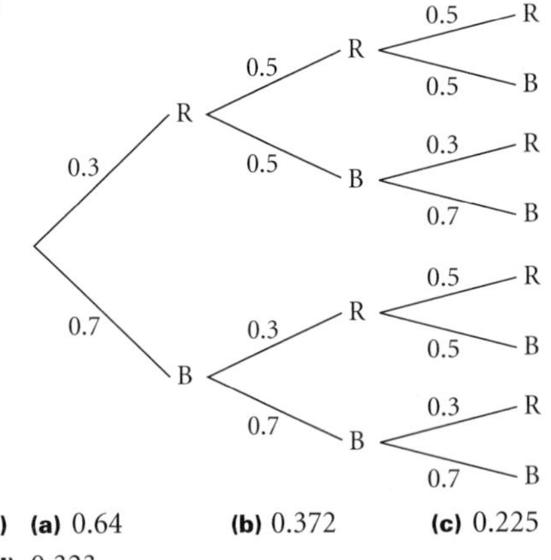

(ii) (a) 0.64 **(b)** 0.372 **(c)** 0.225

(iii) 0.323

Chapter 4

❓ (page 125)

You could conduct a traffic survey at peak times, over fixed periods of time, for example, 1 hour in the morning and 1 hour in the evening, over a period of a working week. You could count both the number of vehicles and the number of people travelling in each vehicle.

❓ (page 125)

A discrete frequency distribution is best illustrated by a vertical line chart.

Using such a diagram you can see that the frequency distribution is positively skewed, see figure 4.1.

Exercise 4A (page 131)

1 (i) 0.1

(ii) 0, 1, 2, 3, 4, 5, 6, 8

(iii) You cannot make 7 by adding two numbers from 0, 1, 2 and 4.

(iv) 0.0004

2 (i) $k = 0.6$

r	0	1	2	3	4
$\mathrm{P}(X = r)$	0	0.1	0.2	0.3	0.4

(ii) 4

3 (i) $k = 0.0005$ or $\frac{1}{2000}$

r	10	20	30	40	50
$\mathrm{P}(X = r)$	0.2	0.3	0.3	0.2	0

(ii) 0.2

4 (i) $k = 0.2$

r	$\mathrm{P}(Y = r)$
0	0.32
1	0.02
2	0.04
3	0.06
4	0.08
5	0.10
6	0.12
7	0.14
8+	0.12

(ii) (a) 0.0144 **(b)** 0.04

(iii) The uniform increase in the probabilities of from one cub to seven cubs seems unlikely.

5 (i) 0, 1 or 2

(ii) $k = \frac{1}{12}$

r	0	1	2
$\mathrm{P}(X = r)$	$\frac{1}{4} = 0.25$	$\frac{1}{3} = 0.33$	$\frac{5}{12} = 0.42$

(iii)

r	0	1	2
$\mathrm{P}(X = r)$	$\frac{16}{25} = 0.64$	$\frac{8}{25} = 0.32$	$\frac{1}{25} = 0.04$

(iv) She puts marks on the backs of the cards.

6 (i) $k = \frac{1}{66}$

r	0	1	2	3	4	5
$\mathrm{P}(N = r)$	$\frac{16}{66}$	$\frac{14}{66}$	$\frac{12}{66}$	$\frac{10}{66}$	$\frac{8}{66}$	$\frac{6}{66}$

(ii) $\frac{4}{11}$

(iii) $\frac{656}{4356} = 0.15$

7 (i) $k[(0+1)! + (1+1)! + (2+1)! + (3+1)!] = 1$

$$k(1! + 2! + 3! + 4!) = 1$$

$$k(1 + 2 + 6 + 24) = 1$$

$$k = \tfrac{1}{33}$$

r	0	1	2	3
$P(X = r)$	$\frac{1}{33}$	$\frac{2}{33}$	$\frac{6}{33}$	$\frac{24}{33}$

(ii)

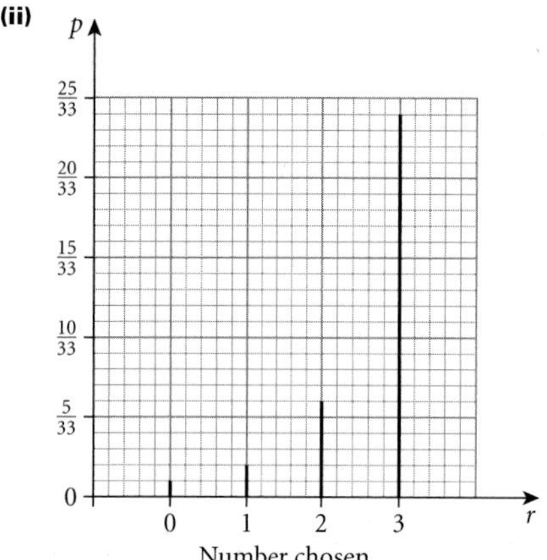

(iii) 0.567

(iv) You might expect most people to choose the middle numbers, or else perhaps to choose all four uniformly, however, the experiment will show whether this is the case.

8 (i) $k = \frac{1}{22}$

r	0	1	2	3	4	5
$P(N = r)$	$\frac{7}{22}$	$\frac{3}{22}$	$\frac{1}{22}$	$\frac{1}{22}$	$\frac{3}{22}$	$\frac{7}{22}$

(ii)

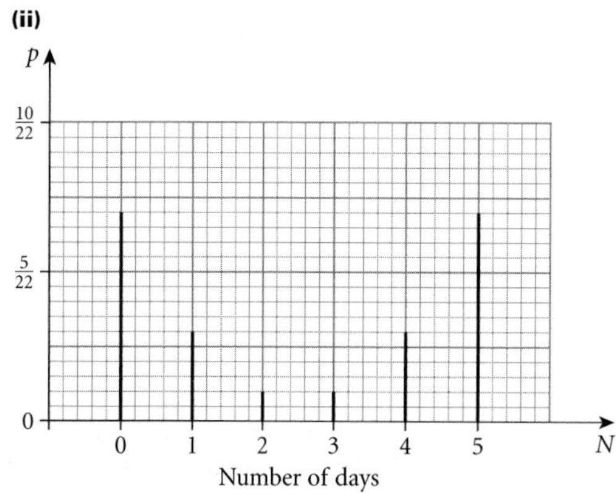

(iii) This distribution is bimodal and the modes tells us that either the train is likely to be on time for the whole week or to be late every day. The expected value for N will be 2.5 and this would be interpreted as 2 or 3 days which is misleading.

9 (i)

r	$P(X = r)$
0	$\frac{1 \times 4 - 3}{8} = \frac{1}{8}$
1	$\frac{2 \times 3 - 3}{8} = \frac{3}{8}$
2	$\frac{3 \times 2 - 3}{8} = \frac{3}{8}$
3	$\frac{4 \times 1 - 3}{8} = \frac{1}{8}$

(ii) It is not symmetrical.

(iii) Let p be the probability of a head.

P(3 heads) $= p^3$

From the table, $p^3 = 0.5$ so $p = 0.794$ or 0.8 to 1 d.p.

10 (i) $k = \frac{1}{35}$

r	0	1	2	3	4	5
$P(X = r)$	0	$\frac{5}{35}$	$\frac{8}{35}$	$\frac{9}{35}$	$\frac{8}{35}$	$\frac{5}{35}$

(ii) 3

(iii) 0.0111

(iv) The model gives the probability of no eggs being laid as 0, which is not realistic.

❓ (page 134)

The Council could have based their claim on the results of traffic surveys. These could be used to calculate summary statistics such as the mean and standard deviation of the number of people per vehicle, as well as the number of vehicles per hour.

❓ (page 134)

By comparing measures of central tendency and spread, it is possible to infer whether or not there is a significant difference between their values. Such tests of statistical inference are introduced in Unit 2. It is also possible to compare statistically the proportion of vehicles with a single occupant.

Activity (page 135)

Mean = 2

Variance = 0.86

Activity (page 136)

Mean = 1.7

Variance = 0.87

The increase in average occupancy, together with a significant reduction in the proportion of vehicles with a single occupant, could be used to infer that the scheme has been successful.

The two measures of spread are almost the same.

? (page 137)

If the expectation, E(X), is not exact in decimal form, then calculations by hand using the definition of Var(X) may be tedious and/or prone to arithmetic errors by premature approximation of E(X). The alternative formulation of Var(X) may be more appropriate in such cases.

Exercise 4B (page 138)

1 (i) 3.6

(ii) $P(1) = P(2) = P(3) = P(4) = P(5) = P(6) = \frac{1}{6}$

Mean $= 1 \times \frac{1}{6} + 2 \times \frac{1}{6} + 3 \times \frac{1}{6} + 4 \times \frac{1}{6} + 5 \times \frac{1}{6} + 6 \times \frac{1}{6} = 3.5$

(iii) 3.5

(iv) The mean is 3.5 but each number is not equally likely to come up so the *astragalos* is not fair.

2 (i) 6.8

(ii) 2.76

(iii) 0.3

(iv) The mean has fallen from 9.5 to 6.8 (there are fewer eels now) but the variance has remained very similar (it was 2.85 and is now 2.76) so the variability in the numbers caught is much the same.

3 (i) $k = \frac{1}{300}$

r	P($X = r$)
0	0.3
1	$\frac{8}{300}$
2	$\frac{14}{300}$
3	$\frac{18}{300}$
4	$\frac{20}{300}$
5	$\frac{20}{300}$
6	$\frac{18}{300}$
7	$\frac{14}{300}$
8	$\frac{8}{300}$
9	0.3

(ii) 0.567

(iii) 4.5 dinosaurs

(iv) 4.5×600 to sell + 600 to give away = 3300

4 (i) $\left(k \times \left(\frac{1}{2}\right)^0\right) + \left(k \times \left(\frac{1}{2}\right)^1\right) + \left(k \times \left(\frac{1}{2}\right)^2\right) + \left(k \times \left(\frac{1}{2}\right)^3\right) = 1$

$k + \frac{1}{2}k + \frac{1}{4}k + \frac{1}{8}k = 1$

$k = \frac{8}{15}$

(ii)

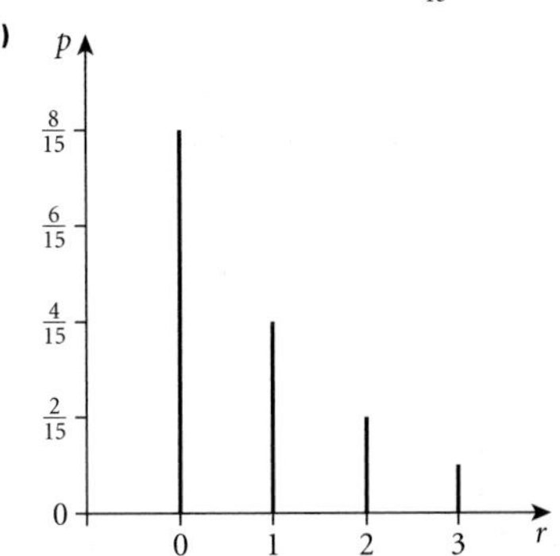

(iii) $E(X) = \frac{11}{15}$ or 0.733, $\text{Var}(X) = \frac{194}{225}$ or 0.862

(iv) Mean daily income = £18.33, variance of daily income = 538.75

5 (i)

r	1	2	3	4
P($X = r$)	k	$\frac{1}{2}k$	$\frac{1}{3}k$	$\frac{1}{4}k$

$k = 0.48$

(ii)

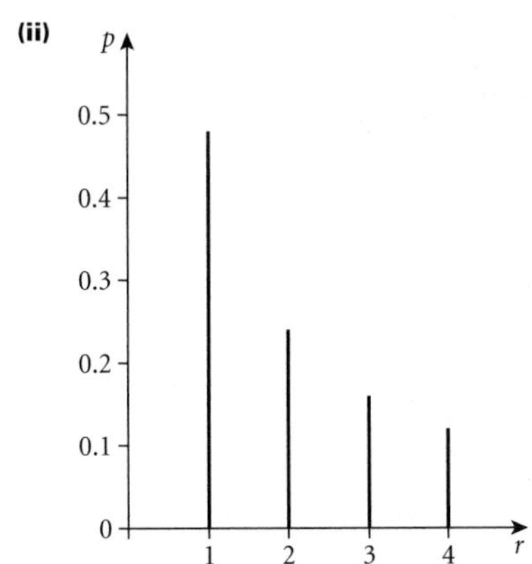

(iii) $E(X) = 1.92$, $\text{Var}(X) = 1.11$

(iv) If single occupant car drivers share, then there will be a smaller proportion of cars in the $X = 1$ category and a greater proportion in the $X = 2$ category, which will increase E(X) and reduce Var(X).

6 (i)

	1	2	3	4	5
1	–	1	2	3	4
2	1	–	1	2	3
3	2	1	–	1	2
4	3	2	1	–	1
5	4	3	2	1	–

From the table it can be seen that the possible values are 1, 2, 3 and 4.

(ii) $X = 1$ occurs 8 times out of $20 = 0.4$.
$P(X = 2) = 0.3$, $P(X = 3) = 0.2$, $P(X = 4) = 0.1$

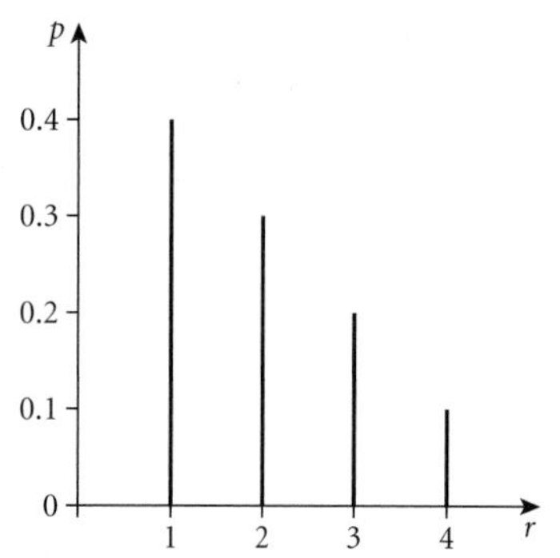

(iii) $E(X) = 2$, $Var(X) = 1$

(iv) $P(\text{wins}) = P(1, 1) + P(2, 2) + P(3, 3) + P(4, 4)$
$= 0.3$

(v) Expected prize per game
$= 1 \times 0.16 + 2 \times 0.09 + 3 \times 0.04 + 4 \times 0.01$
$= £0.50$
So should charge 60p per game.

7 (i)

r	3	4	5	6	7	8
$P(X = r)$	$\frac{2}{112}$	$\frac{6}{112}$	$\frac{12}{112}$	$\frac{20}{112}$	$\frac{30}{112}$	$\frac{42}{112}$

(ii) Mean $= 6.75$, $Var(X) = 1.6875$

(iii)

r	3	4	5	6	7	8
$P(X \leqslant r)$	$\frac{2}{112}$	$\frac{8}{112}$	$\frac{20}{112}$	$\frac{40}{112}$	$\frac{70}{112}$	1

Least value of m is 7.

8 (i)

r	0	1	3	6	10	15
$P(Y = r)$	0.0778	0.2592	0.3456	0.2304	0.0768	0.0102

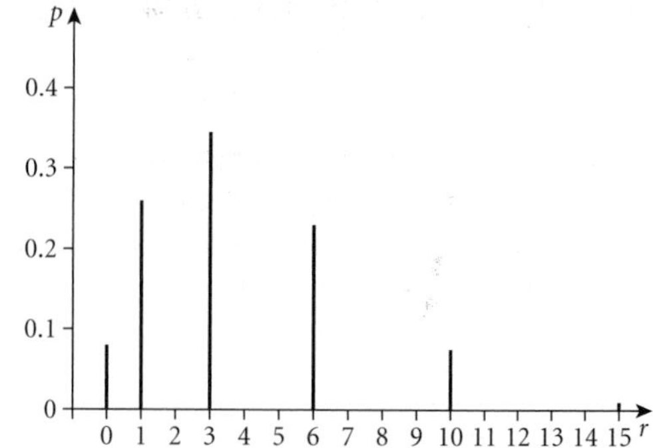

(ii) $E(Y) = 3.60$, $Var(Y) = 8.68$

(iii) 0.0047

(iv) 0.252

9 (i)

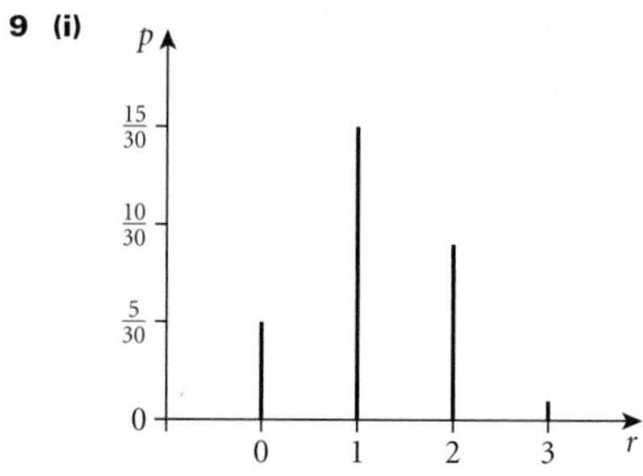

(ii) $E(X) = 1.2$, $Var(X) = 0.56$

(iii) Total cost $= 30(3 - X) + 40X$
$= 90 + 10X$

(iv) $E(\text{cost}) = 102\text{p}$

Exercise 4C (page 141)

1 (i)

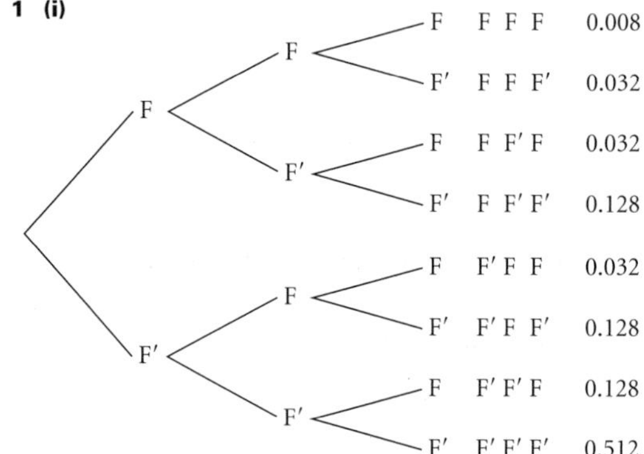

(ii)

Number of successful boreholes	0	1	2	3
Probability	0.512	0.384	0.096	0.008

(iii) £15 million

2 (i)

r	0	1	2	3
$P(X \leqslant r)$	0.1	0.5	0.8	1.0

(ii) $P(L \leqslant 2) = P(X \leqslant 2)^3 = 0.512$ since the largest score will be $\leqslant 2$ when each score is $\leqslant 2$ and this probability is the cube of the probability that one individual score is $\leqslant 2$.
$P(L \leqslant 1) = P(X \leqslant 1)^3 = 0.125$
$P(L = 0) = 0.001$, $P(L \leqslant 3) = 1$

(iii)

r	0	1	2	3
$P(L = r)$	0.001	0.124	0.387	0.488

(iv) $E(L) = 2.362$, $Var(L) = 0.485$

3 (i)

r	0	1	2	3
$P(X = r)$	$25k$	$32k$	$27k$	$16k$

$$25k + 32k + 27k + 16k = 1$$
$$100k = 1$$
$$k = 0.01$$

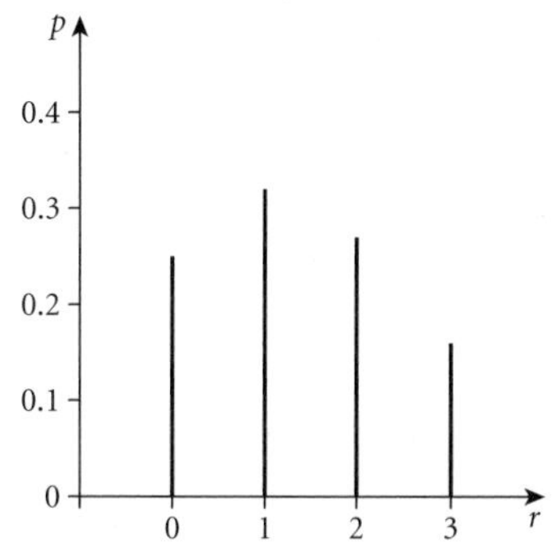

(ii) $E(X) = 1.34$, $Var(X) = 1.04$

(iii) (a) 0.0625 **(b)** 0.1753

You must assume that the number of goals per game is independent.

(iv) Possible reasons include the team members may change, the model is limited to a maximum of three goals, the fixtures may not be the same in the forthcoming year.

4 (i) For $P(X = 0)$, the contestant answers one question only and gets it wrong so
$P(X = 0) = 1 - 0.75 = 0.25$.
For $P(X = 5)$, the contestant gets all five questions correct so
$P(X = 5) = 0.75 \times 0.5 \times \ldots \times 0.25 = 0.011\,25$.

(ii) $E(X) = 1.331$, $Var(X) = 1.27$

(iii) (a) 0.15 **(b)** 0.033 37

(iv) 10 920

5 (i)

r	−5	−4	−3	−2	−1	0	1	2	3	4	5
$P(X = r)$	k	$2k$	$3k$	$4k$	$5k$	$6k$	$5k$	$4k$	$3k$	$2k$	k

$$k + 2k + 3k + 4k + 5k + 6k + 5k + 4k + 3k + 2k + k = 1$$
$$36k = 1$$
$$k = \tfrac{1}{36}$$

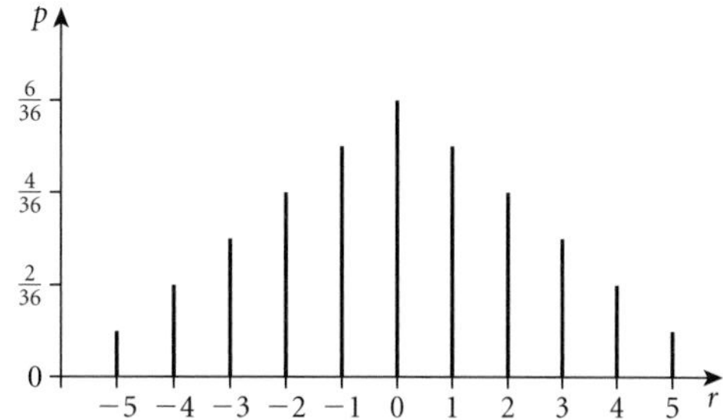

(ii) $E(X) = 0$, $Var(X) = \frac{35}{6}$

(iii) $\frac{5}{12}$

(iv) (a) $1 - \left(\frac{7}{12}\right)^2 = \frac{95}{144} = 0.660$ (to 3 d.p.)

(b) $1 - \left(\frac{7}{12}\right)^4 = 0.884$ (to 3 d.p.)

(v) By taking the exam repeatedly the probability of doing better than their true ability increases. One weakness is that the model assumes the true ability does not change.

6 (i) Let X represent 'gain in tokens'.
When the player loses they lose the token they paid so $r = -1$.
When the player draws they have paid one token but get it back so $r = -1 + 1 = 0$.
When the player wins they have paid one token but receive ten so $r = -1 + 10 = 9$.

(ii) $E(X) = -0.3$, the negative sign indicates that there is a loss.

(iii) 4.71

(iv) 6.3

(v) $0.75^9 = 0.0751$

(vi) $1 - 0.95^9 = 0.3698$

7 (i)

r	0	1	2	3	4
$P(X = r)$	0.66	k	$0.4k$	$0.16k$	$0.064k$

$$0.66 + k + 0.4k + 0.16k + 0.064k = 1$$
$$0.66 + 1.624k = 1$$
$$k = 0.209 \approx 0.21$$

(ii)

r	0	1	2	3	4
$P(X = r)$	0.66	0.21	0.084	0.0336	0.013 44

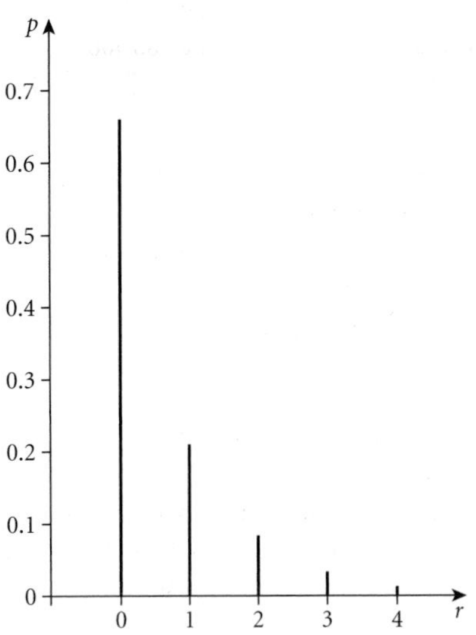

There is a large group of non-offenders. A smaller group who have offended once and then the numbers of motorists who have committed two or more offences are small and get smaller as r increases.

(iii) Mean = 0.53, Var(X) = 0.78

(iv) 1.56

Chapter 5

❓ (page 147)

Gary could have put the bricks in order by chance. A probability of $\frac{1}{120}$ is small but not very small. What would really be convincing is if he could repeat the task whenever he was given the bricks.

Exercise 5A (page 149)

1 **(i)** 720 **(ii)** 120 **(iii)** 240

2 **(i)** 60 **(ii)** 20

3 **(i)** 5! **(ii)** $\frac{6!}{3!3!}$ or $\frac{5!}{3!}$

4 6

5 45

6 **(i)** 120 **(ii)** 24

7 **(i)** 720 **(ii)** 120

8 **(i)** 10 000 **(ii)** 9993 **(iii)** 8100

9 **(i)** 1000
(ii) **(a)** 26 000 **(b)** 24 000
(iii) **(a)** 13 824 000 **(b)** 8 743 680

10 **(i)** 67 600
(ii) $\frac{1}{260}$ or 0.003 85
(iii) A letter, because there are more letters than digits

11 **(i)** $9^8 = 43\,046\,721$
(ii) $9^{13} = 2\,541\,865\,828\,329$

12 **(i)** **(a)** 10 000 **(b)** 100 000
(ii) **(a)** 456 976 **(b)** 1 827 904 **(c)** 7 311 616

Investigation (page 151)

1 When $m = 3$, $n \geqslant 7$.
When $m = 4$, $n \geqslant 8$.
When $m = 5$, $n \geqslant 9$.

2 There are many ways
e.g. $\frac{7!}{5!}$, $\frac{3! \times 7!}{6!}$, $2! \times 4! - 3!$

3 **(i)** $4^4 = 256$
(ii) **(a)** 12 **(b)** 4

❓ (page 152)

No it does not matter.

❓ (page 152)

Multiply top and bottom by 43!

$$\frac{49 \times 48 \times 47 \times 46 \times 45 \times 44}{6!} \times \frac{43!}{43!} = \frac{49!}{6!\,43!}$$

❓ (page 152)

${}^{49}C_6 = 13\,983\,816 \approx 14$ million

❓ (page 153)

By following the same argument as for the National Lottery example but with n for 49 and r for 6.

❓ (page 153)

$${}^nC_0 = \frac{n!}{0!\,n!} = 1 \qquad \text{if } 0! = 1$$

$${}^nC_n = \frac{n!}{n!\,(n-n)!} = 1 \qquad \text{again if } 0! = 1$$

Activity (page 155)

Enter 1 in the cells in column A and on the leading diagonal (B2, C3, etc.).

Enter the formula ‘ = A2+B2’ in cell B3.

Replicate the formula in cells B4, C4, B5, C5, D5, B6, ….

❓ (page 155)

$$\text{R.H.S} = \frac{n!}{r!(n-r)!} + \frac{n!}{(r+1)!(n-r-1)!}$$
$$= \frac{n!}{r!(n-r-1)!}\left[\frac{1}{n-r} + \frac{1}{r+1}\right]$$
$$= \frac{n!}{r!(n-r-1)!}\left[\frac{r+1+n-r}{(n-r)(r+1)}\right]$$
$$= \frac{(n+1)!}{(r+1)!(n-r)!}$$
$$= {}^{n+1}C_{r+1} = \text{L.H.S.}$$

❓ (page 157)

1 The probability is $\frac{1}{24}$, assuming the selection is done at random, so Agnes is not justified when she says 'less than one in a hundred'.

2 As a product of probabilities $\frac{1}{3} \times \frac{1}{2} \times \frac{1}{4} = \frac{1}{24}$

Exercise 5B (page 158)

1 (i) 38 760 **(ii)** 76 904 685

2 (i) 120 **(ii)** 6435 **(iii)** 645 840

3 (i) 847 660 528 **(ii)** 125 970 **(iii)** 2.39×10^7

4 120 selections
${}^6C_5 \times {}^4C_2 = 36$ ways
(i) 4 **(ii)** 60 **(iii)** 20
Getting four chocolates I particularly like is the most likely outcome and has a probability of $\frac{60}{120} = 0.5$.

5 (i) 495 **(ii)** 45 **(iii)** $\frac{1}{11}$
(iv) 210 **(v)** $\frac{4}{35}$

6 (i) 220 **(ii)** 70 **(iii)** $\frac{1}{22}$
(iv) There are $\frac{5!}{2!} = 60$ ways of picking 3 of the 5 numbers. $2 \times 3! = 12$ of these combinations involve 5, 10 and 40 or 5, 8 and 50, which give a product of 2000. So 48 combinations give a prize of £10.
P(winning exactly £10)
= P(revealing 3 numbers) × P(product not 2000)
$= \frac{1}{22} \times \frac{48}{60} = \frac{2}{55}$
(v) (a) 0.069 **(b)** 0.018

7 (i) 5005 **(ii)** 1.25×10^{11}
(iii) 2.13×10^9 **(iv)** 2.10×10^9

8 (i) 40 320
(ii) (a) 1440 **(b)** 5760
(iii) (a) $\frac{1}{7}$ or 0.143 **(b)** $\frac{6}{7}$ or 0.857
(iv) 576 **(v)** $\frac{3}{35}$ or 0.0857

9 (i) 28 **(ii)** 840
(iii) 210 **(iv)** 86 400
(v) 1152 **(vi)** $\frac{840}{4368}$ or 0.192

10 (i) 210
(ii) The number of ways of picking the two odd numbers $= {}^5C_2$.
The number of ways of picking the two other numbers $= {}^5C_2$.
Therefore the number of ways of picking exactly two odd numbers $= ({}^5C_2)^2 = \left(\frac{5!}{3!\,2!}\right)^2 = 100$.
P(correct combination) $= \frac{1}{100} = 0.01$.
(iii) 0.98
(iv) Yes, if five buttons had to be pressed simultaneously, then $r = 5$ and ${}^{10}C_5 = 252$, i.e. there would be 252 possible combinations.
(v) $\frac{1}{2400}$

11 (i) 120
(ii) (a) $\frac{1}{8}$ **(b)** $\frac{1}{120}$
(iii) $\frac{1}{120}$ **(iv)** $\frac{1}{120}$
(v) $\frac{7}{120}$ **(vi)** $\frac{28}{120}$ or $\frac{7}{30}$

12 (i) $\frac{1}{17\,576}$ or 0.000 057 **(ii)** $\frac{6}{17\,576}$ or 0.000 34
(iii) $\frac{75}{676}$ or 0.111 **(iv)** $\frac{6615}{17\,576}$ or 0.376
(v) $\frac{1}{63}$ or 0.0159

Chapter 6

Exercise 6A (page 168)

1 (i) (a) $\frac{1}{32}$ or 0.031 25 **(b)** $\frac{5}{32}$ or 0.156 25
(c) $\frac{10}{32} = \frac{5}{16}$ or 0.3125 **(d)** $\frac{10}{32} = \frac{5}{16}$ or 0.3125
(e) $\frac{5}{32}$ or 0.156 25 **(f)** $\frac{1}{32}$ or 0.031 25
(ii) 1, since the six results are mutually exclusive and a complete set of all possible outcomes.

2 (i) (a) 0.0778 **(b)** 0.2592
(c) 0.3456 **(d)** 0.2304
(e) 0.0768 **(f)** 0.0102
(ii) The total should be 1.

3 (i) (a) 0.4219 or $\frac{27}{64}$ **(b)** 0.4219 or $\frac{27}{64}$
(c) 0.1406 or $\frac{9}{64}$ **(d)** 0.0156 or $\frac{1}{64}$
(ii) Once in three uses is more likely since ${}^6C_2(0.25)^2(0.75)^4 = 0.2966$, which is less than 0.4219.

4 (i) (a) 0.3585 **(b)** 0.3774
(c) 0.1887 **(d)** 0.0754
(ii) 1 is the most likely number of seeds to germinate since $0.3585 < 0.3774 > 0.1887$.

5 **(i)** **(a)** 0.2725 **(b)** 0.3847
(c) 0.2376 **(d)** 0.8948
(ii) 1 is the most likely number to land fully inside a square.

6 **(i)** **(a)** 0.2631 **(b)** 0.7369
(ii) It is more likely that at least one is a female than that none are.

7 **(i)** 0.9 **(ii)** 0.4783
(iii) **(a)** 0.0718 **(b)** 0.1994 **(c)** 0.7288

8 **(i)** **(a)** 0.0020 **(b)** 0.0323 **(c)** 0.1272
(ii) The most likely number is 7 since
$P(X = 6) = 0.1712 < P(X = 7) = 0.1844$
$> P(X = 8) = 0.1614.$

9 **(i)** **(a)** $\frac{15}{64} = 0.2344$ **(b)** 0.3110 **(c)** 0.3292
(ii) Case **(c)** gives the largest probability. It is not simple to predict without doing the calculations.

10 **(i)** 0.2668
(ii) 7, since $P(X = 6) = 0.2001$, $P(X = 8) = 0.2335$ and $P(X = 7)$ lies between these two values.
(iii) The assumption is that the ages of people Joe meets occur randomly and independently. In practice, Joe may well meet people in groups of similar ages.

Activity (page 171)

$$\text{Expectation of } X = \sum_{r=0}^{n} r \times P(X = r)$$

Since the term with $r = 0$ is zero

$$\text{Expectation of } X = \sum_{r=1}^{n} r \times P(X = r)$$
$$= \sum_{r=1}^{n} r \times {}^nC_r p^r q^{n-r}.$$

The typical term of this sum is

$$r \times \frac{n!}{r!(n-r)!} p^r q^{n-r} = np \times \frac{(n-1)!}{(r-1)!(n-r)!} p^{r-1} q^{n-r}$$
$$= np \times \frac{(n-1)!}{(r-1)!((n-1)-(r-1))!} \times p^{r-1} q^{(n-1)-(r-1)}$$
$$= np \times {}^{n-1}C_{r-1} p^{r-1} q^{(n-1)-(r-1)}$$

(using $(n-1) - (r-1) = n - r$)

$$= np \times {}^{n-1}C_s p^s q^{(n-1)-s}$$

where $s = r - 1$.
In the summation, np is a common factor and s runs from 0 to $n - 1$ as r runs from 1 to n. Therefore

$$\text{Expectation of } X = np \times \sum_{s=0}^{n-1} {}^{n-1}C_s p^s q^{(n-1)-s}$$
$$= np(q + p)^{n-1}$$
$$= np \qquad \text{since } q + p = 1.$$

Exercise 6B (page 174)

1 **(i)** 2.55
(ii) **(a)** 0.0282 **(b)** 0.1470 **(c)** 0.3060
(d) 0.3185 **(e)** 0.1657 **(f)** 0.0345

2 **(i)** 1.8
(ii) 0.2835
(iii) $P(X = 1) = 0.3002 > 0.2835$ so most likely number is 1.

3 **(i)** **(a)** 1.75 **(b)** 7
(ii) 0.1719
(iii) The assumptions are that the probability of ‘success’ is constant and ‘successes’ occur randomly and independently. Here, occurrences are not independent because weather-related events tend to be fairly uniform over periods of a few days.

4 **(i)** **(a)** 0.5987 **(b)** 0.3151 **(c)** 0.0861
(ii) **(a)** 0.0345 **(b)** 0.5443

5 **(i)** **(a)** $\frac{32}{81} = 0.3951$ **(b)** $\frac{8}{81} = 0.0988$
(c) 0.0390
(ii) **(a)** $2\frac{2}{3}$ **(b)** $1\frac{1}{3}$

6 **(i)** **(a)** 0.3777 **(b)** 0.2717 **(c)** 0.2805
(ii) AA: 800, Aa: 2400, aa: 1800
(iii) The proportions of A and a are 0.4 and 0.6 respectively.

7 **(i)** **(a)** 0.9999 **(b)** 0.9950 **(c)** 0.9900
(ii) **(a)** Approximately 0.9999, or $\frac{6999}{7000}$
(b) 0.9929
(c) 0.9858
(iii) 0.0080, 0.0114

8 **(i)** **(a)** 0.9282 **(b)** 0.7288
(ii) **(a)** 0.2222 **(b)** 0.0258
(iii) A massive improvement, especially in the frequency of floods in at least two years out of 25.

9 **(i)** 0.6921
(ii) p = mean number of outbreaks per year ÷ 365
$= 0.001\,896\ldots$
≈ 0.0019
(iii) P(at least 1 war) = 1 − P(no wars)
$= 1 - 0.9981^{365}$
$= 1 - 0.499\ldots$
$= 0.500\ldots$
≈ 0.5
(iv) **(a)** 0.031 **(b)** 0.5
(v) 7

10 **(i)** **(a)** 0.4596 **(b)** 0.0988
(ii) **(a)** 0.9992 **(b)** 0.0339
(iii) 0, 5

11 (i) 0.0685

(ii) 0.0017

(iii) The assumption is that the probability remains constant throughout the year. Weather patterns are, however, far from constant so it would not be surprising if certain seasons are almost free from tornadoes and in other seasons they occur much more frequently.

12 (i) 0.2461 **(ii)** 7.383 **(iii)** 0.0020

(iv) 0.0570 **(v)** 0.0554

13 (i) 0.5277 **(ii)** 6 **(iii)** 0.0578

(iv) 0.0069 **(v)** 0.0017

Investigation (page 177)

(i) **(a)** 0.2461 **(b)** 0.1762 **(c)** 0.1254

(ii) As the number of coins doubles the probability multiplies by, approximately, 0.71.

Chapter 7

? (page 180)

Assuming both types of parents have the same fertility, boys born would outnumber girls in the ratio 3 : 1. In a generation's time there would be a marked shortage of women of child-bearing age.

? (page 186)

$0.9629 - 0.8982$ is $P(X \leqslant 6) - P(X \leqslant 5)$ and so is $P(X = 6)$. You will find the number 0.0647 features in the table on page 184 for 6 successes. This is an easy way of working out such binomial probabilities.

Exercise 7A (page 186)

1 (i) H_0: The coin is not biased, $p = \frac{1}{2}$, where p is the probability of the coin coming down heads.
H_1: The coin is biased towards heads, $p > \frac{1}{2}$.

(ii) $P(X \geqslant 15) = 0.0207$
Since $0.0207 < 5\%$, the null hypothesis is rejected.
At the 5% significance level, the evidence supports the claim that the coin is biased towards heads.

(iii) Yes, Alvin should get a new coin.

2 (i) H_0: This type of drawing pin has the same probability as others of landing point down, $p = 0.35$.
H_1: This type of drawing pin has a lower probability than others of landing point down, $p < 0.35$.

(ii) $P(X = 0) = 0.0319$
Since $0.0319 < 5\%$, H_0 is rejected.
At the 5% significance level, the evidence supports the hypothesis that these pins are less likely than others to land point down.

(iii) A longer pin with a heavier head would probably be less likely to land point down.

3 (i) 0.7

(ii) H_0: The probability that an active boxer votes for the Democratic Party is the same as that for the population in general, $p = 0.3$.
H_1: The probability that an active boxer votes for the Democratic Party is less than that for the population in general, $p < 0.3$.

(iii) $P(X \leqslant 2) = 0.035$
Since $0.035 < 5\%$, H_0 is rejected.
At the 5% significance level, the evidence supports the hypothesis that active boxers are less likely to vote for the Democratic Party.

(iv) This comment is not justified since the 'boxing community' is not the same population as 'active boxers'.

4 (i) 0.25

(ii) 0.0139

(iii) H_0: The students in the school are typical of those in the region in terms of sometimes walking to school, $p = 0.25$.
H_1: The students in the school are more likely than others in the region to sometimes walk to school, $p > 0.25$.

(iv) $0.0139 < 5\%$, H_0 is rejected and H_1 is accepted.
At the 5% significance level, the evidence supports the hypothesis that students at the school are more likely than others in the region to sometimes walk to school.

(v) The school could be in a safe area or it could be that many students live close to the school.

5 (i) H_0: The probability that a randomly selected person supports the foreign policy is the same as before, $p = 0.6$.
H_1: The probability that a randomly selected person supports the foreign policy is less than before, $p < 0.6$.

(ii) $0.1423 > 10\%$, H_0 is accepted.
The evidence does not support, at the 10% significance level, the suggestion of a decline in support.

6 (i) H_0: The questions are of the same standard as before, $p = 0.4$.
H_1: The questions have become easier, $p > 0.4$.

(ii) $P(X \geqslant 10) = 0.0583$
Since $0.0583 < 10\%$, H_0 is rejected.
At the 10% significance level, the evidence suggests that the questions have become easier.

(iii) However, at the 5% significance level, there is insufficient evidence to support the claim that the questions have become easier.

7 (i) H_0: The performance is the same as before, $p = 0.35$.
H_1: The performance has improved, $p < 0.35$.

(ii) Since $0.0860 < 10\%$, H_0 is rejected. At the 10% significance level, the company's claim is accepted.

(iii) All the trains in the sample ran in the same week. A better sample would cover a longer period, allowing more possibilities for variable weather and other factors.
The conclusion would have been different at the 5% significance level.

8 (i) For Carol's test:
H_0: Sonya's claimed rate is correct, $p = 0.7$.
H_1: Sonya's claimed rate is too high, $p < 0.7$.
$P(X \leqslant 4) = 0.0473$
Since $0.0473 < 5\%$, H_0 is rejected.
This supports Carol opinion that Sonya's claim is too high.

(ii) In this case the null and alternative hypotheses are the same.
$P(X \leqslant 12) = 0.2277$
Since $0.2277 > 5\%$, H_0 is accepted.
The evidence does not support Carol's opinion.

(iii) Sonya's claim would be expected to apply over time. So the sample tested in part **(i)** is not random because all the shots were on the same day.
It is also the case that Sonya's probability of success may well not be constant. Most sportsmen and sportswomen have good and bad days.
These two considerations taken together mean that the binomial model was not appropriate for Carol's test and so it is invalid.
A further point is that success on one shot will build up Sonya's confidence, possibly making her more likely to succeed on the next. So the results of successive shots are not independent.

9 (i) The probability that both are male is $\frac{1}{2} \times \frac{1}{2} = \frac{1}{4}$.
The probability that both are female is $\frac{1}{2} \times \frac{1}{2} = \frac{1}{4}$.
The probability that both are the same is $\frac{1}{4} + \frac{1}{4} = 0.5$.

(ii) (a) H_0: Same sex dizygotic twins are no more likely among the tribe than in general, $p = 0.5$.
H_1: Same sex dizygotic twins are more likely among the tribe than in general, $p > 0.5$.

(b) $P(X \geqslant 8) = 0.1938$
Since $0.1938 > 10\%$, H_0 is accepted.
The evidence does not support the anthropologist's claim at the 10% significance level.

(c) The sample is not random and may well not be representative of the whole tribe's population; for example, the people in one isolated village may have different genetic characteristics from those of the rest of the tribe.

(iii) $P(X \geqslant 14) = 0.0318$
Since $0.0318 < 10\%$, H_0 is rejected.
The test supports the anthropologist's claim.
However, the non-randomness of the sample, in this case from just two villages, means that the result cannot be treated as valid.

10 (i) (a) ${}^{100}C_{98}(0.95)^{98}(0.05)^2 = 0.0812$

(b) $0.0812 + {}^{100}C_{99}(0.95)^{99}(0.05) + 0.95^{100} = 0.118$

(ii) No. Since $0.118 > 5\%$, there is not enough evidence to claim that the batch is better than the customer's requirement.

? (page 191)

Critical region at 10% significance level is $X \leqslant 4$.

Exercise 7B (page 192)

1 (i) H_0: The drug is successful in 70% cases, $p = 0.7$.
H_1: The drug is successful in less than 70% of cases, $p < 0.7$.

(ii) The critical region is $X \leqslant 7$, since
$P(X \leqslant 7) = 0.0257 < 5\%$
and $P(X \leqslant 8) = 0.0744 > 5\%$.

(iii) 7 is in the critical region so accept H_1, the evidence suggests the drug is not as good as claimed.

2 (i) H_0: The accident has not affected Sunil's ability to solve a puzzle in 30 minutes, $p = 0.75$.
H_1: The accident has reduced Sunil's ability to solve a puzzle in 30 minutes, $p < 0.75$.

(ii) The critical region is $X \leqslant 7$, since
$P(X \leqslant 7) = 0.0383 < 10\%$
and $P(X \leqslant 8) = 0.1117 > 10\%$.

(iii) 6 is in the critical region, so accept H_1, the evidence suggests Sunil's ability to solve the puzzles in 30 minutes has declined.

(iv) $P(X \leqslant 7) = 0.0802 < 10\%$ and
$P(X \leqslant 8) = 0.2060 > 10\%$ so the critical region is unchanged.

(v) The critical region for 5% is altered in the second situation, since
$P(X \leqslant 7) = 0.0802 > 5\%$.

3 (i) H_0: He is equally likely to take either road, $p = 0.5$.
H_1: He is more likely to take the correct road, $p > 0.5$.

(ii) The critical region is $X \geqslant 8$ since $P(X \geqslant 8) = 0.0547 < 10\%$ and $P(X \geqslant 7) = 0.1719 > 10\%$.

(iii) 8 is in the critical region so accept H_1, the evidence suggests Mr Jones' belief is justified.

4 (i) H_0: Plants of the new variety are no more likely to reach maturity, $p = 0.35$.
H_1: Plants of the new variety are more likely to reach maturity, $p > 0.35$.

(ii) Critical region is $X \geqslant 10$, since $P(X \geqslant 10) = 0.0383 < 5\%$ and $P(X \geqslant 9) = 0.0994 > 5\%$.

(iii) 10 is in the critical region so accept H_1, the evidence suggests the new variety is more likely to reach maturity.

(iv) $P(X \leqslant 1) = 0.0067 < 5\%$, so there is sufficient evidence to say that the third variety is less likely to mature than the standard variety.

5 (i) H_0: Prices do not go up after conversion, $p = 0.5$.
H_1: Prices do go up after conversion, $p > 0.5$.

(ii) The minimum number is 12, since $P(X \geqslant 12) = 0.0176 < 5\%$ and $P(X \geqslant 11) = 0.0592 > 5\%$.
So the critical region is $X \geqslant 12$.

(iii) 10 is not in the critical region so accept H_0, there is insufficient evidence that prices have increased.

(iv) Not likely to be valid as the items would most likely have very different prices. An increase in price of more than 50% of the items does not imply the overall cost increases.

6 (i) H_0: Half the employees approve of the new training scheme, $p = 0.5$.
H_1: More than half the employees approve of the new training scheme, $p > 0.5$.

(ii) The critical region is $X \geqslant 14$ since $P(X \geqslant 13) = 0.1316 > 10\%$ and $P(X \geqslant 14) = 0.0577 < 10\%$.

(iii) 14 is in the critical region so accept H_1, there is sufficient evidence to say that more than half the employees approve the new training scheme.

(iv) Yes, they should introduce the scheme.

Exercise 7C (page 197)

1 (i) H_0: The animals in the Siberian colony have the usual survival rate, $p = 0.4$.
H_1: The animals in the Siberian colony have an unusual survival rate, $p \neq 0.4$.
$P(X \leqslant 3) = 0.0464 < 5\%$ so accept H_1, the evidence suggests the Siberian colony has an unusual survival rate.

(ii) They have to find and observe the animals and this may not be a random process. Those they find could be the weaker specimens. Since $P(X \leqslant 3)$ is only just less than 5%, this could certainly affect the outcome.

2 (i) H_0: The probability of success, $p = 0.1$.
H_1: The probability of success, $p \neq 0.1$.
$P(X = 0) = 0.1216 > 2.5\%$, so accept H_0, there is insufficient evidence to say that the probability is different from 0.1.

(ii) A *one-tailed* test would fit better with the charge of cheating. The smallest sample size which yields $P(X = 0) < 5\%$ is 29 (when $P(X = 0) = 0.0471$); with sample size 28, $P(X = 0) = 0.0523$, so he needs to play the game at least 29 times to have any chance, at the 5% level of significance, of demonstrating a *reduction* in probability. So test at the 5% level using a sample size of 30, say, and H_0: $p = 0.1$, H_1: $p < 0.1$.

3 (i) H_0: The earth in the area has the same contamination level as the city, $p = 0.15$.
H_1: The earth in the area has a different contamination level from the city, $p \neq 0.15$.
$P(X = 0) = 0.0874 > 2.5\%$ so accept H_0, there is insufficient evidence to say that the contamination level in the area differs from that of the city.

(ii) H_0: The earth in the second area has the same contamination level as the city, $p = 0.15$.
H_1: The earth in the second area has a greater contamination level than the city, $p > 0.15$.
$P(X \geqslant 5) = 0.0987 > 5\%$ (1-tailed test) so accept H_0, there is insufficient evidence to say that the contamination level in the area exceeds that of the city.

4 (i) H_0: 20% of athletes are taking the banned substance, $p = 0.2$.
H_1: A different percentage of athletes are taking the banned substance, $p \neq 0.2$.
The critical region is $X = 0$ and $X \geqslant 8$, since $P(X = 0) = 0.0180 < 2.5\%$, $P(X \leqslant 1) = 0.0990 > 2.5\%$, $P(X \geqslant 8) = 0.0163 < 2.5\%$ and $P(X \geqslant 7) = 0.0513 > 2.5\%$.

(ii) (a) 0 is in the critical region so accept H_1, the evidence suggests the proportion in the meeting taking the banned substance differs from 20%.

(b) 6 is not in the critical region so accept H_0, there is insufficient evidence to say that the proportion in the meeting taking the banned substance differs from 20%.

(iii) A 1-tailed test with H_1: $p < 0.2$ would make better sense as what the organisers would, no doubt, want to show is that the newspaper is *exaggerating* the problem.

5 (i) H_0: The magazine's claim is correct, $p = 0.6$.
H_1: The magazine's claim is incorrect, $p \neq 0.6$.
$P(X \leqslant 8) = 0.0565 > 2.5\%$ so accept H_0, there is insufficient evidence to dispute the magazine's claim.

(ii) The result is less reliable as the sample is biased by time and place. The fact that it is rush hour might lead more drivers to jump the lights, enhancing significance.

(iii) (a) H_0: 60% of female drivers stop at amber lights, $p = 0.6$.
H_1: The percentage of female drivers stopping at amber lights differs from 60, $p \neq 0.6$.
$P(X \leqslant 3) = 0.0548 > 2.5\%$ so accept H_0, the evidence is consistent with the hypothesis that 60% of female drivers stop at traffic lights.

(b) H_0: 40% of male drivers stop at amber lights, $p = 0.4$.
H_1: The percentage of male drivers stopping at amber lights differs from 40, $p \neq 0.4$.
$P(X \leqslant 2) = 0.1673 > 2.5\%$ so accept H_0, the evidence is consistent with the hypothesis that 40% of male drivers stop at traffic lights.

(c) H_0: 50% of drivers stop at amber lights, $p = 0.5$.
H_1: The percentage of drivers stopping at amber lights differs from 50, $p \neq 0.5$.
$P(X \leqslant 5) = 0.0207 < 2.5\%$ so accept H_1, the evidence does not support the hypothesis that 50% of drivers stop at traffic lights.

6 (i) $P(X \leqslant 3) = 0.0049 < 2.5\%$ so accept H_1, there is sufficient evidence to suggest there has been a change in the proportion intending to vote 'Yes'.

(ii) $P(X \geqslant 8) = 0.1018 > 5\%$ (1-tailed test) so accept H_0, there is insufficient evidence to suggest there has been a change in the proportion of undecided voters.

7 (i) $\frac{2}{3}$

(ii) (a) 0.2143 **(b)** 0.3816

(iii) 0.9919

(iv) H_0: $p = \frac{2}{3}$.
H_1: $p \neq \frac{2}{3}$.

(v) The critical region is $X \leqslant 6$ and $X \geqslant 14$, since
$P(X \leqslant 6) = 0.0308 < 5\%$,
$P(X \leqslant 7) = 0.0882 > 5\%$,
$P(X \geqslant 14) = 0.0194 < 5\%$ and
$P(X \geqslant 13) = 0.0794 > 5\%$.

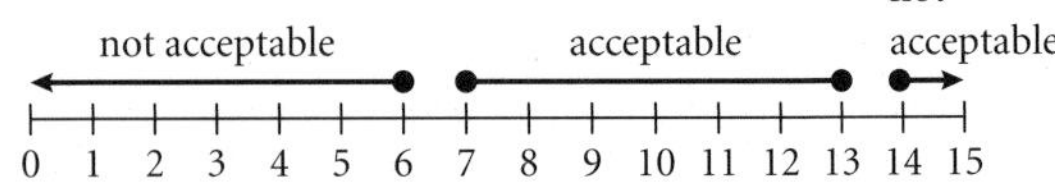

8 (i) H_0: The rainfall still exceeds 60 cm in 5% of months, $p = 0.05$.
H_1: The frequency of monthly rainfall over 60 cm has altered, $p \neq 0.05$.
$P(X \geqslant 3) = 0.0196 < 2.5\%$ so accept H_1, Ingrid's claim that weather patterns have changed is validated.

(ii) (a) $P(X = 0) = 0.5404 > 2.5\%$ so there is no lower (left-hand) critical value.

(b) Let n = smallest sample size. We require $0.95^n < 0.025$, i.e. $n \geqslant 72$ so the smallest sample size is 72.

(iii) The assumption of 'independence' is incorrect.

(iv) Design an experiment based on a sample of future sample data so that it is predictive, and covering a time period of at least 72 months.

Chapter 8

? (page 204)

Given that $\lambda = 0.6$,
the probability of no accidents $= e^{-0.6} = 0.5488$.
The probability of one accident $= 0.6e^{-0.6} = 0.3293$, and so on.
The expected frequency figures are the result of multiplying the probability by the number of days, 720.
So the expected number of days on which there are no accidents is $0.5488 \times 720 = 395.1$, the expected number of days on which there is one accident is $0.3293 \times 720 = 237.1$, and so on.

? (page 204)

The table gives the actual and the expected frequencies.

Number of accidents per day	0	1	2	3	4	5	>5
Actual frequency	395	235	73	17	0	0	0
Expected frequency (1 d.p.)	395.1	237.1	71.1	14.2	2.1	0.3	0

The fit seems to be very close and so the use of the Poisson distribution to model this situation is reasonable.

Activity (page 205)

Occurrences	0	1	2	3
Probability (4 d.p.)	0.0821	0.2052	0.2565	0.2138

❓ (page 206)

To find the probability of there being exactly five accidents in any night you look up the probability of there being five or fewer accidents and subtract it from the previous entry in the table, which is the probability of their being four or fewer accidents.
From the tables the probability of exactly five accidents is $1.0000 - 0.9996 = 0.0004$.
Using the formula the probability of exactly five accidents is $\frac{0.6^5}{5!}e^{-0.6} = 0.0004$ to 4 d.p.

Activity (page 206)

The probabilities will the same as in the table for the activity on page 205.

❓ (page 207)

The probability of no mistakes $= e^{-1.5} = 0.2231$.
The probability of more than two mistakes
$= 1 - \text{P}(0, 1 \text{ or } 2 \text{ mistakes})$
$\text{P(no mistakes)} = e^{-1.5} = 0.2231$
$\text{P(1 mistake)} = 1.5 \times e^{-1.5} = 0.3347$
$\text{P(2 mistakes)} = \frac{1.5^2}{2} \times e^{-1.5} = 0.2510$
So
$\text{P}(0, 1 \text{ or } 2 \text{ mistakes}) = 0.2231 + 0.3347 + 0.2510 = 0.8088$
So $\text{P(more than 2 mistakes)} = 1 - 0.8088 = 0.1912$

Exercise 8A (page 207)

1 $\lambda = 1.8$
(i) 0.1653 **(ii)** 0.2975
(iii) 0.2678 **(iv)** 0.1607
(v) 0.1087

2 $\lambda = 2.2$
(i) 0.1108 **(ii)** 0.2438
(iii) 0.2681 **(iv)** 0.1967
(v) 0.1081 **(vi)** 0.0725

3 $\lambda = 3.5$
(i) 0.0302 **(ii)** 0.1849
(iii) 0.2746

4 $\lambda = 2.9$
(i) 0.0550 **(ii)** 0.1596
(iii) 0.2314 **(iv)** 0.2236
(v) 0.3304

5 $\lambda = 4$
(i) **(a)** 0.0183 **(b)** 0.0733
(c) 0.1465 **(d)** 0.1954
(ii) 0.2149

6 $\lambda = 1$
(i) 0.0613 **(ii)** 0.0190

7 $\lambda = 1.9$
P(0 raisins) = 0.1496
P(1 raisin) = 0.2841
P(2 raisins) = 0.2700
P(3 raisins) = 0.1710
The greatest probability is for $r = 1$ so the most likely number of raisins in a bun is 1.

8 **(i)** The argument assumes that only one particle would ever be found in 1 kg of the molten glass.
(ii) Assuming that the particles occur randomly and independently of each other, then a Poisson model is appropriate with $\lambda = 0.2$.
Then $\text{P}(X \geqslant 1) = 1 - \text{P}(X = 0)$
$= 1 - 0.8187$
$= 0.1813$
So the expected percentage of faulty 1 kg bottles is 18.1% to 3 s.f.

9 $\lambda = 1.5$
(i) P(0 demands) = 0.2231, so in 100 days you would expect there to be 22 with no demands.
(ii) P(more than 2 demands) $= 1 - 0.8088$
$= 0.1912$,
so in 100 days you would expect there to be 19 with more than 2 demands, meaning that there will be 1 or more demands not met.

❓ (page 212)

Points to consider when deciding whether or not the goals scored in a match are independent of each other or not are whether a team is encouraged or demoralised by goals being scored for or against them and whether that changes the probability of another goal being scored.

Exercise 8B (page 213)

1 **(i)** Mean = 0.8, variance = 0.776
(ii) It may be assumed that the bacteria occur randomly and independently.
(iii) **(a)** 0.4493
(b) 0.0014

2 **(i)** Mean = 2.3, variance = 2.23
(ii) The conditions are that the accidents should be random and independent and it is reasonable to assume that these conditions are satisfied.

(iii) 0.0838

So the answer is no (just!).

3 (i)

Number of customers	Frequency
0	13
1	13
2	8
3	5
4	1

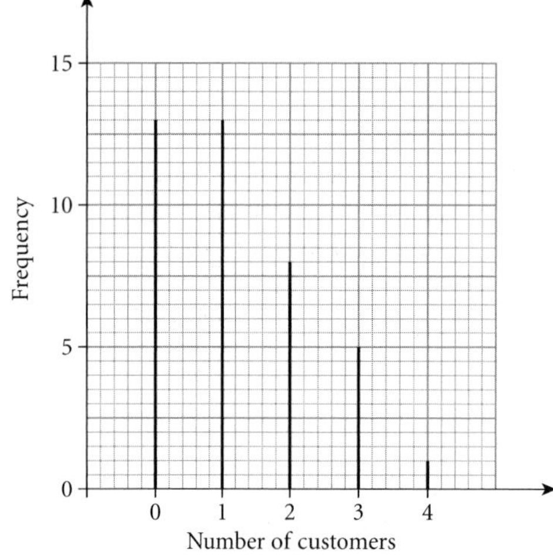

(ii) Mean = 1.2, variance = 1.24

(iii) Take $\lambda = 1.2$

Number of customers	Probability	Expected frequency
0	0.3012	12
1	0.3614	14
2	0.2169	9
3	0.0867	3
4	0.0261	1

There is close agreement except that expected frequencies do not sum to 40.

4 (i) Mean = 1.4, variance = 1.42

(ii) Defective components can reasonably be expected to occur randomly, independently and with a constant probability. Also the mean and the variance are close.

(iii) 0.0143

5 (i) The mean is 0.2 and the variance = 0.234, which are close so the Poisson distribution could be expected to provide a good model. However, the main assumption is that the accidents recorded are random and independent and this may not be so as accidents may involve more than one person.

(ii) (a) 0.001

(b) P(no accidents in a week) = 0.8187.

So P(no accidents in 8 consecutive weeks) $= 0.8187^8 = 0.2$

6 Mean = 7, variance = 6.92

Since the mean and the variance are close and on the assumption that the occurrence of the corpuscles in each compartment was random and independent, a Poisson distribution is a good model.

Expected numbers (to 1 d.p.) = 1.4, 3.3, 5.8, 8.2

7 (i) Mean = 51.3, variance = 1.168

The mean is very different from the variance so a Poisson distribution is not suitable.

(ii) Mean excluding regular commuters = 1.3, variance = 1.168

The mean and the variance are now close in value and so a Poisson model with $\lambda = 1.3$ may be used.

(iii) Bus is full if the number of passengers is 50 regulars + 4.

P(number of non-regular passengers is greater than 4) = 0.0107

? (page 216)

The two orders could arise as:

0 by telephone and 2 online

or 1 by telephone and 1 online

or 2 by telephone and 0 online.

So to find the probability of two orders you add the three probabilities, each of which is the result of multiplying two probabilities.

Exercise 8C (page 217)

1 (i) 0.0067 **(ii)** 0.0337 **(iii)** 0.0843

2 $\lambda_z = \lambda_x + \lambda_y = 3 + 1.3 = 4.3$

(i) 0.0136 **(ii)** 0.1663

3 $\lambda_z = \lambda_A + \lambda_B = 1.3 + 1.6 = 2.9$

(i) 0.0287

(ii) The occurrence of type *A* corpuscles and the occurrence of type *B* corpuscles are independent and random.

4 $\lambda_C = 2.7, \lambda_T = 1.5, \lambda_D = \lambda_C + \lambda_T = 2.7 + 1.5 = 4.2$

(i) P(1 cup of coffee is sold) = 0.1815

P(1 cup of tea is sold) = 0.3347

P(1 of each is sold) = $0.1815 \times 0.3347 = 0.0607$

(ii) 0.1322 **(iii)** 0.2469

5 (i) 0.0996 **(ii)** 5.5

(iii) (a) 0.0041 **(b)** 0.0884

6 $\lambda_T = \lambda_B + \lambda_P = 2 + 1.5 = 3.5$

(i) 0.0302 **(ii)** 0.1424

7 $\lambda_N = 5.0, \lambda_S = 3.0, \lambda_T = \lambda_N + \lambda_S = 5.0 + 3.0 = 8.0$

(i) 0.0067 **(ii)** 0.1912

(iii) 0.8088 **(iv)** 0.1222

8 (i) 0.2

(ii) (a) 0.8187 **(b)** 0.1638 **(c)** 0.0175

(iii) 240 000

(iv) (a) 0.2466 **(b)** 0.2417

Activity (page 220)

B(10 000, 0.0002)

Number of cases	Probability by binomial	Probability by Poisson
0	0.1353	0.1353
1	0.2707	0.2707
2	0.2707	0.2707

B(100 000, 0.000 02)

Number of cases	Probability by binomial	Probability by Poisson
0	0.1353	0.1353
1	0.2707	0.2707
2	0.2707	0.2707

Exercise 8D (page 222)

1 (i) (a) P(0 faulty items) = 0.0052

P(3 faulty items) = 0.1386

(b) P(0 faulty items) = 0.0067

P(3 faulty items) = 0.1403

(ii) The corresponding values are reasonably close so the use of the Poisson distribution to approximate the binomial distribution could be appropriate if accuracy was not critical.

(iii) (a) P(0 faulty items) = 0.0066

P(3 faulty items) = 0.1402

(b) P(0 faulty items) = 0.0067

P(3 faulty items) = 0.1403

(iv) The values here are much closer; the smaller value for p and the greater value for n means that the approximation is valid.

2 0.0166

3 (i) The mean is a reasonable number and it is not possible to determine n or p.

(ii) (a) 0.5340

(b) 0.1007

(iii) $\lambda = 3 \times 2.8 = 8.4$

P(fewer than 3 accidents) = 0.0100

P(more than 15 accidents) = 0.0125

4 0.3840

5 (i) $p = 0.025$, $n = 300$ gives $np = 7.5$

It can be assumed that, when selected, they will be random and independent.

(ii) 0.6218

6 (i) Random, independent events, n large and p small.

(ii) 0.3679

(iii) 0.6321

(iv) 600

(v) 0.5768

(vi) Because part **(iii)** asks for the probability of at least one per day while part **(v)** asks for at least three in three days which allows for none in up to two days.

7 (i) $\lambda = 3$

(ii) (a) 0.0498 **(b)** 0.1991

(c) 0.4232 **(d)** 0.6472

(iii) $P(X \leqslant 5) = 0.9161$

$P(X \leqslant 6) = 0.9665$

So six spares should be carried.

8 (i) $\lambda = 2$

(a) 0.1353 **(b)** 0.5940

(ii) $\lambda = 2$ so same answers.

9 (i) $\lambda = 100 \times 0.02 = 2$ so

P(recruiting at least 1 person) = 0.8647

(ii) $\lambda = 200 \times 0.02 = 4$ so

P(recruiting at least 1 person) = 0.9817

(iii) Require $P(X \geqslant 1) = 1 - P(X = 0) \geqslant 0.99$

$\Rightarrow P(X = 0) \leqslant 0.01$.

From tables you can see that this is when $\lambda = 4.59$.

Since $\lambda = np$ and p is given as 0.02,

$4.59 = 0.02n$

so $n = 229.5$.

He must ask 230 people.

Chapter 9

The answers given in this chapter have been calculated using the Normal distribution table with the z value rounded to 3 decimal places. If you have used a graphic calculator, there may be a slight difference in your answers.

? (page 225)

$$\frac{11.1 - 7.18}{1.21} = 3.240 \text{ standard deviations}$$

❓ (page 228)

Go to row 1.7, column 0.05 then look in column 6 in the right-hand section headed (*add*).
So $\Phi(1.756) = 0.9599 + 0.0005 = 0.9604$.

❓ (page 228)

(i) 0.9893 **(ii)** 0.9850 **(iii)** 0.9729

❓ (page 235)

The shaded area in the diagram below represents $P(Z > z)$.

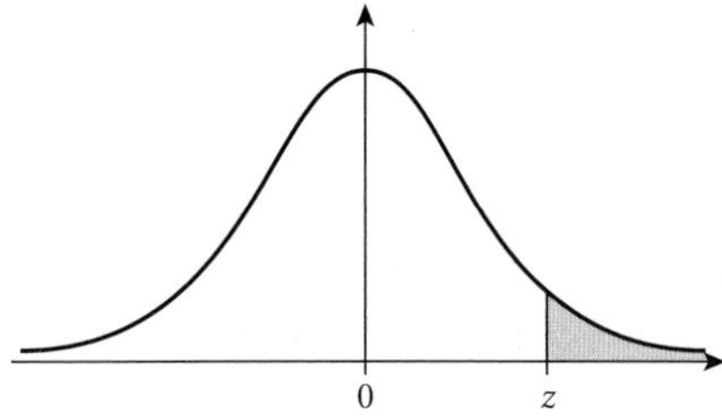

The shaded area in the diagram above is the same as the total area under the curve minus the shaded area, as shown in the diagram below.

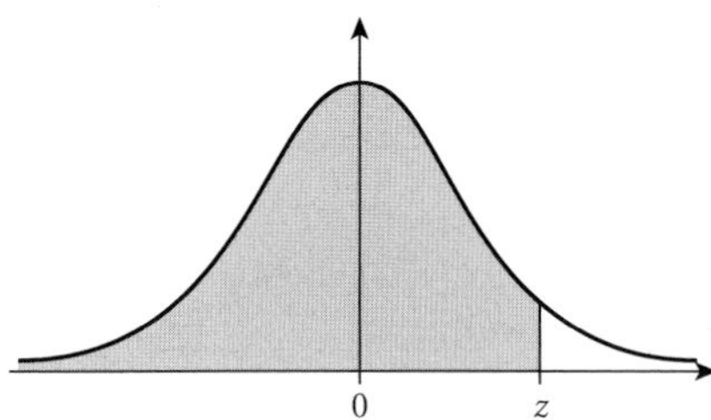

That is $P(Z > z) = 1 - \Phi(z)$.

The shaded area in the diagram below is $\Phi(-z)$.

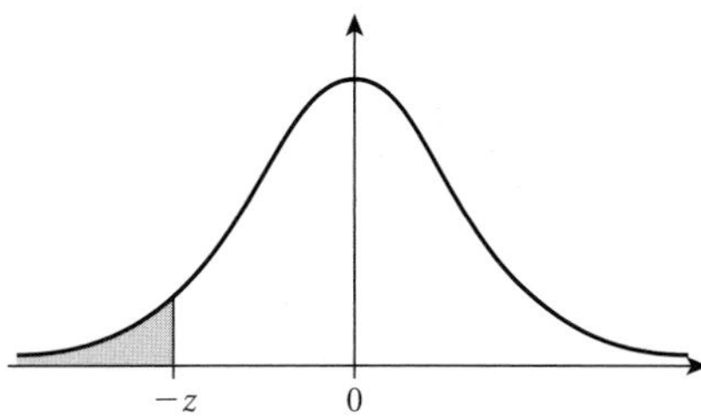

By symmetry, the shaded area in the diagram above is the same as the shaded area in the diagram below.

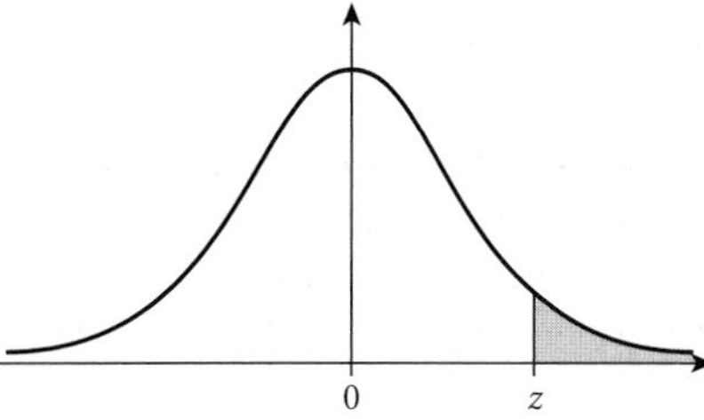

So, using the previous result, $\Phi(-z) = 1 - \Phi(z)$.

❓ (page 238)

Look in the main body of the Normal distribution table for 0.75.
It is in row 0.6 and lies between 0.07 and 0.08.
$\Phi(0.67) = 0.7486$
$\Phi(0.68) = 0.7517$
Use the values in the right-hand part of the table to find the value of the third decimal place.
$\Phi(0.674) = 0.7499$
$\Phi(0.675) = 0.7502$
So the answer lies between 0.674 and 0.675. As the probabilities in the table are given to 4 decimal places, there will be small rounding errors, so it is not possible to give the answer to more than 3 decimal places, in this case 0.674.
Using a table which has more decimal places, the answer given is 0.674 490 which is consistent with the value of 0.674 above and of 0.6745 from the inverse Normal table.

Exercise 9A (page 240)

1 **(i)** 0.7257 **(ii)** 0.1151
(iii) 0.1587 **(iv)** 0.9192
(v) 0.2638 **(vi)** 0.6006
(vii) 0.3087

2 **(i)** 0.0228 **(ii)** 257.4 g
(iii) 253.8 g **(iv)** 0.6826 or 68.26%

3 **(i)** 88.78 **(ii)** 36.13
(iii) 8.20 lb **(iv)** 6.16 lb
(v) 1.63 lb

4 **(i)** 0.6812 or 68.12% **(ii)** 0.2402 or 24.02%
(iii) 0.2758 or 27.58% **(iv)** 9.62

5 **(i)** 0.3050 **(ii)** 0.0934
(iii) 0.3299 **(iv)** 0.7569
(v) 73.47 **(vi)** 6.745 kg

6 **(i)** **(a)** 0.2523 **(b)** 0.3696
(c) 0.2073
(ii) **(a)** 1803 hours **(b)** 2000 hours
(c) 2030 hours

7 **(i)** 11.65 cm **(ii)** 25.0%

8 **(i)** 16.85 minutes **(ii)** 35.1%

9 $\mu = 487$ g, $\sigma = 18.0$ g

10 $\mu = 1023$ hours, $\sigma = 49.3$ hours

11 **(i)** $\mu = 1.84$ m **(ii)** 1.98 m

12 Mean = 15, variance = 35.2

13 **(i)** 187.5 cm **(ii)** $\frac{0.0062}{0.2} = 0.031$

14 Distinction: 83 and over
Merit: 72 to 82
Pass: 62 to 71
Fail: 70 or less

15 **(i)** 0.1056
(ii) 7.57 am

16 **(i)** 24.6%
(ii) 59.9%
(iii) 25.2%
New mean weight = 424.4 grams

17 $\mu + 0.4399\,\sigma = 20.06$
$\mu - 1.175\,\sigma = 20.02$
$\mu = 20.0491$ cm, $\sigma = 0.0248$ cm
Proportion measuring 20.03 cm or more = 0.779
Percentage rejected as being outside the acceptable range = 22.7%

18 Small: 226.6, medium: 614.7, large: 158.7
New mean weight = 47.7 grams
Percentage increase in the number of small eggs = 10.2%

? (page 245)

For 30% to be heavyweight, $\Phi(z) = 0.7$, so $z = 0.5244$.

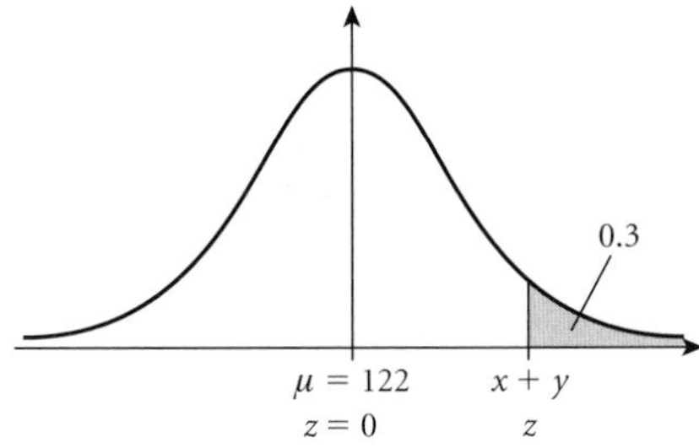

If $z = 0.5244$
then $x + y = 122 + 0.5244 \times 6.403$
$= 125.4$

For 30% to be lightweight, $\Phi(z) = 0.3$, so $\Phi(-z) = 0.7$.
Therefore, $-z = 0.5244$ and $z = -0.5244$.

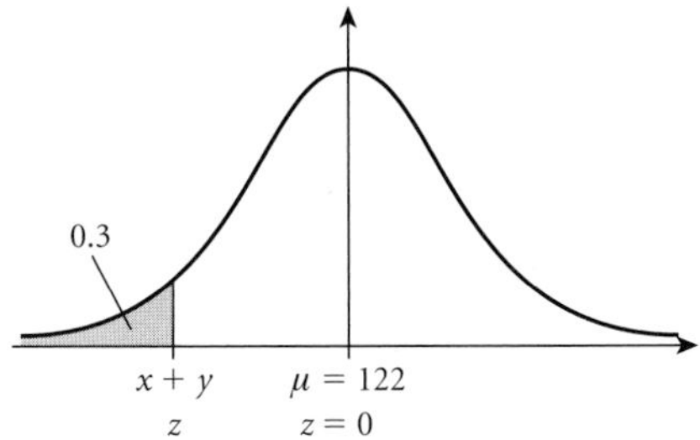

If $z = -0.5244$
then $x + y = 122 - 0.5244 \times 6.403$
$= 118.6$

So the categories should be as follows.
Heavyweight: combined weight greater than 125.4 kg
Lightweight: combined weight less than 118.6 kg.
Middleweight: combined weight between 118.6 kg and 125.4 kg

Exercise 9B (page 251)

1 **(i)** 0.2964 **(ii)** 0.7363
(iii) 0.2703 **(iv)** 0.2073

2 0.0228

3 **(i)** 0.7414 **(ii)** 0.9054

4 **(i)** Mean = 215 g,
standard deviation = $\sqrt{73} = 8.544$ g
(ii) 0.0490

5 P(volume < 0.450) = 0.0401
(i) 0.4593 **(ii)** 0.003 01

6 **(i)**

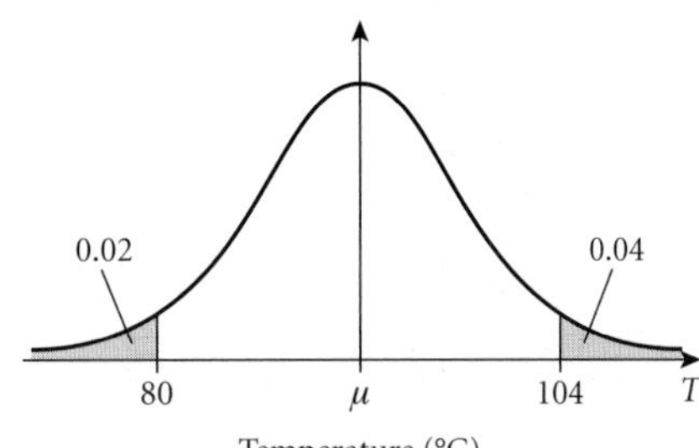

(ii) $\mu = 92.96°$, $\sigma = 6.307°$
(iii) 0.1672 or 16.72% **(iv)** 81.2 °C

7 **(i)**

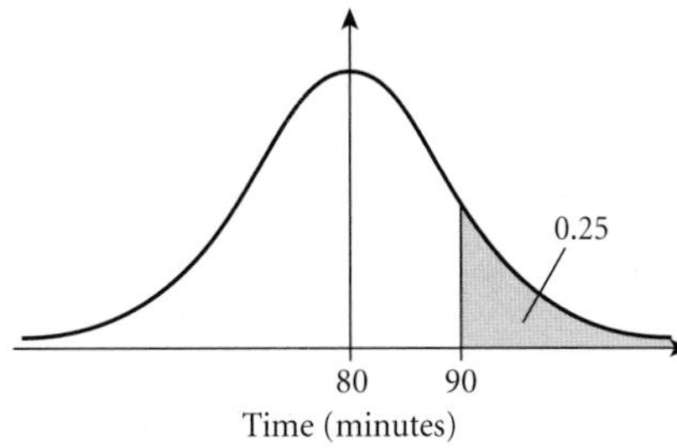

Mean = 80 minutes,
standard deviation = 14.83 minutes
(ii) 0.0038
(iii) 4 pm is only 60 minutes before the play centre closes but the mean length of stay is 80 minutes.
(iv) Assuming that 95% of the lengths of stay are to be satisfied, the latest time of arrival should be 3.15 pm

Chapter 10

? (page 254)

The hospital would be unlikely to be able to operate if everyone refused to go into one of its four wards so it would seem to be irresponsible to suggest that people refuse to use it. On the other hand, if it is genuinely the case that one ward is dangerous then people should be warned about it.

e (page 255)

In most tests the test statistic can take values that are greater or less than a central value and so there are two possible tails. This is not, however, the case with the χ^2 test. The extreme case is that the data fit perfectly and the test statistic, X^2, is a measure of how far the data are away from this ideal in whatever direction. It does not distinguish between cases where the frequency in a particular group is higher than expected, or lower. So, 1-sided is a more appropriate description of the test than 1-tailed.

? (page 258)

The largest entry comes from the Starr ward for infections. Looking at the data shows that the reason for this is that this ward has fewer infections than would be expected.

Exercise 10A (page 260)

In all the questions in this exercise, the null and alternative hypotheses have the same form.
H_0: There is no association between the variables.
H_1: There is an association between the variables.

1 $X^2 = 1.98$, $\nu = 1$ (Yates' correction not used)
Since $2.38 < 3.841$, H_0 is accepted at the 5% significance level.
There is no difference in responses in busy and quiet streets.

2 $X^2 = 12$, $\nu = 1$ (Yates' correction not used)
Since $12 > 6.635$, H_0 is rejected at the 1% significance level.
The evidence supports the hypothesis that there is an association between the sex of a bat and the probability that it has stripes.

3 $X^2 = 19.51$, $\nu = 2$
Since $19.51 > 10.60$, H_0 is rejected at the 0.5% significance level.
The evidence supports the hypothesis that there is an association between the living conditions of hens and the fertility of their eggs.

4 $X^2 = 14.71$, $\nu = 2$
Since $14.71 > 5.991$, H_0 is rejected at the 5% significance level.
The evidence supports the hypothesis that there is a difference between the effectiveness of the two drugs.

5 $X^2 = 1.485$, $\nu = 2$
Since $1.485 < 4.605$, H_0 is accepted at the 10% significance level.
The evidence does not support the hypothesis that there is an association between asthma and how close you live to electricity pylons.

6 **(i)** $X^2 = 37.42$, $\nu = 2$
Since $37.42 > 10.60$, H_0 is rejected at the 0.5% significance level.
The evidence supports the theory that speed cameras affect drivers' subsequent speed.

(ii) The cells relating to serious speeding have the largest effect. The data support Councillor Smith's view.

7 $X^2 = 8.10$, $\nu = 2$
Since $8.10 > 5.991$, H_0 is rejected at the 5% significance level.
The evidence supports the hypothesis that there is an association between attitudes and professional status.

8 **(i)** $X^2 = 18.52$, $\nu = 4$
Since $18.52 > 9.488$, H_0 is rejected at the 5% significance level.
The evidence supports the hypothesis there is an association between smoking habits and attitudes to smoking in restaurants.

(ii) Those who have never smoked.

(iii) Those who have given up smoking and are against smoking in restaurants.
Those who have given up smoking and are in favour of smoking in restaurants.
Current smokers who are in favour of smoking in restaurants.

(iv) The strongest reactions, for or against, come from those who have experienced smoking. Among those who have given up, more than would be expected are against smoking in restaurants and fewer than expected are in favour. The opposite is true among current smokers; more than would be expected are in favour of smoking in restaurants and fewer than expected are against.

9 $X^2 = 12.27$, $\nu = 8$
Since $12.27 < 13.36$, H_0 is accepted at the 10% significance level.
The evidence does not support the hypothesis that there are differences between the composition of lion groups at different locations.

? (page 263)

Jasmine has written down 16 numbers, two for each of the eight interviewers.
She did not need them all. (She only needs 8 of them.)

Activity (page 264)

You can fill in eight numbers freely but you have no choice for the remaining seven if you are to obtain the correct row and column totals. So there are 8 degrees of freedom.
For an $m \times n$ table there are $(m - 1) \times (n - 1)$ degrees of freedom. The number of cells over which you have no choice is given by $m + n - 1$.

? (page 264)

There are seven restrictions.
At first sight it might seem that there should be eight, one for each of the three row totals and one for each of the five column totals. However one restriction is lost since the total of the row totals and the total of the column totals are the same. So the number of restrictions is $8 - 1 = 7$.

Exercise 10B (page 265)

1 (i) 8 **(ii)** 7

2 3
The degrees of freedom
= number of groups − number of restrictions.
There are four groups. There is one restriction, the row total.

3 (i) 25 **(ii)** 15 **(iii)** 10

4 (i) (a) 3
(b) 1
(c) The total number of replies (100)
(ii) (a) 2
(b) 2
(c) The total number of replies (100) and the total of the scores ($100 \times 2.4 = 240$)

Investigation (page 266)

(i) (a) 1 **(b)** 2 **(c)** 5
(ii) (a) 1 **(b)** 2 **(c)** 5
(iii) row 3, column 8
(iv) 5 in all: row 1, column 1; row 6, column 3; row 7, column 9; row 8, column 4; row 9, column 6

? (page 267)

Yes, you have to be very careful about linking cause to effect. You can use statistics to judge how unusual it is to have a given number of snake bites in a year (in this case four) but you have to be much more careful in claiming what caused this. There are many possible explanations, only one of which is global warming, and it could just be random variation.

? (page 268)

The expected frequencies are accurate to one decimal place.

? (page 270)

They are the probabilities in the table on page 268.

? (page 270)

The test would be set up as
H_0: $\mu = 1.27$, the situation is as it always was with the mean number of snake bites per year unchanged.
H_1: $\mu > 1.27$, the mean number of snake bites per year has increased.
1-tailed test
The probability of 0.04 is less than 5% so, at the 5% significance level, the null hypothesis is rejected.
However, 0.04 is greater than 1% so, at the 1% significance level, the null hypothesis is accepted.
Although many tests are carried out at the 5% significance level, you should be aware that when the null hypothesis is true, sometimes (1 time in 20) a test at this level will lead you to reject it incorrectly.

? (page 272)

The groups have been combined because otherwise there would be one group, that for six people with the condition, with a very small expected frequency (much less than 5).

? (page 273)

You would expect a bimodal distribution. The sets of people belonging to families without the genetic link would contain few, if any, people with the condition; by contrast the sets of people belonging to families with the genetic link would contain several people with the condition. So you would expect one mode corresponding to few (if any) people with the condition and another corresponding to several with it. This would not be a binomial distribution.

Exercise 10C (page 276)

1 (i) There are two cells and one restriction, the total, so $\nu = 2 - 1 = 1$.

(ii) H_0: The colours are in the stated proportion of 1 : 3.

H_1: The colours are not in the stated proportion of 1 : 3.

$X^2 = 2.4$

Since $2.4 < 3.84$, H_0 is accepted.

The botanist's theory is accepted at the 5% significance level.

2 Expected frequencies: T_1 17.5, T_2 35, T_3 17.5

H_0: The model applies.

H_1: The model does not apply.

$X^2 = 27.03$, $\nu = 2$

Since $27.03 > 5.991$, H_0 is rejected at the 5% significance level.

The evidence does not support the model.

3 (i) All three possible outcomes have the same probability of $\frac{1}{3}$.

(ii) H_0: The probabilities are $\frac{1}{3}$ when Peter and Jane play.

H_1: The probabilities are not $\frac{1}{3}$ when Peter and Jane play.

$X^2 = 6.2$, $\nu = 2$

Since $6.2 > 5.991$, H_0 is rejected.

The evidence supports Jane's claim at the 5% significance level.

4 (i) Mean = 2.898, variance = 2.882

These are very close together, supporting a Poisson model.

(ii) H_0: The underlying distribution is Poisson.

H_1: The underlying distribution is not Poisson.

$X^2 = 7.83$, $\nu = 9 - 2 = 7$

(The last two groups are combined)

Since $7.83 < 14.07$, H_0 is accepted.

The data support the Poisson model at the 5% significance level.

5 (i) 148, 252

(ii) H_0: There is no change in the level of support for the Green Party.

H_1: There is a change in the level of support for the Green Party.

$X^2 = 3.47$, $\nu = 1$

Since $3.47 < 3.84$, H_0 is accepted.

At the 5% significance level, the evidence does not support the view that there has been a change of support for the Green Party.

6 (i) H_0: The proportions in the different grades are the same as those specified.

H_1: The proportions in the different grades are different from those specified.

(ii)

Grade	Number of apples
A	72.5
B	95.0
C	67.5
D	15.0

(iii) $X^2 = 2.997$, $\nu = 3$

Since $2.997 < 7.815$, H_0 is accepted.

At the 5% significance level, the evidence suggests there has been no change in the proportions in the different grades.

7 (i) H_0: The proportions of late-running trains in the different months are equal.

H_1: The proportions of late-running trains in the different months are not all equal.

$X^2 = 29.63$, $\nu = 11$

Since $29.63 > 19.68$, H_0 is rejected.

At the 5% significance level, the evidence suggests that there are more delays in some months than others.

(ii) The largest contribution to the value of X^2 comes from October suggesting that leaves on the rails may be a major cause.

8 (i)

Band	Expected number of people in sample, f_e
A	13.6
B	86.4
C1	116.4
C2	84.0
D	64.8
E	34.8
Total	400

(ii) H_0: The proportions in the various bands are the same in Avonford as nationally.
H_1: The proportions in the various bands are not the same in Avonford as nationally.
$X^2 = 39.4$, $\nu = 6 - 1 = 5$
Since $39.4 > 16.75$, H_0 is rejected.
At the 0.5% significance level, the evidence suggests that the proportions of people in the different bands in Avonford are different from the national proportions.

(iii) Avonford has more people in the extreme bands, for example A and E, and fewer in the middle bands.

9 (i) Mean = 1.5, variance = 1.617

(ii) H_0: The distribution is Poisson.
H_1: The distribution is not Poisson.
$X^2 = 3.33$, $\nu = 6 - 2 = 4$ (5, 6, 7 and >7 goals are put together as one group)
Since $3.33 < 9.488$, H_0 is accepted.
At the 5% significance level, the evidence suggests that the distribution is indeed Poisson.

(iii)

Number	0	1	2	3	4	5+
Frequency	69.4	118.0	100.3	56.8	24.2	11.3

(iv) In this case the value of the parameter, 1.7, is given and not calculated from the data.

(v) H_0: The distribution is Poisson with parameter 1.7.
H_1: The distribution is not Poisson with parameter 1.7.
$X^2 = 12.87$, $\nu = 6 - 1 = 5$
Since $12.87 > 11.07$, H_0 is rejected.
The evidence suggests that the distribution is not Poisson(1.7). It seems that the football enthusiast is wrong when he claims that the mean number of goals is 1.7.

10 (i)

Number of children	0	1	2	3	4	5+
Number of households	246.6	345.2	241.7	112.8	39.5	14.3

(ii) H_0: The distribution is Poisson with parameter 1.40.
H_1: The distribution is not Poisson with parameter 1.40.
$X^2 = 32.25$, $\nu = 6 - 1 = 5$
Since $32.25 > 11.07$, H_0 is rejected at the 5% significance level.
The evidence suggests that the distribution is not Poisson(1.40).

11 (i) 94 girls and 86 boys, $p = \frac{94}{180} = 0.522$

(ii)

Group	5G 0B	4G 1B	3G 2B	2G 3B	1G 4B	0G 5B
Frequency, f_e	1.398	6.396	11.704	10.708	4.898	0.896

(iii) He combines the groups to avoid those with small values of f_e to get the following.

Group	5G 0B or 4G 1B	3G 2B	2G 3B	1G 4B or 0G 5B
Frequency, f_e	7.794	11.704	10.708	5.794

This reduces the number of groups, k, to 4. There are two restrictions (the total and the observed probability that a randomly selected student is a girl) so $\nu = k - 2 = 4 - 2 = 2$.

(iv) H_0: The distribution is binomial.
H_1: The distribution is not binomial.
$X^2 = 7.424$, $\nu = 4 - 2 = 2$
Since $7.424 > 5.991$, H_0 is rejected.
The test supports the researcher's theory at the 5% significance level.

(v) The experiment assumed that men and women in general will behave in the same way as 15- and 16-year-old boys and girls who do not know each other. This may very well not be the case.

12 (i) It is reasonable to assume that faults occur at random and with a fixed probability.

(ii) $p = \frac{1}{4}$

(iii) H_0: The distribution is binomial.
H_1: The distribution is not binomial.
$X^2 = 10.22$, $\nu = 6 - 2 = 4$ (5, 6 and $\geqslant 7$ are combined into one group)
Since $10.22 > 9.488$, H_0 is rejected.
At the 5% significance level, the data do not support the theory that the distribution is binomial.

(iv) The frequency is greater in the extreme groups, 0 and 5+, than would be expected for a binomial distribution.

Chapter 11

The answers given in this chapter have been calculated using the Normal distribution table with the z value rounded to 3 decimal places. If you have used a graphic calculator, there may be a slight difference in your answers.

Activity (page 283)

Sample results

Size of the sample (n)	5	10	20	40
Minimum value of the sample means	1.40	1.90	2.15	2.60
Maximum value of the sample means	5.80	5.10	4.70	4.275
Mean of the sample means	3.507	3.492	3.506	3.493
Variance of the sample means	0.589	0.295	0.147	0.073

? (page 283)

The mean is approximately 3.5, regardless of sample size, whereas the variance decreases as the sample size increases.

? (page 284)

See the text following this discussion point on page 284.

? (page 286)

Part **(i)** is dealing with a single element drawn from the parent population whereas part **(ii)** is dealing with a sample mean. Sample means are less spread out than the parent population.

Exercise 11A (page 294)

1 **(i)** **(a)** 0.6304 **(b)** 0.6915 **(c)** 0.3219
(ii) **(a)** 0.9087 **(b)** 0.9772 **(c)** 0.8859

2 **(i)** **(a)** 0.3354 **(b)** 0.3821 **(c)** 0.0975
(ii) **(a)** 0.0446 **(b)** 0.1151 **(c)** 0.2853

3 **(i)** 0.1974 **(ii)** 0.1974 **(iii)** 0.2358

4 0.1103

5 **(i)** $z = -1.917$,
critical values $= \pm 2.326$,
not significant
(ii) $z = 1.771$,
critical value $= 1.645$,
significant
(iii) $z = -2.259$,
critical value $= -2.326$,
not significant
(iv) $z = 2.333$,
critical values $= \pm 2.576$,
not significant

6 H_0: $\mu = 11.6$
H_1: $\mu \neq 11.6$
critical values $= \pm 1.960$,
$z = -2$,
significant, so there has been a change in the breaking strength of this type of thread.

7 H_0: $\mu = 67.2$
H_1: $\mu < 67.2$
$z = -2.236$,
critical value $= -2.326$,
not significant, so the population mean is 67.2 kg.

8 H_0: $\mu = 70$
H_1: $\mu < 70$
At the 5% significance level the critical value is -1.645.
$z = -1.766$,
significant, so these students are worse than expected.

9 H_0: $\mu = 100$
H_1: $\mu \neq 100$
critical values $= \pm 1.960$,
$\bar{x} = 109.875$,
$z = 1.862$,
not significant, so the disease has not affected their IQ scores.

10 H_0: $\mu = 15$
H_1: $\mu \neq 15$
As the sample is large σ can be taken as 1.31.
critical values $= \pm 2.326$,
$z = -2.595$,
significant, so the mean diameter of the ball bearings is not 15 mm.

11 **(i)** H_0: $\mu = 63.2$
H_1: $\mu < 63.2$
(ii) $z = -1.460$
(iii) critical value $= -1.645$
(iv) It is not significant, so the mean height of women in Lancashire is the same as that for England overall.

12 **(i)** H_0: $\mu = 900$
H_1: $\mu > 900$
(ii) $z = 1.654$
(iii) critical value $= 1.645$
(iv) It is significant, so the manufacturer's claim is justified.

13 **(i)** $\bar{x} = 65.96$, $s = 13.67$
(ii) H_0: $\mu = 65$
H_1: $\mu \neq 65$

(iii) As the sample is large σ can be taken as 13.67.
$z = 0.471$,
critical values $= \pm 1.960$,
not significant, so this year's intake is another average group.

14 H_1: $\mu \neq 1$,
critical values $= \pm 1.960$,
$\bar{x} = 0.984$,
$z = -1.789$,
not significant, so the mean is 1 lb.
H_1: $\mu < 1$,
critical value $= -1.645$,
$z = -1.789$,
significant, so customers are (on average) sold underweight steaks.

15 H_0: $\mu = 50$
H_1: $\mu < 50$
At the 5% significance level the critical value is -1.645.
$\bar{x} = 49.7$,
$z = -1.875$,
significant, so there is evidence to support the suspicion.

16 The knowledge that it is a new drug could affect the response.
$\bar{x} = 5.14$,
$s = 2.886$ and, as the sample is large, σ can be taken as 2.886
H_0: $\mu = 6.1$
H_1: $\mu < 6.1$
critical value $= -1.645$,
$z = -2.352$,
significant, so the new drug represents an improvement.

17 (i) H_0: $\mu = 1.73$
H_1: $\mu > 1.73$

(ii) $X \sim N\left(1.73, \frac{0.08^2}{8}\right)$

(iii) $z > 1.645$

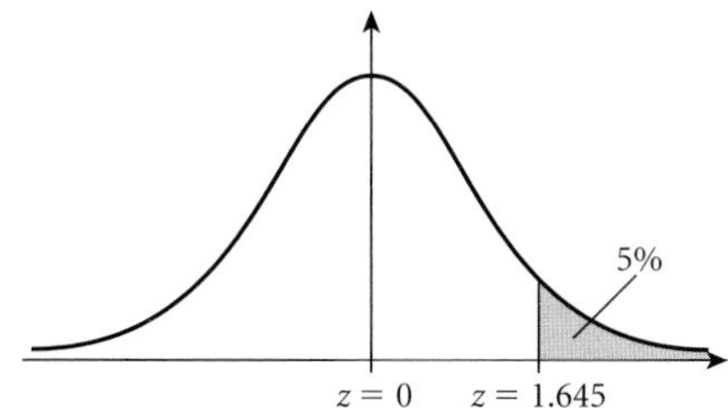

(iv) $z = 1.237$,
not significant, so men who play basketball are the same height as men in general.
Additional assumption: the sample of basketball players is a random sample.

? (page 298)

You would expect the population mean to be close to but not exactly 2.3.

? (page 298)

You would be surprised, and possibly suspicious, if the mean of Richard's sample also turned out to be exactly 2.3. However, it is likely to be quite close to 2.3.
You would probably expect all the means to be quite close together but certainly not all the same.

Exercise 11B (page 304)

1 (i) [0.795, 0.845] **(ii)** [0.787, 0.853]

2 (i) [282.73, 289.84]
(ii) [282.35, 290.22]
(iii) [282.07, 290.51]

3 (i) [0.139, 0.167]
(ii) [0.135, 0.171]

4 As the sample is large you can use $\sigma = 0.13$.
(i) [8.596, 8.644]
(ii) [8.592, 8.648]
(iii) [8.583, 8.657]

5 (i) $\bar{x} = 8.3$ minutes, $s = 2.384$ minutes
(ii) As the sample is large you can use $\sigma = 2.384$.
[7.64, 8.96]

6 (i) [521.6, 524.4] **(ii)** [521.3, 524.7]
(iii) [521.2, 524.8]

7 (i) 67.5 kg **(ii)** 2.37 kg
(iii) [66.7, 68.3]

8 (i) [12.31, 12.89]
(ii) It is likely, as 12.4 lies within the 95% confidence interval.

9 (i) As the sample is large, the value of s^2 can be used as an estimate for σ^2, so an estimate of the variance of the underlying population is 0.004 67.
(ii) [1.113, 1.135] assuming that the sample is a random sample and that, as the sample is large, the distribution of sample means is Normal
(iii) The interpretation given is wrong as the population mean is a *fixed* value; the correct interpretation is that 'the probability is 0.90 that the interval [1.113, 1.135] contains the actual population mean'.
(iv) It appears that the target of 1.136 litres is *not* being met as 1.136 does not lie within the 90% confidence interval.

10 $n \geqslant 54$,
$z = -1.606$,
critical value $= -2.326$,
not significant, so accept H_0 that the mean weight is 1 kg.

11 **(i)** As the sample is large, the value of s^2 can be used as an estimate for σ^2, so an estimate of the variance of the underlying population is 0.4268.
(ii) $\bar{x} = 3.768$, [3.644, 3.892]

12 **(i)** As the sample is large, the value of s^2 can be used as an estimate for σ^2, so an estimate of the variance of the underlying population is 0.126.
(ii) $\bar{x} = 9.82$, [9.77, 9.87] assuming that the sample is a random sample and that, as the sample is large, the distribution of sample means is Normal
(iii) A 95% confidence interval is an interval, based on a random sample, in which the probability is 0.95 that the interval contains the actual population mean.
(iv) **(a)** It is not reasonable to suppose that the mean of the underlying population is 10 litres as 10 does not lie within the confidence interval [9.77, 9.87].
(b) It is reasonable to suppose that the mean of the underlying population is 9.8 litres as 9.8 lies within the confidence interval [9.77, 9.87].

13 **(i)** As the sample is large, the value of s^2 can be used as an estimate for σ^2, so an estimate of σ^2 is 75.
(ii) H_0: $\mu = 0$
H_1: $\mu \neq 0$
critical values $= \pm 1.960$,
$z = 2.191$,
significant, so machine is not correctly calibrated.
(iii) [0.316, 5.684]

Chapter 12

The answers given in this chapter have been calculated using the t distribution table. If you have used a graphic calculator, there may be slight differences in your answers.

? (page 308)

It is difficult to make any judgement without further analysis – the purpose of this chapter.

? (page 312)

In the Normal distribution table 2.326 appears opposite 0.99, so there is 1% at the right-hand tail. As the t distribution table is 2-tailed, the 1% has to be doubled, so 2.326 appears under 2%.

? (page 313)

In order to get 5% for the left-hand tail you have to look up 10% in the t distribution table as it gives the percentage for a 2-tailed test (5% at each end in this case). The degrees of freedom, ν, is $n - 1 = 9$. As it is the left-hand tail you need the negative value.

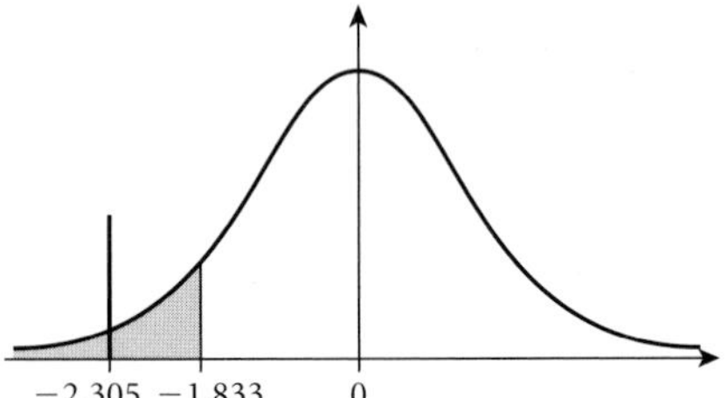

? (page 315)

Unlike the Normal distribution table, you do not have enough information in the t distribution table to enable you to calculate the p value. All you can do is find limits between which it must lie (in this case between 10% and 5%). Many standard computer packages will give you the p value for a t distribution.
As 5.88 is greater than 5, the result is not significant at the 5% significance level, so H_0 is accepted.

Exercise 12A (page 316)

1 **(i)** $\bar{x} = 0.509$, $s^2 = 0.560$
(ii) H_0: $\mu = 0$
H_1: $\mu \neq 0$
$\nu = 9$,
critical values $= \pm 1.833$,
$t = 2.151$,
significant, so mean of population is not zero

2 **(i)** $\bar{x} = 12.7$, $s^2 = 0.0343$
(ii) H_0: $\mu = 12.55$
H_1: $\mu \neq 12.55$
$\nu = 7$,
critical values $= \pm 2.365$,
$t = 2.291$,
not significant, so mean of population is 12.55

3 $H_0: \mu = 0.60$
$H_1: \mu \neq 0.60$
$\nu = 14$,
$t = -2.905$

(i) critical values $= \pm 2.145$,
significant, so there is a change in the setting of the machine

(ii) critical values $= \pm 2.977$,
not significant, so there is no change in the setting of the machine

4 $\bar{x} = 37.2$, $s^2 = 1.7$

(i) $H_0: \mu = 35$
$H_1: \mu > 35$
$\nu = 4$,
critical value $= 3.747$,
$t = 3.773$,
significant, so there has been an increase

(ii) Assume that the sample has been drawn from a Normal population.

5 $H_0: \mu = 1200$
$H_1: \mu < 1200$
$\nu = 11$,
critical value $= -1.796$,
$t = -3.464$,
significant, so mean lifetime of bulbs has decreased

6 $H_0: \mu = 45.0$
$H_1: \mu \neq 45.0$
$\nu = 11$,
critical values $= \pm 2.201$,
$t = 2.896$,
significant, so machine needs to be adjusted
Assumptions: the sample is random and has been drawn from a Normal population.

7 $H_0: \mu = 8.00$
$H_1: \mu > 8.00$
$\nu = 9$,
critical value $= 2.821$,
$t = 3.162$,
significant, so the mean diameter has increased

8 $H_0: \mu = 14.0$
$H_1: \mu > 14.0$
$\bar{x} = 14.98$,
$s^2 = 1.200$,
$\nu = 9$,
critical value $= 1.833$,
$t = 2.829$,
significant, so new diet is an improvement

9 $H_0: \mu = 1000$
$H_1: \mu \neq 1000$
$\bar{x} = 1002\frac{1}{3}$,
$s^2 = 99.25$,
$\nu = 8$,
critical values $= \pm 2.306$,
$t = 0.703$,
not significant, so mean weight for this machine is 1000 g

10 $H_0: \mu = 62$
$H_1: \mu \neq 62$
$\bar{x} = 60.875$,
$s^2 = 5.554$,
$\nu = 7$,
critical values $= \pm 2.365$,
$t = -1.350$,
not significant, so overall mean lateness is 10 minutes
Assume that the sample has been drawn from a Normal population.

11 **(i)** $H_0: \mu = 4$
$H_1: \mu > 4$

(ii) It is a small sample, σ is not known and the population distribution is not known.

(iii) The population distribution is Normal.

(iv) $\bar{x} = 4.4$,
$s^2 = 0.2829$,
$\nu = 7$,
critical value $= 1.895$,
$t = 2.127$,
significant, so supplier is not meeting the stated standard

? (page 319)

(i) 2.776 ($p = 5\%$; $\nu = 4$)

(ii) 2.145 ($p = 5\%$; $\nu = 14$)

(iii) About 2.04 ($p = 5\%$; as $\nu = 29$ is not given directly, use $\nu = 30$ which is very close)

? (page 319)

(i) 2.718 ($p = 2\%$; $\nu = 11$)

(ii) About 1.68 ($p = 10\%$; as $\nu = 49$ is not given directly, use $\nu = 50$ which is very close)

? (page 321)

The alternative hypothesis $H_1: \mu \neq 4.90$ indicates that the mean of the population could be either greater than or less than 4.90, so it is a 2-tailed test.

Exercise 12B (page 322)

1 (i) $\bar{x} = 7.35$, $s^2 = 0.009\,84$

(ii) [7.28, 7.42]

2 (i) $\bar{x} = 36$, $s^2 = 2.857$

(ii) [34.87, 37.13]

3 90% confidence limits: [84.83, 86.37]
98% confidence limits: [84.45, 86.75]
Assumption: The sample is random.

4 (i) $\bar{x} = 14.387$,
$s^2 = 0.0170$,
[14.27, 14.51]
Assumptions: The sample is random and has been drawn from a Normal population.

(ii) 14.25 is not in the confidence interval, so the result is not consistent with the nominal length of the rods being 14.25 cm.

5 (i) $\bar{x} = 19.2$,
$s^2 = 1.671$,
[18.48, 19.92]
Assumptions: The sample is random and has been drawn from a Normal population.

(ii) 95% of the time the confidence interval will include the mean of the population.

6 (i) Possible answer: Give each member a number (starting at 1) and, using random numbers, choose a sample of 10.

(ii) $\bar{x} = 4.74$, $s^2 = 2.738$

(iii) [3.56, 5.92]
Assumptions: The sample is random and has been drawn from a Normal population.

(iv) Increase the sample size; sample size of 14

7 (i) $\bar{t} = 2.36$, $s = 3.060$,
$a = -0.558$, $b = 5.278$
Assumptions: The sample is random and has been drawn from a Normal population.

(ii) This interpretation gives the impression that μ is a variable but it is a fixed (unknown) value.

(iii) As 0 lies within the 90% confidence interval, the commuter's suspicions are not justified; the significance level is 5% (as it is a 1-tailed test).

(iv) The width of the interval will be narrower as the size of the sample is now nine times bigger.

8 (i) H_0: $\mu = 9$
H_1: $\mu > 9$
Assumptions: The sample is random and has been drawn from a Normal population.
$\bar{x} = 9.225$,
$s^2 = 0.0493$,
$\nu = 11$,
critical value = 2.718,
$t = 3.510$,
significant, so the task is taking on average longer than 9 minutes

(ii) [9.084, 9.366]

9 $\bar{x} = 9.15$, $s^2 = 0.249$; [8.748, 9.552]
Assumptions: The sample is random and has been drawn from a Normal population.
For a 95% confidence interval, 95% of the time the confidence interval will include the mean of the population.

10 (i) H_0: $\mu = 23.8$
H_1: $\mu < 23.8$

(ii) $\bar{x} = 23.71$,
$s^2 = 0.0254$,
$\nu = 9$,
critical value = -1.833,
$t = -1.786$,
not significant, so the vitamin content remaining is 23.8 milligrams;
Assumptions: The sample is random and has been drawn from a Normal population.

(iii) [23.60, 23.82]

11 H_0: $\mu = 60.0$
H_1: $\mu > 60.0$
$\bar{x} = 62.54$,
$s^2 = 6.294$,
$\nu = 9$,
critical value = 1.833,
$t = 3.202$,
significant, so the mean yield has increased
Assumptions: The sample is random and has been drawn from a Normal population.
[60.75, 64.33]

12 (i) $\bar{x} = 28.7$, $s^2 = 2.365$

(ii) [27.12, 30.28]

Chapter 13

? (page 327)

The scale of opinions represented by numbers, a rating scale, is an ordered scale where the order has meaning, but the differences between each opinion are not measurable. There are other types of scale where the differences do have meaning. Although it is not sensible to describe a day of 20 °C as being twice as hot as one of 10 °C, the difference in the two temperatures can be measured and has a meaning. This scale is called an interval scale.

If you are measuring snakes you can not only say that one snake is 1 cm longer than another but also describe one snake as being twice, or half, or any ratio of, the length of another. Such a scale is called a ratio scale.
Other examples of ordered scales are where items are judged on merit and placed in order, or where items are grouped, for example, companies placed into one of three groups according to turnover, the three groups being large, medium and small.

? (page 328)

The *t* test needs the assumption that the underlying population is Normally distributed. That is clearly not the case here with a set of responses.

? (page 329)

Not necessarily, provided it is representative of the population being sampled. It is surprising how much research is carried out with small samples, which is what makes the Wilcoxon test so useful. Make a habit of looking for the sample size and, even more importantly, how the sample was chosen when reading any report.

? (page 329)

This is a 1-tailed test because you are only interested in the median being less than 4. If you were interested in it being different from 4, either more or less, it would have been a 2-tailed test.

? (page 335)

Statisticians don't like egg on their face and there is still a possibility, albeit small, that the null hypothesis is not correct. There is only a 5%, or 1 in 20, chance that it is wrong but, by always stating your conclusion with a significance level, you are leaving that possibility open, and your reputation intact. You do not have to stick with a 5% significance level. In some circumstances you might want to be more certain and might go for a 1% significance level.

Exercise 13A (page 336)

1 2-tailed test,
$n = 15$,
$W = W_- = 57.5$,
critical value $= 25$,
accept H_0; the new trainer has made no difference

2 1-tailed test,
$n = 12$,
$W = W_- = 21.5$,
critical value $= 17$,
accept H_0; the student nurses at St Clare's are not consuming more fat than they should

3 1-tailed test,
$n = 16$,
$W = W_- = 27$,
critical value $= 35$,
reject H_0; there are more waders

4 1-tailed test,
$n = 14$,
$W = W_+ = 64.5$,
critical value $= 25$,
accept H_0; listening to Classic FM has not reduced patients' stress levels

5 1-tailed test,
$n = 10$,
$W = W_+ = 10$,
critical value $= 10$,
reject H_0; her staff are taking less than 34 minutes at lunchtimes

6 2-tailed test,
$n = 10$,
$W = W_+ = 8$,
critical value $= 8$,
reject H_0; the rate of pay teenage babysitters receive does not have a median of £6 per hour
1-tailed test,
$n = 10$,
$W = W_+ = 8$,
critical value $= 10$,
reject H_0; the rate of pay teenage babysitters receive has a median of less than £6 per hour

Chapter 14

? (page 341)

It could be. It depends if the companies truly represent the cross-section of local companies and are not just those with the worst (or best) health and safety record.
The first part of the newspaper article is based on one that appeared in the *Independent* a few years ago with the headline 'Illness and accidents cost £16bn a year'. The article followed a detailed government study of illness and accidents at a construction site, a creamery, a transport haulage company, a North Sea oil production platform and an NHS hospital; that is just five companies. The cost of illness and accidents were greatest on the North Sea oil platform, followed by the creamery; they were least in the transport company.

Not all samples are as small. The second part of the article is based on the Self Reported Work Related Illness Survey of 2003/2004 in which 90 000 workers were sampled, but that still only represents 1 in 400 of the total workforce in Great Britain.

? (page 341)

What type of industry or commerce they are engaged in, how many people they employ and how many there are. You can then choose six that represent, as far as possible, the complete picture.

? (page 342)

Possible examples of finite populations include the animals in a zoo, the students in a school, the trees in a wood, the businesses in a town or the machines in a factory.
Possible examples of infinite populations include water in rivers, the air, the bacteria of a certain type, coffee beans in South America, rocks in India.

? (page 345)

'There's no prize for the opinion poll that gets closest to the election result, but from inside a polling company the stakes seem very high,' says Bobby Duffy of Mori. In 2005 they forecast the result based on the voting intentions of 1164 voters, chosen as a representative sample, and did well.

Party	Prediction %	Actual %
Labour	38	36
Conservative	32	32
Liberal Democrats	23	22

www.ipsos-mori.com gives more details of how pre-election polls are carried out.

? (page 346)

Using a control group you can compare the effects of the treatment against non-treatment. By using an appropriate statistical test you can determine whether the results are likely to have occurred just by chance, or otherwise.

? (page 347)

Will it be the left thumb, the right thumb or both. If it is only one thumb, will you measure the right thumb of left-handed people? Where do you start measuring? Top, bottom or middle of joint, or from the wrist. Deciding where to start measuring has a large impact on the measurement. Where will you stop measuring – at the end of the flesh or the end of the nail? What units will you use: centimetres or millimetres? To what degree of accuracy will you be measuring? Have you reliable measuring instruments? Will lots of people be carrying out the survey for you and, if so, will they all be measuring from the same place with the same degree of accuracy?
You get the idea – and that was only thumb sizes.

? (page 347)

Think who you would be most likely to tell the truth to. Most likely it will be an adult who you do not know. Think why people might choose to lie in this situation. Even with an adult they do not know, the truth may not be forthcoming.

? (page 348)

The greatest problem will be getting people to tell the truth. There are ways round this. A bit later in the chapter you will meet the *randomised response technique*, which could be used here.

Investigation (page 348)

You estimate that 40 students answer question H and 40 answer question T.
Of the 40 who answer question T, you estimate that 20 answer Yes.
28 people in total answer Yes, so $28 - 20 = 8$ answer Yes to question H, 'Have you ever smoked cannabis?'
Thus 8 out of the 40, or 20%, who answer question H have smoked cannabis.

Exercise 14A (page 349)

1 Population: all junior hospital doctors.
Sample: junior hospital doctors who work more than 50 hours a week and who have the energy and motivation to write to the national newspaper.
This is a self-selected sample with a vested interested and is unlikely to be representative of all junior hospital doctors.
The size is reasonable.

2 Population: all customers of the town centre shopping complex.
Sample: those using the car park between 09:00 and 16:00 one Wednesday. This sample is not representative as it does not include those normally at work during those hours and who are likely to be customers at the weekend.
Even if the sample were representative, the sample size is rather small; if the staff are going to be at the car park anyway, it would be cost effective to ask more people.

3 Population: all the young people in a particular town. Need to define the age range of 'young'.
Sample: those young people using the local leisure centre.
This sample is likely to be biased as it includes mostly those who visit the leisure centre to exercise and the relatively few who visit to watch or meet people.
The sample size sounds very large for one researcher to cope with. Depending on the size of the town there may not be 2500 different young people using the centre.

4 Population: this is not entirely clear, and the charity may not be clear either. Is it the national adult population or just the adult population of London? It may not be confined to the adult population.
Sample: those whose names appear in the London telephone directories. This will not be representative of the adult population as many people are ex-directory, particularly in London.
The sample size of 200 appears reasonable.

? (page 350)

All three of the samples are equally likely.

? (page 355)

If the business consultant takes a systematic sample of 52 days she will be choosing every seventh day and thus always choosing the same day of the week.

? (page 356)

The third house is always the middle one of a terrace of three, well insulated by the houses on each side.

? (page 356)

As the sample is small, a more representative sample could be obtained by selecting three students from each year group, assuming the year groups are roughly equal in size.

? (page 357)

For a study of smoking habits you might stratify the population by gender or social class but if you were studying mobile phone usage it might be by age.

? (page 357)

There is no sampling frame. Many of the people live in remote communities with little or no contact with the outside world. She would probably choose several such communities, with a suitable geographical spread, visit them, take samples from within them and test these samples for diabetes. In this example the communities are clusters.

? (page 358)

In a random sample there is no bias. Customers would be chosen using some predetermined system so that the probability of picking a particular customer is known. Here the choice of customers to interview is left to the sixth formers. What advantages does it have? It is very simple and quick to operate and there is no problem of non-response, the interviewers just continue to ask people until they have filled their quotas.

? (page 359)

Air pollution data, water table pollution data, dispersal of smoke and soot, effects on local flora and fauna, economic effect, etc.

Exercise 14B (page 360)

1 (i) Population: adult population of Avonford
Variable: opinions
Sample: people interviewed

(ii) (a) People using travel agents tend to be those with higher incomes.

(b) More women than men use supermarkets; if the supermarket is out of town they will be those with cars. Some, more affluent, people have their groceries delivered. Having said that, an appropriate quota sample of supermarket customers is probably not a bad representation of the local population.

(c) Most people coming out of job centres are the unemployed.

(iii) Choose a place where you are likely to find a broad cross-section of the population – a busy high street on a Saturday morning?

2 (i) Population: all hotels in the town
Variable: price of bed and breakfast
Sample: 10 hotels

(ii) Using a random sample will give you a reasonable estimate but, given the numbers of two- and three-star hotels, the sample may well not contain any one-star hotels.

(iii) A more precise estimate would be obtained using a stratified random sample.

3 (i) Population: those eligible to vote in the constituency
Variable: opinions
Sample: people on the electoral roll whose phone numbers were available

(ii) Only those with available phone numbers will be sampled. Many more people these days have ex-directory phone numbers or only have a mobile phone.

(iii) An alternative sample might be to choose small clusters of houses in different socio-economic areas of the constituency to visit and interview all voters in those houses.

4 (i) Population: readers with children
Variable: opinions
Sample: readers who replied

(ii) This is a self-selected sample and, most likely, contains those with strong opinions, so likely to be heavily biased against having children.

(iii) Taking the longer term view, the sample should probably be drawn from over-50s. As no action will follow, an appropriate quota sample taken in a busy town centre would suffice.

5 In a random sample the probability of selecting every possible sample of a given size, and of selecting any member of the population, can be calculated or is known, but the probabilities are not necessarily equal. In a simple random sample every possible sample of a given size is equally likely to be selected from a population. As a consequence of this, every member of the population has an equal chance of being chosen.

6 (i) There are 26 letters in the alphabet. Writing the random numbers in pairs you get 35 33 57 <u>13</u> 29 96 80 32 44 <u>13</u> (ignore) 62 38 53 65 45 59 30 55 99 48 <u>17</u> 23.
A simple random sample of two letters of the alphabet would be the 13th letter, M, and the 17th, Q.

(ii) Writing the random numbers in 3s you get <u>353</u> <u>357</u> 132 996 803 244 136, etc.
The first two students are those numbered 353 and 357.

7 (i) For a simple random sample you need a list of the population. The most appropriate list of adults in Earlsdon is the Electoral Register.

(ii) Selecting 200 households using a simple random sample, does not give every adult an equal chance of being chosen since adults in households containing more than one adult have less chance of being selected.

8 From the table of random numbers, write down the numbers in 3s.
If you start in the top left-hand corner the four numbers less than 224 you obtain are 032, 172, 195 and 141.

9 (i) You could simply number the squares and take a random sample or you could find a random sample of coordinates and use these to identify the squares. (There may be difficulties deciding which square a point is in.)

(ii) Mean number of overcrowded families per square in inner city sampling units is 11.
There are approximately 1964 squares of side 0.2 cm in the inner circle.
Mean number of overcrowded families per square in outer ring is 7. There are approximately 5890 squares of side 0.2 cm in the outer ring.
Estimated total is 63 000 to the nearest 1000.

10 (i) List all the students in the school, allocate each a number and use random numbers to select 10%. Alternatively, use a systematic random sample and choose every 10th person walking through the front door in the morning, having previously used a random number generator to decide on your starting student: first, third, whatever.

(ii) It is possible that there are relatively few sixth formers in the school and that the sample will be over-representative of younger age groups. It is also possible that someone in Year 8, say, is related to a pop star so all of Year 8 are ardent fans of that group. Asking the students as they arrive through the front door may miss those who are very early or very late, or who come in by another entrance.

11 The director should take a stratified sample with factory workers, clerical staff and managerial staff as the three strata, the size of each sample being proportional to the numbers in each group.
There are 600 staff in total, and 500 factory workers so $\frac{500}{600} = \frac{5}{6}$ of the sample should be factory workers.
$\frac{5}{6} \times 120 = 100$ so there should be 100 factory workers in the sample.
There are 70 clerical staff so $\frac{70}{600} = \frac{7}{60}$ of the sample should be clerical staff. $\frac{7}{60} \times 120 = 14$ so there should be 14 clerical staff in the sample.
There are 30 managerial staff, so $\frac{30}{600} = \frac{1}{20}$ of the sample should be managerial staff. $\frac{1}{20} \times 120 = 6$ so there should be 6 managerial staff in the sample.

12 (i) Simple random sample: every elector on the roll has an equal chance of being chosen.

(ii) Not a simple random sample of electors since not all samples of 100 are equally likely to be chosen. The sample is only taken from one road, selected from some or all of the roads in the constituency. It is likely, though not certain, that most people in the same road will have similar voting patterns, which may well not reflect the overall voting intentions of all the electors in the constituency. Such a sample is very likely to invalidate the opinion poll.

(iii) This is a systematic sample. It is not a simple random sample. Nevertheless it is likely to produce a representative sample for the opinion poll.

? (page 366)

If you used a completely randomised design on the ten fields without splitting each one, the amount of variability between one field and another might hide the differences between the yields of the two varieties of strawberry plants. Even if you spilt each field into two plots and then used a completely randomised design, you would have the same problem. You will have less of a problem the more plots each field is split into.

? (page 370)

Read the text that follows this discussion point to discover what actually happened.

Exercise 14C (page 370)

1 There is no control group. It is more than likely that 90% would have recovered within a week even if not given Vitamin C.

2 **(i)** It could be due to differences in the two groups of students; or the different heat in the rooms, or another confounding variable such as the brightness of the light.

(ii) The test would have been better done in the same room.

3 The two identical sets of china should be allocated randomly between the control group and the experimental group, to avoid any hidden differences between the sets.
One dishwasher should be used to avoid differences between machines affecting the outcome.
The washes, of the control group with the old powder or the experimental group with the new, should be allocated randomly.
After the 1000 washes the china should be presented to the assessor in a randomised sequence, the assessor not knowing which china is in the control group.

4 The CD may be of value but there are too many factors at work here for the experiment to be able to tell us much. Most importantly we do not know if the employees used the CD or whether, knowing that they were to retake the test, used a variety of means to ensure that they did better the second time. As it was the same test they could just have learnt the right answers.
A better design would be to pair employees according to perceived mathematical ability and place one of each pair in each of two groups. Before any of them do the test, ask one group to use the CD to help prepare for it. After both groups have taken the test their scores could be compared. It would also be helpful to ask those who used the CD how helpful they felt it had been.

5 To minimise any psychological effect of patients knowing that they are receiving the drug, this should be a blind trial. Because of differences between patients, it should be a paired design with each patient being their own pair. A suggested procedure is that the drug is randomly allocated to half the patients, and the other five patients given an identical-looking placebo, so that no patient knows whether they are receiving the drug or placebo. They are instructed to take the tablets for a month and note the number of migraine attacks. At the end of the month those taking the placebo are given the drug, and vice versa, and the subjects are told to take these for the second month and note the number of attacks as before.
There are two major ethical issues in clinical trials in general. On the one hand you may be deliberately withholding a potentially beneficial treatment from certain patients and, on the other hand, giving a potentially harmful treatment to others. Here the treatment is given to all patients but any treatment can have unknown adverse side effects which these willing volunteers need to be forewarned about.

Chapter 15

? (page 376)

This would indicate that the populations of morning times and of evening times have the same mean.

? (page 377)

The approaches for the single-sample t test and the paired-sample t test are very similar. In the paired-sample t test the variable used is the difference of the two variables that were measured in the sample.

? (page 377)

The data consists of pairs, in this case, married couples.

? (page 378)

The form of the alternative hypothesis, which claims that the difference between the ages of the husbands and wives when they marry is not four years, indicates that a 2-tailed test is appropriate.

? (page 378)

If the test had been significant you would have concluded that the mean difference between the ages of husbands and wives when they marry is not 4 years. You may then decide to go on and do a 1-tailed test.

? (page 379)

This is a reasonable assumption but it is not necessarily the case. In order to check that the differences are Normally distributed you can conduct a test to see whether it is a good fit (see page 267).

Exercise 15A (page 379)

1 H_0: There is, on average, no difference between the performance of Avonford athletes in June and July.
H_1: On average, Avonford athletes are faster in June than in July.
$\bar{d} = -0.4$,
$s = 1.1392$,
1-tailed test,
$\nu = 9$,
critical value $= -1.833$,
$t = -1.110$,
not significant, so no evidence that the athletes are faster in June.
Assumption: the differences are Normally distributed.

2 H_0: There is, on average, no difference between the percentage of impurity as measured by the company and by the supplier.
H_1: On average, there is a difference between the percentage of impurity as measured by the company and by the supplier.
$\bar{d} = 0.04$,
$s = 0.2319$,
2-tailed test,
$\nu = 9$,
critical value $= 2.262$,
$t = 0.5455$,
not significant, it appears that the mean determinations are the same.
Assumption: the differences are Normally distributed.

3 (i) H_0: There is, on average, no difference between the initial weight and the weight after one month.
H_1: On average, the weight after one month is less than the initial weight.
$\bar{d} = 1.422$,
$s = 2.360$,
1-tailed test,
$\nu = 8$,
critical value $= 1.860$,
$t = 1.808$,
not significant, it appears that the weight is unchanged.

(ii) Assumption: the differences are Normally distributed.

4 H_0: There is, on average, no difference between the performance of machine A and machine B.
H_1: On average, there is a difference between the performance of machine A and machine B.
$\bar{d} = 0.725$,
$s = 0.7978$,
2-tailed test,
$\nu = 7$,
critical value $= 2.365$,
$t = 2.57$,
significant, it appears that there is a difference between machines.

5 H_0: There is, on average, no difference between the fuel consumption with the new and the standard tyres.
H_1: On average, the new tyres produce a better fuel consumption.
$\bar{d} = -0.46$,
$s = 0.7199$,
1-tailed test,
$\nu = 9$,
critical value $= -1.833$,
$t = -2.021$,
significant, it appears the consumption is better with the new design of tyre.
Assumption: the differences are Normally distributed.

6 H_0: There is, on average, no difference between the intensity of the reaction before and after therapy.
H_1: On average, the intensity of the reaction after therapy has been reduced.
$\bar{d} = -12.4$,
$s = 17.621$,
1-tailed test,
$\nu = 9$,
critical value $= -1.833$,
$t = -2.225$,
significant, there is evidence that the mean intensity after therapy is lower.
Assumption: the differences are Normally distributed.

7 H_0: There is, on average, no difference between the results using procedure 1 or 2.

H_1: On average, there is a difference between the results using procedure 1 and using procedure 2.

$\bar{d} = 1.8$,

$s = 1.509$,

2-tailed test,

$\nu = 7$,

critical value = 3.499,

$t = 3.374$,

not significant, there is insufficient evidence of a difference between the procedures at the 1% level (but it would have been significant at the 5% level).

? (page 387)

Since the median of the scores without music is 10.5 and the median of the scores with music is 8, the evidence suggests Anita's parents are correct: memory is worse when music is playing.

Exercise 15B (page 387)

1 H_0: There is no difference between the median of the recall of students with no music or with classical music.

H_1: There is a difference between the median of the recall of students.

2-tailed test,

$n = 10$,

$W_+ = 29$, $W_- = 26$,

$W = W_- = 26$,

critical value = 10,

accept H_0; there is no evidence that classical music has an impact on students' recall.

2 H_0: There is no difference between the median amounts of lead before and after traffic calming.

H_1: There is a difference between the median amounts of lead.

2-tailed test,

$n = 10$,

$W_+ = 22.5$, $W_- = 32.5$,

$W = W_+ = 22.5$,

critical value = 8,

accept H_0; there is no evidence that the traffic calming has changed the amount of lead in the air.

3 H_0: There is no difference between the median number of lorries travelling east and west.

H_1: There is a difference between the median number of lorries travelling east and west.

2-tailed test,

$n = 12$,

$W_+ = 52$, $W_- = 26$,

$W = W_- = 26$,

critical value = 13,

accept H_0; there is no evidence that there is a difference in the traffic flows.

4 (i) H_0: There is no difference between the median of weights initially and after one month.

H_1: There is a difference between the median weights, with a reduction after one month. (i.e. There is a positive difference between the medians.)

1-tailed test,

$n = 9$,

$W_+ = 37$, $W_- = 8$,

$W = W_- = 8$,

critical value = 8,

reject H_0; there is evidence that the mean weight has been reduced.

(ii) It is not stated that the differences between the initial weights and the weights a month later are Normally distributed, which is an assumption for a *t* test. The Wilcoxon signed rank test for paired samples is a non-parametric test and does not require the assumption of Normality.

5 H_0: There is no difference between the median level of intensity before and after therapy.

H_1: There is a difference between the median level of intensity, with a reduction after therapy. (i.e. There is a positive difference between the medians.)

1-tailed test,

$n = 10$,

$W_+ = 46$, $W_- = 9$,

$W = W_- = 9$,

critical value = 10,

reject H_0; there is evidence of a reduction in the intensity of the reaction.

6 (i) Each task is performed by two employees, one trained by method A and the other trained by method B.

(ii) H_0: There is no difference between the median of the times.

H_1: There is a difference between the median of the times.

2-tailed test,

$n = 10$,

$W_+ = 10$, $W_- = 45$,

$W = W_+ = 10$,

critical value = 8,

accept H_0; there is no evidence that there is a difference between the times.

Chapter 16

❓ (page 393)

On a practical level most tables of percentage points of the t distribution do not cover the degrees of freedom you are likely to need for large samples. A partial explanation this for this apparent omission is that for large values of ν there is little difference between the t values and the equivalent Normal values. However, there also are theoretical reasons why the Normal test is preferable. Both tests involve approximations. The Normal test relies on the sample variances being very close estimates of the population variances and on the Central Limit Theorem. For large samples this is unlikely to produce as large errors as the assumption required for the t test, that the underlying populations themselves are Normal.

❓ (page 396)

It would not have made any difference since the samples are large. Notice that the test scores are discrete variables so their distribution cannot be exactly Normal.

❓ (page 399)

The form of the alternative hypothesis, which claims that mean difference in lengths is not 3 cm, rather than either it being greater than or it being less than 3 cm, indicates that a 2-tailed test is appropriate.

❓ (page 401)

The form of the alternative hypothesis, which claims that journey times are lower in June than in August rather than that they are unequal, indicates that a 1-tailed test is appropriate.

❓ (page 402)

It is stated that the samples are random samples. It is reasonable to expect Normality in this situation and you might well expect the same variability in journey times as before.

Exercise 16A (page 402)

1 (i) H_0: There is, on average, no difference between the resistances of the components from suppliers A and B.
H_1: On average, there is a difference between the resistances of the components from suppliers A and B.
Assumptions: the two samples are independent random samples of the populations, the variables are Normally distributed and have equal variances.

(ii) pooled $s^2 = 0.009\,855$,
2-tailed test,
$\nu = 15$,
critical value $= -2.131$,
$t = -2.810$,
significant, the null hypothesis is rejected; there is evidence to suggest there is a difference.

2 (i) H_0: There is, on average, no difference between the absence rates.
H_1: On average, factory B has a lower rate of absence.

(ii) 1-tailed test,
critical value $= 1.645$,
$z = 1.2795$,
not significant, the null hypothesis is accepted; it appears that there is no difference between absence rates.

3 (i) H_0: There is, on average, no difference between the cholesterol levels.
H_1: On average, patients treated with the drug have a lower cholesterol level.
Assumptions: the two samples are independent random samples of the populations, the variables are Normally distributed and have equal variances.

(ii) pooled $s^2 = 262.63$,
1-tailed test,
$\nu = 15$,
critical value $= -1.753$,
$t = -1.81$,
significant, the null hypothesis is rejected; the evidence suggests that the drug is successful.

4 H_0: There is, on average, no difference between the cooking times.
H_1: On average, there is a difference between the cooking times.
2-tailed test,
critical value $= 1.96$,
$z = 2.347$,
significant, the null hypothesis is rejected; the evidence suggests there is a difference between the ovens.

5 (i) The two samples are independent random samples of the populations, the variables are Normally distributed and have equal variances.

(ii) H_0: There is, on average, no difference between the volumes before and after overhaul.
H_1: On average, there is a difference between the volumes before and after overhaul.

(iii) pooled $s^2 = 1.278$,
2-tailed test,
$\nu = 15$,
critical value $= -2.131$,
$t = -0.943$,
not significant, the null hypothesis is accepted; there is no difference between volumes before and after overhaul.

6 H_0: The training programme has made no difference to customer satisfaction.
H_1: The training programme has led to a higher level of customer satisfaction.
pooled $s^2 = 114.933$,
1-tailed test,
$\nu = 10$,
critical value $= 1.812$,
$t = 2.047$,
significant, the null hypothesis is rejected; the training programme did improve customer satisfaction.

7 **(i)** H_0: There is, on average, no difference between the amount of light.
H_1: On average, there is a difference between the amount of light.
Assumptions: the two samples are independent random samples of the populations, the variables are Normally distributed and have equal variances.

(ii) pooled $s^2 = 2.3234$,
2-tailed test,
$\nu = 20$,
critical value $= 1.725$,
$t = 1.67$,
not significant, the null hypothesis is accepted; the two designs deliver the same amount of light.

8 H_0: $\mu_2 - \mu_1 = 8$, the difference between the mean noon temperatures in the Hot and Cold seasons is 8 °C.
H_1: $\mu_2 - \mu_1 \neq 8$.
2-tailed test,
critical value $= 1.96$,
$z = 0.797$,
not significant, the null hypothesis is accepted; the data support the meteorologist's theory.

Exercise 16B (page 409)

1 **(i)** H_0: There is no difference between the median levels of stress in males and females.
H_1: There is a difference between the median of levels of stress, with levels in males being higher.

(ii) 1-tailed test,
$m = 8$, $n = 10$,
$W_X = 66$, $W_Y = 105$,
$W = W_X = 66$,
critical value $= 56$,
accept the null hypothesis; there is no difference between the median levels of stress in males and females.

2 **(i)** H_0: There is no difference between the number of items produced when it is cool and when it is warm.
H_1: There is a difference between the number of items produced, with lower numbers in cool conditions.
1-tailed test,
$m = 5$, $n = 6$,
$W_X = 19$, $W_Y = 47$,
$W = W_X = 19$,
critical value $= 20$,
reject the null hypothesis; there is evidence of fewer items being produced when it is cool.

3 H_0: There is no difference between the median length of calls with the different tariffs.
H_1: There is a difference between the median length of calls.
2-tailed test,
$m = 7$, $n = 8$,
$W_X = 39$, $W_Y = 81$,
$W = W_X = 39$,
critical value $= 41$,
reject the null hypothesis; there is evidence of a difference between call lengths.

4 H_0: There is no difference between the median scores achieved in the two statistics tests.
H_1: There is a difference between the median scores.
2-tailed test,
$m = 7$, $n = 10$,
$W_X = 58.5$, $W_Y = 94.5$,
$W = W_X = 58.5$,
critical value $= 42$,
accept the null hypothesis; there is no evidence of a difference between the scores.

5 H_0: There is no difference between the median times in the morning and the evening.
H_1: There is a difference between the median times.
2-tailed test,
$m = 6, n = 7$,
$W_X = 36.5, W_Y = 54.5$,
$W = W_X = 36.5$,
critical value = 27,
accept the null hypothesis; there is no evidence of a difference between the times.

6 H_0: There is no difference between the median scores when questioned by a male or by a female.
H_1: There is a difference between the median scores, with higher scores when questioned by a female.
1-tailed test,
$m = 6, n = 6$,
$W_X = 30.5, W_Y = 47.5$,
$W = W_X = 30.5$,
critical value = 28,
accept the null hypothesis; there is no evidence of a difference between the scores.

Chapter 17

? (page 413)

Yes, the scatter diagram does indicate a fairly strong positive correlation.

? (page 415)

(i) This data pair is genuine and so should be included if it was chosen in the random sample.
(ii) This data pair is also genuine.
(iii) This data pair is for a person who is earning £300 000 and is running a car worth £500. This pair should be questioned, especially given the information about Mr Uncliffe. When data are recorded it is always possible that a mistake is made; in this case it is more likely that Mr Uncliffe's income is £30 000, giving a data pair (30, 0.5). It would be reasonable in this situation to discard the data pair as being unreliable. (Note that you should not make a guess as to what it might be and use that data pair!)

? (page 416)

(i) Both height and weight are random variables with weight being the dependent variable.
(ii) The age in days of the plant is controlled.
(iii) The time of swing of a pendulum is related to its length by a formula.

? (page 420)

In region 2 the value of x in any data pair will be less than $\bar{x}$ and so $x - \bar{x}$ will be negative for all points. Since for every pair the value of y will be greater than $\bar{y}$, $y - \bar{y}$ will be positive. Therefore the product will be negative for each pair.
Likewise, in region 4 $x - \bar{x}$ will be positive for all data pairs while $y - \bar{y}$ will be negative. Therefore the product will again be negative.

Activity (page 421)

(i) $\sum x = 15$
$\sum y = 40$
$\bar{x} = 3$
$\bar{y} = 8$
$\sum x^2 = 61$
$\sum y^2 = 336$
$\sum xy = 133$
$\sum(x - \bar{x})^2 = 16$
$\sum(y - \bar{y})^2 = 16$
$\sum(x - \bar{x})(y - \bar{y}) = 13$

(ii) $S_{xx} = \sum(x - \bar{x})^2 = 16$
$S_{xx} = \sum x^2 - n\bar{x}^2 = 61 - 5 \times 3^2 = 61 - 45 = 16$
$S_{yy} = \sum(y - \bar{y})^2 = 16$
$S_{yy} = \sum y^2 - n\bar{y}^2 = 336 - 5 \times 8^2 = 336 - 320 = 16$
$S_{xy} = \sum(x - \bar{x})(y - \bar{y}) = 13$
$S_{xy} = \sum xy - n\bar{x}\,\bar{y} = 133 - 5 \times 3 \times 8 = 133 - 120$
$= 13$

(iii) $r = 0.8125$

Exercise 17A (page 424)

1 **(i)** 0.5135 **(ii)** 0.0320 **(iii)** −0.7409

2 **(i)**

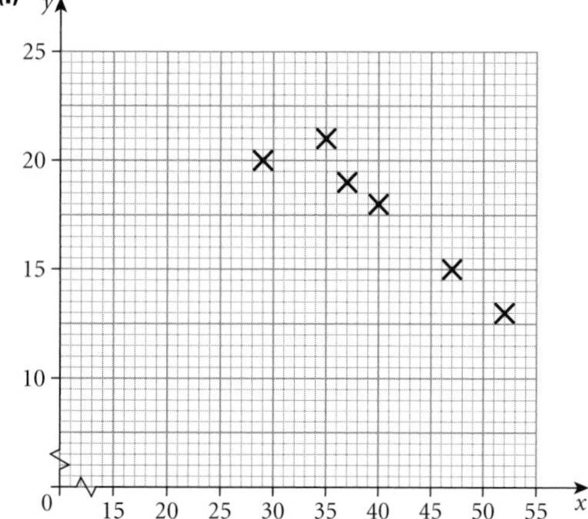

(ii) −0.9428

3 (i)

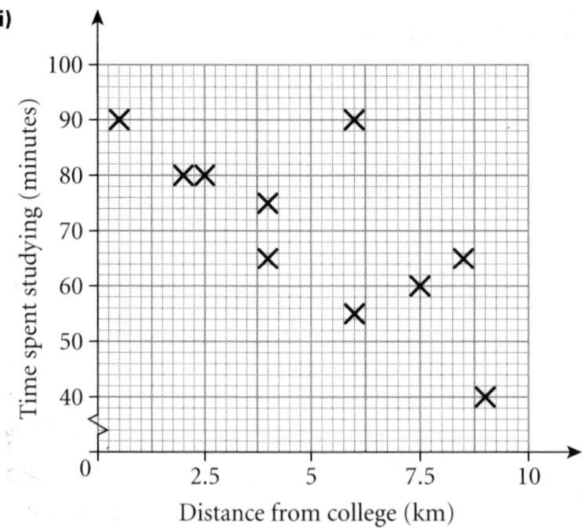

(ii) The data fit approximately to a straight line, both variables are random and it is possible to fit an ellipse round the points.

(iii) −0.7332

4 (i)

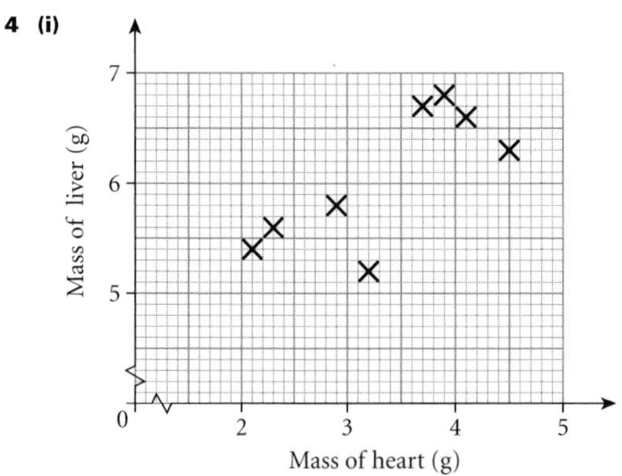

(ii) The data fit approximately to a straight line, both variables are random and it is possible to fit an ellipse round the points.

(iii) 0.7563

5 (i)

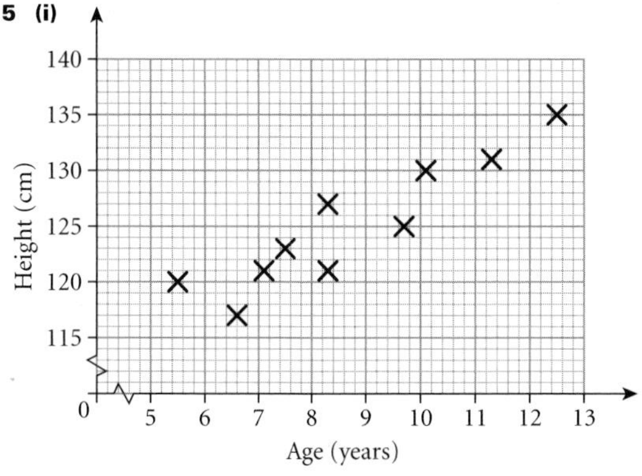

(ii) The data fit approximately to a straight line, both variables are random and it is possible to fit an ellipse round the points.

(iii) 0.9210

? (page 427)

For this 1-tailed test at the 5% significance level with $n = 10$ the critical value is -0.5494.
If $r = -0.3494$ then, since -0.3494 is less extreme than -0.5494 there is no evidence to reject the null hypothesis. The two variables do not seem to be correlated.

? (page 431)

It is impossible to say for sure. That is why you should not make predictions outside the range covered by the data.

? (page 431)

$\sum x = 4, \quad \sum y = 3, \quad \sum x^2 = 10, \quad \sum y^2 = 5, \quad \sum xy = 7$

$\bar{x} = 2, \quad \bar{y} = 1.5$

$S_{xx} = 10 - 2 \times 2^2 = 2$

$S_{yy} = 5 - 2 \times 1.5^2 = 0.5$

$S_{xy} = 7 - 2 \times 2 \times 1.5 = 1$

$r = \dfrac{1}{\sqrt{2 \times 0.5}} = 1$

? (page 431)

Yes

? (page 431)

In this case $r = -1$.

Exercise 17B (page 432)

1 (i) 0.5147

(ii) (a) 1-tailed test,
critical value = 0.4973,
$r = 0.5147$,
reject H_0; there is evidence of positive correlation

(b) 2-tailed test,
critical value = 0.5760,
$r = 0.5147$,
accept H_0; there is no evidence of correlation

2 (i) 1-tailed test,
critical value = 0.2638,
$r = 0.3333$,
reject H_0; there is evidence of positive correlation.

(ii) 1-tailed test,
critical value = −0.3665,
$r = -0.3333$,
accept H_0; there is no evidence of negative correlation.

(iii) 2-tailed test,
critical value = 0.3120,
$r = 0.3333$,
reject H_0; there is evidence of correlation.

3 (i)

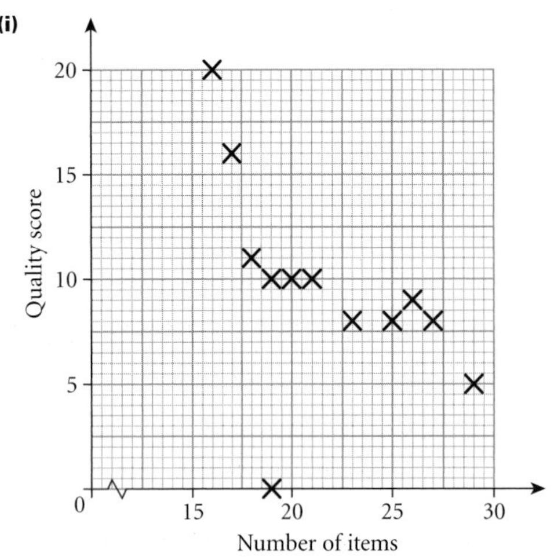

Yes, the data fit approximately to a straight line, both variables are random and it is possible to fit an ellipse round the points.

(ii) H_0: $\rho = 0$, there is no correlation between the number of items finished and the quality.
H_1: $\rho < 0$, there is negative correlation between the number of items finished and the quality.

(iii) $r = -0.5268$

(iv) 1-tailed test,
$n = 12$,
critical value = -0.4973,
reject H_0; there is evidence of negative correlation.
The evidence supports the manager's theory that the faster the craftsmen work the lower the quality of the finished product.

4 (i)

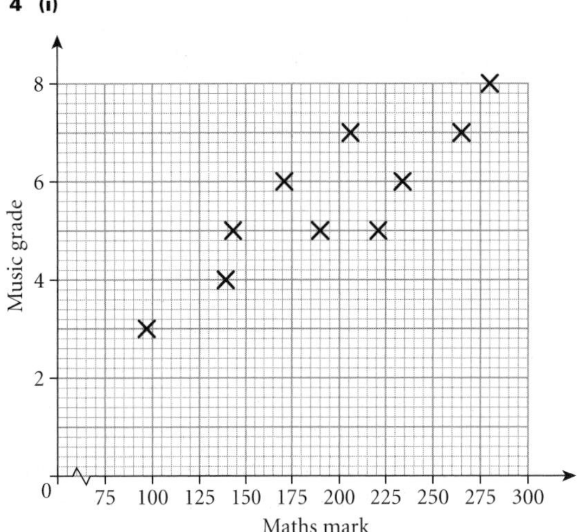

Yes, the data fit approximately to a straight line, both variables are random and it is possible to fit an ellipse round the points.

(ii) H_0: $\rho = 0$, there is no correlation between the maths and music scores.
H_1: $\rho > 0$, there is positive correlation between the maths and music scores.

(iii) 1-tailed test,
$n = 10$,
critical value = 0.5494,
$r = 0.8704$,
reject H_0; there is evidence of positive correlation.
The data support the theory that mathematicians are also good at music.

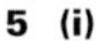

5 (i)

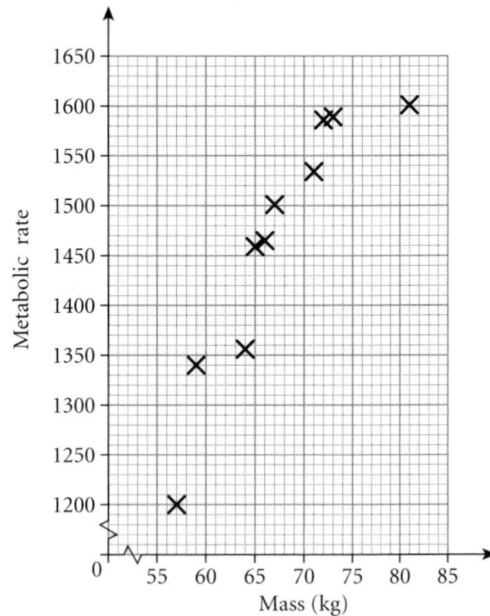

Yes, the data fit approximately to a straight line, both variables are random and it is possible to fit an ellipse round the points.

(ii) H_0: $\rho = 0$, there is no correlation between body mass and metabolic rate.
H_1: $\rho > 0$, there is positive correlation between body mass and metabolic rate.

(iii) 1-tailed test,
$n = 10$,
critical value = 0.7155,
$r = 0.9108$,
reject H_0; there is evidence of positive correlation.
The evidence supports the researcher's theory that body mass and metabolic rate are linearly related.

6 (i)

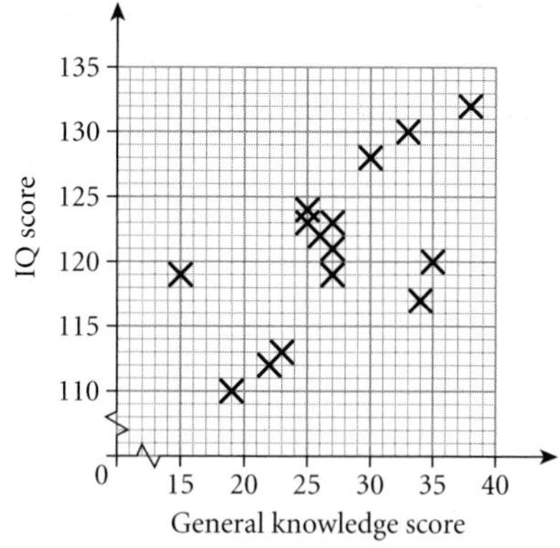

Yes, the data fit approximately to a straight line, both variables are random and it is possible to fit an ellipse round the points.

(ii) H_0: $\rho = 0$, there is no correlation between the scores on the two tests.

H_1: $\rho > 0$, there is positive correlation between the scores on the two tests.

(iii) 1-tailed test,

$n = 15$,

critical value $= 0.4409$,

$r = 0.6168$,

reject H_0; there is evidence of positive correlation.

The evidence supports the statistician's view.

7 (i)

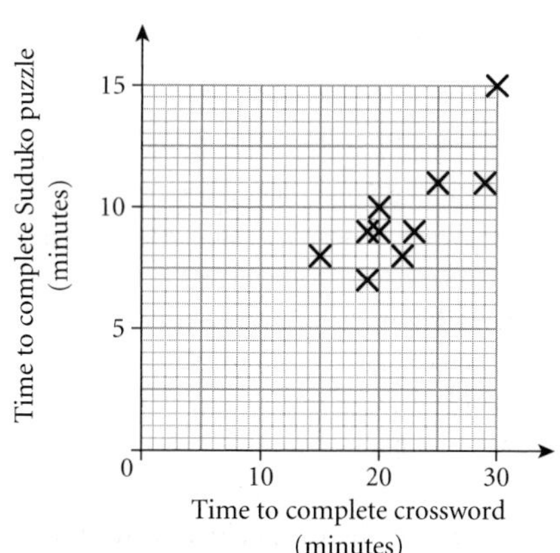

Yes, the data fit approximately to a straight line, both variables are random and it is possible to fit an ellipse round the points.

(ii) H_0: $\rho = 0$, there is no correlation between the times.

H_1: $\rho > 0$, there is positive correlation between the times.

(iii) 1-tailed test,

$n = 10$,

critical value $= 0.5494$,

$r = 0.8131$,

reject H_0; there is evidence of positive correlation.

The evidence suggests that people who are good at crossword puzzles are also good a Suduko puzzles.

8 (i)

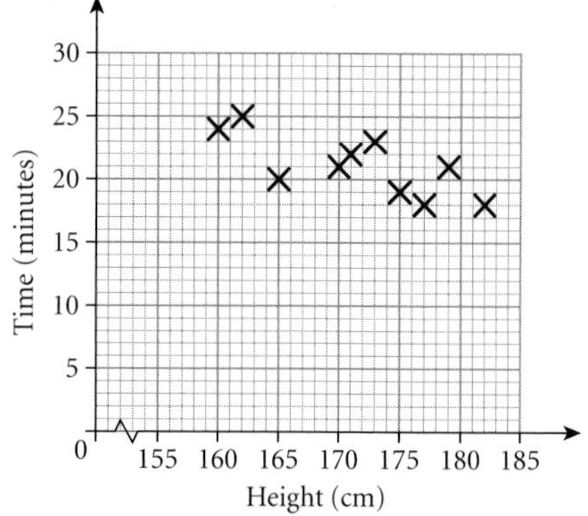

Yes, the data fit approximately to a straight line, both variables are random and it is possible to fit an ellipse round the points.

(ii) H_0: $\rho = 0$, there is no correlation between height and time to run the school cross-country race.

H_1: $\rho < 0$, there is negative correlation between height and the time to run the school cross-country race.

(iii) 1-tailed test,

$n = 10$,

critical value $= -0.5494$,

$r = -0.7443$,

reject H_0; there is evidence of negative correlation.

The evidence supports the games teacher's theory that the taller you are the better you are at long distance running.

9 (i)

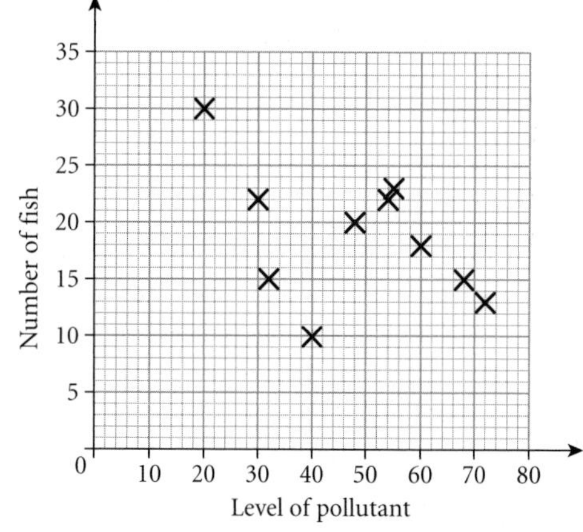

(ii) (40, 10); possibly through a measuring error.

(iii) H_0: $\rho = 0$, there is no correlation between the level of pollutant and the number of fish.

H_1: $\rho < 0$, there is negative correlation between the level of pollutant and the number of fish.

(iv) 1-tailed test,
$n = 10$,
critical value $= -0.5494$,
$r = -0.4640$,
accept H_0; there is no evidence of negative correlation.
The data suggests there is no correlation between the level of pollutant and the number of fish.

(v) 1-tailed test,
$n = 9$,
critical value $= -0.5822$,
$r = -0.6577$,
reject H_0; there is evidence of negative correlation.
The data suggest that the higher the level of pollutant the lower the number of fish.

10 (i)

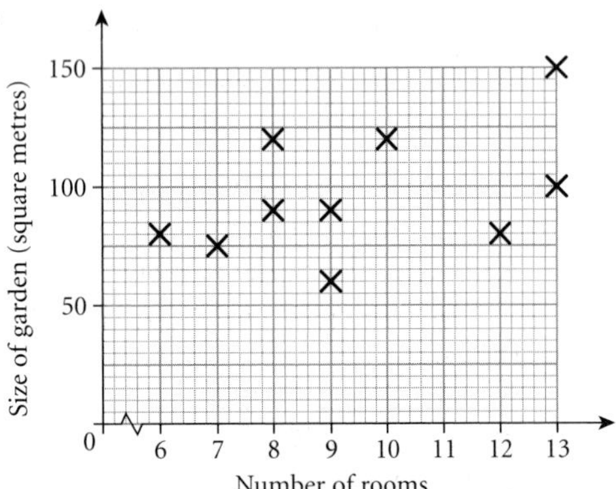

The data should fit approximately to a straight line and it should be possible to fit an ellipse round the points. The data do not conform very well to these restrictions.

(ii) H_0: $\rho = 0$, there is no correlation between the number of rooms and the size of garden.
H_1: $\rho > 0$, there is positive correlation between the number of rooms and the size of garden.

(iii) 1-tailed test,
$n = 10$,
critical value $= 0.5494$,
$r = 0.4698$,
accept H_0; there is no evidence of positive correlation.
The data suggests that there is no correlation between the number of rooms in a house and the size of the garden.

? (page 436)

Yes, it is a standard thing to do providing the judges are using the same criteria.

? (page 436)

The grounds for complaint were that the rankings were so different that she felt it unreasonable to assume that they were using the same criteria.

? (page 436)

In normal circumstances it would seem a reasonable assertion that the judges were marking according to the same criteria. However, the results given do give Maria grounds to be suspicious and to want to do an analysis of the data.

? (page 438)

In this case you get the same value. However, if there are tied ranks the values will not be the same.

Exercise 17C (page 440)

1 2-tailed test
(i) 0.3624
(ii) 0.2545

2 (i) 1-tailed test,
$n = 10$,
critical value $= 0.5636$,
0.60 is significant.
(ii) 2-tailed test,
$n = 10$,
critical value $= 0.6485$,
0.60 is not significant.

3 (i) (a) 0.7143
(b) 0.0857
(ii) Prediction 1 is much closer.

4 (i) H_0: There is no association between the underlying judgements.
H_1: There is positive association between the underlying judgements.
(ii) $r_s = 0.7667$
(iii) 1-tailed test,
$n = 9$,
critical value $= 0.6000$,
reject H_0; there is evidence of positive association.

5 H_0: There is no association between the underlying judgements of the women.
H_1: There is positive association between the underlying judgements of the women.
1-tailed test,
$n = 10$,
critical value $= 0.5636$,
$r_s = 0.8182$,
reject H_0; there is evidence of positive association.
The data suggests that the women are in agreement over the drinks.

6 (i)

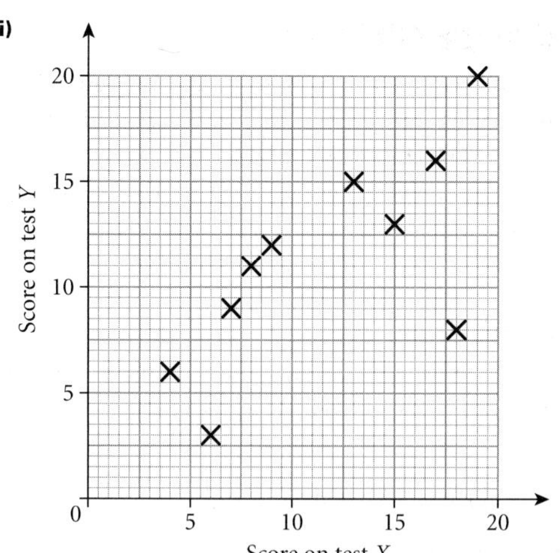

(ii) Student E; no reason

(iii) It does not seem as though there is strong linear association, because of student E.

(iv) H_0: There is no association between the underlying test results.
H_1: There is positive association between the underlying test results.

(v) $r_s = 0.7212$

(vi) 1-tailed test,
$n = 10$,
critical value = 0.5636,
reject H_0; there is evidence of positive association.

7 (i)

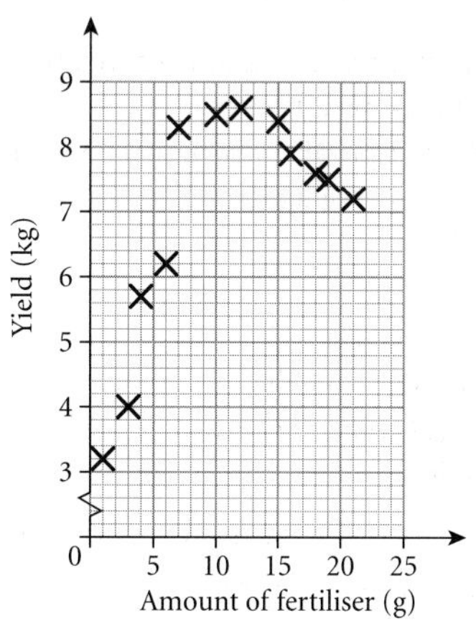

The diagram indicates that the data are not linearly associated.

(ii)

Fertiliser, *x* gram	Rank	Yield, *y* kg	Rank
1	1	3.2	1
3	2	4.0	2
4	3	5.7	3
6	4	6.2	4
7	5	8.3	9
10	6	8.5	11
12	7	8.6	12
15	8	8.4	10
16	9	7.9	8
18	10	7.6	7
19	11	7.5	6
21	12	7.2	5

(iii) H_0: There is no association between the variables in the underlying population.
H_1: There is positive association between the variables in the underlying population.
1-tailed test,
$n = 12$,
critical value = 0.5035,
$r_s = 0.4615$,
accept H_0; there is no evidence of positive association.

(iv) For the first 8 plants, $r_s = 0.9286$

(v) For all 12 the association looks quadratic. It would seem as though there is a maximum amount of fertiliser that should be applied; too much and the yield is adversely affected.

8 For *XY*: $r_{xy} = 0.8788$
For *YZ*: $r_{yz} = 0.7091$
For *ZX*: $r_{zx} = 0.8545$
The coefficient for *X* and *Y* is the nearest to 1, so take the ranks of these two judges.

Contestant	A	B	C	D	E	F	G	H	I	J
Judge *X*	2	7	4	8	9	3	10	1	6	5
Judge *Y*	4	7	3	6	8	2	10	1	9	5
Sum	6	14	7	14	17	5	20	2	15	10
Final position	3	6=	4	6=	9	2	10	1	8	5

9 (i) When ranking greatest time as 1, $r_s = 0.6364$
There is positive association.
When ranking shortest time as 1, $r_s = -0.6364$
There is negative association.

(ii) H_0: There is no association between the variables in the underlying population.
H_1: There is association between the variables in the underlying population.
2-tailed test,
$n = 12$,
critical value = 0.5874,
reject H_0; there is evidence of association at the 5% significance level.
The data indicate that those who took more time were more accurate.

10 (i) $r_s = 0.6121$

(ii) H_0: There is no association between the variables in the underlying population.
H_1: There is positive association between the variables in the underlying population.
The claim is for enhanced growth so the test is if more additive produces more growth. Hence the test is a 1-tailed test.

(iii) 1-tailed test,
$n = 10$,
critical value = 0.5636,
reject H_0; there is evidence of positive association.
The evidence suggests that more additive results in a greater weight.

(iv) Correlation coefficients are dimensionless so the choice of units makes no difference and consequently the result is still valid.
Or: Since the data were ranked, it makes no difference whether the amount of fertiliser is measured in ounces or grams, the rank order is still the same.

Appendices

Exercise A (page 446)

1 (i) $a^2 + 2ab + b^2$

(ii) $c^3 + 3c^2d + 3cd^2 + d^3$

(iii) $e^4 + 4e^3f + 6e^2f^2 + 4ef^3 + f^4$

(iv) $l^5 + 5l^4m + 10l^3m^2 + 10l^2m^3 + 5lm^4 + m^5$

(v) $p^6 + 6p^5q + 15p^4q^2 + 20p^3q^3 + 15p^2q^4 + 6pq^5 + q^6$

(vi) $s^8 + 8s^7t + 28s^6t^2 + 56s^5t^3 + 70s^4t^4 + 56s^3t^5 + 28s^2t^6 + 8st^7 + t^8$

2 (i) $10n^2y^3$

(ii) $210q^6p^4$

(iii) $h^{18} + 18h^{17}k + 153h^{16}k^2 + 816h^{15}k^3$

(iv) $q^{27} + 27q^{26}pt + 351q^{25}p^2t^2 + \ldots + 351q^2p^{25}t^{25} + 27qp^{26}t^{26} + p^{27}t^{27}$

3 (i) 2, 4, 8, 16, 32, 64

(ii) $\sum_{r=0}^{n} {}^nC_r = 2^n$

Index